UNDERGRADUATE TEXTS IN COMPUTER SCIENCE

Editors
David Gries
Fred B. Schneider

Springer
New York
Berlin
Heidelberg
Barcelona
Hong Kong
London
Milan
Paris
Singapore
Tokyo

UNDERGRADUATE TEXTS IN COMPUTER SCIENCE

Oliver Grillmeyer

Exploring Computer Science with Scheme

Springer

Oliver Grillmeyer
Department of Computer Science
University of California at Berkeley
Berkeley, CA 94720
USA

Series Editors
David Gries
Fred B. Schneider
Department of Computer Science
Cornell University
Upson Hall
Ithaca, NY 14853-7501
USA

Library of Congress Cataloging-in-Publication Data
Grillmeyer, Oliver.
    Exploring computer science with Scheme / Oliver Grillmeyer
        p.   cm.—(Undergraduate texts in computer science)
    Includes index.
    ISBN 0-387-94895-3 (hardcover : alk. paper)
    1. Computer science.   I. Title.   II. Series.
  QA76.G723   1997
  004—dc21   97-24294

Printed on acid-free paper.

Production managed by Terry Kornak; manufacturing supervised by Joe Quatela.
Photocomposed copy prepared by the author in TROFF.
Printed and bound by Hamilton Printing Co., Rensselaer, NY.
Printed in the United States of America.

9 8 7 6 5 4

ISBN 0-387-94895-3   SPIN 10789850

Springer-Verlag   New York Berlin Heidelberg
A member of BertelsmannSpringer Science+Business Media GmbH

To my parents, Hans and Maria,
and my wife, Myriam.

PREFACE

1 Computer Science

Most introductory computer science textbooks teach the reader how to write programs in a particular programming language. The student may get the impression that there isn't much more to computer science than just learning different programming languages. Hence, the more languages you know, the more capable you are of solving a greater variety of problems. A student may think that with a number of programming languages under her belt, she can solve most any problem.

As most computer scientists would agree, there is a lot more to the field than just learning different languages—just as architecture involves a lot more than learning how to draw different straight lines and shapes. One of the goals of this book is to present the reader with an understanding of what computer science really is. This is done by presenting the subfields into which computer science is broken, giving explanations and sample programs for each.

It's more than just programming

It is still important to do some programming to get a deeper understanding of computer science. There are books that discuss computer science and give excellent overviews of the field, but do not involve any programming. This approach quite often leaves the reader wondering how the computer actually does all the powerful tasks that it can do. Such books give an idea of what computers are used for and what the areas of study under computer science are, but not how the computer performs these tasks.

This book will mix theory with applications. The reader will learn the "science" of computer science and then see actual applications thereof. This will help demystify the theories and ideas presented.

2   Language Used

Advantages of Scheme

Scheme, a dialect of LISP, will be used. With today's faster, more powerful, and less expensive new machines, languages like Scheme that have typically been in the educational arena in schools of higher education are entering the home user's world. Using Scheme, the programmer can solve many problems much easier and with much less writing and effort than with the more conventional languages used in introductory texts, such as Pascal, BASIC, C, C++, and Java.

The family of LISP languages are sometimes criticized for use as introductory programming languages because they are not used as widely by programmers in the workplace as languages like Pascal, C, or C++. However, it is important to remember that the purpose of an introductory computer science text should be to teach computer science and not just a particular programming language. It is easier to learn programming concepts using Scheme than with these other more popular languages. This is due to the overhead these languages impose on the learner. Scheme is easy to learn, so more time can be spent on programming and computer science concepts than on language idiosyncrasies. Programming techniques and concepts transfer from one language to another, so after learning Scheme students can learn Pascal or C relatively quickly.

3   Functional Programming

Imperative versus functional programming

Typically, students learn to program using an *imperative* approach. This paradigm is used with languages such as FORTRAN, Pascal, C, and BASIC. The imperative approach involves programming by focusing on the sequences of steps that are necessary to perform a task. Such programs tend to consist of interdependent and highly interconnected pieces.

This book uses the *functional* approach to programming. The functional approach concentrates on the creation of simple functions that are applied to values to obtain desired results. These functions are *composed* (combined) to achieve the desired programming goal. Such simple functions are easily tested individually. This greatly helps in producing programs that work right the first time.

One is not limited to imperative programming when using Pascal-like languages, but these languages lend themselves to such techniques. Similarly, one can use imperative programming techniques in Scheme, but the language is better suited to functional programming.

4   Problem Solving

Developing problem solving skills

A major goal of this book is to teach fundamental problem-solving skills. These skills can be applied to any problem-solving task using any programming language. Many new students learn how to program through analogy without ever getting a deep understanding of the concepts. Such students perform very poorly when given new types of problems that cannot be solved using the templates they have been religiously following. Like memorizing recipes in a cookbook, if you can make chocolate chip cookies you can make raisin cookies, but not cheesecake unless you know more of the concepts of cooking.

This book illustrates techniques to aid in the writing of programs. Such techniques include abstracting the problem into the domain of Scheme, creating *pseudo code* as an intermediate solution, using top-down and bottom-up design, building procedural and data abstractions, developing defensive, safe-coding skills, and writing testable, modular programs. In addition, heuristics are given that help determine good test cases to test your code.

5 Pedagogical Techniques

Throughout the book I have tried to present material in a clear, concise manner, using numerous Scheme examples. Common mistakes that students make as they are learning programming are presented in boxes like this:

Aids to understanding the text

Mistakes to Avoid

Remember that `rest` returns a list with all but the first element. A common mistake is to think that

```
(rest '(a (b)))
```

returns `(b)` instead of the true value returned: `((b))`.

Other boxes are used to point out important issues that deserve to be brought to the reader's attention. Margin notes are used throughout the text as a reference tool to help the reader find material in the text and to highlight the important issues presented.

Most programming examples are presented in a case study fashion in which the thought process, design decisions, false starts, and alternative programming choices are presented. This gives the reader a much better understanding of what is involved in programming and helps to make normally tacit programming skills explicit such that the reader can more easily learn them.

Each chapter has numerous exercises to help readers test their understanding of the material. All chapters end with a summary of the entire chapter, which is good for a quick reference or refresher.

Many functions are introduced to augment the built-in functions of Scheme. Most of these functions come from Common LISP and are chosen because they provide useful extensions to Scheme and are used in many of the subsequent programming examples. Wherever possible, these new functions are immediately defined giving the reader a clear understanding of how they work and what they do. Motivation for the creation of the new functions is given to avoid presenting the functions without a context for their use. This helps readers know when to use the functions and how they might consider extending Scheme to meet their needs.

Extensions to Scheme

6   Goals

To recap, the major goals of this text are to:

- Develop an understanding of computer science as a discipline.
- Learn computer programming using the functional programming paradigm and Scheme as the language of choice.
- Develop problem-solving and good programming skills.
- Present the material in a way that facilitates learning.

7   Acknowledgements

First and foremost I thank Michael Clancy for his numerous invaluable suggestions on this book. In addition to commenting on each version of the manuscript, Mike provided help in everything from font selection, layout, and publisher advice to specific examples, functions, and exercises to incorporate in the text. As an author of many textbooks, Mike could empathize with my concerns and difficulties. He was always present to answer a myriad of questions or just listen to my current accomplishments or struggles.

The first ten chapters of this text were used nine terms in courses I taught at U.C. Berkeley. In addition the text is being used in the self-paced courses at U.C. Berkeley. Over the years I received numerous comments from students using this text. I thank all the students who have made suggestions for improvements or just praised the text and brought a smile to my face. Many teaching assistants and readers who have worked with me have commented on the text. I thank them all and give special thanks to Steve Lumetta, Glenn Von Tersch, Mike Schiff, and Tom Boegel.

Thanks to the computer science faculty, graduate students, and support staff at U.C. Berkeley for all the knowledge they have imparted to me over the years. In particular I thank Robert Wahbe, Seth Teller, Paul Hilfinger, Brian Harvey, and Lotfi Zadeh. Kevin Mullally, Fran Rizzardi, and Ruben Zelwer provided technical and formatting support.

Martin Gilchrist from Springer-Verlag was very helpful, giving me encouragement and flexibility in the design and contents of the text. I thank Springer-Verlag's series editor David Gries for his careful and thorough review of the manuscript and the extensive comments and enthusiasm he provided. Thanks to Terry Kornak, production editor, and Chrisa Hotchkiss who proofread the text. They both helped smooth out the rough edges. Karen Phillips was the design supervisor who helped bring my ideas for the cover of the book into reality. Thanks to Chris Dovolis for his helpful review of the text.

Special thanks to Gino Cheng and Brett DeSchepper for providing company and laughs during all the late night trips to Cafe Milano, Triple Rock, and Flint's, and for providing sanity through frisbee therapy. Thanks to Brian Peterson for listening to my concerns and all the slices of Blondies. Thanks to Jean Root, Tedi Diaz, Liza Gabato, and Kate Capps for their constant support. Kathryn Jones provided font examples and suggestions. The layout of the text is due in large part to the suggestions and advice of Yoshiro Soga who also keeps me abreast of all the changes in the worlds of personal computers and football. Thanks to everyone in the U.C. Berkeley Hapkido club who helped me recharge after long days of work on the book.

My family provided support throughout the writing of the book; they were always excited over any progress (even small) that was made. Thanks Robert, Stephen, Maria, and Hans for the encouragement.

Thank you Myriam for bearing all the late nights I spent working on the book and for tolerating me bringing work on our trips to India, Sri Lanka, and Mexico. Thanks for listening to the day-to-day sagas during the book's creation. The book is complete. I'll cook dinner tonight.

CHAPTERS

BRIEF CONTENTS

CONTENTS

13 Compilers and Interpreters 319

13.1   Compilers Versus Interpreters 319
     –translation versus simulation

13.2   Lexical Analysis 320
     –characters to symbols
     13.2.1   Exercises 320
     13.2.2   Tokens and symbol tables 321

13.3   Parsing 321
     –symbols to structure
     13.3.1   Top-Down parsing 323
     13.3.2   Predictive parsing 326
     13.3.3   Bottom-Up parsing 327

13.4   Semantic Analysis 330
     –structure to meaning

13.5   Code Generation 331
     –meaning translated
     13.5.1   Mini Scheme 331
     13.5.2   A simple computer 332
     13.5.3   Assembly language 333
     13.5.4   Conditional expressions in assembly language 336
     13.5.5   Function definitions and calls in assembly language 337

13.6   Historical Background and Current Trends 343
     –early compilers and compiler building tools and techniques
     13.6.1   Compiling the compiler 344

13.7   Implementing a Simple Scheme Compiler in Scheme 346
     –case study: building a code generator for a subset of Scheme
     13.7.1   Generating code for `if` expressions 350
     13.7.2   Generating code for `define` expressions 354
     13.7.3   Generating code for calls to user-defined functions 356
     13.7.4   Generating code for calls to built-in functions 357
     13.7.5   Testing our compiler 359
     13.7.6   Exercises 361

13.8   Extending Our Compiler 362
     –what it would take to incorporate more of Scheme in our compiler
     13.8.1   Adding more data types to our compiler 362
     13.8.2   Adding more functions to our compiler 363
     13.8.3   Adding more special forms and handling scope in our compiler 363
     13.8.4   Code Optimization 364

13.9   Future Trends 365
     –building compilers for parallel machines and for different types of languages

13.10   Summary 365

13.11   Additional Reading 366

13.12   Code Listing 366

CHAPTER 1

INTRODUCTION TO COMPUTER SCIENCE

1.1   What Is a Computer?

A computer can be defined as a machine capable of performing a set of well-defined functions. Modern computers are electronic devices. However, the first computing devices were mechanical in nature.[1] It's the particular set of functions that the computer performs that separates it from microwave ovens or stereos, which are also electronic devices that perform well-defined functions.

A very simple computer that you have probably used is a four-function calculator. These calculators perform a set of well-defined functions, namely basic arithmetic functions ($+, -, \times, \div$). Such calculators may be called simple computers but not general purpose computers. Calculators lack some essential functionality, namely *control functions*. These control functions are used to make decisions based on certain conditions. Many calculators lack the ability to be programmed. You must enter all the necessary key strokes each time you wish to perform any calculation. Programmable calculators are an exception—they allow you to save a sequence of keystrokes that can be recalled. Calculators have limited memory, often just one memory key.[2]

Features important to computers

All of these factors, control functions, programmability, and extra memory are important parts of a general purpose computer. To get a better idea why these features are useful, let's try a simple problem using a calculator.

---

[1] The underlying mechanism (electronic components or gears) of a computer is not important in terms of the computer's abilities. It is important in terms of the speed of the computer.

[2] This does not mean that the calculator can store only one number. Rather, it means that the person using it can save and retrieve only one number.

1.1.1   Example: Balancing your checkbook

You may have done this numerous times already using a calculator. Focus on the differences between using a calculator and using a computer to perform this task.

Using a calculator   With a calculator you might use the following approach:

> Enter your starting balance (since the last time you balanced).
> Call this your current balance.
> For each entry in your checkbook do the following:
> > If it is a deposit,
> > > add it to the current balance.
> > Otherwise, if it is a withdrawal (or finance charge),
> > > subtract it from the current balance.
> > Otherwise, it is a check, so
> > > subtract it from the current balance.
> Your current balance now reflects your final balance.

If you want to get a total of your deposits, withdrawals, and checks paid, you must recompute that information, or modify the above approach to keep running totals of the three amounts. These running totals would be maintained on paper or in other memory keys on the calculator if such existed.

Using a computer   The above steps can be converted into a computer program. Computing the totals of the deposits, withdrawals, and checks paid can be easily incorporated. The computer would *execute* or *run* this program. This means that the computer follows the given steps. We want the computer to make the decisions and calculations so that our job is as easy as possible. Ideally we would only enter the amounts and their types. For example, we might enter

> $5789.25 start balance
> $100 deposit
> $25.37 withdrawal
> $50.67 check
> $120.45 withdrawal
> end

The computer will read this information and decide what calculations to perform based on the transaction type. Once finished, it could give us results like the following:

> Initial balance $5789.25
>
> 1 deposit totaling $100.00
> 2 withdrawals totaling $145.82
> 1 check paid totaling $50.67
>
> Final balance $5692.76

All we had to do was enter the transaction amounts and types. The computer did the right things with them, and then gave us the information we wanted. For the computer to do this, it must have control functions to perform actions based on the type of transaction received—check, deposit, withdrawal, or initial balance. Extra memory is necessary to save the deposit, withdrawal, and checks paid subtotals. Lastly, programmability is necessary to provide the computer with the steps needed. Writing such programs will be the topic of later chapters.

Why computers need control functions, memory, and programmability

Using a computer to balance a checkbook can easily provide more information than using a calculator would. However, using a computer necessitates the creation of a working program. This tradeoff is one that must be considered whenever contemplating the writing of a program to reduce the amount of human work required to perform a certain task. Writing a program does take time and thought, but it can be repaid in saved labor, less boredom (i.e., balancing your checking account), and less human error.

Tradeoffs

1.2 A Look Inside the Computer

The computer can be divided into two parts, *hardware* and *software*. The hardware is the "machine" part of the computer. In an electronic computer, the hardware consists of the electronics that enable the computer to perform its basic functions. This hardware cannot be altered, hence the term *hard*ware. As we have seen in the checkbook example, for a computer to do a specific task, a program is necessary. The programs that one writes are instances of software. Software, unlike hardware, is easily changed.

Hardware versus software

How do we get the hardware to follow the steps dictated by the software? Hardware alone does nothing. It is like a calculator sitting on a desk. Software alone does nothing. It is like a person who has a sequence of calculations in mind but no calculator on which to run them. With the calculator and person, the missing pieces are the numberpad and display. They act as an *interface* between the person and the electronics inside. The picture is more complex with a computer.

An *operating system* is used to run programs on the hardware of the machine. Running a program entails having the computer hardware follow the steps given in the program. The operating system controls the hardware and allows the user of the computer to run programs (software) on that computer. A simplified diagram of a computer system looks like this:

Operating systems

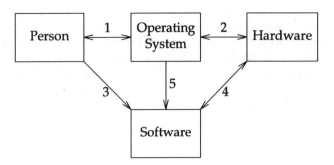

The person (or *user*) sends commands to the operating system, and gets information back [1]. The operating system gives instructions to the hardware and the hardware returns results to the operating system [2]. The person creates programs (software) [3], which can be run on the hardware [4]. The operating system is used to invoke programs such that they may be run on the hardware [5].

The focus of this book is not on machine hardware or operating systems, but on the creation of software. Only a simple version of machine hardware will be shown in the later chapters. Operating systems are covered in Chapter 14.

1.3   Connections Between Computers

Networks

Computers can be connected to other computers in what is termed a *network*. Computers connected together can send and receive information to one another. There are extensive networks linking computers around the world. Users can send *electronic mail* (e-mail) to other users on different machines or read messages over computer *bulletin boards* from people in numerous countries. One such bulletin board forum, USENET, covers thousands of topics and extends to millions of computers around the world.

Internet and World Wide Web

The extensive networking of computers grew into the present day *Internet*, a network that links millions of computers. The Internet was used originally by only a small percentage of computer users primarily for electronic mail and data transfer. This changed with the development of the World Wide Web project in 1990. This project included the creation of a new language, HTML, to create *hypertext documents*—documents that have links to other sections of the document or to other documents. *Browsers* were developed to provide simple access to data on the World Wide Web (also called the Web or WWW) and support multimedia data (pictures, movies, and sounds).

The Web has created an explosive growth in the computer industry by providing a simple means of presenting and receiving information from other people throughout the world. Computer usage on the Web is growing exponentially. Two hundred million people are expected to be using the WWW by the year 2002.

1.4 What Is Computer Science?

Computer science can be defined as the study of computers—their design, capabilities, and limitations. Most of computer science falls into the domains of hardware or software. There is one other domain, *theory*, that is primarily associated with software but can involve hardware. Theory addresses issues of complexity, *algorithms* (ways of doing things), efficiency, and limitations of algorithms and computers, among other things. Some elements of computer theory will be explored in later chapters.

Theory

Teaching you how to create programs is one of the goals of this book. However, do not be misled. Just as there is more to math than arithmetic, and more to music than writing circles and lines on a staff, there is more to computer science than writing computer programs. Computer science is a discipline in its own right with theories, goals, beliefs, and limitations. This text will give the reader a taste of what the discipline of computer science is by going beyond simple programming and looking into problem solving, design, and abstraction. The major subfields of computer science will be explored individually in this text showing each field's accomplishments and goals. The main focus will be on the fields within software.

Going beyond programming

1.5 Subfields Within Software

Within software a number of subfields have arisen as computer science has matured. Below is a list of these subfields:

- Operating systems
- Compilers, interpreters, and programming language design
- Database management systems
- Artificial intelligence
- Soft computing
- Graphics

1.5.1 Operating systems

Operating systems provide a link between the user, the hardware, and the software. The operating system creates an environment with specialized commands that let the user perform various sophisticated actions. Exactly what this environment looks like and what actions are supported depend on the particular operating system. Some of these actions may include

Functions of operating systems

- displaying information on terminals or printing on printers
- sorting, searching, and restructuring information
- hiding or making available information to others using the same computer
- modifying or creating information
- getting instructions on using the operating system itself
- providing access to programs that perform a wide array of tasks
- accessing or sending information to other computers

● sending information to other people on the same or different computers

Peripherals

Operating systems perform other functions. Computers have *keyboards* (or other input devices such as a *mouse* or *writing pad*) and *terminals* that allow people to send and receive information to and from the computer. There are other *peripheral devices*, such as *line* or *laser printers* that produce paper copies of information stored in the computer, and *disk drives* that give the computer access to large amounts of information. The operating system controls all of these resources.

Time sharing

Larger computer systems allow more than one person to use the computer simultaneously. The operating system tries to give each person the illusion that he or she is the only one using the machine. This is termed *time sharing*. This is done by having the computer split its attention among the different users, somewhat like a parent dealing with many children at the same time. The operating system allocates the computer's resources, such as line printers and disk drives, among the people using the computer.

Operating systems may provide support for network features such as electronic mail or access to bulletin boards. Transmitting data across networks to or from other computers is sometimes handled by the operating system as well.

1.5.2   Compilers, interpreters, and programming languages

Hardware performs a limited number of simple functions. This is because hardware design makes a tradeoff between simple, fast functions (or instructions) and complex, slower instructions. Designers have opted for simple, fast instructions due to the performance improvements given to the computer. Having many complex, esoteric functions (like square root or logarithm) built into the hardware is not worthwhile due to their relative infrequency of use and the overall system performance decline they cause.[3]

Machine language versus high-level programming languages

It is possible to write programs using only the instructions that the hardware can perform. This hardware language is called *machine language*. Writing large, sophisticated programs in machine language is a tedious and rather unexciting process. This is due to the simple nature of machine languages. It is like trying to discuss your feelings about something important to you and only using kindergarten-level words. To remedy this, *high-level programming languages* were developed as a link between the hardware and programmers. Human or *natural languages* do not make good programming languages as they are very ambiguous and highly *context sensitive*. Words mean different things depending on their position or use in a sentence. Look at the following sentence's use of the word "can."

[3.] There are, however, custom hardware components like Digital Signal Processors that perform higher-level functions. These components are not for general computing use. For general computing, there has been a movement towards even smaller, simpler instructions. These designs, RISCs (Reduced Instruction Set Computers), are designed to have a small number of commonly used instructions, but run at very high speeds.

> Can the boss can me from the can factory because I can no longer can cans as fast as she can?

High-level programming languages are somewhat of a compromise between human-spoken languages and machine languages.

Compilers (translators) and *interpreters* (simulators) enable the computer to understand programs written in a high-level programming language. Compilers translate programs in these new languages into the machine language that the computer understands. Interpreters do not produce translated programs like compilers, but instead simulate the execution of programs to produce the desired results. This simulation results in slower execution of the programs as compared to a *compiled* program. Compilers and interpreters are programs that are written in a language that the machine already understands. Therefore, one can build languages on top of other existing languages. Look at mathematics for an analogy. Once you know the language of addition, subtraction, and so forth, you can build up to algebra, and then you can build calculus upon your knowledge of algebra and basic math operations.

Compilers and interpreters

The transition of programs to computer "understandable" machine language is diagramed below.

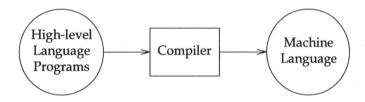

Details on how interpreters and compilers are written will be covered in Chapter 13.

1.5.3 Database management systems

Another subfield of computer science is *database management systems*. One of the major uses of computers is in storing, retrieving, and updating information (data). A collection of data is referred to as a *database*. Just as operating systems act as an environment for users, database management systems are programs that provide an environment that is tailored for the creation, modification, and access of data. This new environment is often less flexible than one that a compiler or interpreter creates with a new language. However, the database management environment has many specialized features that are unique to the problems that you encounter when dealing with large amounts of data. Using such a system, you can easily make complex queries of the data, add new information, or change existing information.

Database systems

For example, you may have a database of all the friends that you have with information on each person indicating their address, phone number, birth date, association to you, and other pertinent information. With a database management system you need not worry about how that information is represented in the machine. There are still some things you must decide about the representation, but they are all on a very high level. You could easily make queries into such a database to print all your friends who have a birthday this month, or print everyone who is between the ages of twenty and twenty-five, in the hiking club, and living in San Francisco or New York. More useful actions can be performed, such as easily removing everyone who lives in Los Angeles.

Database management systems will be covered in Chapter 12.

1.5.4 Artificial intelligence

Artificial intelligence

The most controversial field of computer science is *artificial intelligence*. Artificial intelligence deals with the simulation or modeling of "intelligence" on computers. It comprises many subfields that each address some aspect of intelligence. These include
- Natural language processing:
  Understanding, translating, and paraphrasing spoken languages such as English or German
- Machine learning:
  Learning new information from existing or newly obtained knowledge
- Problem solving:
  Solving tasks within realworld environments
- Expert systems:
  Embodying the knowledge of experts in a particular domain
- Robotics:
  Creating robots that can move about and function in real environments
- Vision:
  Recognizing three-dimensional objects given two-dimensional images
  Chapter 15 will focus on each of these subfields, touching upon their problems and accomplishments.

1.5.5 Soft computing

Soft computing

Soft computing deals with nonexact or *subsymbolic* information. The field comprises various fields, of which *fuzzy logic, neural networks*, and *genetic algorithms* are the most noteworthy.

Fuzzy logic

Fuzzy logic extends familiar, two-value logic that supports only true or false values, and extends it to incorporate *multivalued logic*. Multivalued logic lets one specify degrees of belief such that fuzzy concepts like tall, heavy, and small can be expressed more naturally. Fuzzy logic is primarily used to build fuzzy expert systems that are used often in control devices like antilock car brakes, washing machines, and subways.

Neural networks

Neural networks are loose simulations of neurons in the brain. They offer an alternate way of representing information from that used in traditional artificial intelligence, which uses *symbols* to represent knowledge. Neural networks represent information subsymbolically. Information is distributed throughout the network. This has advantages and disadvantages over symbolic, exact representations.

Genetic algorithms simulate the process of evolutionary change. Information is represented as *chromosomes* that can change through *crosslinking* (two chromosomes splitting to form two new chromosomes) and *mutation* (a piece of a chromosome changing). The chromosomes that perform better are kept, and the system evolves over time to yield a good solution to the problem at hand. Genetic algorithms work by going through a series of evolutionary changes until the system performs at a certain level.

Genetic algorithms

Chapter 16 covers these subfields of soft computing, giving examples of each in Scheme.

1.5.6 Graphics
Computer graphics involves modeling and simulating two- and three-dimensional objects on the computer. Examples of objects that have been modeled in simulated environments include aircraft in flight, ships, automobile aerodynamics, stress and metal fatigue, CAT (Computer Axial Tomography) and MRI (Magnetic Resonance Imaging) for medical examination of bones and tissues.

Computer graphics

The field of computer-aided design (CAD), which helps people with the design of anything from buildings to bolts, depends on computer graphics. Architects use CAD tools to design buildings and show clients how the building will look once it is completed. In fact some of these tools even allow you to do a virtual walk-through of the building to get a feel for the space and the lighting.

Much work is done in graphics for the movie industry. This work may involve augmenting realworld scenes with lifelike, realistic special effects. Another avenue is creating fantastic special effects that would be impossible to create in the physical world, such as flying faster than the speed of light or descending into a black hole.

1.5.7 Exercises
1.1 Describe the following terms in your own words:

> computer
> hardware
> software
> operating system
> compiler
> database management system
> artificial intelligence
> soft computing
> graphics

1.6   Subfields Within Hardware

Hardware

The following list gives some of the major subfields within hardware:

- Integrated circuit design and manufacturing
- Circuit design
- Computer architecture

The electronics of modern day computers are made up of integrated circuits. These are small electronic devices that perform very specialized functions. Integrated circuits are made from silicon that is microscopically etched. The heart of most computers, the *central processing unit*, is typically a single integrated circuit.

Circuit design involves the combination of integrated circuits and simpler electronic components to create electronic circuitry that can perform more sophisticated functions. Computers are made up of integrated circuits and other simpler electronic devices that are joined on a circuit board—sometimes called a *motherboard*.

Computer architecture deals with the design of electronic circuits to create functioning computers. There are numerous design decisions that affect the capabilities, cost, and speed of the computer.

1.7   Subfields Within both Software and Hardware

There are areas within computer science that are closely tied to both hardware and software. These include

- Parallel processing and concurrent programming
- Networks and communication
- Fault tolerance

Parallel programming

The part of the computer that does the calculations and decision making is called the *processor*. Parallel processors are computers that have more than one processor. This enables calculations to occur simultaneously (in parallel). Concurrent programming addresses the problems of creating computer programs that take advantage of these parallel architectures. The parts of programs that can be run simultaneously are sent to different processors, such that they can all be run in less time than if they were run sequentially on a single processor.

Network issues

The widespread growth of networks such as the Internet (introduced in section 1.3) has placed demands on researchers to improve the capabilities of networks. There are both hardware concerns dealing with the electronics and circuitry of the connections between the machines, and software concerns focusing on the communication of information from machine to machine. Speed, security, and information integrity are areas of concern in network hardware and software. In addition, there are theoretical aspects of networks concentrating on efficient routing and layout of the networks.

Fault tolerance

Fault tolerance deals with the creation and testing of hardware and software that can handle erroneous or unexpected situations gracefully. Such robustness is critical with many applications, especially when lives depend on the proper functioning of the system, such as computer-controlled antilock brake systems in cars or air traffic control systems in airports.

1.7.1 Exercises

1.2   List some applications for which computer networks would be useful.

1.3   List some products using computers that must be fault tolerant systems.

1.4   List some applications where parallel processors would be beneficial in improving the performance of the system.

1.8 Summary

- General purpose computers can be programmed, have control functions to make decisions, can perform numerical calculations, and have a great deal of memory.
- Hardware makes up the electronics of computers.
- The programs that can run on computers are referred to as software.
- Operating systems provide a level of abstraction allowing various useful actions to be easily performed.
- Operating systems handle many of the peripheral devices and shared resources of computer systems such as terminals, keyboards, line printers, and disk drives.
- Compilers translate high-level languages into machine language that can be run on the computer.
- Interpreters simulate the execution of programs written in high-level languages.
- Database management systems provide a specialized environment for organizing and searching through large amounts of data.
- Artificial intelligence includes those aspects of software that involve the simulation of some aspect of cognition.
- Soft computing involves the representation of multivalued and subsymbolic information that is needed to handle information that is not sharply definable.
- Computer graphics is concerned with modeling two- and three-dimensional objects.
- Hardware subfields cover the spectrum from the creation of integrated circuits to the design of computers using such components.
- Parallel processing, networking, and fault tolerance are three fields that cross the boundaries into both hardware and software.

1.9   Additional Reading

Brookshear, J.G. (1997). *Computer Science: an Overview, Fifth Edition*, Addison-Wesley, Reading, MA.

Goldschlager, L. and Lister, A. (1988). *Computer Science: a Modern Introduction.* Second edition, Prentice Hall, Englewood Cliffs, NJ.

CHAPTER *2*

PROBLEM SOLVING AND PROBLEM ABSTRACTION

2.1 Problem Solving

People spend a great deal of time solving problems, often without consciously thinking about them. For example, when you go grocery shopping, you may encounter and solve a number of problems without paying attention to them. You might be looking for cream of asparagus soup. You have techniques that you use to find this particular flavor of soup. You probably don't look for it among the frozen pizzas. You may ask someone where it can be found to narrow your search. You might ask, "Where is the cream of asparagus soup?" and be told, "The soups are on aisle four," in which case you would go there and search among the soups. You probably wouldn't respond with, "That's fine, but I want to know where the *cream of asparagus* soup is!"

A typical problem-solving situation

There are countless examples of problem-solving situations that seem trivial. There are other circumstances that we might actually consider problems because they involve more thought. These include solving math word problems, such as "if 12 ounces of soup costs 59 cents and 20 ounces of the same soup costs one dollar, which is a better bargain?"

Computers have less general knowledge than humans do. This is why it is necessary to supply incredibly detailed information to instruct computers to carry out even seemingly simple or obvious tasks. What you should try to develop in this chapter are the skills involved in taking an English problem description and solving it by creating a detailed set of instructions that a machine can follow. The rest of this book will show the specifics of creating computer program solutions to problems, in other words, going from problem descriptions in English to working computer solutions.

Being specific

Understanding the system

The first requirement in problem solving is a thorough knowledge of the capabilities of the system with which you are trying to solve the problem. You typically need not know how the system works, just what it can do. For example, you can instruct a friend to get to your house without having the foggiest idea about how her brain works. You do know, however, the level of instructions she can follow. The instructions that you would give to a two-year-old differ from those you would give to an adult. Similarly, you need to know what computers can do and what they can understand before you begin to instruct them to carry out specific tasks.

2.2   What Computers Can Do

For the most part, computers are stupid machines. They can perform only a limited number of simple operations, usually on the order of fifty to a few hundred. Examples of such computer operations or instructions include addition, subtraction, checking if a number is less than zero, and repeating a collection of instructions. Most of these operations deal with numerical computations or control—deciding what to do next. Even multiplication may not be a standard operation but instead be implemented as a series of additions.

At this point it may seem a wonder computers do the things that they do. After all, computers help people make business decisions, predict the weather, and compute square roots of large numbers in less time than it takes us to write the numbers on a piece of paper. How can this be?

Central processing unit

The picture of the computer that many people have is that of a sophisticated, powerful machine. However, the picture that has been painted here is that of a rather dismal idiot savant. What has been illustrated is the core of the computer, the *central processing unit* or *CPU*. You don't normally see this low level of the machine; instead, you see a much different environment, which is the result of various levels built upon the basic CPU. Each level allows more complex, specialized actions to be performed. As discussed in Chapter 1, an operating system is one such level of abstraction that can be built upon the underlying CPU. This provides a new environment with a new means of communicating with the hardware. Computers such as Macintoshes, PCs, and video games (that have computers) all have environments that are built upon the hardware. These environments make the computer appear powerful and sophisticated.

Our mental development can provide an analogy. As infants, we had fewer capabilities, but each year we learned more and more, adding levels of knowledge. One such level was language, which gave us the ability to communicate and to read this textbook. If we look at the brain as a CPU, as infants, our brains performed only simple actions. The more we learned, the more abstract and powerful our brains became.

2.3 Computer Languages

Machine language

Just as humans understand language, so do computers. And computers, like humans, can understand more than one language. Computers typically use two levels of language. The lowest level is the *machine language*. This language is used to instruct the computer hardware to carry out its basic CPU functions. The next level consists of languages that are built up from the machine language. These languages have particular characteristics and capabilities just as our spoken languages do. Some African languages do not have words for concepts like ownership. Indonesian has many different greetings/blessings to say to someone depending on the time of day. Similarly, each computer language has its areas of specialty and weakness. A computer language has a particular mind set or programming style. If you speak more than one language, you know that there are different ways of thinking or expressing concepts or ideas in each language. Similarly, two solutions to the same problem, each solved using a different computer language, can be different in form and approach.

Computer languages are becoming more powerful and sophisticated; however, no computer language approaches human spoken language. The ambiguity and complexity of our spoken languages has made it extremely difficult to create a computer program that can understand them. This creates a gap that must be bridged. How do we go from English problems to computer language solutions? The next section will focus on this issue.

Summary

Let's review what has been covered:

- CPUs perform only a set of very simple operations.
- Levels of abstraction built upon the CPU make computers more powerful and easier to use.
- Programming languages are a level of abstraction that provide an environment that is closer to the way we think.
- It is from this programming language environment that we will build programs to solve our needs and to extend the computer's capabilities further.

2.4 Problem Abstraction

Knowing the problem domain

The first step in going from English problems to computer solutions is thinking about the problem in terms of the environment in which we will solve the problem. This environment may be some programming language environment. It may be the lowest-level machine language. It may be a database management system. Regardless of the environment, we must think of the problem in terms of what the environment allows and understands. To do this, we need to have a solid understanding of the environment.

The environment in which we will begin problem solving exercises is a robot simulation. This robot, named Bob, lives in an artificial world that contains colored blocks. The blocks are movable and stackable. The robot understands the following commands:

Robot commands

- move forward *distance* meters
- turn left *number* degrees
- turn right *number* degrees
- pick up *object*
- drop *object*
- look
- lower pen
- raise pen
- memorize *sequence-name instruction-sequence*
- perform *sequence-name*

The words in *italics* represent *variables*—actual values would be used in their place in commands to the robot.

The goal is to instruct the robot to carry out simple tasks in this world. The first task is to move one of the objects in this artificial world.

It's a good idea to learn the capabilities and limitations of the system in which you must program. Let's try some of the commands and see what effect they have. In the robot sessions that follow, our requests to the robot will be shown in *italics*. The robot's replies will be shown in **boldface**.

```
request: look
green block at 0 degrees, 3 meters away
yellow block at 90 degrees, 2 meters away
```

The robot returns the position of the blocks in a standard way, telling us the color of the block and its position in degrees and meters from the robot. In this world, 0 degrees is straight up (north), 90 degrees is right (east), 180 degrees is down (south), and 270 degrees is left (west).

The diagram below illustrates the initial robot world. The robot is facing up (north).

green

robot   yellow

Let's try some more commands:

```
request: pick up green block
Error: green block is not reachable

request: drop yellow block
Error: yellow block is not in my possession

request: turn right 90 degrees
right turn complete

request: look
green block at 270 degrees 3 meters away
yellow block at 0 degrees 2 meters away

request: turn left 90 degrees
left turn complete

request: move forward 2 meters
move complete

request: look
green block at 0 degrees 1 meter away
yellow block at 135 degrees 2.83 meters away
```

The memorize command is used to name a sequence of steps that we wish the robot to perform later. This is useful to abbreviate an often-needed sequence or to create a logical collection of steps that help make the overall program more readable. The memorized sequence of commands is performed when a perform command is issued.

Memorized sequences

```
request: memorize go-back-2-turnaround-look
        turn left 180 degrees
        move forward 2 meters
        turn left 180 degrees
        look
        end
okay

request: perform go-back-2-turnaround-look
left turn complete
move complete
left turn complete
green block at 0 degrees 3 meters away
yellow block at 90 degrees 2 meters away
```

The robot world looks the same at the end of this sequence of commands as it did at the start.

The robot was instructed to turn to the right, look, then turn back, then move up towards the green block. After that the robot memorized a sequence to turn around to the left, move two meters, turn back around, and look. Next the robot performed these memorized steps, thereby returning the robot to its starting position.

Now that we have an idea of what the robot can do, let's get back to the task at hand—making the robot move an object.

2.4.1   Example: Move the yellow block up three meters

This problem can be thought of as a sequence of operations:

- move to the yellow block
- pick up the yellow block
- move up three meters
- drop the yellow block

Initially the robot is facing up towards the green block. To move the robot to the yellow block, the robot must face in that direction.
Moving to the yellow block entails the following:

```
turn right 90 degrees
move forward 2 meters
```

Picking up the yellow block can be done with one command:

```
pick up yellow block
```

Moving up three meters is done as

```
turn left 90 degrees
move forward 3 meters
```

Dropping the yellow block is expressed as

```
drop yellow block
```

Putting it all together, we get

```
turn right 90 degrees
move forward 2 meters
pick up yellow block
turn left 90 degrees
move forward 3 meters
drop yellow block
```

2.4.2   Ambiguities

Recognizing ambiguities

The above problem presented a subtle ambiguity. The problem was to move the yellow block up three meters. The ambiguity lies in the problem statement and in the operations of the robot. First, in the problem statement, no mention is made as to whether the yellow block could be shifted to the left or right when it is moved up three meters. Second, the description of how the robot picks up and drops objects was not very detailed. Does the robot need to be touching the object to pick it up? Does the robot need to be facing the object to pick it up? Does the robot drop the object in the reverse manner as it was picked up, or below, behind, or to the side? Before we can respond to any clarification in the problem statement, we must be certain of these questions about the robot.

Let's assume that the robot must be touching and facing the object before it can be picked up and that the object is dropped in front of the robot. We'll refine the problem statement to be moving the yellow block such that it is three meters directly above its previous position; hence, there should be no final left or right shifting of the block. Now do we have enough information to solve the problem?

We can review the steps we took. Moving to the yellow block is still okay, as is picking up the yellow block. Moving up three meters seems okay, but there is an ambiguity lurking here. Does the object stay in front of the robot as it moves and turns?

Let's assume that it does. By turning left, the block is moved so that it is no longer to the right but above the robot. When the robot moves three meters, the block has moved more than three meters from its original position, because the robot's turning the block moved it up an amount equal to the diameter of the robot. The diagram below should help you visualize what is going on. The dotted block labeled *block start* represents the yellow block's initial position. The robot has moved next to it from its initial position. The different dashed shapes represent different positions of the yellow block during its movements.

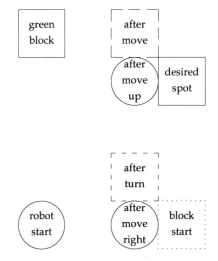

The block moves immediately above the robot to the position labeled *after turn* after the robot rotates left. Next the robot moves up taking the block ahead of it. If the robot drops the yellow block after moving it up three meters, it ends up in the location indicated by the dashed box labeled *after move*. The position where we would like the block to be dropped is labeled *desired spot*. To get to this position, the robot must turn to the right by 90 degrees, effectively undoing the left turn taken before the robot moved up three meters.

The corrected commands are given below:

```
turn right 90 degrees
move forward 2 meters
pick up yellow block
turn left 90 degrees
move forward 3 meters
turn right 90 degrees
drop yellow block
```

2.5   Pseudo Code

Representing solutions in pseudo code

Sometimes a problem is difficult to think of in terms of the commands of the system being used. In this case, we use an intermediary language known as *pseudo code*. Pseudo code lies between English and the environment in which we want our solution to be. There are no definite rules for how pseudo code must look. It is merely a description of the problem that comes closer to the desired solution. In the previous problem, our pseudo code was

```
move to the yellow block
pick up the yellow block
move up three meters
drop the yellow block
```

The following two problems give more examples of using pseudo code.

2.5.1   Example: Draw a two-by-two meter square around the yellow block

Before we begin this problem, we need to know the position of the robot in relation to the yellow block, the size of the robot and the yellow block, and the position of the robot's pen relative to the robot. Assume that the robot is facing up directly in front of the yellow block. Also assume that the blocks are one meter wide by one meter deep, that the robot is one meter in diameter, and that the pen is in the center of the robot. Thus the robot must follow a path immediately around the edge of the yellow box to make a two meter by two meter square. The steps to follow for this problem are

- have the robot lower the pen
- move the robot left one meter
- move the robot up two meters
- move the robot right two meters
- move the robot down two meters
- move the robot left one meter
- have the robot raise the pen

Trace out the robot's movements on the diagram below.

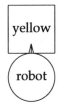

Below are the commands to move the robot. Above each command is a comment (a line beginning with a semicolon ";") that indicates the step involved. Comments are not interpreted as part of the program.

; have the robot lower the pen

```
lower pen
```

; move the robot (currently facing north) left one meter

```
turn left 90 degrees
move forward 1 meter
```

; move the robot (currently facing west) up two meters

```
turn right 90 degrees
move forward 2 meters
```

; move the robot (currently facing north) right two meters

```
turn right 90 degrees
move forward 2 meters
```

; move the robot (currently facing east) down two meters

```
turn right 90 degrees
move forward 2 meters
```

; move the robot (currently facing south) left one meter

```
turn right 90 degrees
move forward 1 meter
```

; have the robot (now facing west) raise the pen

```
raise pen
```

The diagram below shows the trace of the robot's motions. The robot is shown in the end position. He is facing left. The dashed line represents the path the robot followed.

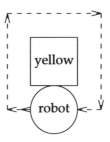

2.5.2   Exercises

2.1   How would you change the above program to have the robot travel counterclockwise?

2.2   Write a sequence of steps that instructs the robot to draw a triangle around the yellow block. Assume that the robot starts in the same position as in the last example. Make the triangle six meters on each side.

2.3   Assume that the robot is between the two blocks with the green block to the immediate left and the yellow block to the immediate right. In other words, the three objects are in a line, with both blocks touching the robot. Write a sequence of steps to command the robot to draw a rectangle around both blocks. What assumptions are you making in your solution?

2.6   Using Memorized Sequences

Simplifying code with memorized sequences

Memorized sequences provide a way to break down a problem into subproblems. This is extremely helpful with larger problems, since they can rapidly become incomprehensible. Also, collections of commands that need to be repeated in the solution can be repeated by invoking the memorized sequence multiple times. This saves a great deal of writing and helps eliminate errors.

2.6.1   Example: Write the robot's name—BOB

For this problem, let's assume that the robot is in an empty world, so we don't need to worry about running into blocks. Also assume that the robot begins at the lower left corner of what will become the "B" and that the robot is facing up. The diagram below shows what the name "BOB" should look like.

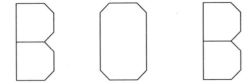

The initial pseudo code for this problem follows:
- draw the first "B"
- move into position for the "O"
- draw the "O"
- move into position for the second "B"
- draw the second "B"

Since we will be drawing two "B"s and they are fairly complex, the commands to draw a "B" should be memorized. Positioning the robot to draw the next letter can be implemented with a single memorized sequence if we design the drawing of letters such that the robot ends up in the same position relative to the letter being drawn each time. This makes it easier to join different parts of the program without having to worry about where the robot is and which direction he is facing. We will make sure that the robot is facing up and is at the left side of the baseline (lower left corner) of the letter at the start and end of printing each letter.

2.6.2 Refinement of pseudo code

Going from the above pseudo code to actual robot commands is more difficult in this problem than in the previous problems. The problem is sufficiently complex that we should do another pass through the pseudo code and refine it, adding more details.

A good place to start is to look for repetition and see whether memorized sequences would help. The top half of the "B" is the same as the bottom, so the commands to draw half a "B" can be a memorized sequence. Similarly, the same sequence can be used to draw the left and right halves of the "O" along a diagonal. Below are diagrams representing these pieces.

Looking for repetition

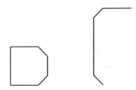

Now we can refine our previous pseudo code:

- draw the first "B"

  - draw the bottom half of the "B"
  - move into position for the upper half
  - draw the upper half of the "B"
  - move to the original starting position and direction

- move right to draw the next letter
- draw the "O"

  - draw the left half of the "O"
  - move into position for the right half
  - draw the right half of the "O"
  - move to the original starting position and direction

- move right to draw the next letter
- repeat the steps for the first "B"

The high-level steps (bulleted steps) can be implemented as memorized sequences. They provide a logical breakdown of the problem and eliminate the repetition in drawing "B"s and moving the robot into position to draw the next letter. Similarly, the commands to draw letter halves can be memorized sequences. We will begin with these half-letter sequences.

Just as we must insure that the robot is in proper position and orientation before drawing each letter, we must assume some standard before each letter half is drawn. Let's assume that the robot is in the proper position and facing the direction of the first line to draw; hence, the first action of a draw half-letter sequence will be to lower the pen and start drawing. It will be the job of the whole-letter drawing sequences to insure that the robot is in the proper position and orientation before invoking each memorized half-letter sequence.

```
; Robot is initially facing north, with the pen up.
memorize draw-half-of-B
    lower pen
    move forward 0.5 meters
    turn right 90 degrees
    move forward 0.4 meters
    turn right 45 degrees
    move forward 0.2 meters
    turn right 45 degrees
    move forward 0.25 meters
    turn right 45 degrees
    move forward 0.2 meters
    turn right 45 degrees
    move forward 0.4 meters
    raise pen
end
```

```
; Robot is oriented to draw the first line, with the pen up.
memorize draw-half-of-O
    lower pen
    move forward 0.2 meters
    turn right 45 degrees
    move forward 0.8 meters
    turn right 45 degrees
    move forward 0.2 meters
    turn right 45 degrees
    move forward 0.4 meters
    raise pen
end
```

Next, we can write memorized sequences to draw the "B" and "O" and move the robot into position for the next letter.

```
; Robot is initially at the lower left corner of the "B"
; facing north, with the pen up.
memorize draw-B
    ; draw lower half of "B" first
        perform draw-half-of-B
    ; set up for upper half of "B"
        turn right 90 degrees
        move forward 0.5 meters
    ; draw upper half of "B"
        perform draw-half-of-B
    ; return to starting position and direction
        turn left 90 degrees
        move forward 0.5 meters
        turn left 180 degrees
end

; Robot is initially at the lower left corner of the "O"
; facing north, with the pen up.
memorize draw-O
    ; set up for left half of "O"
        turn left 45 degrees
        perform draw-half-of-O
    ; set up for right half of "O"
        turn right 45 degrees
        perform draw-half-of-O
    ; return to starting position and direction
        turn right 90 degrees
end
```

Notice that after each letter is drawn the robot ends up facing north, so he must turn to the right to move to the proper position for the next letter and then face north again to draw the next letter. We can write a memorized sequence to implement these steps.

```
; Move robot to draw next letter.
memorize adjust-position
    turn right 90 degrees
    move forward 1 meter
    turn left 90 degrees
end
```

Putting the whole thing together, we have:

```
; Assume that the robot is facing up at the lower left corner
; of the first "B" with the pen up.
perform draw-B
perform adjust-position
perform draw-O
perform adjust-position
perform draw-B
perform adjust-position
```

2.6.3 Exercises

2.4   How could memorized sequences be used in the previous problem (drawing a box around the yellow block) to improve the solution?

2.5   Write pseudo code to write out the numbers zero through nine. Think of how memorized sequences could make the task easier.

2.6   What memorized sequences would be helpful in writing out the letters of the alphabet?

2.7   Write a memorized sequence to stack the yellow block on top of the green block. What assumptions must you make?

2.8   Write commands to switch the order of two blocks that are stacked one upon the other. Try to use memorized sequences to simplify things.

2.9   Think of some other commands that would give the robot more flexibility.

2.7   Adding Parameters to Memorized Sequences

Using parameters to make memorized sequences more general

Some of the robot's commands allow us to specify additional information, such as a distance to move or a number of degrees to turn. By making a simple change to the way we write memorized sequences, we can allow sequences that take such information. These additional values need names by which they can be referred within the definition of the sequence. These names are called *parameters*. For example, imagine the following new version of the sequence `adjust-position` from the previous problem:

```
; Move robot (facing up) distance meters to the right.
memorize metric-move-right (distance) meters
    turn right 90 degrees
    move forward distance meters
    turn left 90 degrees
end
```

This new memorized sequence has a parameter, `distance`, that indicates how many meters to move to the right. To invoke this new sequence to move four meters, use the following command:

```
perform metric-move-right 4 meters
```

This will perform the steps within `metric-move-right`, substituting the value 4 for the parameter `distance`. In this example, 4 is the *argument* to the performed sequence.

To enhance our system further, we can add mathematical functions to our commands. This way we could write sequences like the following:

Mathematical functions

```
; Move robot (facing up) distance feet to the right.
memorize nonmetric-move-right (distance) feet
    turn right 90 degrees
    move forward distance ÷ 3.28 meters
    turn left 90 degrees
end
```

There are approximately 3.28 feet in one meter, so dividing a distance given in feet by 3.28 gives the equivalent distance in meters such that `move forward` (which takes meters) can be invoked with the appropriate value.

The following command results in a move of 3 ÷ 3.28 = 0.915 meters:

```
perform nonmetric-move-right 3 feet
```

2.7.1 Exercises

2.10 Assume that the command `turn left` no longer works. Write a memorized sequence to perform a left turn using the command `turn right`.

2.11 Write a sequence that draws a square around a block in which the length of the side of a square is a parameter to the sequence. Assume that the value given will be large enough to draw a square around the block. Also assume that the robot is immediately below the middle of the block and is facing up.

2.12 Write a version of `draw-B` that takes a parameter for the height of the "B".

2.13 Describe the robot's actions when the following commands are invoked:

```
memorize mystery (number)
    turn left 90 degrees
    move forward number meters
    perform mystery number
end

perform mystery 2
```

2.14 What actions does the robot take when performing the sequence `fractal`?

```
memorize fractal (number)
    move forward number meters
    turn left 45 degrees
    perform fractal number ÷ 3
    turn right 90 degrees
    perform fractal number ÷ 3
    turn left 45 degrees
    move forward number meters
end
```

Hint: assume that the robot ignores the sequence `fractal` when *number* is less than 1. Try starting with *number* equal to 2, then try 6, and then 18.

2.8   Summary

The major issues of this chapter involve the steps to take when solving problems.
- Begin by disambiguating the problem.
  Any aspects that are not clearly defined should be resolved.
- Think of a solution to the problem using a sequence of abstract steps.
  These steps can be expressed as pseudo code.
- Refine the steps to the level of sophistication of the system on which your solution will run. This may involve several passes, each taking the solution closer to the level of the commands understood by the system.

CHAPTER 3

PROGRAMMING THE COMPUTER

3.1 The Scheme Environment

At this point we begin to use a real programming language to perform tasks and solve problems. The programming language used is Scheme, which is a dialect of LISP. LISP is an acronym for **LIS**t **P**rocessing. We will define what a list is and how Scheme goes about processing lists in Chapter 4.

Programming languages were introduced in Chapters 1 and 2 as environments that fill the gap between machine languages and natural languages, like English and Serbo-Croatian. In this chapter, we begin to explore the Scheme environment and what can be done within it. First we must develop an understanding of the Scheme environment.

Let's begin with four basic elements within Scheme: *numbers, symbols, variables*, and *functions*.

Basic components of Scheme

Numbers in Scheme are like the numbers with which you are familiar. Scheme has integers such as 42 and –87, real numbers such as 3.1415 and –2.69, and ratios such as $\frac{2}{3}$ (written in Scheme as 2/3).

Symbols are names. They can have values or can be used merely for their name. For example, john is a symbol. A sentence can be constructed in Scheme by joining symbols together, where each symbol represents a word in the sentence. Scheme is a symbolic processing language, meaning it is good at performing operations on symbols such as creating, transforming, and comparing symbols and collections of symbols.

Variables are symbols that have values associated with them. Remember when you worked on algebra problems that started with "let x be the number of goats in Farmer Bob's ranch"? In Scheme, x would be a *variable*. We can use the symbol myriam as a variable by giving it a value. Later we can reference or change the value of the variable myriam.

Functions perform operations. They are Scheme's equivalent to the commands of the robot world of Chapter 2. Some of the robot commands took arguments (e.g., `move forward` and `turn left`). Scheme functions can take arguments as well. This enables functions to give different results according to their arguments.

Most functions perform operations on values (arguments) and return a result. The basic four operators (+, −, ×, ÷) in calculators are analogous to Scheme functions, and the numbers to which these operators are applied correspond to arguments within Scheme. When we instruct the computer to carry out the actions of a function, we are *invoking* or *calling* the function.

Some texts refer to Scheme functions as *procedures*. Most programming languages use functions to denote objects that return one value when invoked, whereas procedures do not return a value explicitly. This book follows this naming convention, considering functions as objects that return only one value.

Scheme interpreter

The core of Scheme is the *interpreter*. The computer does not directly understand Scheme. It is only by virtue of the Scheme interpreter that the computer can respond to our Scheme requests and return understandable results. Requests are typed on the computer's keyboard. The interpreter receives the requests and sends the appropriate information to the computer, which performs the necessary operations and sends information back to the interpreter. The interpreter prints this information as a result that we can understand on the terminal screen. The following diagram illustrates these components[1]

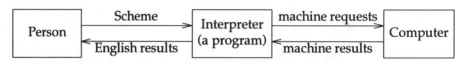

An analogy can be drawn to the way a human interpreter interacts with two speakers who do not speak each other's languages. In the example below an English and a French speaker communicate via an interpreter.

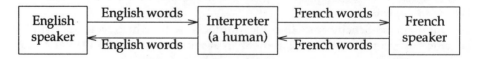

3.1.1   Example: Determining the price of an item with 6% tax added

To compute a tax amount, a function that can multiply numeric arguments together is needed. Fortunately, such a function exists and is called `*`. We need to know how to *invoke* functions with arguments and how to obtain the results.

Calling functions

Invoking (or calling) a function is done by enclosing the function name followed by its arguments in parentheses. Hence, the function call (`* 7.95 1.06`) multiplies 7.95 by 1.06 and returns the product, 8.42.

---

[1] The operating system normally plays a role in this diagram as well, acting between the computer and interpreter. It was left out to keep the focus on the interpreter.

Before function calls can be typed into the computer, the Scheme interpreter must be invoked. Consult your instructor, system administrator, (or Scheme software manual if you have a personal computer and a Scheme interpreter) to determine how to start up Scheme. There is no standard way to exit from Scheme. Try entering (exit) or (quit) or checking if there is a menu command to exit Scheme.

Starting and stopping Scheme

Once the interpreter has been invoked, a *prompt* is displayed. The prompt indicates that the interpreter is ready to receive requests. This book uses the greater-than sign, >, as a prompt. Your prompt may be different. Throughout this book, the prompt and the interpreter's responses will be shown in **boldface**. The user's input will be displayed in *italics*. Comments appear as text following a semicolon. The comments shown are merely to provide information to the reader. They do not need to be entered for these examples to work.

Interacting with Scheme

When (* 7.95 1.06) is entered in the interpreter, the product is printed. What you will see is

> *(* 7.95 1.06)*
8.42

Mistakes to Avoid

Don't forget the space between the function name and its arguments (the values upon which the function acts). Thus,

(*7.95 1.06)

results in an error. Try it on your computer.

3.2 Numerical Functions

Scheme supports the four basic math operators found on calculators, as well as a host of other arithmetic functions. The table below is a partial list of these functions and the operations they perform.

function	arguments	return value
+	0 or more	sum of arguments
-	1 or more	difference of arguments in left to right order
*	0 or more	product of arguments
/	1 or more	quotient of arguments in left to right order
max	1 or more	maximum of arguments
min	1 or more	minimum of arguments
truncate	*num*	integer part of *num* (digits to the left of the decimal)
sqrt	*num*	square root of *num*, $\sqrt{num}$
abs	*num*	absolute value of *num*, $\lvert num \rvert$
expt	*num power*	exponentiation (*num* raised to *power*), num^{power}
remainder	*num1 num2*	remainder of *num1* when divided by *num2*

Simple arithmetic functions

Note: the functions - and / take at most two arguments in some implementations of Scheme. If + and * are called with no arguments, 0 and 1 (the arithmetic and multiplicative identities) are returned respectively. Given one argument, they merely return that argument. If given one argument, - returns its negation, and / returns its reciprocal. When min or max are called with one argument, that argument is returned. To get a better idea of how these functions work, look at the following examples:

```
> (*)
1

> (+)
0

> (+ 3)
3

> (* 4.56)
4.56

> (- 3)
-3

> (/ 4)
1/4                          ; a ratio is returned

> (- 2 3 4)                  ; computes 2 − 3 − 4
-5

> (/ 2 3 4)                  ; computes 2 / 3 / 4
1/6                          ; ratios are always reduced to lowest terms

> (max -24 8 -3 -62)
8

> (min -24 8 -3 -62)
-62

> (truncate 18.5)
18

> (truncate -8.7)
-8

> (sqrt 49)
7.0

> (expt 2 3)
8

> (remainder 5 3)
2
```

```
> (remainder 3 4)
3
```

The last example may be confusing. It involves understanding integer division, which requires that the answer be an integer. This is done by truncating the real division answer. Dividing 3 by 4 gives us 0.75, which when truncated is 0. This means that we must subtract 0×4 from 3, leaving 3; hence, the remainder is 3. If we were to make a diagram of this, it would look like

Integer division and remainders

$$\begin{array}{r} 0 \text{ rem } 3 \\ 4\overline{)\,3} \\ -0 \\ \hline 3 \end{array}$$

3.2.1 Common errors when calling functions

Many types of errors can occur, even at this early stage of learning to program. It is easy to get frustrated thinking that the machine doesn't work when an error message is given. Rather than give up, hit the computer, wish you had never taken a computer class, or try to get your day job back, it's best to take a deep breath and actually read the error message. Not everything in the message may be helpful, but often you can learn what caused the problem. Since each implementation of Scheme has its own way of handling error messages, it is impossible to give all possible errors that you might encounter. The important thing is to be aware of the types of errors that can arise and be familiar with the error messages given by your system.

Some of the more common errors that can occur and the reasons they occur are given below:

Error messages

- Too many arguments:
  This is often caused by having a mistaken understanding of the arguments that the function takes or forgetting a parenthesis after the last argument.
- Too few arguments:
  This can be caused by a mistaken understanding of the arguments that the function takes or by including an extra parenthesis before the last argument.
- Invalid function name:
  This is most often a spelling mistake or simply using the wrong name for a function (e.g., using `power` instead of `expt`).
- Type clash:
  A type clash is a mismatch of the value types (e.g., integer or real) that a function allows. For example, `remainder` works with integers and not real numbers.
- No output:
  This is most likely due to missing right parentheses. Try entering one or more right parentheses until you get a response.

Below are examples of these errors.

```
> (abs 3 4)
Error: Too many arguments: (abs 3 4)

> (-)
Error: Too few arguments: (-)

> (power 3 4)
Error: Unbound variable: POWER

> (remainder 3 4.2)
Error: Expected INTEGER

> (+ 3 (* 4 5)
```

For this last input, the interpreter will not return a value, nor will it print another prompt. This is because it is waiting for the second right parenthesis to end the + function call. As a general rule if you are waiting a long time for a response, try typing in some right parentheses.

Not all error messages are as readable as those given above. Learning how to read complex error messages is an important skill; it can save you a great deal of frustration and wasted time.

3.2.2   Exercises

3.1   What do the function calls below return when typed into the Scheme interpreter?

```
(- 4)

(/ 4)

(+ 4 2 3)

(- 4 2 3)

(- 4 -2 -3)

(/ 24 6 2)

(expt 4 3)

(remainder 7 3)

(remainder 3 7)
```

3.2   What do the function calls below return? Some of them may produce errors.

```
(sqrt 9 16)

(sqrt 9 + 16)

(-2 4)

(*2 3 4)

(+)

(-)

(*)
```

```
(/)
(+ 3)
(remainder 4.2 1.7)
```

3.2.3 Function composition

Functions can be *composed* (combined). For example, the price with 6% tax on the sum of $12.69, $186.34, and $2.74 can be expressed in Scheme as follows:

Composing functions

```
> (* (+ 12.69 186.34 2.74) 1.06)
213.8762
```

The three prices are added first, and then their sum is multiplied by 1.06. Only one value, the product, is returned as the value of the function call. Notice that the sum is not printed; it is only computed as part of the final multiplication calculation.

In most instances, wherever an argument is expected, a function call can take its place. The outermost function is calculated last and its value is printed. This mechanism will be explained in the next section on the evaluator.

3.3 The Evaluator

Function calls, variables, and numbers all can be entered into the interpreter and evaluated. The generic name for anything that can be evaluated is an *expression*. Another name used instead of expression is *s-expression*. This stands for *symbolic* expression.

Expressions and s-expressions

We've already written some simple expressions in Scheme. Now let's get a better understanding of how Scheme works and learn more about existing features of the system.

The Scheme *evaluator* is the heart of every Scheme system. The evaluator gets your input requests and evaluates them according to the following rules:
- numbers evaluate to themselves
- function calls are evaluated in the following manner:
    the arguments are evaluated;
    if errors occur, an error message is printed;
    otherwise,
        the function is applied to the evaluated arguments;
        the result is returned

The workings of the evaluator

Notice that in defining the evaluation of a function, one of the steps is to evaluate the arguments to the function. Evaluating the arguments allows us to use function calls as arguments to functions. If Scheme only allowed numbers as arguments, it could have much simpler evaluation rules. The definition we have used includes the term it is defining; this is a *recursive* definition. We examine recursion in Chapter 6.

Evaluating arguments

Another term to pay attention to in the definition of evaluate is *apply*. Applying a function to its evaluated arguments means that the action of the function is performed on the arguments. This yields a result, which is then returned as the

Applying the function

value of the function call.

Let's use some examples to see what goes on in the evaluator. Once again, the user's input is in *italics*, the computer's output is in **boldface**, and explanations of what the evaluator does is in regular type preceded by semicolons.

> *42*   ; numbers evaluate to themselves
42

> *-18.4*   ; negative and real numbers are numbers too
-18.4

> *(+ 1 2)*   ; this is a function call, and + is a valid function
3   ; 1 evaluates to 1, and 2 to 2
                          ; applying + to 1 and 2 yields 3

> *(+ (* 2 3) 4)*   ; this is a function call, and + is a valid function
10   ; (* 2 3) is the first argument to be evaluated
                              ; * is a valid function
                              ; its arguments 2 and 3 evaluate to 2 and 3
                              ; applying * to 2 and 3 yields 6
                          ; the second argument, 4, evaluates to 4
                          ; lastly, + is applied to 6 and 4, yielding 10

3.3.1 Exercises

3.3   Write out the steps the evaluator takes when evaluating the following function calls:

```
(sqrt (+ 9 7))

(* -3 (+ (* 2 3) 4))
```

3.4   To what do the function calls below evaluate? Some of them may produce errors.

```
(+ 4 (- 3) - 2)

(+ (- 3) (/ 2))

(+ (* 2 3) (- 8))
```

3.3.2 Example: Compute your income tax

To compute income tax, assuming a fixed tax rate of 15%, we'll use the following formula:

$$tax = (work\text{-}income + interest\text{-}income - standard\text{-}deduction\,) \times 0.15$$
$$- (withholding + tax\text{-}credits)$$

Assume the actual values for this formula are

work-income	$25,174.65
interest-income	$132.67
standard-deduction	$6,050.00
withholding	$3,673.83
tax-credits	$125.00

We can write the formula in Scheme in one of two ways. One way is to think of the exact sequence of steps that must be taken, beginning with the first operation, then the second, and so on. Alternatively, we may view the computation more abstractly, beginning with the highest-level operation to be performed, then continuing with a sequence of refinements leading to simple operations that can be entered into the interpreter.

These are such common means for problem solving that they have special names, *bottom-up* and *top-down* design, respectively. One approach is not necessarily better than the other for all problems, but for certain problems one approach may lead to a solution with less mental effort than the other approach would. Often it is a matter of what works best for the individual programmer. For complex tasks, both techniques are often used together. We will see examples of this when we begin writing larger programs.

Design approaches

3.4 Bottom-Up Design

Let's create a bottom-up solution. We start with the bottommost items, in other words, with the first actions that must be performed. The first computation is to determine the taxable income. In Scheme, we would write

```
>  (+ 25174.65 132.67 -6050)
19257.3
```

Notice that we didn't use commas when entering numbers. Commas are never used with numbers in Scheme; however, the decimal point is needed. We entered a negative number for the standard deduction because it is subtracted from the two income amounts. Scheme allows a mixture of real numbers and integers.

Specifying numbers in Scheme

Next, the tax to pay (tax debit) is the product of the total taxable income and the tax rate. Recall that the arguments to a function may be function calls themselves.

```
>  (* (+ 25174.65 132.67 -6050) 0.15)
2888.6
```

The next step is to determine the total credits.

```
>  (+ 3673.83 125)
3798.83
```

Lastly, we subtract the total credits from the total debits.

```
>  (- (* (+ 25174.65 132.67 -6050) 0.15) (+ 3673.83 125))
-910.232
```

We get $910.23 back!

A bottom-up approach involves building up to the solution, using each step along the way as part of the next step toward the solution. We did not have to enter each of these lines into the interpreter. All of the preliminary work could have been done on paper. The partial results returned at each step could have been used directly in obtaining the next result, so that the last step could have been

```
>  (- 2888.6 3798.83)
-910.23
```

A longer approach was shown so that each step along the way could be seen and partial results could be generated to confirm that no mistakes (especially with parentheses) were made along the way.

The parentheses are extremely important. You can't use extra parentheses to make it look nicer, or fewer because it already looks too ugly.

3.5   Top-Down Design

Abstraction

Now let's try the top-down approach. In top-down design, the problem is first looked at from higher levels beginning with the most abstract definition that can succinctly describe the solution. In this case, it breaks down to looking at the amount of tax due as being equivalent to the difference of total debits and total credits. In other words,

tax-due = *total-debits* – *total-credits*

Refinement

Next, a process of refinement is employed to add more details to the solution. We need to define *total-debits* and *total-credits*. *total-debits* is the product of *taxable-income* and the tax rate, 0.15. *total-credits* is the sum of *withholding* and *tax-credits*.

tax-debits = *taxable-income* × 0.15
tax-credits = *withholding* + *tax-credits*

We know what all these values are except *taxable-income*, which is the sum of *work-income* and (*interest-income* minus *standard-deduction*). In the bottom-up example above we simply added three values rather than express a sum and a difference. The same can be done here.

Putting everything together and typing it into the evaluator yields

```
>  (- (* (+ 25174.65 132.67 -6050) 0.15) (+ 3673.83 125))
-910.232
```

Top-down design starts with an abstract definition of the problem. The final solution is reached by refining this to the level of Scheme. This approach lets you ignore the details of the problem at first.

The differences between top-down and bottom-up design and the advantages of one over another will become more apparent as the problems get more complex. Try out both approaches to develop your understanding of them.

3.5.1 Exercises

3.5   What are some of the advantages of bottom-up design?

3.6   What are some of the advantages of top-down design?

3.7   Do you prefer bottom-up or top-down design?

3.8   Develop solutions in Scheme to the problems below. Try using both top-down and bottom-up approaches.
- Quadratic formula:

$$root\,1 = \frac{-b + \sqrt{b^2 - 4ac}}{2a} \quad \text{and} \quad root\,2 = \frac{-b - \sqrt{b^2 - 4ac}}{2a}$$

where $a = 3$, $b = 6$, and $c = 2$.

- Distance between two points:

$$distance = \sqrt{(x_1 - x_2)^2 + (y_1 - y_2)^2}$$

where $x_1 = 5$, $x_2 = -4$, $y_1 = -3$, and $y_2 = 6$.

- Pythagorean theorem:

$$hypotenuse = \sqrt{side1^2 + side2^2}$$

where $side1 = 3.7$ and $side2 = 5.4$.

- Evaluating polynomials:

$$y = 2x^3 - 4x^2 + 8x - 2$$

where $x = 6$.

3.9   Earthquakes are measured using the Richter scale. Values on the Richter scale can be translated into seismic energy (in ergs) using the following formula:[2]

$$10^{(11.8 + 1.5 Richter\_value)}$$

Calculate the strength (in ergs) of the 1906 San Francisco earthquake, which measured approximately 8.25 on the Richter scale.

3.10 Dividing the seismic energies of earthquakes, one finds that an increase of one unit on the Richter scale corresponds to a 31.6 time increase in seismic energy. Thus, an earthquake reading 4.4 on the Richter scale is 31.6 times stronger than a 3.4 earthquake. Another way of looking at this is that it takes 31.6 earthquakes that measure 3.4 on the Richter scale to equal one 4.4

[2.] This formula comes from Bruce A. Bolt's book, *Earthquakes*.

earthquake in seismic energy.

Compute the number of 5.0 earthquakes it takes to equal one 8.25 earthquake. The formula to compute the order of magnitude difference in seismic energy between two earthquakes is:

$$31.6^{(big\_quake - small\_quake)}$$

3.11 Compute the time it would take to reach the moon if you could drive straight there at 130 kilometers per hour. The moon is 384,000 kilometers from the Earth. Assume that you don't need to stop for gas along the way.

3.12 Compute the time it would take to walk around the Earth along the equator. The Earth is 12,640 kilometers in diameter and the circumference of a sphere is the diameter times π, which is approximately 3.1416. Assume an average walking speed of 3 kilometers per hour and that it is possible to walk around the Earth.

3.6   Variables

In a calculator, the memory key stores a value that can be retrieved. In computer programming, it is useful to have many such memory keys; they are called *variables*. To keep track of which variable holds which value, each must be named in some fashion. You can create a virtually unlimited number of variables.[3]

define

To create a variable, use `define`. It takes a variable name and its value as arguments. For example, to create a variable called `tax-rate` with value 0.15, use

```
> (define tax-rate 0.15)
??
```

Binding values to variables

`define` *binds* a variable to a value. Binding associates a value with a variable so that the value can be referenced by name using the variable name. `define` returns an undefined value, which is shown as `??` in this text. Your version of Scheme may return a different value. Some Scheme interpreters return the variable name.

Once a variable has been defined, its value can be retrieved by simply entering the name of the variable.

```
> tax-rate
0.15
```

Evaluator rules for variables
Unbound variables

This extends our definition of the evaluator to include that variables evaluate to their current bound values.

If an unbound variable is evaluated, an error message will occur. It may look like

---

[3] The limitation here is implementation dependent. It depends on such factors as available memory on the computer, and the implementor's design decisions and whims.

```
> taxrate
Error: Unbound variable: taxrate
```

Your version of Scheme may print `Undefined variable` or some similar message.

Mistakes to Avoid

Undefined variable errors are fairly common. If you don't understand why an error message was given, be sure to check the spelling of the variable you are trying to evaluate as well as the call to `define` used to create it. Chances are you misspelled the variable in one of those instances.

It is possible to rebind a variable. This is convenient if you bound it to the wrong value beforehand or want to change the value to get different results. The `define` above bound `tax-rate` to 0.15. We can change this binding as follows:

Redefining variables

```
> (define tax-rate 0.10)
??

> tax-rate
0.10
```

In this case, 0.10 is returned. Each successive `define` to the same variable rebinds that variable.[4]

To get the negative of a variable's value you cannot simply put a - in front of the variable name to make it negative. Instead, use the function - with your variable as in: `(- debt)`. The examples below illustrate what happens:

Negating variables

```
> (define debt 49)
??

> -debt
Error: Unbound variable: -debt

> - debt
<Procedure: ->
49

> (- debt)
-49

> debt
49
```

[4.] The preferred way to change a variable that has already been defined is using the function `set!`. For example:

```
(set! tax-rate 0.10)
```

3.6.1 Symbol and variable names

Rules for symbol names

Symbols are the names of variables. Symbol names can be made up of upper- or lower-case letters, numbers, and any of the characters given below:

```
+ - * / $ % ^ & _ = < > ~ . ! ? :
```

Case insensitive

Scheme is *case insensitive*; it treats upper- and lower-case characters in symbols as the same. Therefore, the names `foo`, `FOO`, and `FoO` all refer to the same symbol. A symbol name cannot begin with a number or a period. For example, `10000maniacs`, `3.14pies`, and `.5bite` are not valid symbol names. However, `all10000maniacs`, `three.14pies`, and `half-a-bite` are legal symbol names.

Keywords

A *keyword* is a symbol that has a special meaning in Scheme; a keyword cannot be used as a variable name. Examples of keywords are `define`, `and`, `or`, `begin`, `case`, `cond`, `if`, `else`, `delay`, `do`, `lambda`, `let`, `quote`, and `unquote`. There are a few others, but they are not English words.

Choosing variable names

It is best to use meaningful variable names, rather than one-letter names or names that do not explain what the variable represents. Such *mnemonic* names help make your Scheme code more readable and understandable. Here are some examples of good mnemonic names:

```
> (define sum-of-squares (+ (expt 3 2) (expt 4 2)))
??

> (define length-of-hypotenuse (sqrt sum-of-squares))
??

> (define the-ultimate-answer 42)
??
```

How variables are evaluated

Mistakes to Avoid

Some beginning Scheme programmers may think that each time a variable is evaluated, the value to which it is bound must be recalculated. For example, if you view `length-of-hypotenuse` above as having the value (`sqrt` `sum-of-squares`) instead of 5.0, then you might believe that each time `length-of-hypotenuse` is evaluated, (`sqrt` `sum-of-squares`) is recomputed. This is not the case. `length-of-hypotenuse` is bound to 5.0. Each time `length-of-hypotenuse` is evaluated, 5.0 is returned regardless of what happens to `sum-of-squares`; no other calculations are necessary. To see this, imagine that the definition of `sum-of-squares` were changed. The variable `length-of-hypotenuse` would maintain its value.

```
> (define sum-of-squares (+ (expt 6 2) (expt 8 2)))
??

> length-of-hypotenuse
5.0
```

Sometimes it is desirable to have a result that changes based on a variable's value. This can be accomplished by writing functions.

3.7 User-Defined Functions

Until now, we've used the built-in functions of Scheme. There are around a hundred built-in functions, but often it is desirable to create our own functions. By creating functions, we in effect extend the language to allow new tasks to be performed easily. Later, more abstract and sophisticated functions can be built upon these newly defined functions. This building up to sophisticated functions provides a convenient means of solving large, difficult programming tasks.

Motivation for creating functions

Another motivation for creating functions is to save a great deal of extra typing. As an example, let's revisit the tax formula

tax = (work-income + interest-income – standard-deduction) × 0.15
– (withholding + tax-credits)

Without having a function to perform this task, each time we would have to enter

```
(- (* (+ work-income interest-income (- standard-deduction)) 0.15)
   (+ withholding tax-credits))
```

where `work-income`, `interest-income`, `standard-deduction`, `withholding`, and `tax-credits` are replaced by their actual values.

If there were a function, `tax-amount`, that took our amounts as arguments and computed the tax, we could write

```
(tax-amount work-income interest-income standard-deduction
   withholding tax-credits)
```

wherever we wished the tax to be computed, again substituting the real values in place of the variable names above.

Using functions not only saves a great deal of typing, it reduces the potential for errors and makes the program more readable and understandable. Someone can read the code and surmise that a tax amount is being computed. If uncertain, the reader can always examine the comment or code in the function `tax-amount` itself. Using mnemonic, meaningful function names further clarifies your programs. Calling the above function `t` or `c-t` would not be as understandable as naming it `tax-amount`.

Functions are defined using a variation of **define**. This variation needs three items: the *name* of the function being defined, the names of the *parameters* of the function, and the *body* of the function. The body consists of the action(s) that the function is to perform and specifies what the function will return when invoked (called). Parameters are names that correspond to the arguments given in a call to the function. The names of the parameters are the names by which these argument values are referenced inside the body of the function. Another way of saying this is that parameters are place holders for argument values.

Defining functions and function parameters

Another analogy comes from the sequences presented in Chapter 2. The command `memorize` performs the same task for robot commands as **define** does for

Scheme expressions. `perform` is used to call memorized sequences with arguments that are passed to parameters. The same thing happens when a Scheme function is called. The arguments are evaluated and their values are passed to the parameters, binding the parameters to the evaluated argument values.

The general form of a `define` for functions is

define syntax

(**define** (*function-name parameter-list*)

     $\boxed{body}$)

where *parameter-list* is zero or more symbols (naming parameters) and *body* is one or more expressions.

In a `define`, the first argument consists of the function name and the parameter names enclosed in parentheses. The remaining arguments make up the body of the function.

To illustrate definitions and invocations of functions, we'll define a simpler function that computes the square of a value. To begin, the number of parameters and their meaning should be made explicit, as well as what the function does and what it returns. This function, called `square`, will have one parameter, called `number`; it represents the value we wish to square. This result is the return value of `square`.

The definition of `square` along with a brief comment describing the function follows:

```
; Return the square of a number.
(define (square number)
  (* number number) )
```

When you type this into the interpreter, the return value is undefined.

When a function is called, each expression in the body of the function is evaluated. The return value is the evaluated result of the last expression. In the case of `square`, there is only one expression defining the body:

```
(* number number)
```

This expression is evaluated and that result is the return value of the function call.

Evaluating function calls

An example function call to `square` is

```
> (square 3)
9
```

The number 3 is the argument that is sent to the function. It is evaluated before that function uses it. This result, 3, is the value to which the parameter `number` is bound. Next, the body of the function is evaluated using the new binding of `number`. Hence, when

```
(* number number)
```

is evaluated, `number` evaluates to 3 and `*` is applied to 3 and 3. This results in 9, which is the return value of the function call, and is what the interpreter prints.

The call

```
(square (+ 1 2))
```

also results in 9. The argument `(+ 1 2)` evaluates to 3, so `number` is bound to 3. The rest of the evaluation is the same as in the example above.

Mistakes to Avoid

Don't confuse function definitions with function calls (invocations). To define (create) a function, use `define`. To call (invoke) a function, enclose the name of the function and the arguments in parentheses.

Mistakes to Avoid

Don't confuse function definitions with variable definitions.

```
(define (length-of-hypotenuse) (sqrt sum-of-squares))
```

is a function definition. To get the length, use `(length-of-hypotenuse)`. The answer depends on the **current** value of `sum-of-squares`. Contrast that with the following:

```
(define length-of-hypotenuse (sqrt sum-of-squares))
```

This `define` sets the variable `length-of-hypotenuse`. To access that value later, use `length-of-hypotenuse`. The return value is based on the value `sum-of-squares` had when the `define` was made. This was illustrated previously at the end of section 3.6, "Variables."

Function definitions versus variable definitions

Mistakes to Avoid

When defining functions, be sure to enclose the function name and all the parameter names in one set of parentheses. The function `sum-abs`, which takes two numbers and returns the sum of their absolute values, would be written as:

```
(define (sum-abs num1 num2)        ; proper heading
   (+ (abs num1) (abs num2)) )
```

not as:

```
(define sum-abs (num1 num2)        ; improper heading
   (+ (abs num1) (abs num2)) )
```

The function and parameter names in a function definition look like function calls in terms of the placement of the parentheses and the number of items. For example, to find the sum of the absolute values of -3 and 4, we would write `(sum-abs -3 4)`. This has the same form as the function definition `(sum-abs num1 num2)`.

The next example shows the function definition for the tax problem presented previously. Recall that the three elements needed for a function definition are

the name of the function
the parameter list
the body of the function

The name of the function is `tax-amount`. The parameter list contains names for the numbers needed, as shown below:

`work-income`	income from jobs
`interest-income`	income from interest
`standard-deduction`	standard deduction
`withholding`	withholding tax already paid
`tax-credits`	any credits to be deducted from the tax to pay

The body of the function looks like

```
(- (* (+ work-income interest-income (- standard-deduction))
      0.15)
   (+ withholding tax-credits))
```

The entire function is

```
; Return amount of tax given income, deductions, and tax credits.
(define (tax-amount work-income interest-income standard-deduction
                    withholding tax-credits)
  (- (* (+ work-income interest-income (- standard-deduction))
        0.15)
     (+ withholding tax-credits)) )
```

To invoke this new function with the values below

`work-income`	$25,174.65
`interest-income`	$132.67
`standard-deduction`	$6,050.00
`withholding`	$3,673.83
`tax-credits`	$125.00

use the function call

```
(tax-amount 25174.65 132.67 6050.00 3673.83 125.00)
```

The parameters in the function definition are bound to the values of the arguments in the function call. These bindings are shown below:

parameter	is bound to
`work-income`	25174.65
`interest-income`	132.67
`standard-deduction`	6050.00
`withholding`	3673.83
`tax-credits`	125.00

Using these bindings, what gets computed is

```
(- (* (+ 25174.65 132.67 (- 6050)) 0.15) (+ 3673.83 125))
```

The result of the above computation is –910.232.

Order of function definitions

User-defined functions can be used within other user-defined functions, as long as the functions are *defined* before they are *invoked*. In other words, before a call to a function can be made, both the function and all functions used within it must be defined. If `tax-amount` calls another function (say `tax-rate`, to compute a tax rate based on the income), both `tax-rate` and `tax-amount` would have to be defined before `tax-amount` can be called. The order in which functions are defined is not important aside from this restriction. Thus, `tax-amount` can be defined before any of the functions that it calls are defined.[5] We will take advantage of this fact throughout this book, especially when using top-down design.

Tax brackets

Let's illustrate this with a concrete example. Suppose we wanted to build a more complex tax model in which the taxable income is taxed at different levels depending on the amount of income. The first $20,000 is taxed at 15%. The next $30,000 at 25%, and anything above $50,000 is taxed at 50%. It seems like we need some way of making decisions to solve this problem, but we can write this function using `max` and `min`.

Let's look at this problem in a top-down fashion. The idea is to add up three products. Each product is the amount of income in a particular tax bracket (e.g., $20,000–$50,000) times the tax rate for that bracket. The amount of income in the lowest bracket ($20,000 or less) is the minimum of the income and 20,000.

```
(min income 20000)
```

The income in the $20,000–$50,000 bracket is more complicated to compute. The calculation

```
(min income 50000)
```

returns a maximum of 50,000. Subtracting 20,000 from this gives the income over $20,000. But what if the income is less than $20,000? We would get a negative amount.[6] To remedy this we can take the maximum of the difference we just computed and zero. The entire calculation is

```
(max (- (min income 50000) 20000) 0)
```

The remaining value is the income above $50,000. We don't need to worry about a limit on the income; the only concern is that there is income over $50,000. Subtracting 50,000 from the income and taking the maximum of that difference and zero gives us the desired value:

```
(max (- income 50000) 0)
```

Now that we have determined how to compute the amounts in the three brackets, we must multiply each by the corresponding tax rate and add up the three products to get a total tax amount. This will be the body of our function. The function has a single parameter, the taxable income:

[5.] In some programming languages this is not allowed—whenever a function is called or used within another function, it must be defined beforehand. Such a language would require `tax-rate` to be defined before `tax-amount`.

[6.] This would give a negative tax reducing the total tax we must pay. A novel plan to help low-income people, but something the government would surely object to.

```
; Compute tax based on three income brackets.
(define (tax-rate income)
   (+ (* (min income 20000) 0.15)
      (* (max (- (min income 50000) 20000) 0) 0.25)
      (* (max (- income 50000) 0) 0.5)) )
```

Here are some example calls to show that this function works:

```
> (tax-rate 10000)
1500.0

> (tax-rate 20000)
3000.0

> (tax-rate 30000)
5500.0

> (tax-rate 50000)
10500.0

> (tax-rate 80000)
25500.0
```

The final step is to modify `tax-amount` to use `tax-rate`. Here is the new version:

```
; Return amount of tax given income, deductions, and tax credits.
(define (tax-amount work-income interest-income standard-deduction
                    withholding tax-credits)
  (- (tax-rate
        (+ work-income interest-income (- standard-deduction)))
     (+ withholding tax-credits)) )
```

The tax on our old figures is now

```
> (tax-amount 25174.65 132.67 6050.00 3673.83 125.00)
-910.232
```

This is the same amount we got with the previous function. Notice, however, that the taxable income is less than $20,000, so it is taxed at 15%.

3.8 Scope and Extent

Each time `square` is called, its parameter `number` is bound to the value of the argument. When `square` returns, `number` is no longer defined. To illustrate this, observe the following example:

```
> (square 4)
16

> number
Undefined variable - number
```

We have previously seen that by creating a variable with **define**, that variable can be later accessed. However, in the above case, `number` cannot be accessed outside of the function.

Two important aspects of a variable must be understood: its *scope* and its *extent*. The scope of a variable refers to that part of the program in which a variable may be accessed; its extent refers to the times during the execution of a program when a variable may be accessed. In simpler terms, scope is *where* a variable can be used, and extent is *when* a variable can be used.

We have seen two types of variables: *global variables* and *parameters*. The variable `tax-rate` used in section 3.6, "Variables", is an example of a global variable. It was created by calling `define`, as shown below:

```
> (define tax-rate 0.15)
??
```

Scope and extent of global variables

Global variables can be accessed anywhere or any time after they have been created. The scope of a global variable is the part of the program after the point of its creation. The extent of a global variable is any time after its creation while the interpreter is still active.

Scope and extent of parameters

Parameters are created when a function is defined and can be accessed only within the body of that function. They have a more limited scope, namely the body of the function. The extent of a parameter is not limited to the time that the function is being invoked. However, accessing a parameter outside the normal call to that function is a somewhat tricky process. It will be covered in Chapter 11, when lexical closures are introduced. To simplify the picture without creating a false story, we'll concern ourselves with scope only. Thus, the reason why the variable `number` could not be accessed in the previous example is that its scope is the body of the function `square`. Therefore, it cannot be accessed outside of the body of the function.

3.9   Shadowing

Shadowing also affects the scope of variables. Global variables with the same name always refer to the same variable and its one current binding. In Scheme, if the same name is used for a global variable and a function parameter, then that name refers to different variables and they each have their own unique bindings. Look at the example below to get a better understanding of the implications of this.

```
> (define number 4)          ; number is a global variable
??

> number                     ; access the global variable number
4

> (define (double number)    ; number is a parameter
    (* 2 number) )
??

> (double 7)
14
```

```
> number                                    ; access the global variable number
4
```

The first two expressions, (**define** number 4) and number, refer to the global variable number. The third expression, a function definition, refers to number as a parameter. When the function is called with (double 7), the parameter number is bound to 7. The body of the function evaluates to 14, which is the return value of the function. The last expression, number, returns the value of the global variable number, which is still 4. There is no way in this example to access the parameter number from outside the function double. This is what *scope* defines.

Precedence of parameters over global variables

How was it that Scheme decided to use the parameter number within the function and not the global variable number? Within functions, parameters take precedence over global variables with the same name. This is what is meant by shadowing. The parameter number *shadows* the global variable number inside the function double.

If number had not been defined as a parameter in double, then the following would have happened:

```
> number                                    ; access the global variable number (still 4)
4

> (define (new-double)                       ; a function with no arguments
    (* 2 number) )                           ; use the global variable number
??

> (new-double)
8

> number                                    ; access the global variable number
4
```

Functions taking no arguments

Notice that new-double has no parameters. To create a function that takes no arguments, simply put a right parenthesis after the function name in the definition. A call to a function taking no arguments is made by enclosing the function name within parentheses.

In this example, number refers to the global variable throughout. When new-double is called, the global variable number is used, so 8 is returned.

Shadowing of functions

Typically, shadowing is the effect that is desired; in other words, the parameter's value is the desired one and not a global variable with the same name. However, be careful when choosing parameter names not to use the name of a Scheme function. Look at what happens in the following example, which computes the difference between the largest and smallest of three numbers with the constraint that they must be between a certain minimum and maximum threshold range. To get the largest number we use the function max. Calling max with the minimum threshold value in addition to the three numbers assures that the numbers aren't too small. Otherwise, the minimum threshold value is returned. The same is done in finding the minimum value.

```
; Return difference between the largest and smallest of three
; numbers within the range min to max.
(define (difference num1 num2 num3 min max)
    (- (max num1 num2 num3 min) (min num1 num2 num3 max)))
```

> `(difference 24 13 20 0 100)`
> **Error: Operator is not a function**

This tells us that one of the functions we used was not legal. One version of Scheme gave the following error message:

Wrong type to apply: 100

This is a rather confusing error message. It sounds like a type clash—100 is used, but some other type (noninteger) is expected. The error also mentions "apply." Functions are applied, so the error message means that the wrong type was given when a function was expected.

At a first glance the code looks okay; however, we are using min and max as parameters. Just as parameters shadow global variables, they shadow functions. Instead of using the function max, we wound up using the number 100 as a function. This caused the error.

Mistakes to Avoid
Be sure not to use parameter names that are also function names.

3.10 Programming Style

Before continuing with further examples of function definitions, the issue of good programming practice should be discussed. The examples given throughout this book will adhere to "good" programming practice. This is measured by readability, modifiability, conciseness, robustness, and other factors. A common programming-style error occurs when misusing `define`. Below is such an example:

Good programming practices

```
; Redefine number to be twice as large.
(define (bad-double)
    (define number (* 2 number)) )
```

The violation is in the use of `define` in the function `bad-double`. The `define` has a *side-effect* of making a change elsewhere in the program: the value of the global variable number is changed. If this weren't expected, for example, if new-double had been written by someone else, and you were not aware of this particular side-effect, then tracking down the cause of the change in number's value could be a difficult task, especially if the program involved was lengthy.

Problems with `define` inside functions

If `bad-double` had been written with number as a parameter, only that parameter would have changed. The global variable number would not have changed since it would have been *shadowed* by the parameter number, and there would be no effect outside of the function. This is relatively harmless. However, if all we want is a function that doubles its argument, the first version of the function, `double` on page 49, is the preferred one.

As a simple rule to avoid problems, remember the following:

> Don't use `define` within functions.

3.10.1   Exercises

3.13 Write a function that takes three numbers and returns their average.

3.14 Write a function that takes five numbers and returns the average of the middle three (dropping the highest and lowest values).

3.15 Write a function that returns the result of converting a temperature in Fahrenheit to its equivalent in Celsius. Use the formula

$$Celsius = (\,Fahrenheit - 32\,) \times 5/9.$$

3.16 Write a function that returns the result of converting a temperature in Celsius to Fahrenheit. See the previous problem for the Fahrenheit to Celsius formula.

3.17 Chinese years correspond to animals in a twelve-year cycle. Write a function that returns the next year of the dragon. To compute this year you will need to know a previous year of the dragon. 1964, 1976, and 1988 were all previous years of the dragon. Your function will take one previous year of the dragon and the current year as arguments. Write your function so that it does not matter with which previous year of the dragon you call it.

3.18 Assume you have calculated your spending by how much you typically spend daily (food and daily needs), weekly (transportation costs, entertainment, etc.), and monthly (rent, loans, credit cards, etc.). Write a function to compute your annual spending. Your function should have three parameters corresponding to the three spending amounts.

3.19 Write a function that computes how many years you could live on a quantity of money. This quantity will be the one parameter of this function. You should use the function you defined in the previous problem to solve this problem.

3.20 One Thai Baht is worth about 4 U.S. cents. Write a function that takes an amount in Baht and converts it into dollars. How expensive is a 400 Baht shirt? How many dollars are there to one Baht?

3.11   Using `let` to Create Local Variables

Parameters are one way to create variables that have limited scope—the body of   *Local variables*
the function in which they are defined. `let` expressions are another means of
creating variables with limited scope. Such variables are often called *local vari-*
ables, because their scope is *local* to a certain part of the program. `let` expressions
are often used within functions to create additional local variables. As an example, recall the tax computation presented earlier in this chapter. In the top-down
solution, the tax amount was

```
(- total-debits total-credits)
```

This eventually led to the complete solution given below:

```
; Return amount of tax given income, deductions, and tax credits.
(define (tax-amount work-income interest-income standard-deduction
                 withholding tax-credits)
  (- (* (+ work-income interest-income (- standard-deduction))
        0.15)
     (+ withholding tax-credits)) )
```

This solution is not as readable as the first step in the top-down approach above.
We could make the function more readable by using the variables `total-debits`
and `total-credits`, and somehow binding them to the proper values. These
variables act as abbreviations for the values that they hold. The variables must be
bound within the function because they get their values

```
(* (+ work-income interest-income (- standard-deduction)) 0.15)
```
and
```
(+ withholding tax-credits)
```

from the parameters, `work-income`, `interest-income`, `standard-deduction`,
`withholding`, and `tax-credits` of the function.

Using a **define** within the function violates the principle of programming
style discussed in the previous section, namely another global variable with that
same name would lose its binding. To get around this problem, a `let` expression
is used.

The general form of `let` is as follows:

```
(let  ( (variable-1  value-1 )                               let syntax
        (variable-2  value-2 )
                  .
                  .
                  .
        (variable-N  value-N )  )
     body   )
```

The first argument to `let` is a list of *variable-value pairs.* Each of these pairs con-   *Variable-value pairs*
sists of a variable name and a value (some expression) for that variable. The *body*
of the `let` is like the body of a function—it can be any number of expressions and
the value returned by the `let` is the return value of the last expression.

The variables defined in the `let` can be used only within the body of the   *Scoping of* `let`
`let`—their scope is the body of the `let`. `let` variables shadow global variables   *variables*
and parameters defined outside of the `let`.

Evaluation rules for
`let`

A `let` expression is evaluated as follows. The values (*value-1 ... value-N*) are evaluated (in some undefined order) and the results are saved. The local variables (*variable-1 ... variable-N*) are then bound to the saved results. The expressions in the body of the `let` are evaluated and the result of the final expression is returned.

Mistakes to Avoid

Since a `let` expression evaluates the values (*value-1 ... value-N*) first and then binds the variables (*variable-1 ... variable-N*) to those results, the values should not refer to other variables defined within the `let`. In other words, the variables in a `let` are valid only within the body of the `let`.

The new function to compute the tax is

```
; Return amount of tax given income, deductions, and tax credits.
(define (tax-amount work-income interest-income standard-deduction
                    withholding tax-credits)
  (let ( (total-debits (* (+ work-income interest-income
                             (- standard-deduction))
                          0.15))
         (total-credits (+ withholding tax-credits)) )
    (- total-debits total-credits)) )
```

The values

```
(* (+ work-income interest-income (- standard-deduction)) 0.15)
```
and
```
(+ withholding tax-credits)
```

are evaluated and then `total-debits` and `total-credits` are bound to the results. The expression

```
(- total-debits total-credits)
```

makes up the entire body of the `let`. Its return value is the return value of the `let`.

You could add the variable `taxable-income` to represent the sum of the work and interest incomes minus the standard deduction. This would reflect the thought process of the bottom-up design of the code, namely

Determine the taxable income.
Determine the total debits by multiplying the taxable income by the tax rate.
Determine the total credits.
Subtract the total credits from the total debits.

The new `let` would be

```
(let ( (taxable-income (+ work-income interest-income
                          (- standard-deduction)))
       (total-debits (* taxable-income 0.15))
       (total-credits (+ withholding tax-credits)) )
   (- total-debits total-credits) )
```

Evaluating this code produces an undefined variable error message indicating that `taxable-income` is undefined. This is because variables defined in a `let` cannot be used as values that define subsequent variables in a `let`. The variable-value pair that causes this problem is

```
(total-debits (* taxable-income 0.15))
```

To get around this difficulty, Scheme provides a variant of `let` called `let*`. `let*` evaluates the values of the variable-value pairs one at a time like `let`; however, `let*` binds each variable to its corresponding value, once that value is determined, then proceeds to the next variable-value pair. Therefore, the expressions that represent the values of variables can refer to variables previously defined within the variable-value pair list.

Using `let*` *to reference previously defined local variables*

Below is a working version of the function `tax-amount`, using `let*`:

```
; Return amount of tax given income, deductions, and tax credits.
(define (tax-amount work-income interest-income standard-deduction
                    withholding tax-credits)
  (let* ( (taxable-income (+ work-income interest-income
                            (- standard-deduction)))
          (total-debits (* taxable-income 0.15))
          (total-credits (+ withholding tax-credits)) )
     (- total-debits total-credits)) )
```

This solution is closer to an *imperative approach* to programming in which partial results leading to a solution are saved in variables, which are combined to yield a final result. This approach has the advantage in this case of being somewhat more readable than the original definition of `tax-amount` given at the start of this section. The disadvantage is that this new solution is somewhat longer. However, in a tradeoff between readability and length of code, you should favor readability.

Imperative programming

In general, `let` and `let*` expressions should be used

When to use `let` *and* `let*`

- To make a function more readable by breaking the final result into partial computations with results saved in mnemonic variable names.
- To avoid computing the same values several times within a function.
- To save values that cannot be recomputed (for example, calls to `read` or `random`).[7]

[7.] The function `read` gets a value from the user—it is discussed in Chapter 9. `random` is used to generate random numbers—it is discussed in Chapter 4.

Mistakes to Avoid

Forgetting the parentheses around the variable-value pairs of a `let` expression is a very common syntactical mistake. This is easily done when there is a single variable-value pair as the example below shows.

```
(let (number 16)          ; improper code
   (sqrt number) )
```

To fix this code, another set of parentheses is needed around the variable-value pair.

```
(let ( (number 16) )      ; correct code
   (sqrt number) )
```

3.11.1 Exercises

3.21 Write a function that takes a single number that represents a century. Your function should return the year in that century that is a palindrome—something that reads the same forward as it does backward. For example given 20, your function should return 1991. Use a `let` or `let*` expression in your solution. Does your function work for centuries beyond the 101st? What about the first century?

3.22 The function `piggy-bank` takes a number that represents how many pennies we have. It should return the equivalent number of quarters, nickels, and pennies as a number where the last digit is the number of pennies, the second to last digit is the number of nickels, and the first digits are the number of quarters. The amounts of quarters and nickels should be maximized (i.e., there shouldn't be more than 4 nickels or 4 pennies in the answer). `(piggy-bank 42)` should return `132`.

```
(define (piggy-bank pennies)
  (let ((quarters (truncate (/ pennies 25)))
        (nickels (truncate (/ pennies 5)))
        (left-over-pennies (remainder pennies 1)))
   (+ (* quarters 100) (* nickels 10) left-over-pennies)))
```

What does `piggy-bank` return when called with 42? If this is the wrong answer, fix `piggy-bank` but keep as much of the structure of the program as possible.

3.12 Writing Styles

The code examples in this text follow one particular style. There are many other styles. Discussions about which programming styles and languages are the best often turn into religious arguments, in which the parties argue furiously over the merits of their style or language. People have debated over issues as trivial as whether one should indent three spaces or four. No one style is the "right" style.

You should choose a style that is the most readable to you and use it consistently. Here are some possibilities:

```
(define (this-books-style arg1 arg2)
  (let ( (var1 value1)
         (var2 value2) )
    (+ (some-very-long-function with lots of arguments)
       3)) )

(define (line-up-parens-style2 arg1 arg2)
  (let ( (var1 value1)
         (var2 value2)
       )
    (+ (some-very-long-function with lots of arguments)
       3
    )
  )
)

(define
  (arguments-on-lines-below-style arg1 arg2)
  (let
    ( (var1 value1)
      (var2 value2) )
    (+
      (some-very-long-function
        with
        lots
        of
        arguments)
      3)) )
```

3.13   Summary

- Function calls are made by enclosing the function name followed by the arguments to the function in parentheses.
- Bottom-up design is a means of solving problems in which you begin with the small details that must be computed first. These first computations will be the innermost arguments of the final Scheme expression.
- Top-down design, another means of problem solving, entails thinking of the problem in abstract terms and then refining these terms to Scheme functions. This approach results in the creation of Scheme code in much the same order as it is written in the final solution.
- Numbers evaluate to themselves.
- Variables evaluate to the values to which they are currently bound.
- Function calls are evaluated by first evaluating the arguments. Then the function is applied to the evaluated arguments and the result is displayed. If the function is not builtin or defined previously, an error message is printed.

- Variables are bound to values using `define`.
- Functions are defined using `define`.
- The scope of a variable is the part of the program in which the variable is defined.
- The scope of a global variable is from its creation point to the end of the program.
- The scope of a parameter is the body of the function in which it is defined.
- Extent is the time during the execution of a program in which a variable is defined.
- Shadowing occurs when a parameter's scope supersedes the scope of a global variable with the same name.
- `let` and `let*` expressions can be used to create local variables. Creating such variables can make a program more readable since they provide names for partial results in the final computation. The scope of a `let` variable is the body of the `let` or `let*`. A `let` variable shadows parameters and global variables of the same name defined outside the `let` or `let*` expression.
- Summary of functions introduced in this chapter:

function	arguments	return value
+	0 or more	sum of arguments
-	1 or more	difference of arguments in left to right order
*	0 or more	product of arguments
/	1 or more	quotient of arguments in left to right order
max	1 or more	maximum of arguments
min	1 or more	minimum of arguments
truncate	*num*	integer part of *num* (digits to the left of the decimal)
sqrt	*num*	square root of *num*, $\sqrt{num}$
abs	*num*	absolute value of *num*, $\lvert num \rvert$
expt	*num power*	exponentiation (*num* raised to *power*), num^{power}
remainder	*num1 num2*	remainder of *num1* when divided by *num2*

- Summary of other objects introduced in this chapter:

object	arguments	return value
define	*variable value*	binds *variable* to *value*
define	(*function params*) *body*	creates *function*
let	*var-value-pairs body*	binds *vars* to *values* and evaluate *body*
let*	*var-value-pairs body*	binds *vars* to *values* in order and evaluate *body*

- The syntax of `define` for function definitions is as follows:

```
(define (function-name parameter-list)
    body )
```

- The syntax of `let` and `let*` is as follows:

```
(let ( (variable-1  value-1)
       (variable-2  value-2)
                .
                .
                .
       (variable-N  value-N) )
       body  )
```

CHAPTER *4*

LISTS:
THE BASIC DATA STRUCTURE

4.1 Lists in Scheme

Information stored within a computer system is called *data*. The types of data we have seen are numbers and symbols. Collectively, these are called *atoms*.

Atoms

When a collection of data is organized in some fashion, it is referred to as a *data structure*. The fundamental data structure used in Scheme is the *list*. A list specifies an ordered collection of information. Lists are written in Scheme as a left parenthesis followed by the information desired in the list and closed with a right parenthesis. The list of even numbers between 1 and 7 is written in Scheme as

Data structures and lists

```
(2 4 6)
```

The numbers 2, 4, and 6 are the *elements* of the list. The order of the elements within the list is important; the lists (6 4 2) and (2 4 6) are different.

The elements of a list can be any atoms (numbers or symbols) or lists. The following lists are all legal within Scheme:

Elements of lists

list	contains
(are you my mother)	four elements, all symbols
(4 score and 7 years ago)	six elements, all atoms
()	no elements, an empty list
((a b c) (1 2 3))	two elements, both lists of three elements
(() 18.54 1/2 ((3)))	four elements: two lists and two numbers
(sqrt 4)	two elements: a symbol and a number

Sublist

*Function calls versus
lists as data*

A list that is an element of a list is a *sublist*. In section 4.4 we look at the advantages of lists of sublists.

The list (sqrt 4) has two elements: the symbol sqrt, which is the name of a built-in Scheme function, and the number 4. We have been using lists to make function calls all along. This brings up an interesting dilemma. How do we differentiate function calls from lists of information? After all, in Scheme they look the same. However, if you were to enter a list that was not a valid function call, you would see something like the following:

```
> (a b c)
Error: Unbound variable: a
```

4.2 Stopping Evaluation with quote

quote

To force the evaluator not to evaluate a list as a function call, use quote, as in

```
> (quote (a b c))
(a b c)
```

quote takes one expression and returns it. Therefore, it prevents the evaluation of its argument. This is the case even if the argument is a list that looks like a function call:

```
> (quote (+ 2 3))
(+ 2 3)
```

quote is used so often that a special shorthand (the " ' " symbol) exists for it.

```
> '(+ 2 3)
(+ 2 3)
```

This notation is functionally equivalent to (quote (+ 2 3)). It saves a lot of typing and helps reduce the number of parentheses, which is always a blessing in Scheme[1].

A common mistake is to overquote lists. Since quote stops the evaluation of its one argument, it is not necessary to quote lists within other quoted lists as in the following example[2].

```
> '('(a b c) '(1 2 3))
('(a b c) '(1 2 3))
```

Notice how this differs from

```
> '((a b c) (1 2 3))
((a b c) (1 2 3))
```

The empty list must be quoted as well.

---

[1] Scheme is a dialect of LISP, which has been facetiously referred to as standing for Lots of Irritating Single Parentheses.

[2] Your version of Scheme may return the function quote instead of the shorthand " ' " as shown. This would produce the return value ((quote (a b c)) (quote (1 2 3))).

> `'()`
`()`

As we have already seen, typing the name of a variable into the interpreter returns the value to which the variable is currently bound. Sometimes we wish to refer to the variable name, and not its value. In this case, we are interested in the symbol itself, so we `quote` it:

> `(quote num)`
`num`

The " **'** " shorthand can be used, as in

> `'num`
`num`

Mistakes to Avoid

Don't quote variables that you wish to bind using `define`. For example,

`(define 'value 2112)`

results in an error. `define` does not evaluate its first argument. The next section discusses the cases when the normal evaluation rules are not used.

4.3 Special Forms

`quote` simply returns its argument. Yet how does this argument escape from the normal evaluation that happens to arguments of functions? Applying the rules of function evaluation to the example above, the argument `num` must be evaluated before `quote` is applied to it. This evaluation should result in the value to which `num` is currently bound. `quote` would then be applied to that value.

The normal evaluation mechanism is not used for `quote`. Instead, the argument to `quote` is not evaluated but simply returned. Objects that look like functions but do not obey the normal evaluation rules are called *special forms*. As you can guess, `quote` is a special form. Special forms are not functions.

Special forms use special evaluation rules

For each special form, the evaluator has a rule for how it should be evaluated. One of the goals of Scheme is to minimize the number of special forms. We have encountered four special forms already: `define`, `let`, `let*`, and `quote`.

4.3.1 Exercises

4.1   Why are `define`, `let`, and `let*` implemented as special forms instead of regular functions?

4.2   Which arguments to `define` and `let` are evaluated and which arguments are not evaluated?

4.3   What do the following expressions evaluate to? Some of them may produce errors. Test your answers on the computer.

```
''(a b c)

('a 'b 'c)

'('a 'b c)

(quote a (1 2))

(quote '(1 2))

()

((+ 1 2))
```

4.4   Using Lists as Data Structures

Lists can be used to represent sets of values such as the prime numbers less than 10:

```
(1 2 3 5 7)
```

Lists can represent more complex data structures, like an address:

```
( (John Doe)
  (14 Main Street)
  (Anytown Anystate 12345) )
```

Nested lists

This structure uses *nested lists* (lists that contain lists as elements) to break up the address into three parts: name, street, and city-town-zip. It need not be entered into the computer on multiple lines as shown; this is merely for readability.

Nested lists provide a natural way of organizing data, or creating hierarchies. Suppose you want a list of the titles of your compact disk collection. You could create a large non-nested structure like

```
(Rolling_Stones Its_Only_Rock_and_Roll Pat_Metheny First_Circle
    Rolling_Stones Black_and_Blue Andy_Narell The_Hammer)
```

Such a list would be difficult to understand, especially if it were long. The data structure does not separate the artists from the CDs, nor does it provide any categories by which you might wish to organize music. It also has unnecessary repetition (Rolling Stones twice).[3]

A much better data structure for a CD collection might be

[3.] Some may argue that there is no such thing as too much Rolling Stones.

```
(rock
   (Rolling_Stones
      (Black_and_Blue
       Its_Only_Rock_and_Roll))
 jazz
   (Pat_Metheny
      (First_Circle)
    Andy_Narell
      (The_Hammer)))
```

CD data structure

This data structure can be illustrated with the following hierarchy:

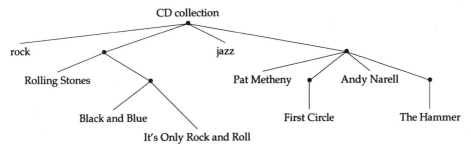

With such a data structure, the CDs are arranged according to musical category, (e.g., rock, jazz, classical). Each category of music is followed by a list of artists and their works. These artists-works lists are lists of artist-name and CD-list pairs. This ensures no ambiguity as to artist or CD name and eliminates repetition of artist names.

This is by no means the only representation that could be used to maintain such information.

4.4.1 Exercises

4.4   What other ways can you think of to organize a collection of CDs?

4.5   What advantages and/or disadvantages does your data structure have compared to this one?

4.6   Design a data structure that you could use to maintain information on students: name, student ID number, year in school, address, grades, grade point average, etc.

4.5   Taking Lists Apart

Many of the functions that will be introduced in this chapter perform operations on the top-level elements of lists only. The atoms and lists that make up a list are the top-level elements of that list. For example,

Counting top-level elements

```
((a list) an-atom (a (nested list)))
```

has three top-level elements: two are lists and one is an atom.

To determine the number of top-level elements in a list, use the function `length`.

length

function	**argument**	**return value**
length	*list*	the number of elements in *list*

Here are some example function calls using `length`.

```
> (length '(1 two (three (not-four nor-five))))
3

> (length '((just an) ((ordinary)) (((list) not))))
3

> (length '())
0
```

The elements in the first example are 1, two, and (three (not-four nor-five)) which is considered one element even though it contains a symbol and a list of two symbols itself. When counting top-level elements, a list up to its closing right parenthesis is considered a single top-level element. The three elements in the second example are (just an), ((ordinary)), and (((list) not)).

Simple list functions

In Chapter 3, we said that LISP, of which Scheme is a dialect, is an acronym for **LIS**t Processing. This is because LISP has a number of functions to take apart, create, sequence through, and even restructure lists. The built-in functions car and cdr are the fundamental functions used to return parts of lists. car returns the first element of a list, and cdr returns the list without the the first element.

History of car *and* cdr

The names car and cdr date back to the first implementation of LISP on the IBM 704 computer. A computer consists of a large collection of numbers, called *words*. On the IBM 704 computer, each word could be accessed by specifying its location (*address*) in one of a number of *index registers*. Each word had different components that could be individually examined. Two of these, the address and decrement parts, could be used to reference other words. These parts were used to hold the first element and the rest of a list. The names car and cdr come from abbreviations of the instructions used to get these different components. car stands for Contents of the **A**ddress part of **R**egister number and cdr for Contents of the **D**ecrement part of **R**egister number. These names have stuck through time, although many versions of LISP now have additional, more mnemonic names for these functions such as `first` and `rest`.

We can easily write the functions `first` and `rest` as follows:

```
; Return the first element of a list.
(define (first a-list)
   (car a-list) )

; Return the rest of a list.
(define (rest a-list)
   (cdr a-list) )
```

In addition, we can use combinations of `car` and `cdr` to create functions to extract the second, third, fourth, and fifth elements of a list:

```
; Return the second element of a list.
(define (second a-list)
   (car (cdr a-list)) )

; Return the third element of a list.
(define (third a-list)
   (car (cdr (cdr a-list))) )
```

You get the idea. Each subsequent `cdr` returns a list with one less element. The implementation of the functions `fourth` and `fifth` is left as an exercise for the reader.

Below is a table of the functions used to return parts of lists. All these functions take a single argument that must be a list.

function	argument	return value
first	*list*	first element of *list*
rest	*list*	rest of *list* without the first element
car	*list*	same as `first`
cdr	*list*	same as `rest`
second	*list*	second element of *list*
third	*list*	third element of *list*
fourth	*list*	fourth element of *list*
fifth	*list*	fifth element of *list*

first → fifth, rest, car, cdr

The following examples illustrate uses of these functions:

```
> (first '((z e r o) 1 (2) ((3))))
(z e r o)

> (rest '((z e r o) 1 (2) ((3))))
(1 (2) ((3)))

> (second '((z e r o) 1 (2) ((3))))
1

> (third '((z e r o) 1 (2) ((3))))
(2)

> (fourth '((z e r o) 1 (2) ((3))))
((3))

> (fifth '((z e r o) 1 (2) ((3))))
Error: Pair expected

> (car (cdr '((z e r o) 1 (2) ((3)))))
1

> (cdr (car '((z e r o) 1 (2) ((3)))))
(e r o)
```

```
> (cdr (cdr '((z e r o) 1 (2) ((3)))))
((2) ((3)))
```

The call to `fifth` above resulted in an error because the list has only four elements. Similarly, if `car`, `cdr`, `first`, or `rest` is applied to `'()`, an error will result.

Mistakes to Avoid

Remember that `rest` returns a list with all but the first element. A common mistake is to think that

```
(rest '(a b))
```

returns b instead of the actual value returned: (b). Similarly,

```
(rest '(a (b)))
```

returns ((b)) and not (b).

The simplest way to determine the return value of `rest` is to cross out the first element of the list. What's left is the `rest` of the list.

Getting any element from a list

Scheme provides a more general means of extracting elements from lists. This is useful when the exact element number is not known beforehand; for example, when it is the result of some computation.

list-ref

function	arguments	return value
list-ref	*list position*	element at *position* in *list*

`list-ref` takes two arguments: a list and the position of the desired element in the list. The position of elements in a list is numbered, in order, starting at zero and continuing up to one less than the length of the list. Thus, the positions of the elements in a list of three elements are 0, 1, and 2.

If `list-ref` is called with a position larger than or equal to the number of elements in *list*, an error will result.

Mistakes to Avoid

Positions are not the same as element numbers used in functions like `first` and `second`. The first element of a list is at position 0 and not 1. Thus, to return the fifth element of the list *my-list*, use

```
(list-ref my-list 4)
```

Finding the last element of a list

Let's write a function that returns the last element of a list. We can use `list-ref` with the length of the list minus 1. Here is an attempt at this function:

```
; Return the last element in a-list.
(define (last a-list)
  (list-ref 'a-list (- (length 'a-list) 1)) )

> (last '(the buck stops here))
Error: Pair expected
```

By quoting a-list, the literal symbol a-list is used instead of the parameter. Here is another attempt:

```
; Return the last element in a-list.
(define (last a-list)
  (list-ref (a-list) (- (length (a-list)) 1)) )

> (last '(the buck stops here))
Error: Wrong type to apply: (the buck stops here)
```

This error occurred because the value of a-list, (the buck stops here), was treated like a function. It is a list and cannot be applied as a function. Quoting it will get rid of that error as seen below:

```
; Return the last element in a-list.
(define (last a-list)
  (list-ref '(a-list) (- (length '(a-list)) 1)) )

> (last '(the buck stops here))
a-list
```

No error this time, but we didn't get the answer we wanted either. By quoting (a-list), we get the literal list (a-list). The length of that list is 1, so we end up taking **list-ref** of the list (a-list) and 0, which is the symbol a-list. To fix this, we need to use the value of the parameter a-list. This is obtained by using a-list directly without parentheses or quotes.

```
; Return the last element in a-list.
(define (last a-list)
  (list-ref a-list (- (length a-list) 1)) )

> (last '(the buck stops here))
here
```

It works! It is essential in Scheme to understand the meaning of quotes and parentheses. Quoting a symbol or list returns its literal value. Putting parentheses around a symbol treats that symbol as if it were a function. A symbol without quotes or parentheses is a variable (or parameter) and it returns its current value. If you understand these ideas, you will reduce the number of errors you get when writing Scheme code.

When to use quotes and parentheses and when not to

Scheme has a built-in function that returns the tail end of a list, **list-tail**. It would be nice to have a more general function that returns a variable-sized, contiguous piece from the head, tail, or middle of a list. We'll call this function **subseq** (short for subsequence). **subseq** returns a contiguous subsequence from anywhere within a list. It can be used to return the tail end of a list so the function **list-tail** isn't necessary. You'll be able to write **subseq** in Chapter 6.

Getting sections of a list

The following table shows different ways that **subseq** can be used to return different parts of a list:

subseq

function	arguments	return value
subseq	*list*, 0, *end*	left part of *list* up to element *end*
subseq	*list*, *start*	right part of *list* starting at element *start* + 1
subseq	*list*, *start*, *end*	*list* with elements *start* + 1 through *end*

Understanding subseq

subseq can be used with two or three arguments. With two arguments subseq uses the length of the list as the value for *end*. With three arguments subseq takes a list, a start element number, *start*, and an end element number, *end*, and returns a list starting with element number *start* + 1 up to element number *end*. *start* must be an integer between 0 and the number of elements in the list. *end* must be an integer between *start* and the number of elements in the list. The list returned will have *end* minus *start* elements. An alternate way of looking at subseq is that *start* indicates the number of elements to skip from the front of the list and *end* is the last element number to include in the list.

Below are examples to help clarify these functions:

```
> (length '((z e r o) 1 (2) ((3))))
4

> (list-ref '((z e r o) 1 (2) ((3))) 0)    ; position 0 is the first element
(z e r o)

> (list-ref '((z e r o) 1 (2) ((3))) 3)
((3))

> (list-ref '((z e r o) 1 (2) ((3))) 4)    ; position 4 is too large
Error: Pair expected

> (subseq '((z e r o) 1 (2) ((3))) 0)      ; list of the first element onward
((z e r o) 1 (2) ((3)))

> (subseq '((z e r o) 1 (2) ((3))) 3)      ; list of the fourth element
(((3)))

> (subseq '((z e r o) 1 (2) ((3))) 5)      ; start value is too large
Error: Improper start value for subseq

> (subseq '((z e r o) 1 (2) ((3))) 0 1)    ; list of the first element
((z e r o))

> (subseq '((z e r o) 1 (2) ((3))) 1 3)    ; list of the 2nd and 3rd elements
(1 (2))

> (subseq '((z e r o) 1 (2) ((3))) 2 2)    ; list of 2–2 = 0 elements
()

> (subseq '((z e r o) 1 (2) ((3))) 1 0)    ; end is less than start
Error: Improper end value for subseq

> (subseq '((z e r o) 1 (2) ((3))) 1 5)    ; end is too large
Error: Improper end value for subseq
```

Mistakes to Avoid

The list functions we've examined don't change their arguments. The functions `rest` and `cdr` return the tail end of lists, leaving the original lists intact. The function `subseq` actually creates a new list without altering the list supplied as an argument in the function calls. Thus, if `subseq` is called with a symbol that is bound to a list, a new list is returned and the symbol is still bound to the original list. This can be seen in the following example:

```
> (define my-list '(this is my very own list))
??

> (subseq my-list 2 4)
(my very)

> my-list
(this is my very own list)
```

Mistakes to Avoid

In determining the starting element of a return list, `subseq` starts with the element that follows the value of *start* given. But the ending element is included. Therefore, to get the list of the second through fifth elements of `my-list`, use

```
(subseq my-list 1 5)
```

Another device that you can use to help get the *start* argument to `subseq` straight is to think of it as the number of elements that will be skipped from the head of the list. Thus, `(subseq my-list 1)` skips the first element returning the second element onward.

You may have wondered why `subseq` uses such a strange scheme for its arguments. Part of the reason for this is to reduce the number of *off-by-one* situations that arise. When a value is one away from its desired value, it is called off-by-one. As it is written, `subseq` requires few off-by-one adjustments to be made.

Method in the madness—reducing off-by-one situations

Functions that return element positions can be used with `subseq`. The function `position` (which is presented in section 4.10) returns the position of an element in a list. We can use the result from a call to `position` to specify a start value for `subseq`. This means that `subseq` would need to use positions of elements like `list-ref` does instead of element numbers. The *start* argument to `subseq` does this. The *end* value to `subseq` doesn't, however. This is to make it easier to refer to end positions relative to the last element of the list. The element number of the last element is the length of the list.

The following chart should help clarify the above explanation by showing how few off-by-one situations arise. You can use it as a quick reference for templates when using `subseq`.

Templates for subseq	

part of list desired	call to subseq
First N elements	`(subseq a-list 0 N)`
Last N elements	`(subseq a-list (- (length a-list) N))`
List without first N elements	`(subseq a-list N)`
List without last N elements	`(subseq a-list 0 (- (length a-list) N))`
List of elements N through M	`(subseq a-list (- N 1) M)`
List from position P onwards	`(subseq a-list P)`
List from position P through Q	`(subseq a-list P (+ Q 1))`

When to use which list function

To summarize, use `first` (or `car`) through `fifth` to return a particular element from a list. There are times when the element number must be computed. In this case, use the function `list-ref`. To return a list with all but the first element, use `rest` (or `cdr`). To return a section of a list (the head, tail, or middle of a list), use `subseq` following the chart above for specific guidance.

4.5.1   Example: Extracting random elements from a data structure

Modeling bureaucratic responses

Those of you Arnold Schwarzenegger fans who saw *Terminator* know that the Terminator had lists of responses from which he could choose to decide the most appropriate retort for any given situation. If you've ever dealt with a true bureaucrat you know that they too seem to be functioning by virtue of simply responding to anything you say with one of a few responses. This type of behavior can easily be modeled in Scheme. Suppose that you have a list containing responses to be used by a particular person such as a bank teller, post office clerk, or police officer. To simplify references to this response list, imagine that it has been bound to the symbol `retort`, using `define` as shown below:

```
(define retort
  '((i am sorry but we are closed now)
    (talk to the person at the end of the hall)
    (you need form 1044-tx8 and not 1044-fg4)
    (we cannot take personal checks)
    (i am sorry we need exact change)
    (oh you only had to fill out this one form not those 20 others)))
```

Getting a random element from a list

The task is to write a function that randomly chooses a retort from a retort list. An extension to Scheme called `random` will be helpful; `(random num)` returns a random number between 0 and num − 1. Thus,

```
(random 3)
```

returns either 0, 1, or 2.

This result works very nicely in conjunction with `list-ref`, which takes a number between 0 and the length of a list minus one. The call

```
(list-ref '(a b c) (random 3))
```

returns a, b, or c.

In general, to return a random element from any list, the following function can be used:

```
; Return a random element from the list a-list.
(define (get-random-element a-list)
  (list-ref
    a-list
    (random (length a-list))) )
```

get-random-element can be applied to retort to get a random retort. Each call to **random** generates a new random number, so each time get-random-element is called, a potentially different retort will be returned.

Mistakes to Avoid

Scheme does not attach any semantics (meaning) to parameter or variable names. The way a parameter is used dictates its type requirements. Thus, naming the parameter above a-list does not mean that it must be a list. However, the way we use a-list as arguments to **length** and **list-ref** means that a-list must be a list. If not, we will get an error when the function is called. It is the responsibility of the person who calls get-random-element to assure that it is called with the proper argument types.

This does not make for secure code that you would want to let just anybody use. To remedy this, there are ways of doing *type-checking*: checking the types of variables. This is covered in Chapter 5.

Mistakes to Avoid

Don't confuse arguments to a function with elements of a list. Look at the following examples, which compute the average of three values:

```
(define (average1 num1 num2 num3)
  (/ (+ num1 num2 num3) 3) )

(define (average2 num-list)
  (/ (+ (first num-list) (second num-list)
        (third num-list)) 3) )
```

The first function average1 takes three arguments (which should be numbers) and returns their average. The second function average2 takes one argument (which should be a list of at least three numbers) and returns the average of the first three numbers in the list.

4.5.2 Exercises

4.7   What do the following expressions return? Test your answers on the computer. Some of them may produce errors.

```
(car '())

(cdr '())

(third (subseq '((4 5) 1/3 67.89 (78) value) 1))

(rest (subseq '(how (strange) (((this)) may) seem) 1 4))

(length '('a '(1 2)))

(length '((3 elements here)))

(length '((yet ((another)) strange (list))))

(car '((yet ((another)) strange (list))))

(cdr '((yet ((another)) strange (list))))

(car (car '((yet ((another)) strange (list)))))

(car (cdr (car '((yet ((another)) strange (list))))))

(car (cdr (cdr (car '((yet ((another)) strange (list)))))))
```

4.8   Assume that the function `extract` below will be called with a list of lists of atoms (e.g., `((a b c) (1 2 3))`). Fill in the blank such that the function returns a.) the first list of atoms or b.) the first atom.

```
(define (extract list-of-lists)
  (_____ list-of-lists))
```

4.9   Write an expression that returns the third element of the list *a-list*.

4.10 Write an expression that returns element number (`+ value 2`) of the list *a-list*.

4.11 Write an expression that returns the list of CDs from the second jazz artist in the CD data structure presented earlier.

4.12 Write your own version of `list-ref` using the other list functions we have discussed. Be careful that your function returns item number *num* and not the list of the *num*th item.

4.13 Write a function `but-last` that takes two arguments, *a-list* and *num*, and returns a list of all but the last *num* elements of *a-list*. Use the other list functions from this section in your solution.

4.14 Write a function called `start` that takes two arguments, *a-list* and *num*, and returns the first *num* elements from *a-list*. Use the other list functions from this section in your solution.

4.15 Write a function end that takes two arguments, *a-list* and *num*, and returns the last *num* elements from *a-list*. Use the other list functions from this section in your solution.

4.16 The function month below returns the month corresponding to month-num. Does the function work correctly? If not, fix it.

```
(define (month month-num)
  (list-ref '(January February March April May June July
              August September October November December)
    month-num) )
```

4.17 The function replace-element below takes *a-list*, a list, *position*, a position in *a-list*, and *element*, an atom that will replace the element at *position* in *a-list*. For example,

```
> (replace-element '(this list is very mundane) 4 'exciting)
(this list is very exciting)
```

Find and fix any bugs in the function below. Note: append combines the elements of many lists into one list. See section 4.7 for a detailed explanation.

```
(define (replace-element a-list position element)
  (append
    (subseq a-list 0 position)
    element
    (subseq a-list position)) )
```

4.18 Fill in the blanks with functions and arguments so that the output shown would be produced. Each line may have zero or more arguments.

```
> (_____ '(a list of sorts) _____)
(a list)

> (_____ '(a list of sorts) _____)
(list of)

> (_____ '(a list of sorts) _____)
(of sorts)

> (_____ '(a list of sorts) _____)
list
```

4.6 Combining cars and cdrs

There are times when you have a rather complex list data structure, with many sublists (elements that are lists themselves). To extract particular elements from sublists, combinations of cars and cdrs can be used as shown in exercise 4.7. Because such constructions are used so often in Scheme, abbreviations have been

Abbreviations of car *and* cdr *compositions*

created to compose up to four levels of `car` and `cdr` function calls. The expression

```
(car (cdr '((Sam Smith) 23000 (August 5 1967))))
```

can be abbreviated as

```
(cadr '((Sam Smith) 23000 (August 5 1967)))
```

This particular expression returns the second element from the list given; hence it could be expressed as

```
(second '((Sam Smith) 23000 (August 5 1967)))
```

Abbreviations of `car` and `cdr` combinations are made by taking the a's and d's from up to four adjacent `car` and `cdr` function calls and enclosing them between c and r. This is easier shown than said. Below are more examples of `car` and `cdr` combinations and their abbreviations.

longhand	abbreviation
`(cdr (car my-list))`	`(cdar my-list)`
`(car (car (cdr my-list))`	`(caadr my-list)`
`(car (cdr (car (cdr my-list))))`	`(cadadr my-list)`

One major problem with `car` and `cdr` and the various combinations of abbreviations thereof is their correct pronunciation. The table below should help you with this.

car cdr *pronunciation*

function	pronunciation	rhymes with or sounds like
car	kär	car
cdr	kŭ´-dər	footer
caar	kə-är´	the 'r'
cadr	ka´-dər	fatter
cdar	kŭ-där´	foot tar
cddr	kŭ-di´-dər	could litter
cadar	kə-där´	the tar
cadadr	kə-da´-dər	cadaver
cddadr	kŭ-di-da´-dər	could it matter

ä as in *car*, *ŭ* as in *could*, *ə* as in *the* or *cut*, *a* as in *cat*.

4.7 Creating Lists

We have created lists by writing them out explicitly, as in

```
(this is a list)
```

We have used functions that return parts of lists, possibly creating new lists in the process. Sometimes we need even more flexibility.

Lists can be created using the functions `cons`, `list`, and `append`.

function	arguments	return value
cons	*element list*	*list* with *element* inserted at the start
list	*el1 el2 ... elN*	the list (*el1 el2 ... elN*)
append	*list1 list2 ... listN*	the list formed by concatenating the elements of *list1 list2 ... listN*.

Functions to build lists

cons takes two arguments and returns a new list that has *element* as its first
element and *list* as the rest of the list. The first argument, *element*, can be a list or
an atom, but the second argument, *list*, should be a list[4].

cons

Below are some examples of what cons returns and what the car and cdr of
those return values look like.

```
> (cons 'something '())
(something)

> (car '(something))
something

> (cdr '(something))
()


> (cons 'apples '(and oranges))
(apples and oranges)

> (car '(apples and oranges))
apples

> (cdr '(apples and oranges))
(and oranges)


> (cons '(some list) '(another list))
((some list) another list)

> (car '((some list) another list))
(some list)

> (cdr '((some list) another list))
(another list)
```

Notice in each of the above cases that the first argument to cons is the car of the
resultant list and the second argument is the cdr of the resultant list. This is true
for cons in general.

cons *as opposite of*
car *and* cdr

The first example,

```
(cons 'something '())
```

shows how to create a list of one element by inserting (consing) that element into

----
[4]. If the second argument is not a list, the result will be a dotted list. Dotted lists are discussed in the
optional section on dotted lists at the end of this chapter.

an empty list.

The second example,

> ```
> (cons 'apples '(and oranges))
> ```

shows the addition of an atom to the front of an existing list.

The third example,

> ```
> (cons '(some list) '(another list))
> ```

demonstrates that lists can be added as elements.

Using cons to create a list of three elements involves three calls to cons:

```
> (cons 'a (cons 'b (cons 'c '())))
(a b c)
```

list
list provides a more convenient means of creating lists of many elements. list takes as arguments the elements of the desired list and returns a new list of those elements. The order of the arguments corresponds to the order of the elements in the resultant list. The arguments to list can be atoms or lists. Below are some examples showing how list works. Note that the arguments to list must be quoted if they are lists or symbols and are to be interpreted as such.

```
> (list 'a 'b 'c)
(a b c)

> (list '(a list) 'a-symbol 4 '())
((a list) a-symbol 4 ())
```

append
Another way to create lists is to use append. append takes all the top-level elements of its argument lists and forms a new list of those elements. In other words, append concatenates the top-level elements from all of its arguments into a new list. Internally, append works by performing a series of conses. Elements from all but the last argument list are consed onto the last list. This is easier shown than said. Following each example of append below is the equivalent series of cons function calls:

```
> (append '(first list) '(second list) '(third list))
(first list second list third list)

> (cons 'first
        (cons 'list (cons 'second (cons 'list '(third list)))))
(first list second list third list)


> (append '((32)) '() '(((1 2 3))))
((32) ((1 2 3)))

> (cons '(32) '(((1 2 3))))
((32) ((1 2 3)))
```

```
> (append 4 '(3))
Error: Pair expected
```

The first example above shows how multiple lists appended together result in one new list with the elements of each list as elements of the new list. The second example of append shows that the empty list can be appended to other lists. By doing so, no elements are added. The last append is illegal, since all the arguments to append should be lists.[5]

cons, list, and append perform different tasks and return different lists when given the same arguments. Look at the following examples:

Differences with cons, list, *and* append

```
> (cons '(1) '(a))
((1) a)

> (list '(1) '(a))
((1) (a))

> (append '(1) '(a))
(1 a)
```

It may seem strange to have the functions cons, list, and append when it is easier to create lists by writing them out explicitly, as in

Literal versus constructed lists

```
'(this ((list is) easy to make))
```

Sometimes the elements of a list are not known beforehand, since they must be computed. These computations may be numerical or may involve extracting information from other lists. These lists may be the values of variables, since variables can be bound to lists using define or used in functions as parameters. In these cases, such lists must be created using cons, list, or append. The following example shows the creation of a new list consisting of the first element of the list employee-list, and the value of salary increased by 10%.

```
(list (first employee-list) (* salary 1.10))
```

Here is another example showing the necessity of these functions. Let's write a function, add-to-end, that takes an item and a list and returns the list with item added to the end. For example,

Adding to the end of a list

```
> (add-to-end 'period '(end a sentence with a))
(end a sentence with a period)

> (add-to-end '(parenthetical remark) '(end a sentence with a))
(end a sentence with a (parenthetical remark))
```

To do this we'll have to append the elements in the list to a list of the item to add:

---

[5] The last argument to append can be an atom. If so, the result will be a dotted list. Dotted lists are discussed in the optional section on dotted lists at the end of this chapter.

```
; Return a-list with item added to the end.
(define (add-to-end item a-list)
  (append a-list (list item)) )
```

Mistakes to Avoid

Suppose the variable `people` has the value 842. To make a list of that number, the call

```
(people)
```

won't work, as it will treat `people` as a function. Instead use **list** as follows:

```
(list people)
```

Mistakes to Avoid

Don't use `list` as the name of a parameter to a function. The parameter will shadow the function **list**.

```
> (define (add-to-end item list)
    (append list (list item)) )
??

> (add-to-end 'bang '(end a sentence with a))
Error: Wrong type to apply: (end a sentence with a)
```

4.7.1 Exercises

4.19 What do the following expressions evaluate to? Some of them may produce errors.

```
(cons 3 '(4))        (list 3 '(4))        (append 3 '(4))

(cons '(3) '(4))     (list '(3) '(4))     (append '(3) '(4))

                     (list 3 4)

                     (list '(3) 4)
```

4.20 Assume that the following `defines` have been made:

```
(define numbers '(2 4 6))
(define letters '(q e d))
(define deep-list '(((13))))
```

Using only these three variables and the functions `cons`, `list`, and `append`, write expressions that will return the following lists:

```
(2 4 6 q e d ((13)))

((2 4 6) (q e d) ((13)))

(2 4 6 (q e d) ((13)))

((2 4 6) (q e d) (((13))))

((2 4 6) q e d ((13)))
```

4.21 Fill in the blanks with functions and arguments so that the output shown would be produced.

```
> (_____ _____ '(not created equal))
(alas all lists are not created equal)

> (_____ _____ '(not created equal))
((alas all lists are) not created equal)

> (_____ _____ '(not created equal))
(lists (not created equal))

> (_____ _____ '(not created equal))
((lists) (not created equal))
```

4.22 Write a function that takes a list *a-list* and returns a list of only the first element of *a-list*. Note: this is not the same as `first` or `car`. For example, given the list (an apple a day), your function should return (an).

4.23 Write a function `add-third` that takes two arguments, *element* and *a-list*, and returns *a-list* with *element* as the new third element. The original third element of *a-list* becomes the new fourth element, and so on for the remaining elements in *a-list*. For example, given the symbol eaten and the list (an apple a day), your function should return (an apple eaten a day). Assume that *a-list* has at least three elements.

4.24 Write a function `remove-third` that takes a list and returns the list without its third element. For example, given the list (an apple a day), your function should return (an apple day). Assume that the list has at least three elements.

4.25 Write a function `switch-first-and-second` that takes a list and returns the list with the first and second elements switched. For example, given the list (an apple a day), your function should return (apple an a day). Assume that the list has at least two elements.

4.8   Representing and Manipulating Text with Lists

Using lists to represent sentences

Lists are a natural data structure to represent text. Sentences can be represented as lists of words, and words as symbols; thus, the sentence "Kim likes to dance to Aretha Franklin tunes" can be represented by

```
(kim likes to dance to aretha franklin tunes)
```

If we wanted to play around with this sentence, we should first bind it to a symbol, as in

```
> (define sentence '(kim likes to dance to aretha franklin tunes))
??
```

To produce the sentence "Kim likes to dance in the dark" we can use the following expression:

```
> (append (subseq sentence 0 4) '(in the dark))
(kim likes to dance in the dark)
```

To produce the sentence "Kim dances to Aretha Franklin tunes," use the expression

```
> (cons (first sentence) (cons 'dances (subseq sentence 4)))
(kim dances to aretha franklin tunes)
```

or

```
> (append (list (first sentence) 'dances) (subseq sentence 4))
(kim dances to aretha franklin tunes)
```

Sentence data abstraction

The problem with these solutions is that they require prior knowledge of what the original sentence looks like. To work properly, the calls to subseq require knowledge of the number of words at the end and beginning of the sentence. A better solution would be to organize the sentence into parts—a noun phrase, verb phrase, and object phrase. The original sentence would be represented as

```
> (define noun-phrase '(kim))
??

> (define verb-phrase '(likes to dance))
??

> (define object-phrase '(to aretha franklin tunes))
??
```

To make the entire sentence, use

```
> (append noun-phrase verb-phrase object-phrase)
(kim likes to dance to aretha franklin tunes)
```

The other two sentences can be produced as follows:

```
> (append noun-phrase verb-phrase '(in the dark))
(kim likes to dance in the dark)

> (append noun-phrase '(dances) object-phrase)
(kim dances to aretha franklin tunes)
```

To make these solutions more general, functions could be made as follows:

```
; Return a sentence with noun-phrase, verb-phrase,
; and "in the dark."
(define (in-the-dark-sentence noun-phrase verb-phrase)
  (append
    noun-phrase
    verb-phrase
    '(in the dark)) )

; Return a sentence with noun-phrase, "dances,"
; and object-phrase.
(define (dances-sentence noun-phrase object-phrase)
  (append
    noun-phrase
    '(dances)
    object-phrase) )
```

These functions could be called with other phrases to produce new sentences.

```
> (in-the-dark-sentence '(little green creatures)
                        '(are often seen))
(little green creatures are often seen in the dark)

> (dances-sentence '(a little purple creature)
                   '(on her fingertips in my dreams))
(a little purple creature dances on her fingertips in my dreams)
```

Such sentences could not have been produced with the original solutions to this problem. By creating a more generic representation of a sentence, we ended up with more general and useful solutions.

4.8.1 Exercises

4.26 Why was the list (kim) used to represent a noun phrase instead of the symbol kim, which could be consed onto the verb and object phrases?

4.27 How might you further define a generic sentence to allow more variation in the sentences that could be produced?

4.28 Write a function add-words that takes *sentence*, a list representing a sentence, *words*, another list representing words to add to *sentence*, and *position*, a number denoting a position in *sentence*. add-words should return a list made by adding the words in *words* to *sentence* immediately before the word at *position* in *sentence*. For example,

```
> (add-words '(the dog barks loudly) '(with huge fangs) 2)
(the dog with huge fangs barks loudly)
```

4.8.2   Computer-Generated sweepstakes

How many times have you received mail telling you something like this:

OLIVER GRILLMEYER

will receive $1,000,000

in the ``Aren't We Cool´´ Sweepstakes

to be paid in yearly installments of $100,000
over the next 10 years or $50,000 over the next 20 years
if you are the one-in-a-billion lucky person chosen in our random drawing.

If you have gotten this letter, what are you doing with my junk mail?

Creating form letters   Scheme can be used to create such form letters, given a list of names to send them to. To begin we need a representation for the names. One simple solution is to represent names as symbols in a list like

```
(John Q. Public)
```

The problem with such an approach is that our form letters may wish to extract the last name to print something like

> Imagine your response when our representative comes to your door to say "Congratulations Mr. Grillmeyer, you have won $1,000,000."

Representing names   To do this we need to extract the last name from a list. It may seem simple enough using `subseq` as follows:

```
> (subseq '(John Q. Public) 2)
(Public)
```

But what if the person has no middle name? Again you can be clever and just extract the last element of the list by determining how many elements to skip from the front based on the length of the list.

```
> (subseq '(Jane Doe) (- (length '(Jane Doe)) 1))
(Doe)
```

As an exercise, write a function that takes a list and returns the last name based on this approach. Does your function work on lists with any number of first or middle names?

Difficulties with names   There is another potential problem lurking here. The last symbol in a name list may not be the person's last name. For example,

complete name	last name
Ludwig van Beethoven	van Beethoven
Myriam Roxanna Haynal M.D.	Haynal
Dr. Gino Cheng Esq.	Cheng
Carla Juanita de la Cruz III	de la Cruz

A seemingly simple problem has opened up into a can of worms. To get around our current dilemma we can do one of three things:

1) Write Scheme code to deal with all of these special cases.
2) Represent names in a different way to disambiguously represent last names.

3) Ignore the issue and have our letters only print the person's entire name.

The third approach may seem like an invalid solution, but there are times when tasks just get too difficult and it is better to simplify the problem rather than implement it as originally desired. The pioneers in language translation learned this lesson the hard way. More on that in Chapter 15.

The first approach is possible if we have a handle on all the possible titles and prefixes to last names we may run across, and there are no ambiguities. It is left as an exercise to the reader.

The second approach is easiest, assuming we have control over the form of the data. This is not always the case for programmers. However, when it is an option, it is best to design your data representation to simplify your task. This is a frequently used technique in programming. In fact, there are entire texts devoted to program design as a split between data representation and algorithms[6].

Data representations to simplify coding

Another advantage is that we don't have to worry about future names that don't follow the conventions of which we are currently aware. There are plenty of nonconventional names you are probably aware of such as Madonna, Sting, the Edge, Plato, Socrates, and Aristotle (the ancient Greeks didn't have last names).

We can represent names as a list of five lists denoting the prefix, first, middle, last name, and suffixes of the person. Thus, Miss Carla Juanita de la Cruz III becomes

```
((Miss) (Carla) (Juanita) (de la Cruz) (III))
```

And Sting becomes

```
(() (Sting) () () ())
```

The last name is the fourth element of a name list. Below is a *selector* function to extract the last name from a name list:

Selector functions

```
; Return the last name, fourth element, from a name list.
(define (last-name name-list)
  (fourth name-list) )
```

It may seem pointless to create a function as simple as this, but it is worthwhile because it makes our final program more readable. It is clearer what is happening when we use a function called last-name rather than fourth. Also, if we should decide to change the data representation, we need only change the selector function. We don't have to search through the entire program looking for calls to fourth and decide if they are extracting the last name or doing something else.

Let's return to the problem of writing form letters. A form letter can be viewed as a template in which the person's name is to be inserted in certain parts. One such form letter may be the following:

[6.] Niklaus Wirth's text *Programs = Algorithms + Data Structures* is a classic example and is a good text, despite the fact that the title is an equation.

Dear Mr. Grillmeyer

This is your last chance to receive our mailings at
the Grillmeyer residence. By ordering your personalized
ceramic utensil set, we will enter the Grillmeyer family
in our sweepstakes giveaway. Don't think any more,
just do it.

To produce such a form letter we can generate a list of symbols for each line
of actual text. An entire form letter will be a list of these lists. Here is an attempt
to produce the above form letter:

```
; Return the prefix (first element) from a name list.
(define (prefix name-list)
  (first name-list) )

; Produce a form letter addressed to name-list.
(define (make-form-letter name-list)
  (list
    (list 'Dear (prefix name-list) (last-name name-list))
    '()
    '(This is your last chance to receive our mailings at)
    (list 'the (last-name name-list) 'residence. 'By 'ordering
          'your 'personalized)
    (list 'ceramic 'utensil 'set, 'we 'will 'enter 'the
          (last-name name-list) 'family)
    '(in our sweepstakes giveaway. Don't think any more,)
    '(just do it.)) )
```

However, when we enter this code into the Scheme interpreter, we get the following error:

```
Error: Comma not inside a quasiquote.
```

Recall from Chapter 3 that commas are not allowed in symbol names. Their
use will be shown in the next section on quasiquoted lists. If we remove the commas from our lists and reenter the function, no error results. So let's try it out.

```
> (make-form-letter '((Mr.) (Michael) (Phillip) (Jagger) '()))
((DEAR (MR.) (JAGGER)) () (THIS IS YOUR LAST CHANCE TO RECEIVE OUR
MAILINGS AT) (THE (JAGGER) RESIDENCE. BY ORDERING YOUR PERSONALIZE
D) (CERAMIC UTENSIL SET WE WILL ENTER THE (JAGGER) FAMILY) (IN OUR
SWEEPSTAKES GIVEAWAY. DON 'T THINK ANY MORE) (JUST DO IT.))
```

This output is far from desirable. In Chapter 9 we cover a means of getting
around this problem. For now, we can print one line at a time using functions
like first or list-ref.

```
> (first (make-form-letter '((Mr.) (Michael) (Phillip) (Jagger) ())))
(DEAR (MR.) (JAGGER))
```

The remaining problem is to eliminate the extra parentheses. This can be done
using append instead of list when creating our lists. Simply changing list to
append will introduce another problem, because all the arguments to append

should be lists. Below is the correct solution:

```
; Produce a form letter addressed to name-list.
(define (make-form-letter name-list)
  (list
    (append '(Dear) (prefix name-list) (last-name name-list))
    '()
    '(This is your last chance to receive our mailings at)
    (append '(the) (last-name name-list)
            '(residence. By ordering your personalized))
    (append '(ceramic utensil set we will enter the)
            (last-name name-list) '(family))
    '(in our sweepstakes giveaway. Don't think any more,)
    '(just do it.)) )
```

4.8.3 Exercises

4.29 Does the above solution give reasonable output when called with names like Sting or Madonna?

4.30 Write a function that generates your own personalized form letter.

4.9   Optional Section: Quasiquoted Lists

Building lists with quasiquote

Another means of creating lists is to use the special form `quasiquote`. Rather than specifying the structure and contents of a list using combinations of `cons`, `list`, and `append`, `quasiquote` allows you to indicate the form of the list directly. `quasiquote` (abbreviated as "`` ` ``") is an extension of the special form `quote`. It can be used to produce literal lists such as

```
> `(mary had a little lamb (or so the story goes))
(mary had a little lamb (or so the story goes))
```

Evaluating parts of quasiquoted *lists*

To create lists that contain the values of variables or the results of computations, simply precede any expressions that you wish to be evaluated by a comma. This is a shorthand for `unquote`. Assume that the definitions below have been made:

```
(define person 'mary)

(define object '(a little lamb))
```

The list `(mary had a little lamb (or so the story goes))` can be created with

```
`(,person had a little ,(third object) (or so the story goes))
```

Notice what happens when a list is inserted.

```
> `(,person had ,object (or so the story goes))
(mary had (a little lamb) (or so the story goes))
```

unquote-splicing

There is an operator similar to comma—comma followed by the at-sign "@". This is a shorthand for **unquote-splicing**. The expression following the comma-at-sign pair should evaluate to a list, and this list is appended to the rest of the **quasiquoted** list. Thus,

```
> `(,person had ,@object (or so the story goes))
(mary had a little lamb (or so the story goes))
```

In summary, to add an evaluated expression to a list, use

  , *expression*

where you wish the evaluated expression to go. To insert the elements of a list obtained from evaluating an expression, use

  , @*expression*

in the **quasiquoted** list at the position where these elements should go.

4.9.1   Exercises

4.31 Assume that the following **defines** have been made:

```
(define number 8.31)
(define name '(gino as in pizza))
```

What do the following expressions evaluate to?

```
`(number ,number name ,name)

`((+ number 100) ,@name)

`(,(+ number 1) ,@(cdr name))
```

4.32 Using the symbols defined in the previous exercise, write expressions that would produce the following lists:

```
(gino as in 8.31)

(gino as in (gino as in) pizza)

((8.31 gino (as in pizza)) 10.31)
```

4.33 Write a function that uses **quasiquoted** lists to create form letters as shown in the previous section.

4.10   Miscellaneous List Functions

A number of other functions work with lists. Below are some of these functions, the arguments that they take, and the values they return. **member** and **reverse** are built-in Scheme functions. The other functions will be defined in this section or in the appendix. They are given as exercises in Chapter 6. Other functions allow you to apply a function to each element in a list. These functions will be covered in Chapter 8.

function	arguments	return value
position	*element list*	the position of *element* in *list* (counting from zero), #f if *element* is not in *list*
member	*element list*	the rest of *list* starting with the first occurrence of *element*, #f if *element* is not in *list*
count	*element list*	the number of occurrences of *element* in *list*
remove	*element list*	*list* with all occurrences of *element* removed
reverse	*list*	the reverse of the top-level elements of *list*

The functions `position`, `member`, `count`, and `remove` search for elements within *list*. These elements can be numbers, symbols, or lists. This behavior can be seen in the following examples that show sample calls of the function `position`:

Which elements get matched

```
> (define my-list '(this list (will help) explain 6 list functions))
??

> (position 'list my-list)
1

> (position 6 my-list)
4

> (position 'word my-list)
#f

> (position '(will help) my-list)
2

> (position 'will my-list)
#f
```

The functions that search for the occurrence of *element* within *list* do not search sublists within *list*. The last function call resulted in #f because `position` does not look within sublists to find matches. Calling `member` with 'will and the same list as arguments will yield #f. Calling `count` with 'will and the same list as arguments will yield 0. Similarly, calling `remove` with the same arguments will return the original *list* (no elements are removed).

Certain elements don't get matched

Here are examples of the other functions:

```
> (member 6 my-list)
(6 list functions)

> (member 'list my-list)
(list (will help) explain 6 list functions)

> (count 6 my-list)
1

> (count 'list my-list)
2
```

```
> (remove 6 my-list)
(this list (will help) explain list functions)

> (remove 'list my-list)
(this (will help) explain 6 functions)

> (reverse my-list)
(functions list 6 explain (will help) list this)
```

Notice that in the call to **reverse**, the sublist (will help) was not reversed. **reverse** only reverses the top-level elements.

Writing count

We don't know enough to write the function **remove**; that material is covered in the sections on creating lists and filters in Chapter 6. We can write the function **count** (using **remove**) and we can write a simplified version of **position**. The number of times an item occurs in a list can be determined by subtracting the number of elements in the list from the number of elements that are left in the list after all occurrences of the item are removed. The number of items in a list is the **length** of that list. The function **count** follows:

```
; Return the number of times item occurs in a-list.
(define (count item a-list)
  (- (length a-list)
     (length (remove item a-list))) )
```

Writing position

The position of an item in a list can be determined using a similar technique as used in **count**. Taking **member** of the item and the list will return the list from item onwards. The difference between the length of the entire list and the list from **member** is the number of elements that occur before the item, which is the same as the position of the item. Here is the code to do this:

```
; Return the position of item in a-list.
(define (position item a-list)
  (- (length a-list)
     (length (member item a-list))) )
```

Note: this version of **position** does not work if item does not occur in a-list.

4.10.1 Exercises

4.34 Using the symbol my-list defined as

```
(this list (will help) explain 6 list functions)
```

and the functions in this section, write expressions that will return the following lists. You may use more than one function in each answer.

```
(explain 6 list functions)
```

```
3
```

```
((will help) explain 6 functions)
```

```
(explain (will help) list this)
```

```
(this list (will help))

((will help) explain)

(functions explain this)
```

4.35 Write a function with two parameters, *element* and *a-list*, that returns the position of the last occurrence of *element* in *a-list*. Assume that *element* is in *a-list*. Watch out for *off-by-one errors*—those in which the answer you get is one away from the answer you want.

4.36 Write a function that takes a list and returns the list with the first and last elements switched.

4.37 Write a function `count-both` that takes two atoms and a list and returns the number of times either of those atoms occurs in the list. Write two versions of this function: one using the function **+** and one without **+**. For example,

```
> (count-both 'a 'b '(a b r a c a d a b r a))
7
```

4.38 Suppose the following expressions have been entered into Scheme:

```
(define months
  '(jan feb mar apr may jun jul aug sep oct nov dec))
(define days
  '( 31  28  31  30  31  30  31  31  30  31  30  31))
```

Write a function `num-days` that takes a symbol representing a month and returns the number of days in that month. For example,

```
> (num-days 'jul)
31
```

4.39 Write a function `whos-there` that returns the names of people working on a certain day and time. `whos-there` has two parameters: *schedule*, a list representing the work schedule for some day, and *time*, an hour of the day (in military time, 0–23). Here is a sample schedule for Monday:

```
(10 hiro 11 madelaine elizabeth 12 13 kessie lou 14)
```

Given this schedule and the time 11, `whos-there` should return the list (`madelaine elizabeth`). Called with the time 12, an empty list should be returned.

Hint: think how you can extract part of the schedule from a certain time till one hour past that time (e.g., that part of the list from 11 to 12), and then adjust this to get the names only. What assumptions about the schedule and hour passed in do you have to make to avoid getting errors when the function is called?

4.11   Representing a Database with Lists

Let's return to the example given earlier of maintaining a database of CDs. Recall that the data structure looked like the following:

CD database

```
(rock
    (Rolling_Stones
        (Black_and_Blue
         Its_Only_Rock_and_Roll))
 jazz
    (Pat_Metheny
        (First_Circle)
     Andy_Narell
        (The_Hammer)))
```

4.11.1   Selecting items from the database

Finding the jazz artists

Let's write an expression to return all the jazz artists and CDs in the collection. We'll assume that the CDs may not be in the order shown above (i.e., rock CDs first, then jazz CDs). The order may be different or other music types may exist. Assume that the CD list has been bound to the symbol CD-list. The jazz artists and CDs are in the list following the top-level symbol jazz within CD-list. To get this list, a combination of **list-ref** and **position** can be used. **position** can be used with jazz to find the location of jazz in CD-list:

```
> (position 'jazz CD-list)
2
```

list-ref can use this result (with one added to it) to get the list of jazz artists and CDs:

```
> (list-ref CD-list (+ (position 'jazz CD-list) 1))
(Pat_Metheny (First_Circle) Andy_Narell (The_Hammer))
```

A slightly simpler solution uses **member**:

```
> (member 'jazz CD-list)
(jazz (Pat_Metheny (First_Circle) Andy_Narell (The_Hammer)))
```

Taking **second** of this list gives us the same list we got above:

```
> (second (member 'jazz CD-list))
(Pat_Metheny (First_Circle) Andy_Narell (The_Hammer))
```

Finding a particular list of CDs

We can go a level deeper and write an expression that returns Andy Narell's CDs. The technique used to return the jazz artists and CDs can be used to find the CDs of a particular artist. This is due to the the similarities between CD-list and the artist-CD lists. CD-list consists of pairs; each pair is a category and an artist-CD list. The artist-CD lists are similar in that they are pairs, where each pair has an artist name and a CD list. To illustrate this parallel, observe the following:

```
> (define jazz-artist-CD-list (second (member 'jazz CD-list)))
??
```

```
> jazz-artist-CD-list
(Pat_Metheny (First_Circle) Andy_Narell (The_Hammer))

> (second (member 'andy_narell jazz-artist-CD-list))
(The_Hammer)
```

Now let's write a general function that takes a musical category (e.g., rock, jazz) and an artist, and returns all the CDs from that artist. This can be accomplished by generalizing what we did above through the use of parameters instead of specific values. To improve the readability of the solution, the composition of second and member can be made into a function as follows:

Generalizing what we've done

```
; Return the element that follows selector in a-list.
(define (element-after selector a-list)
  (second (member selector a-list)) )
```

Here are two example calls to this new function:

```
> (element-after 'rock CD-list)
(Rolling_Stones (Black_and_Blue Its_Only_Rock_and_Roll))

> (element-after 'Pat_Metheny jazz-artist-CD-list)
(First_Circle)
```

The main function can now be written:

```
; Return the CDs by artist and type in CD-list.
(define (artist-CD-list type artist CD-list)
  (element-after
    artist
    (element-after type CD-list)) )
```

Extracting a list of CDs

Here are some sample calls to this new function:

```
> (artist-CD-list 'jazz 'pat-metheny CD-list)
(First_Circle)

> (artist-CD-list 'rock 'rolling_stones CD-list)
(black_and_blue its_only_rock_and_roll)
```

4.11.2 Adding elements to the database

Now let's write a function to add new CDs to the above structure. The function will take four parameters: the CD to add, the category of music, the artist name, and the CD data structure. This problem involves taking apart and rebuilding lists. It can be thought of in the following steps:

- Get the list of existing CDs from CD-list, the CD data structure
- Add the new CD to the head of that list
- Create a new artist-CD list using the new list of CDs
- Create a new overall CD list using the new artist-CD list

Pseudo code to add CDs

Let's refine these steps:

- Get the list of existing CDs from CD-list, the CD data structure:
  This is exactly what the function artist-CD-list written above does.
- Add the new CD to the head of that list:
  This involves calling **cons** with the new CD and the result from the above step.
- Create a new artist-CD list using the new list of CDs:
  Before we refine this step, we should think of it in general terms to combine it with the next step.
- Create a new overall CD list using the new artist-CD list:

Changing an element in a list

The last two steps involve creating a new list that has one element changed from the original list. A new element replaces the element immediately after the category or artist name in the list. The task is to write a function that takes a list, a-list, an element to add, element, and a category or artist name, selector, and returns a new list with element inserted in the position following selector in a-list. For example, the value returned from

```
(new-element jazz-artist-CD-list '(We_Live_Here First_Circle)
          'Pat_Metheny)
```

is

```
(Pat_Metheny (We_Live_Here First_Circle) Andy_Narell (The_Hammer))
```

This function combines three lists:

- the items before the element to be added—the left side of the list
- the list of the new element
- the items after the element to be added—the right side of the list

Now our task is to refine these three steps.

- Step 1: the items before the element to be added—the left side of the list

Getting the elements before the item to be added

To get the left side of a list, use **subseq**. **subseq** needs the position of the category or artist name to denote the last element (the *end*) of the left side. The *start* value is 0. Putting this together in a function we get

```
; Return the elements up to and including selector in a-list.
(define (items-before a-list selector)
  (subseq
    a-list
    0
    (position selector a-list)) )
```

Testing this new function yields

```
> (items-before jazz-artist-CD-list 'Pat_Metheny)
()
```

We wanted to have the list

```
(Pat_Metheny)
```

Remember that `subseq` does not include the element at position *end*. We made an off-by-one error, which is easily fixed by adding one to the value that `position` returns. The corrected code is

```
; Return the elements up to and including selector in a-list.
(define (items-before a-list selector)
  (subseq
    a-list
    0
    (+ (position selector a-list) 1)) )
```

Testing this new function yields

```
> (items-before jazz-artist-CD-list 'Pat_Metheny)
(Pat_Metheny)
```

- Step 2: the list of the new element

This is easily done using `list`. We must use the list of the element to add and not just the element because we are using `append` to build up the new list, and `append` takes lists of the elements that will be in the resulting list.

- Step 3: the items after the element to be added—the right side of the list

To return the tail end of a list, `subseq` can be used. Once again we know the position of the category or artist that is before the element that gets added. This position could be used with `subseq`. Since we want the tail end of the list, we can leave off the third argument, *end*, to `subseq`. The *start* value is the position of the first element that is returned. This is the position of the element that is two elements beyond the *selector* (we want to skip the selector and its matching value—either a CD list or the remaining artist/CD list pairs). The code to return the elements after the new element added is

Getting the elements after the item to be added

```
; Return the elements following the artist selector and her CDs.
(define (items-after a-list selector)
  (subseq
    a-list
    (+ (position selector a-list) 2)) )
```

A test of this function yields

```
> (items-after jazz-artist-CD-list 'Pat_Metheny)
(Andy_Narell (The_Hammer))
```

This is correct. Putting the three pieces together we can write the function `new-element`:

```
; Return a-list with element replacing the item after selector.
(define (new-element a-list element selector)
  (append
    (items-before a-list selector)
    (list element)
    (items-after a-list selector)) )
```

Putting an element into a list

A test of this function yields

```
> (new-element jazz-artist-CD-list '(We_Live_Here First_Circle)
                'Pat_Metheny)
(Pat_Metheny (We_Live_Here First_Circle) Andy_Narell (The_Hammer))
```

The final step is to put all the pieces listed below together to produce the function `add-new-CD`:

- Get the list of existing CDs from `CD-list`
- Add the new CD to the head of that list
- Create a new artist-CD list using the new list of CDs
- Create a new overall CD list using the new artist-CD list

Putting a CD in the CD data structure

```
; Return a new CD-list with a new CD added for artist in
; category.
(define (add-new-CD CD category artist CD-list)
  (new-element
    CD-list
    (new-element
      (element-after category CD-list)
      (cons
        CD
        (artist-CD-list category artist CD-list) )
      artist)
    category) )
```

Let's test this function:

```
> (add-new-CD 'Tattoo-you 'rock 'Rolling_Stones CD-list)
(rock
    (Rolling_Stones
        (Tattoo-you
         Black_and_Blue
         Its_Only_Rock_and_Roll))
 jazz
    (Pat_Metheny
        (First_Circle)
     Andy_Narell
        (The_Hammer))))
```

The actual output will not be indented as shown.

Why so many functions?

Each step in the pseudo code was carried out by a function. We did not need to use this many functions in the solution to this problem. The advantage to such an approach, however, is that each function can be tested individually. Then, when all the parts are put together, the chances of the entire solution being correct are much greater.

If the code is written as one large function and contains some error, a *bug*, it may be in any part of the function, and there is no easy way to narrow it down without looking through the entire large function.

Another advantage to having so many functions is they can act as building blocks to a larger program. Selecting or creating parts of the data structure can be done with these generic functions. Another real advantage is lurking here: should the data structure change, all that needs to be changed are these selector and creator functions. This topic is covered in depth in Chapter 7.

4.11.3 Exercises

4.40 Write `items-before` and `items-after` using **member** and some of the other functions presented earlier instead of **subseq**.

4.41 Write a function `delete-CD` that has the same parameters as `add-new-CD`, but instead of adding a new CD, `delete-CD` returns a CD list with CD removed. Does your solution work if CD is not in the CD list?

4.12 Optional Section: Internal Representations of Lists

Scheme represents lists as sequences of *cons cells*. A cons cell has two components: the first indicates the next element of the list and the second indicates the rest of the list. The list (a b c) consists of three cons cells. It can be drawn as follows:

Cons cells: the building blocks of lists

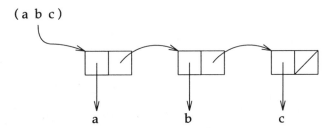

Each box represents a cons cell. The left half of the box has an arrow that points to an element of the list. The right half of the box has an arrow that points to the rest of the list. In the case of the third cons cell, the rest of the list is ( ). This is represented as a box with a line through it. Scheme denotes the end of a list by having the right half of a cons cell point to ( ).[7] The arrows are called *pointers*. A pointer represents a location in the computer's memory. A pointer to a symbol is the location of that symbol in the computer. A list is represented as a pointer to the first cons cell in a cons cell chain. The pointer on the upper left in the above diagram represents the list (a b c). Scheme prints out lists by sequencing through the chain of cons cells until a cons cell with a ( ) right side is encountered. For each cons cell, the element pointed to by the left side pointer is printed out.

Pointers

[7.] In the case of dotted lists, the end of a list is a cons cell whose right side points to an atom. Dotted lists are covered in the next section.

How cons cells make lists

Cons cells are created and combined to make lists. The function `cons` creates a single cons cell. The two arguments to `cons` are the objects to which the left and right pointers of the new cons cell will point. Again, think of a list as being represented by a pointer to the first cons cell in the chain of cons cells that make up that list. This tells us that `car` is obtained by returning what the left half of that first cons cell points to, and `cdr` returns what the right half points to.

Examples of cons cell diagrams

The diagrams below are illustrations of the lists shown in section 4.7. , "Creating Lists." Notice that the left side of the first cons cell points to the `car` of the list and the right side points to the `cdr`.

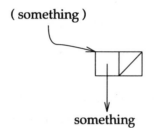

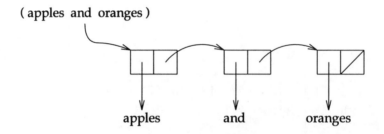

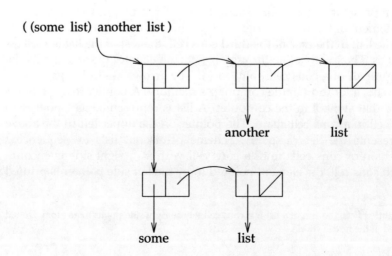

Thinking in terms of the internal representations of lists, `cons`, `list`, and `append` perform the following actions:

What `cons`, `list`, *and* `append` *really do*

- `cons` adds a new cons cell to the front of the list.
- `list` creates a chain of cons cells—one for each argument with which it is called.
- `append` creates new cons cells that are connected to the list representing the last argument given to `append`. One cons cell is created for each element in each of the lists that is supplied as an argument to `append`, with the exception of the last argument.

4.13   Optional Section: Dotted Lists

If an object is `consed` onto an atom, a *dotted list* is returned.

Dotted lists

```
> (cons 'something 'strange)
(something . strange)

> (cons '(some list) 'strange)
((some list) . strange)
```

The example,

```
(cons 'something 'strange)
```

shows what happens when a symbol is `consed` onto a symbol. The resultant object,

```
(something . strange)
```

is called a dotted list. The dot notation is used to differentiate a normal list—one with `()` as its final `cdr`—from a dotted list. The final `cdr` of a dotted list is not a cons cell or `()`. The diagram below shows the internal representation of this dotted list:

Representation of dotted lists

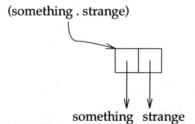

(something . strange)

something strange

The final `cdr` points to the symbol `strange`.

The `cars` and `cdrs` of the results from the above calls to `cons` are the same as the arguments that were applied to `cons`:

```
> (car '(something . strange))
something

> (cdr '(something . strange))
strange


> (car '((some list) . strange))
(some list)

> (cdr '((some list) . strange))
strange
```

Dotted lists can be produced by **append** when the last argument is an atom:

```
> (append '(4) 3)
(4 . 3)
```

This is equivalent to

```
> (cons 4 3)
(4 . 3)
```

Dotted lists can produce somewhat strange results when applied to some of the previously illustrated list functions:

```
> (first '(3 . 4))
3

> (second '(3 . 4))
Error: Pair expected

> (length '(3 . 4))
Error: Pair expected

> (member 3 '(3 . 4))
(3 . 4)

> (member 4 '(3 . 4))
Error: Pair expected
```

Using dotted lists with list functions

Most of the list functions will produce errors if they try to go beyond the final cons cell in a dotted list. This is what happened in all of the cases that resulted in errors above. The call to **first** and the first call to **member** were successful because they did not attempt to go past that final cons cell. This may not be true in all implementations of Scheme.

As a general rule, you should avoid using most list functions with dotted lists. The list functions that will work with dotted lists are **car**, **cdr**, **first**, and **rest**.

4.14 Summary

- The three basic data structures in Scheme are numbers, symbols, and lists. Collectively, numbers and symbols are called atoms. Lists are ordered collections of atoms or lists. The items in lists are called the elements of the list.
- The empty list, one with no elements, is written as `'()`.
- To stop the normal process of evaluation, the special form `quote` is used. `quote` is frequently used to stop the evaluation of lists as functions.
- Special forms are like functions, but they do not follow the evaluation rules for functions.
- To find the number of elements in a list, use `length`.
- To extract an element from a list whose position is known, use one of `first` through `fifth`.
- To extract elements from lists when their positions must be computed beforehand, use `list-ref`.
- To return all but the first element of a list, use `rest` or `cdr`.
- To return the head of a list, use `subseq` with 0 and *end*, where *end* is the last element number you want to include.
- To return the tail of a list, use `subseq` with *start* − 1, where *start* is the first element number you want to include.
- To return any contiguous section of a list, use `subseq` with *start* − 1 and *end*, where *start* is the first element to include and *end* is the last.
- Compositions of `car` and `cdr` can be abbreviated by surrounding the as and ds in the `car` and `cdr` calls with c and r.
- To return a list with a new first element, use `cons`.
- To create a list of many elements, use `list`.
- To put the elements of lists together into one list, use `append`.
- `quasiquote` can be used to create lists by specifying templates of the list. The elements are not evaluated unless they are preceded by a comma or a comma and at-sign, "`,@`". Forms preceded by a comma are evaluated and their return value used. Forms preceded by a comma-at-sign pair should evaluate to lists, and the elements of those lists are used.
- To return the position of an element, the number of times an element occurs, or the rest of the list starting from the element, use `position`, `count`, or `member`, respectively.
- To remove all occurrences of an element from a list, use `remove`.
- To get the reverse of a list, use `reverse`.
- The functions `position`, `count`, `member`, and `remove` do not search within sublists.
- Lists are composed of cons cell chains. Each cons cell has two pointers, which point to the next element in the list and the rest of the list.
- A dotted list is produced when an object is `cons`ed or `append`ed onto an atom.

- Summary of functions introduced in this chapter:

function	arguments	return value
length	*list*	the number of elements in *list*
first	*list*	first element of *list*
rest	*list*	rest of *list* without the first element
car	*list*	same as `first`
cdr	*list*	same as `rest`
second	*list*	second element of *list*
third	*list*	third element of *list*
fourth	*list*	fourth element of *list*
fifth	*list*	fifth element of *list*
list-ref	*list position*	element at position *pos* in *list*
subseq	*list 0 end*	left part of *list* up to element *end*
subseq	*list start*	right part of *list* starting at element *start* + 1
subseq	*list start end*	*list* with elements *start* + 1 through *end*
random	*num*	randomly generated number between 0 and *num* − 1
cons	*element list*	*list* with *element* inserted at the start
list	*el1 el2 ... elN*	the list (*el1 el2 ... elN*)
append	*list1 list2 ... listN*	the list formed by concatenating the elements of *list1, list2, ..., listN*.
position	*element list*	the position of *element* in *list* (counting from zero), #f if *element* is not in *list*
member	*element list*	the rest of *list* starting with the first occurrence of *element*, #f if *element* is not in *list*
count	*element list*	the number of occurrences of *element* in *list*
remove	*element list*	*list* with all occurrences of *element* removed
reverse	*list*	the reverse of the top-level elements of *list*

- Summary of special forms introduced in this chapter:

special form	arguments	return value
quote	*expression*	*expression* unevaluated
quasiquote	*expression*	*expression* unevaluated except for items preceded by "," or ", @"

CHAPTER 5

CONDITIONALS

5.1 Control Through Conditional Expressions

In addition to operations performed upon numbers, symbols, and lists, Scheme has control operations. Recall from Chapter 1 that control operations are an important element that separates computers from simpler computational devices. Control operations allow decisions to be made. Different actions are taken based on the given conditions. Let's look at how Scheme handles control.

Control operations

Scheme has a built-in special form, `if`, that checks a condition and returns one value if it's true and a different value if it's false.[1] The general form of `if` is as follows:

`if`

```
(if condition
    action
    else-action)
```

where *else-action* is optional. To use this function, we need to learn how to create conditions that return true or false values in Scheme.

Predicates are functions that return *true* / *false* values. They can be used as conditions within `if` special forms. Many of these functions are easily identifiable because their names end in `?`. Below is a list of some of the common predicate functions that work on numbers and their meanings:

Predicates

---

[1]. This is termed an *if-then-else statement* in many other programming languages.

predicate	arguments	returns true if and only if
<	*num1 ... numN*	$num1 < num2 < ... < numN$
>	*num1 ... numN*	$num1 > num2 > ... > numN$
=	*num1 ... numN*	$num1 = num2 = ... = numN$
<=	*num1 ... numN*	$num1 \le num2 \le ... \le numN$
>=	*num1 ... numN*	$num1 \ge num2 \ge ... \ge numN$
zero?	*num*	$num = 0$
positive?	*num*	$num > 0$
negative?	*num*	$num < 0$
even?	*num*	*num* is an even number
odd?	*num*	*num* is an odd number
number?	*num*	*num* is a number (integer, real, or ratio)
real?	*num*	*num* is a real number
integer?	*num*	*num* is an integer

False values

In Scheme, the built-in symbol `#f` represents *false*; anything else represents *true*. `#f` is predefined in the language and cannot be changed. Such a symbol is called a *constant*.

True values

There is another predefined constant, `#t`, which is often used to represent *true*; however, any non-`#f` value is considered *true* in Scheme.

Type-checking

As a simple example, suppose you want to add one to some value; yet that value may not be a number, in which case you want to return the value. This type of test is called *type-checking*. Type refers to the kind or type of value to which a variable may be bound (e.g., number, symbol, list). To test if something is a number, use the predicate `number?`. Below are some examples illustrating the use of `number?`:

```
> (number? -1)
#t

> (number? 'an-atom)
#f

> (number? '(some list))
#f
```

We can use this predicate as the condition of an `if` expression.

```
(if (number? item)              ; item is the value being tested
    (+ item 1)
    item)
```

If `item` is a number, `(+ item 1)` is evaluated and `item` plus one is returned; otherwise `item` is evaluated and its value is returned.

if is a special form

An `if` is a special form because not all of its arguments are evaluated. The *condition* is always evaluated. Depending on the return value of *condition*, only one of *action* or *else-action* is evaluated and that value is returned as the return value of the `if`. If *else-action* is not included and *condition* is *false*, an undefined value is returned.

To see why this evaluation method is important, let's look at what happens if we evaluate all of the arguments to the previous `if` expression when called with a non-numerical value, `(a list)`, for `item`. `'(a list)` will be substituted for `item` in the following expressions:

expression	return value
`(number? '(a list))`	`#f`
`(+ '(a list) 1)`	`Error: Expected INTEGER`
`'(a list)`	`(a list)`

If all the arguments to `if` were evaluated, we would have a problem if `item` were not bound to a number. Since `if` is a special form,

```
(+ item 1)
```

will be evaluated only if `item` represents a number, in which case it is safe to perform the addition.

The actions of an `if` can be any expression, even another `if` as the next example *Nested* `ifs` will illustrate. To test if a number, `num`, is greater than 1 but less than 100, the following expression can be used:

```
(if (> num 1)
    (if (< num 100)
        #t
        #f)
    #f)
```

If `num` is not greater than 1, the condition of the first `if` fails and the else-action, `#f` (the second `#f`) is evaluated. `#f` evaluates to itself, thus `#f` would be returned. If the first condition is satisfied, the action to evaluate is the inner `if`:

```
(if (< num 100)
    #t
    #f)
```

If the condition of this `if`,

```
(< num 100)
```

is satisfied, `#t` is returned; otherwise `#f` is returned. Thus, in order for `#t` to be returned, both conditions must be true.

5.1.1   Exercises

5.1   Write an `if` expression that returns the value of the greater of two symbols, `num1` and `num2`.

5.2   Write a function that returns the smaller of its two arguments.

5.3   What does the following expression return?

```
(if (= 3 4)
    3
    (if (= 2 2)
        2
        1))
```

5.4 The following list represents pets and their qualities:

```
(define qualities '(cat (independent lazy sleepy)
  dog (needy loyal) fish (wet slimy colorful) lion (dangerous)))
```

Complete the function `characteristic` that indicates if a certain animal has a particular characteristic according to the data in the list `qualities`. For example,

> *(characteristic 'dog 'loyal)*
> **(yes a dog is loyal)**

> *(characteristic 'lion 'dull)*
> **(no a lion is not dull)**

```
(define (characteristic animal quality)

   (let ((animal-quality-list _____))

     (if (_____)   ; animal has quality

         (_____)   ; yes message

         (_____)))) ; no message
```

5.5 Write a function that takes three numbers representing the lengths of the sides of a triangle. It should return true if the sides represent a right triangle—if the sum of the squares of the first two equals the square of the third. Assume that the arguments are in the proper order, in other words, that the third argument will represent the length of the hypotenuse, the longest side of the triangle.

5.6 Could you solve the above problem if you had to determine the longest side? If so, give a solution; if not, indicate why.

5.7 Write a function that takes two arguments and returns true if both arguments are equal to 0.

5.8 Write a function that returns true if its one argument is equal to 1 or 0.

5.9 Write a function that takes two arguments, *num1* and *num2*, and returns the result of dividing *num1* by *num2* if *num2* is a nonzero number. If *num1* or *num2* are not numbers, your function should return the symbol `non-number`.

If `num2` is zero, your function should return the symbol `zero-divisor`. What happens if you divide a number by zero in Scheme?

5.10 Write a function that takes one argument, *number*, and returns its square root if it is non-negative. If *number* is negative, your function should return the symbol `negative`. What happens if you take the square root of a negative number in Scheme?

5.11 If you divide two integers, the result will be an integer or a ratio (such as 2/3). For example, dividing 2 and 3 results in 2/3. Write a function that takes two integer arguments and returns their quotient as an integer or a real number (floating point number). If the first integer is evenly divisible by the second, your function should return an integer, otherwise it should return a real number. Called with 2 and 3, your function should return the real number 0.667.

5.2　Cond **Expressions**

The special form `cond` is used as a more generalized means of testing conditions in Scheme. `cond` takes multiple condition-action pairs as arguments. Each condition is tested, in the order given, until a condition evaluating to *true* (a non-`#f` result) is encountered. The action associated with this condition is then evaluated and that value is returned. Below is an example to clarify this rather involved special form:

cond

```
(cond ((< num 10) (* num num))
      ((< num 100) (* num 2))
      ((< num 1000) (+ num 10))
      (else (/ num 3)))
```

In the following examples, the current condition-action pair will be in a ⌐box¬.

Evaluation example with cond

```
(cond ┃((< num 10) (* num num))┃
      ((< num 100) (* num 2))
      ((< num 1000) (+ num 10))
      (else (/ num 3)))
```

The condition, `(< num 10)`, is evaluated. If it is *true*, then the action, `(* num num)`, is evaluated, and the product is returned as the value of the `cond`. If the condition is *false*, evaluation continues with the next condition-action pair:

```
(cond ((< num 10) (* num num))
      ┃((< num 100) (* num 2))┃
      ((< num 1000) (+ num 10))
      (else (/ num 3)))
```

which is evaluated like the previous pair.

If the first three conditions are false, we arrive at the final pair:

```
(cond ((< num 10) (* num num))
      ((< num 100) (* num 2))
      ((< num 1000) (+ num 10))
      (else (/ num 3))))
```

else: the fallout condition within cond

The condition `else` is always true; therefore, `(/ num 3)` is returned as the value of the `cond`. This is the standard way of having an *otherwise* clause within a condition. It effectively means if all the above conditions are false, then perform this action.

The above `cond` can be expressed in English as

If `num` is less than 10, return `(* num num)`
otherwise, if `num` is less than 100, return `(* num 2)`
otherwise, if `num` is less than 1000, return `(+ num 10)`
otherwise, return `(/ num 3)`

The order of the condition-action pairs is important, because they are evaluated in the order listed. The location of any *otherwise* clause—one with `else` as its condition—is important. If it is the first pair, then its action is always performed and none of the other conditions are evaluated.

Mistakes to Avoid

Do not put condition-action pairs after an `else` clause. The condition `else` is true, so once it is encountered, its action will be evaluated and returned and no further conditions will be examined. An `else` clause should always be the last condition-action pair in a `cond`.

5.2.1 Exercises

5.12 Assume that the `cond` expression in the section above had been written as

```
(cond ((< num 1000) (+ num 10))
      ((< num 100) (* num 2))
      ((< num 10) (* num num))
      (else (/ num 3)))
```

What value would be returned if `num` were equal to 37? What would the original `cond` have returned? What value(s) of `num` will yield the same results for both `cond`s?

5.13 Write a function `date-compare` that takes two lists, each representing a date and returns the symbol `less` if the first is before the second, and `#f` otherwise. A date is represented as a list of three elements: the month, day, and year. For example,

```
> (date-compare '(1 3 1984) '(1 4 1984))
less
```

5.14 Write a function that takes a single numerical parameter, *num*, and returns the symbol `positive` if *num* is greater than zero, `negative` if *num* is less than zero, and `zero` otherwise. Your function should use a single `cond` expression.

5.15 The previous "Exercises" section had a number of problems that asked you to write functions using `if`. Which of these could be more succinctly written using `cond` instead?

5.16 Modify your solution to exercise 5.4 so that it also tests if the animal is present in the list `qualities`. If it isn't, return a message indicating so. For example,

```
> (characteristic 'platypus 'strange)
(sorry a platypus is not a pet)
```

5.3   Testing Multiple Conditions and Negations

To test multiple predicates, the special forms `and` and `or` are used. Both of these take any number of arguments. When an `and` expression is evaluated, each argument is evaluated one at a time from left to right. If an argument is encountered that evaluates to `#f`, the evaluation of the `and` stops and `#f` is returned. If all the arguments evaluate to *true*, the result of the last argument is returned. In other words, an `and` returns a *true* value only if all of its arguments do not evaluate to `#f`.

and evaluation rules

An `or` expression is evaluated in a similar fashion to `and`. If all the arguments to an `or` return `#f`, `#f` is returned. If any of the arguments, evaluated from left to right, returns a *true* value, evaluation stops and that value is returned.

or evaluation rules

To test for the opposite, or negation, of a condition, use the function `not`. `not` takes one argument and returns `#f` if the argument is *true*, and `#t` if it is *false*, `#f`.

not

The special forms `and` and `or` can be used like conditional expressions. The previous `if` expression

```
(if (> num 1)
    (if (< num 100)
        #t
        #f)
    #f)
```

can be written using an `and` expression as follows:

```
(and (> num 1)
     (< num 100))
```

Evaluation of the `and` begins by testing if num is greater than 1. If it's not, `#f` is returned. Otherwise evaluation continues by testing if num is less than 100. If it's not, `#f` is returned. Otherwise `#t` is returned because it is the return value of the last condition, (< num 100).

This **and** condition can be more simply expressed as

```
(< 1 num 100)
```

which is *true* if 1 is less than `num` (same as `num` is greater than 1) and `num` is less than 100.

Below are some examples of conditions and their Scheme representations using **and**, **or**, and **not**.

Expressing complex conditions in Scheme

Condition	Scheme version
num is odd and divisible by 3	`(and (odd? num)`
	`      (= (remainder num 3) 0))`
num = 3 or num = 4	`(or (= num 3) (= num 4))`
num is even and (77 < num < 100)	`(and (even? num) (< 77 num 100))`
value is not a number	`(not (number? value))`
num is not in 10, 11, ... , 20	`(not (<= 10 num 20))`

This last example could be expressed as `num` is less than 10 or `num` is greater than 20. In Scheme this would be written as

```
(or (< num 10) (> num 20))
```

Using if, cond, and, *or* or

Not all **if** and **cond** expressions are easily written as **and** or **or** expressions, especially if they return values other than #t or #f. For example, the previous **if** expression

```
(if (number? item)
    (+ item 1)
    item)
```

can be written as

```
(or (and (number? item) (+ item 1))
    item)
```

The **or** has two arguments: one **and** expression and the expression

```
item
```

The **and** expression is evaluated first. The condition

```
(number? item)
```

is evaluated. If it returns a non-#f value, evaluation continues with

```
(+ item 1)
```

which evaluates to a non-#f value, and this value is the result of the **and** expression. This value will be the result of the **or** expression as it is a non-#f result of the first argument to **or**. If the **and** expression evaluates to #f, because the expression

```
(number? item)
```

evaluates to #f, the final argument to **or**,

```
item
```

is evaluated. It evaluates to the value of the symbol `item`, and this value is returned as the return value of the **or**.

The original `if` expression is more understandable and readable, and would be preferred to the `or` / `and` equivalent.

In general, an *if-then* or *if-then-else* expression with an else part returning `#f` can be written using `and`. Similarly, nested *if-then-else* expressions can be written using an `and` if all the *else* parts return `#f`. Other simple and nested *if-then-else* expressions are best written using `if`, `cond`, or nested `if`s.

When to use `if`, `cond`, *or* `and`

Mistakes to Avoid

The opposite of "less than," `<`, is `>=`, not `>`. A simpler alternate is to use

```
(not (< num1 num2))
```

to express the opposite of "less than."

Mistakes to Avoid

English typically uses "or" to indicate an alternative, as in: "You can have ice cream or beer for dessert." This is called an *exclusive or*—one of the two items is true, but not both. Scheme uses an *inclusive or*. One or both items must be true for the `or` to be true. To test if either of two numbers is zero, but not both,

```
(or (zero? num1) (zero? num2))
```

will not work, as it will be true if both numbers are zero as well. Instead use

```
(or (and (zero? num1) (not (zero? num2)))
    (and (zero? num2) (not (zero? num1))))
```

or

```
(and (not (and (zero? num2) (zero? num1)))
     (or (zero? num1) (zero? num2)))
```

This second form is used in situations in which you want to return one value if both items are true, another value if one but not both are true, and another value if both are not true. This can be expressed nicely using a `cond`:

```
(cond ((and condition1 condition2) 'both)
      ((or condition1 condition2) 'only-one)
      (else 'neither))
```

Exclusive versus inclusive or

Mistakes to Avoid

Be careful in translating English to Scheme. For example, the condition *"number is neither greater than 20 nor less than 10"* is written in Scheme with an **and**, not an **or** as the English inclusive or statement implies. The correct interpretation is as follows:

```
(and (not (> number 20))
     (not (< number 10)))
```

Similarly, it could be written as

```
(and (<= number 20))
     (>= number 10)))
```

which can be simplified as

```
(<= 10 number 20)
```

De Morgan's laws

De Morgan, a nineteenth century logician, created laws that give equivalences for **and**s and **or**s with **not**s. They show that

```
(not (and condition1 condition2))
```

is the same as

```
(or (not condition1) (not condition2))
```

and that

```
(not (or condition1 condition2))
```

is the same as

```
(and (not condition1) (not condition2))
```

Thus the above **and** expression

```
(and (not (> number 20))
     (not (< number 10)))
```

can be written as

```
(not (or (> number 20)
         (< number 10)))
```

Sometimes it is preferable to transform a condition using De Morgan's laws to make it easier to read. For example, to test *"if value is not a number or not zero,"* use

```
(or (not (number? value))
    (not (zero? value)))
```

which can be written as

```
(not (and (number? value)
          (zero? value)))
```

which reads *"if value is not the number zero."*

5.3.1 Exercises

5.17 Rewrite the `if` expressions below without using `if` or `cond`. You may use
`and` and `or` expressions, but try to use the fewest `ands` and `ors` possible.

```
(if (positive? number)
    #t
    #f)

(if (positive? number)
    'positive
    #f)

(if (positive? number)
    'positive
    'negative)
```

Which of these is more readable using `and` and `or` expressions?

5.18 Rewrite the following `and` and `or` expressions using `if` or `cond` expressions.
In each case, use just a single `if` or `cond` expression.

```
(and (even? num) 'even)

(or (even? num) 'odd)

(or (and (zero? number) 'zero)
    (and (negative? number) 'negative)
    'positive)
```

5.19 Write a function that takes three arguments, *element1* and *element2*, which
are both bound to atoms, and *a-list*, a list. Your function should return true
if *element1* occurs before *element2* in *a-list*. You may use the list functions
from Chapter 4.

5.20 Write a function to perform your own tests for `subseq` (from Chapter 4) that
takes three arguments, a list, *a-list*, and the *start* and *end* element numbers of
the list. Your function should compare the values of *start* and *end* against the
length of *a-list* and each other, and return some helpful error message if they
are not legal. Otherwise your function should call `subseq` to return the
appropriate sublist. Your error message should indicate which value is bad
and what is wrong with it.

5.4 List and Atom Predicates

In addition to numerical predicates, Scheme provides predicates that work on
lists and atoms. Below is a collection of some of the more common of these predicates:

List and atom predi-
cates

predicate	arguments	returns true if and only if
`list?`	*arg*	*arg* is a list
`atom?`	*arg*	*arg* is an atom
`symbol?`	*arg*	*arg* is a symbol
`null?`	*arg*	*arg* is `()`
`equal?`	*arg1 arg2*	*arg1* is the same as *arg2*
`member`	*element list*	*element* occurs in *list*

The predicate `atom?` is not built into Scheme, but is easily defined as follows:

```
; Return true if item is a symbol or a number, false otherwise.
(define (atom? item)
   (or (symbol? item) (number? item)) )
```

There are other functions that return *true* if an element occurs in a list (e.g., `position`). Usually `member` is used, as it is more readable in the context of a predicate, as in

```
(if (member 'anchovies pizza-toppings)
    '(sorry i am not hungry)
    '(sure i will have a slice))
```

Study the following evaluations to see how the above functions work:

```
> (list? '(this is a list with anchovies))
#t

> (atom? 'word)
#t

> (atom? 37)
#t

> (atom? '(this is a list with anchovies))
#f

> (symbol? 'word)
#t

> (symbol? 37)
#f

> (equal? 'linguica 'linguica)
#t

> (equal? 'linguica 'anchovies)
#f

> (equal? 13 (+ 10 3))
#t

> (equal? '(a (hidden (anchovy))) '(a (hidden (anchovy))))
#t
```

```
> (equal? '(a (list)) '(a list))
#f

> (null? '())
#t

> (null? '(this list is not empty))
#f
```

5.4.1 Exercises

5.21 Exercise 4.16 from Chapter 4 asks you to debug the following function that takes a number and returns the month that corresponds to that number:

```
(define (month month-num)
  (list-ref '(January February March April May June July
              August September October November December)
    month-num) )
```

Modify the debugged version of this function such that if called with an invalid value for month-num, the function returns the symbol bad-month.

5.22 Write a function element-after that takes two parameters, *element* and *a-list*, and returns the element that follows *element* in *a-list*. If *element* does not occur in *a-list*, *element-after* should return the symbol no-match. If *element* is the last element in *a-list*, your function should return the symbol at-end-of-list. For example, the call

```
(element-after 'your '(what is your favorite color))
```

should return the symbol favorite.

5.23 Write a version of **position** using the other built-in list functions from Chapter 4. It should return #f if the element is not in the list.

5.5 Optional Section: All Equality Predicates Are Not Equal

The function = is used to test for numerical equivalence, and the function equal? is used to test for equivalence of atoms or lists. There are other equality predicates. Below is a list of the common ones. Each of these predicates takes two arguments, with the exception of = which takes two or more arguments.

Equality predicates

predicate	returns true if and only if the arguments are
equal?	numbers or symbols that are the same; lists that are or look the same
eqv?	numbers, symbols, or lists that are the same
=	numbers that are the same

equal? is the most general of these. If two objects are = or eqv?, they are also equal?. Next in generality is eqv?, which is true for numbers that are = or symbols or lists that are identical. The most specific equality predicate is = which is true if the two objects being compared are the same numbers. = cannot be used

Equality predicates used with lists

with symbols or lists.[2]

The functions `eqv?` and `equal?` differ in their comparisons with lists. `eqv?` is not true for lists or cons cells unless they refer to the same cons cell. The empty list, `()`, is always `eqv?` to itself. These functions compare the pointers that point to the first cons cell that describes a list. If these pointers point to the same cons cell, then the lists are `eqv?`. Cons cells are discussed in "Optional Section: Internal Representation of Lists" in Chapter 4. In order for two lists to be `equal?` they must look the same—have the same elements in the same order.

Creation of `cons` cells

To understand `eqv?`, it is important to know when new cons cells get created, or when existing ones are used. Whenever a list is explicitly mentioned through `quote` or `quasiquote` as in

```
'(this is a new list that i am creating now)
```

a new set of cons cells is created. The following functions also create new cons cells: `cons`, `list`, `append`, `subseq`, `remove`, and `reverse`. When these functions are used the new cons cells that are created will not be `eqv?` to other lists even if they look the same.

When to use the different equality predicates

Study the examples below carefully to get a better understanding of the differences between the equality predicates, especially when comparing lists. Remember symbols that are the same are `equal?` and `eqv?`. Numbers that are the same are `=`, `equal?`, and `eqv?`. Lists that are the same (same cons cells) are `equal?` and `eqv?`. Lists that look the same (not the same cons cells) are `equal?`.

```
> (equal? 3 (+ 1 2))
#t

> (eqv? 3 (+ 1 2))
#t

> (eqv? 'word 'word)
#t

> (equal? '(a list) '(a list))
#t

> (eqv? '(a list) '(a list))          ; each '(a list) creates new cons cells
#f

> (define my-list '(a list))
??

> (eqv? my-list my-list)              ; both lists refer to the same cons cell
#t
```

[2] A fourth equality predicate, `eq?`, is identical to `eqv?` except when comparing numbers, in which case they may or may not be `eq?` depending on the implementation of Scheme used. This predicate is used when comparison speed is important and only symbols or lists are being compared.

```
> (eqv? my-list '(a list))              ;'(a list) creates new cons cells
#f

> (eqv? (cdr my-list) (cdr my-list))    ; no new cons cells are created
#t

> (eqv? (reverse my-list) (reverse my-list))  ; new cons cells are created
#f

> (eqv? (cons 4 my-list) (cons 4 my-list))    ; new cons cells are created
#f

> (equal? (cons 4 my-list) (cons 4 my-list))  ; the two lists look the same
#t
```

5.6   A Musical Offering

In western music, the notes of the musical scale can be represented with the list

```
(A A-sharp B C C-sharp D D-sharp E F F-sharp G G-sharp)
```

Musical scale

Each two consecutive notes are one half-step apart. There are names for the *intervals* or distances that any two notes are from one another. These names, in half-step increments between two notes, are given in the list below beginning with a zero half-step interval.

```
(unison minor-second major-second minor-third major-third
   perfect-fourth diminished-fifth perfect-fifth augmented-fifth
   major-sixth minor-seventh major-seventh)
```

Names of note increments

From this table we see that a one half-step interval is called a minor-second, and a perfect-fifth is a 7 half-step interval.

5.6.1   Computing the intervals between notes

Using the two lists above we can construct a function that takes two notes and returns the interval between them. To do this, determine the number of half-steps between the two notes, then determine the interval that corresponds to that number of half-steps. There is one problem to avoid. The order in which the notes are given is important. The interval between C and G is a perfect-fifth (7 half-steps); however, the interval between a G and the next higher C (after G-sharp the notes continue with A again) is 5 half-steps, or a perfect-fourth. This makes the problem slightly more difficult. The number of half-steps between two notes is the difference in their positions in the scale-list if the second note comes after the first in the scale-list. If the first note comes after the second, then the interval is twelve minus the distance in their positions.

To make the code easier, we'll save the distance between the notes in a let variable. The code follows:

```
; Return the musical interval between note1 and note2.
(define (interval note1 note2 scale-list interval-list)
  (let ( (distance (- (position note2 scale-list)
                      (position note1 scale-list))) )
    (if (positive? distance)
        (list-ref interval-list distance)
        (list-ref interval-list (- 12 distance)))) )
```

Let's test this function. If we call the function with the notes C and D, and the above scale and interval lists, the `let` variable, `distance`, is bound to 2. Taking `list-ref` of `interval-list` and 2 returns `major-second`. If we call the function with D and C, and the same scale and interval lists, `distance` is bound to –2, and the function returns `list-ref` of `interval-list` and 12 – –2, which is an error because there is not an element at position 14 in the list. The problem is that `distance` is negative and we should subtract the absolute value of `distance`. This bug is fixed by changing the else-action of the `if` expression to

```
(list-ref interval-list (- 12 (abs distance)))
```

or to

```
(list-ref interval-list (+ 12 distance))
```

Another good test to make is calling the function with the same note for `note1` and `note2`. This would give `distance` a value of 0, which is not true when applied to `positive?`; thus `list-ref` of `interval-list` and 12, or an error is returned. To fix this bug, the condition of the `if` should be changed to

```
(or (positive? distance) (zero? distance))
```

or the then and else actions can be switched and the condition changed to

```
(negative? distance)
```

A correct solution is

```
; Return the musical interval between note1 and note2.
(define (interval note1 note2 scale-list interval-list)
  (let ( (distance (- (position note2 scale-list)
                      (position note1 scale-list))) )
    (if (negative? distance)
        (list-ref interval-list (+ 12 distance))
        (list-ref interval-list distance))) )
```

5.6.2   Computing the note an interval beyond another note

Another useful function is one that takes a note and an interval and returns the note that is that interval amount above the original note. This function must determine the number of half-steps that defines the interval desired, then add that value to the position of the note in the scale, giving the position of the new note. The actual new note is computed by taking `list-ref` with this position and the scale-list.

If we try out this algorithm to determine the note a perfect-fifth above C, we find a perfect-fifth to be 7 half-steps, and C to be in position 3 in the scale-list.

Adding 7 and 3 gives 10, and the note at position 10 is G. Thus, G is a perfect-fifth above C. This is correct.

However, what happens when we try to compute the perfect-fourth of G—it should be C. The number of half-steps in a perfect-fourth is 5 and the position of G is 10, adding these yields 15, but there is no note at position 15 in the scale-list. To keep the position between 0 and 11, take the remainder of the position and 12. This treats our scale-list as a circular list. Taking the remainder of 15 and 12 gives 3, and the note in position 3 in the scale-list is C, which is correct.

The Scheme code for this function is

```
; Return the note an interval above note.
(define (higher-note note interval scale-list interval-list)
   (let ( (half-steps (position interval interval-list))
          (note-position (position note scale-list)) )
      (list-ref scale-list
                (remainder (+ note-position half-steps) 12))) )
```

5.6.3 Exercises

5.24 The next two problems use a different approach than the previous functions did to handle the problem of exceeding the boundaries of the scale-list. This approach is to represent the scale-list as a longer list, as follows:

```
(A A-sharp B C C-sharp D D-sharp E F F-sharp G G-sharp
 A A-sharp B C C-sharp D D-sharp E F F-sharp G G-sharp)
```

Below is an alternate solution to the function `interval`:

```
(define (interval-alt note1 note2 scale-list interval-list)
   (let ( (distance (- (position note2 (reverse scale-list))
                       (position note1 scale-list))) )
      (list-ref interval-list distance)) )
```

Will this solution work? Why or why not?

5.25 Below is an alternate solution to the function `higher-note` using the scale-list given in the previous problem:

```
(define (higher-note-alt note interval scale-list interval-list)
   (let ( (half-steps (position interval interval-list))
          (note-position (position note scale-list)) )
      (list-ref scale-list (+ note-position half-steps))) )
```

Will this solution work? Why or why not?

5.7 Determining the Value of Poker Hands

Poker is a multiplayer card game in which each person has a total of five cards. These can be represented as a list, as in

```
(jack queen queen jack three)
```

The order of the cards does not matter. The value of a player's cards (their *hand*) is based on the following ordering:

name	example hand
four-of-a-kind	`(seven seven seven two seven)`
full house	`(two eight eight two two)`
three-of-a-kind	`(ace ace king four ace)`
two pairs	`(six seven two two seven)`
one pair	`(three five three king ace)`

This is a simplification of the actual game of poker, which has other winning hands like straights and flushes. In this version of poker, four-of-a-kind is worth the most and one pair the least. A full house consists of one pair and three-of-a-kind.

To determine a hand value, we must count the number of times that each card occurs in the player's hand. Given the list

```
(jack seven queen jack jack)
```

we need to count the number of jacks, queens and sevens. Yet we don't know beforehand what cards exist in the hand. In reality what we will have to do is count the number of times the first card occurs in the hand, and the number of times the second card occurs, and so on. This gives us five totals. For the above example, we would get the totals 3, 1, 1, 3, and 3 for the first, second, third, fourth, and fifth elements of the list, respectively. The first 3 tells us that the first element occurred three times in the card list. From this information we can determine what the value of the hand is. For example, if any of the totals is 4, then the hand is a four-of-a-kind. Rather than keeping these totals in five separate variables, or recomputing them each time they are needed, we can save them in a list and take advantage of the list predicates like **member** to determine if a particular total exists.

The highest value hands should be checked for first to avoid problems like calling a full house a pair or three-of-a-kind because that condition was satisfied first. The pseudo code for this function can be expressed as follows:

- compute and save the totals of each card in the hand in the variable `count-list`
- check for four-of-a-kind
- check for full house
- check for three-of-a-kind
- check for two pair
- check for one pair

The checks can be refined as follows:

- check for four-of-a-kind:
    check if 4 is in `count-list`
- check for full house:
    check if 3 and 2 are in `count-list`

- check for three-of-a-kind:
  check if 3 is in count-list
- check for two pair:
  check if 2 occurs four times in count-list
  The reason 2 must occur four times in count-list is that if it occurs just twice, that denotes a single pair.
- check for one pair:
  check if 2 is in count-list

Expressing this in Scheme gives

```
; Return the value of a poker hand.
(define (poker-value hand)
  (let ( (count-list (list
                        (count (first hand) hand)
                        (count (second hand) hand)
                        (count (third hand) hand)
                        (count (fourth hand) hand)
                        (count (fifth hand) hand))) )
    (cond
      ((member 4 count-list)
        'four-of-a-kind)
      ((and (member 3 count-list) (member 2 count-list))
        'full-house)
      ((member 3 count-list)
        'three-of-a-kind)
      ((= 4 (count 2 count-list))
        'two-pair)
      ((member 2 count-list)
        'one-pair)
      (else 'nothing))) )
```

5.7.1 Exercises

5.26 Suppose we had written the code to check the conditions in reverse order starting with one pair. What input hands to this new function would give erroneous results? What input hands would give correct results?

5.27 Write a function that takes two hands as arguments and returns the winning hand—that with the higher value. If the card values are the same, your function should return the symbol tie.

5.28 Modify the function poker-value so that it returns the names of the cards that participated in the pairs, full houses, etc. For example, if given

```
(king queen eight one queen)
```

your modified function should return

```
(one-pair queen)
```
If called with
```
(king queen king king queen)
```
your modified function should return
```
(full-house king queen)
```
This is tricky for the case of two pair. Hint: use `remove` in your solution.

5.29 Combine your solutions to the previous two exercises so that your new function can pick the winning hand for similar hands by comparing the cards used in the hand. For example, your solution should be able to tell that three jacks would beat three nines.

5.8 Summary

- Predicates are functions that can be used as conditions in `and`, `or`, `if`, and `cond` expressions. Such predicates return `#f` if they are *false*, and some non-`#f` value if they are *true*.
- `#f` and `#t` represent *false* and *true*, respectively, in Scheme.
  They are constants and cannot be changed.
- To test a condition and then take one of two actions depending on the outcome, use `if`.
- To test multiple conditions, use `cond`.
  `cond` can perform multiple actions for each condition. As with functions, the return value of the `cond` is the result of the last action evaluated.
- To form compound conditions, use `and` or `or`.
- To test the negation of a condition, use `not`.
- To test if an expression evaluates to a list, an atom, a symbol, or the empty list, use `list?`, `atom?`, `symbol?`, or `null?`, respectively.
- To test if an atom occurs in a list, use `member`.
- To test if two atoms are the same or two lists look the same, use `equal?`.
- To test if two atoms (symbols or numbers) or two lists are the same, use `eqv?`.
- To test if two symbols or two lists are the same, use `eq?`.
- To test if two numbers are the same, use `=`.

- Summary of predicates introduced in this chapter:

predicate	arguments	returns true if and only if
not	*arg*	*arg* is #f
<	*num1 ... numN*	$num1 < num2 < ... < numN$
>	*num1 ... numN*	$num1 > num2 > ... > numN$
=	*num1 ... numN*	$num1 = num2 = ... = numN$
<=	*num1 ... numN*	$num1 \leq num2 \leq ... \leq numN$
>=	*num1 ... numN*	$num1 \geq num2 \geq ... \geq numN$
zero?	*num*	$num = 0$
positive?	*num*	$num > 0$
negative?	*num*	$num < 0$
even?	*num*	*num* is an even number
odd?	*num*	*num* is an odd number
number?	*num*	*num* is a number (integer, real, or ratio)
real?	*num*	*num* is a real number
integer?	*num*	*num* is an integer
list?	*arg*	*arg* is a list
atom?	*arg*	*arg* is an atom
symbol?	*arg*	*arg* is a symbol
null?	*arg*	*arg* is ( )
member	*element list*	*element* occurs in *list*
equal?	*arg1 arg2*	*arg1* looks the same as *arg2*
eqv?	*arg1 arg2*	*arg1* is the same as *arg2*
=	*num1 num2*	*num1* is the same as *num2*

- Summary of special forms introduced in this chapter:

> (if *condition*
>   *action*
>   [*else-action*])

If *condition* is true, returns *action*. If *condition* is false, returns *else-action*. If *condition* is false and there is no *else-action*, returns an undefined value.

> (cond (*condition action1 action2 ... actionN*)
>   (*condition action1 action2 ... actionN*)
>   .
>   .
>   .
>   (else *action1 action2 ... actionN*)

Evaluates *condition*s in order and returns the last action, *actionN*, corresponding to the first *condition* that is true. If the are no *action*s, *condition* is returned. If all *condition*s are false, returns *actionN* corresponding to else. If all *condition*s are false and there is no else clause, cond returns an undefined value.

> (and *condition1 condition2 ... conditionN*)

Evaluates *condition*s until a false *condition* is found or all *condition*s are true. Returns #f if a false *condition* is found, otherwise returns *conditionN*.

(`or` *condition1 condition2 ... conditionN*)

Evaluates *condition*s until a true *condition* is found or all *condition*s are false. Returns first true *condition* found or #f if all *condition*s are false.

CHAPTER 6

REPETITION
THROUGH RECURSION

6.1   Recursion

There are times when a sequence of actions should be repeated. We may want to apply a function to all the elements of a list. We may want to add the first twenty numbers in a list. We may want to return the first symbol in a list. To carry out such actions the technique of *recursion* can be used. It is essential to master recursion, as it is commonly used in Scheme programming. There are different types of recursion that we will explore individually. The important thing is not to just memorize the general form for each type of recursion illustrated, but to get a thorough understanding of the process of writing recursive functions. Recursion is a skill that you improve on with practice. Use the examples to guide you, then *practice, practice, practice.*

6.1.1   Example: Finding a number in a list that exceeds a threshold value

Recursion is often used with lists. The following example illustrates many of the basic ideas used when recursing through lists. Recursion involves having some code that needs to be repeated and some way of deciding when you are done.

Recursion through lists

The code to repeat for this first example is a test if a number in a list exceeds some threshold. We are done when we find a value that exceeds the threshold, and we return that number.

This can be expressed in Scheme as

```
(if (> (first a-list) threshold)
    (first a-list)
    else-action)
```

If the above condition is met, (`first` a-list) is evaluated and the desired element is returned. The *else-action* is the important missing piece. It must find the element we are looking for if it's not the first element of the list. This can be viewed as finding the element that exceeds the threshold in the `rest` of the list, which can be expressed as

```
(if (> (second a-list) threshold)
    (second a-list)
    ; Find the element that exceeds threshold in the rest of the rest of a-list
```

and so forth.

If we attempted to write this in Scheme, we would get the neverending sequence

```
(if (> (first a-list) threshold)
    (first a-list)
    (if (> (second a-list) threshold)
        (second a-list)
        (if (> (third a-list) threshold)
            (third a-list)
                .
                .
                .
```

Writing such code that works for any length list would be impossible. Yet so far, the only means we have seen of invoking a section of code is by typing it into the interpreter or by calling a function that embodies that code. The first choice is impractical, as we have just seen. If we attempt the second alternative, wouldn't we run into the same senseless repetition as above?

The key here is to look back at the earlier definition of the problem.

> To return the element in a list that exceeds the threshold:
>   if the first element of the list is greater than the threshold
>   return that first element
>   otherwise,
>   return the element in the rest of the list that exceeds the threshold

Recursive definitions

This definition is *recursive* because it uses the term being defined within its definition, namely the step in the otherwise clause that tells us to perform a problem identical to the one being defined, except with the rest of the list instead of the entire list. The definition has an indication of when to stop—when an element greater than the threshold is found.

Recursive functions and recursive calls

The function can be written using an `if` expression that implements the above pseudo code in Scheme. This function has two parameters, `threshold` and `a-list`. The otherwise clause has a call to the function we are defining; thus, it is a *recursive call*, which makes this a *recursive function*. This recursive call is with a different value for *a-list*—(`rest` a-list). This breaks the problem into a smaller, similar problem: namely, finding the element exceeding the threshold in the rest of the list. Defining the problem in terms of smaller, similar pieces is an important aspect of writing recursive functions. The resulting function would be

```
; Return the first number greater than threshold in a-list.
(define (first-greater threshold a-list)
  (if (> (first a-list) threshold)
      (first a-list)
      (first-greater threshold (rest a-list))) )
```

If first-greater is called with a value of (first a-list) greater than the value of threshold, (first a-list) is returned. Otherwise, first-greater is called again, but this time (and this is the key point) with the rest of a-list. When this recursive call is evaluated, it checks the first of the list (which is the rest of the original a-list). Thus the second of the original list is checked. Each element in the list is checked in this fashion until we find an element that exceeds the threshold. That element is returned and the recursive repetition stops.

In the trace below a series of recursive calls is made. This is called a *recursive descent*.

Recursive descent

```
(first-greater 3 '(1 2 4 3 5))
             ↓
; The first condition fails since 1 isn't > 3.
; The otherwise clause is performed.
; The result of the call to (first-greater 3 '(1 2 4 3 5)) is
; the result of this otherwise clause.
             ↓
(first-greater 3 '(2 4 3 5))
             ↓
; Again the condition is false and the return value is
; the result of the otherwise clause.
             ↓
(first-greater 3 '(4 3 5))
             ↓
; The condition is true as 4 > 3, thus 4 is returned.
             ↓
             4
```

The interpreter's output will be as follows:

```
> (first-greater 3 '(1 2 4 3 5))
4
```

Let's try another example:

```
> (first-greater 5 '(1 2 4 3 5))
Error: Pair expected
```

What happened? What should the function have returned? In this case there are no values in the given list that are greater than the threshold value, 5. We wind up recursing through the list until we hit the end of the list. Yet we continue to make a recursive call with the empty list. This results in an error when we try to take the first of the empty list.

Recursing too far

To fix this bug, we must add a test for an empty list and not recurse further. If we hit the end of the list, we should return some reasonable value. #f is a good choice in this case. Below is the new code with the added test:

```
; Return the first number greater than threshold in a-list.
(define (first-greater threshold a-list)
  (cond ((> (first a-list) threshold)
             (first a-list))
        ((null? a-list)
             #f)
        (else
             (first-greater threshold (rest a-list)))) )
```

Let's try this new code out.

```
> (first-greater 5 '(1 2 4 3 5))
Error: Pair expected
```

Putting exit cases in the proper order

We get the same error. In such situations be sure that you used the proper spelling of the function in its definition and all its calls. Sometimes what looks like a bug is just a renaming problem in which you end up defining a new function that calls your old function and produces the same error. Since we didn't make these mistakes, the function must have an error. The first thing the function does is compare the `first` of the list with the threshold value. After that we test if the list is empty. These two tests are in the wrong order. We must first check if the list is empty before comparing the first element. Below is the correct function and a sample call:

```
; Return the first number greater than threshold in a-list.
(define (first-greater threshold a-list)
  (cond ((null? a-list)
             #f)
        ((> (first a-list) threshold)
             (first a-list))
        (else
             (first-greater threshold (rest a-list)))) )

> (first-greater 5 '(1 2 4 3 5))
#f
```

Mistakes to Avoid

Before taking the `first` or `rest` of a list, be sure that the list is not empty (check if (`null?` `a-list`) is not true). In recursive functions that take lists, a check for an empty list is usually the first condition that should be tested.

By evaluating recursive calls as we have evaluated nonrecursive function calls, the outcome of a sample invocation can be traced easily. The important observations to make in the case of `first-greater` are

- Whenever the exit condition is not met, the function is called recursively with a new value for `a-list`.
- Eventually one of the exit conditions (> (`first` `a-list`) threshold) or (`null?` `a-list`) will be met and the recursion will end.

In general, recursive functions have

- exit or termination cases that return values that do not involve recursive calls.
- recursive cases in which a recursive call is made.

In these recursive cases, the recursive call is made with a smaller part of the problem to be solved. Recursion works by breaking the problem down into smaller pieces that eventually lead to exit conditions that terminate the recursion.

6.1.2 Example: Investing in your best interest

This example explores your monetary growth when investing a fixed amount monthly over many years with interest compounded daily. You can use this to do financial planning for your retirement or to calculate how much you would have to invest each month to put a kid through college.

To model these investment scenarios we will need to repeat a section of code a certain number of times. Three important elements are needed:

- The block of code to repeat
- A counter to indicate how many repetitions have been made
- A check to determine if we are done

The block of code to repeat must determine the new balance (balance plus balance times daily interest rate). In addition, every month we add an additional amount to the balance.

To model interest compounded daily, we must perform 365 repetitions (we'll ignore leap years). A counter variable can keep track of the current day we are calculating. We'll need to examine the counter variable to determine if we must add the additional amount to our balance (every 30 days to model making an increment once each month). This counter will get incremented with each repetition of the code. The termination check will be a simple `if` or `cond` expression checking the value of the counter.

Let's refine what we have above and let the counter, which will be called `counter`, start with the value one and increment until it is greater than the number of days `days`. This means we are done when `counter` is greater than `days`. The refined pseudo code follows:

> if `counter` is greater than `days`,
>   return the current balance
> otherwise,
>   make a recursive call with `counter` plus 1 and
>   a new balance (based on the old balance `balance`
>   and the interest rate `rate`) and a possible
>   increment `increment`.

The function has five parameters, `balance`, `counter`, `days`, `rate`, and `increment`. The recursive call breaks the problem into a smaller problem by passing different values for `counter` and `balance`. The recursive call computes the new balance for the days `counter` plus 1 to `days`. Eventually `counter` will exceed `days` and the recursion will stop. Expressing this in Scheme gives

```
; Compute growth of investment given start balance, time period,
; and daily interest rate with increment added every 30 days.
(define (new-balance balance counter days rate increment)
  (cond ((> counter days)
         balance)
        ((zero? (remainder counter 30))
         (new-balance
           (+ (* balance rate) balance increment)
           (+ counter 1) days rate increment))
        (else
         (new-balance
           (+ (* balance rate) balance)
           (+ counter 1) days rate increment))) )
```

Helper function to reduce the number of parameters

This function has two parameters that are only needed for the recursive computations (`counter` and `balance`), and three parameters that make the function general but do not change in the recursive calls (`days`, `rate`, and `increment`). This screams for a helper function that takes fewer arguments and calls `new-balance` with initial values for `counter` and `balance`.

We can go a step further and write a function `investment` that will make it easier to model investments over many years. Rather than take the number of days we are investing and the daily interest rate, it will take the number of years we'll invest and the annual interest rate. We'll need one extra parameter, the amount to invest each month. Here is the code for `investment`:

```
; Compute annual investment given annual interest rate, years,
; and monthly investment amount.
(define (investment years rate increment)
  (new-balance 0 1 (* 365 years) (/ rate 365) increment) )
```

Below is a trace of the function `new-balance` to model 1% interest gained each day over three days on an initial investment of $1000.

```
(new-balance 1000 1 3 0.01 0)
```
↓
; The exit condition fails, as 1 isn't > 3.
; The otherwise clause is performed and its action is evaluated.
↓
```
(new-balance 1010 2 3 0.01 0)
```
↓
; The exit condition fails again.
↓
```
(new-balance 1020.1 3 3 0.01 0)
```
↓
```
(new-balance 1030.301 4 3 0.01 0)
```
↓
; The exit condition is true, as 4 > 3
↓
1030.301

The next example is a call to calculate how much we'd make investing $100 a month for three months, with an initial investment of $1000 with 1% interest daily (don't we wish).

```
> (new-balance 1000 1 90 0.01 100)
2865.09
```

Now let's call `investment` to model some more realistic, long-term investments:

```
> (investment 10 0.05 200)   ; invest $200 monthly over 10 years
31372.45

> (investment 20 0.05 100)   ; invest $100 monthly over 20 years
41690.72
```

In both of these examples the same amount is invested (about $24,000) but the gains are much larger by starting earlier. So start investing now.

6.1.3   Example: Summing digits

Let's write another recursive function. This function returns the sum of the digits within *number*, where *number* is an argument to the function.

Some examples will help to illustrate what the function should do:

the sum of the digits in 1 is 1
the sum of the digits in 342 is 9
the sum of the digits in 1989 is 27

To solve this problem, think of the *definitional pseudo code*[1] to the function. Definitional pseudo code is pseudo code that provides definitions for what the function should return based on the arguments with which it is called. Such a description takes on the following form:

Definitional pseudo code

If *condition-1* is true, the function returns *return-value-1*.
Otherwise, if *condition-2* is true, the function returns *return-value-2*.

.
.
.

Otherwise, the function returns *return-value-N*.

From such a description, the actual Scheme code can be easily written using `if` or `cond` conditional expressions. Part of the definitional pseudo code to a recursive function is a recursive call that breaks the problem into smaller parts. In addition, there should be return values that do not involve recursive calls. These are the actions matching the exit conditions.

Below is the definitional pseudo code to the sum of the digits problem:

---

[1] This is a term I have coined and is not standard in computer science.

Pseudo code for
adding digits

The sum of the digits in *number* is
   number if *number* has only one digit
   otherwise, the sum of the digits is
      the first (leftmost) digit of *number* **plus**
      the sum of the rest of the digits in *number*.

Another possible definition is

The sum of the digits in *number* is
   number if *number* has only one digit
   otherwise, the sum of the digits is
      the last (rightmost) digit of *number* **plus**
      the sum of the rest of the digits in *number*.

Both of these solutions have the same terminating condition—when *number* has only a single digit. In the recursive case, they both break the problem into smaller pieces, namely considering the sum of the digits to be the sum of one digit and the sum of the rest of the digits. Computing the sum of the rest of the digits will be the recursive call in our solution. Eventually this will yield a one-digit number, satisfying the exit condition.

In deciding which of the two above definitions to use, we should look into which is easier to do: extract the first (leftmost) digit and all but the first digit of a number, or extract the last (rightmost) digit and all but the last digit. Without knowing how many digits the number is, the first digit is difficult to extract, whereas the last digit is the remainder of the number when divided by ten. The rest of the digits (the remaining digits to the left) are obtained by dividing the number by ten and then removing any fractional part. This is done with the function `truncate`, which returns the integer part of real numbers (the digits to the left of the decimal point).

For example, the last digit of 347 is

```
(remainder 347 10)  →  7
```

and the first digits are

```
(truncate (/ 347 10))  →  34
```

Lastly, a number is one digit long (our exit condition) if dividing it by ten and truncating the result evaluates to zero. The two examples below illustrate this:

```
(zero? (truncate (/ 9 10)))  →  #t
     however,
(zero? (truncate (/ 347 10)))  →  #f
```

At this point we can create the definitional pseudo code to our summing digits problem:

if *number* is a one-digit number, then
   return *number*
otherwise
   return the sum of the last digit in *number*
      and
   the sum of the digits of the rest of *number* without the last digit.

Rewriting this in Scheme, we get

```
; Return sum of the digits in number.
(define (sum-digits number)
  (if (zero? (truncate (/ number 10)))
      number
      (+ (remainder number 10)
         (sum-digits (truncate (/ number 10))))) )
```

To make this function more readable and eliminate the two identical calls to `truncate`, a `let` expression can be used as follows:

```
; Return sum of the digits in number.
(define (sum-digits number)
  (let ( (last-digit (remainder number 10))
         (rest-of-number (truncate (/ number 10))) )
    (if (zero? rest-of-number)
        number
        (+ last-digit
           (sum-digits rest-of-number)))) )
```

Follow the recursive descent in the trace of this code:

```
(sum-digits 526)
     ↓
; last-digit is bound to 6
; rest-of-number is bound to 52, which is not zero, so the else action is evaluated
     ↓
(+ 6 (sum-digits 52))
       ↓
    ; last-digit is bound to 2
    ; rest-of-number is bound to 5
       ↓
    (+ 2 (sum-digits 5))
         ↓
       ; last-digit is bound to 5
       ; rest-of-number is bound to 0, satisfying our exit condition
         ↓
         5
```

Two recursive calls are made, each one embedded as one of the values that must be summed with the current last digit. Once the last recursive call

```
(sum-digits 5)
```

has been made, these sums can be determined. This can be viewed as climbing   *Recursive unwind*
out of the recursive descent. This is called a *recursive unwind*.

```
(sum-digits 526)
       ↓
(+ 6 (sum-digits 52))
            ↓
     (+ 2 (sum-digits 5))
                  ↓
                  5
        ↓
        7
  ↓
  13
```

Starting at the last recursive call in the above diagram, the value of

```
(sum-digits 5)
```

which is 5 is added to 2 to give the value of

```
(sum-digits 52)
```

In a similar fashion, that result, 7, is added to 6, yielding 13, the return value of

```
(sum-digits 526)
```

Future traces will show both the downward recursive calls and the return values from the recursive steps in one diagram, as in

```
(sum-digits 526)
       ↓
```
; `last-digit` is bound to 6
; `rest-of-number` is bound to 52, which is not zero, so the else action is evaluated
```
       ↓
(+ 6 (sum-digits 52))
            ↓
```
     ; `last-digit` is bound to 2
     ; `rest-of-number` is bound to 5
```
            ↓
     (+ 2 (sum-digits 5))
                  ↓
```
            ; `last-digit` is bound to 5
            ; `rest-of-number` is bound to 0, satisfying our exit condition
```
                  ↓
                  5
        ↓
        7
  ↓
  13
```

6.1.4   General rules for writing recursive functions

Prescriptive method for writing recursive functions

Let's review the steps in writing a recursive function:

- Think of the exit cases—the simplest conditions in which an immediate answer is known without taking any recursive steps. What are the return values in these cases?

- Think of the recursive cases—those involving recursive calls. The recursive calls should break the problem up into similar, smaller pieces. How can the results of the recursive calls be used to get the desired return result?
- Write out the definitional pseudo code to the function using the exit and recursive cases.
- Refine any steps so that the ideas can be stated in Scheme.
- Verify that your solution works in a simple example where only one recursive call is needed. If there are problems, rethink your return values for your exit and recursive cases. Examine the exit conditions, as they may not be appropriate either.
- Write the Scheme code using your definitional pseudo code to guide you.
- Test out your code on the computer or by hand using traces.

6.1.5 Example: Testing if the digits in a number are in increasing order

Let's use the guidelines given above to solve the next recursive problem. The problem is to check if the digits in a number are in increasing order from left to right. For example, the number 1234 has digits that are in increasing order from left to right; however, 647 does not.

This problem can be viewed as determining if the digits are in decreasing order from right to left. As we saw in the last problem, it is easier to sequence through a number in a right to left fashion, so the problem will be restated as such.

First the exit cases—one will be when there are no more digits to compare against in the number, in which case we return #t. Another exit case is when a digit is encountered that is greater than the previous digit (the digit to the right of it). In this case #f is returned.

The recursive case occurs when there are more digits to check and the current digit is less than or equal to the previous digit. In this case we need to compare against the remaining digits (those to the left) recursively.

Now put these cases together as the definitional pseudo code to the problem and refine any areas that do not easily translate into Scheme.

if there are no more digits to check, return #t
Pseudo code to test order of digits
otherwise, if the current digit is greater than the digit to the right of it,
   return #f
otherwise, return the result of a recursive call with the leftmost digits.

Some of these steps need refinement. First, how do we know if there are no more digits to check? Presumably we will be stripping off the last digit with each recursive call, and eventually we will reach zero. As was illustrated in the sum-digits function, when a one-digit number is divided by ten and truncated, zero is returned, as in
Refinement of pseudo code

```
(truncate (/ 7 10))  →  0
```

Thus, there are no more digits to examine when the number to check is zero.

Another aspect that needs refinement is the notion of comparing the current digit against the digit to the right of it. This can be viewed as comparing the last digit (rightmost) with the next to last digit (the one to its immediate left).

We can use a `let` expression to name the last digit, next to last digit, and the rest of the number (without the last digit). Since we can use the value of the rest of the number to more easily compute the next to last digit, we'll use a `let*`.

Now that the refinements have been made, we can express the solution in Scheme as follows:

```
; Return true if the digits in number are increasing
; from left to right.
(define (increasing-digits number)
  (let* ( (last-digit (remainder number 10))
          (rest-of-number (truncate (/ number 10)))
          (next-to-last-digit (remainder rest-of-number 10)) )
    (cond ((zero? rest-of-number) #t)
          ((> next-to-last-digit last-digit) #f)
          (else (increasing-digits rest-of-number)))) )
```

Follow the trace below to see how this function works:

```
(increasing-digits 812)
        ↓
```
; `last-digit` is bound to the value of (`remainder` 812 10) $\rightarrow$ 2
; `rest-of-number` is bound to the value of (`truncate` (/ 812 10)) $\rightarrow$ 81
; `next-to-last-digit` is bound to the value of (`remainder` 81 10) $\rightarrow$ 1
; 81 is not zero, nor is 1 > 2, thus the *otherwise* action is performed
```
        ↓
(increasing-digits 81)
        ↓
```
; `last-digit` is bound to the value of (`remainder` 81 10) $\rightarrow$ 1
; `rest-of-number` is bound to the value of (`truncate` (/ 81 10)) $\rightarrow$ 8
; `next-to-last-digit` is bound to the value of (`remainder` 8 10) $\rightarrow$ 8
; 8 is not zero, but 8 > 1, so #f is returned.
```
        ↓
       #f
```

6.1.6 Exercises

6.1 Another way of testing if a number is a one-digit number is by checking if it is less than ten; however, this does not work for negative numbers. Does the function `sum-digits` work for negative numbers? What about the function `increasing-digits`? If not, how would you fix these functions so that they do work when called with negative numbers?

6.2 Write a function `sum-evens` with two parameters, *start* and *end*. The function should return the sum of the even numbers between *start* and *end* inclusive.

6.3 Explain what this modification to new-balance does.

```
(define (new-balance balance counter days rate period increment)
  (cond ((> counter days)
         balance)
        ((zero? (remainder counter period))
         (new-balance
           (+ (* balance rate) balance increment)
           (+ counter 1)
           days rate period increment))
        (else
           (new-balance
             (+ (* balance rate) balance)
             (+ counter 1)
             days rate period increment))) )
```

Give a sample call to show how much is gained if you invest $50 at the end of each week for a year (52 weeks). Then make a call to see how much is made if you invest the same amount, $2600, by quarters ($650 is invested at the end of each quarter—every 13 weeks). Use 7% as the annual interest rate in your calls. How much more do you make with weekly deposits versus quarterly deposits?

6.4 The following modification to the function new-balance allows different types of investment options.

```
(define (newer-balance balance counter days rate day-list
           increment)
  (cond ((> counter days)
         balance)
        ((member (remainder counter 7) day-list)
         (newer-balance
           (+ (* balance rate) balance increment)
           (+ counter 1)
           days rate day-list increment))
        (else (newer-balance
               (+ (* balance rate) balance)
               (+ counter 1)
               days rate day-list increment))) )
```

Write function calls to model the following annual investments with 5% annual interest (assume that the first week of the year begins on a Monday): a.) investing $10 each weekday (Monday through Friday); b.) making equal investments twice a week on Mondays and Thursdays based on an annual investment total of $1000; and c.) investing $5 a day (except Sundays) starting with an initial balance of $250.

6.5 Write a function with two parameters, *digit*, a single-digit number, and a positive number, *number*. The function should return #t if *digit* is one of the digits in *number*, and #f otherwise.

6.6 Write a function with one parameter, *number*, an integer value. The function should return the largest digit in *number*.

6.7 Modify the function increasing-digits to use an alternate approach for comparing the current digit with the previous digit—that of using an additional parameter to hold the previous digit. Each time the function is called recursively, the current digit value can be used as the previous digit argument. What value should this extra parameter be given for the initial call? Does your solution work for one-digit numbers? Do you prefer this new solution or the original one with one parameter?

6.2 Optional Section: Global Variables and Recursion

Free variables

The function new-balance could have been written without using days, rate, and increment as parameters, instead treating them as *free variables* within new-balance. A free variable is a variable used in a function that is not a parameter or a local variable within a let or let*. Using these parameters as free variables may seem more logical because their values are not changed when making recursive calls. The new code to new-balance would look like the following:

```
; Compute growth of investment given start balance, time period,
; and daily interest rate with increment added every 30 days.
(define (alt-new-balance balance counter)
  (cond ((> counter days)
         balance)
        ((zero? (remainder counter 30))
         (alt-new-balance
           (+ (* balance rate) balance increment)
           (+ counter 1)))
        (else
         (alt-new-balance
           (+ (* balance rate) balance)
           (+ counter 1)))) )
```

Each time you want to invoke alt-new-balance, initial values of days, rate, and increment must be defined. The equivalent of the call to new-balance below,

```
(new-balance 1000 1 3 0.01 0)
```

would be

```
(define days 3)
(define rate 0.01)
(define increment 0)
(alt-new-balance 1000 1)
```

This is not as desirable. You have to remember to set all the values each time you want to call `alt-new-balance`. A more serious problem occurs if there already is a variable with any of the names that were bound somewhere else in the code. It would lose its old value. Effectively, this means that you must carefully examine the code to avoid this and hope that the code will not change in the future and introduce problems.

Danger of using free variables instead of parameters

The situation would be worse yet if `counter` were treated as a free variable in `alt-new-balance`. For that function to work as such, the value of `counter` would have to be changed within the function. As we saw in Chapter 3, this would affect the value of `counter` outside of the function, since it is a global variable. Once again, such *side-effects* are not considered to be good programming style and should be avoided. It is better to pass all the values that the function needs as arguments, as in the original function `new-balance`.

6.3   Optional Section: Different Types of Recursion

The functions `first-greater`, `new-balance`, and `increasing-digits` are *tail recursive* functions. Tail recursion is so named because in the recursive cases, when a recursive call is made, the last action taken is the recursive function call. There are no expressions that follow the recursive call, nor is the recursive call an argument to another function to which the result of the recursive call must be applied. In other words, there are no further evaluations necessary after the recursive call is complete.

Tail recursion

Another type of recursion is *embedded recursion*. This is characterized by recursive cases in which the recursive call is placed so that there are more actions to take after the recursive call returns. The function `sum-digits` is an embedded recursive function. This is because the recursive call is used as an argument to the + function:

Embedded recursion

```
(+ last-digit
   (sum-digits rest-of-number))
```

After the recursive call returns its value, that value must be added to the last digit of the number.

6.3.1   Example: Factorial

Below is another example of embedded recursion—computing the factorial of a number:

Embedded recursive
factorial

```
; Return max factorial.
(define (factorial max)
  (if (zero? max)
      1
      (* max
         (factorial (- max 1)))) )
```

Notice that the recursive call

```
(factorial (- max 1))
```

is an argument to the function *, and once it is evaluated it is multiplied by max. This product is the return value of the function. Therefore, there are delayed actions that can only be performed after the recursive call returns its value. A careful exploration of a trace of factorial will help show what this function does.

```
(factorial 3)
    ↓
(* 3 (factorial 2))
        ↓
    (* 2 (factorial 1))
            ↓
        (* 1 (factorial 0))
                ↓
                1
            ↓
            1
        ↓
        2
    ↓
    6
```

The value of (factorial 3) is the product of 3 and (factorial 2). To compute this product, (factorial 2) must first be determined. (factorial 2) is the product of 2 and (factorial 1), and (factorial 1) is 1 times (factorial 0). At this point we reach the exit condition in our recursion, when max equals 0, and we return 1. (factorial 0), 1, is multiplied by 1 to get the value of (factorial 1). Now we return from our recursive descent. 1 is multiplied by 2, giving 2, the value of (factorial 2). This result is multiplied by 3, yielding 6, the value of (factorial 3), and we're done.

Compare the embedded recursion function factorial with the tail recursive function tail-factorial, below.

Tail recursive factorial

```
; Return max factorial (tail recursive).
(define (tail-factorial max total)
  (if (zero? max)
      total
      (tail-factorial (- max 1) (* max total))) )
```

Notice that `tail-factorial` has two parameters; however, it is functionally equivalent to the function `factorial`. It is often necessary to use extra parameters in a tail recursive solution. These parameters are often not necessary with embedded recursive solutions, because that information is contained in the delayed expressions that are evaluated when the recursion returns upon reaching the exit condition. In general, embedded recursive functions can be written as tail recursive functions.[2]

Extra parameters with tail recursion

The first parameter to `tail-factorial`, max, performs the same role as does the parameter max in `factorial`. The second parameter, total, stores the current partial product. In the initial call, total must be 1. At each step through the recursion, total represents the product of all the previous values of max. There are no expressions to return to. Once max is 0, total contains the correct product, and that is the return value. Below is a trace of `tail-factorial`:

```
(tail-factorial 3 1)
        ↓
(tail-factorial 2 3)
        ↓
(tail-factorial 1 6)
        ↓
(tail-factorial 0 6)
        ↓
        6
```

One of the disadvantages of tail recursive solutions is the need for extra parameters to store partial results. There is a nice way to hide these extra parameters so that the user of the function need not worry about them. A *helper function* can be written that has the number of parameters we would like to have. This function calls the actual recursive function (which has additional parameters), filling in the initial values for the other parameters. As an example, the function below allows us to effectively call `tail-factorial` with one parameter:

Helper functions with tail recursion

```
; Return max factorial (helper function).
(define (fact max)
  (tail-factorial max 1))
```

As you can see, these functions are easy to write.

[2.] This is true for a class of embedded recursive functions known as linear recursive functions. These are functions that use only one recursive call in their recursive cases. In contrast, tree recursive functions have more than one recursive call. These recursive calls are combined in some fashion to produce a return value for the function. Tree recursive functions are embedded recursive functions. However, writing tree recursive functions as tail recursive functions often involves going through a good deal of effort, and isn't really that much fun.

6.3.2   Exercises

6.8   Why was `tail-factorial` called with 1 as the initial value for `total`?

6.9   Does the call (`tail-factorial` 0 1) give the desired results?

6.10   What happens if the call (`tail-factorial` –2 1) is made?

6.11   How would you fix the code to handle any problems that may exist in the two exercises above?

6.12   Write a tail recursive function with one parameter, *max*, that computes the sum of the even numbers from 1 to *max*.

6.13   Write a function with a single parameter, *num*, that sums every number between 1 and *num* that is evenly divisible by 4. Write your function without using `remainder`.

6.4   Using Recursion to Sequence Through Lists

Recursive breakdown on lists

Lists and recursion go hand-in-hand. It is fairly simple to create recursive functions that sequence through lists, or create lists. Most recursive functions that take lists terminate (with an exit case) when called with an empty list. In the recursive cases, the problem is usually broken down into performing some action with the first element of the list and the result of the recursive call with the rest of the list.

6.4.1   Example: Adding up numbers in a list

Let's write a function, *sum-list*, that computes the sum of the numbers in a list that only contains numbers. To begin, consider an exit case—if we have an empty list, the sum is zero. In the recursive case we need to break up the problem into a similar, smaller problem. The recursive action can be viewed as adding the first number in the list to the sum of the rest of the numbers in the list. The sum of the rest of the numbers in a list is just a recursive call to this function with the `rest` of the list.

The first element of the list and the rest of the elements in a list were chosen as operations to break the problem down because they are simple, fast operations in Scheme. Computing the `first` and `rest` of a list is much more efficient than computing the last element and taking a `subseq` to get all but the last element of a list. Since the order in which the elements in the list are added doesn't matter, we might as well be efficient about it.

sum-list can be expressed in definitional pseudo code as follows:

if the list is empty, return 0
otherwise, return the sum of the first element and
  sum-list of the rest of the list.

Finally, refinements of this pseudo code should be made:

A list is empty if `null?` of that list is `#t`.

The Scheme solution is

```
; Return sum of numbers in number-list.
(define (sum-list number-list)
   (if (null? number-list)
        0
        (+ (first number-list)
           (sum-list (rest number-list))))) )
```

A trace of the function will show how it works:

```
(sum-list '(-3 4 5))
        ↓
(+ -3 (sum-list '(4 5)))
           ↓
      (+ 4 (sum-list '(5)))
             ↓
          (+ 5 (sum-list '()))
                 ↓
                 0
           ↓
           5
     ↓
     9
 ↓
 6
```

6.4.2 Example: Checking if a list consists entirely of numbers

The function `sum-list` will not work if given a list that has non-numeric elements. To check for that, we will create a predicate function, *all-numbers?*, that sequences through a list and verifies that all the elements are numbers.

One exit condition for such a function is an empty list. If given an empty list, should *all-numbers?* return `#t` or `#f`? To answer this, you must think of how the recursion will work in the recursive case, where the recursive call will be with a smaller list, and eventually with the empty list.

For a list to be all numbers, the first element must be a number **and** the rest of the list must be all numbers. If the function returned `#f` when called with the empty list, the function would always return `#f` because anything `and` `#f` is `#f` in Scheme.

all-numbers? should return `#f` if an element is encountered that is not a number. This should be another exit case—if the first element of the list is not a number, return `#f`.

Our definitional pseudo code looks like the following:

if the list is empty, then return *true*
otherwise, if the first element is not a number, return *false*
otherwise, return *true* if the first element is a number **and**
   the rest of the list is all numbers—the recursive call.

The only detail to refine is testing if the first element of the list is a number. This can be done with the function `number?`, which returns *true* if given a numerical argument, *false* otherwise.

Eliminating redundancy

It's a good idea to review your pseudo code and look for missing pieces, or redundant pieces. In this case, redundancy is the problem. Twice there is a test to determine if the first element of the list is a number. The second test that would be part of an **and** function call is not necessary because once you have reached that point in the code, you know that the first element in the list is a number. Thus, the code can be simplified as

if the list is empty, then return true
otherwise, if the first element is not a number, return false
otherwise, return the result of the recursive call on the rest of the list.

There are some additional observations to make in the above pseudo code. Since there are two conditions to test, and an otherwise clause in case both are false, a `cond` is easier to use than two `if`s. The test to determine if the list is empty should be performed before testing if the first element is a number.

In Scheme, the code would be as follows:

```
; Return true if all elements of a-list are numbers.
(define (all-numbers? a-list)
  (cond ((null? a-list)
            #t)
        ((not (number? (first a-list)))
            #f)
        (else
            (all-numbers? (rest a-list)))) )
```

Below are two traces of this function:

```
(all-numbers? '(3 frogs 4 you))
        ↓
(all-numbers? '(frogs 4 you))
        ↓
     #f
```

Notice how the recursion stopped as soon as a non-number was found. The next trace continues recursing until the empty list is encountered:

```
(all-numbers? '(25 0 624))
         ↓
(all-numbers? '(0 624))
         ↓
(all-numbers? '(624))
         ↓
(all-numbers? '())
         ↓
        #t
```

Now we can use all-numbers? to create a safer version of sum-list:

```
; Add all numbers in a-list unless some are not numbers.
(define (safe-sum a-list)
  (if (all-numbers? a-list)
      (sum-list a-list)
      'bad-list) )
```

6.4.3 Exercises

6.14 Show a sample call to abc that will return a value and one that will enter an infinite loop.

```
(define (abc xyz)
  (cond ((first xyz) (rest xyz))
        (else (abc xyz))) )
```

6.15 Show a sample call to def that will return a value and one that will produce an error.

```
(define (def uvw)
  (or (zero? (first uvw)) (def (rest uvw))) )
```

6.16 Write a function that takes a single list and returns true if *any* elements in the list are numbers.

6.17 Write a function that takes a list of numbers and returns the maximum number in the list.

6.18 Below is an alternate solution to all-numbers?:

```
(define (all-numbers-alt? a-list)
  (if (null? a-list)
      #t
      (and (number? (first a-list))
           (all-numbers-alt? (rest a-list)))) )
```

Does this solution work? If so, will it stop as soon as it encounters a non-number, as all-numbers? did? If not, can you fix it so it does work?

6.19 Below is an alternate solution to `all-numbers?`:

```
(define (all-numbers-alt? a-list)
  (if (null? a-list)
      #t
      (and (all-numbers-alt? (rest a-list))
           (number? (first a-list)))) )
```

Does this solution work? If so, will it stop as soon as it encounters a non-number, as `all-numbers?` did? If not, can you fix it so it does work?

6.20 What does the function below do? Give a meaningful sample call to this function.

```
(define (unknown a-list c1 c2 c3)
  (cond ((null? a-list)
         (list c1 c2 c3))
        ((number? (first a-list))
         (unknown (rest a-list) (+ c1 1) c2 c3))
        ((symbol? (first a-list))
         (unknown (rest a-list) c1 (+ c2 1) c3))
        ((list? (first a-list))
         (unknown (rest a-list) c1 c2 (+ c3 1)))
        (else
         (unknown (rest a-list) c1 c2 c3))) )
```

6.21 Write a function that takes a list consisting of numbers and returns true if the numbers are in increasing order.

6.22 Write a function that takes a list consisting of zeroes and ones and returns true if the zeroes and ones alternate, as in the list (0 1 0 1 0).

6.23 Write a function that takes a list consisting of numbers, symbols, and possibly sublists, and returns the sum of all the numbers in the list. You should ignore numbers that occur within sublists.

6.24 Write your own version of the function `position` using recursion.

6.25 Write your own version of the function `count` using recursion.

6.26 Write your own version of the function `length` using recursion.

6.27 Write your own version of the function `member` using recursion.

6.28 Write your own version of the function `list-ref` using recursion.

6.29 Write your own recursive version of the function `subseq` that takes a list and an integer, *start*, denoting the start position of the resulting list.

6.30 The function below follows a path through a list.

```
(define (mystery a-list)
  (cond ((null? a-list) #f)
        ((atom? a-list) a-list)
        ((symbol? (first a-list)) (first a-list))
        (else
            (mystery (list-ref a-list (first a-list)))))) )
```

What would the following two calls return?

```
(mystery '(3 (a b c) (3 x y z) (2 be or not 2 be) answer))

(mystery '(2 one (1 (3 4 ((2)) (1 short list) bye))))
```

6.31 Given the two functions below

```
(define (abc lst)
  (cond ((null? lst) lst)
        ((>= (def (car lst)) (def (abc (cdr lst))))
            (car lst))
        (else (abc (cdr lst)))) )

(define (def lst)
  (if (null? lst)
      0
      (+ 1 (def (cdr lst)))) )
```

What do the following calls return?

```
(def '(1 2 3 4))

(abc '((1 2 3) (1 2 3 4) (a b)))
```

If the >= in abc were changed to <, what would the following call return? Be careful—this question is deceptively tricky.

```
(abc '((1 2 3) (1 2 3 4) (a b)))
```

6.32 Suppose abc (from the previous exercise) were modified to be:

```
(define (abc lst)
  (cond ((null? lst) 0)
        ((>= (def (car lst)) (abc (cdr lst)))   (def (car lst)))
        (else (abc (cdr lst)))))
```

What would the following call return?

```
(abc '((1 2 3) (1 2 3 4) (a b)))
```

6.33 Write a function that takes a list and returns the first symbol in the list, or #f if no symbols exist in the list.

6.34 Write a function that takes a list and returns the last positive number in the list, or #f if no positive numbers exist in the list.

6.5   Using Recursion to Create New Lists

*Mapping functions
and filters*

Recursion can be used to construct lists. *Mapping functions* and *filters* are common examples of such functions. A mapping function applies a function to each element in a list and returns a list of the results. A filter is a function that sequences through a list and returns a list of only those elements that satisfy a certain condition. Whereas mapping functions return a list of the same size as their argument list, filters may return shorter lists.

The function `cons` is typically used in the recursive cases of functions that create lists to build up the resultant lists.

6.5.1   Example: A mapping function to take the square roots of numbers in a list

Let's begin with a function that takes a list of numbers and returns a list of the square roots of those numbers. We will sequence through the list in the same manner as the functions `sum-list` and `all-numbers?` did; thus, eventually we will reach the empty list.

Build up approach

We can think about the solution to this problem starting with the exit case. Next we look at cases that involve a single recursive call, then two recursive calls, and so on until we are convinced that our idea is sound. Such a *build up* technique—starting with the exit case and building up to larger examples—is a common means of creating recursive solutions.

For the current problem, if we are given an empty list, `()` is the proper return value—the square roots of an empty list of numbers is an empty list. Given a list of one element, the square root of that element can be combined using `cons` with the square roots of the rest of the elements, `()`, to produce a list of one square root. This technique works with larger lists too. With two elements we `cons` the square root of the first element onto the recursive call of the rest of the list, which we just showed is a list of one square root. This produces a list of the two square roots of the argument list in the proper order.

Given any size list, `cons`ing the square root of the first element onto the result of the recursive call with the rest of the list gives us back a list of square roots in the proper order.

Leap of faith

The *leap of faith* method is an alternate means of formulating recursive solutions. Using the leap of faith you begin with a more complicated example input to your function and assume that the recursive call produces the correct output. This is the leap of faith because at this point you haven't written a recursive solution. You just assume it exists and works. Next you determine how to use the result of the recursive call to create the final return value given your input to the function.

Let's try this approach with the current problem. Given the list `(49 16 100)`, assume that the recursive call with the rest of the list, `(16 100)`, produces the list `(4 10)`. To get the desired result, `(7 4 10)`, we `cons` the square root of 49 onto the recursive call. This is the action we take in the recursive case.

Our definitional pseudo code follows:

if the list is empty, return the empty list

otherwise, return the result of consing the square root of the first
    element onto the recursive call of the rest of the elements.

In Scheme, the code is as follows:

```
; Return a list of the square roots of the numbers in a-list.
(define (square-roots a-list)
   (if (null? a-list)
       '()
       (cons (sqrt (first a-list))
             (square-roots (rest a-list)))) )
```

A trace reveals the following:

```
(square-roots '(49 16 100))
        ↓
(cons (sqrt 49) (square-roots '(16 100)))
        ↓                  ↓
       7.0                 ↓
               (cons (sqrt 16) (square-roots '(100)))
                        ↓                  ↓
                       4.0                 ↓
                           (cons (sqrt 100) (square-roots '()))
                                    ↓                  ↓
                                  10.0                 ()
                               ↓
                            ( 10.0 )
                   ↓
               ( 4.0  10.0 )
       ↓
( 7.0  4.0  10.0 )
```

6.5.2   Example: A filter to extract positive numbers from a list

The next example is a filter that constructs a list of all the positive numbers in its
argument list. The exit case for this function is once again the empty list, and the
return value in this case is the empty list. The difference between filters and mapping functions is that an additional test is needed to check if the next element of
the list should be placed in the resultant list or not. For this problem, the test
checks if the number is positive. If so, that element should be added to the resultant list; otherwise, skip that value and return the positive numbers in the rest of
the list.

The definitional pseudo code is

if the list is empty, return the empty list
otherwise, if the first element of the list is a positive number,
     return the cons of the first element and
            the recursive call with the rest of the list
otherwise, return the recursive call with the rest of the list.

In Scheme,

```
; Return a list of the positive numbers in a-list.
(define (positive-filter a-list)
  (cond ((null? a-list)
              '())
        ((positive? (first a-list))
            (cons (first a-list)
                  (positive-filter (rest a-list))))
        (else
            (positive-filter (rest a-list)))) )
```

Here is a trace of positive-filter:

```
(positive-filter '(3 -1 2))
         ↓
(cons 3 (positive-filter '(-1 2)))
                ↓
         (positive-filter '(2))
                ↓
         (cons 2 (positive-filter '()))
                      ↓
                     ()
           ↓
         (2)
    ↓
(3 2)
```

6.5.3 Exercises

6.35 Write a function that takes a list of numbers and returns a list of pairs of
     numbers, where a pair is a list of the number and its square. Given the list

     (3 4 5)

     your function should produce the list

     ((3 9) (4 16) (5 25))

6.36 Write a function that takes a number and returns a list of all the integer mul-
     tiples of that number from 1 to 10. Given the number 3, your function
     should return the list

     (3 6 9 12 15 18 21 24 27 30)

6.37 Write a filter function that takes a list of numbers and two integers, *low* and *high*. The function should return only those numbers that are between *low* and *high*, exclusive.

6.38 Write a function that takes two arguments, *start* and *end*, and returns a list of all the odd integers between *start* and *end*.

6.39 Write a simplified version of the function append that only takes two lists.

6.40 The function switch-em takes a list and should return the list with pairs of top-level elements switched. For example,

```
> (switch-em '((i am) just another (run of the mill) list)
(just (i am) (run of the mill) another list)
```

There are one or more bugs in this function. Find the bugs and fix them.

```
(define (switch-em a-list)
  (if (null? a-list)
      '()
      (append
        (second a-list)
        (first a-list)
        (switch-em (cdr a-list))))) )
```

6.41 Write your own version of the function remove.

6.42 Write your own version of the function reverse.

6.43 Write a function substitute that takes a list and two atoms, *old* and *new*. The function should return a new list with all top-level occurrences of *old* replaced with *new*. For example,

```
(substitute '(me but (not me)) 'me 'you)
```

should produce the list

```
(you but (not me))
```

6.44 Write your own version of the function subseq that takes three arguments, the list, the start, and the end values. Assume that the start and end values are legal.

6.45 Does the function positive-filter work if called with a list in which some elements are not numbers? If not, modify the function so that it does work with such a list.

6.6 Sequencing Through Nested Lists with `car-cdr` Recursion

Linear versus tree recursion

All of the recursive functions shown have been *linear recursive* functions. A linear recursive function is one that has at most one recursive call in any of its recursive cases. Functions can have more than one recursive call in their recursive cases. Such functions are termed *nonlinear* or *tree recursive*. They may be called deep or multiple recursive as well. Tree recursion is a very powerful type of recursion, in that a small amount of code can perform seemingly impossible or difficult tasks. There is a price that must be paid for this power: tree recursive functions are somewhat more difficult to write, trace, and debug than their linear recursive siblings.

`car-cdr` recursion

A common type of tree recursion in Scheme is `car-cdr` recursion. It is so named because a recursive call is made with both the `car` and the `cdr` of the list. This is used when dealing with lists that have sublists, so that all the sublists can be sequenced through. With the linear recursive functions we have used so far, only the top-level elements have been examined.

6.6.1 Example: Counting all the atoms in a list

An example to begin with is the function *count-atoms* that takes a list and counts the number of atoms in that list and all of its sublists. Below are some examples to show what this function returns:

```
(count-atoms '(1 2 a))  →  3
(count-atoms '((1 (2 a))))  →  3
(count-atoms '((1 2 (a b c) d) 10 (((word)))))  →  8
```

We begin by considering the exit cases. Once again, the empty list is an exit condition. The number of atoms in the empty list is zero.

In the recursive cases of some of our previous list recursive functions, we applied the `car` of the list to some function, and called the `cdr` recursively. The results of these two function calls were then combined using some other function. Let's try the same technique with this problem. The `car` of the list may be an atom or a list. If it is an atom, then the number of atoms to return is one. Otherwise, the `car` is a list, and since we are writing a function to count the number of atoms in a list, the function should be called recursively with the `car` of the list. We need to include the `cdr` of the list as well by calling it recursively.

Leap of faith with tree recursion

At this point we can use the leap of faith strategy. If we believe that our recursive function will produce the proper answers for the `car` and the `cdr` of the list, then if we add these results together, we will have the total number of atoms in the list. For example, if given the list

```
((2 3) 4 (5 numbers))
```

the recursive calls with the `car` and `cdr` of the list yield

```
(count-atoms '(2 3))  →  2
(count-atoms '(4 (5 numbers)))  →  3
```

Adding these results yields 5, the number of atoms in the original list. This technique also works with lists in which the `car` is an atom. In this case, the number of atoms is one plus the number of atoms in the `cdr` of the list. Thus,

```
(count-atoms '(2 4 (5 numbers)))  →
    1 + (count-atoms '(4 (5 numbers)))
```

We can express the solution in definitional pseudo code as follows:

> if the list is empty, return 0
> otherwise, if the `car` of the list is an atom, return one plus
>   the recursive call with the `cdr` of the list
> otherwise, return the sum of the recursive calls with the `car` and
>   the `cdr` of the lists.

If you feel uneasy about this solution, perhaps because you didn't buy the leap of faith approach, then you should test out your solution using your definitional pseudo code. Let's test out the solution with the above example list:

```
((2 3) 4 (5 numbers))
```

We really need to verify if the recursive calls with the `car` and the `cdr` of this list work to add faith to our leap of faith. Beginning with the `car`, (2 3),

Verifying the leap of faith

```
(count-atoms '(2 3))  →  1 + (count-atoms '(3))
```

and

```
(count-atoms '(3))  →  1 + (count-atoms '())
```

and

```
(count-atoms '())  →  0
```

This results in 2, which is correct. Notice that since the `car` of the list was an atom in each case, we performed linear recursion to get this partial result.

Moving on to the `cdr` we have

```
(count-atoms '(4 (5 numbers)))  →
    1 + (count-atoms '((5 numbers)))
```

and

```
(count-atoms '((5 numbers)))  →
    (count-atoms '(5 numbers)) + (count-atoms '())
```

Continuing with these two recursive calls

```
(count-atoms '(5 numbers))  →  2
```

because it is a two-atom list like (count-atoms '(2 3)).

Next

```
(count-atoms '())  →  0
```

Adding up these results, 2 and 0, yields 2, which is added to 1 (from the atom 4), yielding 3. Lastly, adding 3 to 2 from (count-atoms '(2 3)) gives 5; thus, our pseudo code performs correctly.

Now we can write out the Scheme function.

```
; Return the number of atoms that occur anywhere in a-list.
(define (count-atoms a-list)
  (cond ((null? a-list)
           0)
        ((atom? (car a-list))
           (+ 1 (count-atoms (cdr a-list))))
        (else
           (+ (count-atoms (car a-list))
              (count-atoms (cdr a-list)))) )
```

Below is a trace of this function:

```
(count-atoms '(a (b (c))))
         ↓
(+ 1 (count-atoms '((b (c)))))
              ↓
     (+ (count-atoms '(b (c)))        (count-atoms '())
                ↓                            ↓
                ↓                            0
       (+ 1 (count-atoms '((c))))
                 ↓
        (+ (count-atoms '(c))        (count-atoms '())
                  ↓                          ↓
                  ↓                          0
          (+ 1 (count-atoms '()))
                   ↓
                   0
            ↓
            1
          ↓
          1
        ↓
        2
      ↓
      2
    ↓
    3
```

6.6.2   Example: Deep reverse of a list

Another function that uses car-cdr recursion is a deep reverse of a list. In a deep reverse, all the atoms, even those within sublists, should be reversed. Given the list

```
((a b) (2 (3 4)))
```

the function should return

```
(((4 3) 2) (b a))
```

Contrast this with the built-in function `reverse`:

```
> (reverse '((a b) (2 (3 4))))
((2 (3 4)) (a b))
```

Once again, as with all the recursive list functions we have created, an exit condition is the empty list. Since we are returning a list, if we are passed the empty list, we should return `()`.

As with the `count-atoms` function, if the first item in the list is a list, its elements must be reversed, and then that list should be put into the resultant list in the proper location. Assembling the lists from the recursive calls can get tricky.

To make matters simpler, we can think about how to do a top-level reverse, as the built-in function `reverse` performs. The first element in the list must become the last element. To do this, imagine appending the reverse of the rest of the list onto the list of the first element. For example, given the list

Top-level reverse

```
(1 2 3)
```

the reverse of the rest of the list is

```
(3 2)
```

and the list of the first element is

```
(1)
```

Appending these together yields

```
(3 2 1)
```

which is the reverse of the original list. Note that the reason we used the list of the first element, as opposed to just the first element, is because `append` constructs lists from lists, so both arguments to `append` should be lists.

We are using the leap of faith strategy and assuming that the recursive step works, and then determining how to use the results from the recursive calls to produce the desired result. We should verify that the leap of faith idea works. This can be done using the build up approach. This approach starts by testing the function with arguments that satisfy an exit condition. Next test the function with a call that requires a single recursive call. Then build up to calls with more recursive calls until you are convinced the function works (or doesn't work).

Verifying code with the build up approach

We will try the build up approach now. First we must create the definitional pseudo code. *Remember, this is for a top-level reverse, not a deep reverse.*

> if the list to reverse is empty, return the empty list
> otherwise, return the result of appending the reverse of the rest of the list onto the list of the first element.

Now the test starting with an exit case

```
(reverse '())
     ↓
    ()
```

With one recursive call, we get

```
(reverse '(2))
     ↓
(append (reverse '()) (list 2))
               ↓           ↓
              ()          (2)
     ↓
    (2)
```

We can go further and try a call that requires an additional recursive step:

```
(reverse '(1 2))
     ↓
(append (reverse '(2)) (list 1))
               ↓           ↓
              (2)         (1)
     ↓
   (2 1)
```

Once again, the proper result is obtained. This adds the faith to the leap of faith.

Deep reverse

The same technique used in a top-level reverse can be used in a deep reverse, with the added condition that the elements within sublists should be reversed using the *deep-reverse* function recursively. If these sublists have sublists, they should be reversed, and so on.

Just as with the `count-atoms` function, we only deal with sublists when checking the `car` of the list. If the `car` is a list, we call it recursively. Combining this idea with the top-level reverse pseudo code we can construct the following definitional pseudo code:

> if the list given to *deep-reverse* is empty, return '( )
> otherwise, if the first item in the list is an atom, return the
>> append of the *deep-reverse* of the rest of the list onto
>>> the list of that atom
>
> otherwise, return the
>> append of the *deep-reverse* of the rest of the list onto
>>> the deep-reverse of the first element (which is a list).

This can be written in Scheme as:

```
; Return the deep reverse of a-list (reverses all sub-lists).
(define (deep-reverse a-list)
  (cond ((null? a-list)
            '())
        ((atom? (car a-list))
            (append (deep-reverse (cdr a-list))
                    (list (car a-list))))
        (else
            (append (deep-reverse (cdr a-list))
                    (deep-reverse (car a-list)))))  )
```

Below is a trace of `deep-reverse`. To keep things clearer, only the boxed recursive calls will be expanded. After this trace the other recursive calls will be traced out individually, and then all the results will be combined.

```
(deep-reverse '((a 3) (b 2) c))
       ↓
(append [(deep-reverse '((b 2) c))]          (deep-reverse '(a 3)))
                ↓
        (append [(deep-reverse '(c))]        (deep-reverse '(b 2)))
                        ↓
                (append [(deep-reverse '())]    (list 'c))
                                ↓                  ↓
                               ()                 (c)
       ↓
      (c)
```

```
        (deep-reverse '(b 2))
              ↓
(append (deep-reverse '(2))                          (list 'b))
                ↓                                        ↓
        (append (deep-reverse '()) (list 2))            (b)
                      ↓              ↓
                     ()            (2)
              ↓
            (2)
   ↓
  (2 b)
```

Similarly,

```
(deep-reverse '(a 3))
```

will return

```
(3 a)
```

Putting it all together, we get

```
(deep-reverse '((a 3) (b 2) c))
       ↓
(append (deep-reverse '((b 2) c))          (deep-reverse '(a 3)))
                ↓                                    ↓
                ↓                                   (3 a)
                ↓
        (append (deep-reverse '(c))        (deep-reverse '(b 2)))
                      ↓                              ↓
                     (c)                            (2 b)
              ↓
            (c 2 b)
   ↓
  (c 2 b 3 a)
```

Oops. What went wrong? We got the proper order of symbols, but lost our nested list structure. Since the order of the symbols is correct, we are probably making the recursive calls in the correct location, but we are combining the results of these recursive calls improperly. Looking back at the code, notice that in the last recursive case, we append the deep-reverse of the rest of the list onto the deep-reverse of the first of the list. Imagine that the first element is

```
(a 3)
```

The deep-reverse of that list will be

```
(3 a)
```

Appending the list (3 a) to another list merely adds the two elements, 3 and a, to that list rather than adding the list (3 a). To preserve the list structure, append the `list` of the deep-reverse of the `car` of the list. This is similar to the recursive case when the `car` is an atom—we append to the `list` of the `car`. Thus our new code is

```
; Return the deep reverse of a-list (reverses all sub-lists).
(define (deep-reverse a-list)
  (cond ((null? a-list)
           '())
        ((atom? (car a-list))
           (append (deep-reverse (cdr a-list))
                   (list (car a-list))))
        (else
           (append (deep-reverse (cdr a-list))
                   (list (deep-reverse (car a-list)))))) )
```

Perform a trace of this code to verify that it works.

6.6.3   Exercises

6.46 Below is an alternate solution to the count-atoms function. Does it work?

```
(define (count-atoms a-list)
  (cond ((null? a-list)
           0)
        ((atom? a-list)
           1)
        (else
           (+ (count-atoms (car a-list))
              (count-atoms (cdr a-list)))) )
```

6.47 Below is another possible solution to the deep-reverse function. Does it work?

```
(define (deep-reverse a-list)
  (cond ((null? a-list)
           '())
        ((atom? a-list)
           a-list)
        (else
           (append (deep-reverse (cdr a-list))
                   (list (deep-reverse (car a-list)))))) )
```

6.48 The function `unknown` takes a nested list as an argument.

```
(define (unknown a-list)
  (cond ((null? a-list) '())
        ((number? a-list) (list a-list))
        ((symbol? a-list) '())
        (else
          (append
            (unknown (car a-list))
            (unknown (cdr a-list)))))) )
```

What would the following call return?

```
(unknown '(2 (3 words) ((4 more))))
```

6.49 Write a function that performs a deep member function on a list. All the atoms, even those within sublists, should be examined. Given the call

```
(deep-member 2 '(((a b 2))))
```

your function should return a *true* value. Do not use the built-in function **member** in your solution.

6.50 Write a function that returns true if two lists look the same in form. The atoms may be different, but the parentheses should be the same. The following two lists look the same:

```
((a b (c) d) e)
((1 2 (3) 4) 5)
```

6.51 Given the function below

```
(define (mystery unknown)
  (if (or (null? unknown) (atom? unknown))
      unknown
      (cons (mystery (car unknown)) (mystery (cdr unknown))))) )
```

What does the call `(mystery '(1 (2) 3))` return?

6.52 Write a function that returns the total sum of all the numbers in all its sublists. Given the list

```
(((4 3) b) (2 a))
```

your function should return 9.

6.53 Write a function that returns the smallest number that occurs anywhere in a list. Given the list

```
(((4 3) b) (2 a))
```

your function should return 2.

6.54 Write a function that takes a list and returns a flattened version of it—one with no sublists. Given the list

```
(((4 3) b) (2 a))
```
your function should return the list
```
(4 3 b 2 a)
```

6.55 Write your own version of the function `equal?`. Use the function `eqv?` to compare atoms.

6.7 Nested Loops or Recursion Within Recursion

Loops and nested loops

Linear recursive functions (those with one recursive call in the recursive case) perform a sequence of similar actions. In many programming languages, such repetition is called a *loop*. This is because the actions are performed, then the computer loops back to the first of those actions and performs the actions again. It is possible to have loops within loops—such code is called a *nested loop*. Nested loops are used to repeat actions that have repeated steps themselves.

6.7.1 Example: Sum of factorials

Inner and outer loops

Calculating the sum of all the factorials from one to *number* is an example of a nested loop. To calculate the factorial of a number, a loop is required. To add up these factorials, another loop is required. The *inner loop* would be the loop computing factorials. The *outer loop* would be the loop summing the factorials.

In Scheme, nested loops are created using two recursive functions. One function, the inner loop, calls itself recursively. The outer loop is another function that calls itself recursively, and calls the inner loop function.

For our example, we'll begin with the inner loop—factorial. The code is as follows:

```
; Return max factorial.
(define (factorial max)
  (if (zero? max)
      1
      (* max
         (factorial (- max 1)))) )
```

The outer function must call itself and `factorial`. It has an exit case when the number of factorials to sum is zero—in this case the sum is zero. The recursive case requires the addition of the current factorial of *number* to the sum of all the factorials less than *number*.

This can be expressed in definitional pseudo code as

if *number* is 0, return 0
otherwise, return the sum of the factorial of *number* and
        the sum of all the factorials from 1 to *number* minus 1

In Scheme, the function is written as

```
; Return sum of 0 through number factorial.
(define (sum-facts number)
  (if (zero? number)
      0
      (+ (factorial number)
         (sum-facts (- number 1)))) )
```

A trace of the function reveals

```
(sum-facts 3)
     ↓
(+ (factorial 3) (sum-facts 2))
        ↓              ↓
        6              ↓
                (+ (factorial 2) (sum-facts 1))
                       ↓              ↓
                       2              ↓
                               (+ (factorial 1) (sum-facts 0))
                                      ↓              ↓
                                      1              0
                                    ↓
                                    1
                     ↓
                     3
     ↓
     9
```

6.7.2 Example: Sequencing through a database using nested loops

Below is an alternate representation for the CD data structure from Chapter 4. This data structure is a list of music categories (rock, jazz, classical, etc.) and the music within them. Each music category is a list of artists and their CDs. These artist and CD lists have the artist's name as the first element of the list, and the CDs make up the rest of the list. The artist names and the CD names are lists. The new data structure looks like the following list:

```
( ( rock
    ( (Rolling Stones)
      (Black and Blue)
      (Its Only Rock and Roll) ) )
  ( jazz
    ( (Pat Metheny)
      (First Circle) )
    ( (Andy Narell)
      (The Hammer) ) ) )
```

New CD data structure

This CD database can be searched to find the CDs composed by a particular artist, or to find the occurrence of a particular CD. We will use a nested loop to find the CDs written by a particular artist. This will be a list of CDs. The outer loop will sequence through the music categories. These categories are elements of

Nested loop to find CDs

the list that makes up our entire database. The inner loop sequences through the artists within a particular category. We need both loops because we are trying to find a particular artist and we may not know which music category the artist is in. Let's build the inner loop first. It will take as an argument a music category list like the following:

```
( jazz
  ( (Pat Metheny)
    (First Circle) )
  ( (Andy Narell)
    (The Hammer) ) )
```

Inner loop to find CDs

To simplify the code in the inner loop, we can write the outer loop so that it calls the inner loop with a list without the category name—the **rest** of the category list, like the following:

```
( ( (Pat Metheny)
    (First Circle) )
  ( (Andy Narell)
    (The Hammer) ) )
```

The pseudo code we need is

> if the list of artists is empty, return #f to signal the outer function that the artist is not in this category
>
> otherwise, if the first artist in the list is the desired one, return the CDs of that artist
>
> otherwise, check the rest of the artists recursively.

To check if the first artist in the list is the one we want, we can use

> (**equal?** (**first** (**first** *artist-list*)) *artist-name*)

The Scheme code for the inner function is

```
; Find the CDs of artist-name within a music category list.
(define (CDs-within-category artist-list artist-name)
  (cond ((null? artist-list)
            #f)
        ((equal? (first (first artist-list)) artist-name)
            (rest (first artist-list)))
        (else
            (CDs-within-category (rest artist-list) artist-name))) )
```

Outer loop to find the artist

The outer loop takes the entire CD database as an argument and sequences through the music categories until a category in which the artist exists is found, or all the categories have been searched. The outer function will call the inner function to determine if an artist occurs within a musical category. The inner function returns the CD list if it finds the artist and #f if not. The outer function needs an exit case to handle the case in which the artist does not occur in the database—it needs to check for an empty database.

The definitional pseudo code for the outer loop is

if the list of categories is empty, return #f—the artist was not found
otherwise, if the first category contains that artist, return the
    CDs of that artist
otherwise, check the rest of the categories recursively.

The Scheme code for the outer function is

```
; Find the CDs of artist-name within the entire CD-collection.
(define (CDs CD-collection artist-name)
  (cond ((null? CD-collection)
           #f)
        ((CDs-within-category (rest (first CD-collection))
                              artist-name)
         (CDs-within-category (rest (first CD-collection))
                              artist-name))
        (else
           (CDs (rest CD-collection) artist-name))) )
```

This could be written more efficiently as

```
; Find the CDs of artist-name within the entire CD-collection.
(define (CDs CD-collection artist-name)
  (cond ((null? CD-collection)
           #f)
        (else
          (or (CDs-within-category
                  (rest (first CD-collection))
                  artist-name)
              (CDs (rest CD-collection) artist-name)))) )
```

This new definition avoids having to call CDs-within-category twice if a match is found[3].

We can go one level further and look for a particular CD in the CD database. This will require a third innermost loop that sequences through a list of CDs of a certain artist. The outer function can stay as it is written with the exception that artist-name should be replaced with CD-name. The inner function will need a slight change—instead of checking for a match in the artist's name and returning a CD list, it should look more like the outer function and have an otherwise clause that returns the or of a call to the innermost function and a recursive call with the rest of the artists in that category.

An innermost loop to find a particular CD

The new inner function will be

---

[3] Another way of doing this is to change the first version of CDs so that the clause that calls CDs-within-category looks like

```
((CDs-within-category (rest (first CD-collection)) artist-name))
```

There is no action associated with this condition. This is legal in Scheme; the return value for a *true* condition without an action is the return value of that condition.

```
; Find CD-name by an artist within a music category list.
(define (CDs-within-category artist-list CD-name)
  (cond ((null? artist-list)
          #f)
        (else
          (or (CD-within-CD-list
                (rest (first artist-list))
                CD-name)
              (CDs-within-category
                (rest artist-list) CD-name)))) )
```

The innermost function gets a CD list like

```
( (Black and Blue)
  (Its Only Rock and Roll) )
```

and looks for a match of the CD being searched for. If the CD is found, it should be returned; otherwise #f should be returned. This function is similar to the original CDs-within-category function.

The innermost function is

```
; Find CD-name within a list of CDs.
(define (CD-within-CD-list CD-list CD-name)
  (cond ((null? CD-list)
          #f)
        ((equal? (first CD-list) CD-name)
          CD-name)
        (else
          (CD-within-CD-list (rest CD-list) CD-name))) )
```

Note: this function could have been implemented using **member**, as follows:

```
; Find CD-name within a list of CDs.
(define (CD-within-CD-list CD-list CD-name)
  (let ( (found-name (member CD-name CD-list)) )
    (if found-name
        (first found-name)
        #f)) )
```

6.7.3   Example: Poker revisited

Straights in poker

Our version of poker from Chapter 5 did not know about straights like

```
(four five six seven eight)
```

A straight is much easier to recognize if it is in order than if it is unordered, as in

```
(six eight five four seven)
```

If we can sort the hand we are passed, we can test if it matches a subsequence of a list of the ordered cards. These cards can be saved in the variable card-ordering.

```
(define card-ordering
        '(two three four five six seven eight nine ten
          jack queen king ace))
```

Sorting data is a frequently performed operation in computer programming. There are books on the subject and numerous sorting algorithms. We will use a method known as *insertion sort*. The idea behind this sort technique is to build a sorted list beginning with an empty list and inserting elements one at a time in the proper place in the list until a complete sorted list is obtained. There are two loops. The inner loop places an element in the sorted list. The outer loop calls the inner loop to place all the elements.

Insertion sort

The inner loop takes two parameters, *sorted-list*, the sorted list, and *element*, the element to insert in *sorted-list*. The definitional pseudo code to the inner loop is as follows:

Adding an element to a sorted list

> if *sorted-list* is empty, return the list of *element*
> otherwise, if *element* is less than the first element in *sorted-list*,
> > return the list obtained from consing *element* onto *sorted-list*
> otherwise, return the cons of the first element of *sorted-list*
> > and the recursive call of *element* and the rest of *sorted-list*.

We must refine what we mean by one card being less than another. A card is "less than" another card if it occurs earlier in card-ordering. This can be determined by comparing the position of the two cards within card-ordering. The function below does this:

```
; Return true if card1 is lower in value than card2.
(define (lower-card? card1 card2)
  (< (position card1 card-ordering)
     (position card2 card-ordering)) )
```

The Scheme code for the inner loop is

```
; Insert card in sorted order into sorted-list.
(define (insert-card element sorted-list)
  (cond ((null? sorted-list)
            (list element))
        ((lower-card? element (first sorted-list))
            (cons element sorted-list))
        (else
            (cons (first sorted-list)
                  (insert-card element (rest sorted-list)))))) )
```

The outer loop that sorts an unsorted list has the following definitional pseudo code:

Outer loop to sort a list

> if the list to sort is empty, return '()
> otherwise, insert the first element of the list into the recursive call
> > of the rest of the list

In Scheme, this is written

```
; Perform insertion sort on a-list.
(define (sort-hand a-list)
  (if (null? a-list)
      '()
      (insert-card
        (first a-list)
        (sort-hand (rest a-list)))) )
```

Let's see how this code works with the trace below:

```
(sort-hand '(seven two three))
  ↓
(insert-card 'seven (sort-hand '(two three)))
                    ↓
          (insert-card 'two (sort-hand '(three)))
                              ↓
                    (insert-card 'three (sort-hand '()))
                                        ↓
                                        ()
                              ↓
                        ( three )
                ↓
          ( two three )
      ↓
( two three seven )
```

And let's trace the final call to `insert-card`:

```
(insert-card 'seven '(two three))
  ↓
(cons 'two (insert-card 'seven '(three)))
              ↓
        (cons 'three (insert-card 'seven '()))
                          ↓
                      ( seven )
            ↓
      ( three seven )
  ↓
( two three seven )
```

Now we can sort our hand and determine if we have a straight. Once the hand is sorted we want to compare it with a subsequence of `card-ordering`, starting with the low card in our hand. To avoid unnecessary testing we can add another test to see if our low card is less than a jack. If it's not, we cannot have a straight.

```
; Return true if hand is a straight.
(define (is-straight? hand card-ordering)
  (let* ( (sorted-hand (sort-hand hand))
          (low-card (first sorted-hand)) )
     (and (lower-card? low-card 'jack)
          (equal?
            sorted-hand
            (subseq
              (member low-card card-ordering)
              0 5)))) )
```

6.7.4 Exercises

6.56 Modify the functions from the CD example so that the entire database is searched when looking for a particular artist, as opposed to the present scheme in which the search stops when the first artist match is found. Return a list of all CDs by the artist from all categories.

6.57 Does the below alternate definition for CDs work? If not, fix it so it does work properly.

```
(define (CDs CD-collection artist-name)
  (or
    (null? CD-collection)
    (CDs-within-category (rest (first CD-collection))
      artist-name)
    (CDs (rest CD-collection) artist-name)) )
```

6.58 Modify the function poker-value from Chapter 4 so that instead of returning nothing for a nonwinning hand, it returns the high card in the hand. For example, if given the hand

```
(seven jack three five two)
```

your function should return jack.

6.59 Write a function tables that produces a list of multiplication tables. For example

```
(tables 3 4)
```

would produce the list

```
((1 2 3 4)
 (2 4 6 8)
 (3 6 9 12))
```

6.8 Summary

- When writing recursive functions, begin by considering the exit cases. Next think about the recursive cases that break the problem down into similar, smaller subproblems that eventually reach exit cases.
- Tail recursive functions have recursive cases in which the return value is a recursive call.
- Embedded recursive functions have recursive cases in which the return value has a recursive call that is an argument to another function. Another type of embedded recursive function is one in which there is an expression that follows the recursive call in the action of a recursive case.
- Recursive functions that sequence through lists typically have an exit case that checks for an empty list. Such functions usually perform some test or action with the `first` of the list and make a recursive call with the `rest` of the list.
- Mapping and filter functions typically construct lists using `cons`.
- `car-cdr` recursion is a type of recursion that involves recursive calls to both the `car` and the `cdr` of a list.
- Nested loops can be written with multiple recursive functions in which the outer loop functions call themselves and the inner loop functions.

CHAPTER 7

DATA STRUCTURES

7.1 Why Data Structures?

We have looked at Scheme's most common data structure, the list. We have seen how ordered lists and hierarchies can be represented. The focus in this chapter is on using data structures like these and other more abstract data structures in programs.

Niklaus Wirth, the creator of the programming language Pascal, wrote a book entitled *Algorithms + Data Structures = Programs*. In this classic computer science text, he shows that algorithms alone do not make programs; data structures play an important role in the design of programs. This is still true today, and is true for the language Scheme. Just as we are able to write complex programs by abstracting the steps or algorithm necessary, we can create elegant programs by creating abstract data structures to represent the information that our program uses.

Importance of data structures

Perhaps the biggest flaw that beginning programmers make is to ignore the importance of data structures in their programs. It is common to see beginners create the simplest structure that comes to mind or no structure whatsoever, and then create large amounts of code to get the program to work. This approach can yield working programs, but usually they are hard to maintain and modify. By spending some time up front carefully considering how the data in your program will be used and designing the best structure to meet those needs, you can save a great deal of time later in coding.

Enough preaching from the soap box. Let's examine some real examples.

7.1.1 Example: Breaking secret codes

Remember when you were a kid and had a secret decoder ring that you got when you mailed in three box tops of *Sugar, Starch, and Sucrose Cereal*? It was effectively a list of letter pairs that you used to translate English words into a secret code or vice versa. It was fun at first, but after a while it just became too tedious. Of course what you really needed was a computer to do the work for you. So we'll create a program that will translate English to secret code and secret code to English. We'll make two functions to do so, `english-to-code` and `code-to-english`. Both functions will take lists of single-letter symbols that represent letters in words and return similar lists. For example,

```
(english-to-code '(a p p l e))
```

might return

```
(f z z y r)
```

In which case,

```
(code-to-english '(f z z y r))
```

would return

```
(a p p l e)
```

Without using data structures other than the lists that are passed as arguments to these functions, we may be tempted to write the code as a large `cond` that matches letters in English to their secret code equivalents. The solution to go from a letter of secret code, `letter`, to its English equivalent might look like this:

```
(cond ((equal? letter 'a) 'f)
      ((equal? letter 'b) 'g)
             .
             .
             .
      ((equal? letter 'z) 'e)
      (else 'unknown-letter))
```

Two such `cond`s would be necessary—one to go from an English letter to code, and another to go from code to the equivalent English letter.

Data integrity

This solution involves a good deal of coding and is difficult to modify. For example, if you wanted to change the secret code, you would have to change both `cond`s. It would be easy to have inconsistencies between the two `cond`s. This creates a *data integrity* problem.

Mapping English to code

The solution is to have only one *mapping* between English and the secret code. Mapping is used in the mathematical sense here—a one-to-one mapping is one that relates one item uniquely to another item. This mapping must be structured in such a way that would allow us to translate either way—English to code, or code to English. A list of two-element lists would do the job. Each of these sublists represents an English letter and its equivalent in the secret code. One reason that a list of sublists is used instead of one large list is that it ensures that we have an even number of elements. Another reason is that it is easier to see which elements match and which are English letters versus code letters without having to count elements.

Below is what the data structure would look like:

```
((a f)
 (b g)
 (c t)
   .
   .
   .
 (z e))
```

To go from English to code involves sequencing through the list recursively, comparing the `first` of each sublist (an English letter) with the English letter to match. When a match is found, the `second` of the sublist is returned. This process is repeated for each letter in the argument list given to the `english-to-code` function.

Translating English to code

To go from code to English is similar, except the `seconds` of the sublists are compared against the code letter to match, and the `first` of the matching pair is returned.

Translating code to English

The function to translate a single English letter to its code equivalent follows. It has two parameters: the letter to search for, `letter`, and the data structure of letter pairs, `match-list`.

```
; Encode the symbol letter.
(define (english-letter-to-code letter match-list)
  (let ( (letter-pair (first match-list)) )
    (if (equal? letter (first letter-pair))
        (second letter-pair)
        (english-letter-to-code letter (rest match-list))))) )
```

This function can be used in the function `english-to-code` that takes a list of English letters and returns the list representing their code equivalent.

```
; Encode letter-list.
(define (english-to-code letter-list match-list)
  (if (null? letter-list)
      '()
      (cons (english-letter-to-code (first letter-list) match-list)
            (english-to-code (rest letter-list) match-list))) )
```

7.1.2 Exercises

7.1 Write functions to translate code to English.

7.2 How would the functions above that translate from English to code have to be modified if you wished to switch the order in the sublists so that each sublist was a code letter followed by an English letter?

7.3 What happens if `english-to-code` is called with a list that has nonletters (i.e., `(t 4 2)`)? Modify the previous functions so that they do something reasonable in such a situation.

7.4 Suppose we eliminated the inner parentheses and made our mapping of English to code one long list as follows:

```
(a f b g c t . . . z e)
```

Does the following version of `english-letter-to-code` work?

```
; Encode the symbol letter.
(define (english-letter-to-code letter match-list)
  (second (member letter match-list)) )
```

If so, write an analogous function that translates code letters into English letters. If not, explain why.

7.2 Association Lists

Association lists and pairs

Another data structure that is used to make a list of related pairs is an *association list*. An association list is a list of nonempty lists. A nonempty list is often called a *cons* or a *pair*.

Scheme has one built-in function that works with association lists: `assoc`. Another function, `rassoc`, is not built-in, but added as an extension.

`assoc` *and* `rassoc`

function	arguments	return value
assoc	*element assoc-list*	the first pair in *assoc-list* whose `car` is *element*
rassoc	*element assoc-list*	the first pair in *assoc-list* whose `cdr` is *element*

With both `assoc` and `rassoc`, if *element* does not match any of the pairs in *assoc-list*, `#f` is returned.

The function `rassoc` can be defined using recursion as follows:

```
; Like assoc but returns the first pair whose cdr matches elt.
(define (rassoc elt assoc-list)
  (cond ((null? assoc-list) #f)
        ((equal? (cdar assoc-list) elt) (car assoc-list))
        (else (rassoc elt (cdr assoc-list)))) )
```

Look at the following examples that use a partial mapping of English to code:

```
> (define eng-to-code
    '((a f) (b g) (c t)))
??

> (assoc 'b eng-to-code)
(b g)

> (assoc 'f eng-to-code)
#f

> (rassoc 't eng-to-code)
#f

> (rassoc '(t) eng-to-code)
(c t)
```

Notice that `rassoc` must be called with the list of the code letter to match the corresponding English letter.

Mistakes to Avoid

Remember that `rassoc` finds matches with the `cdr`s of the pairs. To match the pair (b g), the following call can be made:

```
> (rassoc '(g) '((a f) (b g) (c t)))
(b g)
```

With two-element pairs the `cdr`s are one-element lists, not atoms.

Similarly the function `assoc` must be called with lists to find pairs whose `car`s are lists. For example,

```
> (assoc '(a b) '(((a a) 1) ((a b) 2) ((a c) 3)))
((a b) 2)
```

Since `assoc` returns the pair whose `car` matches the element being searched for, to get the value associated with that `car`, the `cdr` or `second` of the pair is taken. In the case of converting English to code, we would take the `second` of the pair to get the corresponding code letter. The same applies to `rassoc`, except the `car` of `rassoc` is used.

We can write `english-letter-to-code` and `code-to-english-letter` using `assoc` and `rassoc`. Instead of forcing the user to call `code-to-english-letter` with the list of the code letter (to match the `cdr`s of the pairs), we'll write the function to call `rassoc` with the `list` of the letter.

Translation with `assoc` *and* `rassoc`

```
; Encode the symbol letter.
(define (english-letter-to-code letter match-list)
  (second (assoc letter match-list)) )

; Decode the symbol letter.
(define (code-to-english-letter letter match-list)
  (car (rassoc (list letter) match-list)) )
```

7.2.1 Optional section: Association lists with dotted lists

A dotted list is formed when an atom or list is `cons`ed onto an atom. See the section entitled "Optional Section: Dotted Lists" in Chapter 4 for an introduction to dotted lists. An association list can be made up of dotted lists and then used with the functions `assoc` and `rassoc`. For example,

```
> (define complementary-colors
    '((red . green) (blue . orange) (yellow . purple)))
??

> (assoc 'blue complementary-colors)
(blue . orange)

> (cdr (assoc 'blue complementary-colors))
orange

> (rassoc 'purple complementary-colors)
(yellow . purple)
```

```
>  (car (rassoc 'purple complementary-colors))
yellow
```

Notice that `rassoc` is called with an atom because the `cdrs` of the dotted lists are atoms. For relationships between atoms, an association list of dotted lists is often used because it is simpler to use and uses less memory (less cons cells are required).

To create an association list for the English-letter-to-secret-code letter list, the sublists like `(a f)` would be changed to dotted lists like `(a . f)`. The new list would look like the following:

```
((a . f)
 (b . g)
 (c . t)
     .
     .
     .
 (z . e))
```

We can create new versions of the `english-letter-to-code` and `code-to-english-letter` functions that take association lists of this form. To find a code letter, the call to `assoc` is the same, but the code letter is the `cdr` of the result instead of the `second`. To get the English letter, `rassoc` must be called with the code letter as an atom.

```
; Encode the symbol letter from an association list of dotted lists.
(define (english-letter-to-code letter match-list)
  (cdr (assoc letter match-list)) )

; Decode the symbol letter from an association list of dotted lists.
(define (code-to-english-letter letter match-list)
  (car (rassoc letter match-list)) )
```

7.2.2 Exercises

7.5 Write a program that determines the value of a BlackJack hand. The cards can be represented using the symbols below:

```
ace two three four five six seven eight nine ten jack queen king
```

Aces are worth 1, and jacks, queens, and kings are worth 10. The hand can be represented as a list of card names, such as

```
(jack three five)
```

This hand has a value of 18.

Create an association list to match the card names with the card values, which are

```
1 2 3 4 5 6 7 8 9 10 10 10 10
```

respectively. This assumes that aces are always worth one. Your program should include a function that takes a BlackJack hand (a list of card names) and the association list, and returns the value of the hand.

7.6 Modify the program above so that aces are worth either 1 or 11. Choose 11 unless that will make the hand worth more than 21, in which case the ace should be considered worth 1. Your solution should work if given a hand with more than one ace.
Hint: Only one ace can be worth 11 in a hand; two aces worth 11 each would give a hand value of 22. Thus, you need only worry about making one ace worth 11.

7.7 Write a function that takes a card hand (see above problems) and returns #t if you should hit—ask for another card from the dealer. You can use the following simple algorithm: if the hand is worth less than 15, hit. Or use your own algorithm, perhaps based on the one dealer's card that is showing—this card can be passed to your function as an additional parameter.

7.8 Write a function that checks if the mapping from English to secret code is a one-to-one mapping—each letter of the English list maps onto a unique letter of the secret code list.

7.3 Design for Modifiability

The form of the data structures used in programs tends to be modified over time. Sometimes different forms are used to allow new information to be represented in the data structure. Sometimes the change is made to allow improvements in the speed of data retrieval. It would be ideal if there were an easy way to minimize the changes that have to be made in the program when the data structure takes on a new form.

Data structures are dynamic

Imagine that we changed the data structure of the English-letter-to-code example to a single list as shown below:

```
(a f  b g  c t . . .  z e)
```

This would entail changing the existing code, which becomes more of an ordeal if the program is much larger with many parts accessing the data structure. However, there is a way to assure that the data structure and the program can be independent entities. The key is to create functions that access and modify the data structure and use these functions throughout the program instead of directly accessing or changing the data structure. These *selector* and *creator* functions would have to be modified if the database changed; however, the rest of the program would not have to be changed. An example of a selector function for the previous nested list data structure would be the function english-letter-to-code. It represents the simplest form of data access we wish. The function english-to-code uses this function and does not need to be changed if the data structure is changed. Only english-letter-to-code and code-to-english-letter would have to be changed.

Selector and creator functions

If we did change the data structure to the non-nested list form above, we could still use english-to-code if we write a new version of english-letter-to-code, as follows:

```
; Encode the symbol letter.
(define (english-letter-to-code letter match-list)
  (if (equal? letter (first match-list))
      (second match-list)
      (english-letter-to-code letter (cddr match-list))) )
```

7.3.1 Exercises

7.9 Write a new version of the function `code-to-english-letter` that use the above single list of atoms form of the data structure.

7.10 Suppose that instead of an association list for the English-letter-to-code mapping, there were a mapping of English letters to two different codes so that the new data structure looked like the following:

```
((a f s)
 (b g f)
 (c t m)
    .
    .
    .
 (z e g))
```

The first letter in each three-element sublist is the English letter; the second element is the first code letter; and the third is the second code letter. Write a selector function that takes such a mapping list and an English letter and returns a code letter from the first code list. Similarly, write selectors to go from English to the second set of code letters, and from the first code letters to the second code letters.

7.4 Sets

Lists can be used to represent sets of values. A *set* is an unordered collection of elements with no repeated elements. Sets can be used to represent collections of numbers or names, such as the names of all the presidents of the United States. Below is the set of all prime numbers less than 20:

```
(1 2 3 5 7 11 13 17 19)
```

The order of the elements is not important. The same set could be represented by the list

```
(3 7 11 1 19 17 2 5 13)
```

A list is a convenient representation for a set because it can grow and shrink and be examined easily with many of the built-in functions in Scheme.

Sets are used often in mathematics. The most common operations performed on sets are the following:

function	arguments	operation
`member`	*element set*	does *element* occur in *set*?
`union`	*set1 set2*	set of elements in either *set1* or *set2*
`intersection`	*set1 set2*	set of elements in both of *set1* and *set2*
`null?`	*set*	is *set* empty?
`set-difference`	*set1 set2*	set of elements in *set1* that are not in *set2*
`adjoin`	*element set*	add *element* to *set* if it's not already in *set*
`subset?`	*set1 set2*	are all the elements of *set1* in *set2*?
`length`	*set*	the number of elements in *set*—the cardinality

A *valid* set is a list with no repeated elements. If the set functions are called with lists having repeated elements, the return values may have repeated elements as well. The function `adjoin` should be used to add elements to a set, since it only adds an element if it doesn't already exist in the set. The elements of a set are usually atoms, but if they are lists, the set functions will still work properly.

We have used `member` and `null?` to determine if an element is in a list and if a list is the empty list, respectively. These are both useful operations with sets.

Two sets can be combined by creating a set of all items they have in common—their *intersection*. Another combination of sets is the set of all items that exist in either of two sets, not including any items more than once—the *union* of the sets. The elements that exist in one set but not another can be found using `set-difference`. Adding an element to a set can be performed with `adjoin`, which `cons`es the element to the list representing the set if that element is not already in the set. Lastly, `subset?` is used to determine if one set is a subset of another set—every element of the first set must be a member of the second set.

The functions `union`, `intersection`, `set-difference`, `adjoin`, and `subset?` are not built into Scheme, but are added in our extensions. We can define these functions. `adjoin` is the simplest to define.

```
; Return set with item added unless it already exists in set.
(define (adjoin item set)
  (if (member item set)
      set
      (cons item set)) )
```

The remaining functions can be defined using recursion and `member`. For each set function, we recurse through the first set. The following table shows what result should be returned depending on whether the first element of that set is or isn't in the second set.

function	if element is in `set2`	if element isn't in `set2`
`union`	don't include element	include element
`intersection`	include element	don't include element
`set-difference`	don't include element	include element
`subset?`	check remaining elements	return `#f`

Different actions should be taken when `set1` or `set2` are empty. Observe the subtle differences between these function definitions:

union

```
; Return the set of items in either set1 or set2.
(define (union set1 set2)
  (cond ((null? set1)
            set2)
        ((member (car set1) set2)
            (union (cdr set1) set2))
        (else
            (cons (car set1) (union (cdr set1) set2)))) )
```

intersection

```
; Return the set of items in both set1 and set2.
(define (intersection set1 set2)
  (cond ((or (null? set1) (null? set2))
            '())
        ((member (car set1) set2)
            (cons (car set1) (intersection (cdr set1) set2)))
        (else
            (intersection (cdr set1) set2))) )
```

set-difference

```
; Return the set of items in set1 but not in set2.
(define (set-difference set1 set2)
  (cond ((null? set2)
            set1)
        ((null? set1)
            '())
        ((member (car set1) set2)
            (set-difference (cdr set1) set2))
        (else
            (cons (car set1) (set-difference (cdr set1) set2)))) )
```

subset?

```
; Return #t if all elements in set1 are also in set2, #f otherwise.
(define (subset? set1 set2)
  (cond ((null? set1)
            #t)
        ((null? set2)
            #f)
        (else
            (and (member (car set1) set2)
                 (subset? (cdr set1) set2)))) )
```

7.4.1 Example: Using sets to represent locations traveled to

An example application of sets is creating sets of the exotic places that you and your friends have visited. You could create sets as follows:

```
(define places-i-have-been
  '(turkey belize thailand indonesia india))

(define places-brett-has-been
  '(south-dakota thailand))
```

```
(define places-lisa-has-been
  '(yugoslavia thailand belize turkey india))
```

You can compare these sets to determine the places that any two people have both visited using `intersection`.

```
> (intersection places-i-have-been places-brett-has-been)
(thailand)

> (intersection places-i-have-been places-lisa-has-been)
(turkey belize thailand india)
```

Notice that no elements were repeated in the resultant lists. This is true for sets—they do not have repeated elements. The actual order of the elements in the returned lists may differ depending on the implementation of Scheme used. It's not the order of the elements that matters in a set, but the contents of that set.

The function `union` can be used to find all the places that either of two people have visited:

```
> (union places-brett-has-been places-lisa-has-been)
(south-dakota yugoslavia thailand belize turkey india)
```

To determine the places that one person has been and another hasn't, use `set-difference`. For example,

```
> (set-difference places-i-have-been places-lisa-has-been)
(indonesia)

> (set-difference places-lisa-has-been places-i-have-been)
(yugoslavia)
```

Combining these lists with `union` gives the places that either one, but not both, of two people have been to.

```
> (union (set-difference places-i-have-been places-lisa-has-been)
         (set-difference places-lisa-has-been places-i-have-been))
(indonesia yugoslavia)
```

Another possibility is to take the `set-difference` of the `union` and the `intersection`. This deletes the places where two people have both been (the intersection) from the union of the places where they have been. This leaves only those places that either one has gone to, but not both.

```
> (set-difference (union places-i-have-been places-lisa-has-been)
     (intersection places-lisa-has-been places-i-have-been))
(indonesia yugoslavia)
```

To determine if someone has been to a particular place, `member` is used:

```
> (member 'portugal places-brett-has-been)
#f
```

`subset?` can be used to check if one person has been to all the places that another has been. For example, has Brett been to all the places that Lisa has?

```
> (subset? places-brett-has-been places-lisa-has-been)
#f
```

Set equality

`subset?` can be used to determine if two sets have the same elements. This will be the case if both sets are subsets of one another:

```
> (and (subset? places-brett-has-been places-lisa-has-been)
       (subset? places-lisa-has-been places-brett-has-been))
#f
```

The function `equal?` cannot be used to determine set equality, because `equal?` is true only if the lists have the same elements in the same order, whereas set equality is defined by the members of the sets, and not their order.

7.4.2   Exercises

7.11 Write a version of `union` using the other set functions but without recursion, or indicate why it is impossible. Assume that the lists passed as arguments to your function are valid sets. The two lists may have elements in common, yet your resultant list should have no duplicates.

7.12 Write a version of `intersection` using the other set functions but without recursion, or indicate why it is impossible. Assume that the argument lists are valid sets.

7.13 Write a version of `subset?` using the other set functions but without recursion, or indicate why it is impossible. Assume that you are given valid sets.

7.14 Write a version of `set-difference` using the other set functions but without recursion, or indicate why it is impossible. Assume that you are given valid sets.

7.15 `subset?` was used earlier to determine if two sets are equal; in other words, to determine if they have the same elements. Come up with a different means of determining if two sets are the same.

7.16 Assume that you have variables bound to the following values:

seniors	the first names of the students in the senior class
juniors	the first names of the students in the junior class
physics-majors	the first names of the declared physics majors
english-majors	the first names of the declared English majors
german-majors	the first names of the declared German majors
forestry-majors	the first names of the declared forestry majors

Also assume that each student has a unique first name. Give expressions that could be typed into the interpreter to produce the following sets:

- Seniors majoring in physics
- Juniors majoring in both physics and English
- Seniors and juniors majoring in either English or German

- Seniors and juniors majoring in neither English nor German
- Forestry majors who are not juniors

7.5 Trees

Trees are a very common data structure used in computer science. A computer science tree has a root, leaves, and branches, just like a real tree; however, these trees are drawn upside-down. Here is an example:

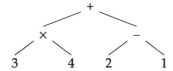

This tree represents the arithmetic expression $(3 \times 4) + (2 - 1)$. To evaluate this expression in Scheme, we would write it as

```
(+ (* 3 4) (- 2 1))
```

which is how this tree may be represented in list form.

Parts of trees

Trees have *nodes* and *branches*. A branch is shown as a / or a \; anything else is a node. There are three types of nodes: *the root*, *inner nodes*, and *leaves*. The root is the uppermost node. There is only one root, and in this example it is +. × and − are inner nodes. A node with no branches below it is called a leaf. 3, 4, 2, and 1 are leaves. The root and inner nodes have branches descending below them. These branches go to smaller sections of the tree which are called the *subtrees*. The roots of these subtrees are the *children* of the node above them. Similarly, the node immediately above a node is the *parent*.

Types of trees

If each node of a tree has two or less branches (or children), it is called a *binary tree*. A *complete binary tree* has zero or two children for each node (as the previous tree does). Trees with nodes having three or less branches are called *ternary trees*. N-ary trees are trees with up to N branches below each node.

Tree representations

A complete binary tree can be represented as a list of three elements. The first element is the root, and the second and third elements are the left and right subtrees. The subtrees may be leaves or complete trees. If the subtrees are trees, then they are represented as lists. Leaves are represented as atoms. This representation may seem recursive in nature, and it is. Recursion provides a wonderful means of dealing with these structures, as we will soon explore.

The previous example tree has root +, and the left and right subtrees are

left subtree   right subtree

```
    ×              −
  /   \          /   \
 3     4        2     1
```

The left subtree has × as its root, and the leaves 3 and 4 are its children. This subtree can be represented as the list (* 3 4). Similarly, the right subtree can be represented as (- 2 1). Thus, the entire tree is represented as

```
(+ (* 3 4) (- 2 1))
```

With such a representation, children that are leaves are represented as atoms, and children that are inner nodes are lists. It may not seem obvious why such a representation is used instead of simpler forms like

```
(+ * 3 4 - 2 1)
```
         or
```
(3 * 4 + 2 - 1)
```

The first representation, (+ * 3 4 - 2 1), can be used if we assume that nonleaf nodes are operators (e.g., +, *) and the leaves are numbers. However, it isn't as easy to access the children with this representation as it is using the representation (+ (* 3 4) (- 2 1)). As the next examples will show, being able to easily access the children of a tree is a very common operation that we will want to perform. The list (3 * 4 + 2 - 1) is ambiguous. It could represent many different trees. Here are some possible examples:

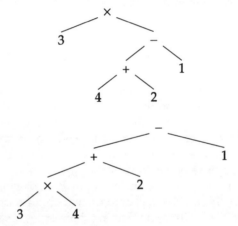

Here is a different tree that is more complex:

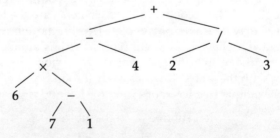

This tree would be represented using the following list:

```
(+ (- (* 6 (- 7 1)) 4) (/ 2 3))
```

The root of this tree is +, the left subtree is (- (* 6 (- 7 1)) 4) and the right subtree is (/ 2 3). These are easily obtained from the list; they are the **second** and **third** elements of the list.

7.5.1 Depth-First search

Trees can be used to hold a collection of values, as shown in the tree below which holds a collection of numbers:

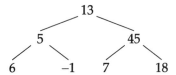

How would we determine if a certain number occurred within a tree? We could start at the root and test it. If it's not the root, then we continue by testing the left and right sides of the tree. A question arises as to which order this traversal through the tree should take. We could test the entire left side before testing the right side; in other words, traverse 13, 5, 6, −1, 45, 7, 18. This is called a *depth-first traversal*.

Depth-first search and depth-first traversal

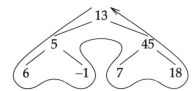

The tree above can be represented with the following list:

```
(13 (5 6 -1) (45 7 18))
```

To perform a depth-first search through such a list, a recursive strategy is employed. Begin by comparing the element being searched for with the root of the tree—this is the first element of the list. If there is no match, continue searching recursively with the left side of the tree. The search is recursive because the left side of the tree may, as in this case, be a tree. If the left side recursive search fails, search the right side recursively. The left and right sides of the tree are the `second` and `third` elements of the list, respectively.

Recursive algorithm for depth-first search

We are missing an exit case to check if the item is not in the tree. This can be added as a test to see if the tree is empty (an empty list), in which case the item being searched for cannot be in the tree, and #f should be returned. Another case to consider is when the tree being examined is a leaf. The tree would be an atom in this case. The return value should be a test checking if that leaf is the item being searched for.

The pseudo code for a depth-first search is

    if the tree is empty, return #f
    otherwise, if we are at a leaf, return the result of comparing that leaf with
            the item we are searching for
    otherwise, if the root matches, return true
    otherwise, if the left side contains the item (recursive call), return true
    otherwise, return the result of checking the right side of the tree recursively

The Scheme code follows:

```
; Use depth-first search to find item in tree.
(define (depth-first-search item tree)
  (cond ((null? tree) #f)                              ; empty tree
        ((atom? tree) (equal? item tree))              ; leaf
        ((equal? item (first tree)) #t)                ; test root
        ((depth-first-search item (second tree)) #t)   ; test left side
        (else
            (depth-first-search item (third tree)))) ) ; test right side
```

Different representations of trees

We have used *prefix* representation for trees. The root of the tree is the first item and it is followed by the children. The root may be between the children (*infix*) or after the children (*postfix*). Each of these representations for a tree is valid and has particular uses.

Function calls in Scheme are expressed in prefix notation:

```
(* (+ 1 2) -4)
```

In typical mathematical notation, infix is used:

```
(1 + 2) * -4
```

Postfix[1] is used in some programming languages and handheld calculators. Parentheses are not needed when the number of operands is fixed according to the operator.[2] This is one reason why some calculators use postfix notation. Our previous mathematical expression is written in postfix as

```
1 2 + -4 *
```

Any of these three representations can be used to represent a tree in Scheme. Extra parentheses (beyond those shown in the above examples) would be needed for the infix and postfix representations. In light of these different tree representations and according to the principle of design for modifiability, we should have selector functions for the root value of the tree and the left and right sides of the tree. This makes the code more readable as well.

Tree selector functions

```
; Return the root of tree.
(define (root tree)
  (first tree))

; Return the left subtree of tree.
(define (left-side tree)
  (second tree))

; Return the right subtree of tree.
(define (right-side tree)
  (third tree))
```

Another change that can be made is in the recursive step of `depth-first-search`; it can be thought of as

---

[1.] Typically postfix is referred to as R.P.N.—Reverse Polish Notation.

[2.] This is true for prefix as well. Scheme needs parentheses because many functions take a variable number of arguments.

item is in tree if it is either in the left or the right side of tree.

The code using this recursive step and the selector functions is

```
; Use depth-first search to find item in tree.
(define (depth-first-search item tree)
  (cond ((null? tree) #f)                    ; empty tree
        ((atom? tree) (equal? item tree))    ; leaf
        ((equal? item (root tree)) #t)       ; test root
        (else                                ; test left and right sides
            (or (depth-first-search item (left-side tree))
                (depth-first-search item (right-side tree)))))) )
```

This solution is equivalent to the previous version. Both versions test the left side of the tree first in the recursive case, and only check the right side if item is not in the left side. Below is a sample trace:

```
(depth-first-search -1 '(13 (5 6 -1) (45 7 18)))
                    ↓
(or (depth-first-search -1 '(5 6 -1))
                        ↓                  (depth-first-search -1 '(45 7 18)))
                        ↓
    (or (depth-first-search -1 6) (depth-first-search -1 -1))
                         ↓                            ↓
                        #f                           #t
     ↓
    #t
 ↓
#t
```

The call (depth-first-search -1 '(45 7 18)) was not expanded because it would not be evaluated. The or evaluates its arguments in left to right order. Since the first argument, (depth-first-search -1 '(5 6 -1)), returns #t, the or doesn't evaluate its second argument.

7.5.2 Breadth-First search

Another way to search through trees is to test the root, then its left child, and then its right child, continuing in the same manner with the children of the sub-trees. Using the previous sample tree, this would be the traversal 13, 5, 45, 6, –1, 7, 18. Such a path is called a *breadth-first traversal*.

Breadth-first search and breadth-first traversal

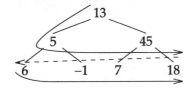

A list is needed to keep track of the subtrees that must be returned to. When a node is reached, it is examined and its subtrees are added to the end of this search list and the search continues. Once the search list is empty, the search is complete. From this definition the pseudo code to perform a breadth-first search through a list can be created.

> if the list of subtrees to search is empty, return #f
> otherwise, if the root of the first subtree in the search list matches the item
> being searched for, return #t
> otherwise, add the subtrees of the current subtree to the end of the search list
> and continue searching with the rest of the subtrees in the search list

The current subtree to search is used a few times in the pseudo code, so we'll save its value in the `let` variable `current-tree`. The code follows:

```
; Use breadth-first search to find item in search-list (a list of trees).
(define (breadth-first-search item search-list)
  (let ( (current-tree (first search-list)) )
    (cond ((null? search-list) #f)
          ((equal? item (root current-tree)) #t)
          (else
            (breadth-first-search
              item
              (append
                (rest search-list)
                (list
                  (left-side current-tree)
                  (right-side current-tree))))))) )
```

The function is called with a list of trees to search; thus, it is initially called with the list of the tree list we want to search. As each node is examined, its immediate subtrees are added to this search list to examine later. Below is a trace of a sample call to this function: The value of `current-tree` is underlined in the argument to `breadth-first-search`.

```
(breadth-first-search -1 '((13 (5 6 -1) (45 7 18)))))
                             ↓
(breadth-first-search -1 '((5 6 -1) (45 7 18)))
                             ↓
(breadth-first-search -1 '((45 7 18) 6 -1))
                             ↓
(breadth-first-search -1 '(6 -1 7 18))
                             ↓
Error: Pair expected
```

Our solution did not handle the case in which we are looking at a leaf. This should be added as another case in the `cond`. If we are examining a leaf, the item is present if it matches that leaf or if it is in the remaining subtrees to be tested. The new solution is

```
; Use breadth-first search to find item in search-list (a list of trees).
(define (breadth-first-search item search-list)
  (let ( (current-tree (first search-list)) )
    (cond ((null? search-list) #f)
          ((atom? current-tree)
            (or (equal? item current-tree)
                (breadth-first-search item (rest search-list))) )
          ((equal? item (root current-tree)) #t)
          (else
            (breadth-first-search
              item
              (append
                (rest search-list)
                (list
                  (left-side current-tree)
                  (right-side current-tree))))) )) )
```

With this new code, we get the following trace:

```
(breadth-first-search -1 '(6 -1 7 18))
                ↓
(breadth-first-search -1 '(-1 7 18))
                ↓
               #t
```

In choosing test data, we should use situations to test all the exit cases. In this function we should test what happens when (null? search-list) is true. This will occur when the item being searched for is not in the tree:

```
(breadth-first-search -1 '((5 6 7)))
                ↓
(breadth-first-search -1 '(6 7))
                ↓
(breadth-first-search -1 '(7))
                ↓
(breadth-first-search -1 '())
                ↓
Error: Pair expected
```

The error occurs when search-list is the empty list. Examining the code, we see that the **let** takes the **first** of search-list, which is (), and an error results. To fix this, either test for an empty list before the **let** or within the **let**. We'll take the second approach and change the **let** to

```
(let ( (current-tree
          (if (null? search-list)
              '()
              (first search-list))) )
```

7.5.3 Exercises

7.17 Is the function below equivalent to `depth-first-search`? Explain your answer.

```
(define (depth-first-search-2 item tree)
  (cond ((null? tree) #f)
        ((atom? tree) (equal? item tree))
        (else
          (or (equal? item (root tree))
              (depth-first-search-2 item (left-side tree))
              (depth-first-search-2 item (right-side tree)))))) )
```

7.18 Is the function below equivalent to `depth-first-search`? Explain your answer.

```
(define (depth-first-search-3 item tree)
  (or (not (null? tree))
      (equal? item tree)
      (equal? item (root tree))
      (depth-first-search-3 item (left-side tree))
      (depth-first-search-3 item (right-side tree))) )
```

7.19 Suppose the recursive call to `breadth-first-search` is changed so that the subtrees are added before the **rest** of `search-list`.

```
(breadth-first-search
  item
  (append
    (list
      (left-side current-tree)
      (right-side current-tree))
    (rest search-list)))
```

How would this affect the traversal through the tree?

7.20 Write a creator function that takes a node value, a left subtree, and a right subtree and returns a tree list of the form discussed in this section.

7.21 Write a Scheme expression that uses the creator function from the above problem to produce the tree below:

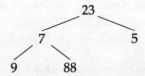

7.22 Write a function that takes a tree and prints out the nodes and leaves of the tree. Print out the root of the tree first, then the left side of the tree, and lastly the right side. Print the values on one line with single spaces between them. Use the selector functions defined in this section in your solution.

7.23 Write a function that takes a tree and prints out only the leaves of the tree. Print the leaves on the left side of the tree first. The leaves should be printed on one line separated by spaces.

7.24 Write a function to determine the depth of a tree. The depth of a tree is the number of branches that must be descended before reaching the bottom-most leaf of the tree. For example, the depth of the tree below is three.

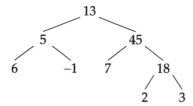

Hints: The depth of a leaf is zero, and the depth of a tree is one plus the larger of the depths of the left and right subtrees of the tree. Use this method to determine the depth of the following trees: 13, (6 7 13), and (6 (1 2 3) 13). Try to simplify your solution using the built-in function max. Recall that max returns the largest of its numeric arguments (e.g., (max 3 4 7 2) → 7).

7.25 The function below takes a binary tree as an argument.

```
(define (who-knows tree)
  (cond ((null? tree) 0)
        ((symbol? tree) 0)
        ((number? tree) tree)
        (else (max
                (who-knows (left-side tree))
                (who-knows (right-side tree)))))) )
```

What does the call below return?

```
(who-knows '(7 (4 3 a) (b 1 d)))
```

7.26 The function is-expression takes a binary tree, *tree*. is-expression should return #t if all the leaves are numbers and all the nonleaf nodes are any of the symbols +, -, *, or /. If not, #f should be returned. For example,

```
> (is-expression '(* (+ 1 2) (- 4 1)))
#t

> (is-expression '(* (+ 1 two) 14))
#f
```

This code was written with too much leap of faith and not enough thought. Fix the code so that it works.

```
(define (is-expression tree)
  (cond ((null? tree) #f)
        ((atom? tree) #t)
        (else (or
                (eq? (first tree) '(+ - * /))
                (number? (second tree))
                (is-expression (third tree)))))) )
```

7.27 The function `path-finder` takes a binary tree, *tree*, and a list, *path*. `path-finder` follows the path through the tree specified in *path*—a list of the symbols `left` and `right` and returns the subtree in *tree* to which *path* takes it. If the path goes beyond the leaves of the tree, return the symbol `error`. For example,

```
> (path-finder '(3 (4 (5 1 2) 7) (6 9 8)) '(right))
(6 9 8)

> (path-finder '(3 (4 (5 1 2) 7) (6 9 8)) '(left left right))
2

> (path-finder '(3 (4 (5 1 2) 7) (6 9 8)) '(right left right))
error
```

Assume that *path* will not contain values other than the symbols `left` and `right` and that the function will not be called initially with an empty tree. Complete the function below.

```
(define (path-finder tree path)
  (cond ((null? _____) _____)
        ((atom? _____) _____)
        ((equal? _____)
          (path-finder _____))
        (else
          (path-finder _____))) )
```

7.6   Sample Exercise with Trees and Sets

Trees as hierarchies

Trees are often used to represent hierarchies of information. A tree can represent a family tree, with the nodes being parents, and the leaves, the current generation of children. Trees can represent the hierarchy of a company, with the president at the top, and the vice presidents, and so on, below.

Trees can be used to help decide to which restaurant to go. In deciding what restaurant you want to go to, you have some notion of conditions like what you want to eat, what you don't want to eat, how much you want to spend, how much time you want to take, what atmosphere you want, etc. Some of these criteria may be important and others may not.

The situation gets more complex when there are numerous people trying to agree on a restaurant. Imagine the following exchange:

CR: Anyone want to go get some spicy food?
Sandy: That sounds good by me, but I can't be gone too long.
Farzad: I don't like it too spicy, and I have to be back soon also.
Craig: How about Japanese food? I feel like splurging on raw fish today.
John: Yeah, we just got paid, let's blow some money, maybe go for margaritas too.
Patty: That doesn't sound quick to me.
Brett: Hey, my boss just left for the day, I'm up for a long lunch.
Paul: I have to finish something tonight, so margaritas are out for me.
Karineh: How about going to a new restaurant?
Dorothy: Are you guys still trying to decide? You need a restaurant expert.

Creating a program that can take such information and return the restaurant that is best suited to meet most of the requests would require a sophisticated, large program. However, we can make some simplifications and create a program that can help narrow the search of which restaurant to choose.

At first we can limit ourselves to the case of a single person deciding what to eat. For any particular type of food, she may be interested in eating it, or may not desire it, or may not care either way. In this program such information will be represented as two lists:

Desired and undesired foods

desired   Things that are desired
undesired   Things that are not desired

Anything not in either of these lists is considered a *don't care* value.

The desired and undesired lists are sets that contain facts about what you want to eat and what you don't want to eat. They might look like the following:

desired-foods: `(ethnic)`
undesired-foods: `(drive-in fast-food)`

It may seem strange to have two lists—one for the desired foods, and one for the undesired foods. An alternative is using a single list, as in

Alternate representations

desired-foods: `(ethnic walk-in sit-down)`

Anything not in this list would be considered a *don't care* value. With a single list, a mapping is needed to match items like `walk-in` and `sit-down` with the internal node values (the questions in the tree) `drive-in` and `fast-food`. This could be implemented using an association list.

```
(define opposites
  '((drive-in walk-in)
    (fast-food sit-down)
    (ethnic domestic)
         .
         .
         .        ))
```

With two lists an association list isn't needed because all the attributes in the lists correspond directly with the internal nodes of the restaurant tree. This will be the approach we use.

Representing restaurants

Another data structure is needed to maintain the restaurants. These restaurants could be the leaves of a tree in which the internal nodes represent questions about what you want to eat. For each question node, the left branch of the tree contains restaurants that pertain if the question is satisfied. The right side of the tree contains restaurants that the person would want to go to if the question is not satisfied.

A restaurant tree may look like the following:

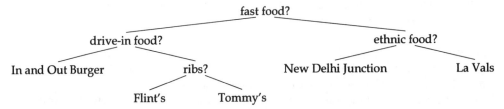

All the restaurants on the left side of the root, *fast food?*, are fast food places, whereas the restaurants on the right side are slower, sit-down restaurants.

A list corresponding to the tree above is

```
(fast-food (drive-in in-and-out-burger (ribs flints tommys))
    (ethnic new-delhi-junction la-vals))
```

When deciding if a question is satisfied, the desired and undesired lists are used. For example, if the program is deciding upon fast-food or non fast-food restaurants, if `fast-food` exists in the desired list, then the program should continue with the questions on the left side of the tree. If `fast-food` is in the undesired list, then continue with the right side of the tree. If `fast-food` doesn't exist in any list, it is a *don't care* value, and both sides of the tree should be examined.

The program works by sequencing through the tree in the following manner:

if you are at a leaf, you've reached a restaurant, return that restaurant,
otherwise, you are at a decision junction,
    if the decision is met (the node occurs in the desired list),
        continue with the left side of the tree
    otherwise, if the decision is undesired (the node occurs in the
        undesired list), continue with the right side of the tree.
    otherwise, continue with both sides of the tree (*don't care* situation).

With the example tree above and the desired and undesired lists below,

desired-foods: `(ethnic)`
undesired-foods: `(drive-in fast-food)`

you begin at the root by checking if you want fast food. Since `fast-food` is in the undesired foods list, the program continues with the right side of the tree—asking if you want ethnic foods. `ethnic` is in the desired list so we go to the left side of the tree. Here we find the leaf `new-delhi-junction` and return it.

Adhering to the principle of design for modifiability, we should use the selector functions we created earlier to access the nodes and subtrees of the tree. The function `root` returns the root of a tree. If it is given a subtree of the original tree, it returns the root of that subtree, which is an inner node in the original tree. The function `left-side` returns the left subtree of a tree, and the function `right-side` returns the right subtree of a tree These functions perform the operations `first`, `second`, and `third`, respectively.

We can add another function to test if we are at a leaf in the tree:

```
; Return true if tree is a leaf (an atom).
(define (leaf? tree)
  (atom? tree))
```

We check both sides of the tree in *don't care* situations. This means that we may find more that one restaurant that satisfies the constraints. Thus, we should return a list of restaurants always. And when the restaurant tree is empty, we should return an empty list. In the case where `restaurant-tree` is an atom (a restaurant), the list of that restaurant is returned. The code for the restaurant advisor can be expressed in Scheme as follows:

```
; Return list of restaurants according to properties in desired
; and undesired lists.
(define (restaurant-advisor restaurant-tree desired undesired)
  (cond ((null? restaurant-tree) '())
        ((leaf? restaurant-tree) (list restaurant-tree))
        ((member (root restaurant-tree) desired)
         (restaurant-advisor (left-side restaurant-tree)
           desired undesired))
        ((member (root restaurant-tree) undesired)
         (restaurant-advisor (right-side restaurant-tree)
           desired undesired))
        (else
          (append
            (restaurant-advisor (left-side restaurant-tree)
              desired undesired)
            (restaurant-advisor (right-side restaurant-tree)
              desired undesired)))) )
```

Handling conflicts of interest

To handle information from multiple people, some means of combining the information is needed. In the case of two people, general desired and undesired lists are needed. These lists should reflect any desires or undesires that the two people have. If we look at the lists as sets, then taking the `union` of the desired lists will yield the set of all desires for those two people. The same can be done with the undesired lists to produce a general undesired list.

With more than one person, conflicts can arise. A conflict would involve having the same item in both the desired and undesired lists. We'll use `intersection` to check if the desired and undesired lists have any elements in common. If the intersection isn't `()`, the two lists have elements in common.

Many techniques can be used to handle conflicts. One way is to create a hierarchy of the people so that certain people's restaurant desires and undesires are given priority over other's desires and undesires.

A more democratic scheme is to give priority to either the desired lists or the undesired lists. If the desired lists have priority, then any conflicting elements in the undesired lists are ignored. As it is written, `restaurant-advisor` gives preference to items that occur in the desired list. This is because decision nodes are compared with the desired list first and the search continues down the left side of the tree if the node is in the desired list. To see this, look at the following trace. Suppose that the variable `restaurants` has been bound to the restaurant list

```
(fast-food (drive-in in-and-out-burger (ribs flints tommys))
   (ethnic new-delhi-junction la-vals))
```

The trace produces the following:

```
(restaurant-advisor restaurants
  '(fast-food drive-in) '(fast-food drive-in))
              ↓
; the root of the tree fast-food is in desired
; so we continue with the left side of the tree
              ↓
(restaurant-advisor '(drive-in in-and-out-burger (ribs flints tommys))
  '(fast-food drive-in) '(fast-food drive-in))
              ↓
; the root of the tree drive-in is in desired
; so we continue with the left side of the tree
              ↓
(restaurant-advisor 'in-and-out-burger
  '(fast-food drive-in) '(fast-food drive-in))
              ↓
; the tree in-and-out-burger is a leaf
; so we return the list of it
              ↓
      (in-and-out-burger)
```

To give the undesired list priority, all the elements in the desired list that are also in the undesired list should be removed. This can be implemented using `set-difference`. The expression

```
(set-difference desired undesired)
```

returns the elements in the desired list that aren't in the undesired list.

Calling the function as

```
(restaurant-advisor restaurant-tree
  (set-difference desired undesired)
  undesired)
```

results in giving the undesired list priority over the desired list. Here is a sample trace using the same desired and undesired lists we used in the last trace.

```
(restaurant-advisor restaurants
  (set-difference '(fast-food drive-in) '(fast-food drive-in))
  '(fast-food drive-in))
```
     ↓

; the set-difference returns '()
     ↓

```
(restaurant-advisor restaurants
  '() '(fast-food drive-in))
```
     ↓

; the root of the tree fast-food is in undesired
; so we continue with the right side of the tree
     ↓

```
(restaurant-advisor '(ethnic new-delhi-junction la-vals)
  '() '(fast-food drive-in))
```
     ↓

; the root of the tree ethnic is not in desired or
; undesired so we continue with both sides of the tree
     ↓

```
(append
  (restaurant-advisor 'new-delhi-junction
    '() '(fast-food drive-in))
  (restaurant-advisor 'la-vals
    '() '(fast-food drive-in)))
```
     ↓

; the trees new-delhi-junction and la-vals are leaves
; so we return their list
     ↓

```
(append
  '(new-delhi-junction)
  '(la-vals))
```
     ↓

(new-delhi-junction la-vals)

7.6.1 Exercises

7.28 Write a function that takes a list of many desired lists and produces one general desired list—the union of all the desired lists.

7.29 The following call to restaurant-advisor is an attempt to eliminate conflicts between the desired and undesired lists without giving priority to one of them.

```
(restaurant-advisor restaurant-tree
  (set-difference desired undesired)
  (set-difference undesired desired))
```

Will this solution work? Why or why not?

7.30 Rather than give preference to desired or undesired lists, conflicts can be resolved by a majority rule. If more people prefer a type of food or restaurant than do not, that type remains part of the desired list, but is removed from the undesired list. Write a function that takes a restaurant tree, desired and undesired lists, and calls `restaurant-advisor` with new desired and undesired lists that have all conflicts removed by majority rule. The original desired and undesired lists are not sets, but rather lists formed by appending various peoples' preferences together.

Hint: You only need to sequence through the desired list and maintain the elements that should be in that list. Then you can form a new undesired list given the new desired list.

7.7 Summary

- Association lists are lists of pairs (nonempty lists) where each pair maps one item with another.
- `assoc` is used to match the `cars` of association lists, and `rassoc` is used to match the `cdrs`. Both functions return the entire pair that was matched.
- Selector and creator functions are used to facilitate code modification and improve code readability.
- Sets are lists of unordered elements with no repeating elements.
- To test for set membership, use `member`.
- To find all the elements two sets have in common, use `intersection`.
- To find all the elements two sets have together, use `union`.
- To find the elements in one set that are not in another, use `set-difference`.
- To find if a set is empty, use `null?`.
- To add an element to a set, use `adjoin`.
- To find if one set is a subset of another, use `subset?`.
- To find the number of elements of a set, use `length`.
- Trees are data structures that have a root value and left and right sides that are trees themselves.
- Depth-first and breadth-first search are two common means of traversing a tree data structure.

- Summary of functions introduced in this chapter:

function	arguments	return value
assoc	*element assoc-list*	the first pair in *assoc-list* whose `car` is *element*
rassoc	*element assoc-list*	the first pair in *assoc-list* whose `cdr` is *element*
member	*element set*	true if *element* occurs in *set*
null?	*set*	true if *set* is empty
length	*set*	the number of elements in *set*—the cardinality
union	*set1 set2*	set of elements in either *set1* or *set2*
intersection	*set1 set2*	set of elements in both of *set1* and *set2*
set-difference	*set1 set2*	set of elements in *set1* that are not in *set2*
adjoin	*element set*	*set* with *element* added if its not already in *set*
subset?	*set1 set2*	true if all the elements of *set1* are in *set2*?

CHAPTER 8

FUNCTIONALS

8.1 Passing Functions as Arguments

In Scheme, functions can be passed as arguments to other functions, in the same fashion that data values like lists and atoms are passed. This enables different actions to be carried out depending on the function passed. Functions that take functions as arguments are called *functionals*. Another term for these functions is *applicative operators*.

Functionals

8.1.1 Mapping functions

Applying a function to every element in a list is called a *mapping*, hence functions that do so are called mapping functions. To get a realworld context of mappings, think of how a map of a city or country is made. Each position in the three-dimensional object (e.g., country) must be projected onto a two-dimensional piece of paper. Another way of saying this is that each position is mapped onto the paper. One of the most common mapping techniques used is the Mercator projection used in making flat world maps that artificially enlarge regions near the poles.

Mapping

`map` is used to apply a function to every element in a list. The function passed to `map` should take one argument and should work when called with any element of the list. `map` returns a list of the results of those function applications.

`map`

A similar function is `for-each`, which is identical to `map` except that it does not return the results of the function applications. Thus, `for-each` is only used for the side-effects that are produced by the function mapped over the elements of the list. `for-each` returns an undefined value. One additional important difference: `for-each` guarantees that it applies the function to elements of the list in a left to right order. `map` makes no such guarantee.

`for-each`

map *and* for-each
syntax

function	arguments	return value
map	*function list*	list of results from applying *function* to elements of *list*
for-each	*function list*	undefined, but applies *function* to elements of *list*

The square-roots function from Chapter 6 is an example of mapping a function over a list. The sqrt function is applied to all the elements in the list given to map, and the resulting list of square roots is returned. square-roots can be rewritten using map, as

```
; Return a list of the square roots of the numbers in a-list.
(define (square-roots-mapping a-list)
  (map sqrt a-list))
```

Below are two sample calls to square-roots-mapping:

```
> (square-roots-mapping '(49 64 100 36))
(7.0 8.0 10.0 6.0)

> (square-roots-mapping '())
()
```

The function deep-reverse from Chapter 6 can be written using map as follows:

```
; Return the deep reverse of a-list (reverses all sub-lists).
(define (deep-rev-map a-list)
  (if (atom? a-list)
      a-list
      (map deep-rev-map (reverse a-list))) )
```

The idea is to use map to invoke the function recursively on all the top-level elements of the reversed list. The check for an atom is very important; without it, the function will be called with atoms, and map will give an error if called with atoms instead of lists. Below are two traces of calls to deep-rev-map. Note that list is used in the expansion of map to simplify the trace:

```
(deep-rev-map '(a apple))
     ↓
(map deep-rev-map '(apple a))
     ↓
(list (deep-rev-map 'apple) (deep-rev-map 'a))
           ↓                        ↓
(list      'apple                  'a))
     ↓
(apple a)
```

Here is a more involved trace:

```
(deep-rev-map '((a apple) b bear))
     ↓
(map deep-rev-map '(bear b (a apple)))
     ↓
(list (deep-rev-map 'bear) (deep-rev-map 'b) (deep-rev-map '(a apple)))
          ↓                      ↓                    ↓
(list      'bear                'b      (map deep-rev-map '(apple a)))
     ↓
(list 'bear 'b (list (deep-rev-map 'apple) (deep-rev-map 'a)))
                          ↓                      ↓
(list 'bear 'b (list      'apple              'a))
     ↓
(list 'bear 'b '(apple a))
     ↓
(bear b (apple a))
```

A nice use of the function `for-each` is a function that prints out the elements of a list one element per line. This function is written in Chapter 9, section 9.1.1.

8.1.2 `apply`: A variation on the normal function application

There are times when you want to apply a function that takes a collection of arguments to a list of arguments. For example, in Chapter 6, we wrote the function `sum-list` that returns the sum of the numbers in a list. We could have written this function using `apply`, as follows:

apply

```
; Return sum of numbers in number-list.
(define (sum-list-alt number-list)
  (apply + number-list) )
```

Here are some other examples using `apply`:

```
> (apply max '(3 1 -5 4 2))
4

> (apply append '((one list) (another) (a third list)))
(one list another a third list)

> (apply list '(1 2 3 4 5))      ; a useless function call
(1 2 3 4 5)

> (apply < '(1 2 3 4 5))
#t

> (apply * (map abs '(3 1 -5 4 2)))
120
```

`apply` does not work when given special forms. This means that we cannot use `apply` to test if all the values in a list are true using the special form `and`. The following example, which attempts to test if all the elements in a list are numbers, illustrates this:

apply doesn't take special forms

```
> (apply and (map number? (-3 4 one 2)))
Error: apply: Wrong type in arg1: macro and
```

8.2   Writing Functions that Take Functions as Arguments

It is possible to create functions that take functions as arguments. Such functions can perform various operations on data depending on the functions with which they are called.

Sometimes you need to invoke the function passed as an argument directly. The function apply-to-7 takes a function as an argument and returns the result of that function applied to the number 7.

```
; Apply 7 to func.
(define (apply-to-7 func)
  (func 7) )
```

Below are some example calls to this function:

```
> (apply-to-7 /)
1/7

> (apply-to-7 number?)
#t
```

Function names are evaluated

To understand how apply-to-7 works, we must refine our simplified model of function evaluation from Chapter 3. Our new model must include one important distinction: when evaluating functions, both the function and its arguments are evaluated. Our previous model only indicated that the arguments were evaluated. The way the function was determined from its name was never addressed. Since we evaluate the item in the function position of a function call, we can do things like the following:

```
; Return a list of elt1 and elt2 using cons or list.
(define (listify elt1 elt2)
  ((if (list? elt2) cons list) elt1 elt2) )

> (listify 'a 'b)
(a b)

> (listify 'a '(b))
(a b)
```

The if expression returns the function cons or list depending on the type of elt2. This function is then applied to the evaluated arguments, elt1 and elt2.

The following function max-of-func takes a list and a function and returns the maximum result obtained when the function is applied to the elements of the list:

```
; Return the largest value of the mapping of function onto a-list.
(define (max-of-func function a-list)
  (apply max (map function a-list)) )
```

This function can be invoked as follows:

```
> (max-of-func abs '(3 -4 2))
4

> (max-of-func length '((73 64 2) ((1 2 3 4)) (a b) ((()))))
3
```

8.2.1 `-if` functions

The functions `count` and `remove` search for elements that match a given item within a list. It is helpful to have a means of searching for elements that satisfy a function. We can do this by creating functions we'll name `count-if` and `remove-if`. These functions are similar to their non `-if` ending counterparts with the exception that elements in the lists passed to these functions are tested against a predicate function, as opposed to being compared to some element. In addition, we'll create a function `find-if` that returns the first element in a list that satisfies the predicate function.

Below are some examples using these functions:

```
> (count-if even? '(3 5 6 4 7))
2

> (remove-if even? '(3 5 6 4 7))
(3 5 7)

> (find-if even? '(3 5 6 4 7))
6
```

The function `count-if` can be implemented using `map`. `map` applies the function to all the elements of the list and returns the results in a list. The number of true values in that return list is what `count-if` returns. To get a better picture of this, look at what `map` returns given the arguments used above to `count-if`.

count-if

```
> (map even? '(3 5 6 4 7))
(#f #f #t #t #f)
```

The number of #ts is what `count-if` should return. If we remove the #fs, we get a list of #ts. Here is the code to `count-if`:

```
; Return the number of elements in a-list that satisfy func.
(define (count-if func a-list)
   (length (remove #f (map func a-list))) )
```

`map` also can be used to write `find-if`. The list element that is in the same position as the first true value from `map` is what `find-if` returns. Expressing this in Scheme, we get

find-if

```
; Return the first element in a-list that satisfies func, else #f.
(define (find-if func a-list)
  (list-ref a-list
     (position #t (map func a-list))) )
```

`remove-if`
remove-if can be implemented using a recursive filter similar to the function `positive-filter` from Chapter 6.

```
; Return a-list without the elements that satisfy func.
(define (remove-if func a-list)
  (cond ((null? a-list)
         '())
        ((func (first a-list))
         (cons (first a-list)
               (remove-if func (rest a-list))))
        (else
         (remove-if func (rest a-list)))) )
```

Let's test these functions. Assume the following function has been defined:

```
; Return true if a-list contain a 3 on the top level.
(define (has-3 a-list)
  (member 3 a-list))
```

```
> (find-if symbol? '((a list) 13 a-symbol five))
a-symbol

> (count-if symbol? '((a list) 13 a-symbol five))
2

> (remove-if symbol? '((a list) 13 a-symbol five))
(a-symbol five)

> (find-if has-3 '((1 one) (2 two) (3 three)))
Error: list-ref: Wrong type in arg2 #f

> (count-if has-3 '((1 one) (2 two) (3 three)))
1

> (remove-if has-3 '((1 one) (2 two) (3 three)))
((3 three))
```

Well, at least count-if works. The problem with remove-if is that it is keeping the items it should remove and vice versa. To fix this, reverse the last two actions so that we do not include (remove) items that satisfy the function and keep those that do not satisfy the function.

find-if works with symbol?, but not with has-3. The error message indicates that list-ref had #f as its second argument. This second argument is the result of a call to position that looks for the first occurrence of #t in the result from map. Let's see what map returns.

```
> (map has-3 '((1 one) (2 two) (3 three)))
(#f #f (3 three))
```

There is no #t in the result, but there is a *true* (non-#f) value. Unfortunately, the functions we know up to this point won't help us to find the first *true* element in a list. We could write a recursive function to do so, but at that point we might as well write a recursive function to implement all of find-if. Let's do that.

The idea is to apply the function passed as an argument to successive elements in the list until a true value is returned. Then we return the list element that satisfied the function. The definitional pseudo code for this follows:

if the list is empty, return #f
otherwise, if the first element satisfies the function, return it
otherwise, recursively check the rest of the list

```
; Return the first element in a-list that satisfies func, else #f.
(define (find-if func a-list)
  (cond ((null? a-list) #f)
        ((func (first a-list)) (first a-list))
        (else (find-if func (rest a-list)))) )
```
Fixed find-if

Testing this on the two examples above, we see that our new solution works:

```
> (find-if symbol? '((a list) 13 a-symbol five))
a-symbol

> (find-if has-3 '((1 one) (2 two) (3 three)))
(3 three)
```

The new version of `remove-if` and sample calls follow:

```
; Return a-list without the elements that satisfy func.
(define (remove-if func list)
  (cond ((null? list)
         '())
        ((func (first list))
         (remove-if func (rest list)))
        (else
         (cons (first list)
               (remove-if func (rest list)))))) )
```
Fixed remove-if

```
> (remove-if symbol? '((a list) 13 a-symbol five))
((a list) 13)

> (remove-if has-3 '((1 one) (2 two) (3 three)))
((1 one) (2 two))
```

8.2.2 Exercises

8.1 Write a function that takes a list of numbers and returns the average of the numbers.

8.2 Write a function that takes a list of numbers and returns the smallest number in the list.

8.3 Write a function associative? that takes a function (taking two arguments) and three additional arguments that could be applied to that function two at a time. associative? should return #t if the function passed to it is associative for the three other arguments. The function is associative if

```
(func (func arg1 arg2) arg3)
```
is equal to
```
(func arg1 (func arg2 arg3))
```

8.4   Write a function `commutative?` that takes a function (taking two arguments) and two additional arguments that could be applied to that function. `commutative?` should return **#t** if the function passed to it is commutative for the two other arguments. The function is commutative if the order of the arguments does not effect the return value. In other words,

```
(func arg1 arg2)  is equal to  (func arg2 arg1)
```

8.5   Write a conditional **map** `map-if` that takes a function and a list just as **map** does, but in addition takes a predicate function. The predicate is applied to each element of the list, and only if a non-**#f** value is returned should the function be applied to the element and that result returned in the answer list. For example,

```
(map-if - '(0 u 8 1 2) number?)
```
returns
```
(0 -8 -1 -2)
```
Notice that the resultant list does not have to be as long as the original list with which `map-if` is called.

8.6   Write a function `deep-abs` that takes a nested list and applies the function **abs** to every atom in the nested list and returns a similarly nested list of results. For example,

```
(deep-abs '((3 -4 (-5)) (6 ((-7 8)))))
```
returns
```
((3 4 (5)) (6 ((7 8))))
```

8.7   Does the following version of **count-if** work?

```
(define (count-if func a-list)
  (count #t (map func a-list)))
```

8.2.3   `-if-not` functions

To find the first nonpositive number in a list of numbers, we might try to use **find-if** with **negative?**, as in the following example:

```
> (find-if negative? '(2 3 0 -3 4 -5))
-3
```

It doesn't return zero because zero is not negative. However, zero is nonpositive and is the answer we wanted. To fix this we could write a function that tests for

negative numbers or zero, and pass that to `find-if`. However, there is a more
general solution.

We can create functions that end in `-if-not` that are identical to their coun-   *if-not functions*
terparts ending in `-if` except that they perform their action on the elements that
do not satisfy *test*. To find the first nonpositive number, we can use

> `(find-if-not positive? '(2 3 0 -3 4 -5))`
0

The function `positive-filter` from Chapter 6 can be written using `remove-if-not`. `positive-filter` takes a list and returns a list of all the positive
numbers in the list. A better name for `remove-if-not` would be `keep-if`—we
keep the elements of the list that satisfy the function.

```
; Return a list of the positive numbers in a-list.
(define (positive-filter-alt a-list)
  (keep-if positive? a-list) )
```

An example call to `positive-filter-alt` follows:

> `(positive-filter-alt '(-5 15 6 -20 0 -1))`
(15 6)

The table below shows the results of applying the `-if` and `-if-not` functions
to the list `(36 three (124))` and the function `atom?`, as in

> `(count-if atom? '(36 three (124)))`
2

function	return value
count-if	2
find-if	36
remove-if	((124))
count-if-not	1
find-if-not	(124)
keep-if	(36 three)

Implementing `count-if-not` and `find-if-not` will be left as exercises. The
first version of `remove-if` we wrote did what `keep-if` should.

Here is a summary of the `if` and `if-not` functions we have created. All the
functions take a function *test* and a list *list*. *test* should take a single argument
whose type matches that of the elements in *list*.

function	arguments	return value	
find-if	*test list*	first element in *list* that satisfies *test*	*Summary of -if and*
count-if	*test list*	number of elements in *list* that satisfy *test*	*-if-not functions*
remove-if	*test list*	*list* without elements that satisfy *test*	
find-if-not	*test list*	first element in *list* that does not satisfy *test*	
count-if-not	*test list*	number of elements in *list* that do not satisfy *test*	
keep-if	*test list*	*list* of elements that satisfy *test*	

Mistakes to Avoid

Remember that `find-if` returns the first element that satisfies the function, not the result of that function call. Similarly, `keep-if` returns a list of elements that satisfy the function, not a list of the return values.

8.2.4   Exercises

8.8   Write expressions to compute the following results using the list `values` that has been bound to some list. Each question refers to the top-level elements in `values`:

      – The numbers in `values`
      – The non-numbers in `values`
      – The number of non-numbers in `values`
      – The first list in `values`
      – The number of elements in the first list in `values`
      – The list `values` without any symbols

8.9   Write the function `find-if-not`.

8.10   Write the function `count-if-not`.

8.11   Anna proposes the following idea to remove duplicate elements from a list to make it a legal set. She suggests combining the list of all the unique elements with the list of all the duplicate elements. The code should work like the example below:

```
> (remove-duplicates '(3 4 3 2 4))
(3 4 2)
```

Here is Anna's code:

```
(define (remove-duplicates a-list)
  (union
    (remove-if (lambda (elt) (> (count elt a-list) 1) ) a-list)
    (keep-if (lambda (elt) (> (count elt a-list) 1) ) a-list)) )
```

Does her solution work. Why or why not?

8.12   Mike looks at Anna's code (from the previous exercise) and says that her idea is right, but her implementation is wrong. If she reversed the two arguments to `union` it would work. He bases this on the way `union` is written. Is Mike right? Why or why not?

8.2.5 `every` **and** `any`

There are times when you want to test if every element of a list satisfies some function. Or you may want to test if some element satisfies a predicate function. Examples of this would be the following: are all the elements of a list even numbers, is a list a valid association list (i.e., it is a list of pairs), and is there a negative number in a list? We can do this by creating two new functions: `every` and `any`.

These functions are similar to `map` in that they apply a function to elements of a list. However, the return value is a true/false value instead of a list of results. One additional difference is that we don't always need to check all the values in the list. For example, if we are testing if all the elements in the list are numbers, and we encounter a non-number, we don't need to check further elements. Similarly, if we are checking if the list contains at least one number, we can stop examining elements once a number is found. In this sense these two functions behave like `and` and `or`.

Here are the complete definitions of the two functions. `every` returns a true value if applying the function to every successive element in the list returns a true value. In this case `every` returns the final true value encountered. If any application results in `#f`, no further elements are tested and `#f` is returned. `any` applies the function to successive elements in the list. If any application returns a true value, no further elements are tested, and that true value is returned. If all applications result in `#f`, `#f` is returned.

function	arguments	return value
`every`	*test list*	final true return value if all elements in *list* satisfy *test*, `#f` otherwise
`any`	*test list*	first true return value from applying *test* to elements in *list*, `#f` otherwise

every *and* any

The following examples illustrate the use of these functions. Assume the function `short-list?` has been defined as follows:

```
; Return true if item is a short list (one or two elements).
(define (short-list? item)
  (and
    (list? item)
    (member (length item) '(1 2))) )

> (every short-list? '((one 1) (two 2) ()))
#f

> (every short-list? '((one 1) (two 2) (3)))
(1 2)

> (every even? '(4 6 2))
#t

> (any even? '(3 6 2))
#t
```

```
> (any even? '(3 9 27))
#f

> (any short-list? '((one 1) (two 2) (3)))
(2)
```

Let's write these two functions. We cannot use **map** because it will always evaluate all the elements in the list. We'll create recursive functions. To return the final true value, **every** should stop when it encounters a one-element list. The definitional pseudo code for **every** is

if the list is empty, return ??
if there is one element in the list, return the function applied to that element
otherwise, return the **and** of the **first** element applied to the function
    and the result of a recursive call on the **rest** of the list.

What shall we return when we have an empty list? You might be inclined to think that **#f** should be returned. However, we should be consistent with how **and** works; it returns **#t** if called with no arguments.

The code for **every** follows:

```
; Return final true return value if all applications of func
; to the elements of a-list are true, otherwise return #f.
(define (every func a-list)
  (cond ((null? a-list) #t)
        ((null? (rest a-list)) (func (first a-list)))
        (else (and (func (first a-list))
                   (every func (rest a-list)))) ) )
```

The code for **any** is very similar. Instead of checking for an item that does not satisfy the function as an exit case, we need a check for satisfying the function. In this case the true value is returned. Reaching the empty list means that none of the elements satisfied the function, so we should return **#f**. We do not need to make a check for a one-element list.

```
; Return first true application of func to the elements of
; a-list, otherwise return #f if no applications are true.
(define (any func a-list)
  (if (null? a-list)
      #f
      (or (func (first a-list))
          (any func (rest a-list)))) )
```

The function all-numbers? from Chapter 6 can be written using **every**. all-numbers? takes a list and returns **#t** if all the elements in the list are numbers, and **#f** otherwise.

```
; Return true if all elements of a-list are numbers.
(define (all-numbers-alt? a-list)
  (every number? a-list) )
```

Below are two example function calls using this function:

```
> (all-numbers-alt? '(3 4 2))
#t

> (all-numbers-alt? '(3 four 2))
#f
```

8.2.6 Exercises

8.13 Given a list `list1`, write expressions to return the following values. You may need to define additional functions.

- true if there is at least one top-level symbol in `list1`
- true if each element of `list1` is a two-element list
- true if `list1` has no sublists

8.14 Explain the differences between `any` and `find-if`.

8.15 Which functional (e.g., `map`, `find-if`, `every`) would you use to find the following values? Note: if none of the functions appear to do the job, indicate how you would determine the value using other techniques.

- the first nested list in a list
- the second atom in a list
- the last number in a list
- the numbers greater than ten in a list of atoms
- a list without any sublists
- the average of a list of numbers
- the first three elements in a list
- the number of negative numbers in a list
- if a list has at least one number
- if a list has at least five numbers

8.2.7 Optional section: Using multiple lists with `map`, `for-each`, `every`, and `any`

`map` can be used to apply functions taking multiple arguments to multiple lists. In this case, `map` takes more than one list. The function used must take the same number of arguments as there are lists passed to `map`. The lists must all be the same length.

The following examples show how `map` can be called with multiple lists:

```
> (map + '(3 6 2) '(4 20 -1))
(7 26 1)

> (map > '(3 6 2) '(4 20 -1))
(#f #f #t)
```

```
> (map list '(3 6 2) '(4 20 -1) '(a b c))
((3 4 a) (6 20 b) (2 -1 c))
```

Note: The last example transposed the elements in the lists. If the lists are viewed as rows of a matrix, then the function call transposes rows into a list of columns.

`every` and `any` can be written to take more than one list just as `map` does. The function given to `every` or `any` must take as many arguments as there are lists given. The function is applied to successive elements in each list:

```
> (every < '(1 3 5) '(2 4 6))
#t

> (every < '(1 3 5) '(2 4 5))
#f
```

`every` and `any` stop evaluating at the end of the shortest list if called with functions taking more than one argument, and given arguments of uneven lengths. The following example shows this:

```
> (every > '(3 9 4 1) '(2 7 2))
#t
```

Rewriting every *and* any *to handle multiple lists*

To write the new versions of these functions, we need to use a variation of **define** that lets us create a function taking a variable number of arguments. This is covered in depth in Chapter 11. In this case we specify one regular parameter (the function), and then use a single parameter name for the remaining lists. That parameter, `lists`, will be a list of the remaining arguments (which should all be lists themselves). To extract the first element from each list, we can use `map` with `first`. Applying the function to the elements is trickier, as the elements are in a list and are not separate arguments. We can use `apply` to get around this problem. Making a recursive call will involve using `apply`, and we need to call the function recursively with the `rests` of all the lists. Before we apply `every` to the list of `rests`, we must add the function to this list because `apply` needs a list of all the arguments to `every`. The new code follows:

```
; every and any each take a variable number of lists as arguments
; and apply func to those lists. apply is used to convert a list of
; arguments into separate arguments.

; Return final true return value if all applications of func to
; successive elements in lists are true, otherwise return #f.
(define (every func . lists)
  (cond ((member #t (map null? lists)) #t)
        ((member #t (map (lambda (lst) (null? (cdr lst))) lists))
            (apply func (map car lists)))
        (else
            (and (apply func (map car lists))
                 (apply every (cons func (map cdr lists))))))) )
```

```
; Return first true value from applying func to successive
; elements in lists, or #f if no elements satisfy func.
(define (any func . lists)
  (if (member #t (map null? lists))
      #f
      (or (apply func (map first lists))
          (apply any (cons func (map rest lists)))))) )
```

The built-in function `equal?` can be written using `every`. This function `new-equal?` must first test the types with which it is called. If the arguments are atoms, it checks if they are `eqv?`. If `new-equal?` is called with two lists, it calls another function that compares the lists. This function uses `every` with `new-equal?` to compare the elements of the two lists. It must check the length of the two lists beforehand because `every` will stop when it hits the end of the shortest list.

Here are the functions that perform the above actions:

```
; Return true if elt1 and elt2 (lists or atoms) are equal.
(define (new-equal? elt1 elt2)
  (cond ((and (atom? elt1) (atom? elt2)) (eqv? elt1 elt2))
        ((or (atom? elt1) (atom? elt2)) #f)
        (else (same elt1 elt2))) )

; Return true if list1 and list2 are equal.
(define (same list1 list2)
  (if (= (length list1) (length list2))
      (every new-equal? list1 list2)
      #f) )
```

We can trace the calls to these functions. Calls to `every` have been represented using **and**.

```
(new-equal? '(a (cat)) '(a (hat)))
    ↓
(same '(a (cat)) '(a (hat)))
    ↓
(and (new-equal? 'a 'a) (new-equal? '(cat) '(hat)))
        ↓                    ↓
(and (eqv? 'a 'a)        (same '(cat) '(hat)))
        ↓                    ↓
(and    #t               (and (new-equal? 'cat 'hat)))
        ↓                         ↓
(and    #t               (and (eqv? 'cat 'hat)))
        ↓                         ↓
(and    #t               (and      #f))
        ↓                    ↓
(and    #t                    #f)
    ↓
    #f
```

8.2.8 Exercises

8.16 Does the following version of `new-equal?` work when called with two lists? Why or why not?

```
(define (new-equal? elt1 elt2)
  (if (atom? elt1)
      (eqv? elt1 elt2)
      (same elt1 elt2)) )

(define (same list1 list2)
  (if (= (length list1) (length list2))
      (every new-equal? list1 list2)
      #f) )
```

8.17 Alexandra proposes that the functions `new-equal?` and `same` can be switched and `new-equal?` will still work when called. Does her switch work like the old version? Why or why not?

```
(define (same elt1 elt2)
  (cond ((and (atom? elt1) (atom? elt2)) (eqv? elt1 elt2))
        ((or (atom? elt1) (atom? elt2)) #f)
        (else (new-equal? elt1 elt2))) )

(define (new-equal? list1 list2)
  (if (= (length list1) (length list2))
      (every same list1 list2)
      #f) )
```

8.18 Here is yet another version of `new-equal`, but this one does not use `same`. Does it work? Why or why not?

```
(define (new-equal? elt1 elt2)
  (cond ((and (atom? elt1) (atom? elt2)) (eqv? elt1 elt2))
        ((or (atom? elt1) (atom? elt2)) #f)
        (else
          (and (= (length elt1) (length elt2))
               (every new-equal? elt1 elt2)))) )
```

8.19 Using functionals, write a function that returns true if two lists look the same in form. The atoms may be different, but the parentheses should be the same. The following two lists look the same:

```
((a b (c) d) e)
((1 2 (3) 4) 5)
```

8.20 Using functionals, write a function that takes two lists of atoms and produces an association list pairing subsequent atoms in each list. Given the lists `(1 2 3)` and `(one two three)`, your function should return

```
((1 one) (2 two) (3 three))
```

8.21 To determine if any of the lists passed as arguments to `every` are empty, we test if any application of `null?` returns `#t` using `member` and `map`. An alternate idea is to use `any` with `null?` as follows:

```
(define (every func . lists)
  (if (any null? lists)
      #t
      (and (apply func (map first lists))
           (apply every (cons func (map rest lists)))))) )
```

Does this new version of `every` work? If `any` were changed in the same manner as `every`, would it work?

8.3 Lambda Expressions

Lambda expressions provide another means of creating functions other than using `define`. A lambda expression is a list whose first element is the symbol `lambda`; the second element is a parameter list; and the remaining elements are the body of the function just as in a `define`. Unlike `define`, `lambda` does not take a name for the function being created; therefore, `lambda` can be looked at as a means of creating nameless functions.

Creating nameless functions on the fly

Lambda expressions can be used in place of function names in functions calls. Thus, in one step we can define and use a function. Look at the following example:

```
> ((lambda (num) (< num 3)) 2)
#t
```

This is functionally the same as doing the following two steps:

```
> (define (small-num num)
    (< num 3) )
??

> (small-num 2)
#t
```

The example above has one important difference from the `lambda` example—it binds the variable `small-num` to a function. We can use that function later referring to it by name.

The `define` above is equivalent to doing the following:

Alternate way of defining functions

```
(define small-num (lambda (num) (< num 3)))
```

The following example shows this equivalence:

```
> (define small-num (lambda (num) (< num 3)))
??

> (small-num 2)
#t
```

We define functions because we can refer to them by name instead of writing an entire lambda expression each time we want to invoke the function. Also, to write recursive functions we need a name to refer to the function.

Lambda expressions are useful as arguments to functionals. This way custom functions do not have to be defined beforehand with `define`, but can be created as one-shot entities.

Below is an example using a lambda expression that returns elements in a list that are greater than or equal to 10:

```
> (keep-if
    (lambda (num)
        (>= num 10))
    '(4 18 7 10))
(18 10)
```

Another common use for lambda expressions is to create functions that combine other functions using `and` or `or`. For example, if you wanted to return the positive numbers in a list that might have non-numbers within it, you would get an error if you wrote

```
(keep-if positive? a-list)
```

This is because `positive?` results in an error if applied to a non-number. One solution is to use a lambda expression, as in

```
(keep-if
  (lambda (element)
     (and (number? element)
          (positive? element)) )
  a-list)
```

The set functions `union` and `intersection` introduced in Chapter 7 can be written using functionals and lambda expressions. The union of *set1* and *set2* is *set2* appended with the elements in *set1* that are not in *set2*.

```
; Return the set of items in either set1 or set2.
(define (union-alt set1 set2)
  (append
    set2
    (remove-if
      (lambda (element)
         (member element set2) )
      set1)) )
```

The `remove-if` sequences through each element of set1 using a lambda expression. The `lambda` uses `member` to determine if the element in set1 being examined is in set2. If so, it is not included in the final list, which is appended to set2.

Mistakes to Avoid

A lambda expression is needed in the above example. The call to `remove-if` could not have been written as

```
(remove-if member set1)
```

This is because `member` needs two arguments. This call would attempt to invoke `member` with one argument—successive elements of `set1`.

Lambda expressions are used to call functionals like `remove-if` (that take one argument functions) with multiargument functions. The lambda expression creates a function taking one argument and calls the multiargument function with fixed values for the other arguments. In the above case, to use `remove-if` with `member`, the lambda expression creates a function that compares successive elements of `set1` with `set2`, the fixed argument to `member`.

We could not have written a separate function to compute the `member`, as in

```
(define (in-list element)
   (member element set2))
```

This is because the scope of the parameter, `set2`, is the function `union-alt`, thus `set2` cannot be referenced outside of that function.[1]

The intersection of *set1* and *set2* is the elements in *set1* that are in *set2*. This is similar to what we did above with `union-alt`. However, in this case we want to **keep** the elements that satisfy the call to `member`, so we use `keep-if`.

```
; Return the set of items in both set1 and set2.
(define (intersection-alt set1 set2)
  (keep-if
    (lambda (element)
        (member element set2) )
    set1) )
```

The function `assoc` can be implemented using `find-if`. The test to apply to `find-if` is one that checks if the `car` of the current pair being examined is equal to the element for which we are searching. `find-if` returns the first pair whose `car` is `equal?` to the element.

```
; Return the first sublist in assoc-list whose car matches element.
(define (alt-assoc element assoc-list)
  (find-if
    (lambda (pair)
        (equal? element (car pair)) )
    assoc-list) )
```

---

[1] Some versions of Scheme allow functions to be defined within other functions. In that case we could define `in-list` within `union-alt`, and call `remove-if` with `in-list`.

> **Mistakes to Avoid**
> It's easy to forget one or more of the following parts of a lambda expression:
> * The parameter list
> * The right parenthesis that closes the lambda expression

> **Mistakes to Avoid**
> When using lambda expressions with applicative operators, it is easy to forget to include the list through which to sequence. Always double check that you have passed in a list and that the elements of the list can be applied to the lambda expression.

8.3.1 Exercises

8.22 Using functionals, write your own version of `set-difference`.

8.23 Using functionals, write your own version of `subset?`.

8.24 Using functionals, write your own version of `rassoc`.

8.25 Using functionals, write a function `substitute` that takes a list and two atoms `old` and `new`. The function should return a new list with all top-level occurrences of `old` replaced with `new`. For example,

```
(substitute '(me but (not me)) 'me 'you)
```

should produce the list

```
(you but (not me))
```

8.26 Write a function that takes a list and returns that list with all the odd numbers replaced with the even numbers one higher. Hint: use `map`. Given the list

```
(1 out of 3 likes U 2 and U B 40)
```

your function should return

```
(2 out of 4 likes U 2 and U B 40)
```

8.27 Write a function `apply-to-atoms` that takes `func`, a function taking one argument, and a list `a-list`. `apply-to-atoms` should apply `func` to all the atoms in `a-list`. All the sublists should be left intact. `apply-to-atoms` returns a new list of these results. For example,

```
> (apply-to-atoms list '(2 (3) four (and (five))))
((2) (3) (four) (and (five)))
```

8.28 Write a function `deep-map` that takes a function and a nested list and applies
the function to every atom in the nested list and returns a similarly nested
list of results. For example,

```
(deep-map positive? '(3 (-14 (2)) 0 (((-7)))))
```

returns

```
(#t (#f (#t)) #f (((#f))))
```

8.4 Combining Results with `accumulate`

We will create a function `accumulate` to apply a *binary* function (one taking two
arguments) to a list of arguments. The binary function is first applied to the first
two elements of the list. Then the function is applied to this result and the third
element of the list, then to this new result and the next element, and so on. The
process continues until all elements in the list have been processed. In short, the
function is applied to all the elements of the list in a left to right order.

`accumulate`

If `accumulate` is called with an empty list, the return value is the result of calling the function with no arguments. If `accumulate` is called with a one-element
list, the return value is the first element of that list.

The general form of `accumulate` is

   (**accumulate** *function* *list*)

The function `sum-list` from Chapter 6, which takes a list of numbers and
returns their sum, can be written using `accumulate` as follows:

```
; Return sum of numbers in number-list.
(define (add-list number-list)
  (accumulate + number-list) )
```

Below is a sample call to `add-list`:

```
> (add-list '(8 2 -1 0 3))
12
```

In this example and many other cases `accumulate` and `apply` are interchange-
able. When used with functions like `+`, `*`, `max`, `min`, and `append`, `accumulate`
yields the same results as `apply`, as the following example shows:

Similarities of
`accumulate` *and*
`apply`

```
> (accumulate append '((one list) (another list)
                       (yet (another list))))
(one list another list yet (another list))

> (apply append '((one list) (another list)
                  (yet (another list))))
(one list another list yet (another list))
```

The order that `accumulate` sequences through the arguments is important
when using nonassociative functions such as `-`, as in

```
> (accumulate - '(1 2 3))
-4
```

The actions performed are

```
(- (- 1 2) 3)
```

┌───┐
│ **Mistakes to Avoid**   │
│ `accumulate` must be called with a function that takes two arguments. │
│ That function should yield a result that can be applied to the function │
│ itself. For example,   │
│   │
│   `(accumulate > '(3 5 -6))`   │
│   │
│ would not work to determine if all the elements of the list were in │
│ increasing order because `>` returns `#t` or `#f`, which cannot be applied to │
│ `>`. In other words, `(> (> 3 5) -6)` produces an error. │
└───┘

Differences between `accumulate` *and* `apply`

There are cases where `accumulate` does more than `apply`. Suppose you want to sum the absolute values of a list of numbers. We can use the function `sum-abs` from Chapter 3 that returns the sum of the absolute values of two numbers:

```
; Return the sum of the absolute values of num1 and num2.
(define (sum-abs num1 num2)
  (+ (abs num1) (abs num2)) )
```

To sum the absolute values of a list of numbers, we pass this function and the list of numbers to `accumulate`:

```
> (accumulate sum-abs '(-2 3 -4 -1))
10
```

Alternatively, we could have done this using `map` and `accumulate` or `apply`:

```
> (accumulate + (map abs '(-2 3 -4 -1)))
10

> (apply + (map abs '(-2 3 -4 -1)))
10
```

Here is a more practical application of `accumulate`. Given `many-lists`, a list of sublists, return the longest sublist:

```
(define many-lists '((1 2 3) (1 2 3 4 5) (1 2 3 4) (1 2)))
```

We can't use `map` with `apply` as follows:

```
> (apply max (map length many-lists))
5
```

This returns the length of the longest sublist. Instead we can write a function that takes two sublists and returns the longest one and then apply this function and `many-lists` to `accumulate`.

```
; Return the longest of list1 and list2.
(define (biggest list1 list2)
   (if (> (length list1) (length list2))
       list1
       list2) )
```

```
> (accumulate biggest many-lists)
(1 2 3 4 5)
```

How do we implement `accumulate`? Let's model the steps that `accumulate`   *Writing* `accumulate`
takes when processing a list. The following call to `accumulate`

```
(accumulate + '(1 2 3 4))
```

is equivalent to the following expression:

```
(+ (+ (+ 1 2) 3) 4)
```

One possibility is to think of the recursive case as follows:

> return the result of applying the function to
>> the recursive call of the list without the last element
>>> and
>> the last element.

Getting the last element and the list without the last element is not as easy or fast to do as getting the rest of the list and the first element of the list. Can we view the recursion in a different fashion?

If we start with the innermost action, `(+ 1 2)`, and then continue outward, we will be traversing the elements of the list in order. At each step we are applying the function to the result of the last computation and the current first element of the list. This value becomes the last computation value to use in the next iteration. We need an extra parameter to hold this last computation. When we reach the end of the list, that parameter should hold the final answer. This approach is tail-recursive. The code looks like

```
; Applies func to answer and first element of a-list, then to that
; result and next element of a-list and so on until a-list is empty.
; Returns final answer.
(define (accum-tail func a-list answer)
  (if (null? a-list)
      answer
      (accum-tail func (rest a-list)
        (func answer (first a-list)))) )
```

What should be the initial value of `answer`? If the function is addition, 0 makes sense, but with multiplication it should be 1, and for `append` it should be `'()`. A better approach is to pick a valid value for any function. The first element of the list will work. Then we recurse on the `rest` of the list. We need to verify the list is not empty first. Otherwise, we return the result of calling the function with no arguments. The helper function to do this follows:

```
; Applies func to first two elements of a-list, then to that result
; and next element of a-list and so on until a-list is empty.
; Returns final answer.
(define (accumulate func a-list)
  (if (null? a-list)
      (func)
      (accum-tail func (rest a-list) (first a-list))) )
```

Using accumulate
properly

Mistakes to Avoid

It is important to think about how the result of a computation will be combined by `accumulate` with other elements of the list. For example, to sum the squares of a list of numbers you might use a function `sum-squares` that returns the sum of the squares of two numbers.

```
; Returns the sum of the squares of num1 and num2.
(define (sum-squares num1 num2)
  (+ (* num1 num1) (* num2 num2)) )
```

And then pass this function to `accumulate` as follows:

```
> (accumulate sum-squares '(-2 3 -4 -1))
34226
```

The result is wrong (it should be 30). The problem is that we take the sum of the first two squares and then square that result and add it to the square of the third number and so on.

The first argument to `sum-squares` should be the total collected so far. Here is a new function that does that:

```
; Returns the sum of total and num squared.
(define (add-num-squared total num)
  (+ total (* num num)) )
```

Calling this new function with `accumulate` yields the following:

```
> (accumulate add-num-squared '(-2 3 -4 -1))
24
```

Another problem. We treated the first number as a total, meaning we added -2 to the sum of the squares of 3, -4, and -1. The first value in the list should be a sum. A quick fix is to add zero to the start of the number list:

```
> (accumulate add-num-squared '(0 -2 3 -4 -1))
30
```

It's probably better to use `apply` and `map` as follows:

```
> (apply +
    (map (lambda (num) (* num num)) '(-2 3 -4 -1)))
30
```

8.4.1 Exercises

8.29 Our first attempt to implement `find-if` failed when we couldn't find the first *true* element in a list. `or` will return the first true argument passed to it. This is almost what we want, except we have a list of values, not a collection of separate arguments. Can `accumulate` help us in this endeavor, as shown below?

```
(define (find-if func a-list)
  (list-ref
    a-list
    (position
      (accumulate
        or
        (map func a-list))
      (map func a-list))) )
```

8.30 Write a function `union-of-many` that takes a list of sets and returns the union of all of those sets.

8.31 Write a function `combine-assoc-lists` that takes a list of association lists and returns one association list containing all the pairs of all those association lists.

8.32 Write a function that takes a list with numbers, symbols, and lists and returns the average of the top-level numbers in the list. For example, given the list (3 (100) 5 ten), your function should return 4.

8.33 Write a function that takes a list of lists of numbers and returns the list with the largest number in it. Given the list

```
((16 43 7) (25 98) (57 2 89 14))
```

your function should return the list (25 98).

8.34 Write a function `smallest` that takes a function and a list and returns the number in the list that has the smallest value when the function is applied to it. For example,

```
(smallest abs '(-3 4 1 -2))
```

returns 1.

8.35 The following function is supposed to flatten a list—remove all the inner parentheses. For example, (1 (2 (3) 4) 5) flattened is (1 2 3 4 5). Does it work?

```
(define (flat a-list)
  (if (atom? a-list)
      a-list
      (map flat (accumulate append a-list))) )
```

8.36 The following function is supposed to flatten a list—remove all the inner parentheses. For example, (1 (2 (3) 4) 5) flattened is (1 2 3 4 5). Does it work?

```
(define (flatten a-list)
  (if (atom? a-list)
      (list a-list)
      (accumulate append (map flatten a-list))) )
```

8.37 Given a database of musical instruments and their prices, as follows,

```
((guitar 600)
 (piano 2000)
 (harmonica 10)
 (trumpet 250)
 (drums 700)
         .
         .
         .
 )
```

write expressions to return the following:

- The average cost of the instruments
- The price of the most expensive instrument
- The name of the least expensive instrument
- The instruments (and their prices) that cost less than $100
- The number of instruments that cost more than $1000

8.4.2   Sorting lists

A general sort function   The function sort-hand was created in Chapter 6 to perform an insertion sort on a list of playing cards. It would be nice to have a sorting routine that could be used for sorting any list. To do so, we can use the structure of sort-hand and its auxiliary function insert-card, but replace the function lower-card? with a function that is passed in as an argument to our generic sorting function. The new sorting function takes a function on which to base its comparison and a list to sort.

```
; Perform insertion sort on a-list based on compare-func.
(define (sort compare-func a-list)
  (if (null? a-list)
      '()
      (insert
        (first a-list)
        (sort compare-func (rest a-list))
        compare-func)) )
```

```
; Insert element in sorted order into sorted-list based on compare-func.
(define (insert element sorted-list compare-func)
  (cond ((null? sorted-list)
            (list element))
        ((compare-func element (first sorted-list))
            (cons element sorted-list))
        (else
            (cons (first sorted-list)
              (insert element (rest sorted-list) compare-func)))) )
```

To sort numbers in increasing order, use

```
> (sort < '(5 3 4 1 2))
(1 2 3 4 5)
```

To sort numbers in decreasing order, use

```
> (sort > '(5 3 4 1 2))
(5 4 3 2 1)
```

8.4.3 Example: Poker revisited, yet again

Our previous versions of poker from Chapters 5 and 6 did not use the cards' suit information. Playing cards have four suits: diamonds, hearts, clubs, and spades. If we include suit information, we can check for flushes, straight flushes, and royal flushes. A flush is a hand in which all the cards are of the same suit (e.g., all diamonds). A straight flush is a straight with all cards of the same suit, and a royal flush is a straight flush with the cards ten through ace.

Card suits and flushes

We can use an association list to represent card values and suits for a hand. Thus a possible hand may be

```
((jack spades) (ace diamonds) (three diamonds) (ace hearts)
 (two clubs))
```

With such a representation our previous code no longer works. We can make it work with some slight modifications and new code to handle flushes, straight flushes, and royal flushes.

Selector and creator functions should be written to get the value and suit of a playing card and to create a card pair.

Selector and creator functions for cards

```
; Return the value of card (e.g., ten or queen).
(define (card-value card)
  (car card) )

; Return the suit of card (e.g., diamonds or hearts).
(define (card-suit card)
  (second card) )

; Construct a card from its value and suit (e.g., (ten hearts)).
(define (create-card value suit)
  (list value suit) )
```

Once again, the ordering of the cards can be saved in the global symbol `card-ordering`.

```
(define card-ordering
  '(two three four five six seven eight nine ten
    jack queen king ace))
```

We can use the new sort from the previous section, and pass it a function that is *true* if the first card comes before the second card. The previous lower-card? function (from Chapter 6) won't work with the new card data structure. The new version should be

```
; Return true if card1 is lower in value than card2.
(define (lower-value? card1 card2)
  (< (position (card-value card1) card-ordering)
     (position (card-value card2) card-ordering)) )
```

We could write this function using member, as follows:

```
; Return true if card1 is lower in value than card2.
(define (lower-value? card1 card2)
  (member (card-value card2)
          (rest (member (card-value card1) card-ordering))) )
```

Testing for straights

The function is-straight? needs some slight modification to reflect the new sorting we are using. We should compare card values only, so we must form a list of card values without the suit information. This is done easily using map. Below is the new version:

```
; Return true if hand represents a straight.
(define (is-straight-new? hand card-ordering)
  (let* ( (sorted-hand (sort lower-value? hand))
          (low-card (first sorted-hand)) )
    (and (lower-value? low-card (create-card 'jack 'any-suit))
         (equal?
           (map card-value sorted-hand)
           (subseq
             (member (card-value low-card) card-ordering)
             0 5)))) )
```

Alternate approaches to test for straights

We could have taken other approaches to determine if a hand is a straight. In these approaches we don't need to sort the cards in the hand, but do need to know the low card in the hand. One approach is to find the low card, and then using recursion or every, test that each subsequently higher card exists in the hand.

Another approach that uses recursion is to find the low card, remove it from the hand, find the low card in the remaining cards, and verify that it is one card higher. We do this until a bad low card is found (it's too high) or all the cards have been examined.

A third approach is to once again begin with the low card and use it to formulate the list of cards needed for a straight based on card-ordering, as we did in our solution above. Then, verify that each card (e.g., using every) in the list of cards needed is in the hand we have. It's important to sequence through the cards needed. If we check that all the cards in our hand are in the list of cards needed, we would get a true answer for hands like (2 2 3 3 5) because they are all in the list (2 3 4 5 6).

A function to check for a flush follows. It checks if the first card's suit matches the suit of the remaining four cards. If so, then that hand is a flush. Alternate techniques for determining if a hand is a flush are given as exercises in the next section.   *Testing for flushes*

```
; Return true if hand represents a flush.
(define (is-flush? hand)
  (= 4
    (count
      (card-suit (first hand))
      (map card-suit (rest hand)))) )
```

`map` is used to return only the suit of each card. These suits are compared with the suit of the first card in the hand. If all of the suits match, `is-flush` returns true.

The next function is used to determine if the hand is a royal flush, assuming that it is known that the hand is a straight flush already. If the hand has an ace and is a straight flush, it must be a royal flush.

```
; Return true if hand represents a royal straight.
(define (is-royal-straight? hand)
  (member 'ace (map card-value hand)) )
```

Lastly, the new `poker-value` function follows. It first computes `hand-values`, the card values of the hand, and then computes `count-list`, the number of times each card appears in the hand. The previous code computed `count-list` by calling `count` five times. We can simplify this using a `map`, which sequences through the hand calling `count` to get the number of cards in the hand that match the current card being examined.

The hands with the highest value should be tested first to avoid problems like calling a full house a pair. The order of the hand values is as follows: *Hand ordering*

> royal flush
> straight flush
> four-of-a-kind
> full house
> flush
> straight
> three-of-a-kind
> two pair
> one pair

Such a testing order can cause some inefficiencies. Namely, royal flushes should be tested for first because they are worth the most; however, to be efficient this test should be nested within tests that check for flushes and straights. Before getting too caught up in this dilemma, it's good to think about the true conflicts that may arise. As it turns out, there are very few. The counting scheme eliminates problems like calling a four-of-a-kind a three-of-a-kind or a pair. The conflicts that arise are listed below: *Testing order conflicts*

hand value	possible conflicts (with hands worth less)
royal flush	straight flush, straight, flush
straight flush	straight, flush
full house	three-of-a-kind, one pair
flush	straight
two pair	one pair

The hand values on the left side of the above table should be tested for before their matching conflicting card values on the right side. One further conflict arises in that we would like to perform all the tests for royal flushes, straight flushes, straights, and flushes within the same nested conditional expression. This will eliminate unnecessary testing. The new function follows:

```
; Return the value of a poker hand.
(define (poker-value-new hand)
  (let* ( (hand-values (map card-value hand))
          (count-list
            (map
              (lambda (card)
                 (count card hand-values) )
             hand-values)) )
     (cond ((is-straight-new? hand card-ordering)
            (if (is-flush? hand)
               (if (is-royal-straight? hand)
                  'royal-flush
                  'straight-flush)
               'straight))
           ((is-flush? hand)
            'flush)
           ((member 4 count-list)
            'four-of-a-kind)
           ((and (member 3 count-list) (member 2 count-list))
            'full-house)
           ((member 3 count-list)
            'three-of-a-kind)
           ((= 4 (count 2 count-list))
            'two-pair)
           ((member 2 count-list)
            'one-pair)
           (else
            'nothing))) )
```

8.4.4 Exercises

8.38 The code above tests for straights before it tests for flushes. Yet flushes are worth more than straights. Does this mean the code has a bug? If so, fix it. If not, why do you think the code was written this way?

8.39 In determining if a hand is a flush, could the expression

```
(accumulate equal? (map card-suit hand))
```

be used?

8.40 Would this function correctly determine if a hand is a flush?

```
(define (is-flush? hand)
  (let ((first-suit (card-suit (first-hand))))
    (every (lambda (card)
             (eqv? first-suit (card-suit card)))
      (rest hand))) )
```

8.41 Would this function correctly determine if a hand is a flush?

```
(define (is-flush? hand)
  (let ((first-suit (card-suit (first-hand))))
    (= 4
      (count-if (lambda (card)
                  (eqv? first-suit (card-suit card)))
        (rest hand)))) )
```

8.42 Write a new version of the function `is-royal-straight?` that uses **find-if** instead of **member** and **map**.

8.43 How would you change the code if the representation for a card were a dotted list like `(queen . hearts)` instead of a two-element list?

8.44 How would you modify the code to allow wild cards (jokers)? There are two jokers in a deck of cards.

8.45 In the game draw poker you are allowed to discard some of your cards and draw new cards once. Write a function that decides which cards to discard based on the value of the existing hand.

8.46 Selection sort is an alternate means of sorting lists. Imagine we are sorting numbers to produce the smallest to the largest numbers. The technique used in selection sort is to find the smallest number in the list and make it the first element in the solution. The rest of the solution is determined recursively using the list with that smallest number removed. Here is a sample call showing how selection sort should work.

```
> (sel-sort '(3 2 1 4) <)
(1 2 3 4)
```

Does `sel-sort` below properly implement selection sort? Does it work with lists that have duplicates (e.g., `(2 4 4 3)`)? If not, fix it so it does.

```
(define (sel-sort a-list compare)
  (if (null? a-list)
      '()
      (let ((next-value (accumulate compare a-list)))
        (cons next-value
          (sel-sort (remove next-value a-list) compare)))) )
```

8.5   Summary

- Below is a table of the functionals covered in this chapter. *function, test*, and *bin-func* are functions that are passed as arguments. *function* and *test* should take a single argument whose type matches that of the elements in *list*. *test* should be a predicate function. *bin-func* must be a function that takes two arguments whose types match those of the elements in *list*. In addition, map, for-each, every, and any can be called with multiple lists. In this case, they should be called with a function that takes multiple arguments. The number of lists must match the number of arguments and the lists must all be the same length.

function	arguments	return value
map	*function lists*	list of results from applying *function* to successive elements of *lists*
for-each	*function lists*	undefined, but applies *function* to successive elements of *lists*
apply	*function list*	result of applying *function* to elements of *list*
every	*test lists*	final true return value if all successive elements in *lists* satisfy *test*, #f otherwise
any	*test lists*	first true value from applying *test* to successive elements in *lists*, #f otherwise
find-if	*test list*	first element in *list* that satisfies *test*
find-if-not	*test list*	first element in *list* that does not satisfy *test*
count-if	*test list*	number of elements in *list* that satisfy *test*
count-if-not	*test list*	number of elements in *list* that do not satisfy *test*
remove-if	*test list*	*list* without elements that satisfy *test*
keep-if	*test list*	*list* of elements that satisfy *test*
accumulate	*bin-func list*	result of applying *bin-func* to the elements in *list* two at a time

- lambda expressions are used to create specialized functions to use with functionals.

CHAPTER 9

INPUT AND OUTPUT

9.1 Input/Output

Information going from the user to the computer is called *input*, and information
from the computer to the user is *output*. We have used the default form of
input/output (often abbreviated as I/O) in Scheme. Input is a product of the
interpreter reading in our requests at the > prompt. Output is the results of
evaluating our input Scheme expressions that the interpreter prints out.

I/O

9.1.1 Printing out additional information

There are times when we wish to get more information from a function call than
the evaluated result of the last expression. To display additional information during the course of the evaluation of a function, calls to output functions are necessary. Below is a list of some of these output functions:

function	arguments	prints out	return value
newline	none	a blank line	undefined
display	*expression*	the value of *expression*	undefined
write	*expression*	the value of *expression*	undefined

newline, display,
and write

Below are some examples of these functions:

```
> (newline)

??

> (display 3)
3??

> (write 3)
3??
```

The return value of `newline`, `display`, and `write` is undefined, and in fact it will probably appear on the same line as the value printed out, as shown in these examples. In actual usage the calls to these output functions would be placed within functions so that they are not the final expression, and thus the return value of the function call will be some other value. Below is an example of this:

```
; Print out num and return num squared.
(define (print-and-square num)
  (display num)
  (* num num) )
```

A call to this function will print the value of the parameter `num` and its square:

```
> (print-and-square 7)
749
```

Use `newline` to get the output to appear on two lines:

```
; Print out num, move to the next line, and return num squared.
(define (print-and-square num)
  (display num)
  (newline)
  (* num num) )

> (print-and-square 7)
7
49
```

Printing a list one element per line

Using `display`, `newline`, and `for-each`, it is possible to write a short function that prints out the elements in a list, one element per line:

```
; Print elements of a-list one per line.
(define (one-per-line a-list)
  (for-each
    (lambda (item)
      (display item)
      (newline))
    a-list) )
```

Here is a call illustrating this handy function:

```
> (one-per-line '(line1 (line 2 here) ((finally (line)) 3)))
line1
(line 2 here)
((finally (line)) 3)
??
```

The final return value is undefined because `for-each` returns an undefined value.

Text strings

Text can be displayed by surrounding the desired text in double quotes, and passing that *string* to `display` or `write`. A string is a sequence of characters surrounded by double quotes. The results can be seen below:

```
> (display "hi there")
hi there??
```

```
> (write "hi there")
"hi there"??
```

`display` and `write` can print out symbol names and lists also:

```
> (display 'symbol)
symbol??
```

```
> (write '(a short list))
(a short list)??
```

The difference between the functions `display` and `write` is that `display` prints out strings without the surrounding double quotes.

9.1.2 Input

To get information to functions, we have used parameters and passed the values as arguments in function calls. There are times when it is desirable to get extra information into a function. This can be done in Scheme with the function `read`. `read` reads in information from the user and returns that information. `read` reads in anything that looks like a Scheme expression—numbers, words, lists, and even strings.

`read`

```
> (read)
42
42
```

```
> (read)
fred
fred
```

```
> (read)
((some (arbitrary list)))
((some (arbitrary list)))
```

```
> (read)
"a string"
"a string"
```

When a `read` function call is evaluated, the interpreter waits for the user to enter a value that is read in and returned as the value of `read`. If more than one value is entered, the following values are interpreted as further commands to the interpreter, and are evaluated in the normal fashion:

```
> (read)
(+ 1 1) (+ 3 4)
(+ 1 1)
7
```

The following example illustrates how a value read in from the user can be used within a function:

```
; Read in a value and return its square root.
(define (read-and-apply)
  (sqrt (read)) )
```

After the function `read-and-apply` is called, the interpreter waits for the user to enter a value, then it continues. Once the value is entered, its square root is computed and displayed:

```
> (read-and-apply)
49
7.0
```

Reading until a number is given

The following function is supposed to ask the user for a number and read in a value. If the user enters a number, its square root should be returned. Otherwise the process repeats.

```
; Read in values until a number is entered; return its square root.
(define (get-number)
  (display "Enter a number: ")
  (if (number? (read))
    (sqrt (read))
    (get-number)) )
```

There is a bug in the above code. Rather than return the square root of the number entered, the call to `read` in

```
(sqrt (read))
```

will force the user to enter another value before execution continues. The value read in when

```
(number? (read))
```

is evaluated is the value desired. To save this value a `let` can be used. The correct function looks like

```
; Read in values until a number is entered; return its square root.
(define (get-number)
  (display "Enter a number: ")
  (let ( (number (read)) )
    (if (number? number)
        (sqrt number)
        (get-number))) )
```

Below is a trace of this function:

```
> (get-number)
Enter a number: foo
Enter a number: (a list will not work either)
Enter a number: 121
11.0
```

9.2 Getting Yes/No Answers

A useful function to create is one to get a "yes" or "no" answer to a question. The function should take a string that is the question to ask the user and print that string, along with an indication to answer *yes* or *no*.

Reading until a yes/no answer is given

```
; Read in values until a yes or no is entered; return #t if
; yes is entered and #f if no is entered.
(define (yes-no query)
  (display query)
  (display " (yes or no) ")
  (let ( (answer (read)) )
    (cond ((eqv? answer 'yes) #t)
          ((eqv? answer 'no) #f)
          (else (yes-no query)))) )
```

Below are examples illustrating this function:

```
> (yes-no "Do you want to continue?")
Do you want to continue? (yes or no) maybe
Do you want to continue? (yes or no) perhaps
Do you want to continue? (yes or no) no
#f

> (yes-no "Are you sure you want to quit?")
Are you sure you want to quit? (yes or no) yup
Are you sure you want to quit? (yes or no) yes
#t
```

9.3 Conditions with Multiple Actions

The condition-action pairs in a cond can have more than one action. They are really condition-action(s) pairs. For the condition that is satisfied, all of its associated actions are evaluated, but only the return value of the last action is returned as the value of the cond. For this reason, just as with function definitions, there is usually only one action associated with each condition.

The usual reason for having more than one action in an action list is to allow *side-effects* to take place. With side-effects, it is not the return value that we are interested in so much as the particular side-effect that it causes. Binding a value to a variable using define is a commonly performed action that produces side-effects. Another often used side-effect is printing out information. Since expressions always print their final return values, we have not used any other means of displaying information. However, there are times when it is desirable to do so.

Side-effects

Suppose you wish to write a cond that returns the number of times *element* occurs in *a-list*. In addition, you want to precede this number with a message.

If *a-list* is empty, return 0 and print the message

```
The list is empty
```

If *element* did not occur in *a-list*, return 0 and print the message

```
The item did not occur in the list
```

Lastly, if *element* did occur in *a-list*, return the number of times it occurred, preceded by the message

```
The number of times item occurs in the list is
```

To get text as displayed above, the simplest way is to call `display` with the desired text surrounded in double quotes (`"`).

Below is the code to do this:

```
; Count the number of times element occurs in a-list; print an
; informative message about the count and return the count.
(define (number-of-times element a-list)
  (cond ((null? a-list)
         (display "The list is empty ")
         0)
        ((not (member element a-list))
         (display "The item did not occur in the list ")
         0)
        (else
         (display "The number of times item occurs in the list is ")
         (count element a-list))) )
```

If *a-list* is an empty list, the two actions

```
(display "The list is empty ")
0
```

are evaluated; the text is displayed, and 0 is returned.

If *element* is not in *a-list*, these two actions are evaluated:

```
(display "The item did not occur in the list ")
0
```

The message gets printed, and 0 is returned.

If *element* is in *a-list*, the actions

```
(display "The number of times item occurs in the list is ")
(count element a-list)
```

are evaluated, the message is displayed, and the value of

```
(count element a-list)
```

is returned.

The sample evaluation of this code illustrates the values that get displayed.

```
> (number-of-times 'word '(word does occur in this word list))
The number of times item occurs in the list is 2
```

9.4 Example: Visualizing Chaos

Ecologists sometimes use formulas to model the growth in a population of organisms in some ecosystem. The *logistic difference equation* is one such formula. It expresses the new population in terms of the old population and some growth rate constant. The formula is

Logistic difference equation

new population = *growth* × *population* × (1 − *population*)

where population is between zero and one. A population of zero means extinction and one means the largest possible population that the ecosystem can support.

For small growth rates, the population typically dies out. Going beyond this threshold, the population reaches some stable value after a number of generations. Larger growth rates produce larger end population values. With a growth rate slightly above three, the population does not stabilize at one value, but jumps back and forth between two values (*bifurcates*). Beyond this, the splitting doubles again and again, but at some point the population jumps around in a seemingly random fashion—chaos emerges.

Population stability and chaos

We can write a recursive Scheme function to model the change in population by printing out population values for a given number of iterations. For each iteration we print out the population and then make a recursive call with the new population. We'll need a counter variable to count the number of iterations. The function new-balance from Chapter 6 provides a model for what we need to do—repeat an action a given number of times. However, we can make one simplification. Rather than count up to the number of iterations, we can count down from the number of iterations to zero. Since we don't need to use the value of the counter, this approach works fine for this problem. It wouldn't have worked in new-balance because we used the counter in the function in deciding when to make incremental deposits.

Modeling population growth

The function takes three parameters: times, growth, and population.

```
; Model the growth of population organisms for times generations.
; growth is the growth rate.
(define (population-growth times growth population)
  (cond ((= 0 times)
         population)
        (else
          (display population)
          (newline)
          (population-growth (- times 1) growth
            (* growth population (- 1 population)))))) )
```

population-growth terminates when times is zero and returns a final population value. This means that times+1 populations are printed: the initial population (generation zero) and the next times generations. The recursive action prints the current population and calls population-growth with counter plus one and the new population value.

Here are some sample calls to `population-growth`:[1]

```
> (population-growth 5 2.0 0.4)
0.4
0.48
0.4992
0.4999
0.4999
0.5

> (population-growth 5 2.0 0.9)     ; same growth rate, larger population
0.9
0.18
0.2952
0.4161
0.4859
0.4996

> (population-growth 5 3.2 0.4)     ; larger growth rate—bifurcation
0.4
0.768
0.5701
0.7842
0.5414
0.7945

> (population-growth 5 4.0 0.4)     ; larger growth rate—chaos
0.4
0.96
0.1536
0.5200
0.9983
0.0064
```

9.4.1 Exercises

9.1 Find growth rates for `population-growth` that lead to bifurcations (alternating sequences of populations). Find growth rates that produce alternating patterns with a period of 4, 8, or 16 (the pattern repeats after 4, 8, or 16 generations).

9.2 At what growth rate does chaos emerge?

9.3 For some growth rates beyond the point of chaos, stable populations with periods of three appear (patterns that repeat after three generations). Find these.

[1.] Only four digits of precision are shown in the output.

9.4 Sometimes it takes a number of generations before the population stabilizes. Modify `population-growth` so that it takes another parameter `start` denoting the number of initial generations to calculate, but not print. Thus, only generations `start`+1 to `times` are printed.

9.5 Write a function to compare the final population given different initial populations and a fixed growth rate. Your function should return true if all the populations are within some value (e.g., 0.0001) of the average population.

9.6 Some of the questions above asked you to find growth rates where period doubling or chaos occurs. Write a function that will help you determine these growth rates.

9.7 Kate wants to change `population-growth` so that it doesn't print the initial (generation zero) population. She proposes the following change:

```
(define (population-growth times growth population)
  (cond ((= 0 times)
         population)
        (else
         (population-growth (- times 1) growth
           (* growth population (- 1 population)))
         (display population)
         (newline))) )
```

Will this work?

9.5 Read-Eval-Print Loop

The central component to the Scheme interpreter is the *read-eval-print loop*. Commands are read in, then evaluated. Finally the evaluated result is printed. In Scheme, the functions **read**, **eval**, and **write** do exactly this.[2] We could write them out to perform a single read-eval-print step:

```
(write (eval (read)))
```

read returns whatever is read in from the user. **eval** takes one argument and returns its evaluated result. **write** takes this result and displays it on the screen. Since **eval** returns the evaluated result, we need not call **write** to print it out. Therefore, we don't need the **write** in the simple case of performing one evaluation. However, the evaluator is doing a read-eval-print *loop*. Because of this we need the **write** function call.

An infinite (nonending) read-eval-print loop could be written as follows:

eval

[2.] It is called a read-eval-print loop instead of a read-eval-write loop because other, older dialects of LISP use the function `print`.

```
; Print prompt, read input, print out evaluation, repeat.
(define (read-eval-print)
  (display "-> ")
  (write (eval (read)))
  (newline)
  (read-eval-print) )
```

The solution below is an improvement, as it allows the user to exit when the symbol quit is entered.

```
; Print prompt, read input, print out evaluation, repeat until
; quit is entered.
(define (read-eval-print-with-exit)
  (display "-> ")
  (let ( (command (read)) )
    (cond ((eqv? command 'quit)
              'bye)
          (else
              (write (eval command))
              (newline)
              (read-eval-print-with-exit)))) )
```

Below is an example call to read-eval-print-with-exit:

```
> (read-eval-print-with-exit)
-> 3
3
-> (* 3 4)
12
-> quit
bye
```

9.5.1 Exercises

9.8   Given the following function,

```
(define (mystery num)
  (cond ((zero? num) 0)
        (else (display num)
              (newline)
              (mystery (- num 1)))) )
```

what will the function call (mystery 3) display? What is the return value?

9.9   Given the following function,

```
(define (unknown num)
  (cond ((zero? num) 0)
        (else (unknown (- num 1))
              (display num)
              (newline))) )
```

what will the function call (unknown 3) display? What is the return value?

9.10 Craig writes the following function to print both the sum and average of a list of numbers:

```
(define (average num-list)
  (/ (display (accumulate + num-list))
     (length num-list)) )
```

Will Craig's function work?

9.6 Summary

- To print a blank line, use `newline`.
- To print out a string (text surrounded by double quotes) without the double quotes, use `display`.
- To print symbols, numbers, or lists, use either `display` or `write`.
- To get a value from the user, use `read`.
  Be sure to save the value read in using a `let` variable if it is used more than once.
- Summary of functions introduced in this chapter:

function	arguments	prints out	return value
newline	none	a blank line	undefined
display	*expression*	the value of *expression*	undefined
write	*expression*	the value of *expression*	undefined
read	none	nothing	value entered by the user

CHAPTER 10

REPETITION THROUGH ITERATION

10.1   Iteration

Iteration is a type of repetition that, like recursion, involves repeating a task a certain number of times, or for every element in a list, or more generally until some condition is met. Iterative functions provide a means of carrying out these commonly performed tasks without having to explicitly create recursive functions. In general, any linear recursive function (a function with a single recursive call in each of its recursive cases) can be written using an iterative function. Most of the examples in this chapter are iterative versions of the functions written using recursion in Chapter 6. You should compare the iterative solutions to their recursive counterparts and decide which seems more natural to you.

The big advantages of iteration over recursion are increased speed and reduced memory requirements. Making a function call is an expensive operation (time- and memory-wise) on a computer. It requires making provisions to save the parameters, the location to return to, and a host of additional information. Chapter 13 goes into the mechanism of function calls in great depth.

Speed and memory considerations

Saving information for function calls requires memory. Once a function returns, that memory can be reused. But a recursive solution that makes a great number of recursive calls may not be able to complete due to memory limitations. You can see this by calling an embedded recursive function with an infinite loop. Here is a very simple example:

```
; Infinite loop with embedded recursion.
(define (infinite)
  (infinite)
  0 )
```

Stack overflow

Calling this function results in a *stack overflow error*, meaning too much memory was used in making recursive calls. However, if you use a tail recursive function, as follows

```
; Infinite loop with tail recursion.
(define (infinite-iter)
    (infinite-iter) )
```

Tail recursion and iteration

you will not have a stack overflow and the program will run until you interrupt it. This is because Scheme internally converts tail recursive functions to iterative loops. Actions are repeated without making recursive calls.

If you are concerned with speed or memory issues, you should use an iterative solution instead of a recursive solution. This means using tail recursive functions or calls to the iterative function do.

The syntax for do is outlined below. The values in square braces "*[ ]*" are optional.

syntax for do

```
(do (  (variable1  initial-value1  [ update-value1 ])
       (variable2  initial-value2  [ update-value2 ])
                         ⋮
       (variableN  initial-valueN  [ update-valueN ])  )
    (test  exit-actions)
    body)
```

exit-actions are zero or more expressions, similar to the actions in a condition-actions pair in a cond expression. *body* is zero or more expressions. The *body* of a do is somewhat analogous to the body of a function definition with one important distinction: none of the expressions in the body are returned. They are all only used for their side-effects, just like any expressions that proceed the final expression in the body of a function.

Evaluation rules for do

do begins by evaluating all the *initial-value*s and then binding all the *variable*s to those values. Thus the *initial-value*s cannot refer to previous *variable*s. This is identical to the way that a let binds its variables.

Next *test* is evaluated. If it returns a non-#f result, the *exit-actions* are evaluated and the value of the last action is returned, much like how a cond with a single condition-actions pair would behave. If there are no *exit-actions*, do returns an undefined value. If *test* returns #f, *body* is evaluated, the *update-value*s are evaluated, and the *variable*s take on those values. Then the entire process continues by evaluating *test* again. If no *update-value* is supplied for a *variable*, the *variable* keeps its current value.

The bindings of variables to the *update-value*s follows the same rules as the bindings to the *initial-value*s. Thus the *update-value*s are all evaluated and then the *variable*s are sequentially bound to those values. Any references to *variable*s in *update-value*s refer to the old bindings of those *variable*s.

do may be better understood by showing its equivalent to other Scheme expressions. The following function, do-loop, is functionally equivalent to a do expression. The items in *italics* represent pieces of the do syntax shown above. The function do-loop would be called initially with the *initial-value*s:

```
; Recursive equivalent to do.
(define (do-loop value1 value2 ... valueN)
  (let ( (variable1 value1)
         (variable2 value2)

                  .
                  .

         (variableN valueN) )
     (cond (test exit-actions)
           (else body
                 (do-loop update-values))))) )
```

*Functional equivalent
of* do

```
(do-loop initial-values)
```

We can model a **do** without using **let**. In this case, imagine we call do-loop-2
with the *initial-value*s of the *variable*s:

```
; Recursive equivalent to do.
(define (do-loop-2 variable1 variable2 ... variableN)
  (cond (test exit-actions)
        (else body
              (do-loop-2 update-values))) )
```

```
(do-loop-2 initial-values)
```

Notice in both of these examples that *body* is the first action of the else clause
of the **cond**. It is evaluated but its results are not returned.

10.2 Repeating Actions a Number of Times

To repeat a body of code *body* a certain number of times, the following **do** template can be used. This template repeats *body num-times* times by incrementing
the **do** variable *counter* with values from 1 to *num-times*.

```
(do ( (counter 1 (+ counter 1)) )
    ((> counter num-times) exit-actions)
    body)
```

*Template to repeat
actions a number of
times*

If we don't need to use the value of *counter* as it increments or we want
counter to decrement (counting backwards), we can use the following template to
repeat *body num-times* times:

```
(do ( (counter num-times (- counter 1)) )
    ((= counter 0) exit-actions)
    body)
```

*Template to repeat
actions counting back-
wards*

10.2.1 Example: Printing changing populations

The function population-growth from Chapter 9 can be implemented easily
using the second template given above. population-growth has three parameters; one is an integer, times, that corresponds to the number of populations to
calculate and print. Here is a new version using iteration:

```
; Model the growth of population organisms for times generations.
; growth is the growth rate
(define (population-growth-iter times growth population)
  (do ( (counter times (- counter 1))
        (pop population (* growth pop (- 1 pop))) )
    ((= counter 0) pop)
    (display pop)
    (newline)) )
```

Notice the use of the variable `pop`, which is initially bound to the starting population and then updated to the new population values. Evaluating this function yields the following:

```
> (population-growth-iter 5 4.0 0.4)
0.4
0.96
0.1536
0.5200
0.9983
0.0064
```

10.3   Repeating an Action for each Element in a List

To repeat a section of code for every element in a list, the following `do` template can be used. This template repeats *body* for each element in *a-list*. The variable *list-remaining* is initialized to *a-list* and then set to successive `rest`s of *a-list* each time through the `do`.

Template to repeat actions for each element in a list

```
(do ( (list-remaining a-list (rest list-remaining)) )
    ((null? list-remaining) exit-actions)
    body)
```

10.3.1   Example: Checking if a list consists of numbers only

do with two exit cases

The template above can be used to implement the function `all-numbers?` from Chapter 6, which takes a list and returns `#t` if all the elements in the list are numbers and `#f` if not. The iteration through the list should stop when a non-number is encountered. This means there will be two exit cases, encountering an empty list (no more elements to process) and encountering an element that is a non-number. The return value depends on the exit case. The *test* and *exit-actions* of the `do` must check for both exit cases and return the proper value accordingly. There is no action to take in the body, so it isn't needed.

```
; Return true if all elements of a-list are numbers.
(define (all-numbers?-iter a-list)
  (do ( (current-list a-list (rest current-list)) )
    ((or (null? current-list)
         (not (number? (first current-list))))
     (if (null? current-list)
         #t
         #f))) )
```

Examine the evaluations below:

```
> (all-numbers?-iter '(3 4 2))
#t

> (all-numbers?-iter '(3 four 2))
#f
```

It is important to put the conditions of the **or** in the order they are given. If not, we may take the **first** of an empty list and get an error. The code above works because if `current-list` is empty, `(null? current-list)` is true and the **or** does not check the second condition. For the same reason, the **if** must check for an empty list instead of an element that is not a number.

Order of conditions in do

Mistakes to Avoid

In this **do** and many others, there is no body. If you are comparing iterative constructions in Scheme with those in other languages like Pascal or C, you may find this strange. In a loop in these languages the body contains the actions. However, in Scheme the body of a **do** loop is only used for side-effects (e.g., printing out values). As an example of this, let's change the function above as follows:

```
; Return true if all elements of a-list are numbers - buggy.
(define (all-numbers?-iter-bad a-list)
  (do ( (current-list a-list (rest current-list)) )
    ((null? current-list) #t)
    (if (not (number? (first current-list)))
        #f)) )

> (all-numbers?-iter-bad '(1 2 three))
#t

> (all-numbers?-iter-bad '(one two three))
#t
```

Regardless of the list `all-numbers?-iter-bad` is called with, it will always return #t. This is because the **if** expression is part of the body of the **do**. It is evaluated, but its return value is never used. The **do** eventually ends when the list has been sequenced through and returns #t, which is the exit action of the **do**.

Improper uses of the body of a do

10.4 General Examples with do Loops

The function do can be used for more than repeating actions a certain number of
times or for each element in a list.

10.4.1 Example: Factorial

An example use of do is the function factorial from Chapter 6, which takes an
argument max and returns the product of the numbers from one to max. The product will be maintained in the variable prod.

```
; Return max factorial (with iteration).
(define (fact-iter max)
  (do ( (number max (- number 1))
        (prod 1 (* number prod)) )
    ((zero? number) prod)) )
```

Below is a trace of the bindings of the variables number and prod for the function call (fact-iter 3):

> number is bound to 3
> prod is bound to 1

number is not zero, so the do continues.

> number is bound to (- 3 1) or 2
> prod is bound to (* 3 1) or 3

Notice that the old value of number is used in the computation of prod. This is
because the values are all evaluated before they are bound to the variables. Continuing on,

> number is bound to (- 2 1) or 1
> prod is bound to (* 2 3) or 6

Continuing further,

> number is bound to (- 1 1) or 0
> prod is bound to (* 1 6) or 6

number is now zero. Thus, *test* is satisfied, and *exit-actions* are performed. In this
case the one action, prod, is evaluated and returned, giving the result 6.

10.4.2 Example: Adding up the digits in a number

Another example using do is a new version of the function sum-digits from
Chapter 6, which adds the digits in a number. The variables within the let in
sum-digits: last-digit and rest-of-number will be used as variables within
the do. last-digit is initialized to the last digit of the parameter number. After
that it is bound to the last digit of rest-of-number. rest-of-number is initially
the leftmost digits of the parameter number, and then the leftmost digits of its
previous value. In addition, the variable answer will be used to accumulate the
sum. answer is initialized to last-digit and updated by adding its old value to
the current value of last-digit.

```
; Return sum of the digits in number.
(define (sum-digits-iter number)
  (do ( (last-digit (remainder number 10)
                    (remainder rest-of-number 10))
        (rest-of-number (truncate (/ number 10))
                        (truncate (/ rest-of-number 10)))
        (answer last-digit (+ answer last-digit)) )
      ((zero? rest-of-number) answer)) )
```

Note that `sum-digits-iter` and `fact-iter` have no *body*. Below is a trace of this function:

```
> (sum-digits-iter 749)
Undefined variable: last-digit
```

Caution with do *variables*

Recall that the variables in a `do` are like the variables in a `let` in that they cannot use the current values of other variables in the variable list. When `last-digit` is being evaluated, it has not been defined yet. This creates an undefined variable error. We can change the code as follows to fix this error:

```
; Return sum of the digits in number.
(define (sum-digits-iter number)
  (do ( (last-digit (remainder number 10)
                    (remainder rest-of-number 10))
        (rest-of-number (truncate (/ number 10))
                        (truncate (/ rest-of-number 10)))
        (answer 0 (+ answer last-digit)) )
      ((zero? rest-of-number) answer)) )
```

Here is a run of the new version:

```
> (sum-digits-iter 749)
13
```

We got rid of the error message, but got the wrong answer. Here is a trace of the bindings of the variables:

`last-digit` is bound to (`remainder` 749 10) or 9
`rest-of-number` is bound to (`truncate` (/ 749 10)) or 74
`answer` is bound to 0

We continue,

`last-digit` is bound to (`remainder` 74 10) or 4
`rest-of-number` is bound to (`truncate` (/ 74 10)) or 7
`answer` is bound to (+ 0 9) or 9

Next,

`last-digit` is bound to (`remainder` 7 10) or 7
`rest-of-number` is bound to (`truncate` (/ 7 10)) or 0
`answer` is bound to (+ 9 4) or 13

Since `rest-of-number` is 0, we exit returning `answer`, 13.

To get around this problem we can change the exit action to return the answer plus the current last digit, (+ answer last-digit). Or we can use the last digits directly by eliminating the variable `last-digit` and just use its value throughout. Let's try this approach:

```
; Return sum of the digits in number.
(define (sum-digits-iter number)
  (do ( (rest-of-number (truncate (/ number 10))
                        (truncate (/ rest-of-number 10)))
        (answer (remainder number 10)
                (+ answer (remainder rest-of-number 10))) )
      ((zero? rest-of-number) answer)) )
```

Let's try this new version using the previous call, (sum-digits-iter 749).

>   `rest-of-number` is bound to (**truncate** (/ 749 10)) or 74
>   `answer` is bound to (**remainder** 749 10) or 9

`rest-of-number` is not zero, so the variables are bound to the update values.

>   `rest-of-number` is bound to (**truncate** (/ 74 10)) or 7
>   `answer` is bound to (**+** 9 (**remainder** 74 10)) or 13

Again the variables are bound to the update values.

>   `rest-of-number` is bound to (**truncate** (/ 7 10)) or 0
>   `answer` is bound to (**+** 13 (**remainder** 7 10)) or 20

`rest-of-number` is now 0, and the value of `answer`, 20, is returned.

10.5   Writing Mapping Functions and Filters Using Iteration

All the different types of linear recursion functions covered in Chapter 6 have been shown, with the exception of functions that produce lists—namely the mapping functions and filters. It is possible to write such functions using an iterative construct, but it requires building up a list of results.

10.5.1   Example: A mapping function to take square roots in a list

The function `square-roots` from Chapter 6 can be written using an iterative function. `square-roots` takes a list of numbers and returns the list of the square roots of those numbers. Since we must build up a list of results, `do` variables will be used to update that list and `cdr` down the list supplied as an argument.

```
; Return a list of the square roots of the numbers in a-list.
(define (square-roots-iter a-list)
  (do ( (current-list a-list (cdr current-list))
        (answer '() (cons (sqrt (car current-list)) answer)) )
      ((null? current-list) answer)) )
```

A trace of the call (square-roots-iter '(1 4 9)) follows:

`current-list` is bound to (1 4 9)
`answer` is bound to ()

Since `current-list` is not (), the iteration continues:

`current-list` is bound to (`cdr` '(1 4 9)) → (4 9)
`answer` is bound to (`cons` (`sqrt` (`car` '(1 4 9))) '()) → (1.0)

`current-list` is bound to (`cdr` '(4 9)) → (9)
`answer` is bound to (`cons` (`sqrt` (`car` '(4 9))) '(1.0)) → (2.0 1.0)

`current-list` is bound to (`cdr` '(9)) → ()
`answer` is bound to (`cons` (`sqrt` (`car` '(9))) '(2.0 1.0)) → (3.0 2.0 1.0)

`current-list` is now () and `answer`, (3.0 2.0 1.0), is returned. This is the reverse of the desired result.

In writing the recursive solution to `square-roots`, **consing** the **sqrt** of the `car` of the list works because the **conses** don't take effect until we unwind from the recursive descent. With an iterative solution, we are building the list starting with the first element. Subsequent elements are **consed** after this. We can fix this by appending the new item onto the end of the current list, as follows:

Using append *to build lists with* do

```
(append answer (list (sqrt (car current-list))))
```

Another, simpler approach is to change the exit action to return the reverse of `answer`. This solution follows:

```
; Return a list of the square roots of the numbers in a-list.
(define (square-roots-iter-correct a-list)
  (do ( (current-list a-list (cdr current-list))
        (answer '() (cons (sqrt (car current-list)) answer)) )
    ((null? current-list) (reverse answer))) )

> (square-roots-iter-correct '(121 169 64 36))
(11.0 13.0 8.0 6.0)
```

10.5.2 Example: A filter to extract positive numbers from a list of numbers

Filters can be written using iteration. The resultant list is created by conditionally **consing** elements onto a solution list. Once again we must reverse the final answer to get the elements in the proper order. The function `positive-filter` from Chapter 6 follows. `positive-filter` takes a list of numbers and returns a list of only the positive numbers in that list:

```
; Return a list of the positive numbers in a-list.
(define (positive-filter-iter a-list)
  (do ( (current-list a-list (cdr current-list))
        (answer '() (if (positive? (car current-list))
                        (cons (car current-list) answer)
                        answer)) )
    ((null? current-list) (reverse answer))) )
```

Below is a trace of (`positive-filter-iter` '(-12 13 14)):

`current-list` is bound to (-12 13 14)
`answer` is bound to ()

`current-list` is not `()`, so evaluation continues

> `current-list` becomes `(13 14)`
> `answer` remains `()` because `-12` is not positive

> `current-list` becomes `(14)`
> `answer` becomes `(13)` because 13 is positive

> `current-list` becomes `()`
> `answer` becomes `(14 13)`

`current-list` is `()`, so the exit action (`reverse` answer), `(13 14)`, is returned

10.5.3   Exercises

10.1   Write your own version of the function `length` using an iterative function.

10.2   Using an iterative function, write a function `substitute` that takes a list and two atoms, *old* and *new*. The function should return a new list with all top-level occurrences of *old* replaced with *new*. For example,

```
(substitute '(me but (not me)) 'me 'you)
```

should produce the list

```
(you but (not me))
```

10.3   Write your own version of the function `union` using an iterative function.

10.4   Write your own version of the function `intersection` using an iterative function.

10.5   Write a function that removes numbers from a list using an iterative function.

10.6   Write your own version of the function `keep-if` using an iterative function.

10.7   Write your own version of the function `count-if-not` using an iterative function.

10.8   Write a function that takes a list and returns a list of the cubes of that list using an iterative function.

10.5.4   Example: Sorting a list

In Chapters 6 and 8 we developed a function to sort a list. We can write a version of the enhanced sort from Chapter 8 using `do`. There are two functions. The main function `sort-iter` is similar to a mapping function, except instead of `cons`ing a function applied to the first of the list onto an answer, we call `insert-iter` to put the first element of the list in the proper position in the answer. This means we won't have to reverse the answer at the very end.

```
; Perform insertion sort on a-list based on compare-func.
(define (sort-iter compare-func a-list)
  (do ( (current-list a-list (rest current-list))
        (sorted-list '() (insert-iter (first current-list)
                           sorted-list compare-func)) )
    ((null? current-list) sorted-list)) )
```

The function `insert-iter` takes an element to add, a sorted list, and a comparison function, and returns a new sorted list with the element added. This function is somewhat like a mapping in that it sequences through the sorted list, and somewhat like a filter in that it must decide what to include in the answer (the element or the current list item). However, it has two exit conditions. If we satisfy the comparison function, we should return the list we have assembled (this time we have to reverse it) and the remaining elements we haven't looked at yet. The other exit condition is reaching an empty list. In this case we simply return the reverse of the answer:

```
; Insert element in sorted order into sorted-list based on
; compare-func.
(define (insert-iter element sorted-list compare-func)
  (do ( (sort-list sorted-list (rest sort-list))
        (new-list '() (if (compare-func element (first sort-list))
                          (cons element new-list)
                          (cons (first sort-list) new-list))) )
    ((or (null? sort-list)
         (compare-func element (first sort-list)))
     (if (null? sort-list)
         (reverse new-list)
         (append (reverse new-list) sort-list)))) )
```

Let's test out these functions:

```
> (sort-iter < '(3 4 2 6 7 1))
()
```

Wow! We lost all the values. Before we look at the code, let's test `insert-iter` individually. Remember `insert-iter` expects a sorted list as an argument.

```
> (insert-iter 3 '(1 2 4 6 7) <)
(1 2 4 6 7)

> (insert-iter 3 '(4 6 7) <)
(4 6 7)

> (insert-iter 3 '(1 2) <)
(1 2)
```

This clarifies the bug. Regardless of where the element must be inserted (middle, start, or end of the sorted list), it is not added. Since we never add elements, we wind up with an empty list when we call `sort-iter`.

The code seems to add the element to the new list in the update value for new-list. However, what winds up happening is that before the update value sees that the element satisfies the comparison function, the exit action is satisfied. This is because the old values for sort-list and new-list are used in the variable binding section of the do, but the new values are used in the test. This is similar to a problem we ran into when writing sum-digits-iter.

To fix the bug we can add element as part of the exit action. We don't need the code that adds the element in the update value, so we can change that to unconditionally add the first item in the sorted list:

```
; Insert element in sorted order into sorted-list based on
; compare-func.
(define (insert-iter element sorted-list compare-func)
  (do ( (sort-list sorted-list (rest sort-list))
        (new-list '() (cons (first sort-list) new-list)) )
    ((or (null? sort-list)
         (compare-func element (first sort-list)))
     (if (null? sort-list)
         (reverse new-list)
         (append (reverse new-list) (list element) sort-list)))) )

> (insert-iter 3 '(1 2 4 6 7) <)
(1 2 3 4 6 7)

> (insert-iter 3 '(4 6 7) <)
(3 4 6 7)

> (insert-iter 3 '(1 2) <)
(1 2)
```

Two out of three of the cases worked. In the last case, we exit because we reach an empty list, and this case needs to add the element to the end of the new list as well. Here is the correct code:

```
; Insert element in sorted order into sorted-list based on
; compare-func.
(define (insert-iter element sorted-list compare-func)
  (do ( (sort-list sorted-list (rest sort-list))
        (new-list '() (cons (first sort-list) new-list)) )
    ((or (null? sort-list)
         (compare-func element (first sort-list)))
     (if (null? sort-list)
         (reverse (cons element new-list))
         (append (reverse new-list) (list element) sort-list)))) )

> (insert-iter 3 '(1 2) <)
(1 2 3)

> (sort-iter < '(3 4 2 6 7 1))
(1 2 3 4 6 7)
```

```
>  (sort-iter > '(3 4 2 6 7 1))
(7 6 4 3 2 1)
```

Not all functions with multiple exit cases are as burdensome to write as *Improvements with* do
`insert-iter`. In fact, most of the difficulties stemmed from the binding of variables after all update values are evaluated. Common LISP gets around this by using a variation of `do` called `do*`, in which the variables are bound immediately as with `let*`. Scheme does not have this function, unfortunately.

Another way to simplify writing these problematic `do` loops is using the function `call-with-current-continuation`, which provides an alternate way to exit from within a `do` loop. This function is presented in Chapter 11 along with examples of how it can be used with `do` loops.

10.5.5   Exercises

10.9   Write your own version of the function `find-if` using an iterative function.

10.10 Write your own version of the function `position` using an iterative function.

10.11 Write your own version of the function `member` using an iterative function.

10.12 Write your own version of the function `assoc` using an iterative function.

10.6   Nested Loops Using Iteration

Nested loops can be written using iterative functions. Each loop is carried out by *Nested loops to* an iterative function. As an example, imagine a data structure that represents the *search within a* structure of a particular company. This company consists of a number of divisions. Each division is a collection of departments. Each department is a collection of employees. *company data structure*

The company is represented as a list of division lists. The first element of each division list is the division name. The remaining elements are departments within that division. Departments are lists where the first element is the department name and the rest of the list is employee names. Below is an instance of such a company:

```
((far-east (engineering gino bill)
           (advertising bernice yoshiro kumi))
 (eastern  (health ximena)
           (technical eric seth))
 (western  (engineering brian ephram robert)
           (investment stephen))
 (european (management maria)
           (sales hans)
           (advertising jutta jurgen tiziana)))
```
Sample company database

To determine the division and department of a particular person in a company, a function `find-employee` can be written that takes a company list and a person. If that person exists in the company list, a list of their division and department is returned. If not, `#f` is returned. The outer loop will sequence through the divisions, and the inner loop will sequence through the employees within a division.

We'll need two exit cases in both the outer and the inner loops. The inner loop should return `#f` if no match is found, or return the department name if a match is found. The outer loop should test the value returned by the inner loop and return the division and department names if the employee was found in the inner loop, or return `#f` if all divisions have been tested and no match was found. If neither of these conditions is true, the outer loop should continue.

Complications in saving the inner loop value

Since the inner `do` loop value will be used twice in the outer `do` loop—once in the test and once in the exit-action to return the department name—we should save the inner loop value in a `let` variable. Unfortunately there is no good way to do this, as the value of the `let` variable must be computed within the outer `do` loop but used in different locations there. We can't compute the inner loop's value at the start of the outer loop; however, we can save the inner loop's value in a `do` variable in the outer loop. Here again we'll need two different calls to the inner loop—one for the initial value and another for the update value. We'll be better off implementing the inner loop as a separate function.

Helper functions to access the division name and department lists from a division, and the department name and employee list from a department, will make the code more readable and easier to update if the database structure changes.

```
; Return the name of division.
(define (division-name division)
  (first division) )

; Return the list of departments in division.
(define (department-list division)
  (rest division) )

; Return the name of dept.
(define (department-name dept)
  (first dept) )

; Return the list of employees in dept.
(define (employees dept)
  (rest dept) )
```

The rest of the code follows. First the outer loop:

```
; Return the division and department of person in company-list,
; #f if person is not in company-list.
(define (find-employee company-list person)
  (do ( (company company-list (rest company))
        (dept
          (find-dept (department-list (first company-list)) person)
          (find-dept (department-list (first company)) person)) )
     ((or (null? company) dept)
      (if (null? company)
          #f
          (list (division-name (first company))
                dept)))) )
```

And the inner loop:

```
; Return the department of person in dept-list, #f if person is not
; in dept-list.
(define (find-dept dept-list person)
  (do ( (dept dept-list (rest dept)) )
     ((or (null? dept)
          (member person (employees (first dept))))
      (if (null? dept)
          #f
          (department-name (first dept))))) )
```

Let's test these functions. Assume that the variable com is bound to the company data structure shown at the start of this example:

```
> (find-employee com 'bernice)
(far-east advertising)

> (find-employee com 'fred)
#f

> (find-dept (rest (third com)) 'stephen)
investment

> (find-employee com 'stephen)
(european investment)
```

The last result should be (western investment). find-dept appears to be working though. The only problem seems to be that the wrong division is returned. The problem is subtle: the value of the do variable company is used when find-dept is called and when division-name is called. However, company has different values for these different calls. When find-dept is called, company still has its old value. It does not take on the new value until all the update-values have been computed. Thus, we wind up looking for the employee in one division and returning the division name of the next division. This does not happen if the person is in the first division, because find-dept is called with company-list.

To fix this bug, we can return to our first approach of calling the inner loop in the test and the exit-action parts of the outer loop. Here is the new version:

```
; Return the division and department of person in company-list,
; #f if person is not in company-list.
(define (find-employee company-list person)
  (do ( (company company-list (rest company)) )
    ((or (null? company)
         (find-dept (department-list (first company)) person))
     (if (null? company)
         #f
         (list (division-name (first company))
               (find-dept (department-list (first company))
                  person)))) )
```

> *(find-employee com 'bernice)*
(far-east advertising)

> *(find-employee com 'fred)*
#f

> *(find-employee com 'stephen)*
(western investment)

> *(find-employee com 'hans)*
(european sales)

Now the code works.

10.6.1   Exercises

10.13 Write an iterative function that takes a company list of the above form and
      returns a list of the departments of the company.

10.14 Write an iterative version of the function sum-facts from Chapter 6. sum-
      facts takes an argument number and returns the sum of the factorials of
      one through number.

10.15 Here is an alternate fix to find-employee that requires a change to find-
      dept as well. It has a subtle bug. Fix it, making as few changes as possible.

```
(define (find-employee company-list person)
  (do ( (company company-list (rest company))
        (dept #f
              (find-dept (first company) person)) )
      ((or (null? company) dept)
       (if (null? company)
           #f
           dept))) )
```

```
(define (find-dept division person)
  (do ( (dept (department-list division) (rest dept)) )
    ((or (null? dept)
         (member person (employees (first dept))))
     (if (null? dept)
         #f
         (list (division-name division)
               (department-name (first dept)))))) )
```

10.7 Summary

- To repeat an action a number of times, use the following template:

```
(do ( (counter 1 (+ counter 1)) )
  ((> counter num-times) exit-actions)
  body)
```

body represents the action(s) to repeat. *numtimes* is the number of repetitions to take. *counter* increments from 1 to *numtimes* through the loop. *exit-actions* are the actions to take at the end of the loop.

- To repeat an action for every element of a list, use the following template:

```
(do ( (list-remaining a-list (rest list-remaining)) )
  ((null? list-remaining) exit-actions)
  body)
```

a-list is the list to sequence through. *list-remaining* is successive **rest**s of that list. *body* represents the action(s) to repeat. *exit-actions* are the actions to take at the end of the loop.

- To perform general iteration, use **do**:

```
(do ( (variable1  initial-value1  [ update-value1 ])
      (variable2  initial-value2  [ update-value2 ])
                         .
                         .
                         .
      (variableN  initial-valueN  [ update-valueN ])  )
  (test  exit-actions)
  body)
```

do sets variables like **let** does.

- Multiple exit cases can be handled by combining the exit cases in an **or** in the *test* of the **do** and then returning the proper value based on the specific condition that caused the exit. This is tested for in the *exit-actions* of the **do**.

ADVANCED USES OF FUNCTIONS

11.1 Writing Functions that Take a Variable Number of Arguments

There are three legal ways to specify parameters in a function definition. We have used the simplest method in which each parameter is given a unique name that matches directly with an argument when the function is called. These functions must be called with a fixed number of arguments. We can create functions that take a variable number of arguments. This is done by specifying one parameter after the function name and a period (making a function heading that looks like a dotted list). When the function is called, the arguments will be in a list that is bound to the single parameter. Here is an example of this method:

Writing functions that take zero or more arguments

```
; Return average of a variable amount of numbers.
(define (avg . nums)
  (if (null? nums)
      'no-average
      (/ (apply + nums) (length nums))) )

> (avg 3 4 5)
4

> (avg 1 2 3 4 5 6 7 8 9 10)
5.5

> (avg)
no-average
```

We can write functions that take some fixed arguments followed by a variable number of optional arguments. This is done by using a mix of the syntax from the method above and the standard syntax we have used to write functions. The required parameter names follow the function name in the header, then a period and a single parameter. The function must be called with at least enough

Writing functions with both fixed and optional arguments

arguments to match each fixed parameter. The final parameter is bound to a list of any additional arguments.

In the next example the function `elts` returns a list of selected elements from a list. It takes the list as a required argument and a variable number of element positions as optional arguments. It is an error to call `elts` with no arguments.

```
; Return list of elements specified by their positions.
(define (elts a-list . positions)
  (map (lambda (pos) (list-ref a-list pos)) positions) )

> (elts '(a b c d e f g) 0 2 4)
(a c e)

> (elts '(a b c d e f g))
()

> (elts)
Error: Too few arguments: (elts)
```

Defining functions with optional arguments using `lambda`

These two additional forms of **define** are not required as part of the Scheme language specification. That means that your implementation of Scheme may not support them. You can get around this by using the following variations of **lambda**, which are required in Scheme. We could specify the above two functions as follows:

```
(define avg
  (lambda nums
    (if (null? nums)
        'no-average
        (/ (apply + nums) (length nums))) ) )

(define elts
  (lambda (a-list . positions)
    (map (lambda (pos) (list-ref a-list pos) ) positions) ) )
```

11.2   Functions that Return Functions

First class objects

Functions are *first class objects*, meaning they can be used in expressions, stored in data structures, bound to variables, passed to functions, and returned from functions. In most programming languages functions are not first class objects, so it may seem that it is not important to give functions such an elevated status. However, there are some nice advantages to having functions as first class objects.

Functions as arguments

We have used functions as arguments in many cases. This allows us to write functions that can be used to perform a variety of tasks. For example, our insertion sort function from Chapter 8 is a big improvement over the original sort function we wrote in Chapter 6. By making the comparison function an argument, the same sort function can be used to sort objects of different types and to sort in increasing or decreasing order.

Allowing functions to return functions opens up more possibilities. In Chapter 16 the function `make-fuzzy-triangle` returns a function based on the arguments with which it is called. This function is created once and then used a number of times. The problem could have been solved without this approach, but it is easier to do this way.

Functions as return values

Let's look at a simple example of a function that returns another function:

```
; Return function encapsulating info about a person.
(define (person-info name birth-date income job)
  (lambda (request)
    (cond ((eq? request 'name) name)
          ((eq? request 'age) (- current-year (third birth-date)))
          ((eq? request 'year) (third birth-date))
          ((eq? request 'month) (first birth-date))
          ((eq? request 'day) (second birth-date))
          ((eq? request 'income) income)
          ((eq? request 'broke) (< income 1000))
          ((eq? request 'rich) (> income 100000))
          ((eq? request 'occupation) job)) ) )
```

The function `person-info` takes information about a person and returns a function that *encapsulates* that information. Encapsulation is maintaining local information within a function. This information is often called *local state* information. `person-info` encapsulates `name`, `birth-date`, `income`, and `job`. The return function has a single parameter, `request`. Let's use these functions:

Encapsulation

```
(define dilbert
  (person-info 'dilbert '(5 12 57) 45000 'programmer))

> (dilbert 'name)
dilbert

> (dilbert 'month)
5

> (dilbert 'rich)
#f
```

The first two examples do not offer much more than a simple data structure with selector functions would offer. The third example goes a bit beyond the simple access of information.

But what happens to `dilbert` if we create another person? Does `dilbert`'s information change? Let's see.

```
(define dogbert (person-info 'dogbert '(7 9 90) 0 'philosopher))

> (dogbert 'name)
dogbert

> (dilbert 'name)
dilbert
```

Dilbert's data remained intact. Each time `person-info` is called, it creates a new function with unique values. This information is maintained in what is

Closures

called a *lexical closure* (typically referred to as a closure). A closure is a function that contains additional information about the environment in which it was created. The environment in this case refers to variables and their bindings that affect the function. These variables are within the scope of the function that is created. Scope in Scheme is determined lexically according to the position in the code in which variables are defined. For example, when `dogbert` is defined by calling `person-info`, the function returned has access to the parameters `name`, `birth-date`, `income`, and `year`. These are maintained in an environment and are not accessible in any way other than through the closure once the function `person-info` finishes.

Extent of closures

A closure stays in existence (its extent) as long as there is some way to access it. In this example that is as long as the variables `dilbert` and `dogbert` are bound to the function, or any other variable or data structure that includes the closures exists. For example, we can create a clone for Dilbert named Studbert:

```
(define studbert dilbert)

> (studbert 'name)
dilbert
```

Studbert has access to Dilbert's values because Studbert is defined to be what Dilbert is. Even if we change `dilbert`'s binding, `studbert` maintain's the values.

```
(define dilbert 'programmer)

> (dilbert 'name)
Error: Operator is not a function: programmer

> (studbert 'name)
dilbert
```

Changing values in a closure

The values within closures can be changed. The following example illustrates this. Notice that the function returned takes one required argument and optional arguments after that:

```
; Return function encapsulating job information.
(define (job-info name income job)
  (lambda (request . value)
    (cond ((eq? request 'name) name)
          ((eq? request 'income) income)
          ((eq? request 'broke) (< income 1000))
          ((eq? request 'rich) (> income 100000))
          ((eq? request 'occupation) job)
          ((eq? request 'raise)
             (set! income (+ income (first value))))
          ((eq? request 'new-occupation)
             (set! job (first value)))) ) )

(define ratbert (job-info 'ratbert 1000 'pest))

> (ratbert 'income)
1000
```

```
>  (ratbert 'raise 100000)
??

>  (ratbert 'income)
101000

>  (ratbert 'rich)
#t
```

We have created a means of changing information stored within a closure. We can represent an entire company and give everyone a raise fairly easily using the function job-info:

```
(define larry (job-info 'larry 10000 'stooge))
(define moe (job-info 'moe 11000 'stooge))
(define curly (job-info 'curly 12000 'stooge))
(define emps (list larry moe curly))

>  (for-each (lambda (emp) (emp 'raise 500)) emps)
??

>  (map (lambda (emp) (emp 'income)) emps)
(10500 11500 12500)
```

The list emps is a list of employees (represented as closures) that can be sequenced through using **for-each** and **map**.

11.2.1 Exercises

11.1 Write a function last that has one required parameter a-list and an optional parameter number. If last is called with a-list alone, it returns the last element of a-list; otherwise, last returns a list of the last number elements of a-list.

11.2 Write a function ncons that takes a variable number of arguments and conses them together into a new list.

```
(ncons 'a 'b '(c d) '(e f))
```

is equivalent to

```
(cons 'a (cons 'b (cons '(c d) '(e f))))
```

11.3 Write a function make-power that takes a number *num* and returns a function that takes a single argument and raises it to the *num*th power. For example,

```
(make-power 3)
```

returns a function that cubes its argument. Show a single expression using make-power that computes 25 to the 6th power.

11.4 Write a new version of **accumulate** that does not take a list of elements to be accumulated, but instead takes them as separate arguments. For example,

```
(new-accum cons 'a 'b 'c)
```

should return the same value as

```
(accumulate cons '(a b c))
```

11.5   What does the following function do?

```
(define (weird func)
   (lambda args (list (apply func args)) ) )
```

What do the following expressions return?

```
((weird abs) 3)
((weird max) 3 4 5 6)
((weird accumulate) list '(3 4 5))
```

11.3   Object-Oriented Programming

Objects

Using closures we have created *objects* like those used in object-oriented programming. An object is a data structure that has data and programs associated with it. It is possible to retrieve the data in an object directly or to get information resulting from computations on the object's data.

Programming paradigms

Object-oriented programming (OOP) is a style or paradigm of programming. There are four major programming paradigms: imperative programming, functional programming, logic programming, and object-oriented programming. Languages like Pascal and C follow imperative programming. Scheme is based on functional programming. PROLOG uses logic programming that involves programming by creating facts, rules, and queries. Object-oriented programming languages include Smalltalk, C++, and Java. Look at each of these as a style of programming. Certain tasks may be easier using a particular style, but any style is general enough such that a program written in one style could be rewritten using another style.

Classes and instances

Objects are just one part of object-oriented programming. In addition there are *classes*, which specify the types of information that objects contain and the operations they can perform. A class is similar to a data type and an object is an *instance* of a class similar to a variable.[1] For example, we may have a class for cars (called auto) and then define some instances of cars, like my-car, your-car, and fast-car.

Instance and class variables

A class defines the information that the instances of the class have. This information is maintained in *instance variables* or *fields*. For example our auto class may have instance variables for the make and model of the car, the number of doors, and the color. *Class variables* represent information that is shared between

---

[1] This is different from what we are accustomed to in Scheme. Scheme does not specify types for its variables, as many other programming languages do. Types are associated with the values themselves.

all instances in a class. This may be a common, fixed piece of information, such as the number of wheels in all cars, or it may be a shared variable such as a counter of the number of cars, in which every time a new car is created the counter is increased.

Classes can be based on other classes. For example, our car class may be based on the class `vehicle`. The class `vehicle` is a *superclass* of `auto`, which is the *subclass*. There may be numerous subclasses of `vehicle` like `motorcycle` and `truck`. Instance variables in the superclass can be used in the subclasses. For example, we could put the instance variables for make, model, and color in the superclass `vehicle` and still access them from the `auto` subclass. A subclass *inherits* the instance variables of its superclass. This simplifies the creation of programs. We can still have instance variables for subclasses if needed. For example, `auto` and `truck` would still have the number-of-doors instance variable, but `motorcycle` wouldn't.

Superclasses, subclasses, and inheritance

Some object systems allow inheritance from more than one superclass. This is called *multiple inheritance*. It gives more flexibility but has more complications in handling situations where conflicts in methods may arise.

Multiple inheritance

Code can be part of objects and it is specified in the class definitions. Such code is called a *method*. For example, our `auto` class could have a method to keep track of miles per gallon. Imagine we had instance variables for the number of miles driven and the number of gallons purchased. A simple method could divide these and return miles per gallon. Methods are invoked by *message passing*. An object is sent a message that invokes a method. The selection of the method is called *dispatching*.

Methods and message passing

Object-oriented programming provides a convenient means for handling *polymorphic functions*—functions that take different types of arguments. The same message can be sent to different types of objects and handled by different methods that perform the proper actions based on the object class. This is one way of handling polymorphic functions. The programmer does not need to worry about the type of the object. She can focus on the messages to the object.

Polymorphism

The benefits of object-oriented programming are in the simplification of complex structures, especially those that are hierarchical in nature and in ease of reuse of code and code modifiability. The methods associated with objects are well defined and easy to use. Through message passing, you can focus on the actions you want performed and not on the details of how they must be done, which allows polymorphic functions to be used easily. If you ask for the color of a vehicle, you don't have to worry if it is a motorcycle or a truck. The language provides features to eliminate a great deal of the overhead.

Object-oriented programming plusses

There is cost associated with the creation of classes, instance variables, methods, and instances. So for small programs, this creation overhead might not be worthwhile. But for large programs it is a big plus. The widespread growth of C++ and the design of Java to be object-oriented are testimony to the advantages that object-oriented programming offers.

11.3.1   How to write in the object style

We will develop a simple example that illustrates some of the things that can be done using object-oriented programming. The creation of the classes and instances in these examples is more complex than you would normally encounter in an object-oriented programming language. This is because Scheme itself does not support objects. Therefore, we have to explicitly take all the steps required to produce classes, instances, methods, inheritance, and dispatching.

Macros

It is not possible to write code that handles the class and instance creation overhead to make an OOP system, as our examples will have. This is because some of the functions that must be created do not follow the normal evaluation rules. They would be passed arguments that are class and instance names and methods that should not be evaluated. Essentially we must create special forms. This can be done by either modifying the interpreter or using an implementation of Scheme that allows the creation of *macros*. Macros are similar to functions except instead of being evaluated, they are translated into equivalent function compositions and then evaluated. Macros can be used to define special forms that do not follow the normal evaluation rules. Without macros we would be unable to write class and instance creation special forms.

Creating code and evaluating it later

The above paragraph is not entirely true. We could write functions to create classes and instances and provide the OOP features we need. But the special information needed by these functions (i.e., instance variable names, methods, superclass names) would have to be quoted or part of quoted lists. Then we build the functions we need, adding all the overhead to support OOP and embedding the information we passed in (e.g., class and instance variable names). Finally, we `eval` this newly created function. Techniques like this are used in some of the later chapters where code is adjusted and then `eval`ed. It is much nicer to be able to use macros where you can more freely design the structure of the function calls and specify special evaluation rules.

Some implementations of Scheme have extensions that support OOP. For example, STK has extensions that support both objects and the graphics toolkit of Tcl/Tk, which provides support for creating graphical user interfaces (GUIs). If you are using a version of Scheme that supports objects, you should learn how to use the functions that are provided to create classes, instances, and methods. Then you can create an example similar to the one given below. You'll most likely find that your version is much shorter and easier to write.

The example we will build will illustrate some of the features of objects, in particular the use of class and instance variables, methods, and inheritance from a superclass. Let's look into these properties individually to see how they can be implemented.

Creating class definitions

To create a class definition, we can define a function that returns another function. The function returned is an instance of that class. So we are combining class definition with instance creation. Most OOP systems make these separate operations. This return function encapsulates the instance variables of the object. Here is an example:

```
; Create simple car class.
(define (auto make model)
  (lambda (req)
    (cond ((eq? req 'make) make)
          ((eq? req 'model) model)
          (else 'bad-request)) ) )
```

This defines a simple class for cars. The return value of `auto` is a function that is used as an instance of the `auto` class. There are two instance variables: `make` and `model`. Here is an example using this function:

Creating instances

```
(define fast (auto 'porsche 928))
(define small (auto 'plymouth 'arrow))
```

```
> (fast 'make)
porsche
```

```
> (small 'model)
arrow
```

The instances are functions and the messages sent as arguments to the functions retrieve instance variables or invoke methods. In some object systems the message names are the functions and their arguments are the objects. This fits in with the idea of viewing functions as action doers and objects as things acted upon, and works nicely with polymorphism especially when it extends over into built-in functions. For example, we could have a `display` method for the `auto` class. With our system we would have to invoke it as

Handling messages

```
(fast 'display)
```

With other object systems we would enter

```
(display fast)
```

Let's add methods to change instance variables. The method `paint` changes the instance variable `color` and the method `add` augments the instance variable `accessories`. These methods will take additional arguments, so we'll modify the return function to take additional, optional arguments:

Creating methods

```
; Create car class with modifiable instance variables.
(define (auto make model color accessories)
  (lambda (req . args)
    (cond ((eq? req 'make) make)
          ((eq? req 'model) model)
          ((eq? req 'color) color)
          ((eq? req 'paint) (set! color (first args)) color)
          ((eq? req 'accessories) accessories)
          ((eq? req 'add)
            (set! accessories (append args accessories))
            accessories)
          (else 'bad-request)) ) )
```

When we create a car, we will specify an initial color and accessory list:

```
(define fast (auto 'porsche 928 'red '(stereo fat-tires)))
(define small (auto 'plymouth 'arrow 'white '())) 
```

> *(fast 'color)*
red

> *(fast 'paint 'bright-red)*
bright-red

> *(fast 'color)*
bright-red

> *(small 'accessories)*
()

> *(small 'add 'radio 'clock 'alarm-system)*
(radio clock alarm-system)

Creating class variables

We can add a class variable to our initial auto class that is shared among all cars. To do this the variable will have to be defined outside of the return function but within the definition of the class so that it is not simply a global variable that can be affected by any part of the program. Putting a let variable between the class definition and the return function will solve this. The shared variable all-repair-cost keeps track of the total repair cost for all the cars.

Instance variables versus class variables

Another variable repaired is unique for each car, but is not a parameter to auto. It acts like an instance variable in that it is unique for each instance; however, it is not specified as an argument when the object is created. The repair method takes an item to be repaired and its cost. It will add the repaired item to the repaired instance variable and update the total cost in the all-repair-cost class variable. Notice the difference in the placement of the two lets:

```
; Create car class with class and instance variables.
(define (auto make model)
  (let ((all-repair-cost 0))
    (lambda (req . args)
      (let ((repaired '()))
        (cond ((eq? req 'make) make)
              ((eq? req 'model) model)
              ((eq? req 'cost) all-repair-cost)
              ((eq? req 'repair)
                (set! all-repair-cost
                  (+ (second args) all-repair-cost))
                (set! repaired (cons (first args) repaired))
                repaired)
              (else 'bad-request)))  ))  )

(define fast (auto 'porsche 928))
(define small (auto 'plymouth 'arrow))
```

> *(fast 'repair 'brakes 129)*
(brakes)

```
> (fast 'cost)
129

> (small 'repair 'fender 300)
(fender)

> (small 'cost)
300

> (fast 'cost)
129
```

Our shared variable isn't being shared. The problem is not with the placement of the `let` outside of the return function. Instead it is in the definition of the `auto` function before the `let`. Each time `auto` is called, it invokes the outer `let` expression which creates a new `all-repair-cost` variable. Each instance created calls `auto` and thus gets a unique `all-repair-cost` variable. To fix this, the `let` must be defined before the `auto` function.

Fixing bugs in our class and instance variables

We should test our second `let` variable, `repaired`, as well:

```
> (small 'repair 'hood 600)
(hood)

> (small 'cost)
900
```

The `repaired` instance variable did not maintain the previous repair, `fender`. Once again this `let` is in the wrong position in relation to the inner `lambda`. The variable `all-repair-cost` is keeping a proper running total for the individual cars. The inner `let` should be relocated to the position where the outer `let` is. Here is a new version of `auto` with both of these bugs hopefully fixed:

```
; Create car class with class and instance variables.
(define auto
  (let ((all-repair-cost 0))    ; class variable
    (lambda (make model)        ; auto function header
      (let ((repaired '()))     ; instance variable
        (lambda (req . args)    ; parameters for methods
          (cond ((eq? req 'make) make)
                ((eq? req 'model) model)
                ((eq? req 'cost) all-repair-cost)
                ((eq? req 'repair)
                  (set! all-repair-cost
                    (+ (second args) all-repair-cost))
                  (set! repaired (cons (first args) repaired))
                  repaired)
                (else 'bad-request)) )) ) )

(define fast (auto 'porsche 928))
(define small (auto 'plymouth 'arrow))
```

```
> (fast 'repair 'brakes 129)
(brakes)

> (fast 'cost)
129

> (small 'repair 'fender 300)
(fender)

> (small 'cost)
429

> (fast 'cost)
429

> (small 'repair 'hood 600)
(hood fender)

> (small 'cost)
1029
```

Creating inheritance

It works! The final object-oriented feature we'll include is inheritance. We will define a superclass to auto called vehicle. It will contain the make and model instance variables that auto had. The auto subclass will contain an instance variable for the number of doors the car has. The make and model information for a car will be inherited from the vehicle superclass. This is done by creating an instance of the superclass whenever an instance of auto is created. Any method requests that the instance of auto does not know about are sent to the superclass.

Passing methods to the superclass

In creating the instance of the superclass, certain arguments may be needed. These can be named explicitly as parameters in the subclass or by using a variable number of arguments. This latter solution makes for code that is easier to write and to modify. Notice how the parameter list of auto specifies its parameters and takes a variable number for the vehicle superclass. Also notice how the instance of vehicle is created and how it is invoked when the subclass cannot handle the request.

```
; Create vehicle superclass.
(define (vehicle make model)
  (lambda (req)
    (cond ((eq? req 'make) make)
          ((eq? req 'model) model)
          (else 'bad-request)) ) )

; Create car subclass.
(define (auto num-doors . args)
  (let ((parent (apply vehicle args)))    ; create vehicle instance
    (lambda (req . args)
      (cond ((eq? req 'num-doors) num-doors)
            (else    ; send message to parent
              (apply parent (cons req args)))) )) )
```

```
(define fast (auto 3 'porsche 928))
(define small (auto 2 'plymouth 'arrow))

> (fast 'make)
porsche

> (small 'model)
arrow

> (fast 'num-doors)
3
```

Now that we have explored some aspects used in object-oriented programming, we can put all the pieces together into a larger example. We will have a vehicle superclass with auto and motorcycle subclasses. These subclasses have instance variables unique to their classes. Most of the instance variables are in the vehicle class including the type of the vehicle, which is automatically passed to the vehicle function when the instance is created. This is done by simply cons-ing the appropriate type (car or motorcycle) onto the list of arguments applied to vehicle. An instance of vehicle can be created directly without going through a subclass. The van object is an example of that.

A large object-oriented example

Another feature that an object system may support is the ability to run some code when an instance is created. We model this to keep track of the total vehicle count. The variable num is used in vehicle to maintain this count. Each vehicle or subclass of vehicle can access the count using the method count. When a vehicle is created, num is incremented to count the new vehicle.

```
; Create vehicle superclass.
(define vehicle
  (let ((num 0))
    (lambda (type make model year color owner)
      (set! num (+ num 1))
      (lambda (req . args)
        (cond ((eq? req 'type) type)
              ((eq? req 'make) make)
              ((eq? req 'model) model)
              ((eq? req 'year) year)
              ((eq? req 'color) color)
              ((eq? req 'owner) owner)
              ((eq? req 'buy) (set! owner (car args)) owner)
              ((eq? req 'count) num)
              (else 'bad-request)) ) )) )

; Create car subclass.
(define (auto num-doors . args)
  (let ((parent (apply vehicle (cons 'car args))))
    (lambda (req . args)
      (cond ((eq? req 'num-doors) num-doors)
            (else (apply parent (cons req args))))) ) )
```

```
; Create motorcycle subclass.
(define motorcycle
  (let ((num-bikes 0))
    (lambda args
      (set! num-bikes (+ num-bikes 1))
      (let ((parent (apply vehicle (cons 'motorcycle args))))
        (lambda (req . args)
          (cond ((eq? req 'num-bikes) num-bikes)
                (else (apply parent (cons req args)))) )) )) )
```

Below are five instances of these classes that are all put into the list `all` so we can send messages to all the instances in a single mapping:

```
(define my-car (auto 4 'vw 'jetta 1984 'blue 'oliver))
(define her-car (auto 3 'mazda 323 1990 'blue 'myriam))
(define old-bike (motorcycle 'yamaha 'XS400 1988 'white 'oliver))
(define new-bike (motorcycle 'kawasaki 'KZ650 1996 'red 'gino))
(define van (vehicle 'utility 'nissan 'quest 1996 'silver 'hans))
(define all (list my-car her-car old-bike new-bike van))
```

```
> (map (lambda (veh) (veh 'make)) all)
(vw mazda yamaha kawasaki nissan)

> (map (lambda (veh) (veh 'count)) all)
(5 5 5 5 5)

> (map (lambda (veh) (veh 'type)) all)
(car car motorcycle motorcycle utility)

> (map (lambda (veh) (veh 'num-bikes)) all)
(bad-request bad-request 2 2 bad-request)

> (map (lambda (veh) (veh 'num-doors)) all)
(4 3 bad-request bad-request bad-request)

> (map (lambda (veh) (veh 'owner)) all)
(oliver myriam oliver gino hans)

> (new-bike 'buy 'alex)
alex

> (map (lambda (veh) (veh 'owner)) all)
(oliver myriam oliver alex hans)
```

Notice that the vehicle counts are the same for all instances, because the count is in a shared variable. The methods `num-bikes` and `num-doors` only work with the motorcycle and auto classes. For all other classes, `bad-request` is returned.

11.3.2   Exercises

11.6   Why is the name `auto` used to define the car class instead of `car`?

11.7 Extend the example above to calculate miles driven and gasoline used for each car. Provide methods to take mileage and gasoline amounts and keep them in running totals for each vehicle. Write another method to compute and return the miles per gallon. Then extend this to support shared variables for total miles driven and gas used by all the vehicles. Provide a method that returns the average mileage per gallon of all the vehicles.

11.8 Design the class structure for a library. For books keep track of their title, author, subject, publisher, page count, and publishing year. For periodicals store some general information about the magazine (title, subject, which years are in the collection) and specific information for each issue (article titles, authors, and subjects). How would you structure the classes to allow inheritance of information from superclasses?

11.9 Given the library class structure from the previous problem, add classes for newspapers and videos. Is this an easy extension or did you have to redesign parts of your structure?

11.10 Build the actual class and instance functions for the library described above, supporting books and periodicals only.

11.11 Create classes, instances, and methods to model a problem of your choosing. Try to use class and instance variables, methods that take multiple arguments, inheritance, and instance or class variables with values that can be updated.

11.4 Forcing Exits with `call-with-current-continuation`

Scheme provides a powerful function that can be used to leave a section of code and jump to a predefined area. This can be used to exit from deep within a composition of functions or within a recursive call or a `do` loop. Any remaining actions that were to be done are left forever. These bypassed actions are a *continuation*. The function that allows us to exit from a continuation is `call-with-current-continuation`. Before we talk about this complex and powerful function, let's look at continuations.

In Chapter 3 we looked at the evaluation of composed (one expression inside another) Scheme expressions. Before we apply the outermost function, we must evaluate its arguments. This sets up a continuation—an action that must be returned to. For example, when the interpreter begins to evaluate the first subexpression,

Continuations

```
(* new 4)
```

in the expression

```
(list (* new 4) old)
```

it makes a continuation to evaluate old and to list the two subexpressions. All actions in Scheme involve continuations, even simple top-level calls: once they are evaluated, the results are printed and the next command is read in. Continuations can be bypassed using call-with-current-continuation.

call-with-current-continuation allows you to exit from a continuation (typically a loop) and return a certain value. Leaving a continuation is done simply by calling a predefined exit function with a value that the prematurely exited continuation will return. Evaluation continues with the expression after call-with-current-continuation.

call-with-current-continuation takes a function of one argument. That argument names the exit function. The body of the function contains the expression(s) from which we wish to be able to exit.[2] call-with-current-continuation is best explained with examples.

The following two recursive functions print strings before and after making recursive calls. Both test their one argument. When the argument exceeds three, vanilla returns done. However, strawberry forces an exit by calling stop (the exit function set by call-with-current-continuation). See how this affects the remaining displays:

```
; Print messages during recursive descent and unwind.
(define (vanilla arg)
  (cond ((> arg 3) 'done)
        (else
          (display "before recursion")
          (newline)
          (vanilla (+ arg 1))
          (display "after recursion")
          (newline))) )

; Print messages during recursive descent only.
(define (strawberry arg)
  (call-with-current-continuation
    (lambda (stop)
      (define (inner-berry arg)
        (cond ((> arg 3) (stop 'done))
              (else
                (display "before recursion")
                (newline)
                (inner-berry (+ arg 1))
                (display "after recursion")
                (newline))) )
      (inner-berry arg))) )
```

---

2. We can exit from a wider range of continuations than those immediately defined in the body of the function argument to call-with-current-continuation. This will be covered in the upcoming examples.

```
> (vanilla 1)
before recursion
before recursion
before recursion
after recursion
after recursion
after recursion
??

> (strawberry 1)
before recursion
before recursion
before recursion
done

> (list (strawberry 1) 'already)
before recursion
before recursion
before recursion
(done already)
```

In `vanilla` three recursive calls are made. The final one, with `arg` equal to four, satisfies the exit condition and `done` is returned. However, this is not the final return value. The recursive call is followed by another **display** and **newline**. These must be done for each recursive call made. The final return value is the return value of the last expression in the `else` action—a call to **newline**. This value is unspecified in Scheme.

Regular recursion

In `strawberry` the exit function `stop` is called when the exit case of the recursion is reached. This means we immediately exit from the `call-with-current-continuation` and do not return to any of the recursive calls (the continuation) like `vanilla` did. `done` is returned as the value of the `call-with-current-continuation` and `strawberry`. The continuation does not include the call to `list` as the last function call shows. So the call to `list` is evaluated and the list `(done already)` is returned.

Exiting from a recursive descent

The exit function can be passed as an argument to other functions. This allows an exit to occur in a function that is not defined within the `call-with-current-continuation`. Look at the following variation of `strawberry`:

Passing exit functions as arguments

```
; Set up exit function and pass to nonberry.
(define (chocolate arg)
  (call-with-current-continuation
    (lambda (stop)
      (nonberry arg stop))) )
```

```
; Print messages during recursive descent only.
(define (nonberry arg exit-func)
  (cond ((> arg 3) (exit-func 'done))
        (else
          (display "before recursion")
          (newline)
          (nonberry (+ arg 1) exit-func)
          (display "after recursion")
          (newline))) )

> (chocolate 1)
before recursion
before recursion
before recursion
done
```

chocolate defines stop as an exit function and then calls nonberry with stop. When exit-func (which is bound to stop) is called in nonberry, it forces an immediate exit from the recursion, and done is returned. chocolate behaves just like strawberry.[3]

Saving the exit function in a global variable

The exit function can be saved in a global variable. The global variable must be set within the call-with-current-continuation. If we use a define, it can't be used outside of the call-with-current-continuation because it creates a variable local to the call-with-current-continuation. To create a global variable, we must first create the global variable using define on the top level outside the call-with-current-continuation, and then change its value inside the call-with-current-continuation using set!. This can be done as follows:

```
(define bail-out 'nothing-yet)

(call-with-current-continuation
  (lambda (stop)
    (set! bail-out stop)))
```

bail-out is now a global exit function. The call-with-current-continuation is defined at the top level, so calling bail-out causes evaluation to continue at the top-level read-eval-print loop. Here are some examples showing how bail-out can be used:

```
> (bail-out 2)
2

> (* 4 (+ 3 (bail-out 2) 5))
2

> (list 'before (bail-out 2) 'after)
2
```

[3.] But it tastes quite different.

> `(list (display "before ") (bail-out 2) (display "after "))`
`before 2`

The second and third examples show how an exit function nested within a function call causes the return value to be that of the exit function. The exit function supersedes the continuation in place. The last example shows that nested functions are called up to the point of the exit function, and then the exit function's value is returned. The string `before` gets displayed, but `after` doesn't because the second `display` (the continuation) does not get evaluated.

11.4.1   Using `call-with-current-continuation` to exit from a do loop

Many iterative functions using `do` can be simplified using `call-with-current-continuation`. This is especially true for `do` loops with multiple exit conditions (e.g., `all-numbers?-iter` and `insert` from Chapter 10).

Writing subset? *with* do *and* call-with-current-continuation

Below is a function that implements **subset?**. It has two exit conditions: testing for a nonmatch and testing for an empty list. We need to check each element of the first list and test if it occurs in the second list. If it doesn't, we needn't test any further and should exit from the testing loop and return #f. Our `do` will use a single exit case testing for an empty list. The `call-with-current-continuation` will set up an exit function for the second exit case—an element that does not occur in the second list.

```
; Return #t if all elements in set1 are also in set2, #f otherwise.
(define (subset?-iter set1 set2)
  (call-with-current-continuation
    (lambda (exit)
      (do ( (test-set set1 (rest test-set)) )
        ((null? test-set) #t)
          (if (not (member (first test-set) set2))
              (exit #f))))) )
```

The return value will be #f if (`first` test-set) is ever not a member of set2, or #t when test-set is empty—all elements have been checked.

Below is a trace of the call (subset?-iter '(2 3 4) '(4 2 5)):

test-set is bound to (2 3 4)

(`first` test-set) is in set2, (4 2 5), so we continue.

test-set is bound to (`rest` '(2 3 4)) or (3 4)

(`first` test-set) is not in set2. Thus exit is called, passing the value #f back to **call-with-current-continuation**, which it returns. Hence subset?-iter returns #f.

Finding employees using do *and* call-with-current-continuation

The function `find-employee` from Chapter 10 can be written using `call-with-current-continuation`. `call-with-current-continuation` sets up an exit function to jump out of either `do` loop. As before, the outer `do` loop sequences through the divisions of the company, and the inner `do` loop sequences through the departments of each division. If a match is found, the division and department of that employee is returned by calling `return`, the exit function, with a list of the division and department names. If none of the people in the departments matches `person`, then the inner `do` loop returns `no-match`. Since the inner `do` loop is the body of the outer `do`, the outer `do` continues with the next division. If the department lists in all divisions do not match `person`, `(null? company)` will be true and `#f` will be returned.

We are using the definitions of `department-list`, `employees`, `division-name`, and `department-name` from Chapter 10.

```
; Return the division and department of person in company-list,
; #f if person is not in company-list.
(define (find-employee company-list person)
  (call-with-current-continuation
    (lambda (return)
      (do ( (company company-list (rest company)) )
        ((null? company) #f)
        (do ( (dept (department-list (first company)) (rest dept)) )
          ((null? dept) 'no-match)
          (if (member person (employees (first dept)))
              (return (list (division-name (first company))
                            (department-name (first dept)))))))) ) )
```

Here are tests of this new version using the definition of `com` from Chapter 10:

```
> (find-employee com 'bernice)
(far-east advertising)

> (find-employee com 'fred)
#f

> (find-employee com 'stephen)
(western investment)

> (find-employee com 'hans)
(european sales)
```

11.4.2   Exercises

11.12 Does the following version of `strawberry` work like the previous one from page 276?

```
(define (strawberry arg)
  (call-with-current-continuation
    (lambda (stop)
      (cond ((> arg 3) (stop 'done))
            (else
              (display "before recursion")
              (newline)
              (strawberry (+ arg 1))
              (display "after recursion")
              (newline))))) )
```

11.13 Write a new version of `all-numbers?-iter` from Chapter 10 that uses `do` and `call-with-current-continuation`.

11.14 Write a new version of `insert` from Chapter 10 that uses `do` and `call-with-current-continuation`.

11.15 Write your own version of the function **any** using `do` and `call-with-current-continuation`.

11.16 Write your own version of the function **every** using `do` and `call-with-current-continuation`.

11.17 Write your own version of the function **find-if** using `do` and `call-with-current-continuation`.

11.18 Write your own version of the function **assoc** using `do` and `call-with-current-continuation`.

11.5 Summary

- To write a function that takes a variable number of arguments (zero or more), use one of the following templates:

```
(define (function . optional-args)
  body)
```

```
(define function
  (lambda optional-args
    body))
```

The arguments are stored in a list named *optional-args*.

- To write a function that takes some required and some optional arguments, use one of the following templates:

```
(define (function required-args . optional-args)
  body)
```

```
(define function
  (lambda (required-args . optional-args)
    body))
```

- Functions are first class objects. They can be used in expressions, stored in data structures, bound to variables, passed to functions, and returned from functions.
- A closure is a function that encapsulates information in existence when the function is created. Closures can be used to keep local state information instead of using global variables.
- Object-oriented programming is a style of programming based on the use of objects that maintain data and code, and messages that send information or make requests of objects.
- Classes specify the type of information in an object. The individual objects are called instances. The information maintained in objects is called instance variables. Class variables hold information that is shared among all the instances of a particular class.
- Methods specify code associated with an object. They may be a function of some of the instance variables or change the values of these variables or even invoke other objects sending them messages.
- Classes can be based on other classes through inheritance. A subclass inherits the instance variables and methods of its superclass. Multiple inheritance is the use of instance variables and methods from more than one superclass.
- Object-oriented programming languages provide support to facilitate the creation of classes, instances, and methods.
- `call-with-current-continuation` is used to create a function that when called returns to the continuation where it was defined. A continuation represents the actions that must be returned to or continued in a composition of functions, recursive call, or `do` loop.
- The exit function created by `call-with-current-continuation` can be used within the body of the `call-with-current-continuation`, or passed as an argument to another function, or bound to a global variable to create a global exit function.
- `call-with-current-continuation` can be used to allow early exits from iterative functions. This is perhaps the simplest way to deal with multiple exit cases when using iterative functions.

11.6   Additional Reading

Booch, G. (1994). *Object-Oriented Analysis and Design with Applications*, Second edition, Benjamin Cummings, Redwood City, CA.

Budd, T. (1997). *An Introduction to Object-Oriented Programming*, Second edition, Addison-Wesley, Reading, MA.

Keene, S.E. (1989). *Object-Oriented Programming in Common LISP: A Programmer's Guide to CLOS*, Addison-Wesley, Reading, MA.

Kiczales, G., Des Rivieres, J., and Bobrow, D.G. (1991). *The Art of the Metaobject Protocol*, MIT Press, Cambridge, MA.

Taylor, D.A. (1990). *Object-Oriented Technology: A Manager's Guide*, Addison-Wesley, Reading, MA.

Wilkinson, N.M. (1995). *Using CRC Cards: An Informal Approach to Object-Oriented Development* SIGS Books, New York, NY.

Winblad, A.L., Edwards, S.D., and King, D.R. (1990). *Object-Oriented Software*, Addison-Wesley, Reading, MA.

CHAPTER 12

DATABASE MANAGEMENT SYSTEMS

12.1 Database Systems

A *database* is a collection of information, such as facts about countries, statistics on demographics, a store's inventory, and phone lists. A database system allows one to access, insert, delete, and modify information stored within a computer system. The term computer system is used as opposed to computer because external memory may be needed. Database systems often require large amounts of memory that greatly exceed the storage capacities of the computer's main memory. The *database management system* (DBMS) performs operations on the information stored within a database. The DBMS is a program that contains a *query language* that allows database updates and retrievals. A DBMS can be viewed as a layer or abstraction built upon the computer system. The diagram below shows the pieces of a database system:

Databases and database systems

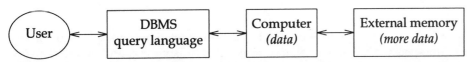

There are many ways in which database systems organize data. A table is one way, as the following example of American beers illustrates. We'll refer to this table as `brew`.

`brew` *relation*

name	type	rating	brewery
Blue Whale	ale	9	Oakland
A.V. Oatmeal	stout	10	Boonville
Sierra Nevada	ale	9	Chico
Big Foot	barley-wine	10	Chico
Liberty	ale	9	San Francisco
Augsburger	lager	4	Milwaukee
Pabst	lager	1	Milwaukee
Schlitz	malt-liquor	2	Milwaukee

Relations, tuples, and attributes

Tables, like the one above, are the primary data structure in *relational database systems*. Tables are called *relations* and rows in a relation are *tuples*. For example,

Liberty   ale   9   San Francisco

is a tuple. The columns in a relation are called *attributes*. Each tuple has information about one member of the relation and each attribute describes one particular aspect of that tuple (e.g., name or rating).

Query languages and SQL

A query language is similar to a programming language except it is tailored to the specific task of handling updates and accesses to data. It is possible to make rather sophisticated retrievals of information using a query language without having to know how the data is stored. The below query retrieves all the beers in the `brew` relation that are from Milwaukee or those that have a rating above nine. It is written in the query language SQL, an acronym for Structured Query Language. SQL is pronounced "sequel."

Sample SQL query

```
SELECT  brew.name
FROM    brew
WHERE   brew.brewery = 'Milwaukee'
        or brew.rating > 9;
```

The result would be

```
brew.name
A.V. Oatmeal
Big Foot
Augsburger
Pabst
Schiltz
```

`SELECT`, `FROM`, *and* `WHERE`

When a query is performed, the tuples in the relation are sequenced through and the specified attributes of those tuples that satisfy the condition are returned. The `SELECT` clause specifies which attributes are desired. Attribute names are formed by joining the relation name to the attribute name with a period making them one symbol. The `FROM` clause specifies the relations to examine. The `WHERE` clause gives the condition against which each tuple is tested.

`INSERT`

New data is added using the `INSERT` clause. To insert Lucky Lager into the database, the following command is used:

```
INSERT
INTO    brew
VALUES ('Lucky', 'lager', 1, 'Milwaukee');
```

More than one relation can be used. For example, a relation of establishments, `bar`, and the beers they serve can be created.

name	beer	location
Pacific Coast	Blue Whale	Oakland
Pacific Coast	A.V. Oatmeal	Oakland
Pacific Coast	Sierra Nevada	Oakland
Brickskeller	Sierra Nevada	Wash. D.C.
Brickskeller	Big Foot	Wash. D.C.
Brickskeller	Liberty	Wash. D.C.
Brickskeller	Augsburger	Wash. D.C.
Brickskeller	Pabst	Wash. D.C.
Bent Elbow	Pabst	Terre Haute
Bent Elbow	Schlitz	Terre Haute

`bar` relation

With the new relation, queries can be made such as the following which finds all bars that serve local beers and lists the names of those locally brewed beers.

Queries with two relations

```
SELECT bar.name, bar.location, brew.name
FROM    bar, brew
WHERE   bar.location = brew.brewery;
```

The name and location attributes of the `bar` relation and the name attribute from the `brew` relation are returned.

```
bar.name         bar.location    brew.name
Pacific Coast    Oakland         Blue Whale
```

Notice that the FROM clause specifies both the `bar` and `brew` relations. These are combined in an operation called a *join*. A join appends each tuple in one relation with all the tuples in another relation. This is one type of join; there are other types which are discussed later in section 12.3, "Implementing a Relational Database in Scheme."

Join operation

Below are two queries that find all the bars that serve beers with a rating of seven or more:

```
SELECT bar.name
FROM    bar, brew
WHERE   bar.beer = brew.name
        and brew.rating >= 7;
```

or

```
SELECT bar.name
FROM    bar
WHERE   bar.beer IN
        (SELECT brew.name
         FROM    brew
         WHERE   brew.rating >= 7);
```

The result from either query is

```
bar.name
Pacific Coast
Brickskeller
```

The first example searches through the tuples in the join of the `bar` and `brew` relations. For each tuple, if the beer attribute in the `bar` relation matches the name attribute in the `brew` relation and the beer has a rating of seven or more, the tuple is eliminated.

Nested queries

The second example is a nested selection. Since selections return relations, they can be used as input to other selections. In this case the inner SELECT

```
(SELECT  brew.name
 FROM    brew
 WHERE   brew.rating >= 7);
```

searches through the `brew` relation and returns a relation of beer names that have ratings of seven or more. This relation is

```
brew.name
Blue Whale
A.V. Oatmeal
Sierra Nevada
Big Foot
Liberty
```

Next the outer SELECT

```
SELECT bar.name
FROM    bar
WHERE   bar.beer IN
    inner SELECT
```

searches through the `bar` relation and returns the names of bars that match beers from the inner selection relation, namely those with ratings of seven or more.

```
bar.name
Pacific Coast
Brickskeller
```

Closure in SQL

Nested queries are possible because SELECTs return relations. In fact, all three of the relational operators we have seen, SELECT, FROM, and WHERE, return relations. When a function or operator returns a type that it accepts as input, it is *closed over that function or operation*.[1] Many Scheme functions such as `+`, `rest`, and `subseq` exhibit this very useful property. The following function calls illustrate how closed functions can be inputs to calls of the same function:

```
(+ (+ 3 4) 5)
```

```
(rest (rest (rest '(many numeric and list functions are closed))))
```

---

[1] This type of closure is an algebraic closure and should not be confused with the *lexical closure of functions* as discussed in Chapter 11.

Another possible structure for the above database of `bar` and `brew` relations is to combine them in one relation, as shown below:

Alternate data structure

name	beer	location	type	rating	brewery
Pacific Coast	Blue Whale	Oakland	ale	9	Oakland
Pacific Coast	A.V. Oatmeal	Oakland	stout	10	Boonville
Pacific Coast	Sierra Nevada	Oakland	ale	9	Chico
Brickskeller	Sierra Nevada	Wash. D.C.	ale	9	Chico
Brickskeller	Big Foot	Wash. D.C.	barley-wine	10	Chico
Brickskeller	Liberty	Wash. D.C.	ale	9	San Francisco
Brickskeller	Augsburger	Wash. D.C.	lager	4	Milwaukee
Brickskeller	Pabst	Wash. D.C.	lager	1	Milwaukee
Bent Elbow	Pabst	Terre Haute	lager	1	Milwaukee
Bent Elbow	Schlitz	Terre Haute	malt-liquor	2	Milwaukee

This may seem conceptually easier than having two separate relations. However, there is a problem with maintaining data values when tuples are deleted. For example, suppose that the Brickskeller stops serving Liberty ale and that tuple is deleted. All the information about Liberty ale would be lost. By having two relations, `bar` and `brew`, the tuple

Disadvantages to large relations

```
Brickskeller   Liberty   Wash. D.C.
```

can be deleted from the relation `bar` and the tuple maintaining information about Liberty ale is retained in the `brew` relation.

```
Liberty   ale   9   San Francisco
```

Thus, queries about Liberty ale can still be made. Much repetition is eliminated when two relations are used. For example, the information about Pabst and Sierra Nevada beers is maintained only once instead of twice.

In general, relations should be set up to reflect simple, complete chunks of information. Another possibility for our database would be to use three relations: one for beers, one for bars and the beers they have, and another for bars and their location. This would eliminate much of the redundancy that currently exists in the `bar` relation. This process of restructuring the form of the database to eliminate redundancy and dependencies is called *normalization*.

Use simple relations

Database theory specifies different degrees of normalization to produce databases of different *normal forms*. The simplest is called first normal form (1NF) and the most rigorous and best from a database design perspective is fifth normal form (5NF). For example, if we restructure the database as mentioned above and split the `bar` relation into two relations: one matching bars with locations and another matching bars to the beers they serve, we would convert the `bar` relation from second normal form to third normal form. Normal forms are covered in depth in C.J. Date's text which is referenced in "Additional Reading" at the end of this chapter.

Normalization and normal forms

12.1.1   Exercises

12.1   Write a SQL query to find the names and brewery locations of beers that are ales.

12.2   Write a SQL query to find the names and locations of bars that serve beers that are lagers with ratings above six.

12.3   Write the query below without using a nested SELECT.

```
SELECT beer.name, beer.rating
FROM   beer
WHERE  beer.name IN
    (SELECT bar.brew, bar.location
     FROM   bar
     WHERE  bar.location = 'Oakland');
```

12.2   Historical Background

Goals of early database systems

Early databases focused on business applications such as banking, record keeping, and reservation systems. These early systems had four major goals:

Efficiency: Fast access and modifications to large amounts of data
Resilience: Survive hardware crashes and software errors
Access control: Simultaneous multiuser access
Persistence: Ensure data exists for long periods without the program running

12.2.1   First generation: Hierarchical and network database systems

Hierarchical database systems and records

The first generation of database systems were hierarchical and network systems. A *hierarchical system* is set up as a collection of trees. Each tree represents an implicit relationship between the parent and its zero or more children. Data is maintained in structures called *records*. The parent is a certain *record type* (holds certain values) and the children are of potentially different types. For example, to represent information about companies, the parent record type might contain information about a company like the name of the company and when it was established. A child type below the company root might represent the different departments within the company where each member holds the department name, working budget, person in charge, etc. Below this department record type there could be different children record types. One child type could hold information about the employees of that department with such facts as the names, dates hired, employee identification numbers, salary, and so on. Another child type might contain information about the products of the department. A picture of this follows:

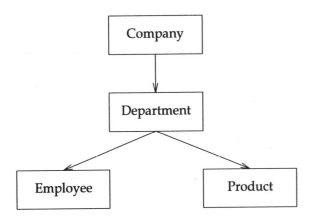

These boxes represent the different record types in the database. The root box, Company, would contain information about a single company. The Department box would be relaced by a number of records containing information about the different departments of the company. Below each department box would be any number of employee and product records, each containing information about employees and products within that department. It is not necessary to specify explicitly which department an employee works in; that fact is implicit from the tree structure of the database.

We would run into problems if we tried to represent our beer/bars relationship as a hierarchical system. We cannot set up a relationship with a hierarchical system in which bars are children of beers (i.e., a beer is available from a number of different bars) and beers are children of bars (a bar serves a number of beers). This will be further explored below.

Limitations of hierarchical systems

In a *network system*, a child can have more than one parent. This is the distinguishing feature between hierarchical and network systems. And this makes the network system more flexible than the hierarchical system. Network databases comprise *records* and *sets*. Records maintain the information about individual items in the database. They are similar to tuples within a relational database. Sets are ordered collections of records. Each set has an owner and various members. In considering our example database of bars and beers, we can imagine having a set of beers for each bar representing the beers that each bar carries. This is a *1 to N* relationship, in which there is one *owner* (a bar) and many *members* (the beers). For such relationships, network systems provide a natural model. Sets are represented as an ordered sequence of records starting at the owner, going through all the members, and ending back at the owner. A picture of such a relation follows. The owner is the bar Brickskeller and the members are the beers that the Brickskeller sells.

Network database systems and sets

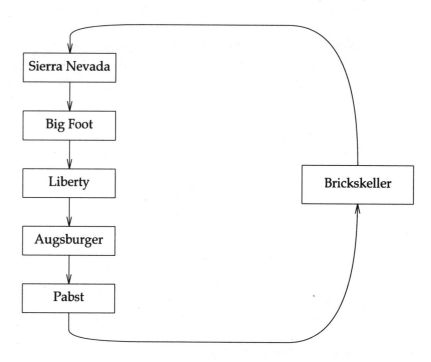

Limitations of network systems

A complication arises if different owners share the same members in the same set type. This would happen in our beer/bar database with the beers Pabst and Sierra Nevada, which are each served in more than one bar. The problem is that multiple paths are needed and there are ambiguities as to which path to follow when sequencing through the set. Such a situation is called an *N to M* relationship (N owners and M members). The following diagram illustrates this more complex database.

The problem with this next database becomes clear when you try to follow a path (see page 293). For example, starting at the Bent Elbow an arrow goes up and left to Pabst. However, two arrows leave Pabst, one to Schlitz, and another to the Brickskeller.

Dummy records

There is a way to get around this ambiguity. Another record type is needed (sometimes called a *dummy record*). Each dummy record represents a beer available at a particular bar. In our database there are eight different beers, two of which are served in different bars; thus there are ten unique beer/bar combinations. This means there will be ten instances of this new dummy record type.

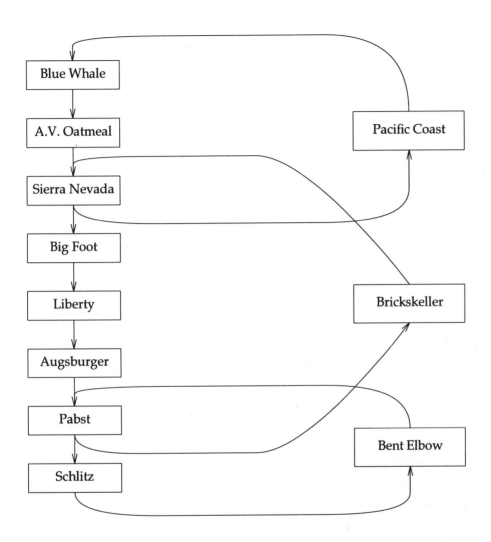

This new record will be called `bar-beers`; it will have two parents, the `bar` and `brew` records. This is not allowed in a hierarchical system where each record can have only one parent. This gives network systems an advantage. Below is a diagram of the record structure for this new database:

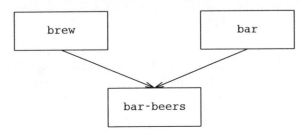

Below is the diagram of this new structure with the actual record values. The empty small boxes are records of the type `bar-beers`. The solid arrows to/from the top and bottom of the boxes connect members of the `bar` set. The dashed arrows to/from the sides of the boxes connect members of the `beer` set.

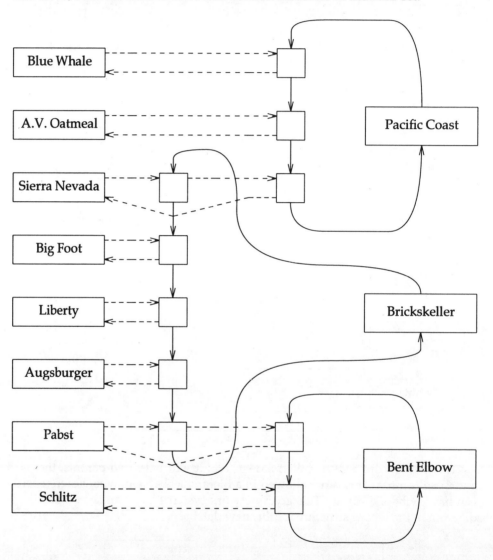

Writing queries in network systems

To make queries in a network system, we can write programs that sequence through sets until the desired information is obtained. The current set and record provide a frame of reference for operations. Certain commands are provided such as the following:

command	action
MOVE	establishes the field name of a record for searches
FIND	finds a record in a set according to the field name established with a MOVE command
FIND-NEXT	go to the next member of the current set
FIND-OWNER	go to the owner (record) of the current set
INSERT	add a new record in the current set
DELETE	delete the current record from the current set
MODIFY	change the contents of the current record
CONNECT	connect the current record to the current set
DISCONNECT	disconnect the current record from the current set

As an example, we'll try to find the beers sold at the Brickskeller that have ratings above seven. To do so we need to sequence through all the beers in the Brickskeller's beer set. This set comprises five bar-beer records that each connect to a beer record containing the rating information we must check. FIND-NEXT is used to sequence through the set. When the end of the set is reached (the owner is reached), FIND-NEXT returns *fail*. Here are the instructions for this query:

```
MOVE "Brickskeller" to name in bar
FIND bar
Loop: FIND-NEXT in bar-beers
      if fail
         exit
      FIND-OWNER in beer
      if rating in beer > 7
         PRINT name in bar
      GOTO Loop
```

The MOVE command specifies that we are interested in the record with the name "Brickskeller." The FIND finds the Brickskeller record in the bar set. Loop specifies a location (*label*) in the program that we can come back to with a GOTO. The FIND-NEXT finds the next record in the bar-beers set. The first time it is called it finds the first record in that set. After the last record has been found, FIND-NEXT returns *fail*. The if statement checks for *fail* and exits from the query if all records have been searched. If there are more records to search, the FIND-OWNER is performed, which finds the record in the beer set that corresponds to the current record in the bar-beers set. If the rating of this record is greater than seven, the name is printed. Next we go back to the statement at the Loop label and continue searching with the next record in the bar-beers set.

Queries are written in an algorithmic fashion in which you must specify how the database is traversed. Therefore you must know how the data is structured, in particular which sets connect to which records.

Relationships between queries and data structures

Setting up the structure of such a database is a difficult task, and it involves having knowledge of how the database will be used to allow queries to be easily and optimally made. If a database is changed, the queries that access the data usually must be changed. This is a major difficulty with network systems.

12.2.2   Second generation: Relational database systems

The second generation of database systems uses the relational approach that we saw in the beginning of this chapter. The relational viewpoint to database systems was proposed as a simplification to network database systems. Rather than view the database as an interconnected collection of sets, the relational view is that a database is a collection of relations.

Separating storage details from the data structure

In relational database systems there are no storage details that are implicit in the structure of the database, as with network databases. All information is made explicitly in the relations. This often requires more effort in entering the data initially, but it doesn't require that queries be rewritten if the data structure changes. The order of the tuples and attributes in any table is not important. How relations are stored internally is invisible to the user; in fact, all the internal storage details are hidden from the user. The result is a simpler system from the user's perspective. The price to be paid is that relational systems require more work in the DBMS, which is more complex. Relational systems tend to be slower as well.

12.2.3   Considerations database systems must address

Data independence

Data independence and *data integrity* are two key problems that all database systems must consider. Data independence involves designing database systems that can perform even when their structure changes via the addition or deletion of information in the database. This is a difficulty in network database systems since the form that a query takes depends on how the data is organized.

Data integrity

Data integrity concerns maintaining consistency in the database so that no items that should be the same are different. This can be solved by eliminating all redundancy in the database. Data integrity is difficult in relational database systems, as relations tend to have redundancy. Normalization techniques can be used to eliminate the redundancy.

12.3   Implementing a Relational Database in Scheme

To get a better understanding of database systems, we'll implement a mini-relational database system in Scheme. Before beginning such an endeavor, it is important to have a good understanding of the commands that must be implemented and the data structures upon which those commands act. In the case of a relational database, the primary data structure is the relation. A relation consists of tuples (rows) and attributes (columns). Before deciding how to represent relations, let's look at how they are used. The commands that we have seen are

```
SELECT
FROM
WHERE
```

The operations that are performed involve both tuples and attributes. SELECT extracts attributes from relations, as in

```
SELECT bar.name, bar.location
```

WHERE chooses certain tuples from relations, as in

```
WHERE  bar.name = "Pacific Coast"
```

Unconstrained join

FROM specifies the relations that will be used in the query. This is important when more than one relation is specified, as those relations must be combined in some fashion. This is done with what is termed a *join*. An unconstrained join (also called a *Cartesian product*) such as

```
SELECT bar.name, brew.name
FROM   bar, brew;
```

forms all combinations of bar and beer names. There are three bars and eight beers. Thus there are $3 \times 8 = 24$ bar/beer combinations altogether. The resulting relation would look like the following:

```
bar.name        brew.name
Pacific Coast   Blue Whale
Pacific Coast   A.V. Oatmeal
Pacific Coast   Sierra Nevada
Pacific Coast   Big Foot
Pacific Coast   Liberty
Pacific Coast   Augsburger
Pacific Coast   Pabst
Pacific Coast   Schlitz
Brickskeller    Blue Whale
Brickskeller    A.V. Oatmeal
Brickskeller    Sierra Nevada
Brickskeller    Big Foot
Brickskeller    Liberty
Brickskeller    Augsburger
Brickskeller    Pabst
Brickskeller    Schlitz
Bent Elbow      Blue Whale
Bent Elbow      A.V. Oatmeal
Bent Elbow      Sierra Nevada
Bent Elbow      Big Foot
Bent Elbow      Liberty
Bent Elbow      Augsburger
Bent Elbow      Pabst
Bent Elbow      Schlitz
```

This example is somewhat misleading, as it gives the impression that all three bars serve all eight beers, which is not the case. An accurate list is formed by explicitly requesting only those beers that are served in the bars, as in the following query:

```
SELECT bar.name, brew.name
FROM   bar, brew
WHERE  bar.beer = brew.name;
```

This will result in a *constrained join* (also called *theta join*), as the WHERE clause specifies a *join condition*. The resulting relation yields the bars and the beers that they serve:

```
bar.name          brew.name
Pacific Coast     Blue Whale
Pacific Coast     A.V. Oatmeal
Pacific Coast     Sierra Nevada
Brickskeller      Sierra Nevada
Brickskeller      Big Foot
Brickskeller      Liberty
Brickskeller      Augsburger
Brickskeller      Pabst
Bent Elbow        Pabst
Bent Elbow        Schlitz
```

This relation is a subset of the previous relation. The WHERE clause restricts the tuples of a relation according to some condition.

12.3.1 Deciding on a data structure

Now that the commands of the SQL subset we have been looking at have been examined, we can start thinking in terms of which Scheme structures would be most effective.

A SELECT is an operation based on attributes—keeping the desired ones. WHERE and FROM are based on tuples—keeping desired tuples and joining tuples. Also printing out relations involves printing a tuple per line. The emphasis is on tuple operations; therefore, a list of tuples will be a good choice for a data structure to represent relations. The attribute names can be placed in the first sublist of each relation. To represent the brew relation, we can use the following list:

```
(define brew '(
  (brew.name       brew.type     brew.rating  brew.brewery)
  (Blue_Whale      ale           9            Oakland)
  (A.V._Oatmeal    stout         10           Boonville)
  (Sierra_Nevada   ale           9            Chico)
  (Big_Foot        barley-wine   10           Chico)
  (Liberty         ale           9            San_Francisco)
  (Augsburger      lager         4            Milwaukee)
  (Pabst           lager         1            Milwaukee)
  (Schlitz         malt-liquor   2            Milwaukee)
))
```

Notice the use of underscores and dashes to tie words together as single symbols. The column indentation is just for our readability.

12.3.2 Implementing the WHERE clause

A WHERE clause is an operation that takes a list of tuples and returns a subset of that list based on some condition. This can be implemented using a `keep-if` with a function that returns true for any of the tuples that are desired and `#f` for those not wanted. To retrieve the ales from the `brew` relation, the following Scheme function call could be made:

```
(keep-if
  (lambda (beer-tuple) (eqv? (second beer-tuple) 'ale))
  brew)
```

A function that performs the operation of a WHERE clause needs a condition and a relation. The condition will have references to attributes such as `brew.name`. These references must be converted to the appropriate attribute values from within the tuple before the condition can be evaluated. This can be done in two ways. One way is to replace the attribute references in the condition with the actual attribute values for each tuple. A second way is to change the condition such that all attribute references are replaced with function calls that extract the correct attribute values when called with a tuple.

Replacing condition attributes with tuple values

The first approach is easier to write; however, it involves an extra step for each tuple. The second method only requires that the condition be changed. Given this new condition, it can be directly called with each tuple to decide if the tuple should remain. In the interest of simplicity, let's try the first approach. The second method will be left as an exercise.

The function `convert` takes a condition and a tuple and returns a new condition with all attribute references replaced with the appropriate tuple values. `convert` is called with each tuple in the relation. The converted condition is then evaluated to determine if that particular tuple should be part of the new relationship or not. As an example, consider the following condition and tuple:

original condition:	`(and (> brew.rating 7) (equal? brew.type 'ale))`
tuple:	`(Liberty ale 9 San_Francisco)`
attribute names:	`(brew.name brew.type brew.rating brew.brewery)`
converted condition:	`(and (> 9 7) (equal? 'ale 'ale))`

The `convert` function needs the condition, the current tuple being examined, and the list of attribute names for that tuple. `convert` sequences through the condition and replaces references to attributes with the actual values from the current tuple. Two additional functions will be helpful: a predicate function `attribute-name?`, that checks for attribute references, and a function `attribute-value`, that returns the appropriate values.

The function `attribute-name?` checks if the element being examined is an attribute—a member of the list of attribute names. The function follows:

Checking for attribute names

```
; Return true if element is an attribute in attrib-names.
(define (attribute-name? element attrib-names)
  (member element attrib-names) )
```

Getting attribute values

The function `attribute-value` gets the value from the tuple that corresponds to the attribute reference. `attribute-value` needs the attribute name list and the tuple being checked. The position of the attribute in the attribute name list is also the position of the actual value in the tuple. For example, given the attribute name list and tuple below,

attribute name list: `(brew.name   brew.type   brew.rating   brew.location)`
tuple: `(Liberty      ale         9             San_Francisco)`

`brew.rating` is the third element in the attribute name list. Thus its value is the third element in the tuple, 9. The code for `attribute-value` follows:

```
; Return the attribute named element within tuple given a list
; of attribute names, attrib-names.
(define (attribute-value element attrib-names tuple)
  (list-ref tuple (position element attrib-names)) )
```

Deep conversion of attributes

Now that the auxiliary functions `attribute-name?` and `attribute-value` have been defined, we can write `convert`. `convert` must look deep inside the condition to find attribute names. A simple mapping will not work, as only the top-level elements would be checked. Instead, either a `car-cdr` recursive function could be built or we could use a `map` that has a conditional clause that checks if the element being examined is a list. If so, we handle it recursively. The code to do this follows:

```
; Given condition, tuple, and attrib-names, a list of attributes,
; return a new condition with attributes replaced by actual values.
(define (convert condition tuple attrib-names)
  (map (lambda (element)
         (cond ((list? element)
                (convert element tuple attrib-names))
               ((attribute-name? element attrib-names)
                (attribute-value element attrib-names tuple))
               (else element)))
       condition) )
```

Let's test this function.

```
> (convert '(and (> brew.rating 7) (equal? brew.type 'ale))
           '(Pabst lager 1 Milwaukee)
           '(brew.name brew.type brew.rating brew.brewery))
(and (> 1 7) (equal? lager 'ale))
```

Evaluating the converted condition

Lastly, the function `where` can be written. `where` sequences through the tuples of the relation comparing them against the condition. For each tuple a new condition is formed based on the values in the tuple. This new condition is tested to determine if the tuple should remain. To test the condition, we need an extra level of evaluation. This is because the function `convert` returns a condition as a list (as the examples above illustrate). To evaluate that condition list, an `eval` is needed. The examples below will help illustrate this important point:

```
> (convert '(> brew.rating 7) '(Pabst lager 1 Milwaukee)
    '(brew.name brew.type brew.rating brew.brewery))
(> 1 7)

> (if (convert '(> brew.rating 7) '(Pabst lager 1 Milwaukee)
        '(brew.name brew.type brew.rating brew.brewery))
      'OK
      'not_OK)
OK

> (eval (convert '(> brew.rating 7) '(Pabst lager 1 Milwaukee)
        '(brew.name brew.type brew.rating brew.brewery)))
#f
```

The function where can be written using a call to keep-if. Only the tuples should be tested and not the attribute name list (the first sublist of the relation); thus, keep-if should be called with the rest of the relation. However, we do want to return a relation with an attribute name list; therefore we must cons the attribute name list onto the resulting relation from the keep-if.

Selector functions for the attribute name lists and the tuples of a relation will make our code more readable and easier to modify if the structure of relations is changed:

Selector functions

```
; Return the attribute names of a relation.
(define (attributes relation)
  (first relation) )

; return the list of tuples of a relation
(define (tuples relation)
  (rest relation) )
```

And finally, the function where:

```
; Return all the tuples in relation that satisfy condition.
(define (where condition relation)
  (cons
    (attributes relation)
    (keep-if
      (lambda (tuple)
        (eval (convert condition tuple (attributes relation))))
      (tuples relation))) )
```

Below are some tests of this function. The resulting relations have been shown one tuple per line with attributes lined up in columns. The real output would look different.

```
>  (where '(> brew.rating 7) brew)
(  (brew.name        brew.type       brew.rating   brew.brewery)
   (Blue_Whale       ale             9             Oakland)
   (A.V._Oatmeal     stout           10            Boonville)
   (Sierra_Nevada    ale             9             Chico)
   (Big_Foot         barley-wine     10            Chico)
   (Liberty          ale             9             San_Francisco) )

>  (where '(and (> brew.rating 7) (equal? brew.type 'ale)) brew)
Undefined variable: ale
```

What happened? It's easy to jump to conclusions and think that the Scheme interpreter made a mistake. After all, ale is quoted and shouldn't be treated as a variable. Let's examine the functions that where calls. First let's see what convert returns for the above condition and the first tuple in the brew relation.

```
>  (convert '(and (> brew.rating 7) (equal? brew.type 'ale))
      '(Blue_Whale ale 9 Oakland)
      '(brew.name brew.type brew.rating brew.brewery))
(and (> 9 7) (equal? ale 'ale))
```

If we try to eval this expression, we get an error because the first reference to ale is not quoted. To get around this problem, we could either change the function convert such that it inserts a call to quote before any replaced value, or we could quote all attribute names in conditions passed to where. The second approach is easier but less intuitive for the user, as attribute names are more like variables than constant symbols. So we'll opt for the first approach and modify convert as follows:

```
; Given condition, tuple, and attrib-names, a list of attributes,
; return a new condition with attributes replaced by actual values.
(define (convert condition tuple attrib-names)
  (map (lambda (element)
         (cond ((list? element)
                 (convert element tuple attrib-names))
               ((attribute-name? element attrib-names)
                 (list 'quote
                   (attribute-value element attrib-names tuple)))
               (else element)))
       condition) )
```

Here are tests of the convert and where functions:

```
>  (convert '(and (> brew.rating 7) (equal? brew.type 'ale))
      '(Blue_Whale ale 9 Oakland)
      '(brew.name brew.type brew.rating brew.brewery))
(and (> (quote 9) 7) (equal? (quote ale) 'ale))
```

```
>  (where '(and (> brew.rating 7) (equal? brew.type 'ale)) brew)
(  (brew.name       brew.type      brew.rating    brew.brewery)
   (Blue_Whale       ale            9              Oakland)
   (Sierra_Nevada    ale            9              Chico)
   (Liberty          ale            9              San_Francisco) )
```

12.3.3   Implementing the SELECT clause

A SELECT clause returns a relation with a subset of the attributes in the original relation. To get a better idea of this, imagine the query

```
SELECT brew.name, brew.rating
FROM   brew;
```

This would return the brew relation without the type and brewery attributes.

```
name            rating
Blue_Whale      9
A.V._Oatmeal    10
Sierra_Nevada   9
Big_Foot        10
Liberty         9
Augsburger      4
Pabst           1
Schlitz         2
```

Forming new tuples

For each tuple in the relation we must return a tuple with just the name and rating attribute values. To do this we can construct a new list from each tuple and then combine these lists to form a new relation. We can sequence through the list of desired attribute names using the attribute-value function to produce a list of attribute values from each tuple.

Another method is to construct tuples using access functions derived from the desired attribute list. For each desired attribute we create an access function. Then we apply these access functions to each tuple to form the list of attributes we want. This can be done with a sequence of maps: one sequences through the attribute list to form access functions; another sequences through the access functions and produces a new tuple; and the third sequences through all the tuples.

Another problem is converting attribute names into access functions, for example converting brew.name into **first** or the equivalent function. This second approach is more involved than the first approach. Both approaches must sequence through the entire relation and the list of desired attributes. The second approach must sequence through the access functions that are formed as well.

Let's make life easier and use the first approach. The desired attributes and the relation are passed directly to select. We can use the selector function attributes to get the attribute list from the relation.

To create the desired tuple from the original tuple, we can use a map that calls attribute-value for each attribute in the list of desired attributes. The code follows:

```
(map
  (lambda (attribute)
    (attribute-value attribute (attributes relation) tuple))
  desired-attributes)
```

`tuple` corresponds to the current tuple. All the tuples will have to undergo this step and be put together to make a new relation. To do this another `map` can be used. `(attributes relation)` is the list of attribute names in the relation. Rather than calling `attributes` many times in the `map`, the result can be saved in a `let` variable. The final function is

```
; Return a relation with only the attributes in desired-attributes.
(define (select desired-attributes relation)
  (let ( (attribute-list (attributes relation)) )
    (map
      (lambda (tuple)
        (map
          (lambda (attribute)
            (attribute-value attribute attribute-list tuple))
          desired-attributes))
      relation)) )
```

Creating a list of tuples

The outer `map` generates a new relation by creating new tuples from the original tuples in the original relation. This `map` sequences through all the sublists of the relation including the first, which is the attribute list.

Creating a single tuple

The inner `map` returns individual tuples by forming a list of attributes; one for each element in the desired attributes list. Each attribute is the result of calling `attribute-value` with the tuple.

Below is a sample call to `select`. Once again, the output is displayed one tuple per line for readability.

```
> (select '(brew.name brew.type) brew)
( (brew.name       brew.type)
  (Blue_Whale      ale)
  (A.V._Oatmeal    stout)
  (Sierra_Nevada   ale)
  (Big_Foot        barley-wine)
  (Liberty         ale)
  (Augsburger      lager)
  (Pabst           lager)
  (Schlitz         malt-liquor) )
```

12.3.4   Implementing the FROM clause

Implementing join

To handle the FROM clause, a join operation must be implemented. To join two relations, each tuple in the first relation is appended to every tuple in the second relation. To join three relations, first join the first two, then join that result to the third relation. This method can be generalized using `accumulate` to join any number of relations. Below is a simple example showing a join of two relations:

```
(join
  '((name    home)
    (pig1    straw)
    (pig2    twigs)
    (pig3    bricks))

  '((disaster    symptoms   effects)
    (earthquake  shaking    bricks)
    (fire        burning    twigs)
    (wolf        puffing    straw)))
```

The result should be the following relation:

```
( (name   home    disaster     symptoms   effects)
  (pig1   straw   earthquake   shaking    bricks)
  (pig1   straw   fire         burning    twigs)
  (pig1   straw   wolf         puffing    straw)
  (pig2   twigs   earthquake   shaking    bricks)
  (pig2   twigs   fire         burning    twigs)
  (pig2   twigs   wolf         puffing    straw)
  (pig3   bricks  earthquake   shaking    bricks)
  (pig3   bricks  fire         burning    twigs)
  (pig3   bricks  wolf         puffing    straw) )
```

The attribute names are appended and all combinations of the tuples from the two relations are made. This is an unconstrained join. Another possibility is to produce a constrained join by combining the join operation with the where operation and conditionally forming tuples. This is more complex and is left as an exercise.

We can use a nested loop to produce these tuples. The inner loop sequences through the tuples in the second relation, appending them onto the end of the current tuple in the first relation. The outer loop sequences through the tuples in the first relation. This nested loop can be built using nested **maps**:

Nested loop to make a join

```
; Return an unconstrained join of relation1 and relation2.
(define (join relation1 relation2)
  (map
    (lambda (tuple1)
      (map
        (lambda (tuple2)
          (append tuple1 tuple2))
        relation2))
    relation1) )
```

Given the previous sample call to `join`, this new function would produce the following list:

```
( ( (name home     disaster    symptoms   effects)
    (name home     earthquake  shaking    bricks)
    (name home     fire        burning    twigs)
    (name home     wolf        puffing    straw) )
  ( (pig1 straw    disaster    symptoms   effects)
    (pig1 straw    earthquake  shaking    bricks)
    (pig1 straw    fire        burning    twigs)
    (pig1 straw    wolf        puffing    straw) )
  ( (pig2 twigs    disaster    symptoms   effects)
    (pig2 twigs    earthquake  shaking    bricks)
    (pig2 twigs    fire        burning    twigs)
    (pig2 twigs    wolf        puffing    straw) )
  ( (pig3 bricks   disaster    symptoms   effects)
    (pig3 bricks   earthquake  shaking    bricks)
    (pig3 bricks   fire        burning    twigs)
    (pig3 bricks   wolf        puffing    straw) ) )
```

We have two problems. The attribute names are included too many times because we treated them like tuples instead of as a special case. Secondly, there is an extra level of nesting. Instead of getting one attribute name list and nine tuples, we got four lists of lists. This is an artifact of the way map works: namely if we call map with a list of four elements, we get a list of four elements back.

What we really want is to call the maps with lists of tuples without the attribute name sublist. Then we convert the list of lists of tuples into a flat list of tuples. This is done by flattening the list one level by appending the tuple lists together. Since there are many tuple lists, the append should be used in conjunction with apply or accumulate. The following example shows how this can work:

```
> (apply append
  '( (tuple1 tuple2 tuple3)
     (tupleA tupleB tupleC)
     (tupleX tupleY tupleZ) ))
(tuple1 tuple2 tuple3 tupleA tupleB tupleC tupleX tupleY tupleZ)
```

The attribute name list should be created outside of the map loops and consed to the new tuples. The resulting corrected join function follows:

```
; Return an unconstrained join of relation1 and relation2.
(define (join relation1 relation2)
  (cons
    (append (attributes relation1) (attributes relation2))
    (apply append
      (map
        (lambda (tuple1)
          (map
            (lambda (tuple2)
              (append tuple1 tuple2))
            (tuples relation2)))
        (tuples relation1)))) )
```

Since `join` takes two relations and returns a single relation, to perform multiple joins `accumulate` can be used. This then fully implements the FROM clause:

Multiple joins

```
; Return an unconstrained join on relations in relation-list.
(define (from relation-list)
  (accumulate join relation-list) )
```

To test the function `from`, assume that the following relations have been defined. The artists Rolling Stones and Grateful Dead have been abbreviated as `Stones` and `Dead`.

name	relation
flower	((flower color) (rose red) (violet blue))
song	((song artist) (Dandelion Stones) (Scarlet_Begonias Dead) (Sugar_Magnolias Dead))
album	((album artist) (Black_and_Blue Stones) (White_Album Beatles))

Below is a sample call to the function `from`:

```
> (from '(flower song album))
Error: Pair expected
```

This error message or something similar, depending on the implementation of Scheme that you are using, occurs when you try to perform an operation that requires a list on a nonlist object. `from` calls `accumulate`, which calls `join` with the first two elements of the list passed to `from`. These two elements are not evaluated, but are passed directly to `join`. This produces the call

```
(join 'flower 'song)
```

and results in an error because `flower` and `song` are symbols, not lists.

To fix this problem we could modify `join` so that it does an **eval** on its two arguments and uses those results throughout. A **let** form would be helpful to do this. A second solution would be to change `from` such that it **evals** the relations before calling `accumulate`. This can be done with a **map** on `relation-list`. A third solution would be to leave the functions as they are and call `from` as follows:

```
(from (list flower song album))
```

This forces the evaluation of the three relations because they are arguments to **list**.

Either solution is viable; however, the first involves the most work, and the third is a bit ugly from the user's perspective when making queries. Thus, we'll opt for the second choice—modifying the function `from`. The new code is

```
; Return an unconstrained join on relations in relation-list.
(define (from relation-list)
  (accumulate join (map eval relation-list)) )
```

Below is the same sample call to the new version of `from`. Note: to get each tuple to fit on a line, some of the attributes have been abbreviated.

```
> (from '(flower song album))
((flower    color    song          artist    album           artist)
 (rose      red      dandelion     stones    black_n_blue    stones)
 (rose      red      dandelion     stones    white_album     beatles)
 (rose      red      scarlet_beg   dead      black_n_blue    stones)
 (rose      red      scarlet_beg   dead      white_album     beatles)
 (rose      red      sugar_magno   dead      black_n_blue    stones)
 (rose      red      sugar_magno   dead      white_album     beatles)
 (violet    blue     dandelion     stones    black_n_blue    stones)
 (violet    blue     dandelion     stones    white_album     beatles)
 (violet    blue     scarlet_beg   dead      black_n_blue    stones)
 (violet    blue     scarlet_beg   dead      white_album     beatles)
 (violet    blue     sugar_magno   dead      black_n_blue    stones)
 (violet    blue     sugar_magno   dead      white_album     beatles))
```

12.3.5   Putting it all together

Translating SQL into Scheme

The final step is to put the pieces together and decide how queries can be made using these new functions. One approach would be to use the existing form of SQL queries and transform the comma-separated lists in SELECT and FROM clauses into lists of attribute and relation names, respectively. The conditions in WHERE clauses will have to be transformed into Scheme conditions. The order in which the operations are performed is important. The FROM clause defining any joins should be done first, then the WHERE clause which eliminates certain tuples from the joined relation. Finally the SELECT, which returns a subset of the attributes from the tuples desired, should be performed. Actually the WHERE and SELECT could be reversed, but due to the order in which they occur in SQL, it is easier to perform the SELECT last. Thus,

```
SELECT  bar.name, brew.rating
FROM    bar, brew
WHERE   bar.beer = brew.name
        and brew.rating > 7;
```

becomes

```
(select '(bar.name brew.rating)
  (where '(and (equal? bar.beer brew.name) (> brew.rating 7))
    (from '(bar brew))))
```

select takes two arguments, the list of desired attributes and the relation from where. where takes two arguments also, the condition to test tuples and the relation from the call to from. from has one argument, the list of relations to join.

Executing the query above produces the following:

```
> (select '(bar.name brew.rating)
     (where '(and (equal? bar.beer brew.name) (> brew.rating 7))
       (from '(bar brew))))
((bar.name        brew.rating)
 (pacific_coast   9)
 (pacific_coast   10)
 (pacific_coast   9)
 (brickskeller    9)
 (brickskeller    10)
 (brickskeller    9))
```

12.3.6 Some extras

Two additional functions would improve our simple relational database program. The first is to pretty print relations such that there is only one tuple per line and the attributes line up in columns. Another function would allow us to insert new tuples into existing relations (implementing the SQL INSERT clause).

Pretty printing relations

A print function is easy to implement using nested calls to **map**. One loop will sequence through the tuples and another will process the attributes within the tuples. To print strings out in a tabular fashion, we can write a function that determines the length of its argument. This can be done by converting symbols or numbers into strings using **symbol->string** or **number->string**, respectively. Then we can count the characters in that string using the function **string-length**. If this is longer than our fixed field width, say sixteen spaces, we just print the first sixteen characters of the string. Otherwise we print the string and enough extra blanks to position the cursor at the start of the next field.

Just as **subseq** returns part of a list, **substring** returns part of a string. **substring** takes a string and start and end position, as **subseq** does. Printing a number of blanks can be done using a loop of some sort, or more simply using the function **make-string**, which takes a number and a character and returns a string consisting of that many repetitions of that character. Use #\space to refer to the space character.

```
; Print out attribute and spaces to fill 16 characters.
(define (fixed-print attribute)
  (let ( (string
           (cond ((symbol? attribute) (symbol->string attribute))
                 ((number? attribute) (number->string attribute))
                 (else attribute))) )
    (cond ((< (string-length string) 16)
           (display string)
           (display
             (make-string (- 16 (string-length string)) #\space)))
          (else (display (substring string 0 16)))))) )
```

Let's try printing out three attributes. To combine multiple calls to fixed-print in one expression, list is used. We are interested in the values displayed before the return value—a list of undefined values.

```
> (list (fixed-print 'left-stuff)
        (fixed-print "more than 16 characters")
        (fixed-print 18))
left-stuff      more than 16 cha18              (?? ?? ??)
```

for-each versus map

Since we are printing out values using `fixed-print` and we don't care what value the function that sequences through the attributes or tuples returns, we can use the function `for-each` to sequence through these lists. `for-each` is identical to `map` in that it applies a function to elements of a list. The exceptions are that `for-each` guarantees that the elements in the list are applied in left to right order and that the return value is undefined. `for-each` is used when we only care about the side-effects that the function produces, such as setting or printing variables.

The complete print function is below:

```
; Print out relation formatted in columns 16 characters wide.
(define (print-relation relation)
  (for-each
    (lambda (tuple)
      (for-each fixed-print tuple)
      (newline))
    relation) )
```

Below is a sample call to `print-relation`:

```
> (print-relation (where '(< brew.rating 7) brew))
brew.name       brew.type       brew.rating     brew.brewery
augsburger      lager           4               milwaukee
pabst           lager           1               milwaukee
schlitz         malt-liquor     2               milwaukee
??
```

Inserting into relations

To implement the INSERT clause, we'll add the new tuple after the first element in the relation. Recall that the first element in a relation is the list of attribute names. To make this addition, it is better to destructively change the list. The reason for this is that we would like to refer to this new relation by name without having to get the result from a call to an insert function each time we want to use the relation.

The list can be changed using `define` or `set!`; however, it is necessary to change the list internally. A subtle mistake to avoid is the following oversimplification:

```
; Return relation with tuple added as the new first tuple.
(define (insert-tuple relation tuple)
  (define relation
    (cons (first relation)
      (cons tuple (rest relation)))) )
```

Local bindings

This results in changing the value of the parameter `relation` and does not affect the actual argument with which the function is called, as the following example illustrates:

```
> (define small-relation '((name favorite-color) (arthur blue)))
??

> (insert-tuple small-relation '(lancelot yellow))
??

> small-relation
((name favorite-color) (arthur blue))
```

To fix this problem the list has to be changed internally. This can be done
using `set-car!` or `set-cdr!`. These functions change the `first` or `rest` of a list.
For example,

<code>set-car! and set-cdr!</code>

```
> (define colors '(red yellow green))
??

> (set-car! colors 'black)
??

> colors
(black yellow green)

> (set-cdr! colors '(and blue))
??

> colors
(black and blue)
```

To add a new element between the first and second elements of a list use
`set-cdr!`. Instead of the original rest of the list, a new list is created comprising
the tuple we wish to add followed by the rest of the original list. The first of the
list is not changed. The correct code is

```
; Return relation with tuple added as the new first tuple.
(define (insert-tuple relation tuple)
   (set-cdr! relation
      (cons tuple (rest relation))) )
```

Below is a sample call to `insert-tuple`:

```
> flower
((flower color) (rose red) (violet blue))

> (insert-tuple flower '(poppies orange))
??

> flower
((flower color) (poppies orange) (rose red) (violet blue))
```

12.3.7 Exercises

12.4   Express the queries below in Scheme.

```
SELECT  brew.name
FROM    brew
WHERE   brew.brewery = 'Milwaukee'
        or brew.rating > 9;

SELECT  bar.name
FROM    bar
WHERE   bar.beer IN
        (SELECT brew.name
         FROM    brew
         WHERE   brew.rating >= 7) ;
```

12.5   The functions `where` and `select` call the function `attribute-value` to retrieve certain attributes from tuples. Another method discussed involved creating an access function that given a tuple returned the desired attribute. Use this method to write new versions of `where` and `select`. `where` will create a general condition that can be used for each tuple rather than converting the condition for each tuple. The idea is to replace attribute names in the original condition with functions and then test each tuple against this general condition. `select` will create access functions for each requested attribute. Think about how and when these access functions are to be evaluated.

12.6   The function `select` can use the idea of removing unwanted attributes from tuples instead of building up new tuples based on the desired attributes. It will be helpful to have a means of finding the position of attributes and having a function, *remove-nth*, that takes a number, *num*, and a list and removes the *num*th element from that list. Write the function *remove-nth* and the new `select` function.

12.7   The function `join` forms the Cartesian product of the two relations it takes as arguments. This creates very large relations especially when many relations are joined together. Write a new version of `join` that is a merger with the `where` function. This new function takes the condition from the `where` function call. Only those tuples that satisfy this condition are appended to the new relation. This is called a *theta-join*. The tricky part is deciding how to deal with attribute names that are not in the two relations that are being joined, but refer to other relations. This is often the case when more than two relations are joined.

12.8   The function below takes a relation and a tuple. Explain what it does.

```
(define (unknown relation tuple)
  (set-cdr! (subseq relation (- (length relation) 1))
    (list tuple)) )
```

12.9 Write a function `delete-attrib` that takes a relation, an attribute name, *name*, and an attribute value, *value*. The function should destructively change the relation such that all tuples are removed whose *name* attribute is *value*. For example, given the original `flower` relation of roses and violets, the call

```
(delete-attrib flower 'color 'red)
```

should change the relation `flower` to be

```
((flower color)
 (violet blue))
```

12.10 Write a function `thin` that takes a relation and an attribute name and returns a new relation such that the attribute specified is removed from all tuples. For example, given the original `flower` relation of roses and violets, the call

```
(thin flower 'color)
```

should return the relation

```
((flower)
 (rose)
 (violet))
```

12.11 Write a function `fatten` that takes a relation and a list comprising an attribute name and values for that attribute for each tuple. The function should return a new relation such that it now includes the extra attribute for each tuple. For example, given the original `flower` relation of roses and violets, the call

```
(fatten flower '(rhyme hose file_it))
```

should return the relation

```
((flower color rhyme)
 (rose   red   hose)
 (violet blue  file_it))
```

12.12 SQL supports a number of aggregate functions that can be used to answer queries such as "what is the average rating of the ales in the `brew` relation?" Aggregates return single values and are implemented as part of the SELECT clause. An aggregate is followed by an attribute to indicate the value to which the aggregate function should be applied. MAX, MIN, SUM, AVG are four aggregate functions that return the maximum, minimum, sum, and average, respectively, of attribute values. The attribute should be a numeric value. For example, the SQL query to find the average rating of ales is

```
SELECT AVG (brew.rating)
FROM    brew
WHERE   brew.type = 'ale'
```

The return value would be 9.

Decide on a means of expressing this query in Scheme and modify the function `select` to support calls to the aggregate functions MAX, MIN, AVG, and SUM. Assume that only one aggregate function with one attribute is allowed in a SELECT clause. You will probably find it helpful to use the existing version of SELECT to get all the attributes desired, a vertical slice of the relation, and then apply the aggregate function to this list.

12.4   Future Trends

New database systems support more sophisticated types of data such as multimedia data like sound, images, video, and graphics. The applications of database systems will be enlarged to include CASE, Computer-Aided Software Engineering, CAD, Computer-Aided Design, CAM, Computer-Aided Manufacturing, graphics, and knowledge representation for artificial intelligence applications. Along with supporting these richer types of data, the query languages will have to be enhanced to allow queries to be made of this data.

Object-oriented database systems

The paradigms for future database systems are *object oriented* and *extended relational*. Object-oriented databases have DBMSs that are extensions of or use the ideas of object-oriented programming languages. This allows the data objects to have procedural attachments (functions) so that they can send and receive messages from one another. It allows inheritance that will let subtypes of objects inherit the properties of their parent types. Extended relational systems add extensions to existing DBMSs.

Another idea is to create PROLOG-like DBMSs based on logic programming. PROLOG supports operations that are similar to database searches. The idea is to extend PROLOG to incorporate other ideas that are important to database environments.

Intelligent databases

Work is being done to create "intelligent" databases in which certain data values have rules associated or built into them. These rules can provide constraints for the values of the data object, for example, a rule that will not allow an employee's salary to be negative or greater than a certain value. Rules can perform management tasks like print a message or update the prices of certain items if a tax amount increases.

Knowledge discovery in databases and data mining

Knowledge discovery in databases (KDD) is a new challenge for large database systems. KDD is the problem of finding associations, gaining insight, or making sense of very large databases that may not be structured. One method of doing this is called *data mining*. The challenges to this field are intelligently handling huge amounts of data that may have little or no structure and finding interesting structure or correlations in the data. These results are often implicit in the data and must be made explicit. Plus the data may not be exact and data mining techniques may have to handle imprecision.

12.5 Summary

- A database is a collection of information that is stored within a computer system.
- A database system comprises a user, software to access a database, a computer and external memory in which the data is stored, and the data itself.
- A database management system, DBMS, is software that accesses a database and provides a language to make queries to the database.
- A relation is a tabular data structure that maintains a collection of information about various objects. Rows in relations are called tuples and columns are attributes. Tuples hold information about a certain member of the database, for example, an employee. Attributes represent the individual values within that tuple, for example, the employee's age.
- Relational databases maintain all information explicitly in relations.
- Hierarchical databases consist of records that are arranged in trees with implicit relations between the parent record and the child records.
- Network databases are like hierarchical databases with the exception that a child record can have more than one parent record. Network databases are thought of as sets of records, where any record can belong to a number of sets. One to many (1 to N) relationships are easily created with network databases, but many to many (N to M) relationships are more difficult to build.
- SQL is a query language used in relational database systems. Queries are made by specifying the attributes desired in a SELECT clause, the relations to examine in a FROM clause, and the tuples in a WHERE clause. If more than one relation is specified, they are combined through a join operation in which all combinations of tuples are appended together.
- Future databases will support multimedia data types and support areas such as CAD, CAM, and CASE. These new systems will incorporate ideas from object-oriented programming.
- Knowledge discovery in databases and data mining techniques can be used to learn more about large, unstructured databases.

12.6 Additional Reading

Date, C.J. (1995). *An Introduction to Database Systems, Volume I, Sixth Edition,* Addison-Wesley, Reading, MA.

Ulman, J.D. (1988). *Principles of Database and Knowledge-Base Systems, Volume I,* Computer Science Press, Rockville, MD.

Ulman, J.D. (1989). *Principles of Database and Knowledge-Base Systems, Volume II: The New Technologies,* Computer Science Press, Rockville, MD.

Special Issue on Database Systems, *Communications of the ACM,* Oct. 1991, Volume 34, Number 10.

12.7   Code Listing

Below is the complete Scheme code for the simple relational database including the `bar` and `brew` relations from this chapter:

```scheme
(define brew '(
   (brew.name        brew.type      brew.rating  brew.brewery)
   (Blue_Whale       ale            9            Oakland)
   (A.V._Oatmeal     stout          10           Boonville)
   (Sierra_Nevada    ale            9            Chico)
   (Big_Foot         barley-wine    10           Chico)
   (Liberty          ale            9            San_Francisco)
   (Augsburger       lager          4            Milwaukee)
   (Pabst            lager          1            Milwaukee)
   (Schlitz          malt-liquor    2            Milwaukee)) )

(define bar '(
   (bar.name         bar.beer          bar.location)
   (Pacific_Coast    Blue_Whale        Oakland)
   (Pacific_Coast    A.V._Oatmeal      Oakland)
   (Pacific_Coast    Sierra_Nevada     Oakland)
   (Brickskeller     Sierra_Nevada     Wash.D.C.)
   (Brickskeller     Big_Foot          Wash.D.C.)
   (Brickskeller     Liberty           Wash.D.C.)
   (Brickskeller     Augsburger        Wash.D.C.)
   (Brickskeller     Pabst             Wash.D.C.)
   (Bent_Elbow       Pabst             Terre_Haute)
   (Bent_Elbow       Schlitz           Terre_Haute)) )

; Return true if element is an attribute in attrib-names.
(define (attribute-name? element attrib-names)
   (member element attrib-names) )

; Return the attribute named element within tuple given a list
; of attribute names, attrib-names.
(define (attribute-value element attrib-names tuple)
   (list-ref tuple (position element attrib-names)) )

; Return the attribute names of a relation.
(define (attributes relation)
   (first relation) )

; return the list of tuples of a relation
(define (tuples relation)
   (rest relation) )
```

```scheme
; Given condition, tuple, and attrib-names, a list of attributes,
; return a new condition with attributes replaced by actual values.
(define (convert condition tuple attrib-names)
  (map (lambda (element)
         (cond ((list? element)
                (convert element tuple attrib-names))
               ((attribute-name? element attrib-names)
                (list 'quote
                  (attribute-value element attrib-names tuple)))
               (else element)))
    condition) )

; Return all the tuples in relation that satisfy condition.
(define (where condition relation)
  (cons
    (attributes relation)
    (keep-if
      (lambda (tuple)
        (eval (convert condition tuple (attributes relation))))
      (tuples relation))) )

; Return a relation with only the attributes in desired-attributes.
(define (select desired-attributes relation)
  (let ( (attribute-list (attributes relation)) )
    (map
      (lambda (tuple)
        (map
          (lambda (attribute)
            (attribute-value attribute attribute-list tuple))
          desired-attributes))
      relation)) )

; Return an unconstrained join of relation1 and relation2.
(define (join relation1 relation2)
  (cons
    (append (attributes relation1) (attributes relation2))
    (apply append
      (map
        (lambda (tuple1)
          (map
            (lambda (tuple2)
              (append tuple1 tuple2))
            (tuples relation2)))
        (tuples relation1)))) )

; Return an unconstrained join on relations in relation-list.
(define (from relation-list)
  (accumulate join (map eval relation-list)) )
```

```scheme
; Print out attribute and spaces to fill 16 characters.
(define (fixed-print attribute)
  (let ( (string
            (cond ((symbol? attribute) (symbol->string attribute))
                  ((number? attribute) (number->string attribute))
                  (else attribute))) )
    (cond ((< (string-length string) 16)
              (display string)
              (display
                (make-string (- 16 (string-length string)) #\space)))
          (else (display (substring string 0 16)))))) )

; Print out relation formatted in columns 16 characters wide.
(define (print-relation relation)
  (for-each
    (lambda (tuple)
      (for-each fixed-print tuple)
      (newline))
    relation) )

; Return relation with tuple added as the new first tuple.
(define (insert-tuple relation tuple)
  (set-cdr! relation
    (cons tuple (rest relation))) )
```

CHAPTER *13*

COMPILERS AND INTERPRETERS

13.1 Compilers Versus Interpreters

A *compiler* is a program that translates statements in one language into equivalent statements in another language. Typically, compilers translate programs written in a high-level language into programs that perform that same task in machine language. These machine-language programs can then be run on the computer. A *cross-compiler* produces machine language that is to be run on a different machine than the one on which the compiler runs. This is helpful when the computer for which the machine language is being produced is not readily available (e.g., a developmental machine).

Compilers and cross-compilers

An *interpreter* interprets statements in a language so that the actions of the statements can be simulated on a computer. An interpreter does not produce results that can be performed on another machine, so cross-interpreters do not exist. Interpreters are easier to produce than compilers; however, interpreted code runs slower than compiled code.

Interpreters

Many applications use ideas that come from compiler research. Such applications include *language-based editors*. These editors are tailored to particular programming languages. They have knowledge of the language and can do simple checks such as counting the number of arguments, examining the structure of the statements, and checking for balanced parentheses. *Pretty printers* print out programs in a standard formatted manner. They need information about the language being printed. *Text formatters* are similar to pretty printers, but they print out text rather than programs. Text formatters have commands embedded in the text. The commands dictate how the text should be printed; certain commands are analyzed using ideas from compiler theory.

A compiler is made up of four basic components: a *lexical analyzer*, a *parser*, a *semantic checker*, and a *code generator*. These different components are joined, as the following diagram illustrates. The compiler in this example takes high-level code as input and produces the machine-language equivalent of that code.

Parts of a compiler

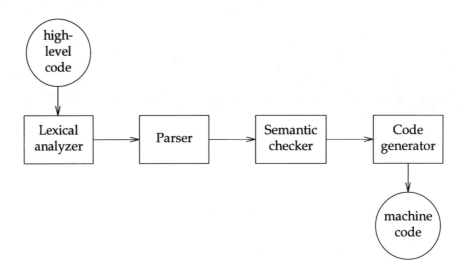

13.2 Lexical Analysis

Tokens

Lexical analysis is the process of reading in a program and classifying its components. A program is read in as a sequence of characters and converted into a sequence of *tokens*. Tokens are the fundamental lexical items of a language. Examples of tokens in Scheme are delimiters such as parentheses, special operators such as the quote symbol, "'", and identifiers such as symbol and function names. A lexical item is one that can be easily identified using simple rules without having to know about its meaning or use in the language.

Regular expressions

Regular expressions can be used to describe the tokens of a language. Regular expressions indicate exactly how tokens are formed out of single-character objects, letters, digits, and punctuation marks or special characters like parentheses. For example, below is a regular expression describing real numbers consisting of an optional plus or minus sign followed by zero or more digits, followed by an optional decimal point and one or more digits:

$$[+|-] \text{ digit}^* \quad [. \text{ digit}^+]$$

Braces, "[ ]", denote optional items. Vertical bars, "|", denote that either of the items surrounding The vertical bar may be used. The notation *item** means that zero or more occurrences of *item* are allowed, whereas the notation *item*$^+$ denotes one or more occurrences of *item*. digit refers to one of the digits 0–9.

13.2.1 Exercises

13.1   Write a regular expression to describe integers.

13.2   Write a regular expression to describe symbol names. Assume that letter represents one of the letters A–Z or a–z.

13.2.2 Tokens and symbol tables

Suppose we have defined the following tokens for a subset of Scheme:

token	meaning
number	a real or integer number
id	a symbol name
define	the symbol `define`
(	a left parenthesis
)	a right parenthesis

Applying lexical analysis to the Scheme function

```
(define (seconds-to-minutes seconds)
   (/ seconds 60.0) )
```

yields the following stream of tokens:

```
( define ( id id ) ( id id number ) )
```

All the blanks, tab indents, and carriage returns are eliminated. The spaces separating the tokens are just for our readability. This simplified form of the original Scheme function makes it easier to do the next phase of compiling: parsing.

One question that arises at this point is how the different `id` tokens are distinguished. Looking at the above list of tokens, it is impossible to surmise their meaning. For parsing, all that is needed is simple tokens such as `id` or `number`. It is only in the last phase of compilation, code generation (or while printing descriptive error messages), that the actual identifier names are needed.

The names that correspond to `id` tokens are saved in a *symbol table*, which is simply a list of symbol names. When a symbol is encountered, the token `id` is returned along with its position in the symbol table. As a new symbol is read in, the symbol table is searched for it. If it is found, the matching position in the symbol table is returned; otherwise, the symbol is added to the symbol table and that position is returned.

Symbol table

13.3 Parsing

Parsing or syntactical analysis is used to check if the tokens formed during lexical analysis represent legal statements within the language. The *grammar* of a language defines the set of legal statements in the language. Looking at English for an analogy, there are grammar rules specifying what constitutes a properly formed sentence in English. Below are three grammar rules for a subset of simple English sentences:

Parsing grammars

sentence → *noun-phrase verb-phrase*

noun-phrase → `article noun`

verb-phrase → `verb`

Terminals and nonterminals

Such rules of a grammar are called *productions* or *rules*. Items in `courier` are *terminals*; they represent tokens from the lexical analyzer. Items in *italics* are *nonterminals*—names that represent a collection of nonterminals or terminals. The statements in a language are *derived* by replacing nonterminals on the *left side* of productions with the terminals and nonterminals on the *right side* of productions. The arrow, "→", separates the left and right sides of productions. The derivation of symbols begins at the *start symbol*, which in this example is the nonterminal *sentence*.

Parse trees

During parsing, tokens are grouped into *parse trees*, which represent the structure of the token group. The start symbol is the root of the parse tree. Given the following tokens,

        `article noun verb`

parsing would yield the parse tree below:

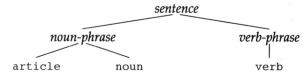

Below are some productions for a Scheme grammar. The start symbol is the nonterminal *expr-list*. The name *expr* stands for *expression*.

Simple Scheme grammar

production	description
1. *expr-list* → *expr*	single expression
2. *expr-list* → *expr expr-list*	more than one expression
3. *expr* → (`if` *expr expr*)	if-then expression
4. *expr* → (`if` *expr expr expr*)	if-then-else expression
5. *expr* → (`define` (`id` *id-list*) *expr-list*)	function definition
6. *expr* → (`id` *expr-list*)	function call
7. *id-list* → `id`	single identifier
8. *id-list* → `id` *id-list*	more than one identifier

Recursive grammars

Most grammars are recursive; they have elements in the left side of productions that also appear in the right side, as in

    expr-list → *expr expr-list*

This production is recursive because *expr-list* appears on both the left and right sides of the production. If many expressions make up an *expr-list*, production 2 must be invoked several times. Production 2 is a *right recursive production*—the left side nonterminal is on the right end of the right side of the production. An equivalent *left recursive production* would be

    expr-list → *expr-list expr*

The next sections illustrate two types of parsing.

13.3.1 Top-Down parsing

There are two major classes of parsers: *top-down* and *bottom-up*. These names refer to the way in which the parse tree is formed. Top-down parsers build a parse tree starting at the root and work down to the leaves. Bottom-up parsers build a parse tree starting at the leaves and work up to the root.

Top-down versus bottom-up parsing

With top-down parsers, at each node the appropriate production is chosen based on the current nonterminal that is being expanded and the *lookahead token*—the current token that is being examined from the input of the lexical analyzer. If the lookahead token can always unambiguously indicate which production is to be applied, then the parser is called a *predictive parser*. If the lookahead token is not sufficient to determine the production to use next, then alternative productions must be tried. This is *backtracking*—backing up to try a different approach. A *recursive descent* parser uses recursive functions to search through different production possibilities and handle *recursive grammars* like the one used above.

Lookahead token. Types of top-down parsers: predictive and recursive descent

Top-down parsers cannot handle left recursive productions, though. They tend to get stuck in infinite loops. For example, parsing *expr-list*, using the left recursive production

> *expr-list* → *expr-list expr*

expands to

> *expr-list expr*

which starts with *expr-list*, which expands to

> *expr-list expr*

which starts with *expr-list* which ... You get the idea. Such productions must be rewritten to eliminate left recursion.

Let's parse the token list that was produced in the previous section after lexically analyzing the function `seconds-to-minutes`. The tokens from this function definition are repeated below:

```
( define ( id id ) ( id id number ) )
```

We begin parsing with the start symbol, *expr-list*. Using production 1, *expr-list* expands to *expr*. The new goal is to derive the parse tree from the nonterminal *expr*. Starting with production 3, the right side is an if-then expression. This matches the first input token, "(." However, the next part of the right side `if` does not match the next input token, `define`. Thus, using production 3 to expand *expr* fails. So we backtrack and return to satisfying the right side of production 1, *expr*. When we backtrack, we reset the lookahead token. In this case we return to the first left parenthesis. We continue, now trying to satisfy production 4. This will fail also, so we backtrack and try production 5. The input matches the right side of production 5 up to the nonterminal *id-list*. This becomes the new subgoal to satisfy. The diagram below represents the steps in parsing the input tokens. The lookahead token (shown as an arrow pointing to the input), current nonterminal to satisfy, and production matched is given at each step of the parse. The unsuccessful steps (as in trying productions 3 and 4 above) have been eliminated

Top-down parsing example

for simplicity.

input and lookahead token	nonterminal	production
(define (id id) (id id number)) ↑	expr-list	1
(define (id id) (id id number)) ↑	expr	5
(define (id id) (id id number)) ↑	id-list	7
(define (id id) (id id number)) ↑	expr-list	1
(define (id id) (id id number)) ↑	expr	6
(define (id id) (id id number)) ↑	expr-list	2
(define (id id) (id id number)) ↑	expr	?

The lookahead token is id, which does not match the expected nonterminal, *expr*. Backtracking to production 2 would fail because it also tries to match *expr*.

At this point an error would be produced saying something to the effect of id found while *expr* was expected. The actual identifier, seconds, would typically be displayed. But we input a valid Scheme expression. What happened?

The production for define looks correct. What about the productions for *expr-list*? The productions indicate that an *expr-list* is one or more expressions. This also seems correct. What about the productions for *exprs*? An *expr* is an if, a define, or a function call. However, recall that symbols and numbers are also valid inputs to the Scheme interpreter; thus, they are valid expressions. We must modify the grammar to include these by adding the following two productions:

production	description
9. *expr* → id	identifier
10. *expr* → number	number

Now we can continue parsing from where we left off:

input and lookahead token	nonterminal	production
(define (id id) (id id number)) ↑	9	expr
(define (id id) (id id number)) ↑	1	expr-list
(define (id id) (id id number)) ↑	10	expr

The second to last right parenthesis matches the end of production 6. The final parenthesis matches the right parenthesis in production 5 and the parse is complete.

Another way to view the process of parsing is to look at the formation of the   *Building a parse tree*
parse tree. The parse tree begins with the start symbol, *expr-list*. After production
1 is performed, the parse tree is

Once the lookahead symbol is `define`, production 5 is selected and the parse
tree is expanded. The parentheses have been eliminated because they are redundant information—the levels of the parse tree itself reflect the same information
as parentheses.

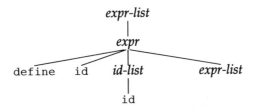

We advance the lookahead as long as it matches the next leaf of the parse tree.
When the lookahead symbol is the second `id`, the nonterminal *id-list* in the parse
tree must be expanded. Production 7 is selected, resulting in the new parse tree
below:

This process continues until the entire input has been processed. The final
parse tree follows:

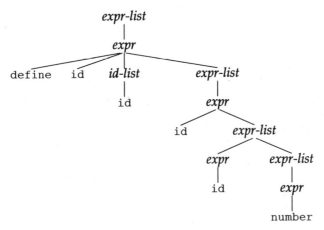

13.3.2 Predictive parsing

Predictive parsers

The above grammar can be modified so that backtracking is not necessary. This greatly speeds up the parsing process. Recall that a top-down parser that can unambiguously decide which production to take based on the current token is called a predictive parser. To change the above grammar so that a predictive parser can be used, all productions that have the same terminal or nonterminal at the start of their right sides must be rewritten.

LL grammars

An *LL(1) grammar* can be used for predictive parsing. A parser for an LL(1) grammar scans the input tokens from left to right, forms a *leftmost derivation* for the input, and uses one lookahead token. A leftmost derivation is one in which the leftmost nonterminal is replaced first. A grammar that can be parsed this way is called an LL(1) grammar. The next example shows how we can transform our previous grammar into an LL(1) grammar. Below is the previous grammar:

production	description
1. *expr-list* → *expr*	single expression
2. *expr-list* → *expr expr-list*	more than one expression
3. *expr* → (if *expr expr*)	if-then expression
4. *expr* → (if *expr expr expr*)	if-then-else expression
5. *expr* → (define (id *id-list*) *expr-list*)	function definition
6. *expr* → (id *expr-list*)	function call
7. *id-list* → id	single identifier
8. *id-list* → id *id-list*	more than one identifier
9. *expr* → id	identifier
10. *expr* → number	number

Productions 1 and 2 both have *expr* as the first nonterminal in their right side. Similarly, productions 3, 4, 5, and 6 all begin with a left parenthesis and productions 7, 8, and 9 begin with the terminal id. Below is a grammar that eliminates these duplicate right side beginnings. The symbol "ε" represents nothing (no token is matched).

Grammar for a predictive parser

production	description
1. *expr-list* → *expr more-exprs*	one or more expressions
2. *more-exprs* → ε	no more expressions
3. *more-exprs* → *expr-list*	more expressions
4. *expr* → (*func*)	function call
5. *expr* → id	identifier
6. *expr* → number	number
7. *func* → if *expr expr rest-of-if*	if expression
8. *func* → define (id *id-list*) *expr-list*	function definition
9. *func* → id *expr-list*	function call
10. *rest-of-if* → ε	if-then expression
11. *rest-of-if* → *expr*	if-then-else expression
12. *id-list* → id *more-ids*	one or more identifiers
13. *more-ids* → ε	no more identifiers
14. *more-ids* → *id-list*	more identifiers

With this grammar it is possible to unambiguously decide which production to use based on the current input tokens. But how does ε get matched? Nothing (ε) is matched if the lookahead token matches the next terminal or nonterminal of the previous right side. For example, suppose the lookahead token is) and the input is

Matching ε

```
( define ( id id ) ( id id number ) )
            ↑
```

At this point the nonterminal *more-ids* must be matched. It can be ε (nothing) or *id-list*. The lookahead token does not match *id-list* (it would have to be id to do so), but it does match the symbol following *id-list* in the right side of the *func* production. That is the production that precedes *id-list*.

To review, a grammar describes the set of legal statements in a language. A grammar comprises productions. Productions have terminals and nonterminals. Terminals (written in courier) represent individual tokens in the input. Nonterminals (written in *italics*) represent zero (matching ε) or more tokens in the input. Each production indicates a transformation rule in which the left side nonterminal is satisfied if the right side (terminals and nonterminals) is matched. This process constructs a parse tree that shows the syntactic structure of the input tokens.

Overview of top-down parsing

13.3.3 Bottom-Up parsing

The second major class of parsers is the *bottom-up parsers*. Bottom-up parsers also generate parse trees, but from the leaves up to the root and not from the root to the leaves, as with top-down parsers. A general method of bottom-up parsing is through *LR parsers*, which read the input tokens from left to right, but produce a rightmost derivation—the rightmost nonterminal is replaced first when processing a production with several nonterminals. A grammar is LR if it can be parsed with an LR parser.

Bottom-up and LR parsers

Shift-reduce parsing is a frequently used type of LR parsing in which the input tokens are *reduced* to the start symbol of the grammar. Shift-reduce parsers get their name because they either reduce a sequence of tokens to a nonterminal symbol or they read another token (a shift in the input). A reduce operation occurs when the right side of a production has been found and can be collapsed to the left-side nonterminal.

Shift-reduce parsers

A table is used to decide which operation to make (shift or reduce) based on the current input token and *state*. The state of a parsing system depends on the input that has been seen before that. *Shift-reduce tables* are usually generated using programs that take as input the grammar of the language being parsed. One such tool is called *yacc*.[1]

Shift-reduce tables

Let's look at a very simple grammar and its shift-reduce parsing table. The grammar is a subset of our prior Scheme grammar.

[1.] *yacc*, Yet Another Compiler Compiler, is available under the UNIX operating system. The shift-reduce table in this example was produced using yacc.

production	description
1. *id-list* → id	single identifier
2. *id-list* → id *id-list*	more than one identifier

Here is the shift-reduce parsing table for this grammar:

Shift-reduce table for a simple grammar

state	input		goto
	id	end	*id-list*
0	shift 2		1
1		accept	
2	shift 2	reduce 1	3
3		reduce 2	

This shift-reduce table shows that there are two inputs: id and nothing (end of input). Depending on the state and the input, a shift, reduce, or accept action is taken. The number after the shift is the new state. The number after reduce is the production to use when reducing. The goto column is used with reduce operations to determine the next state. There is a goto column for each nonterminal in the grammar.

Bottom-up parsing example

The table below shows the steps taken in parsing the input id id. The parser maintains a stack of the states and shifted and reduced values. Each step either shifts a new value and state onto the stack, or reduces one or more values to a nonterminal value and state. The values and new states at each step are shown together in parentheses:

input	stack	action
id id	0	shift 2
id	0 (id 2)	shift 2
	0 (id 2) (id 2)	reduce 1
	0 (id 2) (*id-list* 3)	reduce 2
	0 (*id-list* 1)	accept

Parsing begins at state 0. The input token is the first id, which in state 0 corresponds with the action shift 2. This means the parser shifts to the next token and goes to state 2. Now the input token is the second id, which in state 2 is a shift 2 operation. There is no more input, so the action corresponding to "end" in state 2 is done, which is reduce 1. The number after the reduce is the production that gives the reduce step. In this case id is reduced to *id-list*. The second id entry and its state, (id 2), are removed from the stack. The next state is determined by the goto column. This state is looked up according to the nonterminal reduced to (*id-list*) and the state on the top of the stack (state 2). Looking across the state 2 row and down the *id-list* column, state 3 is found. Continuing from state 3 with "end" as input, the action is reduce 2. Production 2 replaces id *id-list* with *id-list*. (id 2) and (*id-list* 3) are removed from the stack. Now the goto state for *id-list* is looked up under state 0; it is state 1. State 1 gives an accept action for the end of the input. This terminates the parsing.

The entire ten production grammar from the prior section on top-down parsing can be represented with a shift-reduce table with 26 states.

With shift-reduce parsers, ambiguities can arise when deciding whether to reduce values or shift the next token. Such errors are called *shift/reduce conflicts*. Similarly there are *reduce/reduce conflicts* in which multiple productions may be applied and one must be chosen. The parser must disambiguate these or the grammar must be changed to eliminate these problems.

Shift/reduce conflicts

Scheme makes extensive use of parentheses to group objects and provide structure to the language. Because of this, Scheme is not prone to shift/reduce conflicts. A classic shift/reduce conflict that occurs in other programming languages is the dangling else clause in nested if-then-else statements. If Scheme allowed `if` expressions to be written without the surrounding parentheses, we could recreate this shift/reduce conflict.

Dangling else clause

The ambiguity begins to arise when the first action of an `if` expression is another `if` expression. Imagine the following statement, which returns the largest of two numbers after first verifying that they are both numbers:

```
if (and (number? num1) (number? num2))
    if (> num1 num2)
        num1
        num2
```

Alternatively, `num2` could be interpreted as the else action for the first condition. The following indentation shows this:

```
if (and (number? num1) (number? num2))
    if (> num1 num2)
        num1
    num2
```

These two interpretations return different values when the first condition is false or when the first condition is true but the second isn't. However, while parsing, spaces (indentation) do not matter in the input. The parser only sees tokens such as `if`, `(`, and `)`. This means that to a parser the two examples above look identical. To which `if` expression does `num2` belong? When the `num2` expression is reached, there is not enough information to decide whether to reduce the inner `if` expression to an `if` without an else action or to shift and consider `num2` the else action. This is a shift/reduce conflict.

Shift/reduce conflicts are resolved by modifying the grammar of the language to specify explicitly which action to take when a shift/reduce conflict arises. Most parsers will have a default action to take if this isn't specified. In the case of nested `if` expressions, the usual action is to associate the dangling else with the innermost `if`. This means a shift action would be performed.

Resolving shift/reduce conflicts

A reduce/reduce conflict could come about if we used the grammar below, which treats function calls as it does special forms, namely as an `id` followed by an *expr-list*.

Reduce/reduce conflicts

1. *expr-list* → *expr*
2. *expr-list* → *expr expr-list*
3. *expr* → id
4. *expr* → number
5. *expr* → *function-call*
6. *expr* → *special-form*
7. *function-call* → (id *expr-list*)
8. *special-form* → (id *expr-list*)

Productions 7 and 8 have identical right sides, so given the same input, it is ambiguous as to which reduction should be made. In other words, if (id *expr-list*) is encountered, the productions do not indicate whether they should reduce to a *function-call* or to a *special-form*. This is a reduce/reduce conflict.

Resolving reduce/reduce conflicts

Reduce/reduce conflicts are removed by fixing the grammar or by relying on the default behavior of the parser, which is usually to choose the first reduction specified in the grammar.

Advantages of bottom-up parsers

In general, LR (bottom-up) parsers are used for the following reasons:

- they can recognize almost all programming languages where a grammar can be written to describe the language;
- they require no backtracking (as recursive descent top-down parsers do);
- they can parse a larger set of grammars than predictive (top-down) parsers;
- they can detect syntax errors as soon as possible while scanning the input tokens;
- parser building tools exist to automatically construct a parser given a grammar;
- LR grammars can describe more languages than LL grammars.

13.4 Semantic Analysis

The third phase of compiling is *semantic analysis*. The input to the semantic analyzer is a parse tree and the output is a refined parse tree. The refinements that are made involve *type-checking* and checking the validity of the location of certain statements in the program, such as the use of parameters or let variables outside of their scope. Other tasks are carried out by semantic analyzers; however, many do not apply to Scheme. In general, semantic analysis performs the checks that parsing could not make because parsing does not look into the meanings (semantics) of the tokens being read.

Type checking

For example, a semantic analyzer might check the types of the arguments given in a call to the function remainder to make sure that they are both integers. In Scheme this cannot be done always at compile time, since a symbol or function call may be given as an argument to remainder, and that value is not known until the program runs.

Polymorphism

Semantic analysis is used to handle *polymorphic functions*: functions that take arguments of different types. The arithmetic functions +, -, *, and / are all polymorphic. These functions take arguments that are integers or real numbers or a mixture of the two. Scheme supports rational numbers like 4/5 and complex numbers like (2 + 3i). The four functions above accept rational and complex numbers as well.

Many polymorphic functions are *overloaded*; that is, they perform different operations depending on the types of the arguments given or the context in which the functions are used. The function + is overloaded. If called with integers, + performs integer arithmetic. If called with real numbers, + performs real arithmetic producing real number results. Another example of overloading occurs in some languages in which function calls and array[2] accesses are both performed using the parenthesis operator, as in F(n). During semantic analysis, the type of the token preceding the parentheses is checked and the parse tree is modified to indicate whether the operation is an array access or a function call.

Overloading

To summarize, semantic analysis adds information to the parse tree to assist with code generation. This information specifies the operations that overloaded functions must perform in that particular instance. Semantic analysis looks at the types of the objects to disambiguate parts of the language that parsing cannot.

13.5 Code Generation

The final phase of compilation is *code generation*. Code generation involves the creation of statements in the language being compiled to. The input to the code generator is the parse tree that has been updated by the semantic analyzer. As stated at the start of this chapter, most compilers produce machine language code. To clarify this point somewhat, what is actually produced is *assembly language* code that uses mnemonic names to express the same information that machine language does with numbers. Assembly language is much easier for us to read and can be joined (*linked*) with other assembly language programs.

Producing assembly language

13.5.1 Mini Scheme

In this chapter we will create a Scheme compiler. Building a compiler for all of Scheme would be a rather formidable task. Instead we will develop a compiler for a small subset of Scheme consisting of the following functions:

category	functions
arithmetic	+ (with two arguments), - (with one or two arguments)
comparison	=, /= (not equal), >, <, >=, <= (with two arguments)
conditional	if (with *then* and optional *else* action)
definition	define of functions (allowing recursive functions)

Scheme functions supported by our compiler

Function calls to user-defined functions are allowed. The only type of data allowed is integer.

---

[2] An array can be viewed as a fixed length list with elements all of the same type.

13.5.2   A simple computer

To understand code generation it is necessary to understand assembly language, and to understand assembly language you should understand some basics of computer hardware. The following diagram shows a very simple computer:

These pieces make up the core of a computer. Below are brief descriptions of the functions they perform:

Parts of a compiler

machine part	operation performed
Data	Numerical information
Instructions	Instructions for the computer to perform
Registers	Store temporary values or results from computations for rapid access
Arithmetic Logic Unit (ALU)	Performs the mathematical and logical functions
Comparator	Indicates if the last arithmetic computation is equal to, not equal to, less than, or greater than 0
Program Counter	Location of the current instruction being executed
Data Stack	A section of data reserved for programs to save information
Stack Pointer	Location of the top of the data stack

Memory: RAM and ROM

Programs are placed in the data and instructions area. This area is part of the main memory of the computer. It is memory that can be read or changed (written). Such memory is called RAM, random access memory. There is also ROM, read-only memory, which can be read but not changed. Each memory location has a unique *address* which specifies its location. A computer address is similar to a house address.

The registers comprise a special set of memory locations that can be accessed very rapidly. However, there are a limited number of registers. Careful use of registers can produce assembly code that runs faster. Most modern machines have a special area of memory called *cache* that is rapidly accessible like registers, but much larger in storage potential.

Registers

The program counter contains the address of the next instruction to run. Before a program can be run, its instructions must be loaded into the machine's main memory and the program counter set to the location of the first instruction of the program. That instruction is executed and the program counter is incremented. Then the next instruction is executed. This process continues until the program completes. The operating system plays a major role in this process; it is discussed in depth in Chapter 14.

Program counter

The stack pointer is the address of the top of the stack. The stack is used to hold information for short periods of time. One of the most common uses is to save the values of registers and parameters to functions. Before a function is called, the registers in use can be saved on the stack. When the function ends, the registers can be restored by retrieving their values from the stack. To pass arguments to a function, they can be put on the stack and when the function is called it can access its parameters from the stack values. When the function finishes, the stack pointer is moved past the arguments to effectively remove the arguments from the stack.

Stack and stack pointer

The ALU does arithmetic and logical operations like addition, subtraction, and logical *and*, *or*, and *not* operations. The ALU and comparator are used to make comparisons. When an arithmetic operation is performed, information about the result is saved. This information includes if the result of the computation is zero, less than zero, greater than zero, or negative. This data is examined when branching instructions are made. A *branch* is a conditional jump to a different instruction. If the condition is true the program counter is changed. For example, if two numbers are subtracted and the result is negative and the next instruction is branch if less than, the branch is done. The output from the ALU can be stored in a register or the main data.

ALU and comparator

13.5.3 Assembly language

An assembly language program is an ordered collection of instructions that are executed in sequence. In this sense assembly language is similar to Scheme, in which expressions are evaluated in order. The similarity ends there. Instead of evaluating functions and passing results to other functions, assembly instructions save results of computations in registers or in the machine's RAM. Thus both data and instructions coexist in the computer's main memory. This is an important idea that dates back to the earliest computers. Such a design in which the machine memory comprises data and instructions is called a *Von Neumann architecture*, named after the creator of the idea. Von Neumann was a pioneer in the early years of computer science.

Von Neumann architecture

Operands and literals

Our hypothetical machine will use an assembly language with only eleven instructions. Most computers have more instructions, but this sparse set is adequate for our needs. The *operands* (items upon which the instructions work) *src*, *des*, and *loc* stand for source, destination, and location, respectively. These represent addresses in the computer's memory. *src* may represent a *literal*, a numeric value. This is written as a pound sign, "#", followed by a number, as in #42.

Our assembly language

name	operands	description
MOV	*src, des*	copy (move) *src* to *des*
ADD	*src, des*	add *src* to *des*, saving the result in *des*
SUB	*src, des*	subtract *src* from *des*, saving the result in *des*
NEG	*des*	negate *des*, saving the result in *des*
JMP	*loc*	jump to *loc* in the computer's memory
BEQ	*loc*	branch to *loc* if comparator is equal to zero
BNE	*loc*	branch to *loc* if comparator is not equal to zero
BLT	*loc*	branch to *loc* if comparator is less than zero
BGT	*loc*	branch to *loc* if comparator is greater than zero
JFN	*loc*	jump to *loc* (to call a function)
RET		return from a function

The instructions ADD, SUB, and NEG set the comparator for subsequent branching instructions.

Addressing modes

Memory locations can be referenced in many ways; the three our assembly language uses are *absolute*, *indirect*, and *indexed*. These are *addressing modes*. An absolute reference specifies the address of the data to use. In other words, the contents of the given memory location are used. An indirect reference specifies a location whose contents are the location of the data. This means that an extra level of address lookup is used. An indexed reference adds an index value to the contents of a location and uses that as the address of the data.

Representing memory and addressing

To understand this better, look at the computer's memory as a long list of integers. Each element is a unique value, which can be accessed or modified. Each of the elements has an address specifying its location. Addresses are numbers, just as the contents of the addresses (the value of the elements in our list) are numbers.

Any piece of memory can be accessed using list-ref. The call

    (list-ref memory SP)

is an absolute reference. SP is the address, and the value returned is the contents of the location at that address.

    (list-ref memory (list-ref memory SP))

is an indirect reference. The address is (list-ref memory SP). An indexed reference would be

    (list-ref memory (+ index (list-ref memory SP)))

In addition to these three modes, we will use two variations on indirect addressing: *post-increment* and *pre-decrement* indirect addressing. Post-increment and pre-decrement modes do two levels of address lookup. In addition, they increment or decrement the contents of the address given. This means that the next indirect address request using the same address will retrieve the neighboring data value. Post-increment gets the location from the address given and then increments the address. Pre-decrement decrements the address given first and then uses the contents of the decremented address as the location.

The table below shows how these addressing modes are written in assembly language. A literal value is referred to as an *immediate address*.

mode	example
immediate	#42
absolute	SP
indirect	(SP)
indexed	3(SP)
post-increment	(SP)+
pre-decrement	-(SP)

Addressing modes in assembly language

SP is the address of the top of the stack and (SP) is the contents of the location at that address, or the value at the top of the stack. -(SP) decrements the stack pointer before a value is added to or read from the stack. And (SP)+ reads or puts a value on the stack and then increments the stack pointer.

Below are some examples that use our assembly language. Assume that these commands are performed in sequence and that memory location 4 contains the value 100, location 5 contains 25, and location 7 contains 86. VALUE and TEMP are addresses.

assembly	actions
MOV #4, VALUE	store 4 into VALUE
MOV VALUE, TEMP	store 4 into TEMP
MOV (VALUE), TEMP	store 100 into TEMP
MOV 3(VALUE), TEMP	store 86 into TEMP
MOV (VALUE)+, TEMP	store 100 into TEMP and 5 into VALUE
MOV -1(VALUE), TEMP	store 100 into TEMP
MOV (VALUE), TEMP	store 25 into TEMP
MOV -(VALUE), TEMP	store 4 into VALUE and 100 into TEMP

Sample assembly instructions

Literal addresses can be used with *src* addresses only. The other addressing modes are allowed with *src*, *des*, and *loc* addresses.

An example will help show how assembly language is written. Suppose we wish to add 4 and number and save the result in answer. In Scheme we could express this as

```
(define answer (+ number 4))
```

Mathematical expressions and variable binding in assembly

In assembly language, the same code is expressed as

```
MOV NUMBER, ANSWER
ADD #4, ANSWER
```

The first instruction copies the contents of the memory location labeled NUMBER to memory location ANSWER. The next instruction adds the literal value 4 (written as #4) to the contents of the memory location labeled ANSWER. Below is a variation of these operations:

```
ADD #4, NUMBER
MOV NUMBER, ANSWER
```

Creating assembly code that is functionally equivalent to the Scheme code

At first, it might seem that these two sets of instructions are equivalent, but there is an important difference. The value of memory location NUMBER is not changed in the first example, whereas in the second example it is incremented by four. The Scheme expression does not change the value of number, so the first assembly language version is the preferred choice.

In general, to produce a value such as

```
(+ number 4)
```

the result of the computation should be saved in a separate memory location, preferably a register. By storing such partial results in registers, additional memory locations are not needed, and there is a speed improvement because it is faster to access and update a register than a memory location in RAM. Thus,

```
(+ number 4)
```

could be expressed in assembly language as

```
MOV NUMBER, R0
ADD #4, R0
```

R0 is register 0, which is where the result of the computation is held.

Function composition in assembly

If the result of this computation were needed for another computation, for example if the actual Scheme expression were

```
(- (+ number 4) 2)
```

the sum (+ number 4) is obtained from R0. The assembly language for this Scheme expression would be

```
MOV NUMBER, R0
ADD #4, R0
SUB #2, R0
```

The final result is once again in register 0, R0.

13.5.4   Conditional expressions in assembly language

Branching instructions

To express a Scheme if expression in assembly language, a *conditional branch* is used. A conditional branch jumps to a different section of code if a condition is met. For example, to express the following Scheme expression,

```
(if (< num 3)
    (- num 1)
    (- num))
```

in assembly language, the commands below can be used. A brief explanation in English follows each instruction. These comments, preceded by semicolons, are optional.

```
        MOV NUM, R0      ; store NUM in R0
        SUB #3, R0       ; subtract 3 from R0 and set the comparator
        BLT THEN         ; if less-than-0 is set (num < 3) jump to THEN
        MOV NUM, R0      ; else part: store NUM in R0
        NEG R0           ; negate R0
        JMP DONE         ; skip then part of if-then-else
THEN    MOV NUM, R0      ; store NUM in R0
        SUB #1, R0       ; subtract 1 from R0
DONE    next instruction
```

At the end of this sequence, the return value of the `if` expression is in register 0, R0. The words THEN and DONE are *labels*. They represent addresses in the computer memory. The assembly language version only performs one of the *then* or *else* parts of the `if`, just like the actual Scheme expression would.

Labels

13.5.5 Function definitions and calls in assembly language

Function definitions are performed by creating the code for the function and then associating the start location of those instructions with the function name. A call to a function is a jump to the function's start location. Function arguments and return values are covered later in this section.

Below is a function definition in Scheme:

```
(define (the-ultimate-answer)
  (+ 21 21) )
```

The instructions JFN and RET are used to call and return from functions. JFN saves the location of the following address on the stack and then jumps to the address that specifies the start of a function. RET is called at the end of the function. It uses the address saved on the stack to return to the instruction after the function call. The function `the-ultimate-answer`, abbreviated TUA, is called with

JFN and RET

```
        JFN TUA          ; call the-ultimate-answer
```

The function `the-ultimate-answer` is expressed in assembly as

```
TUA     MOV #21, R0      ; store 21 in R0
        ADD #21, R0      ; add 21 to the contents of R0
        RET              ; return to the caller
```

The first statement is labeled TUA. Following the function's instructions a RET instruction is performed to return to the location following the one from which the function call was made. The return value of the function is held in register 0, R0. This may seem fine, but there are some important details that have been left out. First, what happens if register 0 is being used at the time this function is being called? It is impossible to know at compile time exactly which functions will be active when another function is called. This is illustrated in the following example, where the number of functions called depends on a value passed to `two-choices`.

Saving return values

```
(define (two-choices num)
  (if (> num 0)
      (+ num (the-ultimate-answer))
      (+ (another-function) (the-ultimate-answer))) )
```

Maintaining values on the stack

If both `another-function` and `the-ultimate-answer` use R0 as their return values, then both return values cannot be maintained. As a further complication, function `two-choices` might use R0, in which case that value is lost when the other functions are called. To get around this problem, all the registers can be saved before a function is called and then restored when the function returns. This storage happens on the *stack*—a space within main memory that can be viewed as a pile of numbers in which numbers are added and removed. The last number to be added to the stack is the first number that will be removed. For an analogy, think of a stack of plates in which you always place and take plates from the top of the stack.

Saving register values

Saving all the registers is time consuming. Other solutions exist, such as saving only those registers currently in use. Either the caller of the function or the function being called is given the responsibility of saving and restoring any registers that it needs. Another possibility is to use *register windows*, in which sections of memory represent different collections of registers, which can be switched by changing the address holding their starting location. Hybrid solutions exist in which certain registers are allocated to the caller and certain ones to the callee (the function that is called). Any of these solve the basic problem of saving values in a limited number of registers when functions are called.

We will have the caller assume responsibility of saving the registers it uses before it calls a function and then restoring those values when the function finishes. This way the function being called is free to use any registers without conflicts arising. An alternate strategy would be to have the callee push the register values for the registers it will use. This requires an initial pass through the callee's code to determine which registers it will use. In general, it is better to give the callee more responsibility during a function call, because the callee's code is only generated once, whereas the caller's code is generated for each function call.

Dedicating register 0 for return values

The return value from functions can be placed on the stack. A simpler solution would be to place the value in a register, but as we saw earlier we cannot know beforehand which registers will be free. However, a register could be dedicated to hold the return value from function calls. Register number 0 will be used for this purpose.

If multiple function calls must be made, prior return values can be moved to other registers. For example, if the function that calls `the-ultimate-answer` must save the return value in register 2, it must include a MOV instruction after the JFN to copy the return value of the function into R2.

```
JFN TUA        ; call function the-ultimate-answer
MOV R0, R2     ; copy the return value into R2
```

Functions that take arguments need space for the parameters within the function that hold the argument values. The arguments cannot be kept in specific registers because the function may be called recursively, in which case multiple copies of those arguments must be maintained. The arguments should be held on the stack. Each time the function is called recursively, the new arguments are added to the top of the stack.

Saving space for parameters

When parameters are referenced in the function being called, they can be fetched relative to the stack pointer. However, subsequent function calls shift the position of the stack pointer so we can no longer look up values relative to the stack pointer. Instead, the values are held relative to the *frame pointer*. The frame pointer is similar to the stack pointer except that it points to the bottom of the current stack of parameters on the stack. When a function is called, the parameters are pushed on the stack and the frame pointer is set to the address of the first parameter. The stack pointer moves as parameters and other values are added to the stack, but the frame pointer stays. All references to parameters made in the function are relative to the frame pointer. The indexed addressing mode is a convenient means of doing this.

Frame pointer

As functions terminate, their parameters are no longer needed and they can be deleted from the stack. The previous frame pointer must be restored then. This means the old frame pointer should be saved on the stack as well. In addition, the return address is needed on the stack when making recursive calls. The JFN instruction and RET push and pop the return address from the stack.

To clarify all these steps, here is a table summarizing the steps that the caller and callee take:

location	action performed
caller	save registers in use
caller	push arguments
caller	JFN pushes return address
callee	push frame pointer
callee	set frame pointer to first argument
callee	execute code in callee routine
callee	put return value in register 0
callee	restore (pop) old frame pointer
callee	RET pops return address
caller	save return value in proper register
caller	increment stack pointer past arguments
caller	pop registers

Summary of caller and callee responsibilities

The following diagrams show the stack at each step taken by the caller and callee as a function is called and returned from. Imagine a function is being executed and it is about to call another function. Before the call is made, the stack contains the values shown in diagram 1. SP and FP refer to the stack and frame pointers, respectively. The frame pointer points to the location of the first argument of the function and the stack pointer points to the return address, which is the last value added on the stack.

Diagram 1
SP→return address
    argumentN
FP→argument1

Before the function is called, the caller saves the registers it is using.

Diagram 2
SP→registerM
    register1
    return address
    argumentN
FP→argument1

Then the caller evaluates the arguments and saves them on the stack. The callee will access these relative to the frame pointer which the callee will move to the first argument.

Diagram 3
SP→argumentL
    argument1
    registerM
    register1
    return address
    argumentN
FP→argument1

The call to JFN pushes the return address on the stack and the callee code is executed.

Diagram 4
SP→return address
    argumentL
    argument1
    registerM
    register1
    return address
    argumentN
FP→argument1

Before the callee executes any of the code specific to its actions, it must save the frame pointer used by the caller on the stack and then move the frame pointer for its uses to the first argument to the callee. The callee accesses the arguments relative to the frame pointer. When the callee has computed its return value, it stores it in R0.

Diagram 5

SP→frame pointer
   return address
   argumentL
FP→argument1
   registerM
   register1
   return address
   argumentN
   argument1

Once the callee has executed its code, it must restore the old frame pointer. The stack looks like diagram 4 then. Lastly the callee calls RET to return to the caller. The return address is on top of the stack. Now the stack looks like diagram 3.

The caller continues; it must adjust the stack pointer past the arguments. The stack looks like diagram 2 now. Then the caller pops the saved registers from the stack, returning the stack to diagram 1.

Let's try a function with arguments: *Sample function*

```
(define (pints-to-cups pints)
  (+ pints pints) )
```

The arguments and the frame pointer will be saved on the stack. The equivalent of this function in assembly language is

```
PTC    MOV FP, -(SP)     ; push frame pointer on the stack
       MOV SP, FP        ; set frame pointer to the stack pointer
       ADD #2, FP        ; adjust frame pointer to first argument position
       MOV (FP), R0      ; store parameter pints in R0
       ADD R0, R0        ; add pints to pints saving result in R0
       MOV (SP)+, FP     ; restore old frame pointer
       RET               ; return to the caller
```

The calling instructions for the expression   *Sample function call*

```
(+ (pints-to-cups 2) 3)
```

are

```
       MOV #2, -(SP)     ; push argument value, 2, on the stack
       JFN PTC           ; call function pints-to-cups (result will go into R0)
       ADD #1, SP        ; skip past argument on stack
       ADD #3, R0        ; add 3 to R0, (pints-to-cups 2), saving result in R0
```

R0 contains the return value of this expression.

We can execute this program by hand, simulating the actions of the machine, by writing out the stack and register values as we go through the assembly code. Assume that R0 and FP are initially 100 and 200. Going through the instructions for (+ (pints-to-cups 2) 3) up to JFN PTC (including pushing the return address on the stack but before executing the code at PTC) yields the following values:

Trace of the stack and register values

stack contents
SP→return address
        2
_____

register   value
R0   100
FP   200

The stack and registers look as follows after the instructions in `pints-to-cups` up to and including the ADD instruction are executed:

stack contents
SP→200
        return address
FP→2
_____

register   value
R0   initially 2 from (FP), then 4 after the ADD instruction

Once the function has finished and the RET instruction is executed, the stack and registers are as follows:

stack contents
SP→2
_____

register   value
R0   4
FP   200

Continuing with the instructions after JFN PTC, the stack is empty and the registers are

register   value
R0   7
FP   200

Sample recursive
function and call

Now let's try a recursive function definition and a call to it. The function below multiplies two positive numbers using a sequence of additions. Following the definition is a call to the function:

```
(define (mult num1 num2)
  (if (= num1 1)
      num2
      (+ num2 (mult (- num1 1) num2))) )


(mult 2 3)
```

Putting all the ideas from this section in mind, let's write the assembly code for `mult`. The function has two parameters: the first will be at the frame pointer and the second will be in the address preceding the frame pointer. A recursive function will contain the instructions for both the caller and callee. Notice that R0 is used in this function before the recursive call, but its value is not saved on the stack. This is because the value is not needed after the recursive call. A good optimizing compiler will make such tests to reduce the amount of code generated.

```
MULT    MOV FP, -(SP)      ; push frame pointer on the stack
        MOV SP, FP         ; set frame pointer to the stack pointer
        ADD #3, FP         ; adjust frame pointer to first argument position
        MOV (FP), R0       ; initialize R0 to the first parameter—num1
```
evaluate condition → (= num1 1)
```
        SUB #1, R0         ; subtract 1 from R0, num1, to test for equality
```
test condition
```
        BEQ THEN           ; if that value is 0, (num1 = 1), so jump to THEN
```
else action → (+ num2 (mult (- num1 1) num2))
```
        MOV R0, -(SP)      ; push (- num1 1) on stack (first argument)
        MOV -1(FP), -(SP)  ; push num2 on stack (second argument)
        JFN MULT           ; call mult function
        ADD #2, SP         ; skip past arguments on stack
        ADD -1(FP), R0     ; add second parameter num2 to return value from mult
        JMP DONE           ; skip then part of if-then-else
```
then action → num2
```
THEN    MOV -1(FP), R0     ; store return value, num2, in R0
DONE    MOV (SP)+, FP      ; restore old frame pointer
        RET
```

The following assembly code is for the call (mult 2 3):

```
        MOV #2, -(SP)      ; push 2 on stack (first argument)
        MOV #3, -(SP)      ; push 3 on stack (second argument)
        JFN MULT           ; call mult function; result saved in R0
        ADD #2, SP         ; skip past arguments on stack
```

To see how this works, produce a stack and register trace like the one made above for the call to (+ (pints-to-cups 2) 3).

13.6 Historical Background and Current Trends

The first compilers marked the advent of high-level computer languages. Before compilers existed, programs were written in machine language or assembly language, which is easily translated into machine language. FORTRAN was one of the first languages for which a compiler was written. This was considered a monumental task; it took eighteen person-years to complete. The FORTRAN compiler was an existence proof that it was possible to write programs in high-level languages and have them run on machines. This radically changed the productivity of programmers and made way for the current proliferation of programming languages.

FORTRAN compiler

Much has been learned since the late 1950's, when compilers started appearing. Tools have been created that generate lexical analyzers and parsers. In the UNIX environment, lex and yacc are two such tools. *Lex* takes descriptions of the

Lex

input in regular expression form, rules to indicate how the different tokens should be handled (e.g., identifiers should be added to the symbol table), and auxiliary functions that are needed (such as a function to install an identifier in the symbol table). This description is input to lex, which produces a lexical analyzer program in the language C. This can then be linked with the rest of the compiler.

Yacc

Yacc stands for Yet Another Compiler Compiler. It produces a parser program that can be linked with the rest of the compiler in the same fashion as lex is linked. Yacc takes the names of the tokens from the lexical analyzer, translation rules describing grammar rules and the actions to take based on those inputs, and lastly the lexical analyzer and any error recovery functions. Yacc produces an LR parser complete with a shift-reduce table as described in the section on bottom-up parsers. Yacc has built-in rules for disambiguating shift/reduce and reduce/reduce conflicts, which can be superseded if needed.

Using these two tools, all that is left is semantic analysis and code generation. Here, too, shortcuts can be made. For example, if compilers were needed to translate a high-level language into three assembly languages for three different computers, the same lexical analyzer, parser, and semantic analyzer could potentially be used. Even the majority of the code generation could be used by all three compilers if an intermediate form of assembly language were used. The three different compilers would share those pieces. A program taking the intermediate assembly code and translating it to the final assembly language would have to be written for each machine. Such practices simplify the task of updating compilers for multiple machines when language specifications change.

13.6.1   Compiling the compiler

Perhaps the most powerful form of compiler creation involves a technique known as *compiling the compiler*. In this technique a compiler program itself is given as input to another compiler. To illustrate this idea we'll use a concrete example. It is important to keep the following three components straight:

- the language being compiled (translated)
- the language produced
- the machine on which the compiler runs

Let's suppose we have a compiler that runs on a Pentium machine and compiles the language C into Pentium assembly language. The Pentium is a microprocessor built by Intel. If we want to produce a Scheme compiler for the Pentium, we could write the compiler in Pentium assembly language. This would be extremely tedious. A simpler way would be to write a compiler in C that takes Scheme code as input and produces Pentium assembly language. Then, use this compiler as input to the existing C compiler to produce a compiler that runs on the Pentium that takes Scheme as input and produces Pentium assembly as output. The diagram below illustrates this:

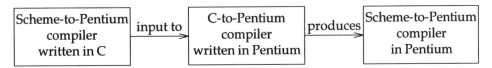

Now suppose we want a Scheme compiler for the PowerPC (PPC)—a microprocessor made by Motorola. To complicate matters, let's assume that we don't have a C compiler for the PowerPC. Thus, we cannot take the path used above. To further complicate matters, let's assume that we have no compilers for the PowerPC. Where do we start? It looks like we have to build a compiler in PowerPC assembly language.

This is where the true power of compiling compilers comes through. We begin by writing a compiler in Scheme that takes Scheme and produces PowerPC code. Next, we give this compiler as input to the compiler created above that takes Scheme and produces Pentium code. This compiler runs on a Pentium. The result is a *cross-compiler* that runs on a Pentium, takes Scheme, and returns PowerPC assembly code. A cross-compiler is a compiler that produces assembly code for a different machine than the one on which it runs. The diagram below illustrates this:

Cross-compilers

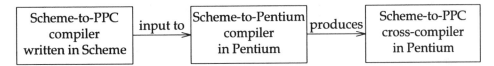

Now repeat the process, but this time the Scheme compiler we wrote is input to the cross-compiler produced above. The cross-compiler runs on a Pentium, but produces PowerPC code; thus, sending it a Scheme-to-PowerPC compiler will produce a Scheme-to-PowerPC compiler that runs on a PowerPC. This is illustrated in the diagram below:

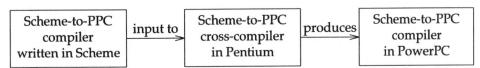

To recap, start with a C-to-Pentium compiler that runs on a Pentium. Write a Scheme-to-Pentium compiler in C and compile that compiler to produce a Scheme-to-Pentium compiler that runs on a Pentium. Next, write a Scheme-to-PowerPC compiler in Scheme and compile that compiler once (on the Scheme-to-Pentium compiler) to produce a Scheme-to-PowerPC cross-compiler running on a Pentium, and again (on the cross-compiler) to give a Scheme-to-PowerPC compiler running on a PowerPC machine.

13.7   Implementing a Simple Scheme Compiler in Scheme

Lexical analysis

To implement a Scheme compiler in Scheme we will take many shortcuts. For example, we do not need to read in the input as individual characters, but can read in Scheme objects like numbers, symbols, and lists directly. This eliminates the majority of the work done by the lexical analyzer. All that is left is to convert numbers into the token `number`, and symbol and function names into the token `id`, and store their names in a symbol table. In fact, we can even bypass some of these steps.

Parsing

The majority of the parser's task is not needed because Scheme code has an extremely simple syntax. This structure provides a natural parse tree for Scheme statements. The only change to the structure of basic Scheme is adding nodes to label the subtree types, for example, adding *expr* as the parent node to a Scheme expression, or *id-list* as the parent to parameter lists. In our mini-Scheme version, we can get by without the extra nodes and simply use the existing structure of Scheme expressions.

Semantic analysis

Semantic analysis is needed to deal with the types of arguments given to overloaded functions, assuming that we can determine the types at compile time (when the compiler processes the code). In a strongly typed language, where all variables must be declared, this can be done. However, in Scheme or other languages where variables are not typed, the compiled code must include tests for the types and then perform the appropriate actions. This makes for slower execution times and is one of the major criticisms of Scheme. Some dialects of LISP allow the programmer to specify the type of a variable to improve runtime speed.

We will need semantic analysis to properly interpret calls to the negation-subtraction function, "-." If - is called with one argument, negation should be performed instead of subtraction. In assembly language, this translates into using NEG instead of SUB.

Error checking

Error checking is done during lexical analysis, parsing, and semantic analysis. We will perform minimal error checking, making the assumption that we are given valid input so that we can ignore fully robust error checking. If we make this assumption and ignore the addition of extra nodes in the parse tree, we can skip lexical analysis, parsing, and semantic analysis altogether. We will include the tests for negation/subtraction in the code generation section.

Code generation

Code generation is the remaining task. It involves sequencing through Scheme expressions and producing assembly language. To make things simpler we will only allow the simple set of Scheme functions previously shown in section 13.5.1 and only support integer typed values. This provides a reasonable idea of what is involved in code generation without getting bogged down in all the details that would arise in compiling the full set of Scheme functions and allowing multiple types.

Section 13.5, "Code Generation," gives examples of assembly code broken down by different expression types. Using a similar approach we can address each type of expression allowed in our mini-Scheme and generate the assembly code for that expression. We won't always produce code that is as streamlined as that shown in the examples from section 13.5. Producing efficient assembly code is one of the most difficult elements of compiler design.

One issue that will come up throughout the process of code generation is the use of registers. Registers are a finite resource and should be used as much as possible, as they are rapidly accessible by the CPU. Whenever registers can be re-used, we should try to do so. This involves realizing when values must be saved and when they need not be saved.

Efficient use of registers

Another issue that will come up is the return value of expressions. A complex expression may involve many subexpressions, whose values must be combined to produce a final return value. We will need a mechanism to save these different return values.

Return values

A final theme is handling symbols. The values of symbols used as parameters must be saved somewhere. We will use the stack to do so, along with a symbol table that links symbols with their location on the stack.

Symbols

Employing top-down design, we start with the top-most function, which compiles a list of expressions. This function takes the list of expressions, a list of register names that the computer supports, and the symbol table. For each expression in the expression list, this function simply calls another function that generates code for a single expression. Since each expression is independent and the results computed by each expression need not be saved, except for the last one, the register list for each expression can be reused.

Compiling expression lists

```
; Generate code for a list of expressions.
(define (code-gen-expr-list expr-list reg-list symbol-table)
  (for-each
    (lambda (expr)
      (code-gen-expr expr reg-list symbol-table) )
    expr-list) )
```

The function code-gen-expr, the heart of the code generator, generates code or calls functions to generate code for each type of expression with which it might be called. The return value of an expression may be required in another computation. For example, when evaluating a function call, code-gen-expr must be called recursively to generate the code for the arguments. The results for each argument must be saved somewhere and then applied to the function being called. The first register in the register list can be used to represent the location where the result of the current expression should be put. The remaining registers are free for use in computing that value.

Compiling single expressions

Error handling may occur deep within our code. Rather than try to recover from errors, we'll immediately bail out of the code generation process and return a string indicating what caused the error. The easiest way to bail out from anywhere in a collection of functions is by calling an exit function established with **call-with-current-continuation**. Examples of this function are covered in Chapter 11, "Forcing Exits with **call-with-current-continuation**." The following two expressions establish fatal-error as an exit function.

Error handling

```
(define fatal-error 'not-yet)
```

```
(call-with-current-continuation
  (lambda (stop)
    (set! fatal-error stop)))
```

Printing out assembly instructions

To output assembly instructions, we use a function `output` that takes a symbol representing the instruction and optional arguments representing additional information that may be needed, such as the *src*, *des*, and *loc* values. Instructions are indented so that labels (which aren't indented) stand out. The tricky part is dealing with the commas that precede all but the first optional argument.

```
; Print out instruction and operands.
(define (output instruc . addrs)
  (display "  ")
  (display instruc)
  (cond ((not (null? addrs))
         (display " ")
         (display (first addrs))
         (for-each
           (lambda (addr)
             (display ", ")
             (display addr) )
           (rest addrs)))))
  (newline) )
```

Symbol lookup

We need another function to look up the symbol in the symbol table (an association list) to find the register or position on the stack (in the case of parameters) holding its value. If the symbol does not exist in the symbol table, code generation terminates.

```
; Lookup address of symbol in symbol table.
(define (symbol-address symbol symbol-table)
  (let ( (address (assoc symbol symbol-table)) )
    (if address
        (cdr address)
        (fatal-error
          (string-append
            "Undefined variable:"
            (symbol->string symbol)))))) )
```

Finally, here is the code to handle a single expression. It handles six different types of expressions: symbols, numbers, if-then-else expressions, function definitions, calls to built-in functions, and calls to user-defined functions. The result from each expression is saved in the first register in `reg-list`. To deal with symbols, this function will need the symbol table, so it is a parameter.

```
; Generate code for a single expression saving return value in the
; first register of reg-list.
(define (code-gen-expr expr reg-list symbol-table)
  (let ( (result (first reg-list)) )
    (cond ((symbol? expr)
              (output 'MOV (symbol-address expr symbol-table) result))
          ((number? expr)
              (output 'MOV (literal expr) result))
          ((is-if? expr)
              (code-gen-if expr reg-list symbol-table))
          ((is-func-def? expr)
              (code-gen-func-def expr reg-list symbol-table))
          ((is-built-in-func? expr)
              (code-gen-built-in-func expr reg-list symbol-table))
          (else ; otherwise it's a user-defined function call
              (code-gen-user-func expr reg-list symbol-table)))) )
```

The auxiliary functions used in code-gen-expr must be written. We'll start with the functions that check the expression type:

```
; Test if expr is an if expression.
(define (is-if? expr)
  (eqv? (first expr) 'if) )

; Test if expr is a function definition.
(define (is-func-def? expr)
  (eqv? (first expr) 'define) )

; Test if expr is a call to a built-in function.
(define (is-built-in-func? expr)
  (member (first expr) '(+ - < > = /= <= >=)) )
```

We could have placed the code for these conditions directly in code-gen-expr. Writing separate functions adheres to data abstraction principles, which minimize changes that have to be made to the code when the data structure changes. For example, our data structure would change if a parser were used that produced a parse tree with a different form than the Scheme input we presently receive.

Data abstraction

When a number is evaluated, its literal value, an immediate address (represented as the character "#" followed by the number), must be produced. The function literal does this by appending the string "#" to the string representation of the number.

Forming literals

```
; Generate a string representing a literal.
(define (literal number)
  (string-append "#" (number->string number)) )
```

While we are dealing with addresses, let's create functions to generate different addresses. These functions will be given a symbol and possibly a number (indexed address).

Forming different addressing modes

```
; Generate a string representing an indirect address.
(define (indirect address)
  (string-append "(" (symbol->string address) ")") )

; Generate a string representing an indexed address.
(define (indexed address index)
  (string-append (number->string index) (indirect address)) )

; Generate a string representing a post-increment address.
(define (post-inc address)
  (string-append (indirect address) "+") )

; Generate a string representing a pre-decrement address.
(define (pre-dec address)
  (string-append "-" (indirect address)) )
```

13.7.1   Generating code for `if` expressions

For an `if` expression, the basic steps in generating assembly code are as follows:

Steps to produce an
`if` expression

1. Generate code for the conditional test.
2. Create a branch to the *then* label if the test passes (jump to *then* action).
3. Generate code for the *else* action.
4. Create a branch to a label following the *then* action (end of `if` expression).
5. Insert a label for the *then* action.
6. Generate code for the *then* action.
7. Insert a label for the end of the `if` expression.

Mutual recursion

This can get complex if the conditions or actions are themselves complex collections of function calls or even other `if` expressions. This is not as bad as it may sound if we take advantage of the powers of recursion. Each step that generates code can be handled by making a call to `code-gen-expr`. This is a type of recursion known as *mutual recursion* in which one function calls another, which in turn calls the first.

Selector functions for
`if`

As mentioned earlier, data abstraction is important in writing compilers. We have written functions to test the types of expressions. We should write selector functions to access the different parts of expressions. For an `if` expression, data selector functions for the condition, then-action, and else-action are needed. These are written below:

```
; Return the condition of an if expression.
(define (get-condition if-expr)
  (second if-expr) )

; Return the then-action of an if expression.
(define (get-then-action if-expr)
  (third if-expr) )
```

```
; Return the else-action of an if expression.
(define (get-else-action if-expr)
  (fourth if-expr) )
```

Making recursive calls to code-gen-expr will take care of parts 1, 3, and 6 of handling an if expression. Parts 2 and 4 involve jumping to labels and parts 5 and 7 involve inserting those labels in the assembly code produced. Creating labels has a subtle difficulty associated with it: each label must be unique. In the previous examples we had a rather cavalier attitude toward label names. If there are several if expressions, the label ELSE cannot be used to signify the start of each else action. Labels produced by compilers are often written as a letter followed by a number (e.g., L7). Each label that is needed gets a larger number. Thus, we need a counter as either a global variable that is updated each time we create a label or as a variable in a lexical closure in a label-producing function that is incremented each time the closure is invoked. This technique is presented in Chapter 11 in the section called "Functions that Return Functions."

Creating labels

The first approach is not desirable stylistically because it uses a global variable that gets redefined in different functions throughout the code generator. The second approach is more complex but is better from a programming style viewpoint. We'll use it. We need two functions. The primary function gentemp produces a unique symbol given a prefix string, like "L." gentemp is produced by the second function make-gentemp, which maintains the local state (using a let variable) of the counter variable used to produce the unique symbols.

```
; Return a function that generates unique address labels.
(define (make-gentemp)
  (let ( (n 0) )
    (lambda (prefix)
      (set! n (+ n 1))
      (string->symbol
        (string-append prefix (number->string n))) )) )

(define gentemp (make-gentemp))
```

Below are some examples:

```
> (gentemp "L")
L1

> (gentemp "L")
L2
```

Since both labels will have to be used twice in the assembly code—once as a jump instruction and once as a label—their values should be saved in a let expression. To output labels, we use a function output-label, which we will write later.

The condition (part 2) uses the register list first, and the registers don't need to be saved for the *then* or *else* actions (parts 3 and 6), so the actions will use the entire register list as well. Since only one action will be performed, there is no conflict here. The *then* and *else* actions define the return value of the if expression.

Part 2 requires a conditional branch. This could be BEQ, BNE, BGT, BLT, or a combination of these. For example, the assembly equivalent of Scheme's >= is

```
BEQ then-label
BGT then-label
```

If either condition is met, a jump is made to the *then-action*. Producing the branching instructions will be done by the function conditional-test.

At this point, we can put the entire *if-then-else* function together. The auxiliary functions will be defined later.

```
; Generate code for an if expression.
(define (code-gen-if if-expr reg-list symbol-table)
  (let ( (then-label (gentemp "L"))
         (end-label (gentemp "L")) )
```
; 1. generate code for conditional test
```
    (code-gen-expr (get-condition if-expr) reg-list symbol-table)
```
; 2. create a branch to label if test passes (jump to *then* action)
```
    (conditional-test (get-condition if-expr) then-label)
```
; 3. generate code for the *else* action
```
    (code-gen-expr (get-else-action if-expr) reg-list symbol-table)
```
; 4. create a branch to a label following *then* action (end of if expression)
```
    (output 'JMP end-label)
```
; 5. insert a label for *then* action
```
    (output-label then-label)
```
; 6. generate code for *then* action
```
    (code-gen-expr (get-then-action if-expr) reg-list symbol-table)
```
; 7. insert a label for end of if expression
```
    (output-label end-label)) )
```

The function conditional-test produces code for comparison functions such as = and >. An association list *condition-assem* is used to map Scheme conditions with assembly instructions:

```
; Generate conditional branch to label.
(define (conditional-test condition label)
  (let ( (assem (assoc (first condition) *condition-assem*)) )
    (if (not assem)
        (fatal-error (string-append "bad-instruction: "
                       (symbol->string (first condition))))
        (for-each
          (lambda (instruction)
            (output instruction label) )
          (cdr assem)))) )
```

```
(define *condition-assem* '(
  (>  BGT)
  (<  BLT)
  (=  BEQ)
  (/= BNE)
  (>= BGT BEQ)
  (<= BLT BEQ)) )
```

The function `output-label` follows. It prints out a label without indentation.   *Printing labels*

```
; Generate a label for a subsequent instruction.
(define (output-label label)
  (display label) )
```

The code we have created is for `if` expressions with *else* actions. What about   *Handling `if`*
`if` expressions without *else* actions? Let's see what happens if we try the existing   *expressions without*
function with an *if-then* expression. The test is generated and a branch is made to   *else actions*
the *then* label if the test passes. Next, the code for the *else* action is generated. The
function `get-else-action` will return an error if called with an *if-then* expression. To allow for *if-then* expressions, we modify `get-else-action` to return `#f` if
no *else* action exists and modify `code-gen-if` to test the return value of `get-`
`else-action`.

```
; Return the else-action of an if expression or #f if none exists.
(define (get-else-action if-expr)
  (if (not (null? (cdddr if-expr)))
      (fourth if-expr)
      #f) )
```

```
; Generate code for an if expression.
(define (code-gen-if if-expr reg-list symbol-table)
  (let ( (then-label (gentemp "L"))
         (end-label (gentemp "L"))
         (else-action (get-else-action if-expr)) )
```
; 1. generate code for conditional test
```
    (code-gen-expr (get-condition if-expr) reg-list symbol-table)
```
; 2. create a branch to label if test passes (jump to *then* action)
```
    (conditional-test (get-condition if-expr) then-label)
```
; 3. generate code for the *else* action if one exists
```
    (if else-action
        (code-gen-expr else-action reg-list symbol-table))
```
; 4. create a branch to a label following *then* action (end of `if` expression)
```
    (output 'JMP end-label)
```
; 5. insert a label for *then* action
```
    (output-label then-label)
```
; 6. generate code for *then* action
```
    (code-gen-expr (get-then-action if-expr) reg-list symbol-table)
```
; 7. insert a label for end of `if` expression
```
    (output-label end-label)) )
```

13.7.2   Generating code for `define` expressions

To create a function, we must put all the assembly code that makes up the function into the memory space of the virtual machine and then label the start of those instructions with the symbol name for the function, so that when the function is called, JFN jumps to that label and begins executing the function's instructions.

To refine this further, the assembly code needed for a function definition is as follows:

Steps to handle function definitions

1. Generate label for the start of the function, using function name.
2. Save (push) the current frame pointer on the stack.
3. Set the new frame pointer to the first parameter.
4. Generate code for the body of the function.
5. Save the return value in register 0.
6. Restore (pop) the old frame pointer from the stack.
7. Generate a RET instruction.

The first step can be implemented using `output-label`. The second, third, and sixth steps are conditional; if the function has no parameters, these steps can be ignored. To set the frame pointer to the location of the first parameter in the third step, set the frame pointer to the top of the stack and then increment it past the return address and the other parameters. The fourth step can be handled by calling `code-gen-expr-list` with the expressions comprising the body of the function, the available registers, and a symbol table mapping the parameters to their addresses. The fifth and seventh steps are straightforward.

Selector functions to extract the function name, parameter list, and body from a function definition will be useful, and we'll define them later.

Getting return value into register 0

There is an additional subtlety to step five. We must know which register holds the function's return value. Each expression uses the entire register list when calling `code-gen-expr`, and the return value of the expression is saved in the first register of that list. Since the return value of a function is the result of the final expression, the function's return value will be in the first register. If the first register is R0, then we can skip this instruction to avoid creating the useless instruction

```
MOV R0, R0
```

Making an association list for parameter names and values

The parameter names must be saved in the symbol table. There they are matched with locations on the stack relative to the frame pointer. The function `make-table` will create the table, taking a list of parameter names and returning a symbol table (an association list) that maps parameters to their offsets from the frame pointer. Recall that the first parameter is at the frame pointer, the second parameter is one address preceding the frame pointer, and so on. For example, given the parameter list

```
(size width height)
```

`make-table` should produce the following association list:

```
((size . "(FP)")
 (width . "-1(FP)")
 (height . "-2(FP)"))
```

Notice how the offset from the frame pointer is the negative of the position of the parameter in the parameter list. We will use this relationship in writing `make-table`:

```
; Create a symbol table for the parameters to a function.
(define (make-table parameter-list)
  (if (null? parameter-list)
      '()
      (cons
        (cons (first parameter-list) (indirect 'FP))
        (map
          (lambda (parameter)
            (cons
              parameter
              (indexed 'FP (- (position parameter parameter-list))))) )
          (rest parameter-list)))) )
```

Here is the code for `code-gen-func-def`:

```
; Generate code for a function definition.
(define (code-gen-func-def expr reg-list symbol-table)
  ; 1. Generate label for the start of the function, using function name.
  (output-label (get-func-name expr))
  (cond ((not (null? (get-params expr))) ; if function has parameters
         ; 2. Save (push) the current frame pointer on the stack.
         (output 'MOV 'FP (pre-dec 'SP))
         ; 3. Set the new frame pointer to the first parameter.
         (output 'MOV 'SP 'FP)
         (output 'ADD
            (literal (+ (length (get-params expr)) 1)) 'FP)))
  ; 4. Generate code for the body of the function.
  (code-gen-expr-list (get-body expr) reg-list
    (make-table (get-params expr)))
  ; 5. Save the return value in register 0.
  (if (not (eq? (first reg-list) 'R0))
      (output 'MOV (first reg-list) 'R0))
  ; 6. Restore (pop) the old frame pointer from the stack.
  (if (not (null? (get-params expr)))
      (output 'MOV (post-inc 'SP) 'FP))
  ; 7. Generate a RET instruction.
  (output 'RET) )
```

The selector functions are defined below:

Selector functions for function definitions

```
; Return function name from function definition.
(define (get-func-name func)
  (caadr func) )
```

```
; Return parameter list from function definition.
(define (get-params func)
  (cdadr func) )

; Return body from function definition.
(define (get-body func)
  (subseq func 2) )
```

13.7.3   Generating code for calls to user-defined functions

Before a user-defined function (one created using `define`) is called, a number of operations must be performed:

Steps to take before calling functions

1. Save (push) the registers currently in use on the stack.
2. Generate code for the arguments and push the results on the stack.
3. Call the JFN instruction.

After the function returns, the following steps must be taken:

Steps to take after returning from functions

4. Save the return value in the first register if it's not already there.
5. Increment the stack pointer past the arguments.
6. Restore (pop) the registers from the stack.

Pushing and popping values onto the stack

We could simplify things if we had functions that pushed values onto the stack and popped values from the stack. These functions will take a list that indicates which addresses to pop the stack values into or which values to push onto the stack. These functions, `push-vals` and `pop-vals`, are defined below:

```
; Generate code to push values in address-list on stack.
(define (push-vals address-list)
  (for-each
    (lambda (address)
      (output 'MOV address (pre-dec 'SP)) )
    address-list) )

; Generate code to pop values from stack into address-list addresses.
(define (pop-vals address-list)
  (for-each
    (lambda (address)
      (output 'MOV (post-inc 'SP) address) )
    address-list) )
```

Be careful when pushing and popping values onto the stack. If registers R0, R1, and R2 are pushed on the stack using

```
(push-vals '(R0 R1 R2))
```

the top of the stack is R2. Hence, the registers should be popped in the reverse order like this:

```
(pop-vals '(R2 R1 R0))
```

Most of the steps outlined above involve pushing or popping values or producing simple instructions. Step two requires generating code for the arguments. We cannot use `code-gen-expr-list` to do this because each argument's value must be pushed on the stack after it is determined. Instead we can use multiple calls to `code-gen-expr` and `push-vals` to push the results onto the stack.

One further complication exists: how do we know which registers should be saved? `reg-list` indicates the registers that can be used. We need a complete list of registers with which to compare `reg-list`. A global variable can do this:

```
(define *all-regs* '(R0 R1 R2 R3 R4 R5 R6 R7))
```

Below is the code to call user-defined functions, `code-gen-user-func`. Once again, selector functions are used to get the arguments and function name.

```
; Generate code to call user-defined functions.
(define (code-gen-user-func expr reg-list symbol-table)
  ; 1. Save (push) the registers currently in use on the stack.
  (push-vals (set-difference *all-regs* reg-list))
  ; 2. Generate code for the arguments and push the results on the stack.
  (for-each
    (lambda (arg)
      (code-gen-expr arg reg-list symbol-table)
      (push-vals (subseq reg-list 0 1)) )
    (get-args expr))
  ; 3. Call the JFN instruction.
  (output 'JFN (get-call-name expr))
  ; 4. Save the return value in the first register if it's not already there.
  (if (not (eq? (first reg-list) 'R0))
      (output 'MOV 'R0 (first reg-list)))
  ; 5. Increment the stack pointer past the arguments.
  (if (not (null? (get-args expr)))
      (output 'ADD (literal (length (get-args expr))) 'SP))
  ; 6. Restore (pop) the registers from the stack.
  (pop-vals (reverse (set-difference *all-regs* reg-list))) )
```

Our selector functions are defined below:

```
; Return arguments from a function call.
(define (get-args expr)
  (rest expr) )

; Return function name from a function call.
(define (get-call-name expr)
  (first expr) )
```

13.7.4   Generating code for calls to built-in functions

The final step is to write a function that generates assembly language for calls to built-in functions. We have to handle the following function calls:

category	functions
arithmetic	+ (with two arguments), - (with one or two arguments)
comparison	=, /=, >, <, >=, <= (with two arguments)

Predicate functions that test for the type of function call will be helpful. These will be defined later. To call a built-in function, the steps are as follows:

1. Generate code for the arguments, saving the results in registers.
2. Perform the operation of the function using the values (saved in registers) from the above step.
3. Save the result in the appropriate register.

The function that carries out these actions will be given an expression and a list of available registers. The first register in this list denotes the location of the return value. All other registers can be used to hold temporary values such as argument values. Examine the following call:

```
(+ 4 num)
```

Code would first be generated for the arguments. Assuming that the result of this addition operation is saved in register 1, the argument values could be placed in registers 2 and 3. The final step would be to do an ADD instruction and a MOV to put the result in register 1 as follows:

```
ADD R2, R3
MOV R3, R1
```

This MOV instruction can be avoided if registers 1 and 2 hold the values of the arguments. Then a single instruction can do the same operation.

```
ADD R2, R1
```

Conveniently, this works for subtraction too. Given the call

```
(- 4 3)
```

and storing 4 in register 1 and 3 in register 2, the assembly instruction to save the result in register 1 is

```
SUB R2, R1
```

This properly subtracts 3 from 4, leaving 1 in register 1.

Below is the code for generating assembly language for calls to built-in functions:

```
; Generate code for calls to built-in functions.
(define (code-gen-built-in-func expr reg-list symbol-table)
  (code-gen-expr (get-first-arg expr) reg-list symbol-table)
  (if (has-two-args? expr)
      (code-gen-expr
        (get-second-arg expr) (rest reg-list) symbol-table))
  (cond ((is-negation? expr)
         (output 'NEG (first reg-list)))
        ((is-addition? expr)
         (output 'ADD (second reg-list) (first reg-list)))
        ((or (is-subtraction? expr) (is-comparison? expr))
         (output 'SUB (second reg-list) (first reg-list)))) )
```

Below are the auxiliary functions to test the type of function call being made and extract the arguments:

```
; Test if function call has two arguments.
(define (has-two-args? expr)
  (= (length expr) 3) )

; Test if function call is a call to unary - (negation).
(define (is-negation? expr)
  (and (eqv? (first expr) '-)
       (= (length expr) 2)) )

; Test if function call is a call to + (addition).
(define (is-addition? expr)
  (and (eqv? (first expr) '+)
       (= (length expr) 3)) )

; Test if function call is a call to binary - (subtraction).
(define (is-subtraction? expr)
  (and (eqv? (first expr) '-)
       (= (length expr) 3)) )

; Test if function call is a call to a comparison function.
(define (is-comparison? expr)
  (and (member (first expr) '(> < >= <= = /=))
       (= (length expr) 3)) )

; Return first argument to function call.
(define (get-first-arg expr)
  (second expr) )

; Return second argument to function call.
(define (get-second-arg expr)
  (third expr) )
```

13.7.5 Testing our compiler

As an example to test out the preceding code, let's try to compile the recursive function `mult` and a call to it. This will test most pieces of our compiler. The call

```
(code-gen-expr
  '(define (mult num1 num2)
     (if (= num1 1)
         num2
         (+ num2 (mult (- num1 1) num2)))) )
  *all-regs* '())
```

produces the following assembly instructions. English explanations of the assembly are given as well but are not produced by our compiler.

assembly	description
`mult  mov fp, -(sp)`	push frame pointer on stack
`mov sp, fp`	set frame pointer to
`add #3, fp`	location of first argument
`mov (fp), r0`	move `num1` into register 0
`mov #1, r1`	
`sub r1, r0`	produce `(- num1 1)`
`beq L1`	if `(= num1 1)` go to *then* action
`mov -1(fp), r0`	move `num2` into register 0
`mov r0, -(sp)`	push R0 on stack (save register)
`mov (fp), r1`	move `num1` into register 1
`mov #1, r2`	
`sub r2, r1`	produce `(- num1 1)`
`mov r1, -(sp)`	push this value on the stack (first argument)
`mov -1(fp), r1`	move `num2` into register 1
`mov r1, -(sp)`	push it on the stack (second argument)
`jfn mult`	jump to `mult` function
`mov r0, r1`	save return value from `mult` in R1
`add #2, sp`	increment past the two arguments on the stack
`mov (sp)+, r0`	restore register 0, `num2`
`add r1, r0`	add `num2` to return value
`jmp L2`	jump past *then* action
`L1  mov -1(fp), r0`	move `num2` into register 0
`L2  mov (sp)+, fp`	restore old frame pointer
`ret`	

Comparing our hand-coded assembly with the computer-generated assembly

This is quite a bit longer than our hand-coded version. There are some steps where two instructions could be reduced to one. The value `(- num1 1)` was computed twice, requiring an additional two instructions. Register 0 was used to hold the value of `num2` as the first argument to the function `+`. This forced register 0 to be saved on the stack before calling the function and to be restored afterwards.

Calling `mult` yields better results, but the arguments could have been put onto the stack in two instructions instead of four:

```
(code-gen-expr '(mult 2 3) *all-regs* '())
```

assembly	description
`mov #2, r0`	
`mov r0, -(sp)`	push first argument, 2, on the stack
`mov #3, r0`	
`mov r0, -(sp)`	push second argument, 3, on the stack
`jfn mult`	jump to `mult` function
`add #2, sp`	increment past the two arguments on the stack

13.7.6 Exercises

13.3 Could `make-gentemp` be defined as a variable instead of as a function, as follows?

```
(define make-gentemp
  (let ( (n 0) )
    (lambda (prefix)
      (set! n (+ n 1))
      (string->symbol
        (string-append prefix (number->string n))) )) )
```

If so, what are the advantages/disadvantages of this approach? If not, why not?

13.4 The function `code-gen-if` does not produce code for an *else* action if one does not exist. What will the generated code return in this case when the condition is false? Does this value make sense? If not, modify the function to return a more meaningful value.

13.5 No checks are made in this compiler to determine if registers are left in `reg-list`. What happens when all the registers are used up? Or is this a situation that can never arise? Indicate why all the registers cannot be used up or give an example expression that uses up all the registers and indicate how to modify the code to deal with this situation in some reasonable way.

13.6 Build a simulator that models the actions of a machine running assembly language instructions. This is a big but very useful exercise in verifying our compiler. The simulator will be a virtual machine that models the main memory, stack space, frame and stack pointers, registers, ALU, and comparator. The simulator will take a list of instructions where each instruction is a list, such as

```
((START MOV (literal 21) R0)
 (SUB (literal 20) R0)
 (BLT L1)
 (MOV (literal 3) R0)
 (JMP L2)
 (L1 MOV (literal 4) R0)
 (L2 HALT))
```

The first instruction to simulate is labeled START, and instructions should be processed until a HALT instruction is encountered. This way instructions that make up functions can exist in the instructions. Addressing modes (other than absolute) will be specified using lists like

```
(indexed FP -3)
```

Everything else is represented with symbols.

You'll need to create data structures for the registers, data stack, and stack and frame pointers. You'll also need to simulate the actions of the ALU and comparator. You will need a controller that sequences through the instructions, determines the type of instruction, and takes the appropriate actions. After each instruction, print out the values of the registers.

13.8   Extending Our Compiler

We have created a compiler for a simple subset of Scheme. Our mini-Scheme has two special forms (`if` and `define`), one data type (integer), and two arithmetic and six comparison functions. Let's explore what must be done to extend our compiler to incorporate more of Scheme. The focus is on five major areas: data types, functions, special forms, scope, and code optimization.

13.8.1   Adding more data types to our compiler

Representing different types

In this text, we have looked at six types of Scheme objects: numbers (which are further divided into integers, reals, ratios, and complex numbers), symbols, lists, booleans (`#t` and `#f`), functions, and strings.[3] All of these are represented as numbers in digital computers. This brings up two big questions: How are they represented and how are they distinguished? Floating point numbers, ratios, and complex numbers can be represented as two numbers. Symbols are addresses pointing to a symbol table entry giving the value of the symbol and its name. Booleans are represented as numbers (0 can be false and anything else is true). Functions are a collection of assembly language instructions. These instructions can be written in machine language (numbers). Strings are a series of numbers. Each number represents one or more characters of the string. A character can be represented as a number between 0 and 127.

Discerning objects of different types

But this brings up some ambiguities, namely how do we know if a number refers to an integer, part of a string, a machine language function, or something else? We can address this problem by representing each data type as two numbers; one number indicates what type the data is and the other is the data itself. For example if 0 denotes a number, then "0 2364" would represent the number 2,364. Such a structure is called a *record* and the individual parts of it are called *fields*.

Representing lists

How do we represent a list using numbers? Before answering this, review "Optional Section: Internal Representations of Lists" from Chapter 4. This section presents lists as sequences of cons cell structures. A cons cell comprises two pointers: one to the first element of the list and a second to the rest of the list.

We can represent a cons cell as two records (the `car` and `cdr` of the list). This is a new data type, so we will have to extend our types to include a cons cell type that has three fields: the type, the `car` record, and the `cdr` record. For example, if a cons cell type is denoted by the number 7, the series of numbers "7 0 4 0 2" would represent the dotted list `(4 . 2)`.

[3.] Scheme has two additional types: vectors and characters. Vectors are like lists but they cannot change size after they are created. Vectors typically require less memory space than lists and have faster access times for individual elements than lists do. Strings are made up of characters.

Another data type is needed to represent a list. A list is a pointer to the first cons cell in the cons cell chain making up the list. The list record has two fields, the list type and the address of the first cons cell. The address 0 can represent an empty list. If 8 denotes the list type, "8 0" is an empty list. The sequence "8 12463" represents a list with a cons cell at address 12463. If this address is the start of the series "7 0 2 8 0," that represents the list (2). "8 23489" is the list (4 2) if address 23489 starts the series "7 0 4 8 12463."

13.8.2 Adding more functions to our compiler

The function `car` returns the `car` field of the cons cell record; `cdr` returns the `cdr` field. The functions `first` through `fifth`, `list-ref`, and `rest` can be written using `car` and `cdr`. To create lists, `cons` is the fundamental function. `cons` takes two records and creates the series "7 record1 record2" in some memory locations in the machine. `list`, `append`, and `subseq` can be written using `cons`.

Adding list functions

The various type-checking predicate functions such as `null?` and `number?` are easily written by checking the type field of the record with which they are called. `eq?` compares the type and value of records and, if they are the same, returns true. `eqv?` is a subtle variation on this that doesn't apply to our compiler but would to one that represents numbers as an address of their location. Two identical numbers may not be `eq?` because they are not at the same location even though both locations hold the same value. They should be `eqv?`, however. `equal?` can be written using a recursive function that uses `eq?`.

Adding type checking

Applicative functions such as `map` and `accumulate` can be implemented using recursive functions and the primitives mentioned above.

Adding functionals

13.8.3 Adding more special forms and handling scope in our compiler

Each special form has its own evaluation rules, so we will have to write a function to handle each one. Some of these, like `define` for defining a variable and `quote`, are fairly easy to implement. Others (like `let`, `cond`, or `do`) are more involved. Special forms like `let` and `do` define variables with limited scope. `define` defines global variables if used on the top level. We will have to see how our scoping rules allow for these situations. A global variable can be created by adding an entry to the symbol table. `let` can be handled by treating it as a function definition followed by a function call. For example,

Scoping issues

```
(let ((a 1) (b 2)) (* a b))
```

is the same[4] as the two expressions

---

[4]. There is one important distinction: defining a function creates code that can be jumped to, so the function should be given a name that is not likely to be used by the programmer.

```
(define (temp a b)
  (* a b))


(temp 1 2)
```

Chapter 10 shows how a do can be written as a recursive function with a let and a cond.

In Scheme functions are *first class objects*. This means they can be assigned to a variable (function definition), passed to a function (as in applicative operators), and returned by a function. We can pass a function by passing its label. Returning a function created by a lambda can be done by creating an internal name for the nameless lambda function and returning that name. When creating functions that aren't on the top level, scope issues are important when functions use variables that aren't parameters. The variables in the scope of a function must be maintained. This is called an *environment*.

13.8.4   Code Optimization

Our compiler could produce more streamlined code. This is known as *code optimization*. Code is optimized to reduce the number of statements or to reduce the time required to run the code. These are both measures of how effective an optimizer is.

Peephole optimization

There are many methods used to improve the code generated by a compiler. Some of these look at a few neighboring instructions at a time. This is called *peephole optimization*, because only a small part of the code is being examined at any time, like looking at the world through a peephole. Peephole optimization can handle reducing two instructions like

```
MOV #3, R0
MOV R0, -(SP)
```

to one instruction:

```
MOV #3, -(SP)
```

Saving results from prior computations

Other global optimization techniques require examining large segments of the code. Such techniques can handle cases like saving partial results that are used more than once in registers. For example, our code for the function mult generated (- num1 1) twice. In the hand-generated version, this computation was computed once and then saved in a register.

One should play close attention to loops (sections of code that are repeated) to assure there are no unnecessary instructions. Registers should be used frequently to improve the time to run since it is typically much faster to access a value held in a register than in main memory. Careful attention to addressing modes and the time taken to access the actual address they refer to can result in improved code performance.

13.9 Future Trends

Many pieces that make up a compiler are well understood and stable. With tools like lex and yacc, lexical analyzers and parsers are fairly easy to create. Code generation and optimization techniques are subject to change as new generations of hardware are introduced. For example, early computer systems ran much slower than today's computers, so if a computation could be saved by storing it in memory, that was done. Nowadays many processors are so fast compared to memory accesses that it's quicker to compute a value twice than to compute it once, save it in memory, and look it up.

Other hardware advances have radically changed the way compilers are created. *Parallel machines* that have more than one processor should have compilers that take advantage of the extra processors and keep as many of them occupied as possible. This can be done by executing different instructions in parallel as long as it is not necessary to run them sequentially. For example, the instructions

Parallel machines

```
(define a (* b c))
(define d (/ e (* f g)))
```

can be executed in parallel, but

```
(define a (* b c))
(define b (/ a (* f g)))
```

can be partially run in parallel. (* b c) and (* f g) can be run in parallel, but (* b c) must be computed and saved in the variable a before a is divided by (* f g). Compilers must detect these dependencies.

New programming languages that embody new ideas or paradigms in programming involve new ideas in compiler creation. Object-oriented and logic programming languages have ideas and features that must be implemented in assembly language by the compiler writer. Some parallel languages are designed to run on parallel machines. New languages will always be created and compiler writers will always have new challenges in implementing these on different machines.

13.10 Summary

- A compiler translates code in one language into functionally equivalent code in another language.
- An interpreter simulates the execution of code in some language on a machine.
- A cross-compiler translates code into a language that is understood by a different machine than the one on which the cross-compiler runs. It typically produces assembly language for a different machine.
- Lexical analysis (scanning) converts the individual characters that compose a program into a sequence of tokens (like number, identifier, define).
- Parsing takes the sequence of tokens and organizes them into a parse tree according to the syntax (structural rules) of the language.

- Semantic analysis checks the semantics (meaning) of the parse tree to disambiguate things that look the same but mean different things based on the types of the identifiers.
- Code generation takes the modified parse tree and produces a sequence of statements in the language being compiled into (target language).
- Machine language is a numeric language—each instruction is a number—that runs directly on the hardware.
- Assembly language is a symbolic representation of machine language.
- The program counter is the location of the next instruction to be executed.
- The stack is a space in the machine where values are added to or deleted from one at time at the top of the stack.
- The stack pointer indicates the top of the stack.
- The frame pointer indicates the location on the stack of the first parameter to a function.
- Registers are locations that can be quickly accessed; they are useful for storing results of computations.
- The arithmetic logic unit (ALU) does the computations (e.g., addition or negation).
- The comparator is used to examine the status of the last computation (e.g., was the result negative or zero).

13.11   Additional Reading

Aho, A.V., Sethi, R., and Ullman, J.D. (1986). *Compilers, Principles, Techniques, and Tools*, Addison-Wesley, Reading, MA.

Aho, A.V. and Ullman, J.D. (1977). *Principles of Compiler Design*, Addison-Wesley, Reading, MA.

Wilhelm, R. and Maurer, D. (1995). *Compiler Design*, Addison-Wesley, Harlow, England.

Wirth, N. (1996). *Compiler Construction*, Addison-Wesley, Harlow, England.

13.12   Code Listing

```
; Generate code for a list of expressions.
(define (code-gen-expr-list expr-list reg-list symbol-table)
  (for-each
    (lambda (expr)
      (code-gen-expr expr reg-list symbol-table) )
    expr-list) )

(define fatal-error 'not-yet)
```

```scheme
(call-with-current-continuation
  (lambda (stop)
    (set! fatal-error stop)))

; Print out instruction and operands.
(define (output instruc . addrs)
  (display "  ")
  (display instruc)
  (cond ((not (null? addrs))
          (display " ")
          (display (first addrs))
          (for-each
            (lambda (addr)
              (display ", ")
              (display addr) )
            (rest addrs))))
  (newline) )

; Lookup address of symbol in symbol table.
(define (symbol-address symbol symbol-table)
  (let ( (address (assoc symbol symbol-table)) )
    (if address
        (cdr address)
        (fatal-error
          (string-append
            "Undefined variable:"
            (symbol->string symbol))))) )

; Generate code for a single expression saving return value in the
; first register of reg-list.
(define (code-gen-expr expr reg-list symbol-table)
  (let ( (result (first reg-list)) )
    (cond ((symbol? expr)
            (output 'MOV (symbol-address expr symbol-table) result))
          ((number? expr)
            (output 'MOV (literal expr) result))
          ((is-if? expr)
            (code-gen-if expr reg-list symbol-table))
          ((is-func-def? expr)
            (code-gen-func-def expr reg-list symbol-table))
          ((is-built-in-func? expr)
            (code-gen-built-in-func expr reg-list symbol-table))
          (else ; otherwise it's a user-defined function call
            (code-gen-user-func expr reg-list symbol-table)))) )

; Test if expr is an if expression.
(define (is-if? expr)
  (eqv? (first expr) 'if) )
```

```scheme
; Test if expr is a function definition.
(define (is-func-def? expr)
  (eqv? (first expr) 'define) )

; Test if expr is a call to a built-in function.
(define (is-built-in-func? expr)
  (member (first expr) '(+ - < > = /= <= >=)) )

; Generate a string representing a literal.
(define (literal number)
  (string-append "#" (number->string number)) )

; Generate a string representing an indirect address.
(define (indirect address)
  (string-append "(" (symbol->string address) ")") )

; Generate a string representing an indexed address.
(define (indexed address index)
  (string-append (number->string index) (indirect address)) )

; Generate a string representing a post-increment address.
(define (post-inc address)
  (string-append (indirect address) "+") )

; Generate a string representing a pre-decrement address.
(define (pre-dec address)
  (string-append "-" (indirect address)) )

; Return the condition of an if expression.
(define (get-condition if-expr)
  (second if-expr) )

; Return the then-action of an if expression.
(define (get-then-action if-expr)
  (third if-expr) )

; Return the else-action of an if expression or #f if none exists.
(define (get-else-action if-expr)
  (if (not (null? (cdddr if-expr)))
      (fourth if-expr)
      #f) )

; Return a function that generates unique address labels.
(define (make-gentemp)
  (let ( (n 0) )
    (lambda (prefix)
      (set! n (+ n 1))
      (string->symbol
        (string-append prefix (number->string n)))) ) )

(define gentemp (make-gentemp))
```

```
(define *condition-assem* '(
  (>   BGT)
  (<   BLT)
  (=   BEQ)
  (/=  BNE)
  (>=  BGT BEQ)
  (<=  BLT BEQ)) )

; Generate conditional branch to label.
(define (conditional-test condition label)
  (let ( (assem (assoc (first condition) *condition-assem*)) )
    (if (not assem)
        (fatal-error (string-append "bad-instruction: "
                        (symbol->string (first condition))))
        (for-each
          (lambda (instruction)
            (output instruction label) )
          (cdr assem)))) )

; Generate a label for a subsequent instruction.
(define (output-label label)
  (display label) )

; Generate code for an if expression.
(define (code-gen-if if-expr reg-list symbol-table)
  (let ( (then-label (gentemp "L"))
         (end-label (gentemp "L"))
         (else-action (get-else-action if-expr)) )
```
; 1. generate code for conditional test
```
    (code-gen-expr (get-condition if-expr) reg-list symbol-table)
```
; 2. create a branch to label if test passes (jump to *then* action)
```
    (conditional-test (get-condition if-expr) then-label)
```
; 3. generate code for the *else* action if one exists
```
    (if else-action
        (code-gen-expr else-action reg-list symbol-table))
```
; 4. create a branch to a label following *then* action (end of if expression)
```
    (output 'JMP end-label)
```
; 5. insert a label for *then* action
```
    (output-label then-label)
```
; 6. generate code for *then* action
```
    (code-gen-expr (get-then-action if-expr) reg-list symbol-table)
```
; 7. insert a label for end of if expression
```
    (output-label end-label)) )
```

```
; Create a symbol table for the parameters to a function.
(define (make-table parameter-list)
  (if (null? parameter-list)
      '()
      (cons
        (cons (first parameter-list) (indirect 'FP))
        (map
          (lambda (parameter)
            (cons
              parameter
              (indexed 'FP (- (position parameter parameter-list)))) )
          (rest parameter-list)))) )
```

```
; Generate code for a function definition.
(define (code-gen-func-def expr reg-list symbol-table)
```
  ; 1. Generate label for the start of the function, using function name.
```
  (output-label (get-func-name expr))
  (cond ((not (null? (get-params expr))) ; if function has parameters
```
         ; 2. Save (push) the current frame pointer on the stack.
```
         (output 'MOV 'FP (pre-dec 'SP))
```
         ; 3. Set the new frame pointer to the first parameter.
```
         (output 'MOV 'SP 'FP)
         (output 'ADD
           (literal (+ (length (get-params expr)) 1)) 'FP)))
```
  ; 4. Generate code for the body of the function.
```
  (code-gen-expr-list (get-body expr) reg-list
    (make-table (get-params expr)))
```
  ; 5. Save the return value in register 0.
```
  (if (not (eq? (first reg-list) 'R0))
      (output 'MOV (first reg-list) 'R0))
```
  ; 6. Restore (pop) the old frame pointer from the stack.
```
  (if (not (null? (get-params expr)))
      (output 'MOV (post-inc 'SP) 'FP))
```
  ; 7. Generate a RET instruction.
```
  (output 'RET) )
```

```
; Return function name from function definition.
(define (get-func-name func)
  (caadr func) )
```

```
; Return parameter list from function definition.
(define (get-params func)
  (cdadr func) )
```

```
; Return body from function definition.
(define (get-body func)
  (subseq func 2) )
```

```
; Generate code to push values in address-list on stack.
(define (push-vals address-list)
  (for-each
    (lambda (address)
      (output 'MOV address (pre-dec 'SP)) )
    address-list) )

; Generate code to pop values from stack into address-list addresses.
(define (pop-vals address-list)
  (for-each
    (lambda (address)
      (output 'MOV (post-inc 'SP) address) )
    address-list) )

(define *all-regs* '(R0 R1 R2 R3 R4 R5 R6 R7))

; Generate code to call user-defined functions.
(define (code-gen-user-func expr reg-list symbol-table)
  ; 1. Save (push) the registers currently in use on the stack.
  (push-vals (set-difference *all-regs* reg-list))
  ; 2. Generate code for the arguments and push the results on the stack.
  (for-each
    (lambda (arg)
      (code-gen-expr arg reg-list symbol-table)
      (push-vals (subseq reg-list 0 1)) )
    (get-args expr))
  ; 3. Call the JFN instruction.
  (output 'JFN (get-call-name expr))
  ; 4. Save the return value in the first register if it's not already there.
  (if (not (eq? (first reg-list) 'R0))
      (output 'MOV 'R0 (first reg-list)))
  ; 5. Increment the stack pointer past the arguments.
  (if (not (null? (get-args expr)))
      (output 'ADD (literal (length (get-args expr))) 'SP))
  ; 6. Restore (pop) the registers from the stack.
  (pop-vals (reverse (set-difference *all-regs* reg-list))) )

; Return arguments from a function call.
(define (get-args expr)
  (rest expr) )

; Return function name from a function call.
(define (get-call-name expr)
  (first expr) )
```

```
; Generate code for calls to built-in functions.
(define (code-gen-built-in-func expr reg-list symbol-table)
  (code-gen-expr (get-first-arg expr) reg-list symbol-table)
  (if (has-two-args? expr)
      (code-gen-expr
        (get-second-arg expr) (rest reg-list) symbol-table))
  (cond ((is-negation? expr)
           (output 'NEG (first reg-list)))
        ((is-addition? expr)
           (output 'ADD (second reg-list) (first reg-list)))
        ((or (is-subtraction? expr) (is-comparison? expr))
           (output 'SUB (second reg-list) (first reg-list)))) )

; Test if function call has two arguments.
(define (has-two-args? expr)
  (= (length expr) 3) )

; Test if function call is a call to unary - (negation).
(define (is-negation? expr)
  (and (eqv? (first expr) '-)
       (= (length expr) 2)) )

; Test if function call is a call to + (addition).
(define (is-addition? expr)
  (and (eqv? (first expr) '+)
       (= (length expr) 3)) )

; Test if function call is a call to binary - (subtraction).
(define (is-subtraction? expr)
  (and (eqv? (first expr) '-)
       (= (length expr) 3)) )

; Test if function call is a call to a comparison function.
(define (is-comparison? expr)
  (and (member (first expr) '(> < >= <= = /=))
       (= (length expr) 3)) )

; Return first argument to function call.
(define (get-first-arg expr)
  (second expr) )

; Return second argument to function call.
(define (get-second-arg expr)
  (third expr) )
```

CHAPTER 14

OPERATING SYSTEMS

14.1 Operating Systems

The *operating system* serves a number of functions in a computer system. It acts as an abstraction level between the hardware and the software to facilitate access to programs existing in the computer system. The operation system provides a simpler means of dealing with the resources that programs must use such as memory, printers, and input and output (I/O) devices (terminals, keyboards, and mouse). The operating system handles the information stored within the computer system; this information is typically maintained as a *file system*. The operating system takes care of the computer system memory, handling its distribution to programs running on the computer, and protection such that one program cannot corrupt another program. The operating system manages the programs running on the computer system to best utilize the resources of the computer; this is called *process management*. Each of these areas is discussed in more depth below. However, to better understand the workings of an operating system, it is important to understand the different pieces composing a computer system.

Role of the operating system

Computer systems consist of various interconnected parts each serving a specialized purpose. Let's review some of these pieces that were introduced in earlier chapters. The *central processing unit*, or *CPU*, is the "brains" of the computer system. It does all the arithmetic and logical computations, comparisons, and jumps to different instructions. The CPU understands machine language instructions only. It is directly connected to the *main system memory*, consisting of *RAM* (random access memory) and *ROM* (read only memory). RAM can be read from and written to, but ROM can be only read from. Both RAM and ROM can be randomly accessed meaning any location can be jumped to quickly. There are also sequential access memory devices in which the memory must be accessed in a sequence. Think of the difference in going to the start of a song using a CD player versus with a tape deck. A tape deck has sequential access only, whereas the CD player has random access allowing you to jump to the start of another song.

Computer systems

In addition to main memory, the CPU is connected to *secondary storage*, which consists of *tape drives* (usually used for backups) and *disk drives*, which are like CDs that can be read from and written to. The CPU can access *peripheral devices*, like printers, keyboards, mice, and terminals for displaying information. A computer system comprises all of these different components. It is important not to confuse the CPU with the entire computer system. The operating system exists in main memory, runs on the CPU, and controls the entire computer system.

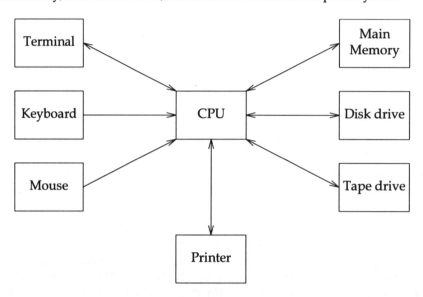

14.2   Historical Background

Early computers

The first computers were programmed by entering binary instructions directly into the machine one instruction at a time. With such a computer system, an operating system was not necessary. Only one person could use the computer at a time running only one program. There were no terminals, keyboards, window systems, or mice (except fuzzy ones). There were no files or directories. All memory was accessible to the programmer and there were no other peripheral devices that an operating system would have to handle. The machine would display results via a row of lights representing one binary word in the machine's memory. Each light corresponded to one bit; if it was on it was a 1, otherwise a 0.

Peripheral devices and device drivers

As advances in computers began, the need for operating systems arose. Toggling instructions directly into the computer gave way to paper card readers that used punch cards to hold instructions. Line printers were developed to facilitate getting output from the computer. Tape drives were used to save programs so they didn't have to be loaded in from cards each time. Each of these peripheral devices required programs called *device drivers* that enabled the CPU to access and use the devices. At first these device drivers were loaded in with the programs to be run. Later they became part of the operating system.

With card readers came the advent of *batch processing* in which users would submit their programs (a stack of cards) and then come back later to get the results (output from the line printer). The cards contained the program as well as special *job control cards*. Job control cards indicated the start and end of different *jobs* (user programs) and the start of the data for the programs (if any). A program called a *monitor* recognized these control cards, loaded the programs into the computer, and started running the programs. The monitor contained device drivers to handle peripheral devices.

Batch processing and monitors

Disk drives provided a more flexible means of data storage than magnetic tape. Tape is read and written sequentially and one cannot rapidly jump to a particular section of a tape. Disks, on the other hand, give *random access*. Information can be read from one part of the disk by a program, and new information can be written to another part of the disk in a rapid manner. Random access allows one to move rapidly to a new memory location, for example jumping from song to song on a CD versus using the (not so) fast forward button on a tape deck.

Disk drives

Another big improvement in computer throughput came about through the use of *multiprogramming* and *timesharing* in computer systems. Multiprogramming involves switching between jobs when the CPU is idle. A computing system spends its time doing CPU work and I/O work. CPU work is the time that that CPU is executing instructions (e.g., doing computations, comparisons, and jumping to different instructions). I/O work is reading and writing information from and to sources like card readers, keyboards, line printers, and terminals. A job is termed *I/O-bound* if it does a great deal of I/O work and *CPU-bound* if it primarily does CPU work. When a job is doing an I/O operation the CPU sits idle while the I/O device waits for the desired information to be input or displayed. This can involve seconds or much longer in the case of an I/O-bound job with a great number of I/O operations. This is a very long period of time for a CPU, which may be capable of executing hundreds of millions of instructions per second. Even a slow processor (by today's standards) performs on the order of ten million instructions per second[1]. In the few seconds it takes to respond to a query, this relatively slow CPU could have performed millions of instructions.

Multiprogramming

Rather than wait for I/O events to finish or arrive, a multiprogramming system will switch to a different job and let that job run until it finishes or gets an I/O event. This gives better usage of the CPU and means that more jobs can be run in the same amount of time.

Timesharing is an extension of multiprogramming. With multiprogramming and batch processing, jobs are submitted and the output is ready some time later when the job finishes. In a timesharing system each user has a terminal where they can communicate with the operating system and submit jobs directly. The job's output can be seen on the terminal as the job is being run, instead of at the end of the job in batch systems.

Timesharing

---

[1] The instructions per second of a machine is a function of the CPU's clock speed in cycles per second (typically given in megahertz) and the number of cycles per instruction, which varies depending on the CPU and maybe even the instructions themselves.

To provide more equity among CPU-bound jobs, timesharing systems switch jobs after a job has run for a certain period of time without an I/O request. This time period is called a *quantum*. Even with many people using the computer at a time, multiprogramming gives each job some CPU time while the other jobs are waiting for I/O requests to finish or have used their quantum. If there aren't too many jobs contending for the CPU at a time, the user has the illusion that she is the only person using the computer. This illusion rapidly disappears as the number of users and jobs grows.

Network operating systems

With the advent of networks interconnecting computers, *network operating systems* developed. At first simple changes were made to the operating system to support networks. These changes allowed users to send messages to other machines via e-mail, copy files to or from other machines, and remotely log on to machines. Later more sophisticated systems like SUN's network file system (NFS) were developed to make remote file acquisition invisible to the user. With NFS, computers with no local disks (*diskless nodes*) could be used in a network. These diskless nodes would get all their files from a file server.

Access to other CPUs in a network is typically not allowed without special permission or a password. And even if you can access another computer on the network you are on, you are in effect running a job on that computer just as a user who is connected directly to that computer would.

Distributed operating systems

Distributed operating systems make the use of multiple CPUs in a network as invisible as network file systems make remote file access. A distributed operating system decides on which CPU (or CPUs) to run your job. This involves a great deal of changes to the operating system. The process scheduler (which decides which job to run) must be changed to support multiple CPUs. This gets more complex if different CPUs have specialized hardware or resources (for example, a fast floating point unit or high resolution color laser printer). If a job is run on multiple CPUs at the same time, the operating system must know where a job can be split to run in parallel and which parts must be run serially, or when one CPU must wait for another to finish before starting. The way that memory in a job is handled is tricky as well. Some distributed systems use the idea of shared memory and others use a message passing system.

Now let's look at the jobs that the operating system does in more detail.

14.3 Resource Allocation

The resources of a computer system are devices that the operating system or programs may use. These include printers, tape drives, I/O devices, and memory. The CPU is a resource as well. The goals associated with resource allocation are outlined below:

Resource allocation goals

- Get the best usage of the system resources.
- Provide a simple means of allowing programs to get access to resources.
- Provide protection such that one program cannot interfere with another program's use of nonshareable resources.

- Assure that the system avoids *deadlock*, which occurs when two or more programs cannot continue because they are waiting for resources being used by other programs.

One commonly used technique to increase CPU utilization is *spooling*, which involves writing information for peripheral devices to areas of memory (*buffers*). The CPU is much faster than most peripheral devices and to best utilize it, we should keep it occupied at all times, not waiting for slower devices to finish doing what they need to do. For an analogy, imagine a teacher in an introductory foreign language class giving the class an exercise to translate a sentence. She can go to each student one at a time giving each a few words and then patiently wait for their slow response before giving more words. Or she can write the sentence on the board (a buffer) where each student can read and translate the words at their own rates. The students can write their translations on paper (more buffers), whereupon the teacher can check the translations, examining many words at a time rather than the slow one-word-at-a-time stream from each student as they are translating.

Spooling to buffers

Rather than have the CPU wait for peripheral devices to be ready to receive data, it is best to send that data to a buffer. The CPU can write information to a disk or RAM buffer much faster than to most peripheral devices. Then the device can read the data from the buffer directly at its own leisurely rate. Some devices that take input also produce output. These devices may spool their output to a buffer as well. This reduces the number of times the device must interrupt the CPU for each little part of the output it produces. Imagine how wasteful it would be if the teacher had to run to each student every time they produced a single word to verify it was correct. It is much more efficient to process many words at a time. These spooling techniques are used for devices that are slow and nonshareable, like printers and tape drives.

The operating system provides a means to access system resources. This saves programmers a great deal of headaches and hassles. Dealing with peripheral devices involves knowing a lot of specialized *communication protocols*, rules for how to "talk" to the device. If the operating system takes care of these low-level communication details and provides functions that the programmer can use to access the peripheral devices, the programmer's job is much easier and less prone to error.

Simplifying programming

Using functions provided by the operating system to access peripherals helps make programs more portable. A program that runs on the Macintosh operating system can run on many different types of Macintosh and Macintosh-clone computers. The machines must have the same CPU or the same family of CPU because the programs are delivered in the *object code* of the CPU. The object code is what the compiler produces and is what the underlying machine understands. The operating system can handle the differences between the various types of printers, monitors, keyboards, and hard drives that exist on these systems.

Portability

Protection is another advantage of using operating system functions for resource access. If programs had complete access to all of the system's memory, or to printers and tape drives, chaos and possibilities of corruption would ensue.

Protection

One could write a program that could write into the same memory space that another program was using. Or if two programs were using the printer at the same time, the output of both programs would be interspersed. The operating system can prevent this by only allowing programs to use the part of the memory that they have been allocated, and to control access of peripheral devices such that nonshareable devices (like printers and tape drives) cannot be used by more than one process at a time.

Deadlock

Deadlock is a subtle but crippling problem that the operating system must prevent. Deadlock can happen when two or more processes are in contention for the same nonshareable resources. Imagine that process1 is using the printer and process2 is using the tape drive, hence each process has acquired a nonshareable resource. Now suppose that process1 needs to use the tape drive and process2 needs the printer. They will both request these resources, which, of course, are being used. Both processes will wait until those resources are available, but in waiting they cannot continue. Thus they cannot release the resources they have already acquired. Since each process is waiting for resources that cannot be freed, the system is locked up—deadlock.

The classic example of deadlock is the dining philosophers problem from Edsger Dijkstra. Here is a slight variation on that problem. The situation is this: There are five philosophers sitting at a round table in a Chinese restaurant doing what philosophers do, namely eating food and thinking. This restaurant has cut down costs and only gives each philosopher one chopstick instead of two. To eat, a philosopher must pick up the chopstick to her left and then the one to her right. When done eating the philosopher replaces the chopsticks. If her neighbors are thinking instead of eating, this works fine, but if one or both are eating, then she must wait. A deadlock situation arises when all philosophers are hungry at the same time and each picks up the chopstick to their left and then wants to grab the right chopstick. All five philosophers will be stuck waiting for a second chopstick.

Critical sections

There are a number of means to prevent deadlock. One method is to require that processes acquire all the resources that they will need before they begin running. This can make for a very inefficient system, however. Another means is to try to stop deadlock before it occurs. This can be done by defining certain regions of the code as *critical sections*, those in which shared resources are used. By only allowing one process in a critical section at a time and carefully structuring the way that requests for resources are allowed, deadlock can be avoided. For example, deadlock can be avoided in the dining philosophers problem by only allowing one philosopher at a time to decide if the two neighboring chopsticks are available. If they are, then the philosopher takes them and eats. Any neighboring philosopher who attempts to eat then will have to wait because both chopsticks are not available.

In general, preventing deadlock is more involved and requires some trade-offs. One solution is to numerically order all the resources and require processes to acquire resources in order. This means that a process can never obtain a resource and then request one numbered less. Making all nonshareable resources shareable through techniques such as spooling, where devices write to disk rather than the device itself, is another way of preventing deadlock.

14.4 Process and Memory Management

The CPU is the most valuable resource of the computer system, and a good operating system will try to keep the CPU in use at all times. Getting the best usage of the CPU is handled primarily by the part of the operating system that deals with *process management*. A *process* is a program or application running on the computer. The term *job* is often used for processes. Process management techniques vary depending on the hardware and type of the operating system. The heart of process management is the *scheduler*, which decides when processes are run and temporarily stopped (*blocked*). Different scheduling algorithms are shown in sections 14.8 and 14.9.

Process management: improving CPU utilization

Processes can be in one of three states: running, ready to run, or waiting (or blocked) for some I/O request to finish. Process management concerns itself with the movement of processes between these three states. The following diagram illustrates this:

Process states

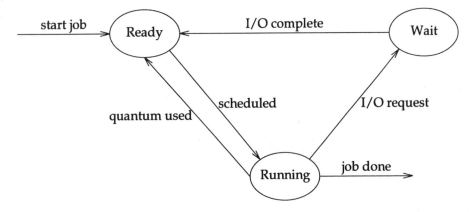

When a user submits a job to be run it goes to the ready queue. The scheduler picks jobs from the ready queue so they are run. A job stays running until it requests I/O or uses up its quantum.[2] If a job requests I/O it moves to the wait state until its I/O request has been serviced. Once serviced the job is moved to the ready queue. If a job uses up its quantum, it returns to the ready queue.

Process scheduling can be measured using many criteria. Some of these criteria are mutually exclusive—improving one diminishes another. Seven criteria are summarized in the table below:

Measuring process scheduling

---

[2] A job stays running based on these reasons in a preemptive scheduler. In a nonpreemptive scheduler there are no quantum time outs, and in a batch scheduler, there is no blocking for I/O.

criterion	measures
response time	the time a job waits before it gets to start running
wait time	the time that each job spends waiting to be run
CPU usage	percent of time that the CPU spends executing jobs
turnaround time	the time it takes for a job to finish
priorities	the turnaround time of high priority jobs
equality	the variation in turnaround time between jobs
throughput	the number of jobs run in a given time

Response time, wait time, and CPU usage

Minimizing *response time* is important in timesharing systems because the sooner a job starts, the sooner some output can be seen. The CPU can produce output faster than it can be displayed and much faster than it can be read, so giving users at least a little output early on keeps them happy and busy. *Wait time* measures the response time from the time a job is loaded into memory ready to be run and all the additional times it is waiting in the ready queue to be run again after using its quantum or blocking for an I/O request. These are really the times that are affected by the scheduler, rather than the time spent doing processing or handling I/O. Wait times should be minimized. *CPU usage* looks at the time the CPU spends processing jobs. The time spent servicing I/O requests or waiting to be run is not included in this measurement. CPU usage should be maximized.

Turnaround time and throughput

Turnaround time is the sum of the wait time, CPU time, and I/O time of a job. It is the measurement that the users are aware of as they wait for their jobs to finish in either a batch or timesharing system. Turnaround should be minimized. There are three variations on how turnaround figures can be used: focusing on high-priority jobs at the expense of low-priority jobs; keeping turnaround as constant as possible in a no-priority environment; and *throughput*. Throughput is a good overall measurement of a scheduler. Throughput is the number of jobs that complete in a certain time period. Dividing this overall time by the throughput gives an average turnaround figure. Throughput should be maximized.

Memory management

Processes exist in the main memory (RAM) of the computer when they are run. The simplest approach to handling the memory of a process is to load all of a process into the memory before it starts running and keep it there until the process finishes. However, this means that no process can be larger than the available memory on the machine. This approach becomes more problematic if the operating system allows more than one process to be run at the same time.

Virtual memory and demand paging

Virtual memory allows programs that do not fit in their entirety in the computer's main memory to be run on the computer. In a computer system that supports virtual memory, the operating system must support *demand paging*. With demand paging, an entire process is not loaded into memory. Instead only part of the process is loaded; other parts are loaded only if they are needed and are not present. This may require that part of the same or another process be moved out of the computer's memory to make room. The operating system must take care of this movement (*swapping*) as well, deciding what is best to *swap out* to keep the system performing well and avoid *thrashing*. Thrashing occurs when the operating system spends all of its time switching between parts of processes in memory. The parts of a program that are moved are called *pages*, which is where the term *demand paging* comes from.

14.5 File Systems

Information saved on the computer is organized into *files* and *directories*. Together, these make up the computer's *file system*. The operating system usually maintains the file system. Files represent information such as a cooking recipe, a Scheme program, a list of addresses, a letter to a friend, a saved screen image, a digitally encoded song, or even part of an operating system.

The file system and files

Files are organized into structures called directories. Directories can be viewed as drawers in a file cabinet and files as file folders in those drawers. What is written on the papers in a file folder is the contents of the file. The name on the tag of the file folder is the name of the file. Directories are used to organize collections of files into groups just as you might organize file folders into different drawers of a file cabinet. The file cabinet metaphor falls apart, though, as directories can have other directories within them. This would be like opening up a file cabinet drawer and finding other file cabinet drawers within it.

Directories

Files can be created from scratch, added to, changed (*edited*), merged with other files, searched through, sorted, shared, and printed (just to name a few operations). Some of these are operations that the operating system performs and some are operations that programs that work with files support. With many microcomputer operating systems, certain file operations (such as searching, creating, editing, and printing) are performed by separate software applications, such as word processors or database management systems. The operating system performs organizational operations like creating directories, moving files within directories, copying files, and deleting files. In larger computer systems like workstations or minicomputers, the operating system is usually more sophisticated and provides many file and directory functions. These operating systems usually have editors, text processing systems, and tools to search for patterns in files or make changes to files based on matched patterns.

Operations on files

Most files are collections of characters (*text files*) or binary information (*binary files*). Text files are used to hold human readable information. Each character is represented internally as a number using some standard that specifies a mapping between numbers and characters. ASCII or EBCDIC are two such standards. Binary files hold computer code that the CPU can understand. When a program is compiled into machine language, the result is a binary file (an *object file*) that can be executed on a machine.

Logical representations of files

Files can take on other forms as well. Files can hold information in some special proprietary format—many programs save their data this way. Files can be encrypted such that they are secure. Files can be encoded according to some standard such that they can be made available to other computer systems that use different operating systems or CPUs and have different text and binary representations. Files can be compressed using compression programs to take up less disk space, and entire directory structures can be represented as single files. All of these different representations serve particular needs and have advantages and

Physical representations of files

disadvantages.

All of the above differences aside, there is a distinction between how a user views a file and how the computer system stores a file. The user sees the file as text, a movie, a screen display, or music. The computer system represents the file in a very different form. The vast majority of today's computers are binary computers. They only deal with binary numbers, thus the representation of files is as binary information (a collection of zeroes and ones). A single zero or one is called a *bit*. A single character is represented using eight bits (a *byte*).

The human view of the file represents pieces of the file as *logical records*, and the machine's representation is as *physical records*. These physical records are stored as *blocks*. A block is a fixed amount of space, typically 512, 1,024, or 2,048 bytes long.[3] In most instances the logical record differs in size from the physical record. A text file uses a character (one byte) as its logical record. In a system that uses 1,024-byte blocks, each block holds 1,024 characters and a file with one character in it would use one block of space—as much as a thousand-character file would.

14.6   Utilities

Example utilities

Most operating systems provide a great number of *utility programs*. One set of commonly available *utilities* let the user create and manipulate information stored on the computer. We have discussed some of these in section 14.5 above. File utilities allow users to create files from scratch, edit existing files, concatenate (join) files, sort files, merge sorted files together, search for patterns in files, compare files, share files with other users, and print files. Some operating systems provide utilities that are miniature programming languages (UNIX's *awk* and *perl*) to perform complex operations on files.

Operating systems usually provide operations to display information on terminals and print to printers. These seemingly simple-sounding operations are complicated because there are few standards for terminals or printers. The operating system must know how to "talk to" different terminals and printers to produce the desired results. Ideally, the difficult parts are kept invisible from the user.

Synchronous and asynchronous communication

Facilities to communicate with other users are another commonly provided operating system feature. Communication can be synchronous or asynchronous. The telephone is an example of a synchronous communication device. Both parties are actively participating in the dialogue at the same time. Writing letters and sending them via the postal service is an example of asynchronous communication. Communication happens at a slower speed, but both parties need not be present at the same time to get messages across. Electronic mail (e-mail) uses asynchronous communication. There are utilities (e.g., *talk* in UNIX) that allow users to talk to one another at the same time (synchronous communication) even

---

[3.] These numbers are based on the size of sectors in the disk. Sectors are physical sections of disks that are typically 512, 1,024, or 2,048 bytes long. These numbers are all powers of 2.

across the planet.

Other communication protocols exist like USENET—a huge collection of special interest groups to which individuals can read and write—and other bulletin boards and information sources like Gopher, WWW (World Wide Web), and WAIS (Wide Area Information Service). *Browsers* are programs that enable users to retrieve information and search through large databases. Netscape Navigator and Microsoft Internet Explorer are two popular browsers to search through the World Wide Web. This network allows images, movies, sound, and text to be retrieved. Browsers may not be part of an operating system, but the operating system takes care of many of the communication details that browsers use to link to different machines.

14.7 Types of Operating Systems

The simplest type of operating system is a *single-user/single-job system*. Such a system only allows one person to use the computer at a given time and run only one job at a time. The earliest computers and the early microcomputers used this type of system. In the case of early computers, there was no operating system at all.

Single-job system

Another type of operating system is a *batch system*. In a batch operating system there may be many users who have access to the computer, but the computer runs only one job at a time. Jobs are typically run in a first-come, first-served fashion, and the turnaround time, the time between submitting your job to the computer and getting the results back, can vary dramatically (anywhere from minutes to hours to days).

Batch systems

Interactive operating systems are systems that support many users running many jobs at roughly the same time. The operating system switches between jobs to best utilize the CPU and share it among all the jobs waiting to be run.

Interactive systems

Realtime operating systems guarantee that jobs will run at a certain speed. Such systems are important whenever timing issues are critical. If you need to measure the time it takes for an event to occur, you need to guarantee that your process is not interrupted. In a timesharing system an interrupt may happen. Music environments, control systems, and medical systems are examples where realtime systems are needed.

Realtime systems

A computer network is created by connecting computers together with cables, allowing information to be sent and received between computers. There are both short-range networks called *local area networks* or *LANs*, and long-distance networks called *wide area networks* or *WANs*. The computers hooked up to such networks need some way to communicate and share information with other computers on the networks. The network operating system typically provides some level of support for this. In network operating systems each machine is autonomous, having its own unique running operating system.

Networks and Network operating systems

Messages (e-mail) and files may be sent between machines in networked systems. To exchange files with remote machines, a network operating system provides a mechanism to explicitly send files. In addition to file access, networked operating systems typically support remote access to other machines such that a

File server and clients

user can connect directly via the network to a remote machine.

The exact location of a user's files can be made invisible to the user. They may exist on a different machine from the one the user is connected to, the same machine, or even on a collection of machines. File access is sometimes explicitly made or can be invisible to the user such that the operating system gives the illusion that files are on the local machine when in reality they are on a different machine or *file server*. A file server maintains files for other machines (*clients*). The advantage of such a system is that files only need to be maintained on the file server so each client has smaller local disk storage requirements. In the case of the latter, from the user's perspective the files are all local.

Each computer does not need to be connected to all the other computers in the network. Information may go from one computer to another through various other computers along the way to its destination. A *network operating system* supports the transmission of information among computers connected to one another via some type of network.

Distributed operating systems

Distributed operating systems work with many machines connected together via a network or through shared memory. In distributed systems the user has the illusion of using the local machine when in reality she may be using a remote machine or many at once. As in network systems, files can be accessed remotely. In addition, processes may run on any machine(s) on the network to best utilize the available CPU resources. Performance from the user's point of view is greatly enhanced when a job is run on the least loaded CPU or split up to run on many CPUs at the same time.

Distributed systems are a lot more complex than single CPU systems and creating operating systems, compilers, and software that best utilize multiple CPUs is a challenge. However, distributed systems offer great improvements in speed (splitting the job load among many processors), reliability (if one CPU fails, there are still others that can be used), and division of labor or resource handling (each CPU can specialize on certain tasks or handle certain peripherals that can be shared among all the CPUs in the distributed system).

14.8   How a Scheduler Works

Before running a job, the operating system must load the job into memory and then put that job into the ready queue of jobs waiting for the CPU. Once the job is started, a timer must be set allocating the maximum time limit, quantum, for that job until the next job waiting may run. If the job makes any I/O requests, the operating system must handle them. While the job is being serviced with an I/O request, it is blocked until the I/O request is complete. Once complete, the job is put into the ready queue again.

Scheduling algorithms

Let's examine the internals of the scheduler in a *multitasking operating system*. Multitasking is another term used for multiprogramming and typically refers to an operating system with the ability to switch between processes (also called *tasks*) that are initiated by a single user. In a multitasking system the scheduler decides which job in the ready queue should be run next. The scheduler must make its decision to provide the highest degree of throughput possible. Many different algorithms can be used. The simplest approach is *first-come, first-served scheduling*. In this approach the job that is first in the ready queue is the one the scheduler chooses. This approach is easy to implement, but tends to be inefficient as it is a *nonpreemptive* algorithm. A nonpreemtive scheduler does not allow another job to replace (or preempt) an existing, running job unless it requests I/O. This means that other jobs in the queue will wait if a large CPU-bound job comes before them in the ready queue.

Another scheduling algorithm is to base the choice of which job to run next upon *job priority* or type of job. If a job is given a high priority, it will be run before other jobs. A low-priority job will not be run unless the system is relatively empty. This is beneficial in terms of getting better performance for those users who have high-priority jobs, but certain jobs may wait a long time if their priority is set too low.

Choosing a job based on its type (CPU- or I/O-bound) can result in overall system performance improvement. If I/O-bound jobs are chosen first, the average response time and turnaround time improves. I/O-bound jobs will be blocked when they do I/O requests, enabling other jobs to run while the I/O request is being serviced. If CPU-bound jobs are run first, the I/O-bound jobs must wait for their completion before starting, and then the CPU will sit idle while the I/O-bound jobs are getting their I/O requests serviced. The average waiting time will be greater. For CPU-bound jobs, choosing shorter jobs first will result in shorter average *response times*—the time it takes for a job to get started.

Round-robin scheduling is another technique that is like first-come, first-served scheduling, except it is *preemptive*; it adds a time limit to the CPU time. Each job is given a time slice (quantum), and once that has been used up, the job times out and another job runs. This approach works well in timesharing operating systems.

14.9 Implementing a Scheduler in Scheme

We will implement two schedulers in Scheme. One is for batch jobs and the other for multitasking environments. The scheduling algorithm will be a function that is passed (as a parameter named `select`) to our schedulers. This way we don't have to write a different scheduler for each algorithm we wish to use. We need only write a different scheduling algorithm function. Part of the scheduler's job will be to measure the efficiency of the scheduling algorithm used. This will enable us to compare different scheduling algorithms.

We will need a representation for jobs that are waiting to be run. These job descriptions will be arguments to our scheduler function. They should provide enough information about the jobs such that the different scheduling algorithms can be used. We need to indicate job priority and CPU and I/O times used.

To measure job timing we will need time constants for the quantum used (`*quantum*`), and the time it takes to do a switch from one job to another, *context switch* (`*context-switch*`). The context switch involves saving and restoring

Quantum and context switch times

registers and certain data structures used in the operating systems to keep track of processes and their memory. It also includes the time that the scheduler takes in making the choice of which job to run next. We'll use one tenth of a second (100,000 microseconds) for our quantum and 100 microseconds as the time to do a context switch.

14.9.1   Deciding on a data structure

Representing jobs

The main data structure is for jobs. Each job can be represented as a list—a job description. A collection of jobs can be represented as a list of job descriptions. We should have some means of indicating when jobs arrive (are ready to run) at the computer system. Let's make the *ready time* the first item in the job description list. The second element is the priority of the job ranging from 1 to 10, with 10 being the highest priority. If the priority is not needed, #f will be used instead of a priority number. The next items in the job description are the times required for CPU and I/O. I/O times will be prefaced with the symbol io. In general, a job description looks like the following.

(ready-time priority times)

Loops

Many jobs have loops, and rather than repeat CPU and I/O times in the loops, we can use a list to represent a loop. The first element of the list is the number of iterations of the loop. The remaining elements are the CPU and I/O times. All CPU and I/O times are expressed in microseconds. One second is one million microseconds and one millisecond is one thousand microseconds. For example, the list

```
(2000000 #f 1000 io 1000000 600 (4 io 100000 500))
```

represents a job arriving (ready) after 2 seconds with no priority. The job spends 1 millisecond of CPU time and then 1 second of I/O time, followed by 600 microseconds of CPU time, and then enters a loop 4 times. Each time through the loop the job performs a 100 millisecond I/O request followed by 500 microseconds of CPU time.

Such job descriptions, along with a scheduling algorithm, are passed to our scheduler which returns performance measurements of the scheduling algorithm. We can make use of applicative operators to run job lists against a variety of scheduling algorithms to test which scheduling algorithm works best for those jobs. Another useful thing would be to test each scheduling algorithm against different job lists. We can determine if certain scheduling algorithms work best in general or work best for CPU-bound jobs or I/O-bound jobs.

Measuring the effectiveness of our scheduler

Section 14.4 presented various ways of measuring scheduling algorithm effectiveness. Response time (the time a job waits to be run) and wait time (the total of all times a job spends in the ready queue waiting to be run) are good measures because they don't take into account the CPU and I/O times of the jobs, like turnaround time and throughput do. However, these measures don't tell us about CPU utilization. CPU utilization is a good measure because it focuses only on the CPU, which is the resource for which the scheduler is trying to maximize usage. However, CPU utilization can be high but the overall system performance can be suboptimal if the scheduling algorithm switches between jobs too often by using a low quantum. Ideally, most jobs should finish their CPU bursts within the given quantum for improved efficiency. Throughput (the number of jobs completed in some amount of time) is a convenient measure to use because it gives an overall picture of the operating system's performance. Given a fixed job list, we can use throughput as a measure of scheduling algorithm efficiency because the CPU and I/O times are constant, so they won't affect the results when doing comparisons between scheduling algorithms.

14.9.2   Building a batch scheduler

The scheduler, as we have been describing it, takes a list of job descriptions and a scheduling algorithm. The scheduling algorithm decides which job to choose given a job description list, whereas the goal of the scheduler is to handle the timing. The scheduler must keep track of the time the CPU and I/O devices spend handling parts of a job and the time that each job spends waiting to be run. The exact time figure we return depends on which measure of scheduler performance we choose, or we can be flexible and return different performance measures. Our scheduler will be flexible and return a list of CPU, I/O, and wait times. These times can be used to compute the average wait time, CPU utilization percentage, percent of time spent handling I/O, and total time spent to complete all the jobs. In addition, the scheduler will print out each job as it is run, along with its start time and the amount of CPU, I/O, and wait time the job used. This information is useful in verifying that the scheduler is working properly.

Maintaining CPU, I/O, and wait times

To save the running totals for wait, CPU, and I/O times, we can use different variables that we change using `set!`. We can avoid setting global variables by using variables defined in a `let`. Another way would be to use additional parameters in our function and change these as we make recursive calls with smaller portions of the job lists. This final solution is cleaner.

To start we'll create a batch scheduler that takes a job description list and decides which job to invoke based on the scheduling algorithm, which uses information like the order in which the jobs arrive in the ready queue and the priority of the jobs. Once a single job has been chosen, it can be processed by a separate function. This provides a nice breakdown of our overall problem. The function that processes a job takes a job description list and recurses through it adding the job's CPU and I/O times to running totals. It is best to call this function using a job description with the ready time and job priority stripped off, since we will recurse only on the CPU and I/O times. The function `times` will do this.

Processing a single job

The extra parameters for the total CPU and I/O times must be incremented based on the current time value being processed in the job description list. This is complicated by loops that are represented as sublists. However, if we take advantage of the recursion, we can handle such sublists.

Below is a first attempt at the code to run a batch job to completion.

```
; Simulate running a batch job - version 1.
(define (run-batch-job job-times CPU-time I/O-time)
  (cond ((null? job-times) (list CPU-time I/O-time))
        ((number? (car job-times))    ; CPU time
         (run-batch-job (cdr job-times)
           (+ CPU-time (car job-times)) I/O-time))
        ((symbol? (car job-times))    ; I/O time
         (run-batch-job (cddr job-times) CPU-time
           (+ I/O-time (second job-times))))
        (else   ; loop
         (run-batch-job (car job-times) CPU-time I/O-time))) )
```

Let's test this code:

```
> (run-batch-job '(700 io 3000 550 (3 1000 io 4000) 500) 0 0)
(2253 7000)
```

The answer we wanted is (4750 15000). One problem with the code is that times that follow a loop are ignored. We must make a recursive call with the cdr of the job list as well. The tricky part then is how we combine these results, as both will be lists. We must add the corresponding elements of each returned list and return a list of the sums. This can be done using map.

Preprocessing loops   Another problem is that the loops aren't handled properly. The first element of the loop list is the number of repetitions of the loop. We are treating this value as a CPU time. If we compute the CPU and I/O times for one pass through the loop and then multiply each time by the number of iterations through the loop, we get the CPU and I/O times we need. We can do this by treating lists as a special case in run-batch-job. Another approach is to preprocess the job description lists and eliminate the loops (sublists). For example, the job description

```
(700 io 3000 550 (3 1000 io 4000) 500)
```

should be translated to

```
(700 io 3000 550 3000 io 12000 500)
```

We'll take the approach of preprocessing the list in the interest of keeping run-batch-job simple. Here is the code for these functions:

```
; Return a job time list without loops (the times in a loop are
; multiplied by the number of repetitions of the loop).
(define (no-loops job-times)
  (cond ((null? job-times) '())
        ((atom? (car job-times))
         (cons (car job-times) (no-loops (cdr job-times))))
        (else
         (append
          (map (lambda (time) (if (number? time)
                                  (* time (caar job-times))
                                  time) )
               (cdar job-times))
          (no-loops (cdr job-times)))))) )
```

```
; Simulate running a batch job - version 2.
(define (run-batch-job job-times CPU-time I/O-time)
  (cond ((null? job-times) (list CPU-time I/O-time))
        ((number? (car job-times))    ; CPU time
          (run-batch-job (cdr job-times)
            (+ CPU-time (car job-times)) I/O-time))
        ((symbol? (car job-times))    ; I/O time
          (run-batch-job (cddr job-times) CPU-time
            (+ I/O-time (second job-times)))))
        (else   ; ignore other items
          (run-batch-job (cdr job-times) CPU-time I/O-time))) )
```

Let's try these new functions:

```
> (no-loops '(700 io 3000 550 (3 1000 io 4000) 500))
(700 io 3000 550 3000 io 12000 500)

> (run-batch-job
    (no-loops '(700 io 3000 550 (3 1000 io 4000) 500)) 0 0)
(4750 15000)
```

The batch scheduler must choose the most appropriate job based on the scheduling algorithm it uses. This algorithm is passed in as an argument. Only the jobs that are currently ready to run should be examined by the scheduling algorithm. The function `ready-jobs` will filter out the jobs ready to run. It compares the time the job is ready to run (obtained from the selector function `ready-time`) with the current time, which is maintained as the parameter `time` in the scheduler.

Choosing a job

Once a job has been chosen, it is run using `run-batch-job` to compute its CPU and I/O times. The time a job had to wait before it was run can be determined by taking the difference of the job's ready time and the time it was chosen. This time is appended to the CPU and I/O times that are returned from `run-batch-job`. The scheduler returns a list of these three times.

The scheduler must be called recursively on the remaining jobs. When we recurse, the current time is incremented adding the CPU and I/O times of the last job. The recursive result is combined with the times from the current job using `map`. After a job runs, it must be removed from from the job queue. We shouldn't use the function **remove** to do so, as it will remove all jobs that are identical to the last one run. Instead we'll write a function `remove1` that returns a list without the first occurrence of an item. To help us understand our scheduler, we'll call the function `info` to print out the job selected, its start time, and the times the job took to run. Here is the code for the scheduler and its auxiliary functions:

```scheme
; Simulate running a collection of jobs in batch fashion using
; select as the scheduling algorithm.
(define (batch-scheduler job-collection select time)
  (if (null? job-collection)
      '(0 0 0)    ; zero times
      (let* ( (next-job (select (ready-jobs job-collection time)))
              (wait-time (- time (ready-time next-job)))
              (time-spent
                (append
                  (run-batch-job (no-loops (times next-job)) 0 0)
                  (list wait-time))) )
        (info next-job time time-spent)
        (map +
          time-spent
          (batch-scheduler
            (remove1 next-job job-collection)
            select
            (+ time (first time-spent) (second time-spent)))))) )

; Print job description and job timing information.
(define (info job start-time time-spent)
  (display job)
  (newline)
  (display "   start: ")
  (display start-time)
  (display ", spent: ")
  (display time-spent)
  (newline) )

; The time when a job is first ready to run.
(define (ready-time job-desc)
  (first job-desc) )

; The job's priority.
(define (priority job-desc)
  (second job-desc) )

; Job description without the ready-time and priority.
(define (times job-desc)
  (subseq job-desc 2) )

; The collection of jobs that is ready to run.
(define (ready-jobs job-collection time)
  (keep-if
    (lambda (job) (<= (ready-time job) time) )
    job-collection) )
```

```
; Remove the first occurrence of job from job-collection.
(define (remove1 job job-collection)
  (let ( (pos (position job job-collection)) )
    (append (subseq job-collection 0 pos)
            (subseq job-collection (+ pos 1)))) )
```

We can test out this scheduler with a collection of jobs. We'll create these jobs with various priorities and times in which they are ready to run. Here are some CPU- and I/O-bound jobs:

```
(define cpu1 '(0 8 50000 io 1000 30000 io 1000))
(define io1 '(0 6 1000 io 500000 10000 io 30000))
(define cpu2 '(30000 10 200000))
(define io2 '(60000 7 10000 io 250000 (2 5000 io 10000) 7000))
```

We can use the function **first** as the scheduling algorithm, meaning jobs are selected according to the order in which they enter the ready queue. As described earlier, this is called first-come, first-served scheduling.

First-come, first-served batch scheduling

```
> (batch-scheduler (list cpu1 io1 cpu2 io2) first 0)
(0 8 50000 io 1000 30000 io 1000)
   start: 0, spent: (80000 2000 0)
(0 6 1000 io 500000 10000 io 30000)
   start: 82000, spent: (11000 530000 82000)
(30000 10 200000)
   start: 623000, spent: (200000 0 593000)
(60000 7 10000 io 250000 (2 5000 io 10000) 7000)
   start: 823000, spent: (27000 270000 763000)
(318000 802000 1438000)
```

The final list is the total CPU, I/O, and wait times. Adding the CPU and I/O times gives the turnaround time of all the jobs. This totals to 1,120,000 microseconds or 1.12 seconds. Dividing the total CPU time by this figure gives us the CPU utilization: about 28.4%. This is not that good.

14.9.3 Building a multitasking scheduler

The above scheduler is a batch-oriented scheduler; once a job is selected it is run in its entirety. This is contrasted with multiprogramming, in which a job is blocked when it makes an I/O request and another job is started. This tends to keep the CPU occupied. Multiprogramming systems have nonpreemptive and preemptive schedulers. Jobs run in a nonpreemptive scheduler get run in their entirety unless they make I/O requests. With a preemptive scheduler jobs can be switched after an I/O request or after a job has used up its time slice in a timesharing environment.

To handle preemptive multiprogramming schedulers (multitasking schedulers), we need to be able to switch jobs after I/O requests or after time slices have elapsed. The function that runs the jobs, `run-mt-job`, will run a job until it is blocked (does an I/O request or uses up its quantum) or finishes. If a job blocks, it must be returned to the ready queue by the scheduler. A function passed as a parameter `insert` will be used to put the job back in the ready queue. To do this,

Multitasking schedulers

`run-mt-job` will return the new job description to the scheduler along with the elapsed CPU and I/O times for that job. The scheduler then calls itself recursively with this new job description, saved in the `let` variable `returned-job`, replacing the old job description that was just run.

Jobs waiting for I/O are returned to the ready queue using the length of time for the I/O requested as the time to wait until the job is ready to run (the first element of the job description list). This makes the assumption that I/O requests are handled in the time given in the job description list. In reality it may take longer due to multiple jobs competing for the same resources. Jobs that have *timed out* (exhausted their quantum) are put onto the ready queue immediately ready to run again. The function `make-job` takes the remaining CPU and I/O times of a job and adds the ready time and priority back to reform a proper job description list.

```
; Return a job description to be inserted back in the ready queue.
(define (make-job time time-spent priority new-job-times)
  (cons (+ time (first time-spent) (second time-spent))
    (cons priority new-job-times)) )
```

Handling loops in the multitasking scheduler

We must create a new function to preprocess loops, as `no-loops` simply multiplies the CPU and I/O times by the number of repetitions. We need to model the exact sequence of CPU and I/O events. We'll need a function that takes a list like

```
(100 (3 200 io 1000) 500)
```

and produces the list

```
(100 200 io 1000 200 io 1000 200 io 1000 500)
```

The function `expand` does this with the help of `repeat`, which repeats an item a given number of times.

```
; Return job times without loops (loops are replaced with a series
; of the times in the loop).
(define (expand job-times)
  (cond ((null? job-times) '())
        ((atom? (car job-times))
          (cons (car job-times) (expand (cdr job-times))))
        (else
          (append
            (repeat (caar job-times) (cdar job-times))
            (expand (cdr job-times)))))) )
```

```
; Return a list of the times in time-list repeated number times.
(define (repeat number time-list)
  (if (<= number 0)
      '()
      (append time-list (repeat (- number 1) time-list))) )
```

In a multitasking system, wait times are indicators of how well the scheduling algorithm is performing. Just as with the batch scheduler, wait times are added to a running total each time a process gets scheduled to run. The `multitask-`

`scheduler` **function follows:**

```
; Simulate running a collection of jobs in a multitasking fashion.
; select is the scheduling algorithm. insert indicates how jobs are
; to be replaced in the ready queue.
(define (multitask-scheduler job-collection select insert time)
  (if (null? job-collection)
      '(0 0 0)   ; zero times
      (let* ((next-job (select (ready-jobs job-collection time)))
             (wait-time (- time (ready-time next-job)))
             (job-vals
               (run-mt-job (expand (times next-job)) 0 *quantum*))
             (returned-job (first job-vals))
             (time-spent
               (append (rest job-vals) (list wait-time))))
        (info next-job time time-spent)
        (map +
          time-spent
          (multitask-scheduler
            (if (null? returned-job)    ; if job is done
                (remove1 next-job job-collection)
                (insert
                  (make-job time time-spent
                    (priority next-job) returned-job)
                  (remove1 next-job job-collection)))
            select insert
            (+ time (first time-spent)   ; add CPU time and
               *context-switch*))))) )   ; context switch time
```

With multitasking, jobs may not run to completion. Thus, `run-mt-job` must be written such that when a job exceeds its quantum or does an I/O request, it is blocked and exits `run-mt-job`. This routine calls itself recursively until the job blocks. It returns a list of a new job description (to be added to the ready queue) and the elapsed CPU and I/O times.

Running a job in the multitasking scheduler

```
; Simulate running a job in a multitasking environment returning
; a list of the remaining job times and elapsed CPU and I/O times.
(define (run-mt-job job-times CPU-time quantum)
  (cond ((null? job-times) (list '() CPU-time 0))   ; job is done
        ((number? (car job-times))   ; CPU-time
          (if (< (car job-times) quantum)   ; enough time
              (run-mt-job (cdr job-times)
                (+ CPU-time (car job-times))
                (- quantum (car job-times)))
              (list (cdr job-times) (+ CPU-time quantum) 0)))
        ((symbol? (car job-times))   ; I/O-time
          (list (cddr job-times) CPU-time (second job-times)))
        (else   ; ignore other items
          (run-mt-job (cdr job-times) CPU-time quantum))) )
```

All that is left to do is define the scheduling algorithms. The simplest algorithm to define is first-come, first-served scheduling. Given a list of jobs, this
algorithm simply returns the first job in the job list. That job is run to completion,
meaning first-come, first-served scheduling is nonpreemptive; time limits are not
used. A running job will only block if it requests I/O. We cannot use our batch
processor to implement this because it never blocks; we can use the multitasking
scheduler if we choose a very large quantum. If a job blocks on I/O, it should be
added to the end of the ready queue so the next job is selected to run. Adding a
job to the end of a list will be implemented with the following function:

```
; Add a job to the end of the ready queue.
(define (to-end job job-collection)
  (append job-collection (list job)) )

(define *quantum* 1000000000)


; First-come, first-served scheduling algorithm.
(define (fcfs-scheduling job-collection)
  (multitask-scheduler job-collection first to-end 0) )
```

We must define the context switching time as well:

```
(define *context-switch* 100)
```

Now we can try our multitasking scheduler with the first-come, first-served
scheduling algorithm:

```
> (fcfs-scheduling (list cpu1 cpu2 io1 io2))
(0 8 50000 io 1000 30000 io 1000)
   start: 0, spent: (50000 1000 0)
(30000 10 200000)
   start: 50100, spent: (200000 0 20100)
(0 6 1000 io 500000 10000 io 30000)
   start: 250200, spent: (1000 500000 250200)
(60000 7 10000 io 250000 (2 5000 io 10000) 7000)
   start: 251300, spent: (10000 250000 191300)
(51000 8 30000 io 1000)
   start: 261400, spent: (30000 1000 210400)
Error: Pair expected
```

The scheduler went through all the jobs at least partially. The second job
finished, and the other three blocked waiting for I/O. The first job ran again and
blocked for another I/O request. But look at the I/O times of the third and fourth
jobs. They are much longer than the elapsed time. Unfortunately, the code in
`multitask-scheduler` does not handle the situation when no jobs are ready to
run. It will try to pick the first (our scheduling selection) job from an empty list,
and here lies the bug. To fix this bug, we should have the scheduler update its
elapsed time parameter `time` to the minimum ready time of the jobs in the ready
queue when there are no jobs that are ready to run.

The other change we should make to the scheduler is printing the elapsed
time. For our batch scheduler we used the sum of the total CPU and I/O times. In
a multitasking scheduler this will most likely not be the turnaround time for all

the jobs, since CPU times can happen in parallel with I/O times (when jobs block for I/O), and there may be dead time in which no jobs are ready to run (because they are waiting for their I/O requests to be serviced). The elapsed time value is the time in which the next process could run. It does not include the final I/O times to be serviced. Here is the new multitasking scheduler:

```
; Simulate running jobs in a multitasking fashion. select is the
; scheduling algorithm. insert replaces jobs in the ready queue.
(define (multitask-scheduler job-collection select insert time)
  (cond ((null? job-collection) (display "elapsed time -> ")
            (display time) (newline) '(0 0 0))   ; return zero times
         ((null? (ready-jobs job-collection time))
            (multitask-scheduler job-collection select insert
              (apply min (map ready-time job-collection))))
         (else
           (let* ((next-job
                    (select (ready-jobs job-collection time)))
                  (wait-time (- time (ready-time next-job)))
                  (job-vals (run-mt-job (expand (times next-job))
                              0 *quantum*))
                  (returned-job (first job-vals))
                  (time-spent
                    (append (rest job-vals) (list wait-time))))
             (info next-job time time-spent)
             (map + time-spent
               (multitask-scheduler
                 (if (null? returned-job)   ; if job is done
                     (remove1 next-job job-collection)
                     (insert (make-job time time-spent
                               (priority next-job) returned-job)
                       (remove1 next-job job-collection)))
                 select insert
                 (+ time (first time-spent)   ; add CPU time and
                   *context-switch*)))))) )   ; context switch time
```

```
> (fcfs-scheduling (list cpu1 cpu2 io1 io2))
(0 8 50000 io 1000 30000 io 1000)
   start: 0, spent: (50000 1000 0)
(30000 10 200000)
   start: 50100, spent: (200000 0 20100)
(0 6 1000 io 500000 10000 io 30000)
   start: 250200, spent: (1000 500000 250200)
(60000 7 10000 io 250000 (2 5000 io 10000) 7000)
   start: 251300, spent: (10000 250000 191300)
(51000 8 30000 io 1000)
   start: 261400, spent: (30000 1000 210400)
(511300 7 5000 io 10000 5000 io 10000 7000)
   start: 511300, spent: (5000 10000 0)
(526300 7 5000 io 10000 7000)
   start: 526300, spent: (5000 10000 0)
```

```
(541300 7 7000)
   start: 541300, spent: (7000 0 0)
(751200 6 10000 io 30000)
   start: 751200, spent: (10000 30000 0)
elapsed time -> 761300
(318000 802000 672000)
```

The CPU utilization is 318,000/761,300 or 41.77%, which is quite better than with batch scheduling. Another big improvement is in wait time reduction. If there were more CPU processes waiting to be run, we would see an even bigger improvement in CPU utilization in the multitasking scheduler than in the batch scheduler.

Round-robin scheduling

The preemptive version of first-come, first-served scheduling in multitasking environments is round-robin scheduling. Recall that in round-robin scheduling, once a job has used up its quantum it is moved to the end of the job queue and the next job is started. It is called round-robin because long jobs each get a turn in sequence, round-robin. This algorithm is the same as first-come, first-served but uses a much smaller quantum so jobs with long CPU bursts will be preempted to allow other jobs to run.

```
(define *quantum* 100000)

; Round-robin scheduling algorithm.
(define (round-robin job-collection)
  (multitask-scheduler job-collection first to-end 0) )

   > (round-robin (list cpu1 cpu2 io1 io2))
(0 8 50000 io 1000 30000 io 1000)
   start: 0, spent: (50000 1000 0)
(30000 10 200000)
   start: 50100, spent: (100000 0 20100)
(0 6 1000 io 500000 10000 io 30000)
   start: 150200, spent: (1000 500000 150200)
(60000 7 10000 io 250000 (2 5000 io 10000) 7000)
   start: 151300, spent: (10000 250000 91300)
(51000 8 30000 io 1000)
   start: 161400, spent: (30000 1000 110400)
(411300 7 5000 io 10000 5000 io 10000 7000)
   start: 411300, spent: (5000 10000 0)
(426300 7 5000 io 10000 7000)
   start: 426300, spent: (5000 10000 0)
(441300 7 7000)
   start: 441300, spent: (7000 0 0)
(651200 6 10000 io 30000)
   start: 651200, spent: (10000 30000 0)
elapsed time -> 661300
(218000 802000 372000)
```

Looking at the final result, notice that the total CPU time (218 milliseconds) is less than the total CPU time returned by the first-come, first-served scheduler (318 milliseconds). Also notice that the second job ran for half of its CPU burst

(100 milliseconds) and then was preempted, but the second half was never finished. This accounts for the missing 100 milliseconds.

Something is wrong with our code. It is probably in the section where we have CPU times that are greater than the quantum. This happens in run-mt-job. When the CPU time is greater than or equal to the quantum, we return the rest of the job times and the elapsed CPU and I/O times for that burst. This means that the remaining CPU time (that exceeding the quantum) is silently eliminated. We should make the recursive call with a modified CPU time subtracting the quantum from the original CPU time. If the quantum is equal to the CPU time, we don't want to return a CPU time of 0, so we should change the test condition to be <=. The new code follows:

```
; Simulate running a job in a multitasking environment returning
; a list of the remaining job times and elapsed CPU and I/O times.
(define (run-mt-job job-times CPU-time quantum)
  (cond ((null? job-times) (list '() CPU-time 0))    ; job is done
        ((number? (car job-times))   ; CPU-time
         (if (<= (car job-times) quantum)   ; enough or exact time
             (run-mt-job (cdr job-times)
               (+ CPU-time (car job-times))
               (- quantum (car job-times)))
             (list
               (cons (- (car job-times) quantum) (cdr job-times))
               (+ CPU-time quantum) 0)))
        ((symbol? (car job-times))   ; I/O-time
         (list (cddr job-times) CPU-time (second job-times)))
        (else   ; ignore other items
         (run-mt-job (cdr job-times) CPU-time quantum))) )

> (round-robin (list cpu1 cpu2 io1 io2))
(0 8 50000 io 1000 30000 io 1000)
   start: 0, spent: (50000 1000 0)
(30000 10 200000)
   start: 50100, spent: (100000 0 20100)
(0 6 1000 io 500000 10000 io 30000)
   start: 150200, spent: (1000 500000 150200)
(60000 7 10000 io 250000 (2 5000 io 10000) 7000)
   start: 151300, spent: (10000 250000 91300)
(51000 8 30000 io 1000)
   start: 161400, spent: (30000 1000 110400)
(150100 10 100000)
   start: 191500, spent: (100000 0 41400)
(411300 7 5000 io 10000 5000 io 10000 7000)
   start: 411300, spent: (5000 10000 0)
(426300 7 5000 io 10000 7000)
   start: 426300, spent: (5000 10000 0)
(441300 7 7000)
   start: 441300, spent: (7000 0 0)
(651200 6 10000 io 30000)
   start: 651200, spent: (10000 30000 0)
```

```
    elapsed time -> 661300
    (318000 802000 413400)
```

The elapsed time dropped by 100 milliseconds because we broke up the large CPU job into two bursts. This allowed the other I/O-bound jobs to start earlier and once they block, the waiting CPU processes can start earlier resulting in an overall turnaround savings. This can be seen in the reduced wait time as well. Now the CPU utilization is 318,000/661,300, or 48.09%, which is an improvement over first-come, first-served scheduling.

Priority scheduling

A different approach is to choose jobs based on their priority. Recall that a job's priority is obtained using the selector function `priority`. Priorities are numbers in which the largest number represents the highest priority. We can extract the job priorities as a list of numbers from the job collection using **map** with **priority**. Applying **accumulate** to **max** and this priority list will return the highest priority. However, we need to get the job that has that highest priority, not just the number. Instead of writing a function that searches through the job collection list to find the job that matches the largest priority number, we can use **accumulate** with the job collection list and a comparison function that matches the priorities of jobs. The job with the highest priority is returned at each comparison. When **accumulate** finishes, it returns the job with the largest priority. Jobs with no priorities are given a #f as their priority. These will be considered as the lowest priorities. If two jobs with no or identical priorities are compared, the first one wins. The function follows:

```
; Return the job with the highest priority value.
(define (pick-highest job-collection)
  (accumulate
    (lambda (job1 job2)
      (cond ((not (priority job2)) job1)
            ((not (priority job1)) job2)
            ((>= (priority job1) (priority job2)) job1)
            (else job2)) )
    job-collection) )

; Priority scheduling algorithm.
(define (priority-scheduling job-collection)
  (multitask-scheduler job-collection pick-highest cons 0) )

    > (priority-scheduling (list cpu1 cpu2 io1 io2))
    (0 8 50000 io 1000 30000 io 1000)
      start: 0, spent: (50000 1000 0)
    (30000 10 200000)
      start: 50100, spent: (100000 0 20100)
    (150100 10 100000)
      start: 150200, spent: (100000 0 100)
    (51000 8 30000 io 1000)
      start: 250300, spent: (30000 1000 199300)
    (60000 7 10000 io 250000 (2 5000 io 10000) 7000)
      start: 280400, spent: (10000 250000 220400)
    (0 6 1000 io 500000 10000 io 30000)
```

```
    start: 290500, spent: (1000 500000 290500)
(540400 7 5000 io 10000 5000 io 10000 7000)
    start: 540400, spent: (5000 10000 0)
(555400 7 5000 io 10000 7000)
    start: 555400, spent: (5000 10000 0)
(570400 7 7000)
    start: 570400, spent: (7000 0 0)
(791500 6 10000 io 30000)
    start: 791500, spent: (10000 30000 0)
elapsed time -> 801600
(318000 802000 730400)
```

The CPU utilization dropped to 39.67% and the wait time increased significantly compared to the round-robin scheduling. Our jobs are ranked positively by CPU demand and negatively by I/O usage. So with these priorities we favor the CPU-bound jobs. Let's see what happens if we favor the I/O-bound jobs.

Another scheduling algorithm is to choose the job with the shortest CPU time *Shortest CPU times*
demand. In the case where jobs consist of only CPU times, choosing the shortest jobs will reduce the average response and wait times for all the jobs. If jobs contain a mixture of CPU and I/O bursts, we can still choose the job with the shortest upcoming CPU time requirement. If there is a job waiting for I/O, it can take priority to free up the CPU for another process to run while the I/O request is being serviced. This algorithm can be implemented as follows:

```
; Return the first job requesting I/O or the job with the
; shortest CPU request.
(define (shortest-CPU-time job-collection)
  (accumulate
    (lambda (job1 job2)
      (let ((time1 (third job1))
            (time2 (third job2)))
        (cond ((symbol? time1) job1)    ; if i/o job, choose it
              ((symbol? time2) job2)
              ((<= time1 time2) job1)    ; else use shortest CPU job
              (else job2))) )
  job-collection) )

; I/O or shortest CPU first scheduling algorithm.
(define (short-CPU-scheduling job-collection)
  (multitask-scheduler job-collection shortest-CPU-time cons 0) )

  > (short-CPU-scheduling (list cpu1 cpu2 io1 io2))
  (0 6 1000 io 500000 10000 io 30000)
    start: 0, spent: (1000 500000 0)
  (0 8 50000 io 1000 30000 io 1000)
    start: 1100, spent: (50000 1000 1100)
  (30000 10 200000)
    start: 51200, spent: (100000 0 21200)
  (60000 7 10000 io 250000 (2 5000 io 10000) 7000)
    start: 151300, spent: (10000 250000 91300)
```

```
(52100 8 30000 io 1000)
    start: 161400, spent: (30000 1000 109300)
(151200 10 100000)
    start: 191500, spent: (100000 0 40300)
(411300 7 5000 io 10000 5000 io 10000 7000)
    start: 411300, spent: (5000 10000 0)
(426300 7 5000 io 10000 7000)
    start: 426300, spent: (5000 10000 0)
(441300 7 7000)
    start: 441300, spent: (7000 0 0)
(501000 6 10000 io 30000)
    start: 501000, spent: (10000 30000 0)
elapsed time -> 511100
(318000 802000 263200)
```

This is a big improvement over all the other scheduling algorithms. CPU utilization increased to 62.22% and wait times dropped 263.2 milliseconds. Favoring I/O and short CPU jobs is very beneficial.

14.9.4   Exercises

14.1   The function `expand` could be written without using `repeat`. The idea is to break a job time list like

```
(3000 (3 io 5000 500) 7000)
```

into this

```
(3000 io 5000 500 (2 io 5000 500) 7000)
```

This process continues until the number of repetitions is 0. Write a new version of `expand` using this idea.

14.2   Write new versions of `no-loops` and `expand` that support loops that are nested within loops, such as

```
(5000 (3 200 (4 io 3000 5000) io 2000))
```

Write your functions so that they work with arbitrarily deep nesting.

14.3   To compute the CPU usage of the batch scheduler, we divided the total CPU time by the sum of the total CPU and I/O times. This is problematic in that it assumes that there is no dead time in which no jobs are ready to run. Fix `batch-scheduler` so that it can properly handle dead time and have it print the true elapsed run time.

14.4   Create your own scheduling algorithm and write functions to implement it. Test it using the four jobs used above.

14.5   Modify `multitask-scheduler` and/or `run-mt-job` so that they also display the CPU utilization, average turnaround time, average response time, and average wait time for the jobs entered.

14.6 Make some experiments with the multitasking scheduler to see the effects that different quantum and context switch times have on the different scheduling algorithms. You may want to create some different job description lists to test against.

14.10 Future Trends

Computer networks are becoming more prevalent and larger. More and more information is being transmitted over local and wide area networks. Operating systems must provide some level of support to handle the increasing traffic in terms of not just more people sending more information, but multimedia information that is much larger in size than simple text.

With a distributed operating system, transparent computational operations are allowed just as networked operating systems allow transparent file access. Computations may be run on other machines or perhaps multiple machines without having to explicitly request this. Running computations on other machines is often easier and quicker than transferring the files to the local machine. For example, if you wanted to find the sizes of all the files and directories on a remote machine, it would be quicker to run the command on the other machine instead of transferring all the files and directories over to the local machine.

Distributing jobs over a network

If processes can be run on other machines, then this can create a large savings in speed. If the operating system can pick the machine with the lightest load and run the next job there, the job will execute faster, resulting in better turnaround time. The machines in a network may be of different types or configurations, so a job that was invoked on one machine may run faster on a different machine that has more appropriate hardware for that process (e.g., faster processor or more main memory). Even if all the machines in a network are of the same type and configuration, they may have different software; a distributed operating system may use this knowledge to direct processes to the most appropriate machine in the network.

Creating distributed operating systems is a difficult endeavor. There are communication issues: should the machines send messages to one another or interact through some shared memory space? There are timing issues: each machine has its own CPU with its own clock. This creates difficult synchronization and deadlock problems. Handling deadlock on distributed systems is much more complicated than on single CPU systems. It is not practical to prevent, so it must be detected and then recovered from. Scalability is a question: is it possible to add CPUs to a distributed operating system in a simple fashion, and what happens when the number of CPUs grows very large (e.g., in the billions)? Can reliability be provided? Can a distributed system be built that degrades gracefully as CPUs go down? Distributed systems with central control will fail at this, as the entire network of machines may be crippled when the controlling CPUs go down. Can true transparency of files and computations be given? There are solutions to file transparency but this is on networks with machines running the same

Building distributed operating systems

or a few operating systems. It would be nice to have simple access to nonprotected files existing on a variety of hardware platforms across the network. Can computation be handled similarly such that jobs are dispatched to the most appropriate machines in a network to maximize turnaround? A huge software infrastructure must be built: software that utilizes multiple CPUs in distributed systems is very difficult to create. Compilers that produce code that takes advantage of multiple CPUs is a good example of this.

Multiprocessor systems

As CPUs get cheaper and cheaper, the number of multiple CPU systems grows. Such *multiprocessor systems* have special requirements that the operating system must meet. In multiprocessor systems, operating systems have many of the same issues to address as in networked systems. Distributed operating systems are more the norm in multiprocessor systems; in fact, there is typically only one copy of the operating system running. It must decide how to best allocate jobs to the different processors to get the highest throughput. There has been research in how individual jobs may be split up and run on different processors. Some jobs lend themselves to this splitting up, or *parallelization*, as they have separate, autonomous segments that can be run independently in parallel on different processors. Other jobs are more sequential in nature and difficult to parallelize. The goal is to automate this process to best make use of multiprocessor systems.

Multithreaded processes

Using multiple *threads* is one way to parallelize a process. Before defining threads, let's take a closer look at processes. A process is a program that can be run on a machine. It has its own set of instructions that it executes, its data stack, register values, and program counter.[4] Each process may have a part of the main memory set aside for its use as well. Such a process is called a *heavyweight process*. A heavyweight process cannot be broken up into smaller entities that can run on the CPU.

There are tasks in which we would like to be able to split a process into smaller processes that can independently handle subtasks. Such a miniature process is called a thread. The threads of a single process all use the instructions and memory of that process; however, each thread has its own program counter, register values, and data stack. This way a thread acts as a separate process with some shared memory in common with other threads from the same parent process. A thread is a *lightweight process*—it is easy and fast to switch from one thread to another.

For an example of an application where threads would be nice, imagine an interactive program in which the user makes requests and the system performs them. This may be a library query system where someone requests information about books or periodicals. These requests may be time-consuming searches, and waiting for the user to enter a request is also slow. To speed things up we can have one thread handle requests while another gets requests from the user. The operating system will switch from one to another just as jobs are switched in a multitasking environment. However, the context switch time for threads is less

---

[4.] These terms were introduced in Chapter 13.

than for heavyweight processes, so they are more efficient. Also the threads all share the same memory (variables and data structures), so the thread that gets a request from a user reads that request into the same variable that the thread that processes the request uses.

As more programmers see the usefulness of threads, more operating systems will support them. There are some difficulties associated with threads, however. Multithreaded operating systems need schedulers that handle different types of context switches (switching between threads of the same process versus switching between threads of different processes). The same problems that arose with shareable resources also exist with threads because they share a process's memory space. For example, one thread may set a variable and be preempted, and then another thread may reset that variable before the first thread is able to use it. Some means of handling such critical section problems must be implemented and supported by the operating system.

14.11 Summary

- Operating systems handle resource allocation, process and memory management, provide access to the file system, and provide various utilities to perform a myriad of tasks.
- The first computers had no operating systems. Instead programs were loaded directly into the computer.
- Peripheral devices such as line printers and card readers were added to computers. These devices were controlled with programs called device drivers.
- Batch systems were used in the early operating systems. They ran one job at a time to completion.
- To better utilize the CPU, multiprogramming schedulers were built that switched between jobs when the running job was doing an I/O operation.
- Multiprogramming led to multitasking, where jobs would be preempted if they ran beyond some time limit, quantum. This allowed timesharing systems to come about in which multiple users could each share one CPU.
- Computer networks brought about network operating systems, which added support for file transmission between computers and remote access to computers.
- Distributed operating systems extend the ideas of transparent file access to transparent computer usage in which jobs are run on local, remote, or a combination of machines to best utilize the network CPU resources.
- Spooling involves sending or receiving information from a memory buffer instead of waiting for a slow device to be ready. It helps keep the CPU better-used.
- Deadlock occurs when two or more processes are unable to continue because they are both waiting for resources that the other already has and won't give up. It is typically either detected and recovered from or prevented by not allowing the conditions that lead up to deadlock to occur.

- Process management is the control of job sequencing to best utilize the CPU.
- The scheduler chooses which job to run according to the scheduling algorithm. There are various criteria for making this choices, including maximizing CPU usage and throughput (the number of jobs completed in a given time), and minimizing the response time (the time before a job starts) and the turnaround time (the time a job takes to complete).
- Some common scheduling algorithms include first-come, first-served (jobs are run in the order in which they reach the scheduler until they block for I/O); round-robin (jobs are run in order until they are preempted for I/O or using their CPU quantum); and I/O-bound jobs first (jobs with I/O demands or small CPU demands are run first).
- Batch schedulers run jobs until they finish. Multiprogramming schedulers run jobs until they block for I/O only (nonpreemptive schedulers) or either I/O or quantum expiration (preemptive schedulers).
- Memory management deals with providing and securing the computer's main memory among the running processes.
- Virtual memory allows jobs to run even if they need more memory than is available.
- Demand paging is the process of bringing sections (pages) of memory that have been held on the disk back into the main memory when they are needed.
- A file is a collection of information.
- File systems are collections of files that can be accessed by one or more computers.

14.12   Additional Reading

Nutt, G.J. (1992). *Centralized and Distributed Operating Systems*, Prentice Hall, Englewood Cliffs, NJ.

Silberschatz, A. and Galvin, P.B. (1994). *Operating System Concepts*, Fourth edition, Addison-Wesley, Reading, MA.

Tanenbaum, A.S. (1992). *Modern Operating Systems*, Prentice Hall, Englewood Cliffs, NJ.

Tanenbaum, A.S. (1995). *Distributed Operating Systems*, Prentice Hall, Englewood Cliffs, NJ.

14.13   Code Listing

Job collection:

```
(define cpu1 '(0 8 50000 io 1000 30000 io 1000))
(define io1 '(0 6 1000 io 500000 10000 io 30000))
(define cpu2 '(30000 10 200000))
(define io2 '(60000 7 10000 io 250000 (2 5000 io 10000) 7000))
```

Batch scheduler:

```
; Return a job time list without loops (the times in a loop are
; multiplied by the number of repetitions of the loop).
(define (no-loops job-times)
  (cond ((null? job-times) '())
        ((atom? (car job-times))
         (cons (car job-times) (no-loops (cdr job-times))))
        (else
         (append
          (map (lambda (time) (if (number? time)
                                  (* time (caar job-times))
                                  time) )
               (cdar job-times))
          (no-loops (cdr job-times))))) )

; Simulate running a batch job - version 2.
(define (run-batch-job job-times CPU-time I/O-time)
  (cond ((null? job-times) (list CPU-time I/O-time))
        ((number? (car job-times))    ; CPU time
         (run-batch-job (cdr job-times)
           (+ CPU-time (car job-times))
           I/O-time))
        ((symbol? (car job-times))    ; I/O time
         (run-batch-job (cddr job-times) CPU-time
           (+ I/O-time (second job-times)))))
        (else   ; ignore other items
         (run-batch-job (cdr job-times) CPU-time I/O-time))) )
```

```scheme
; Simulate running a collection of jobs in batch fashion using
; select as the scheduling algorithm.
(define (batch-scheduler job-collection select time)
  (if (null? job-collection)
      '(0 0 0)    ; zero times
      (let* ( (next-job (select (ready-jobs job-collection time)))
              (wait-time (- time (ready-time next-job)))
              (time-spent
                (append
                  (run-batch-job (no-loops (times next-job)) 0 0)
                  (list wait-time))) )
        (info next-job time time-spent)
        (map +
          time-spent
          (batch-scheduler
            (remove1 next-job job-collection)
            select
            (+ time (first time-spent) (second time-spent)))))) )

; Print job description and job timing information.
(define (info job start-time time-spent)
  (display job)
  (newline)
  (display "   start: ")
  (display start-time)
  (display ", spent: ")
  (display time-spent)
  (newline) )

; The time when a job is first ready to run.
(define (ready-time job-desc)
  (first job-desc) )

; The job's priority.
(define (priority job-desc)
  (second job-desc) )

; Job description without the ready-time and priority.
(define (times job-desc)
  (subseq job-desc 2) )

; The collection of jobs that is ready to run.
(define (ready-jobs job-collection time)
  (keep-if
    (lambda (job) (<= (ready-time job) time) )
    job-collection) )
```

```
; Remove the first occurrence of job from job-collection.
(define (remove1 job job-collection)
  (let ( (pos (position job job-collection)) )
    (append (subseq job-collection 0 pos)
            (subseq job-collection (+ pos 1)))) )
```

Multitasking scheduler:

```
; Return a job description to be inserted back in the ready queue.
(define (make-job time time-spent priority new-job-times)
  (cons (+ time (first time-spent) (second time-spent))
    (cons priority new-job-times)) )

; Return job times without loops (loops are replaced with a series
; of the times in the loop).
(define (expand job-times)
  (cond ((null? job-times) '())
        ((atom? (car job-times))
          (cons (car job-times) (expand (cdr job-times))))
        (else
          (append
            (repeat (caar job-times) (cdar job-times))
            (expand (cdr job-times)))))) )

; Return a list of the times in time-list repeated number times.
(define (repeat number time-list)
  (if (<= number 0)
      '()
      (append time-list (repeat (- number 1) time-list))) )

; Simulate running a job in a multitasking environment returning
; a list of the remaining job times and elapsed CPU and I/O times.
(define (run-mt-job job-times CPU-time quantum)
  (cond ((null? job-times) (list '() CPU-time 0))    ; job is done
        ((number? (car job-times))   ; CPU-time
          (if (<= (car job-times) quantum)   ; enough or exact time
              (run-mt-job (cdr job-times)
                (+ CPU-time (car job-times))
                (- quantum (car job-times)))
              (list
                (cons (- (car job-times) quantum) (cdr job-times))
                (+ CPU-time quantum) 0)))
        ((symbol? (car job-times))   ; I/O-time
          (list (cddr job-times) CPU-time (second job-times)))
        (else    ; ignore other items
          (run-mt-job (cdr job-times) CPU-time quantum))) )
```

```
; Simulate running jobs in a multitasking fashion. select is the
; scheduling algorithm. insert replaces jobs in the ready queue.
(define (multitask-scheduler job-collection select insert time)
  (cond ((null? job-collection) (display "elapsed time -> ")
         (display time) (newline) '(0 0 0))    ; return zero times
        ((null? (ready-jobs job-collection time))
         (multitask-scheduler job-collection select insert
           (apply min (map ready-time job-collection))))
        (else
          (let* ((next-job
                   (select (ready-jobs job-collection time)))
                 (wait-time (- time (ready-time next-job)))
                 (job-vals (run-mt-job (expand (times next-job))
                             0 *quantum*))
                 (returned-job (first job-vals))
                 (time-spent
                   (append (rest job-vals) (list wait-time))))
            (info next-job time time-spent)
            (map + time-spent
              (multitask-scheduler
                (if (null? returned-job)    ; if job is done
                    (remove1 next-job job-collection)
                    (insert (make-job time time-spent
                              (priority next-job) returned-job)
                      (remove1 next-job job-collection)))
                select insert
                (+ time (first time-spent)    ; add CPU time and
                   *context-switch*))))))) )    ; context switch time
```

Scheduling algorithms:

```
; Add a job to the end of the ready queue.
(define (to-end job job-collection)
  (append job-collection (list job)) )

(define *quantum* 1000000000)

; First-come, first-served scheduling algorithm.
(define (fcfs-scheduling job-collection)
  (multitask-scheduler job-collection first to-end 0) )

(define *context-switch* 100)

(define *quantum* 100000)

; Round-robin scheduling algorithm.
(define (round-robin job-collection)
  (multitask-scheduler job-collection first to-end 0) )
```

```
; Return the job with the highest priority value.
(define (pick-highest job-collection)
  (accumulate
    (lambda (job1 job2)
      (cond ((not (priority job2)) job1)
            ((not (priority job1)) job2)
            ((>= (priority job1) (priority job2)) job1)
            (else job2)) )
    job-collection) )

; Priority scheduling algorithm.
(define (priority-scheduling job-collection)
  (multitask-scheduler job-collection pick-highest cons 0) )

; Return the first job requesting I/O or the job with the
; shortest CPU request.
(define (shortest-CPU-time job-collection)
  (accumulate
    (lambda (job1 job2)
      (let ((time1 (third job1))
            (time2 (third job2)))
        (cond ((symbol? time1) job1)    ; if i/o job, choose it
              ((symbol? time2) job2)
              ((<= time1 time2) job1)    ; else use shortest CPU job
              (else job2))) )
    job-collection) )

; I/O or shortest CPU first scheduling algorithm.
(define (short-CPU-scheduling job-collection)
  (multitask-scheduler job-collection shortest-CPU-time cons 0) )
```

CHAPTER 15

ARTIFICIAL INTELLIGENCE

15.1 Artificial Intelligence

Artificial intelligence is perhaps the most talked about field within computer science. This is not due to the number of researchers or proponents within the field, or to number of accomplishments. Artificial intelligence, or AI as it is usually referred to, is so popular because it is the most controversial field within computer science. AI is threatening to some people and exciting to others. Some say it is an idea that is a few years away from becoming reality, while others say it will never be a possibility. Some say it's hip; others, hype. How can one field elicit such disparate beliefs? The answer lies in what AI attempts to do.

The controversy of AI

Artificial intelligence is the study of creating computers and software that can perform intelligent actions. This very broad definition might not seem worthy of the controversy that it has stirred. It is the nature and degree of the intelligent actions that causes the problems. If by "intelligent" we mean programs that can multiply 20-digit numbers faster than humans can, then that goal has been met and most people are not bothered or impressed. If we are talking about a program that can recognize a joke, that is an extremely difficult and impressive endeavor. Many people find the notion of a machine embodying such intelligence a frightening prospect. Intelligence is revered; it is the thing that separates us humans from the rest of life on the planet. When AI researchers started making claims that programs would exist that could outperform humans, it made many people uncomfortable. Others became excited and enthusiastic. Still others felt it could not and would not ever happen.

Intelligence

What really defines the intelligence that AI is trying to embody in computers? The answer depends on whom you ask. Most researchers in AI focus on specific problems or commercial applications. The days of claiming that computers will outsmart humans in so many years are over. Modeling human intelligence is a tough problem.

Rather than existing as a single unified field, AI is a collection of subfields, each with its own unique problems and accomplishments. We'll look at these subfields and some general themes that exist across them, such as searching and knowledge representation.

15.1.1   Subfields of artificial intelligence

The major subfields of AI include the following:

*   Natural Language Processing
    Natural language processing (NLP) addresses the problems of understanding human spoken languages (natural languages) so that they can be translated, summarized, used in communication between humans and computers, and used in tasks that involve some degree of language comprehension.
*   Machine Learning
    Machine learning studies how computers can learn new information from existing knowledge and beliefs.
*   Problem Solving and Planning
    Problem solvers and planners solve tasks within realworld environments.
*   Expert Systems
    Expert systems are programs that embody the knowledge of experts in a particular domain.
*   Robotics
    Robotics is the creation of robots that can move about and function in real environments.
*   Vision
    Vision involves recognizing three-dimensional objects given two-dimensional images from still or motion pictures.

15.2   Historical Background

Different perspectives of AI

The history of AI can be looked at through many lenses. A philosophical viewpoint is shown in the dialogue between AI advocates and protagonists. Books like *What Computers Can Do*, *What Computers Can't Do*, and *What Computers Still Can't Do* exemplify the disparate beliefs between the different camps. A businessperson might look at the introduction and growth of AI in the marketplace. A sociologist will look at changes in a population's views and beliefs of AI. A linguist may look at how machine intelligence is used in text and speech. An engineer will see how AI techniques can be used to solve problems or improve designs.

In all these areas, there has been a growth in the interest and awareness of AI. However, the big question of whether it is possible to create machines that are as intelligent as humans still remains. Some of the early AI pioneers thought that machines would outperform humans in a short period of time. Now AI researchers are more modest in their claims. Some AI researchers believe that machines will never reach human mental capabilities but still do research because a lot of improvement can be made that will result in higher quality and easier-to-use computers.

Let's look at some of the early work in AI. Allen Newell and Herbert Simon, two of the pioneers of AI, built two well-known AI programs. Their Logic Theorist (LT) could prove logic theories and even produced a proof shorter than one Bertrand Russell had in his classic logic text *Principia Mathematica*. Newell and Simon's General Problem Solver (GPS) was intended to solve any type of problem. It modeled human problem solving methods using *means-ends analysis*, in which the system looked at which operator could be applied to achieve the end result. If the conditions of that operator were not present, then they became new subgoals to be solved recursively. Later programs were built to solve algebra word problems and prove theorems in geometry.

Logic Theorist and General Problem Solver

Some programs could "understand" some amount of human language. Terry Winograd's SHRDLU[1] could answer questions about a world consisting of colored blocks. It could answer questions like "Can the red block be moved on top of the yellow block?" The answer to this depended on whether the blocks had objects above them.

SHRDLU

There were failures in natural language processing as well. A large effort in translating Russian to English in the early cold war period from the mid 1950s to the mid 1960s was one of AI's biggest blunders. Researchers thought the task was possible using grammar parsing techniques and dictionary lookup. Words in Russian would be searched in a Russian-to-English dictionary built into the program, and the English equivalent was returned. Translating English to Russian and then back into English resulted in transformations like

Failures in AI

> "Out of sight, out of mind" → "Invisible insanity"
>   and
> "The spirit is willing but the flesh is weak" → "The vodka is strong but the
>   meat is rotten"

After ten years of research, a study reported that the language translation efforts, even with human assistance to clean up the translations, were not effective. Even with foreseeable increases in computing power, translation efforts were seen as impossible.

Many fields within AI were running into limits. The toy problems that the AI programs could solve so well did not scale up to realworld domains. Programs like GPS turned out to be not so general after all.

AI made its recovery by limiting its research agenda to solving particular aspects of problems. Rather than translate entire natural languages, work was done on modeling small aspects of language understanding, like inference or planning. Problem solvers moved from general problems to specific problems. This brought about the field of expert systems, which saw a large degree of commercial success.

AI moves to attainable goals

---

[1] The letters in SHRDLU are the seventh through twelfth most common letters used in English words. The letters in ETAOIN are the first through sixth most common letters. These twelve letters make up a row in a popular typesetting terminal.

Expert systems

Work on expert systems started at Stanford in the late 1960s with DENDRAL. Hundreds of large expert systems were developed. The table below lists some of the early, well-known expert systems:

DELTA	aids in troubleshooting and repairing diesel electric locomotive engines, (Diesel Electric Locomotive Troubleshooting Aid)
DENDRAL	determines the molecular structure of chemicals given mass spectrometry data, (DENDRitic ALgorithm)
MACSYMA	simplifies, solves, and integrates algebraic expressions using symbolic manipulation, (MIT's Project MAC—Machine-Aided Cognition—SYmbolic MAthematics)
MYCIN	diagnoses and treats infectious diseases, (from the suffix of antibiotics like erythromycin, streptomycin, and neomycin)
PROSPECTOR	finds mineral deposits
SOPHIE	teaches students how to troubleshoot faulty electric circuits, (SOPHisticated Instructional Environment)
XCON	determines the layout of VAX computer systems, (eXpert CONfigurer)

Many expert system businesses grew in the early 1980s and then faded almost as quickly in the late 1980s and early 1990s.

AI hardware

As AI software grew, so did AI hardware. Specialized LISP workstations were built that helped speed up what was then a rather slow language in comparison to other commonly used languages. Symbolics, Texas Instruments, LISP Machines Inc., and Xerox all made custom LISP computers that ran LISP code faster than general purpose computers. However, with the advent of faster, general purpose computers and LISP compilers and optimizers, many of these specialized LISP workstations have become a thing of the past.

15.2.1   Game playing and puzzle solving programs

Some of the earliest AI programs were game playing programs in which a person competed against a computer or in puzzle solving programs, where a program tried to solve some type of logic or reasoning puzzle. Many of these problems have become "classic" AI problems and are used to test new searching or problem solving algorithms for their generality, expressiveness, speed, and efficiency.

Chess

One of the oldest and hardest problems is to create a program that can play chess at the grand master level. The journal *ACM* (*Association for Computing Machinery*) sponsors an annual contest in which different chess programs compete against one another. Programs are pitted against people quite often as well. At the writing of this book, some programs could occasionally beat grand masters in chess, but no program could do this consistently.

Most chess programs pick moves based on a success measure that compares all possible moves (assuming the opponent makes the best counter move). To be successful, these programs must look ahead many moves of play. This involves a lot of reduction in the space of possibilities (pruning of the search tree). Successful AI programs check many moves in parallel and eliminate poor moves early on in the search. Only the most promising moves are searched further.

Other games and puzzles are easier than chess and are often used as benchmarks for testing new searching algorithms. Here are some of these.

The 8-queens problem is played on a chessboard. The goal is to place all 8 queens on the chessboard with the constraint that no queens can attack one another.

8-queens

The 8-puzzle is a game played on a 3-by-3 square with sliding tiles. Each tile is numbered from 1 to 8. One part of the puzzle has no tile and is the spot in which a neighboring tile can be moved. The goal is to arrange the numbered tiles in some sequence, such as

8-puzzle

The 15-puzzle is a larger variation on this puzzle with 15 numbered tiles on a 4-by-4 square.

15-puzzle

Cryptarithmetic is a puzzle in which letters represent single digit numbers. The letters are arranged like a math equation. For example,

Cryptarithmetic

```
    S E N D
  + M O R E
  ---------
  M O N E Y
```

Here, the sum of the digits represented by the letters in SEND plus the digits in MORE equals the digits in MONEY. The goal is to figure out which digits match which letters in the puzzle. It breaks down into solving a series of equations with many variables. For example,

```
D + E = Y
N + R + carry from above = E
etc.
```

The traveling salesman problem exists in many businesses. The goal is to find the least expensive route that visits a collection of locations. Imagine having to fly to twenty different cities. Each flight costs some amount, and there is a best route that hits every city at the smallest total cost.

Traveling salesman problem

This problem is well known in computer science theory. It is an *NP-hard* problem, meaning that no known algorithm can solve this problem in polynomial time.[2] Polynomial time grows according to some polynomial equation such as the sum of the cube plus double the square of the number of cities to visit. NP-hard problems take exponential time to solve. In the case of the traveling salesman problem, this means the time is some amount raised to the number of cities to visit. As the number of cities grows, the time to solve the problem grows

Polynomial versus exponential time problems

---

[2] This is the current belief. However, someone may create such an algorithm, which would be a major find, since then the entire class of NP-hard problems would be solvable in polynomial time.

extremely large.

The traveling salesman problem is a good test case to measure the quality of new search techniques used in AI. Problems that grow exponentially can be solved using AI techniques, but they require a great deal of pruning of the search space or making choices that might not produce the best solution, but a reasonable one. With NP-hard problems, a fairly good solution is an excellent realworld compromise, since no one wants to wait an eternity for the best solution.

Missionaries and cannibals

Another puzzle is the missionaries and cannibals problem. The goal is to get three missionaries and three cannibals across a river using a boat that can hold only one or two of them at a time. There is a constraint: at no time can the cannibals outnumber the missionaries on either shore or in the boat. We will solve this puzzle in a later section of this chapter.

15.3   Common Problems

A number of problem areas exist in most, if not all, the subfields of AI. We'll look at them individually before focusing on the different subfields. The four problems we'll look at are searching, knowledge representation, reasoning, and world or commonsense knowledge.

15.3.1   Searching

Searching involves finding a path from an initial state to a final or goal state. A state is a description of the environment at some point in time. In addition, there are operators that describe transformations from one state to another; these are the actions that can be taken to change the state.

Search paths

Sometimes the path taken to the goal is the information that is needed. For example, in the missionaries and cannibals problem, we are looking for a sequence of moves to get all the people across the river. Each move affects the arrangement of people and therefore changes the state in this puzzle. Sometimes we only care about reaching the goal state and not how it was reached. In chess, if we know that a move will result in a win, we want to take that move. We don't care about the path there because it makes estimates of what the opponent will do and we must recalculate each move based on the exact move the opponent took. Some problems have many paths to the goal, but we want to find the cheapest one or a relatively inexpensive solution even though it may not be the absolute best one. The traveling salesman problem is an example of this. The same is true if you are shopping around for a good price. You will call some places, but not every single store that may carry the item even though it may be cheaper elsewhere. It just takes too much time.

Traversing the search space

Search is often discussed in terms of movement through a search space that is a tree or network of some sort. Each node in the tree or network represents some state, and branches from the node represent operators that can be taken to move to another node. With a search tree, the initial state is the root of the tree and the goal state is typically one of the leaves. There are numerous ways to search. Two of the simplest search algorithms were presented in Chapter 7: depth-first and breadth-first search. Both of these are exhaustive search approaches since they can search the entire search space. Depending on how the information is represented and where the goal is in the search tree, one approach will yield better results than the other. Depth-first moves quickly toward the leaves, whereas breadth-first covers a wider space of initial moves earlier on.

Uniform-cost search, a variation of breadth-first search, chooses the node with the least expensive cost from the start state to that node. Hence, it follows the cheapest alternative at all times. If that path gets more expensive than another path, the cheaper path is followed. This process continues until the goal is found. The idea is that if the cheapest path is followed and a solution is found, there cannot be a cheaper path that leads to the solution.

Hill-climbing, a variation of depth-first search, involves always choosing the best node to search next. This is akin to climbing a hill by always moving along the steepest path at every junction of many alternative paths. Hill-climbing is often faster than depth-first search because it limits the number of paths it searches (it is not exhaustive). However, hill-climbing can get stuck at *local maxima* and not find the desired *global maximum*. A local maxima is a high point relative to other points, but is not necessarily the overal maximum which is called the global maximum. If a path takes us to the top of a side hill that is lower than the overall hill we want to climb, we get stuck there. Hill-climbing does not back up and try another path.

Best-first search is like hill-climbing in that it has a means of ranking the nodes to determine their distance to the goal state. Rather than following only one path and choosing the best child from the current node of that path, many alternative paths are considered. The most promising path is followed. If that path fails, best-first search can backtrack, thereby avoiding the problem hill-climbing has of getting stuck at a local maxima.

A* search (pronounced A star) looks at the overall search picture to make decisions of which path to follow. A* search combines the cost that has already been incurred from the start state to the current state with the predicted cost of following a given path to the goal state. Thus A* search is a mix of uniform-cost search and best-first search. If the predicted cost from the current node to the goal doesn't overestimate the actual cost, A* will find the minimal cost path to the goal. Ideally, to reduce the amount of unnecessary searching, the predicted cost should be close to the actual cost. If the predicted-cost function underestimates too much, then A* starts to perform like uniform-cost search, which bases its decisions only on the cost of the path taken so far.

A* search is expressed using the following equation, where f is the overall cost (to be minimized), $g(n)$ is the cost incurred so far to get to node n, and $h(n)$ is the estimated cost of going from node n to the goal.

$$f = g(n) + h(n)$$

The following table shows the different search strategies of the above search methods. The table differentiates the strategies with two categories: the cost of the path taken so far and the cost to the goal. The costs are expressed as either not used (shown as an underscore), measured by the next node, or measured by the

Uniform-cost search

Hill-climbing

Best-first search

A* search

path cost or estimate.

method	cost so far	cost to goal
depth-first	–	–
breadth-first	–	–
hill-climbing	–	node
uniform-cost	path	–
best-first	–	path
A*	path	path

Comparison of search strategies

Minimax search

For game search, *minimax searching* is used. Minimax involves using one tree to represent moves by both players. The first player tries to maximize its situation, while the second player tries to minimize the first player's situation. In light of this, the first player must always think ahead to what the second player can do in response to its move. For example, in tic-tac-toe, if the first player makes a move to get two pieces in a row, but neglects to block a column in which the second player already has two pieces, the first player will end up loosing. Similarly, in chess, moving the queen to put the other player's king in check may seem like a good move, but if the other player can respond by capturing the queen, the move was not good.

Alpha-beta pruning

To reduce the search space of two-player game problems like the minimax search above, *alpha-beta pruning* is used. Alpha-beta pruning involves keeping track of best-case and worst-case situations at different nodes in the search space and removing paths that are too costly. As the minimax search tree is examined, there are times when a given move would be too costly because of an opponent's response. There is no point in checking alternative responses by the opponent or checking the following moves we could make. For example, a move that would cause a valuable piece to be lost is not worth exploring further. The search continues exploring other safe or less costly moves. By keeping track of the costs already evaluated at different levels in the tree, it is possible to know when other paths are worthwhile for further exploration or not.

Heuristic search

A *heuristic* is a strategy or rule-of-thumb that is applicable in certain situations. Using heuristics in addition to straight search methods may lead to a solution more quickly. Heuristic search uses additional information about the tree or certain nodes that enables pruning the search tree or making decisions to pursue a given node ahead of alternative nodes. For example, the first move may be defined by a heuristic because it is known to be a strong move. This may be done in tic-tac-toe or chess. Rather than search through the space of possible moves, a heuristic defines a move to take in a certain situation. Search can be done purely with heuristics. Expert systems are an example of this.

To better understand search, let's explore two search algorithms in detail. First, here is a function that implements best-first search:

```
; Parameters: goal-func, a function returning true if a goal has
; been met; choices, a list of paths to search; cost-func, a cost
; function to order new states; and next-states, a function that
; generates new states from a current path.
; Return the first path encountered that satisfies goal-func.
; The list of path choices is printed each time through the code.
(define (best-first-search goal-func choices cost-func next-states)
  (display choices)
  (newline)
  (cond ((null? choices) #f)     ; no more choices
        ((goal-func (first choices)) (first choices))
        (else
          (best-first-search goal-func
            (add-paths
              (rest choices)
              (make-paths (next-states (first choices))
                (first choices))
              cost-func)
            cost-func
            next-states))) )
```

The function `next-states` takes the current path from `choices` and returns
the possible valid states below that. These should be returned in a list, which will
be empty if there are no further states below the current state. These states are
converted into paths by `make-paths`. Then `add-paths` joins them to the existing
paths in the proper order based upon the cost function `cost-func`. Paths are
formed by adding the new state to the end of the list representing the current
path. The function `make-paths` removes empty lists from the list of new states
from `next-states`. This is to allow more flexibility and ease in writing `next-states`. For example, empty branches of a tree can be represented as empty lists.
Rather than test and conditionally add these to the list of new states to process,
we can always add them and they will be removed by `make-paths`. The function
`add-paths` calls `insert` (from section 8.4.2, "Sorting lists" in Chapter 8). It is
included here to ease the burden of jumping through the text.

```
; Return a new sorted list with element inserted into sorted-list
; based on compare-func.
(define (insert element sorted-list compare-func)
  (cond ((null? sorted-list)
           (list element))
        ((compare-func element (first sorted-list))
           (cons element sorted-list))
        (else
           (cons (first sorted-list)
             (insert element (rest sorted-list) compare-func)))) )
```

```
; Add paths in new-choices to old paths, old-choices, in sorted
; order based on cost-func.
(define (add-paths old-choices new-choices cost-func)
  (if (null? new-choices)
      old-choices
      (insert (first new-choices)
              (add-paths old-choices (rest new-choices) cost-func)
              cost-func)) )

; Given a list of new states, remove the empty lists and convert
; the states into complete paths.
(define (make-paths new-states current-path)
  (map (lambda (state) (append current-path (list state)))
    (remove '() new-states)) )
```

Using best-first search to write depth-first and breadth-first search

The function best-first-search can be used to perform a depth-first or breadth-first search. The initial choice is a path representing the starting state, the root of the tree. To make the root a path we make it a list, and since we need to pass a list of path choices, we must apply list once again. To add new paths to the start of the list of path choices, we use a cost function that always returns true. Lastly, the next states are the left and right children of the current node in the tree, which can be found by following the current path to get there. The function find does this by traversing through a tree based on the search path.

```
; Depth-first search implemented using best-first search.
(define (depth-first-alt goal-func tree)
  (best-first-search goal-func (list (list (root tree)))
    (lambda (path1 path2) #t)
    (lambda (path)
      (list (left-child (find path tree))
            (right-child (find path tree)))))) )
```

Breadth-first search is similar except the new states are added to the end of the path choices, so the cost function must always return false. The function passed to the parameter next-states must form a list with the right child first to work properly for breadth-first search, because the new paths are added to the end of the list in reverse order. The last child in the list is added to the end of the search path list first. The first child in the list of new states will be the final value added to the end of the path list.

```
; Breadth-first search implemented using best-first search.
(define (breadth-first-alt goal-func tree)
  (best-first-search goal-func (list (list (root tree)))
    (lambda (path1 path2) #f)
    (lambda (path)
      (list (right-child (find path tree))
            (left-child (find path tree)))))) )
```

```
; Return the subtree in tree based on path.
(define (find path tree)
  (cond ((null? tree) #f)    ; problem
        ((and (null? (cdr path))
              (equal? (root tree) (car path))) tree)
        ((null? (cdr path)) #f)     ; problem
        ((equal? (left-child tree) (second path))
          (find (cdr path) (left-side tree)))
        ((equal? (right-child tree) (second path))
          (find (cdr path) (right-side tree)))
        (else #f)) )     ; problem

; Selector functions for parts of trees.
(define root first)
(define left-side second)
(define right-side third)
(define (left-child tree)
  (if (null? (second tree)) '() (caadr tree)))
(define (right-child tree)
  (if (null? (third tree)) '() (caaddr tree)))
```

Let's make calls to these functions to see how they work. First we'll define a tree to traverse:

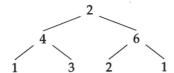

```
(define tree '(2 (4 (1 () ()) (3 () ())) (6 (2 () ()) (1 () ()))))
```

Now we call our functions with the tree and a goal function that tests for a path with nodes that add up to more than seven.

```
> (depth-first-alt (lambda (path) (> (apply + path) 7)) tree)
((2))
((2 4) (2 6))
((2 4 1) (2 4 3) (2 6))
((2 4 3) (2 6))
(2 4 3)

> (breadth-first-alt (lambda (path) (> (apply + path) 7)) tree)
((2))
((2 4) (2 6))
((2 6) (2 4 1) (2 4 3))
(2 6)
```

The function best-first-search prints the available choices in each iteration through the search. Notice how the two search techniques use a different search ordering and produce different results in this example.

A* search through trees

Next let's explore A* search beginning with a variation on A* search that works only on trees. Our A* search is an extension of best-first search.

```
; A* search of tree implemented using best-first search.
; g is a function that returns the cost incurred so far and
; h is a function returning the expected cost to reach the goal.
(define (a*-tree-search goal-func tree g h)
  (best-first-search goal-func (list (list (root tree)))
    (lambda (path1 path2)
      (<= (+ (g path1) (h path1)) (+ (g path2) (h path2))))
    (lambda (path)
      (list (left-child (find path tree))
            (right-child (find path tree)))))) )
```

A* search in general

Here is another version of A* search that works on data structures other than trees or in situations where it is easier to express the successor states with a function rather than by creating a tree. This is the case in many problems, such as the two problems in the following sections:

```
; General a* search implemented using best-first search.
; start-path is the path to the start state.
; successors is a function that returns the next states.
; g is a function that returns the cost incurred so far and
; h is a function returning the expected cost to reach the goal.
(define (a*search goal-func start-path successors g h)
  (best-first-search goal-func (list start-path)
    (lambda (path1 path2)
      (<= (+ (g path1) (h path1)) (+ (g path2) (h path2))))
    successors) )
```

15.3.2 Scheduling problem solved with A* search

Let's look at an example of how A* search works. Imagine the following problem. We are trying to fill time slots during the day with people who are available to work at those times. Each person can work a maximum of two hours in a day. We'll represent the times we want to fill as a list of numbers representing the hour of the day (each time slot is one hour long starting and ending on the hour). For each person in our problem, we have a list representing the times that they are available to work listed in order of their preferences. We'll use a twenty-four hour clock to avoid dealing with A.M. and P.M.

There are two variations of this problem. One is to return a solution that merely fills all the time slots. As long as all the time slots get filled and no one works more than two hours, this problem is satisfied. The second solution fills up all the required time slots but also attempts to give each person their preferred time requests. The first problem has potentially many solutions, whereas the second has one optimal solution (or some number of ties).

To solve the first variation of the problem, we have to fill a collection of time slots. In A* search we are trying to minimize the function

$$f = g(n) + h(n)$$

Here, the function $g(n)$ represents the number of time slots already filled. If the path has one node for each time slot, the length of the path corresponds to g. The function $h(n)$ is an estimate of the number of slots that remain to be filled. At best, the remaining time slots will be filled by making the proper choices each time. Since h should not overestimate the number of steps, we can use this simple measure for h: the number of slots remaining.

Calculating g and h functions for A* search

Here is the list of times to fill and hours people can work:

```
(define times-to-fill '(8 9 10 11 12 13 14 15 16 17))

(define people '(
  (myriam 8 9 10 11 12)
  (nate 12 13 14 16 17)
  (alisa 8 9 10 15 16 17)
  (wayne 11 13 14 15)
  (therese 9 10 11 14 15 16)))
```

The function `possible-choices` returns a list of people who can work at a given time given the current schedule. It limits each person to two hours of work.

```
; Given list of times, people, and people already scheduled, path,
; return list of people who can work at time.
(define (possible-choices time path)
  (map car
      (keep-if (lambda (person-times)
                  (and (member time (cdr person-times))
                       (< (count (car person-times) path) 2)))
          people)) )
```

Here is the call to `a*search` to solve the first version of our problem:

```
(a*search
  (lambda (path) (= (length path) (length times-to-fill)))
  '()
  (lambda (path)
    (possible-choices (list-ref times-to-fill (length path)) path))
  length
  (lambda (path) (- (length times-to-fill) (length path)))))
```

This call returns

```
(myriam myriam alisa wayne nate nate wayne therese therese alisa)
```

Take a look at the values returned. The first seven people are the first choices in the list `people` for those times (remember that each person can only work two hours). For 3:00 P.M. (15) Alisa is the first person who can work and the first choice made by the program. This path fails, since Thérèse cannot work the final hour. The next alternative is to have Thérèse work at 3:00 P.M. This path has one problem when the first choice, Alisa, is chosen to work at 4:00. The next alternative is having Thérèse work at 4:00, and then the final step can be reached in which Alisa works at 5:00.

Scheduling with priorities

For the second version of this scheduling problem, we want to optimize the choice based on the work preferences given by each person. This changes the functions g and h, which must now reflect the quality of the times chosen. The new functions are based on the position of the times in the time-preference lists, where the lower the position, the better the choice. The function g is the sum of the costs incurred so far. For each person in the path, the position of the time they work is computed. This list of numbers is added to get the total cost of the path so far.

Creating a good h function

For the function h we can compute the sum of the costs of the people who will work in the remaining time slots to fill. Since there can be many people who can work at a given time slot, we can compute the costs for each available person and use the minimum cost. Finally, we sum all the minimum costs for each remaining time to get the cost to reach the goal. This will not take into account the true list of those who can work because that would involve knowledge of all the people working earlier. So the function h underestimates the actual cost.

Using the h function from the first version of this scheduling problem (that doesn't look at time preferences) will not work, because it may overestimate the cost function. For example, if there are two slots to fill, the first h function returns a cost of 2. However, if there are people available whose first choice matches those times, then the actual cost is 0. If the converse is true and the remaining times slots are all later choices in the preference lists, then the first h function will greatly underestimate the actual cost, and A* search will behave more like uniform-cost search instead.[3]

Here is the call to `a*search` to choose people according to their time preferences. The function g totals the list from a mapping across the people in the current path and the corresponding times that they work. The function mapped computes the position of the given time in the person's time preference list. The function h is more complex. For the remaining times to find people to work, h computes a list of the preferences for the people who can work then. The minimum of these preferences is used, and all the preference minimums for each time to fill are added:

[3.] I tried using the first h function, and the search to fill the ten time slots took a lot longer to return a final answer. It took around one hour as opposed to one to two minutes! The return value was a different (but still optimal) list:

```
(myriam myriam therese wayne nate wayne therese alisa alisa nate)
```

```
(a*search
  (lambda (path) (= (length path) (length times-to-fill)))
  '()
  (lambda (path)
    (possible-choices (list-ref times-to-fill (length path)) path))
  (lambda (path)
    (apply +
      (map (lambda (person time)
             (position time (cdr (assoc person people)))) )
        path (subseq times-to-fill 0 (length path)))))
  (lambda (path)
    (apply +
      (map (lambda (time)
             (apply min
               (map (lambda (person)
                      (position time (cdr (assoc person people)))) )
                 (possible-choices time path))) )
        (subseq times-to-fill (length path))))))
```

There is a bug, which can lead to an error when no one can work in a given time slot. We cannot take the minimum cost of no costs. The `apply` with `min` will return an error with an empty list. To fix the bug, we can test the result of the call to `possible-choices` and return some large cost if nobody can work then (we don't want to take a path that is a deadend). An alternative solution is to use a custom version of `min` that can handle no arguments, in which case it returns a very large value. Opting for the first fix, here is the new call to `a*search`:

```
(a*search
  (lambda (path) (= (length path) (length times-to-fill)))
  '()
  (lambda (path)
    (possible-choices (list-ref times-to-fill (length path)) path))
  (lambda (path)
    (apply +
      (map (lambda (person time)
             (position time (cdr (assoc person people))))
        path (subseq times-to-fill 0 (length path)))))
  (lambda (path)
    (apply +
      (map (lambda (time)
             (if (not (null? (possible-choices time path)))
                 (apply min
                   (map (lambda (person)
                          (position time
                            (cdr (assoc person people))))
                     (possible-choices time path)))
                 1000))   ; return a large cost
        (subseq times-to-fill (length path))))))
```

The result of this call is

```
(myriam therese myriam wayne nate wayne therese alisa nate alisa)
```

15.3.3 The missionaries and cannibals problem solved with A* search

Data representation for missionaries and cannibals

We can use A* search to solve the missionaries and cannibals problem. We need a data representation for the problem. The most obvious representation (in terms of matching the mind's eye picture of the problem) is three lists. The first list represents the people on the initial river bank, the second list represents people in the boat and the boat's location, and the third list represents people on the opposite shore. The initial state can be represented as the list

```
((m m m c c c) (left) ())
```

Refining the data representation

The m's are missionaries and c's are cannibals. The left denotes that the boat is at the left bank, where the people are. Of course the order of the people does not matter, so to make life easier in verifying that we haven't violated the conditions of the puzzle or in generating new states, we can use numbers instead. The first number is the number of missionaries. Now our initial state is

```
((3 3) (left) (0 0))
```

We don't need to keep track of the people in the boat with a list. There are at most five possible configurations of people in the boat and they are all legal (i.e., the missionaries are never outnumbered). All we really need to keep track of is where the boat is. Here is a new representation for the initial state:

```
((3 3) left (0 0))
```

The goal state is the list

```
((0 0) right (3 3))
```

This process of refinement of the data structure is common during the design phase of computer programs. We could even go further and eliminate the list representing the people on the right bank. It can be computed from the numbers in the first list (the people on the left bank). For now we'll skip that change to the data structure and keep both left and right bank lists.

Before reading the solution to this problem, take some time and try to solve the problem by hand. Do this now.

Problem characteristics

You may have noticed some interesting things about the problem. First, it's not that easy. Second, most states don't have many possible moves because they are illegal (i.e., the missionaries get eaten) or they return to a previous state visited earlier. Third, it's a slow process taking two steps forward and then one step backward.

Now let's build a solution using A* search. We'll be dealing with paths in which each path is a list of the states taken to get to that point in the solution. New moves are a function of the current state, which is the last entry in the path list. The function last (repeated from Chapter 4) returns the last element in a list; we will use it to get the current state:

```
; Return the last element in a-list.
(define (last a-list)
  (list-ref a-list (- (length a-list) 1)))
```

The function `move-people` generates a list of legal moves that can be taken from the current state. We can check both lists (each side of the river) or take a quicker approach and test only the first list (the left bank) by making the following realizations:

Legal configurations

> a move is legal if the number of missionaries on the left side is zero
>> (because the other side has three missionaries and they aren't outnumbered)
> or there are three missionaries
>> (the other side will have zero)
> or the number of missionaries equals the number of cannibals
>> (the numbers will be equal on the other side as well)

Otherwise the move is illegal. For example, two missionaries and one cannibal on the left side means one missionary and two cannibals are on the right side, which is illegal.

To test for valid states, `keep-if` is used to individually check each possible state. To generate all possible successor states, `map` is called to perform a transformation of the current state to the successors. This transformation is done by adding and subtracting the number of missionaries and cannibals that can be moved. The list below represents the numbers of missionaries and cannibals that can go in the boat:

Generating successor states

```
((1 0) (0 1) (2 0) (0 2) (1 1))
```

The first element denotes one missionary and no cannibals going across in the boat. If we map across this list with the current state, we can form a list of the successor states. We need to check which side the boat is on to decide if we must add or subtract the people in the boat.

```
; Given state, the current position of people, return a list of
; legal successor states.
(define (move-people state)
  (keep-if
    (lambda (new-state)
      (or (= (caar new-state) 0)
          (= (caar new-state) 3)
          (= (caar new-state) (cadar new-state))) )
    (map (lambda (trans)
           (if (eq? (second state) 'left)
               (list (map - (first state) trans)
                     'right
                     (map + (third state) trans))
               (list (map + (first state) trans)
                     'left
                     (map - (third state) trans))) )
         '((1 0) (0 1) (2 0) (0 2) (1 1)))) )
```

Here is a sample call to `move-people`:

```
> (move-people '((3 3) left (0 0)))
(((3 2) right (0 1)) ((3 1) right (0 2)) ((2 2) right (1 1)))
```

This shows that there are three legal states from the initial state. The other two possible states from the initial state are illegal since the missionaries are outnumbered on one side of the river. The function `move-people` must be augmented to not include states that already have been visited in the path. Calling `set-difference` with the states from `move-people` and the current path can handle this.

g and h functions for missionaries and cannibals

Lastly, we must write the functions *g* and *h* for A* search. The cost *g* already incurred is the length of the path. The estimated cost *h* to the goal can be represented as the number of people remaining to add to the other side. This is the number of people on the left bank, which is determined easily by adding the elements in that list using `apply`.

The call to `a*search` follows:

```
(a*search
  (lambda (path) (equal? (last path) '((0 0) right (3 3))))
  '(((3 3) left (0 0)))
  (lambda (path) (set-difference (move-people (last path)) path))
  length
  (lambda (path) (apply + (first (last path))))))
```

The results (formatted to look nice) are as follows:

```
(((3 3) left (0 0))    ((2 2) right (1 1))    ((3 2) left (0 1))
 ((3 0) right (0 3))    ((3 1) left (0 2))    ((1 1) right (2 2))
 ((2 2) left (1 1))    ((0 2) right (3 1))    ((0 3) left (3 0))
 ((0 1) right (3 2))    ((1 1) left (2 2))    ((0 0) right (3 3)))
```

The answer is found in eleven steps. This took less than a second to run. Taking out the check for states that have already been encountered in the path (the `set-difference` of the call to `move-people`) produces the same result, but it takes about six minutes to run! A* search should internally test for repeated states. In the interest of simplicity this was left out, but for the missionaries and cannibals problem it is important to include.

15.3.4   Exercises

15.1   Show a call to `a*search` that calculates a variation on the missionaries and cannibals problem with four missionaries and four cannibals. You may have to make changes to `move-people`.

15.2   Create a data representation and *g* and *h* functions for the 8-puzzle.

15.3   Think of what constitutes a state in 8-puzzle and write a function that computes the next states that are allowed from a given state.

15.4   Design a data representation for cryptarithmetic. It should be general so it works for any cryptarithmetic problem.

15.5   Describe *g* and *h* functions for cryptarithmetic.

15.6   Indicate what states in cryptarithmetic look like and write a function that returns all possible successor states of a given state.

15.3.5   Knowledge representation

One of the most important decisions to make in programming is deciding the form of the data structure. Chapter 7 presented examples to help illustrate this concept. Data structures are important in AI programming as well. Here data structures are often used as representations of knowledge within the program. *Knowledge representation* is the problem of designing a structure for data that represents knowledge in a program. Below are some common choices.

Conceptual dependencies are used to represent sentences. They are presented in section 15.7, "Natural Language Processing."

Semantic networks are graphs (a collection of connected nodes) in which each node represents some object and the connection between the nodes represents the relationship between the objects it connects. A graph is more general than a tree, in that a graph can have connections to any node, not just the ones immediately above or below it.

Semantic networks

Here is an example of a semantic net that represents information about animals:

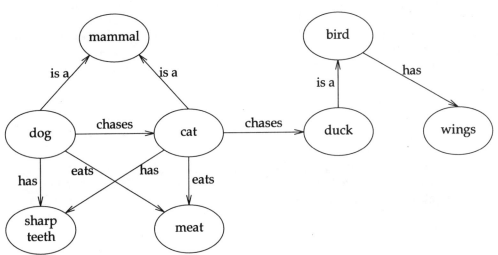

The ellipses represent nodes and the arrows between them are the connec-tions. The connections represent the relationship that a node has to the node to which it is pointing. For example, "dog is a mammal" is represented by an arrow labeled "is a" that goes from the dog node to the mammal node. The "is a"

Relations in semantic networks

relationship specifies that a node is a subset of another node to represent facts like all dogs are mammals. *Property inheritance* gives the subset the same properties as the superset, thus dogs will have all the properties of mammals. To indicate the properties that a node may have, the "has" relation is used. Another relationship is "instance," which says that a particular object is a member of a node. For example, we could specify the cat "Ruby" as an instance of the node cat. For other specific relationships, the nature of the association between the nodes is used (e.g., chases or eats).

Frames

Frames are similar to semantic networks. Instead of a collection of nodes with labeled arrows, a frame has objects and their properties (called *slots*). A frame may have code (procedural information) as well. For example, there may be code specifying how to compute the value for a given slot.

Here is an example of a frame for dogs. Below the frame name is a list of slots and their values:

> dog frame
>   is-a mammal
>   has sharp-teeth
>   eats meat

Inheritance

Frames support inheritance, in which a frame inherits the properties of the frame of which it is a member. For example, if there is a mammal frame, then, since dogs are mammals, they would inherit all the properties of mammals.

First-order predicate calculus

With a few extensions from first-order logic,[4] *predicate calculus* provides an expressive form of representing information. A predicate is a relation between objects that is either true or false. Predicate calculus defines a language for describing and using predicates. Predicates represent facts about the data being modeled. We can combine predicates with the logical operators *and, or, if-then, equivalence,* and *not*. We can also use functions that we define that return information about objects.

Below is a list of predicates and their arguments representing the animal structure defined above:

> is-a (dog, mammal)
> is-a (cat, mammal)
> is-a (duck, bird)
> has (bird, wings)
> has (dog, sharp-teeth)
> has (cat, sharp-teeth)
> eats (dog, meat)
> eats (cat, meat)
> chases (dog, cat)
> chases (cat, duck)

---

4. These additions include functions that return values that aren't necessarily true or false and the predicate "equals" to test if two things are the same.

Predicate calculus includes a means of *quantifying* predicates, which allows us to form statements like

Existential and universal quantifiers

some dogs chase ducks

This would be represented as

There exists an x such that: is-a (x, dog) and chases (x, ducks)

This quantifier is called an *existential quantifier*. There is also a *universal quantifier* that can be used to represent statements like

all dogs are mammals

This statement is expressed as

For all x, if is-a (x, dog) then is-a (x, mammal)

Since we can define general rules with predicate calculus, we can put in information about the system we are modeling and then ask questions or perform calculations based on particular examples. For example, if we have established the rules

all mammals have hair, and
all cats are mammals

and then determine that Ruby is a cat, we can determine that Ruby has hair by first realizing that she is a mammal and then since she is a mammal, she must have hair. The next section goes into more detail into the reasoning process.

15.3.6 Reasoning

A dictionary definition of reasoning may mention logical thought, decision making, inference, rational thought, and judgment as part of reasoning. Reasoning is important in AI because it provides a means to obtain new information or make conclusions given information. Reasoning provides not only a means, but an ability to explain how the new information or conclusions were obtained. The simplest type of reasoning involves drawing a conclusion based on direct facts that match the desired goal. Unfortunately, many problems involve combining information in some way using different types of reasoning. Below are four of the commonly used reasoning techniques.

Induction is a type of reasoning that involves generalization. If we have enough examples of some phenomenon, we may induce that it is generally applicable. Medicine often works by induction. If researchers see enough cases of some symptom along with some disease, they start believing that it is more than correlation, but causation. Inductive reasoning may go as follows:

Inductive reasoning

Twenty-five sailors didn't eat any form of vitamin C and contracted scurvy.
Ten patients didn't get vitamin C in their diets and contracted scurvy.

Therefore, if one doesn't get vitamin C, they'll contract scurvy.

This type of reasoning is not always correct and can lead to false conclusions.

Deductive reasoning

Deduction is one of the most powerful forms of reasoning. Syllogisms are examples of deduction. For example,

"All men are mortal,"
"Socrates is a man,"
Therefore, "Socrates is mortal."

This type of deduction involves specification. We go from a general statement, "All men are mortal," to a specific conclusion: "Socrates is mortal."

Deduction is most easily shown with if-then statements in which we know the antecedent (the condition part of an if-then statement) is true, so we can deduce the consequent (the *then* part). For example, parents often tell their children statements like

If you eat your dinner, then you'll get dessert.

If the child eats her dinner, then we deduce that she will get dessert.

Abductive reasoning

Abduction is similar to deduction, except it works by taking an if-then statement and its consequent (the *then* part), and concluding that the antecedent (the condition) is true. Taking the above example, we begin with

If you eat your dinner, then you'll get dessert.

Given the knowledge that the child got dessert, we conclude that the child must have eaten her dinner. This seems reasonable, but is not logically true. If the consequent in an if-then is true, the antecedent need not be true in order for the if-then statement to be logically true.

The opposite is not the case. If the antecedent in an if-then is true, the consequent *must* be true in order for the if-then statement to be true. Deduction works by knowing the antecedent is true, and then logically concluding that the consequent must be true. Abduction takes the consequent as its true information and tries to explain why it is true. If there is a causality between the consequent and the antecedent, abduction may be correct to some degree. If no other antecedent causally leads to the consequent, then that relationship becomes an if-and-only-if relation in which case abduction holds. For example,

If and only if you eat your dinner, then you'll get dessert.

If we know that the child got dessert, then we can conclude that the child ate her dinner.

Probabilistic reasoning

It is often the case that many relationships exist with probabilities of one event occurring or *conditional probabilities* of one event occurring given knowledge that another event occurred. The probability that a child ate dinner given the fact that she got dessert is a conditional probability, and is written as $P(dinner \mid dessert)$. We can calculate this conditional probability given the *unconditional probability* that the child gets dessert (written as $P(dessert)$), the unconditional probability that the child eats dinner, $P(dinner)$, and the conditional probability that the child gets dessert given that the child ate dinner, $P(dessert \mid dinner)$. This is calculated using Bayes' rule, as follows:

$$P(dinner \mid dessert) = \frac{P(dessert \mid dinner)P(dinner)}{P(dessert)}$$

Given the statement "if you eat your dinner, then you'll get dessert," we know that the child will get dessert if she ate dinner (from deductive reasoning), so $P(dessert \mid dinner)$ is 1. Let's assume that $P(dinner)$ is 0.6 and $P(dessert)$ is 0.8. The conditional probability that the child ate dinner given the fact that she got dessert is 0.75.

If there are other probabilities we know about, such as the conditional probability that the child gets dessert given the fact that she cleaned her room and the probability that the child cleans her room, we can calculate which event (eating dinner or cleaning the room) is more likely to have explained why the child got dessert. Techniques like this are used to find the most likely causes of events given only probabilistic knowledge of the world.

15.3.7 World or commonsense knowledge

Most AI programs are first developed within a small domain. Within such "toy" worlds, or microworlds, the programs perform impressively. The difficulty lies in scaling the worlds up to the real world in which we live. In a small or abstract domain it is possible to encode all the details and information about the domain that the program must know. Trying to encapsulate all the information about the world is a different matter altogether. This is the problem of representing world knowledge or commonsense knowledge.

Scaling up to the real world

World knowledge or commonsense knowledge is very large and is something that we learn with years of growing up in the world, observing the behavior and actions of objects around us. To get an idea of how difficult it is to learn such general knowledge, think about learning the culture of a foreign country or of a different age or socioeconomic group in your own country. In fact, just try to understand the opposite sex and you find that the interpretations and viewpoints of the world can be very different. This confounds the problem of gathering world knowledge as well, since there is a context associated with it. One person's humor is another person's insult. For example,

Knowledge context

> Question: What do lawyers use for birth control?
> Answer: Their personalities.

may be humorous to many but offensive to lawyers. Of course, a great deal of world knowledge is constant across all people and places. We are all affected by the laws of physics. Gravity and friction exist in all countries throughout the planet.

A program whose domain is the world has to deal with any type of situation that the world and the laws of physics can throw at it, so it must understand how the world and physics work. We may think that understanding how the world works isn't that difficult. We deal with it every day and do just fine (more or less). But physics, now that is hard stuff. For a program however, it's the other way around. Newtonian physics can be explained fairly nicely, given a handful of rules and some constants. For most realworld problem solving, our program won't have to try to perform a grand unification of all the forces of nature or deal with relativity, quarks, superstrings, or any of a host of issues that nuclear and high energy physicists deal with. As long as it knows about simple physics (e.g., gravity, force, inclined planes, pulleys, electricity, and magneticism), then it is in good shape.

Explaining what happens in a television show is much more complex. The program would have to know about family relationships, economics, sociology, romance, appropriate and inappropriate behavior, and so on. We have learned this over the course of many years of watching and being in the world. If we spent as much time studying physics or Scheme, we may find that they come as naturally and simply as watching television.

Even if one could create a set of all the minute facts about the world, how would one represent them in a computer program? How would all the interconnections be made? How would inferences be made? Would one have to represent all facts, such as humans cannot walk through walls, or it's a bad idea to eat anything larger than your head?

CYC

A team lead by Doug Lenat is developing a system called CYC[5] that is trying to amass world and commonsense knowledge. CYC is a huge knowledge base of concepts, assertions, and heuristics for reasoning over them. An assertion in CYC is a commonsense fact about the world such as "you have to be awake to eat." In just over ten years CYC has grown to include millions of assertions based on a hundred thousand fundamental concepts.[6]

About a million assertions were entered by people and coded in CYC's representation language, which is based on first-order predicate logic with some extensions. Other assertions have been produced by the system based on how it reasons and infers with its knowledge base. This has resulted in the addition of millions of new assertions. The hope is that more and more of the system will be self-generated.

CYC's assertions are assumed to be true in some given context.[7] For example, in the context of naive physics there would be an assertion about objects coming to rest eventually. In the physicist context, we would find a different assertion about objects tending to stay in motion if they are in motion. CYC reasons within a specific context or contexts. This helps to reduce the search space of assertions dramatically and also handle contradictions between assertions. The two motion assertions are contradictory but wouldn't pose a problem to CYC because only one would apply, given a question like "Would a physicist have difficulty understanding how an air hockey game works?"

CYC is still in its development phase but is being linked with other programs to extend their capabilities. At this point, it is too early to tell if a project like CYC

[5.] The name CYC comes from enCYClopedia.

[6.] These numbers are somewhat deceptive, since CYC contains some general assertions that encompass many individual assertions.

[7.] When CYC was first developed, its assertions were weighted (given a degree of belief). This proved to be problematic and the notion of assertions dependent on context was developed.

will succeed. No one knows if CYC will be able to solve AI problems where they have not scaled up due to a lack of world knowledge.

15.4 Problem Solvers and Planners

Problem solving is one of the fundamental goals of AI. Most AI programs are attempts at solving some problem, whether it is medical diagnosis, object or speech recognition, grasping an object, or playing a game of chess. Much of AI's early work centered around building systems that could solve a class of problems (e.g., the Logic Theorist) or general problems (GPS). What emerged from this was a series of programs that focused on planning to reach some end goal.

We already introduced GPS, Newell and Simon's General Problem Solver. It did solve problems, but it was far from general. The big problem with any attempt at building a general problem solver is dealing with world knowledge. And as we saw above and could have imagined before, this is no easy task.

Putting world knowledge aside, let's take a closer look at how GPS works. *GPS operators and* GPS uses a collection of operators that each represent some action that can be *preconditions* taken in the world being modeled. For example, an operator might represent moving from one location to another, picking something up, or putting something down. Each operator has preconditions that must be satisfied before the operator can be applied and effects that the operator produces. For example, to pick something up the preconditions may be that your hands are empty, that you are at the object, that the object is not under other objects, and that the object is not too heavy. The effects of carrying out the operation are that the object's location has moved and that your hands are no longer empty.

GPS uses *means-ends analysis* to reach its goal by trying to reduce the differ- *Means-ends analysis* ences in its current state and its goal state. If some action produces the desired goal but cannot be performed because its preconditions have not been met, then those preconditions become the new goals. This hopefully reduces the difference between the current state and the goal state. If the goal can be solved, then eventually all the preconditions will be met and the sequence of steps taken defines a means to the goal. If a condition is reached that is not met and no goal specifies it as its outcome, then the goal cannot be reached with those operators.

The original GPS was modified by Richard Fikes and Nils Nilsson in 1971. *STRIPS* Their version was called STRIPS (Stanford Research Institute Problem Solver). STRIPS had a more restricted language for defining operators and had *add* and *delete lists* to model the effects of actions. To model an operation, the items in the add list would be added to the current state and the items in the delete list would be removed from the current state. For example, the operation of moving from location1 to location2 would involve adding the state `at-location2` and deleting the state `at-location1`.

Further refinements were made to problem solvers. One was to add *critics* that help in the selection of actions or reduce the amount of backtracking needed by making the correct decisions early on. Another strategy was to abstract the problem such that it could be solved in a hierarchical fashion, ignoring the details at first. These models improved the original GPS, but none wound up producing a true general problem solver.

15.5   Expert Systems

The grandiose claims made about general problem solvers were never realized. Instead of trying to continue along that path, some AI researchers shifted to solve more limited and specialized problems. Out of this arose expert systems. The early expert systems were in the areas of chemical structure analysis from mass spectroscopy data (DENDRAL, 1965) and identification of infectious diseases (MYCIN, 1976).

Production systems

The foundation for expert systems came from the idea of *production systems*, developed by Emil Post in the early 1940s. A production system is a collection of production rules, current state information, and an interpreter. Production rules are situation-action pairs. They model some specific fact about the world as a rule in the form of

"if some situation is true, perform the following actions"

The current state information is called *working memory* since production systems started as a psychological model of the mind. The interpreter chooses productions whose situations match the current working memory and performs the corresponding actions. The actions add information to working memory, remove information, print information, or indicate that the system should stop.

Conflict resolution and conflict resolution strategies

When more than one rule is applicable, *conflict resolution* is used to choose one to apply. There are many possible conflict resolution schemes. One scheme chooses a rule according to some priority. The rules can be prioritized or the situations or actions of the rules can be prioritized. For example, the situation `engine-overheating` and the action `engage-brake` may have very high priorities. Another typical conflict resolution scheme is to choose the most specific of the applicable rules. For example, consider the following two rules:

```
if pan-is-hot then add-oil-to-pan
if pan-is-hot and garlic-is-golden-brown and onions-are-golden then
   add-vegetables-to-pan
```

The second rule should have priority over the first; otherwise, we will keep adding oil to the pan and end up with a vat of hot oil instead of a vegetable stir-fry.

Choosing the rule whose situations were most recently satisfied can be used to influence some control over the sequence of rules that are chosen. Not choosing a rule if it has been recently chosen is used to avoid having rules run continuously. Perhaps the simplest conflict resolution scheme is to choose the first rule encountered that is satisfied and then continue evaluating rules starting with the next rule. This allows the rule writer to sequence rules to have a great degree of control and understanding of the interaction of rules.

The conflict resolution scheme has a large impact on the order in which rules are chosen. Sometimes the rule writer wants control over the rule ordering, but there are times when this is not wanted. In fact, expert systems started as a move away from traditional control. The problem with controlled systems is that it is difficult to model highly interconnected domains. Think of a medical system. Even though the body comprises various systems (e.g., circulatory and respiratory), it is highly interconnected. If we wrote separate rules for each system, many rules would be repeated in the rulebases for different body systems, or jumps from one rulebase to another would be needed. In the end, the control would look like a tangled web of rules. In programming this is referred to as *spaghetti code*.

Control in production systems

Production systems offer a different approach: Produce rules that ideally can stand alone, each representing some independent fact about the system. The rule ordering no longer matters. Rules are invoked when their conditions are met. Conflict resolution gives an ordering to rules so that the most important rule happens first. For example, given a collection of rules for an object avoidance system in an aircraft, we might want to have the rules invoked in the following order:

```
if on-collision-course then turn left
if on-collision-course then light "fasten seat belt" sign
if on-collision-course then send message to other aircraft
```

Some expert systems give an explanation of their reasoning process. These explanations are useful in debugging the rulebase. They are essential in a field where someone is using an expert system to augment their own expertise. For example, a doctor receiving advice from a program will want to know why the advice was given. This can be done fairly easily by producing a trace of the rules that were evaluated. Some expert systems have a question/answer interface in which the user can ask for explanations about the expert system analysis.

Explanatory abilities

An expert system has three parts: the *rulebase*, the *database*, and the *inference engine*. The rulebase is the collection of rules that represent the expert knowledge. The database is a collection of known facts about the system being modeled. It may change as the rules are evaluated to reflect changes in the system. The inference engine sequences through the rules and finds those that are satisfied according to the information in the database. The inference engine includes the conflict resolution mechanism that chooses one rule from those that are satisfied. Then that rule's actions are performed. This is called *firing a rule*.

Parts of an expert system

Just as software engineering is the process of developing, testing, debugging, and maintaining programs, *knowledge engineering* is the process of creating, verifying, and refining expert systems. Two pieces of an expert system must be created: the inference engine and the rules that make up the knowledge base. The inference engine makes up the shell of an expert system. In fact expert system shells can be purchased to simplify the creation of an expert system; you just add the rules. The real knowledge is in the rulebase.

Knowledge engineering

The process of obtaining the rules is called *knowledge acquisition*. This is a process of interviewing experts and trying to formulate concrete, independent rules

Knowledge acquisition

from their explanations. This process can be extremely difficult because much of human reasoning is tacit. The expert has spent years forming knowledge, which typically is not in the form of neat, concise rules. During knowledge acquisition, the expert's knowledge must be brought out and manipulated into rules compatible with the inference engine.

15.6   Implementing an Expert System in Scheme

Forward and backward chaining expert systems

There are two general kinds of expert systems: *forward chaining* and *backward chaining*. A forward chaining (also called *data driven*) expert system iteratively chooses a rule from the rulebase with conditions that are satisfied, and performs its actions. A backward chaining (or *goal driven*) expert system looks at the actions of the rules in search of one that will satisfy the desired goal. If the conditions corresponding to the action are true, the system finishes. Otherwise those conditions become new goals to satisfy. This is the same idea behind means-ends analysis.

We will build a generic expert system shell that does forward chaining. It can be an expert in many domains depending on the rulebase and database it is given. Rather than having a fixed conflict resolution scheme, we'll allow a function to handle that. Given a list of applicable rules (those with conditions that have been met), this function will choose one to apply.

Stopping rules from being continuously chosen

We need to assure that once a rule is chosen, it does not get chosen constantly. This can be handled by having the rules put or remove something in the database that is tested in the condition. However, this makes the rule writing an uglier process. Another way is to test if the rule's actions have already occurred; in other words, if the items that the rule adds to the database are already in the database, the rule is ignored. The parameter `redundant?` will take a function that checks for this.

We also need some way of knowing when to stop sequencing through rules. The parameter `finished` takes a function that takes the database as an argument and determines if the system should terminate.

To make our code more readable, we'll create `let` variables to hold the list of satisfied rules, the satisfied rules that haven't already been invoked (the non-redundant ones), and the rule chosen by the conflict resolution function. We won't include the database as a parameter because during the processing of the rules it must be changed. It could be changed as a parameter, but it is a lot more work than treating it as a global variable and destructively changing it. This global database is named `database`.

```
; Given rule-list, a list of rules, redundant?, a function to test
; if a rule is redundant (i.e., its actions have already occurred),
; conflict-func, to handle conflict resolution, and finished, to
; test for termination, iteratively choose an applicable rule and
; apply it until finished is true.
(define (expert-shell rule-list redundant? conflict-func finished)
  (let* ( (satisfied-rules (keep-if satisfied? rule-list))
          (valid-rules (remove-if redundant? satisfied-rules))
          (rule-to-apply (conflict-func valid-rules)) )
    (apply-rule rule-to-apply)
    (if (finished database)
        'finished
        (expert-shell rule-list redundant? conflict-func
          finished))) )
```

Our expert system shell needs the following additional functions:

```
; Test if condition of rule is true.
(define (satisfied? rule)
  (eval (condition rule)) )

; Apply all the actions of rule.
(define (apply-rule rule)
  (for-each eval (actions rule)) )

; Selector function to return condition of rule.
(define (condition rule)
  (first rule) )

; Selector function to return actions of rule.
(define (actions rule)
  (rest rule) )
```

15.6.1 An expert in Mille Bornes

We have created an expert system shell. It is generic in that it can be given rules dealing with a variety of problem domains. The real expert knowledge is in the rulebase. Let's take the next step and define a rule base. The rules will provide moves in playing the card game Mille Bornes.

The object of Mille Bornes is to drive a car 700 miles before your opponent does. You gain distance by playing mileage cards if you are able to drive. There are hazard cards, which affect your ability to drive (e.g., stop, speed limit, and out-of-gas), repair cards that fix hazards (e.g., go, end-of-limit, and gasoline), and safety cards that prevent you from receiving hazards (e.g., right-of-way or driving ace).

Mille Bornes description

Players hold six cards in their hand. To play, a player draws a card from the deck and then plays a card or discards a card. The goal is to play enough mileage cards to total exactly 700 miles. Mileage cards can be played only if you do not have a hazard and you have played a go or right-of-way safety. There are five different mileage amounts: 200, 100, 75, 50, and 25. If your opponent puts a speed limit on you, you are limited to 50 or 25 mile distances. The hazards have corresponding repairs and protection (safeties). The table below shows these:

hazard	repair	safety
flat tire	spare tire	puncture proof
accident	repairs	driving ace
out of gas	gasoline	extra tank
speed limit	end of limit	right of way
stop	go	right of way

The scoring of the game is somewhat complicated. This is saved as one of the exercises at the end of this section. A true Mille Bornes expert system would include rules to maximize the score earned per game. Our simplified rulebase will try only to win the game by getting 700 miles before the opponent does.

Playing the game is fairly simple, but certain strategies can be used to improve the chances of winning. For example, a player may be aggressive by playing hazard cards on the opponent whenever possible or focus on gaining distance by playing large mileage cards. A player may not play a go card to move until she has accumulated, in her hand, the mileage needed to win (toward the end of the game). By keeping track of the played and discarded cards, a player can make good decisions about which cards to discard when none in her hand can be played.

There are two players: a person and the computer driven by the expert system. The database of the expert system is the cards in the computer's hand and the player's hand (the computer won't "look" at the player's cards), the computer's and player's state (e.g., accident or go), the computer's and player's accumulated mileage, the cards that the computer has seen (those that it has drawn and those that the person has played or discarded), and a repository for miscellaneous information used in the rulebase, which we'll call the blackboard (abbreviated as bb).[8] Each of these different miniature databases is a category of our big database. Here is a snapshot of how the database may look during the game. It is represented as an association list of categories and their values.

```
((hand1 go stop 25 50 100 end-of-limit)
 (hand2 stop 75 75 100 extra-tank accident)
 (state1 flat-tire)
 (state2)
 (mileage1 . 150)
 (mileage2 . 0)
 (deck go go go go go go go go go go go go stop stop ...)
 (seen go stop 25 25 50 75 75 100 ...)
 (bb))
```

We'll need functions to access the database. The function pair will return a pair from the database (e.g., (state1 flat-tire)). The function pair is called by the function data to access the data alone (e.g., flat-tire) and by add-to

---

8. Some expert systems used the idea of a blackboard as a place to store generally accessible and pertinent information.

and `delete` to change the data. Since `pair` is used in all of these functions, it will do the error checking for a bad category. When such an error is encountered, the program will stop running. This can be handled using `call-with-current-continuation`, which is covered in Chapter 11 under "Forcing Exits with `call-with-current-continuation`." The following two expressions establish `error` as an exit function:

```
(define error 'not-yet)

(call-with-current-continuation
  (lambda (stop)
    (set! error stop)))
; Return the pair associated with name.
(define (pair name)
  (let ((data-pair (assoc name database)))
    (if data-pair
        data-pair
        (error (append '(bad category given) (list name)))))) )
; Return the data associated with name.
(define (data name)
  (cdr (pair name)) )
```

The functions `add-to` and `delete` add and delete cards destructively from the database. To restore a category to an empty value, `reset` is used:

```
; Add a card to a category pair in the database.
(define (add-to category card)
  (set-cdr! (pair category) (cons card (data category))) )

; Remove a card from a category in the database.
(define (delete category card)
  (set-cdr! (pair category) (remove-one card (data category))) )
```

The function `remove-one` is like `remove1` from Chapter 14 except it tests if the item occurs in the list.

```
; Remove one occurrence of item from a-list.
(define (remove-one item a-list)
  (let ((location (position item a-list)))
    (if location
        (append (subseq a-list 0 location)
                (subseq a-list (+ 1 location)))
        a-list)) )

; Reset category to an empty list.
(define (reset category)
  (set-cdr! (pair category) '()) )
```

To simplify the rules, we use a couple additional functions that test if a certain set of cards (e.g., our hand) contains a particular card or one of a set of cards. We can then inquire if the opponent's state is stop or if we have any mileage cards.

```
; Return true if value occurs within the category name.
(define (contains? name value)
  (member value (data name)) )

; Return true if any element in set occurs within the category
; name.
(define (contains-any? name set)
  (not (null? (intersection set (data name))))) )
```

Testing for redundant actions

We can now create the function that tests for redundant actions (those that have already taken place) to avoid endlessly repeating the same action. We can do this by testing all the add-to actions of a rule. If the category contains the value to be added, the action has already taken place. We must apply eval to the category and its value because they are quoted in the rules, and the quote must be eliminated. See what happens when you leave out the eval in repeat-action?.

```
; Test if the add-to actions in a rule have already been performed.
(define (repeat-action? rule)
  (every
    (lambda (action)
      (if (eq? (first action) 'add-to)
          (contains? (eval (second action)) (eval (third action)))
          #f) )
    (actions rule)) )
```

Testing if a move is complete

The expert shell function needs a function to test if the selection of rules is complete. In Mille Bornes, a move is complete when a card is played or discarded. These are the actions in the rules. When we write the code to handle these actions, we can include a step to add the symbol done to the blackboard to denote that the move is complete. Our function to test when a move is finished simply tests for done in the blackboard.

```
; Test if a single move in mille bornes is complete.
(define (move-done? database)
  (contains? 'bb 'done) )
```

Handling cards for the player and computer

The following functions take care of the actions of drawing, discarding, and playing cards for the computer and player. Both will need to take similar actions, but there will be some differences. For example, when the computer draws a card, it should mark it as seen; however, only when the player discards or uses a card can the computer see it. The computer must add done to the blackboard when it plays or discards.

```
; Computer picks a card from the deck and marks it as seen.
(define (draw-card)
  (add-to 'seen (draw 'hand1)) )
```

```scheme
; Computer discard: remove card from hand and mark move as done.
(define (discard card)
  (display "Computer discards ")
  (display card)
  (newline)
  (add-to 'bb 'done)
  (delete 'hand1 card) )

; Computer play: process card and mark move as done.
(define (play-card card)
  (display "Computer plays ")
  (display card)
  (newline)
  (add-to 'bb 'done)
  (play card 'hand1 'state1 'state2 'mileage1) )
```

To play a card, the actions taken depend on the card type (mileage, hazard, repair, or safety). The player and computer can share the following function:

```scheme
; Perform the actions needed when playing a card.
(define (play card hand state1 state2 mileage)
  (cond ((member card '(200 100 75 50 25))
           (set-cdr! (pair mileage) (+ card (data mileage))))
        ((member card '(stop accident flat-tire out-of-gas))
           (delete state2 'go)
           (add-to state2 card))
        ((eq? card 'speed-limit)
           (add-to state2 card))
        ((eq? card 'go)
           (delete state1 'stop))
        ((eq? card 'end-of-limit)
           (delete state1 'speed-limit))
        ((eq? card 'right-of-way)
           (delete state1 'stop)
           (delete state1 'speed-limit)
           (delete state1 'go))
        ((member card '(repairs driving-ace))
           (delete state1 'accident))
        ((member card '(spare-tire puncture-proof))
           (delete state1 'flat-tire))
        ((member card '(gasoline extra-tank))
           (delete state1 'out-of-gas))
        (else
           (display (append '(illegal card:) (list card)))))
  (if (member card '(go right-of-way driving-ace puncture-proof
                        extra-tank))
      (add-to state1 card))
  (delete hand card) )
```

The player and computer can share the following function as well, which picks a card from the deck:

```
; Pick a card at random from the deck and add it to hand.
(define (draw hand)
  (let* ((card-num (random (length (data 'deck))))
         (card (list-ref (data 'deck) card-num)))
    (add-to hand card)
    (delete 'deck card)
    card) )
```

15.6.2   The Mille Bornes rulebase

Here is a rule set that covers some of the previously mentioned strategies. It is not the best possible player that can be created, but it should give you an idea of how an expert rule base looks. The rules are in sections, and each section is prefaced with a brief description of what it tries to accomplish.

Mille Bornes rules

```
(define mille-rules '(
```

Draw cards if needed.

```
( (< (length (data 'hand1)) 7)
  (draw-card))
```

Go if not going and no hazard exists.

```
( (and (not (contains-any? 'state1
              '(go right-of-way accident out-of-gas flat-tire)))
         (contains? 'hand1 'go))
  (play-card 'go))
```

Play big mileage if possible.

```
( (contains-any? 'state1 '(go right-of-way))
  (add-to 'bb 'can-go))

( (and (contains? 'hand1 200)
        (<= (data 'mileage1) 500)
        (not (contains? 'state1 'speed-limit)))
  (add-to 'bb 'use-200))

( (and (contains? 'hand1 100)
        (<= (data 'mileage1) 600)
        (not (contains? 'state1 'speed-limit)))
  (add-to 'bb 'use-100))

( (and (contains? 'bb 'can-go)
        (contains? 'bb 'use-200))
  (play-card 200))

( (and (contains? 'bb 'can-go)
        (contains? 'bb 'use-100))
  (play-card 100))
```

Attacking moves.

```scheme
( (and (contains-any? 'state2 '(go right-of-way))
       (not (contains-any? 'state2
         '(out-of-gas flat-tire accident)))
       (contains-any? 'hand1
         '(out-of-gas flat-tire accident stop)))
  (add-to 'bb 'attack))

( (and (contains? 'bb 'attack)
       (contains? 'hand1 'out-of-gas)
       (not (contains? 'state2 'extra-tank)))
  (play-card 'out-of-gas))

( (and (contains? 'bb 'attack)
       (contains? 'hand1 'flat-tire)
       (not (contains? 'state2 'puncture-proof)))
  (play-card 'flat-tire))

( (and (contains? 'bb 'attack)
       (contains? 'hand1 'accident)
       (not (contains? 'state2 'driving-ace)))
  (play-card 'accident))

( (and (contains? 'bb 'attack)
       (contains? 'hand1 'stop)
       (not (contains? 'state2 'right-of-way)))
  (play-card 'stop))

( (and (contains? 'hand1 'speed-limit)
       (not (contains-any? 'state2 '(right-of-way speed-limit))))
  (play-card 'speed-limit))
```

Play smaller mileage if possible.

```scheme
( (and (contains? 'hand1 75)
       (<= (data 'mileage1) 625)
       (not (contains? 'state1 'speed-limit)))
  (add-to 'bb 'use-75))

( (and (contains? 'hand1 50)
       (<= (data 'mileage1) 650))
  (add-to 'bb 'use-50))

( (and (contains? 'hand1 25)
       (<= (data 'mileage1) 675))
  (add-to 'bb 'use-25))

( (and (contains? 'bb 'can-go)
       (contains? 'bb 'use-75))
  (play-card 75))
```

```
( (and (contains? 'bb 'can-go)
       (contains? 'bb 'use-50))
  (play-card 50))

( (and (contains? 'bb 'can-go)
       (contains? 'bb 'use-25))
  (play-card 25))
```

Apply remedy or safety if stopped.

```
( (and (contains? 'statc1 'out-of-gas)
       (contains? 'hand1 'extra-tank))
  (play-card 'extra-tank))

( (and (contains? 'state1 'flat-tire)
       (contains? 'hand1 'puncture-proof))
  (play-card 'puncture-proof))

( (and (contains? 'state1 'accident)
       (contains? 'hand1 'driving-ace))
  (play-card 'driving-ace))

( (and (contains-any? 'state1 '(stop speed-limit))
       (contains? 'hand1 'right-of-way))
  (play-card 'right-of-way))

( (and (contains? 'state1 'out-of-gas)
       (contains? 'hand1 'gasoline))
  (play-card 'gasoline))

( (and (contains? 'state1 'flat-tire)
       (contains? 'hand1 'spare-tire))
  (play-card 'spare-tire))

( (and (contains? 'state1 'accident)
       (contains? 'hand1 'repairs))
  (play-card 'repairs))

( (and (contains? 'state1 'stop)
       (contains? 'hand1 'go))
  (play-card 'go))

( (and (contains? 'state1 'speed-limit)
       (contains? 'hand1 'end-of-limit))
  (play-card 'end-of-limit))
```

Play safeties if can't play another card.

```
( (contains? 'hand1 'extra-tank)
  (play-card 'extra-tank))

( (contains? 'hand1 'puncture-proof)
  (play-card 'puncture-proof))
```

```
( (contains? 'hand1 'driving-ace)
  (play-card 'driving-ace))

( (contains? 'hand1 'right-of-way)
  (play-card 'right-of-way))
```

Discard card if can't move. First try to discard unnecessary cards.

```
( (and (contains? 'hand1 'end-of-limit)
       (or (contains? 'state1 'right-of-way)
           (= (count 'speed-limit (data 'seen)) 3)))
  (discard 'end-of-limit))

( (and (contains? 'hand1 'go)
       (or (contains? 'state1 'right-of-way)
           (= (count 'stop (data 'seen)) 4)))
  (discard 'go))

( (and (contains? 'hand1 'repairs)
       (or (contains? 'state1 'driving-ace)
           (= (count 'accident (data 'seen)) 2)))
  (discard 'repairs))

( (and (contains? 'hand1 'gasoline)
       (or (contains? 'state1 'extra-tank)
           (= (count 'out-of-gas (data 'seen)) 2)))
  (discard 'gasoline))

( (and (contains? 'hand1 'spare-tire)
       (or (contains? 'state1 'puncture-proof)
           (= (count 'flat-tire (data 'seen)) 2)))
  (discard 'spare-tire))

( (and (contains? 'hand1 'stop)
       (contains? 'state2 'right-of-way))
  (discard 'stop))

( (and (contains? 'hand1 'speed-limit)
       (contains? 'state2 'right-of-way))
  (discard 'speed-limit))

( (and (contains? 'hand1 'accident)
       (contains? 'state2 'driving-ace))
  (discard 'accident))

( (and (contains? 'hand1 'flat-tire)
       (contains? 'state2 'puncture-proof))
  (discard 'flat-tire))

( (and (contains? 'hand1 'out-of-gas)
       (contains? 'state2 'extra-tank))
  (discard 'out-of-gas))
```

```
(  (and (contains? 'hand1 200)
        (> (data 'mileage1) 500))
   (discard 200))

(  (and (contains? 'hand1 100)
        (> (data 'mileage1) 600))
   (discard 100))

(  (and (contains? 'hand1 75)
        (> (data 'mileage1) 625))
   (discard 75))

(  (and (contains? 'hand1 50)
        (> (data 'mileage1) 650))
   (discard 50))
```

If no cards are unnecessary, try to discard cards with the least value.

```
(  (and (contains? 'hand1 75)
        (contains? 'state1 'speed-limit))
   (discard 75))

(  (and (contains? 'hand1 100)
        (contains? 'state1 'speed-limit))
   (discard 100))

(  (and (contains? 'hand1 200)
        (contains? 'state1 'speed-limit))
   (discard 200))

(  (contains? 'hand1 25)
   (discard 25))

(  (contains? 'hand1 50)
   (discard 50))

(  (contains? 'hand1 75)
   (discard 75))

(  (contains? 'hand1 100)
   (discard 100))

(  (contains? 'hand1 200)
   (discard 200))

(  (contains? 'hand1 'go)
   (discard 'go))

(  (contains? 'hand1 'stop)
   (discard 'stop))

(  (contains? 'hand1 'end-of-limit)
   (discard 'end-of-limit))
```

```
( (contains? 'hand1 'speed-limit)
  (discard 'speed-limit))

( (contains? 'hand1 'gasoline)
  (discard 'gasoline))

( (contains? 'hand1 'spare-tire)
  (discard 'spare-tire))

( (contains? 'hand1 'repairs)
  (discard 'repairs))

( (contains? 'hand1 'out-of-gas)
  (discard 'out-of-gas))

( (contains? 'hand1 'flat-tire)
  (discard 'flat-tire))

( (contains? 'hand1 'accident)
  (discard 'accident)) ) )
```

15.6.3 Building a driver for Mille Bornes

Controlling the play

The current set of rules represent the strategic aspects of the game—those things that involve "expertise" in deciding which actions to take. We need some control features to handle the play between each player. We have two choices when building the rest of the Mille Bornes system. One choice is to build additional rules to take care of the sequencing of moves (e.g., stopping the game when one player wins) and the details of shuffling, dealing, and discarding cards. The other approach is to build functions that handle these actions. The second approach will be easier, especially in terms of handling the flow of control of the play. Rule-based systems don't lend themselves to handling complex flow of control. They work best with large collections of independent rules, which may apply at any time.

The additional functions will act as a *driver* calling the expert system, which will sequence through the rules until an action (play or discard) is performed. Then the driver will read a move from the second player. This sequence of actions continues until one player wins.

```
; Main driver to alternate computer's and player's move until
; game is complete.
(define (mille)
  (reset 'bb)
  (expert-shell mille-rules repeat-action? first move-done?)
  (cond ((= (data 'mileage1) 700)
         '(sorry the computer beat you))
        (else
          (get-action)
          (if (= (data 'mileage2) 700)
              '(congratulations you won)
              (mille))))) )
```

As a variation we could change the driver to invoke another expert system for the second player with a different strategy and compare the two strategies.

The function `get-action` will display information to the user, showing her hand, state, and mileage and the computer's state and mileage. It calls `play-or-discard` to get a move from the user.

```
; Print current state and get a move from the user.
(define (get-action)
  (draw 'hand2)
  (newline)
  (display "Your mileage: ")
  (display (data 'mileage2))
  (display "    Your state: ")
  (display (data 'state2))
  (newline)
  (display "Computer mileage: ")
  (display (data 'mileage1))
  (display "    Computer state: ")
  (display (data 'state1))
  (newline)
  (display "Your hand: ")
  (display (data 'hand2))
  (newline)
  (play-or-discard) )

; Read in a play or discard move from the user.
(define (play-or-discard)
  (newline)
  (display "What would you like to do: ")
  (let* ((input (read))
         (card (if (member input '(discard play))
                   (read))))
    (cond ((eq? input 'discard)
           (add-to 'seen card)
           (delete 'hand2 card))
          ((eq? input 'play)
           (add-to 'seen card)
           (play card 'hand2 'state2 'state1 'mileage2))
          (else
           (display "Illegal move. ")
           (display "Please 'discard card' or 'play card'")
           (newline)
           (play-or-discard)))) )
```

Representing the card deck   The cards are entered as a list, and multiple cards are sublists containing the card name and the number of occurrences of that card. This makes it easier to enter the cards and to make changes if we decide to. The functions `expand-deck` and `repeat-card` (based on the functions `expand` and `repeat` from Chapter 14) will turn this compressed list into a flat list from which we can choose random elements. Contrast `repeat-card` which is written using **do** with `repeat`.

```scheme
; The mille bornes deck in compressed form.
(define compressed-cards
  '((go 14) (stop 4) (200 4) (100 12) (75 10) (50 10) (25 10)
    (gasoline 6) (out-of-gas 2) extra-tank (spare-tire 6)
    (flat-tire 2) puncture-proof (repairs 6) (accident 2)
    driving-ace (end-of-limit 6) (speed-limit 3) right-of-way))

; Expand a compressed list into a flat list with repeated elements.
(define (expand-deck compressed)
  (cond ((null? compressed) '())
        ((list? (car compressed))
          (append (repeat-card (caar compressed) (cadar compressed))
                  (expand-deck (cdr compressed))))
        (else
          (cons (car compressed) (expand-deck (cdr compressed)))))) )

; Return a list of times occurrences of card.
(define (repeat-card card times)
  (do ((count 0 (+ count 1))
       (ans '() (cons card ans)))
    ((= count times) ans)) )
```

We can test `expand-deck` with a small sample list:

```scheme
> (expand-deck '((go 3) stop (gasoline 2)))
(go go go stop gasoline gasoline)
```

We'll save the actual list of cards in the variable `mille-cards`.

```scheme
(define mille-cards (expand-deck compressed-cards))

> (length mille-cards)
101
```

Lastly, we need to initialize the database so that the deck is a full set of cards and that both players begin with six cards. This should be done before each game, so a function to do this is handy. We need to define the database on the top level and then redefine it in this function using `set!`.

Initializing the database

```scheme
(define database '())

; Reset initial database.
(define (initialize)
  (set! database '(
    (hand1)  (hand2)
    (deck)  (seen)
    (mileage1 . 0)  (mileage2 . 0)
    (state1)  (state2)
    (bb)))
  (set-cdr! (pair 'deck) mille-cards)
  (do ((count 1 (+ count 1)))
    ((> count 6) 'done)
      (draw-card)
      (draw 'hand2)) )
```

Testing the game　　　　After getting the program running, I tried a game against the computer. I easily beat it. In fact, the computer never got started. After looking more carefully at its actions I noticed that it had discarded go cards. I realized that one rule said if you are stopped, play a go, but no rule said that you need to initially play a go to get moving in the first place. I added this one rule, and then played another game. The computer won. This felt good in that the program was working well, but also rather strange in that a machine I had programmed with my knowledge and strategy beat me. Of course there is an element of luck, so I got up my nerve and tried it again. This time the machine shut me out! I did finally manage to beat it, but many games turned out like the one shown in the trace below. Notice the series of attacks the computer made to keep me from gaining mileage.

```
> (initialize)
done
```

Sample game
```
> (mille)
Computer plays go

Your mileage: 0     Your state: ()
Computer mileage: 0     Computer state: (go)
Your hand: (end-of-limit 75 200 end-of-limit go 50 50)

What would you like to do: play go
Computer plays flat-tire

Your mileage: 0     Your state: (flat-tire)
Computer mileage: 0     Computer state: (go)
Your hand: (repairs end-of-limit 75 200 end-of-limit 50 50)

What would you like to do: discard end-of-limit
Computer plays 75

Your mileage: 0     Your state: (flat-tire)
Computer mileage: 75     Computer state: (go)
Your hand: (100 repairs 75 200 end-of-limit 50 50)

What would you like to do: discard 50
Computer plays 75

Your mileage: 0     Your state: (flat-tire)
Computer mileage: 150     Computer state: (go)
Your hand: (gasoline 100 repairs 75 200 end-of-limit 50)

What would you like to do: discard 50
Computer plays 200

Your mileage: 0     Your state: (flat-tire)
Computer mileage: 350     Computer state: (go)
Your hand: (25 gasoline 100 repairs 75 200 end-of-limit)
```

```
What would you like to do: discard 25
Computer plays 25

Your mileage: 0    Your state: (flat-tire)
Computer mileage: 375    Computer state: (go)
Your hand: (100 gasoline 100 repairs 75 200 end-of-limit)

What would you like to do: discard 75
Computer plays 200

Your mileage: 0    Your state: (flat-tire)
Computer mileage: 575    Computer state: (go)
Your hand: (100 100 gasoline 100 repairs 200 end-of-limit)

What would you like to do: discard 100
Computer plays 100

Your mileage: 0    Your state: (flat-tire)
Computer mileage: 675    Computer state: (go)
Your hand: (50 100 gasoline 100 repairs 200 end-of-limit)
```

Time passes.

```
Your mileage: 0    Your state: (flat-tire)
Computer mileage: 675    Computer state: (driving-ace right-of-way)
Your hand: (puncture-proof go go gasoline 100 repairs 200)

What would you like to do: play puncture-proof
Computer plays speed-limit

Your mileage: 0    Your state: (speed-limit puncture-proof)
Computer mileage: 675    Computer state: (driving-ace right-of-way)
Your hand: (100 go go gasoline 100 repairs 200)

What would you like to do: play go
Computer plays out-of-gas

Your mileage: 0    Your state: (out-of-gas speed-limit puncture-proof)
Computer mileage: 675    Computer state: (driving-ace right-of-way)
Your hand: (50 100 go gasoline 100 repairs 200)

What would you like to do: play gasoline
Computer discards repairs

Your mileage: 0    Your state: (speed-limit puncture-proof)
Computer mileage: 675    Computer state: (driving-ace right-of-way)
Your hand: (100 50 100 go 100 repairs 200)

What would you like to do: play go
Computer discards repairs
```

```
Your mileage: 0     Your state: (go speed-limit puncture-proof)
Computer mileage: 675    Computer state: (driving-ace right-of-way)
Your hand: (gasoline 100 50 100 100 repairs 200)

What would you like to do: play 50
Computer plays stop

Your mileage: 50    Your state: (stop speed-limit puncture-proof)
Computer mileage: 675    Computer state: (driving-ace right-of-way)
Your hand: (gasoline gasoline 100 100 100 repairs 200)

What would you like to do: discard gasoline
Computer discards 200

Your mileage: 50    Your state: (stop speed-limit puncture-proof)
Computer mileage: 675    Computer state: (driving-ace right-of-way)
Your hand: (go gasoline 100 100 100 repairs 200)

What would you like to do: play go
Computer discards 100

Your mileage: 50    Your state: (go speed-limit puncture-proof)
Computer mileage: 675    Computer state: (driving-ace right-of-way)
Your hand: (stop gasoline 100 100 100 repairs 200)

What would you like to do: discard stop
Computer plays accident

Your mileage: 50    Your state: (accident speed-limit puncture-proof)
Computer mileage: 675    Computer state: (driving-ace right-of-way)
Your hand: (gasoline gasoline 100 100 100 repairs 200)

What would you like to do: play repairs
Computer discards go

Your mileage: 50    Your state: (speed-limit puncture-proof)
Computer mileage: 675    Computer state: (driving-ace right-of-way)
Your hand: (go gasoline gasoline 100 100 100 200)

What would you like to do: play go
Computer discards 75

Your mileage: 50    Your state: (go speed-limit puncture-proof)
Computer mileage: 675    Computer state: (driving-ace right-of-way)
Your hand: (50 gasoline gasoline 100 100 100 200)

What would you like to do: play 50
Computer discards 75

Your mileage: 100    Your state: (go speed-limit puncture-proof)
```

```
Computer mileage: 675    Computer state: (driving-ace right-of-way)
Your hand: (extra-tank gasoline gasoline 100 100 100 200)

What would you like to do: play extra-tank
Computer plays 25
(sorry the computer beat you)
```

15.6.4 Exercises

15.7 Try your hand at knowledge engineering. Choose someone you know who is an expert in some domain. This person does not have to be an expert in a technical area with a wall full of degrees. Pick someone who has a good deal of experience doing some task (e.g., fixing bikes, moving lawns, baking cookies, changing diapers). Interview this expert and build a set of rules to represent their expert knowledge.

15.8 Modify the expert system shell so that it stops if no rules are applicable and returns the symbol no-matches.

15.9 Change the Mille Bornes code and data structures so that it uses the functions expand and repeat from Chapter 14 instead of the new versions expand-deck and repeat-card.

15.10 The real game of Mille Bornes awards a bonus for playing a safety immediately after receiving the corresponding hazard and before drawing a card. This is called a coup foure. Also, whenever a safety is played (whether it qualifies as a coup foure or not), the player gets an extra turn. Modify the rules to incorporate this. You may need to make changes to some of the functions that drive the Mille Bornes program.

15.11 The Mille Bornes player's moves are not checked, so the player can make illegal moves, like playing mileage when stopped. Add tests to disallow illegal moves.

15.12 Modify the rules to improve the discard policy. Some rules test if cards are unnecessary (e.g., a repair card is not needed if two accidents have been seen or if we have a driving ace card). Other rules unconditionally eliminate cards according to some ordering in the rules. Create more discard rules that test for things like discarding go if the player has many of them in her hand or discarding additional repairs if one is already in the hand and an accident has been played (there are only two accidents in the deck and if one has been played, only one is needed as protection).

15.13 Each safety played is worth bonus points. Modify the rules to play any safeties still in the hand just before winning the game (assuming the opponent isn't too close to winning).

15.14 Modify the rules and driver to support extensions to the game. A player with 700 miles can choose to extend the game to 1000 miles. Then the first player to 1000 miles wins the game.

15.15 Modify the Mille Bornes functions to keep track of special bonuses that are included in the real game. These are

bonus	points	explanation
safety	100 each	playing a safety
coup foure	300 each	playing safety immediately after hazard
trip completed	400	getting 700 or 1000 miles first
safe trip	300	completing trip without using 200 mile cards
delayed action	300	completing trip after the deck is finished
extension	200	completing 1000 mile trip
shut-out	500	completing trip before opponent plays mileage

15.16 Modify the rules to improve the strategy for playing mileage near the end of the game. Instead of immediately playing miles, wait until the exact mileage to win is held in the hand. This avoids problems like getting 675 miles and then having to wait for 25 miles to win (this is what happened to the computer in the game shown).

15.7 Natural Language Processing

Natural language processing (NLP) was introduced in section 15.2, "Historical Background." To recap, the early work in NLP attempted language translation based on syntactical rules and dictionary lookup of words. This failed miserably, and for many years little was done in NLP research. One of the lessons learned is that semantics are necessary for understanding. This can be seen in examples such as

The importance of semantics

"The pen is in the box"
     versus
"The box is in the pen"

These two sentences are syntactically equivalent, but the usual interpretation of "pen" is different in each sentence. In the first sentence one pictures a pen like a ballpoint writing pen. In the second sentence "pen" becomes a large containment pen, like a playpen. Syntax alone cannot give us this insight, but the semantics of what being in another object requires tells us that the pen cannot be a writing pen in the second sentence (unless we picture a very small box).

When NLP resurfaced, researchers didn't make big claims but instead worked on smaller, specific problems. Rather than attempting complete language translation, work was done on translation within specific domains of discourse such as traffic reports or database queries.

SAM

The focus in NLP changed to the individual pieces of human language abilities that make up full understanding. One such ability is making inferences given incomplete information. This work was done with a program called SAM (script applier mechanism). For example, you might be told the following:

Sam goes to Sante Fe Bar and Grill
He orders a salad
He leaves Sante Fe Bar and Grill

After a program receives this information, it can answer questions like the following:

Did Sam eat a salad?
Did Sam pay for a salad?

The program can infer the answers to these questions even though the story never explicitly indicated that Sam ate a salad (only that he ordered a salad) or that Sam paid for the salad. The program can make inferences by having knowledge of what typically happens in restaurants. This knowledge is represented as scripts (like movie or story scripts), which dictate a specific sequence of actions that are usually taken. These scripts are abstracted using variables instead of specific people, places, and items. A simple restaurant script may look like the following:

Inference

person goes to *restaurant*
person orders *food*
person eats *food*
person pays for *food*
person leaves *restaurant*

Restaurant script

SAM has a collection of such scripts representing events like eating in restaurants, driving to work, and buying clothes. When given some sentences as input, SAM tries to match these with the scripts in its script database. The specific instances (names, places, items) are matched with the variables in the script. For example, given our previous sentences

Sam goes to Sante Fe Bar and Grill
He orders a salad
He leaves Sante Fe Bar and Grill

these match with the first, second, and last lines of the script

person goes to *restaurant*
person orders *food*
person leaves *restaurant*

The variable *person* matches Sam, *restaurant* matches Sante Fe Bar and Grill, and *food* matches a salad. The remaining lines of the script are changed to reflect the variable values as follows:

Sam eats a salad
Sam pays for a salad

Now it is easy to answer questions like

Did Sam eat a salad?

Did Sam pay for a salad?

SAM was written in the mid 1970s. However, the idea behind scripts resurfaced in the world-knowledge program CYC (presented in section 15.3.7). CYC's contexts, when reduced to specific events, can be viewed as scripts. Instead of writing a list of sentences of the events within a script, CYC maintains a collection of assertions that are typically true in a given context. CYC might have a restaurant context with assertions like "people typically pay for the food they order and eat."

15.7.1   Representing natural languages

Conceptual dependency

SAM did not use English to represent its scripts and sentences. A simplified language called Conceptual Dependency (CD) was used. In CD, about a dozen different primitive actions are defined. These actions correspond roughly to English verbs. Many possible actions are not included because they are modeled by combining two or more actions or they are represented as changes to an object's state. For example, "Mickey upset Minnie" would be represented as a change in Minnie's state, becoming upset, caused by some action that Mickey did. The actions are outlined below.

Actions in CD

action	description	example
ATRANS	transfer of possession of object	Fred gave Fran a rose
MTRANS	information is transferred	Fred read a book
PTRANS	physical transformation	Fred went to the store
PROPEL	applying a force	Fran kicked the ball
MBUILD	creating mental information	Fran thought about the game
ATTEND	to focus attention on something	Fred looked at the rock
SPEAK	to make a sound	Fran yelled "Duck!" at Fred
GRASP	to grasp an object	Fred grabbed the bag
MOVE	to move a body part	Fred lifted his arm
INGEST	to take an object into the body	Fran sipped her Chardonnay
EXPEL	to release an object from the body	Fred cried

Sentences in CD

In addition to actions, there are actors (the things that do the acting), objects (the things that are acted upon), and directions (the orientation of the action). These are represented as *slots* in a data structure. Together they represent one *event*. For example, the sentence "Sam went to Santa Fe Bar and Grill" can be represented as follows:

```
((actor Sam)
 (action PTRANS)
 (object Sam)
 (direction (to Santa Fe Bar and Grill) (from unknown)))
```

The sentence "Sam eats a salad" would be

```
((actor Sam)
 (action INGEST)
 (object salad)
 (direction (to Sam's mouth) (from plate)))
```

We could add other events to represent the movement of the salad to Sam's mouth, Sam grasping a fork to grab the salad, and the movement of Sam's hand to move the fork and salad from the plate to his mouth. Such events are not necessarily correct, however. Sam may be eating the salad with a spoon (it could be a potato or fruit salad), or with his hands and injera (an Ethiopian pancake-like bread) at an Ethiopian restaurant. The salad may not be on a plate but could be in a bowl. Sam may be a baby and "eating" the salad by wiping it in the general vicinity of his face, his clothes, and the most expensive furniture in the room.

One of the advantages of CD representations is that different sentences with the same fundamental meaning can be represented with identical CDs. The following sentences can all be represented with the same CD.

Canonical representation

John gave Mary a book.
John handed a book to Mary.
Mary received a book from John.
A book was given to Mary by John.
John presented Mary with a book.
John transferred a book from his possession to Mary's.
Mary, hereinafter known as the recipient, came into possession of said book, exhibit A, given to her by the defendant, John.
A transferral of a book initiated by John directed toward Mary resulted in the set of items constituting Mary's possessions being augmented to include a book that previously was a member of the set of John's possessions.

The CD representation clearly labels all the different parts of the sentence: the actor, the recipient, the action, and so on. This helps in the process of summarizing, paraphrasing, answering questions, and in translation. Look at the following two sentences. The first is in the active voice and the second in the passive voice.

The fish ate the shrimp.
The shrimp was eaten by the fish.

Both sentences would be represented as the same CD event diagram

```
((actor the fish)
 (action INGEST)
 (object the shrimp)
 (direction (to the fishes' mouth) (from unknown)))
```

With such a representation, it is easy to answer questions like "What ate the shrimp?" or "What did the fish eat?" It is clear that the fish did the eating and not the shrimp. Translation is partially a matter of looking up the corresponding word knowing its context.

The context of the word is important because it dictates the meaning to use when a word has more than one meaning. For example,

Context in NLP

> Look at all the stars!

means different things depending on the context. It could be an utterance made while gazing at the heavens on a cloudless night away from the city. Or it could be a comment made at the Academy Awards presentations. The meaning of such a sentence cannot be determined outside of its context.

World knowledge in NLP

Many sentences cannot be translated or understood without semantic information. For example,

> He went wild, charging everything in sight: the cologne, the suit, the watch.
> He went wild, charging everything in sight: the matador, the picador, the walls.

It is clear that in the first sentence "charging" refers to buying items with a credit card. In the second example, the subject is most likely a bull who is charging at its antagonists in the bullring. The semantics can explain this without knowledge of the surrounding context in which the sentence occurs. One does not normally charge into cologne, suits, or watches, nor does one buy matadors, picadors, or walls with a credit card. To know this requires knowledge of objects in the world and the typical behavior of actors in the world.

Plans and goals

We have looked at how scripts can assist in making inferences about unspecified events in a story. Having a model that includes plans and goals is also important. A story contains a goal or goals that the actor or actors are attempting to achieve. To meet these goals a script may be followed or plans may be used. Recognizing goals, scripts, and plans facilitates understanding.

A script is a stereotypical solution to achieve a goal. The restaurant script meets the goal of satisfying hunger. Planning is a more fundamental and general mechanism that is necessary because not all goals can be met using scripts. A plan defines some course of action that attempts to achieve some goal. In addition, plans are used to link scripts or parts of a dialogue together to support goals. Here is a simple story with a goal and a plan:

> Tom was getting hungry.
> He picked up the book *Yummy, Yummy, Yummy Quick Dishes*.

Tom's goal is to satisfy his hunger, but its clear from the second sentence that the restaurant script is not being followed. Instead Tom is following a plan to find a recipe in a cookbook and make food. We know, or at least hope, that Tom isn't picking up the cookbook to eat it. An NLP system would need knowledge of typical goals, plans, and the outcomes of plans. The system would need to know that a cookbook provides recipes that are used to prepare food and that the cookbook itself is not edible.

Sometimes goals and plans are not obvious, as this next story illustrates.

> A man went to bar and asked for a glass of water.
> The bartender pulled a gun on him.
> The man thanked the bartender and left.

To understand stories like this that don't have scripts because they aren't common events, one must understand goals and plans. Goals may not be readily apparent, or an incorrect goal may be surmised. The goal of the man appears to be to quench his thirst. He makes a plan to ask for a glass of water to meet that goal. Instead of giving him water, the bartender pulls a gun on him. This seems like the bartender does not understand the man's goal. However, the man thanks the bartender, so it appears that his goal is satisfied. The task now is to think of a goal that makes sense in the context of the whole story. In this case that goal is to stop the man's hiccups. The man had the plan of drinking water to stop the hiccups. The bartender, hearing the hiccups, had a different plan of scaring the man to stop the hiccups. This plan worked and the man showed appreciation.

One other mechanism was used in understanding the above sentence— coherence. Stories must be coherent to be understood. The above story was not, until we discovered a new plan. Coherency checks help us in verifying that our goals, plans, and understanding are going well. These checks can happen within a sentence. Take the following example:

Coherence

> The old man's glasses were filled with sherry.

As we read or listen to this sentence, a common interpretation upon hearing the noun phrase "the old man's glasses" is to first think that "glasses" refers to spectacles or reading glasses. Then, when we encounter the rest of the sentence, we realize that spectacles cannot hold sherry (incoherence) so we change them to drinking glasses[9].

15.7.2   Current uses of NLP

The complete goal of natural language processing has not been attained, and the immediate future offers no promise of doing so. In the meantime, NLP research continues but often with smaller scale projects. There are many domains in which the discourse is usually limited and language understanding systems can be built. NLP techniques have been used to provide front-ends to databases so that queries can be made in English rather than in the query language of the database system. These front-ends translate the English query into a query suitable for the database system. The result from the query can be translated to an English answer. Another example is generating reports from information stored in some fairly typical form with a limited vocabulary. For example, the U.S. Geological Service provides weather information. This can be translated into a more readable form or into a format for a database on weather information.

NLP front-ends

Digital libraries present a large area of research and NLP promise. With the growing number of texts digitally encoded, we are able to rapidly search for information from a huge number of sources. This data is in a database that is readily accessible through the proper queries. Information retrieval and filtering techniques are used to extract information. The difficulty is often in knowing how to simplify requests for information so that they are not too specific or too general. NLP techniques may offer some improvement here.

Digital libraries, information retrieval, and information filtering

---

[9] Another possible interpretation (the one that I made upon first hearing this example) is to maintain the spectacles interpretation of "glasses," but view "sherry" as a woman named Sherry who is being ogled by the old man so intently that all he sees is Sherry.

Intelligent spell checkers

Word processors can use NLP techniques to improve their spelling and grammar checkers. An intelligent spelling checker may be able to correct words that are spelled correctly but used improperly. For example, the sentence

Marry through there bawl threw the whole in the read wall.

produces no spelling errors but makes no sense. Given knowledge of words that are similar and typical misuses of words, a program may be able to find the sentence

Mary threw their ball through the hole in the red wall.

This would take a very sophisticated program that had extensive knowledge of English grammar rules and knowledge about the semantics of words. For example, you can throw a ball through a hole, but it makes no sense to throw a bawl through a whole.

Speech recognition

Two fields related to natural language processing are *speech recognition* and *speech synthesis*. Speech recognition is the process of producing written text from spoken text. Read the above two sentences about Mary/Marry aloud—both sound the same. To understand which of many homonyms to use requires an understanding of the semantics of the words. Sometimes it's not a matter of deciding between homonyms but between groups of words that have the same pronunciation. For example,

"It's hard to recognize speech"
versus
"It's hard to wreck a nice beach"

The words "recognize speech" sound the same as "wreck a nice beach" when spoken fast and slurred a bit. In speech recognition, individual syllables must be processed to determine if they are part of the current word or the next. Gaps in speech cannot always be used because sometimes the gaps between syllables in a word are bigger than the gaps between words. This is made very dramatic if you record a sentence and then play it backwards. You'll notice the true gaps in sound more clearly, because you won't have recognizable words to give you mental word gaps.

Speech synthesis

Speech synthesis is challenging as well. Its task is to take text in some language and produce the corresponding sounds of the text. This may sound easy but is complicated, especially in the case of a nonphonetic language like English, in which identical spellings are pronounced differently, like

You must read the book
versus
Yesterday he read the book

wild
versus
wilderness

Most pronunciations can be handled with less than 1,000 rules that map spellings to sounds. To do a perfect job would require a degree of language understanding to discern, as in the above example, the proper pronunciation of the word "read" based on its use as a command in the present tense or a past tense action.

Additionally, *prosody* is important when speaking text. Prosody is the use of intonation, timing, and sound intensity when speaking. When asking a question, the last word often ends on a rising tone. For example,

> You did what?

Prosody

A sequence of numbers is often ended with the final number voiced over a longer period of time. Phone number information services (dialing 411) use speech synthesis, and the final number in the prefix and suffix are elongated. Ignoring prosody results in stale and strange-sounding speech. Tone is critical for understanding—actually producing different words and meanings—in tonal languages like Thai.

15.8 Robotics

Robots are machines that interact with the real world to carry out particular tasks. Many robots are autonomous in that they can act without human intervention. Much of what robots do involves recognition, planning, and acting. Robots must recognize their world to grab objects or know when to stop moving toward an object. They must make plans to deal with going from a given initial state to the desired goal state, for example to determine how to grab a nut and later tighten it onto a bolt that is moving along an assembly line. Lastly, the robot must take action to carry out the task.

Recognition is extremely important because of all the difficulties entailed in being in the real world. Even a robot doing a task as seemingly simple as stapling a stack of papers will run into problems if the papers are not lined up properly or are not where the robot expects them to be. Robots can never rely 100% on receiving the material they will work on at a given location. Think of how a xerox machine can get stuck when the paper jams.

Recognition

Recognition is not necessarily done only through visual systems. It may be a tactile input to pressure-sensitive devices. A robot that picks up objects may need tactile feedback to know if it is grabbing the object tightly enough and also that it is not grabbing it too tightly. The robot must be aware of its location and the location of all of its moving parts. This *proprioceptive sense* is one we don't think about too much, but it is crucial for robots, since they must know where they are in the three-dimensional world to avoid colliding with other objects or themselves.

We often think of robots in two ways: either as sophisticated futuristic devices that can communicate, reason, move about, and interact with the world (like the robots from the movie *Star Wars*) or as machines that simply follow the same sequence of actions tirelessly and endlessly like welding robots in an automobile factory. For certain robots that take on the same task without ever adjusting to a changing environment, there is no need for planning. The robot is really just a mindless machine. However, if the robot is taking in inputs about its world and is supposed to be able to respond to changes in its world, planning is necessary. Robots interacting with the real world must deal with a constantly changing

Planning

environment. This makes planning much more difficult since the world conditions are dynamic. Imagine a robot that is supposed to follow an object that is also moving. The robot must constantly adjust its actions according to the change in relative position between it and the object it is following and the surrounding objects.

Movement and degrees of freedom

Robots move in a variety of ways: they have treads, wheels, and legs. They have appendages that can move independently. These may move linearly (back and forth or up and down) or by rotating. Each movement (linear or rotational) effects a degree of freedom. With six degrees of freedom, a robot or robot arm can be at any position and orientation to grab or move an object. To plug in a toaster, the end of the electrical cord must be directly in front of the outlet. This position component has three subcomponents: distance to the outlet, height relative to the outlet, and horizontal position left or right of the outlet. The cord has an orientation in three axes. The cord can be pointing up or down instead of toward the outlet, it can be pointing left or right as well, and finally the cord can be rotated along its length. Once the cord is in the proper position and orientation, it can be plugged into the outlet. More sophisticated robots have more degrees of freedom. This allows the robot more flexibility in taking action in an environment with a lot of obstacles. More degrees of freedom comes at a price, however. It requires more moving parts and the control and sensing mechanisms for them. It also complicates calculating if part of the robot will collide with another object because more movements and potential collisions are possible.

Actions and effectors

Once a plan of action has been made, a robot must take action. The robot needs some way of interacting with the world by using *effectors*, things that have an effect on the world. Devices that grab, push, screw, cut, and weld are all effectors. The robot must move using legs, wheels, and motors that extend limbs and effectors and rotators that rotate all or parts of the robot. The movements are initiated by instructions from the robot's "brain"—the program that controls the robot. These instructions are converted into electrical signals to control the motors that perform the mechanical activity of moving the robot.

15.9   Vision

Recognizing objects

The challenge of computer vision is to find the location, orientation, distance, color, and size of objects in an image; in short, to recognize objects. The input to a vision system is a two-dimensional image that is a representation of our three-dimensional world. These images may be from a photograph, drawing, or TV screen. From this we must determine three-dimensional objects in the view and information about the objects, such as the surfaces, textures, sizes versus distances, and whether they are obscuring or obscured by other objects. Doing this is not simple and involves getting information in many ways.

Edge detection

Vision begins by taking the output from some device that captures an image (such as a CCD—charge-coupled device—from a video camera) and finding the edges. Edges define boundaries between different objects in the image or can indicate where an object changes shape or has a certain texture. An edge may denote an area where one object occludes another object. Further analysis is required to determine the meaning of edges. For example, edges may denote shadow regions of objects.

Much of the low-level recognition work involves mathematical analysis of the two-dimensional (2-D) image. David Marr, the late vision researcher, took an approach that involved a series of steps going from a 2-D representation to a *primal sketch* or *2.5-D representation* to a 3-D representation. The primal sketch determines some of the edges and information about how edges relate to one another.

Knowledge about objects in the physical world is used in visual systems. A visual system can make interpretations that are not physically possible. Many of M.C. Escher's paintings use the fact that it is possible to draw objects in two dimensions (what a visual system would perceive) that are impossible in three dimensions (or only possible with cleverly constructed models viewed from particular angles and with a carefully chosen light source). Escher plays with depth and perspective to give the illusion that water runs uphill or a rooftop can be circumnavigated in either a neverending upward climb or a downward descent. If a visual system does not know how to perceive angles and corners as convex or concave based on physical world possibilities, improper visual analysis will be the result.

World knowledge in vision

The Necker cube in the diagram below has two legal interpretations. One has the face labeled "back" (with vertices A, B, C, and D) as the nearest face and the other has it as the furthest face from the observer. A visual system may interpret corners in ways that are impossible. For example, the vertex near the label "back" may be viewed as closer than the vertex labeled "A" and the vertex labeled "B" may be seen as being in front of the vertex "back." This is impossible with a three-dimensional cube shown from this perspective. Given knowledge about what types of shapes are possible in the real world and how vertices that share edges relate, these misinterpretations can be avoided.

Necker cube

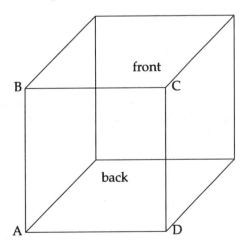

Depth and stereo disparity

Additional information is used to determine more about the objects in an image. Depth information can be obtained from *stereo disparity* clues. Stereo disparity refers to the differences in the perceived location of the same object when viewed from different vantage points by separate lenses. Our eyes provide a perfect tool for doing this task. They are separated by a small distance, but this is large enough to produce disparity. You'll easily notice this by holding a pen or a book in front of you, looking at it with one eye only and then observing how it jumps when you rapidly switch eyes to view it with the other eye. The pen hasn't moved, only our perception of its location. The closer the object, the larger the disparity, and this is how depth information is computed from the inputs of both eyes. The brain combines the two disparate images into one cohesive image with depth information.

Light information

Light color (hue), brightness, surface material, texture, and angle of the light with respect to the viewer and the object are all used in determining the actual color of objects. Factors such as angles of light, texture, and surface material may not seem important, but the perceived hue varies with all of these factors. Think of the glitter of a shiny new car or the shaded area that is darker in perceived hue than the color in direct light.

Objects can be discovered using texture, hue, and motion information. Many objects tend to have the same texture and/or color. So the borders of textures or colors often are the borders of objects. Motion against a constant background can indicate the outline of objects.

Shading and highlighting

Shading can give clues as to the contours of an object. If we know from other analysis that an object is constant color, then perceived differences in color will be due to changes in the contour of the object. Changes in angles of reflectance from the light source result in various degrees of shading. Direct line of sight reflection causes specular highlights, which are bright and may reflect the color of the light source back to the observer. Varying degrees of partial reflection give varying degrees of light intensity and hence perceived color. The completely shaded regions will be dark. Using this information and the rates of change over the object, the contours of the object can be analyzed. A sharp change in light intensity usually means an edge of the object; a gradual change would denote a curved object.

Vision on the highway

Visual systems have become sophisticated enough to take on tasks like recognizing lanes on a highway scene and the location and distance of other vehicles. With systems like this and robotic controls to guide the vehicle, unmanned cars on the highway are a reality!

15.10   Is Artificial Intelligence Possible?

Hopefully, this chapter has given you a sense of what AI researchers have done. It is a long way from full intelligence. Will AI ever fully succeed in its end goals? Some researchers think so and some do not. The arguments for point to the progress that has been made and feel that scaling up to larger problems is just a matter of time and addition of more information into AI systems. The arguments against point to the failures of AI and indicate that no major changes have taken place to get around the big problems of world knowledge and combinatorial explosions of data.

In addition to these arguments, there is the philosophical outlook. One philosophical argument in favor of AI follows a functionalist view of the mind. This view holds that it's the functions of the mind that matter, not the means in which they are realized. Given this viewpoint, it doesn't matter whether intelligence comes from neuronal activity in a brain or electrical activity in a computer. This is a viewpoint that computer scientists can relate to because of the idea that programs can run on many different computer platforms. A program may compile into different instructions on different machines (see Chapter 13), but the running program behaves the same.

Philosophical views

A philosophical argument against AI claims that a computer is just a simulation of intelligence, but there is no real intelligence there. The only thing that is really happening in an AI program is that symbols are being manipulated, and there is no grounding of those symbols to reality. This grounding issue is a sticky one, since some argue that it is the relationships that symbols have with one another that define grounding, whereas others argue that no matter how many relationships are specified, the emotional content is lost in a symbol manipulation system. In other words, a computer cannot feel or experience emotions, and this is necessary for true intelligence.

Is a simulation of intelligence good enough or is it lacking? Music from a CD player can be viewed as a simulation of the original sounds. The CD does not have a physical representation of sound waves like a record or cassette tape does via grooves or a magnetized tape. It is just a collection of *samples*—numbers that represent the sound amplitude at specific instances in time. Given enough of these samples of the sound, a reasonable equivalent of the original sound is produced. For most of us, a CD is perfectly adequate. For some audiophiles it isn't. If the sample rate is dropped, the sound does diminish to a point where most would feel it is not adequate, and if the sample rate increases, even the audiophiles are happy. Is intelligence the same—just a matter of degree of the quality of the simulation of mental activity?

Simulation versus the real thing

The philosopher John Searle created the following thought experiment, known as the Chinese room. Imagine being in a sealed room and given a Chinese text. Also imagine that you do not read Chinese,[10] so to you the Chinese text is completely meaningless. Later you are given more Chinese text and some English instructions that explain how to relate the two Chinese texts to one another without translating the texts into English. Later you get another Chinese text and more English instructions explaining how to formulate responses in Chinese based on the three texts you have received. You follow the instructions and write down some Chinese characters and pass them to the people outside the room.

Searle's Chinese room experiment

The three Chinese texts represent a script (a la SAM), a story that is pieces of a script with real objects instead of variables (e.g., "Marcy went to Rivoli," "Marcy

---

[10.] If you do read Chinese, pick an alphabet you don't read to make this experiment more meaningful.

ate Ahi tuna," ...), and questions (e.g., "What did Marcy order?"). The English instructions represent the rules the program SAM uses. Searle's argument is that to an outside observer the person in the room appears to understand Chinese, since she can respond to questions in Chinese with responses in Chinese. To the person inside, the Chinese is just meaningless squiggles and she is merely following the English instructions, which only explain which symbols to write given the symbols that are shown. Or to summarize Searle's point—symbol manipulation is not understanding.

Many people have argued against Searle, giving reasons such as it is the system composed of the person and the room along with the texts that understands. Another argument says if the English program given to the person in the room were a true simulation of the actions that take place in a human brain that understands Chinese, then the person would understand Chinese just as a Chinese speaker would. Yet another argument says that if, instead of a person in the room, there were a robot or a program that actually learned the rules of how the symbols are to be manipulated, then it would have the same knowledge as a Chinese reader because it had internalized the knowledge to produce Chinese output. Others have argued that Searle is missing the whole point and has confused different conceptual levels. You must decide for yourself who is correct.

Neuron replacement thought experiment

Another thought experiment is to imagine that an electronic device exists that can carry on the same activity as a single neuron in the brain. We replace a single neuron in someone's brain with this device. Does this affect the person's intelligence? Now replace some more neurons with additional copies of this device. At some point does the person start loosing intelligence or the grounding of concepts or the emotional quality of thoughts?

Obviously the neuron replacement test cannot be done. Would you volunteer? Even if it could, how could we know if we were observing a simulation of intelligence where after a while, the person would slowly loose her sense of self. Another test is needed to measure intelligence. The classic test is the Turing test named after Alan Turing, one of the pioneers of computer science.

Turing test

The Turing test works as follows. Two computer terminals are used. One is connected to a computer running the AI program being tested and the other is connected to a person. Another person (the experimenter) types in text to either of the terminals and gets responses from the computer or person. The computer program tries to convince the experimenter that it is the human. The premise of the Turing test is that if the experimenter cannot tell which terminal is connected to the computer and which to the person, then that computer program has passed the Turing test and exhibits intelligence. To date, no program has passed the Turing test.

Eliza and Parry

One program, Eliza or Doctor, has fooled some people briefly. It simulates a psychologist using the Rogerian method of analysis, which involves rephrasing the patient's comments into questions to force introspection. Another program called Parry has been more successful. It emulates a paranoid schizophrenic patient and it has fooled some psychiatrists who could not discern Parry from a real paranoid schizophrenic. While it has fooled people, Parry does not truly pass the Turing test, because paranoid schizophrenia is a somewhat limited type of behavior. Parry and Eliza were once connected to one another over the Internet. The resulting conversation is quite hilarious. Parry was much more convincing than Eliza.

15.11 Summary

- Artificial intelligence is a collection of subfields that share a common interest in trying to build systems that model some aspect of natural intelligence.
- The early work in AI consisted of small, fairly well-defined problems. Its success gave false hopes of solving bigger problems, but the solutions to these "toy" problems did not scale up to realworld problems.
- Searching is important in many fields within AI. There are numerous search algorithms including uninformed methods (breadth-first and depth-first search), algorithms that look at the cost incurred so far (uniform-cost search), algorithms that look at the cost to reach the goal (hill-climbing, best-first search) and A* search, which looks at the cost already incurred and the expected cost to the goal.
- Knowledge representation is another fundamental issue in AI. The knowledge in an AI system is often maintained in data structures. These must be constructed in a fashion that facilitates the types of queries and reasoning that AI systems make. Semantic networks, frames, and first-order predicate calculus are commonly used representations for knowledge.
- AI systems often must reason with the information they have to formulate an answer to a question. Inductive, deductive, and abductive reasoning methods can be used.
- The difficulty that many AI programs have in scaling up to solve larger problems is handling world or commonsense knowledge. To reason properly in the world, a program must know about the world. The problem is that there is a lot to know and the information is highly interconnected and often context-specific. CYC is a project to collect all world knowledge in one huge database and provide a means to query and reason within the database.
- Problem solvers are programs that have knowledge about items in the world and their effect on other items, and can indicate how to use these items to reach certain goals. Programs that can solve any problem have been unsuccessful in large part due to the world-knowledge problem. Some problem solving techniques are used in AI, in particular planning is used in robotic and natural language processing systems.
- Expert systems embody the knowledge of an expert in a given field to carry out specific tasks. Expert systems are typically built on a model in which the expertise is encoded in if-then rules that are examined to determine which are applicable. One rule is chosen and its actions are performed. This process continues until a solution has been found or no rules are applicable.
- Natural language processing attempts to understand human spoken languages so they may be translated, paraphrased, or used as a frontend to

systems as a more natural interface. Early efforts in machine translation did syntactical transformations and dictionary translation of words. They did not scale up however, because to do complete translation, semantics (the meaning of words) is necessary. Later NLP systems attempted simpler parts of language understanding such as making inferences or handling limited domains of discourse.

- Robotics involves the control of mechanical objects that interact with the world. It requires recognition of the world and the robot's position, planning to carry out a sequence of steps that will attain the desired goal, and acting out the necessary steps.

- Vision entails recognizing objects given a two-dimensional representation of them (e.g., a photograph or video information). Vision systems begin with very low-level analysis of the image (line and edge detection) and reason about which edges make up parts or boundaries of shapes. Shapes can appear quite different depending on their orientation, lighting, and occlusion by other objects. This complicates the task of computer vision.

15.12   Additional Reading

Norvig, P. (1992). *Paradigms of Artificial Intelligence Programming: Case Studies in Common LISP*, Morgan Kaufmann, San Mateo, CA.

Rich, E. and Knight, K. (1991). *Artificial Intelligence*, Second edition, McGraw-Hill, New York, NY.

Russell, S.J. and Norvig, P. (1995). *Artificial Intelligence: A Modern Approach*, Prentice Hall, Englewood Cliffs, NJ.

Winston, P.H. (1992). *Artificial Intelligence*, Third edition, Addison-Wesley, Reading, MA.

AI references and historical coverage

Barr, A. and Feigenbaum, E.A., editors (1981). *The Handbook of Artificial Intelligence*, Volume 1, William Kaufman Inc., Los Altos, CA.

Barr, A. and Feigenbaum, E.A., editors (1982). *The Handbook of Artificial Intelligence*, Volume 2, William Kaufman Inc., Los Altos, CA.

Barr, A., Cohen, P.R., and Feigenbaum, E.A., editors (1989). *The Handbook of Artificial Intelligence*, Volume 4, Addison-Wesley, Reading, MA.

Cohen, P.R. and Feigenbaum, E.A., editors (1982). *The Handbook of Artificial Intelligence*, Volume 3, William Kaufman Inc., Los Altos, CA.

Shapiro, S.C., editor (1992). *Encyclopedia of Artificial Intelligence*, Second edition, Volumes 1 and 2, John Wiley & Sons, New York, NY.

Books specific to AI subfields

Gazdar, G. and Mellish, C.S. (1989). *Natural Language Processing in LISP: An Introduction to Computational Linguistics*, Addison-Wesley, Reading, MA.

Horn, B.K.P. (1986). *Robot vision*, MIT Press, Cambridge, MA.

Marr, D. (1982). *Vision: A Computational Investigation into the Human Representation and Processing of Visual Information*, W.H. Freeman, San Francisco, CA.

Murray, R.M., Li, Z., and Sastry, S.S. (1994). *A Mathematical Introduction to Robotic Manipulation*, CRC Press, Boca Raton.

Parsaye, K. and Chignell, M. (1988). *Expert Systems for Experts*, John Wiley & Sons, New York, NY.

Schank, R.C. and Riesbeck, C.K. (1981). *Inside Computer Understanding: Five Programs Plus Miniatures*, Lawrence Erlbaum Associates, Hillsdale, NJ.

Waterman, D.A. (1986). *A Guide to Expert Systems*, Addison-Wesley, Reading, MA.

Philosophical issues

Dreyfus, H.L. (1992). *What Computers Still Can't Do: A Critique of Artificial Reason*, MIT Press, Cambridge, MA.

Hofstadter, D.R. and Dennett, D.C. (1981). *The Mind's I*, Basic Books, New York, NY.

Minsky, M.L. (1986). *The Society of Mind*, Simon and Schuster, New York, NY.

Penrose, R. (1989). *The Emperor's New Mind: Concerning Computers, Minds, and the Laws of Physics*, Oxford University Press, New York, NY.

Searle, J.R. (1984). *Minds, Brains, and Science*, Harvard University Press, Cambridge, MA.

15.13   Code Listing

Code for searching:

```
; Parameters: goal-func, a function returning true if a goal has
; been met; choices, a list of paths to search; cost-func, a cost
; function to order new states; and next-states, a function that
; generates new states from a current path.
; Return the first path encountered that satisfies goal-func.
; The list of path choices is printed each time through the code.
(define (best-first-search goal-func choices cost-func next-states)
  (display choices)
  (newline)
  (cond ((null? choices) #f)      ; no more choices
        ((goal-func (first choices)) (first choices))
        (else
          (best-first-search goal-func
            (add-paths
              (rest choices)
              (make-paths (next-states (first choices))
                (first choices))
              cost-func)
            cost-func
            next-states))) )

; Return a new sorted list with element inserted into sorted-list
; based on compare-func.
(define (insert element sorted-list compare-func)
  (cond ((null? sorted-list)
          (list element))
        ((compare-func element (first sorted-list))
          (cons element sorted-list))
        (else
          (cons (first sorted-list)
            (insert element (rest sorted-list) compare-func)))) )

; Add paths in new-choices to old paths, old-choices, in sorted
; order based on cost-func.
(define (add-paths old-choices new-choices cost-func)
  (if (null? new-choices)
      old-choices
      (insert (first new-choices)
              (add-paths old-choices (rest new-choices) cost-func)
              cost-func)) )

; Given a list of new states, remove the empty lists and convert
; the states into complete paths.
(define (make-paths new-states current-path)
  (map (lambda (state) (append current-path (list state)))
    (remove '() new-states)) )
```

Depth-first and breadth-first search using best-first search:

```scheme
; Depth-first search implemented using best-first search.
(define (depth-first-alt goal-func tree)
  (best-first-search goal-func (list (list (root tree)))
    (lambda (path1 path2) #t)
    (lambda (path)
      (list (left-child (find path tree))
            (right-child (find path tree)))))) )

; Breadth-first search implemented using best-first search.
(define (breadth-first-alt goal-func tree)
  (best-first-search goal-func (list (list (root tree)))
    (lambda (path1 path2) #f)
    (lambda (path)
      (list (right-child (find path tree))
            (left-child (find path tree)))))) )

; Return the subtree in tree based on path.
(define (find path tree)
  (cond ((null? tree) #f)     ; problem
        ((and (null? (cdr path))
              (equal? (root tree) (car path))) tree)
        ((null? (cdr path)) #f)      ; problem
        ((equal? (left-child tree) (second path))
          (find (cdr path) (left-side tree)))
        ((equal? (right-child tree) (second path))
          (find (cdr path) (right-side tree)))
        (else #f)) )      ; problem

; Selector functions for parts of trees.
(define root first)
(define left-side second)
(define right-side third)
(define (left-child tree)
  (if (null? (second tree)) '() (caadr tree)))
(define (right-child tree)
  (if (null? (third tree)) '() (caaddr tree)))
```

A* search through trees using best-first search:

```scheme
; A* search of tree implemented using best-first search.
; g is a function that returns the cost incurred so far and
; h is a function returning the expected cost to reach the goal.
(define (a*-tree-search goal-func tree g h)
  (best-first-search goal-func (list (list (root tree)))
    (lambda (path1 path2)
      (<= (+ (g path1) (h path1)) (+ (g path2) (h path2))))
    (lambda (path)
      (list (left-child (find path tree))
            (right-child (find path tree)))))) )
```

Generic A* search:

```
; General a* search implemented using best-first search.
; start-path is the path to the start state.
; successors is a function that returns the next states.
; g is a function that returns the cost incurred so far and
; h is a function returning the expected cost to reach the goal.
(define (a*search goal-func start-path successors g h)
  (best-first-search goal-func (list start-path)
    (lambda (path1 path2)
      (<= (+ (g path1) (h path1)) (+ (g path2) (h path2))))
    successors) )
```

Expert system shell code:

```
; Given rule-list, a list of rules, redundant?, a function to test
; if a rule is redundant (i.e., its actions have already occurred),
; conflict-func, to handle conflict resolution, and finished, to
; test for termination, iteratively choose an applicable rule and
; apply it until finished is true.
(define (expert-shell rule-list redundant? conflict-func finished)
  (let* ( (satisfied-rules (keep-if satisfied? rule-list))
          (valid-rules (remove-if redundant? satisfied-rules))
          (rule-to-apply (conflict-func valid-rules)) )
    (apply-rule rule-to-apply)
    (if (finished database)
        'finished
        (expert-shell rule-list redundant? conflict-func
          finished))) )

; Test if condition of rule is true.
(define (satisfied? rule)
  (eval (condition rule)) )

; Apply all the actions of rule.
(define (apply-rule rule)
  (for-each eval (actions rule)) )

; Selector function to return condition of rule.
(define (condition rule)
  (first rule) )

; Selector function to return actions of rule.
(define (actions rule)
  (rest rule) )
```

CHAPTER 16

SOFT COMPUTING: FUZZY LOGIC, NEURAL NETWORKS, AND GENETIC ALGORITHMS

16.1 Soft Computing

Soft computing is a relatively new field within computer science. It is a conglomeration of fuzzy logic, neural networks, and probabilistic reasoning. Probabilistic reasoning is further divided into belief networks, genetic algorithms, and chaos theory. What all of these subfields share is an adherence to nonexact computation. Up until now, we have been using formal Boolean logic, which says that something is either true or false, yes or no, black or white. There are no shades of gray with this type of logic.

Soft computing supports degrees of precision, certainty, belief, and truth. Instead of using Boolean logic with two truth values, *multivalued logic* is used in which something can have more than a true or false value. The difficulty lies in how multivalued items can be combined logically. For example, suppose we represent information dealing with a washing machine. We want to be able to ask questions like the following:

Multivalued logic

- In a washing machine, how long should the clothes be rinsed if they are still fairly soapy and the rinse water is very hot?
- How much additional soap or agitation time during the wash cycle should be used if the clothes are moderately dirty and the water is slightly soapy?

To make statements like these, we need a way of logically expressing and combining descriptions like "long," "fairly soapy," "very hot," and "moderately dirty." Each subfield in soft computing has a way of handling this.

This chapter will not address all the subfields that compose soft computing, but instead focus on those that have been most influential recently. Of these, fuzzy logic has had perhaps the biggest success due to its growing role in our day-to-day life.

16.2   Fuzzy Logic

Fuzzy logic provides a formal way to represent multivalued logical values—values that aren't just 0 or 1, but represent degrees of belief, fit, or agreement. Fuzzy logic provides a way to express notions like *very high*, *fast*, and *comfortable*. These are not *crisp* values, but fuzzy values. The notion *tall* cannot be simply represented as true for anyone 6′ 2″ (or 1.88 meters) tall and false for those who are shorter. There is a spectrum of values and they have different degrees of satisfying the notion *tall*. To represent such notions, fuzzy sets are used.

Fuzzy sets and membership grades

For example, if we want to represent a fuzzy set like *tall* we could do so with a table, as shown below. Each height has a corresponding *membership grade* or degree of fit in the fuzzy set. The larger the membership grade, the better the height describes or fits the notion of tall. A membership grade of 0 means definitely not tall and a membership grade of 1 means definitely tall.

actual height	membership grade
5′ 3″ or less	0
5′ 6″	0.25
5′ 9″	0.5
6′	0.75
6′ 3″ or more	1

Fuzzy set functions

Fuzzy sets can be represented as functions that represent thresholds (as above), triangles, or trapezoids. These are called L (decreasing threshold), Γ (increasing threshold), Λ, and Π functions due to the similarity the name of the function has with the actual shape of the function.

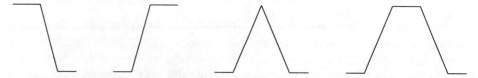

For example, *tall* could be expressed as an increasing threshold (Γ) function as follows (*h* represents the actual height value):

actual height	membership grade
$h < 5′ 3″$	0
$5′ 3″ <= h <= 6′ 3″$	$(h − 5′ 3″) / 12″$
$h > 6′ 3″$	1

Fuzzy sets are clearly subjective. A tall person might have a very different fuzzy set for *tall* than a short person would. However, a fuzzy set like the above fuzzy set would be more agreeable to most people than a crisp set would. A crisp set would have a single cut off point with everyone shorter than that considered as definitely not tall, and everyone above that considered definitely tall.

Linguistic variables are variables that take on fuzzy sets as values instead of numerical or logical values. *Height* can be a linguistic variable that can take values such as *short, tall, medium, huge,* etc.

Linguistic variables

A *hedge* is a modifier that can be applied to a fuzzy set. *Very* is a hedge that can modify a fuzzy set like *tall* to produce a new fuzzy set, *very tall. Somewhat, rarely,* and *more or less* are other examples of hedges. A hedge reduces or increases the membership grades of a fuzzy set. For example, the hedge *very* reduces the membership grades of a fuzzy set by squaring them. Look at the difference between the fuzzy set *tall* and the fuzzy set *very tall*:

Hedges

actual height	*tall* **membership grade**	*very tall* **membership grade**
5′ 3″ or less	0	0
5′ 6″	0.25	0.0625
5′ 9″	0.5	0.25
6′	0.75	0.5625
6′ 3″ or more	1	1

16.2.1 Fuzzy expert systems

Most often fuzzy sets are used in conjunction with rule-based systems forming fuzzy expert systems. With fuzzy expert systems, one can express statements like

if the temperature is *very high*, then set the fan speed to *fast*
if the temperature is *fine*, then turn the fan *off*

In addition, fuzzy expert systems provide a means of combining conditions such that rules like the following can be expressed:

if the temperature is *fine* and the humidity is *high*, then set the fan speed to *medium*
if the temperature is *very high* or the humidity is *high*, then set the fan speed to *fast*

These rules can be acted upon as well. Here is an overview of a fuzzy expert system that controls the speed of a fan. Imagine we have fuzzy sets to represent the following linguistic variables: temperature, humidity, fan speed. These fuzzy sets represent temperatures like *cool* and *hot*, humidities such as *high* and *very low*, and speeds: *medium* and *fast*. Sensors will measure crisp input values (temperature and humidity). These are fuzzified—for each applicable fuzzy set, the membership grade is calculated. Next the rules are evaluated based on the fuzzy values. All the rules with fuzzy sets with membership grades greater than 0 are applicable. If there are multiple conditions in a rule, these are combined to get an overall rule strength. All the applicable rules are combined to produce a final fuzzy set that represents each applicable rule's effect on the action. Lastly, this new fuzzy set is *defuzzified* to produce a crisp output value—a fan speed like 325 revolutions per minute.

Fuzzy fan controller

To summarize, the steps are

- Fuzzify crisp inputs
- Find applicable rules
- Combine rules according to membership grades to produce output fuzzy set
- Defuzzify output fuzzy set to get crisp value

Fuzzify inputs

Now let's look at a fuzzy system in more detail. The inputs to the system are usually crisp values. In our example we'll have a temperature and humidity percentage. We compare these inputs with our fuzzy sets. For example, look at the following five fuzzy sets:

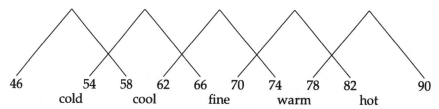

46   54   58   62   66   70   74   78   82   90
cold   cool   fine   warm   hot

Given an input temperature of 71 degrees, we compare this value with our fuzzy sets and we see that it is within the *fine* and *warm* fuzzy sets. Computing the membership grades for these two fuzzy sets, we find that 71 degrees has a degree of membership of 0.5 in *fine* and 0.167 in *warm*. For all other temperature fuzzy sets, the membership degree is 0.

Let's assume that there are three humidity fuzzy sets (*low*, *medium*, and *high*), and that the humidity is 65%, which has a 0.8 degree of membership in *medium* and 0.3 in *high*.

Rule inferencing

All the rule premises are examined one at a time. For example, suppose we have the following four fuzzy rules:

if the temperature is *cool*, then set the fan speed to *slow*
if the temperature is *warm*, then set the fan speed to *fast*
if the temperature is *fine* and the humidity is *high*, then set the fan speed to *medium*
if the temperature is *warm* or the humidity is *medium*, then set the fan speed to *medium*

The first rule is not satisfied because *cool* has a membership degree of 0. The second rule applies, but the action (set the fan speed to *fast*) is weighted according to the membership degree of *warm*, 0.167. The third rule has two conditions joined with an and. We use the minimum membership degree in this case. Seventy-one degrees has membership grade of 0.5 in *fine* and 75% humidity is *high* with membership grade of 0.3. We use the minimum value 0.3 to weigh the action (set the fan speed to *medium*). Lastly, the fourth rule has two conditions joined with or, so the maximum of the membership grades is used. The temperature's membership grade in *warm* is 0.167 and the humidity in *medium* is 0.8. Thus the strength of this action (set the fan speed to *medium*) is 0.8.

Each rule's actions take effect according to the degree of membership of the premise. The second rule specifies setting the fan speed to *fast* by 16.7%. The third rule sets the speed to *medium* by 30% and the fourth rule also sets the fan speed to *medium*, but by 80%. This percentage adjustment is performed by either multiplying the fuzzy sets by the percentage or by using the percentage as a cut-off on the fuzzy set. Here are the three fuzzy sets for the fan speed. The speeds are in revolutions per minute (RPM).

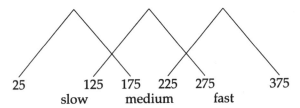

When the fuzzy sets are weighted, we get three new fuzzy sets that look like this:

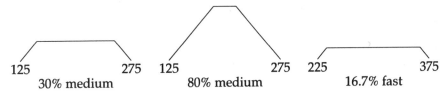

Combining fuzzy sets

The final step in the evaluation of fuzzy rules is to combine the fuzzy sets produced by each rule into one fuzzy set. This is done by either summing all the fuzzy sets, or choosing the maximum value among each fuzzy set for each possible input, and constructing a new fuzzy set from that. We'll use the maximum method to get the following fuzzy set:

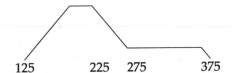

Defuzzifying output

Most fuzzy systems need to produce a crisp value. In this case we want an amount for the fan speed. There are a number of schemes to do this. The most common technique is to find the *center of mass* or *center of gravity* of the fuzzy set and return the crisp value that corresponds to it. Another technique to defuzzify a fuzzy set is to choose the weighted average of the output values that yield the largest degree of membership values. This technique is called *average of maximums*. It is computationally simpler than the *center of mass* method, so we will use it. In the example above the fan speed with the largest membership grade for the *medium* fuzzy set is 200 RPM and 300 RPM for the *fast* fuzzy set. The weighted average is

$$\frac{\sum_1^n maxValue_i \times strength_i}{\sum_1^n strength_i}$$

In this example, it is

$$\frac{200 \times 0.8 + 300 \times 0.167}{0.8 + 0.167}$$

The result is 217.233 RPM.

Possibility versus probability

Notice that the sum of the three membership grades (80%, 30%, and 16.67%) is greater than 100%. This would not be allowed in a *probability* system. With probability, the *rule of extended middle* says that the individual outcome probabilities of an event must not add up to greater than 1.0 or 100%. They must be exclusive of one another. Fuzzy logic systems do not have this restriction; they can and do overlap. Grade of membership should not be looked at as being the probability that a linguistic variable (e.g., *fan speed*) equals a certain crisp value (e.g., 200 RPM), but rather the possibility or degree of fit that the linguistic variable can take on that crisp value. In other words, it does not make sense to say that the probability that 57 degrees is *cool* is 70% and the probability that 57 degrees is *cold* is 40%, because the probabilities of the possible outcome states must not exceed 100%. However, it is acceptable to say that 57 degrees feels 70% *cool*, and at the same time it feels 40% *cold*. This is what is meant by a possibility value in fuzzy logic.

16.2.2   History of fuzzy logic

Fuzzy logic got its beginnings in the 1920s through the work of Jan Lukasiewicz in multivalued logic. In 1965, Lotfi Zadeh published a paper that laid the groundwork for fuzzy logic. Zadeh defined a working mathematics for fuzzy sets that provided a formalism upon which fuzzy systems could be built. Ten years later the first application of fuzzy systems, a fuzzy controller for a steam engine, was developed. The first major industrial application of fuzzy systems was established in 1982. This is a fuzzy expert system that controls the mixing and grinding of cement for a cement kiln. The most celebrated fuzzy system is a fuzzy controlled subway system that outperforms humans. It went into production in 1986 in Japan and has improved rider comfort and decreased ride times and running costs.

Applications of fuzzy logic

The number of fuzzy systems has grown dramatically in recent years. In 1986, there were eight commercial and industrial applications of fuzzy systems. That has more than doubled each year to reach 300 applications by 1991 and 1500 applications in 1993. Fuzzy systems are used mainly in control systems ranging from cars to commercial/industrial uses to household applications. In cars, fuzzy systems were first used for cruise controls in 1991. Now they are used in transmissions, brakes, and engines. Fuzzy controlled helicopters have been built that respond to voice commands to hover, turn, go up, and land. Video cameras use fuzzy logic for auto-focus, exposure settings, and anti-jitter stabilization. Fuzzy washing machines adjust the wash cycle using about ten rules. Fuzzy vacuum cleaners measure dust flow for energy savings. There are fuzzy microwave ovens, refrigerators, and even rice cookers. Fuzzy systems have been used to evaluate credit applications for lenders, estimate performance on the stock market, and design plans for patients in hospitals.

To speed up fuzzy applications, custom microprocessors, or *chips*, have been built that process fuzzy rules (make fuzzy inferences). The first such fuzzy microprocessor built in 1985 could process 80,000 rules per second, or 0.08 million rules per second. Fuzzy chips are measured in terms of *FLIP*s, fuzzy logic inferences per second. In 1993, chips capable of 2 million FLIPs had been built. That corresponds to a performance increase of 25 times in speed in just eight years, or more than a doubling of performance every two years.

Fuzzy microprocessors

16.2.3   A fuzzy expert system in Scheme

To build a complete fuzzy expert system, we need to represent fuzzy sets or membership functions, linguistic variables, hedges, and fuzzy rules. We must provide some type of inference engine that evaluates rules and determines fuzzy outcomes. Lastly, if we want to input or output crisp numbers, we'll need a way to fuzzify inputs and defuzzify outputs.

We've seen two different representations of membership functions, as lists of pairs or as functions. Membership functions are typically represented as functions modeling triangular or trapezoidal shapes (Λ and Π functions). This system will represent membership functions as functions that correspond to triangles. The input to such a function should be simple. We can represent a triangle as three numbers corresponding to the position on the x-axis where the triangle hits 0 and 1 membership degree values (in other words the left, middle, and right parts of the triangle). For example, to represent a triangle that is 0 below 40, reaches 1 at 60, and then returns to 0 at 80, we could use the three numbers 40, 60, and 80.

Representing fuzzy sets

The function that creates a triangular fuzzy set should return a function that we can plug crisp numbers into and get membership grade values back. For inputs below the left or above the right values, the function should return 0. For values between left and right, the function should return a value corresponding to the input's height along the triangle.

In addition to computing membership grades, we will need to return the maximum value of a fuzzy set (the value that has a membership grade of 1). We'll need this when we defuzzify the final actions of the rules. We can use the ideas of message passing to do this. If we call the fuzzy set with the message `max`, it will return the middle value of the triangle.

Returning maximum of fuzzy sets

```scheme
; Create a function returning the membership grade of a crisp value.
(define (make-fuzzy-triangle left mid right)
  (lambda (crisp-num)
    (cond ((eq? crisp-num 'max) mid)
          ((or (< crisp-num left) (> crisp-num right)) 0)
          ((< crisp-num mid) (/ (- crisp-num left) (- mid left)))
          (else (/ (- right crisp-num) (- right mid)))) ) )
```

To fuzzify a crisp number, we simply have to invoke the function that the fuzzy set represents with that crisp number. This is easily implemented as follows:

```
; Fuzzify crisp-number based on fuzzy-set.
(define (fuzzify crisp-number fuzzy-set)
  (fuzzy-set crisp-number))
```

Here is an example creating a fuzzy set for the *fine* temperatures:

```
(define fine (make-fuzzy-triangle 62 68 74))
```

Calling this new function with a temperature yields its membership grade:

```
> (fuzzify 71 fine)
0.5

> (fuzzify 61 fine)
0

> (fuzzify 'max fine)
68
```

Working with fuzzy sets

All of the details of the method outlined before are somewhat difficult to model, as the functions we are using are not continuous functions. They compute different functions depending on the range of inputs given. This makes it difficult to compute minimum, maximum, sums, and products of fuzzy sets. Computing the center of mass to defuzzify is rather difficult, as it involves computing integrals. However, if we don't produce a representation of the final output fuzzy set and we defuzzify our output using the average of maximums method instead of the center of mass method, we can avoid these problem areas.

Representing rules

Fuzzy rules can be represented in two parts in lists. The first element represents the condition of the rule. Each condition is a pair—a list of the linguistic variable and its fuzzy set value. Multiple conditions can be combined using and and or. The rest of the rule list is the rule's actions. It is a list of pairs of linguistic variables and their fuzzy set values. Here are two rules and their representations. Note: symbols beginning with "?" represent linguistic variables that will be replaced by actual input values when the rules are inferenced.

if the temperature is *cool*, then set the fan speed to *slow*
if the temperature is *warm* or the humidity is *medium*, then set the fan speed to *medium*

```
((?temperature cool) (?fan-speed slow))
((or (?temperature warm) (?humidity medium)) (?fan-speed medium))
```

Representing the actual inputs into the rules

The rules have variables that must be replaced with the actual crisp input values. We can create a variable to input value mapping that can be represented as an association list. Here is an example mapping of the temperature 71 degrees and the humidity 75%:

```
((?temperature . 71) (?humidity . 75))
```

Evaluating rules

The next step is to sequence through the rules and get a list of all actions that apply, along with the corresponding degree to which they should be applied. Given a list of fuzzy rules, we want to find those with conditions that have been satisfied and the overall membership degree of the condition. We don't need the complete rules, only the actions and the membership degrees. Therefore, we'll return a list of sublists with these values. Each sublist consists of a membership degree followed by the rule's actions. In addition, let's create two selector functions to get the condition and actions of the rules:

```
; Return the condition of a rule.
(define (condition rule)
  (first rule))

; Return the actions of a rule.
(define (actions rule)
  (rest rule))

; Return list of applicable actions and the degree to which they
; should be applied.
(define (outputs rule-list input-values)
  (keep-if
    (lambda (evaled-rule)
      (not (zero? (car evaled-rule))))
    (map (lambda (rule)
           (cons
             (membership-grade (condition rule) input-values)
             (actions rule)))
         rule-list)) )
```

The function `membership-grade` takes a condition and the input values and returns the overall membership grade:

```
; Return overall membership grade of condition based on input-values.
(define (membership-grade condition input-values)
  (cond ((eq? (car condition) 'and)
         (apply min (map (lambda (clause)
                           (membership-grade clause input-values))
                         (rest condition))))
        ((eq? (car condition) 'or)
         (apply max (map (lambda (clause)
                           (membership-grade clause input-values))
                         (rest condition))))
        (else
         (fuzzify (cdr (assoc (first condition) input-values))
           (second condition)))) )
```

Let's test these functions. We'll create some fuzzy sets, rules, and inputs first: *Testing our code*

```
(define warm (make-fuzzy-triangle 70 76 82))
(define cool (make-fuzzy-triangle 54 60 66))
(define medium (make-fuzzy-triangle 69 74 79))
(define rule1 '((?temperature cool) (?fan-speed slow)))
(define rule2 '((or (?temperature warm) (?humidity medium))
                (?fan-speed medium)))
(define input '((?temperature . 71) (?humidity . 75)))

> (membership-grade (condition rule1) input)
Error: Wrong type to apply: cool
```

The function `cool` is passed to `fuzzify`. This seems to be okay. Let's try some more explicit calls:

```
> (fuzzify (cdr (assoc (first (condition rule1)) input))
           (second (condition rule1)))
Error: Wrong type to apply: cool

> (cdr (assoc (first (condition rule1)) input))
71

> (second (condition rule1))
cool

> (fuzzify 71 cool)
0
```

This probably seems strange unless you have figured out the bug. Calling `fuzzify` directly with the arguments 71 and `cool` works, but not when the arguments are evaluated based on `rule1`. The problem here is a subtle one. Here is a hint:

```
> (fuzzify 71 'cool)
Error: Wrong type to apply: cool
```

We managed to replicate the bug. The issue is the difference between a symbol and a function. Quoting `cool` returns the symbol `cool`, not the function. Without the quote, `cool` returns the function bound to the variable `cool`. Since `rule1` is a quoted list, none of its elements are evaluated, so the `cadar` of `rule1` is the symbol `cool`. There are two ways we can fix this. One is to define the rules using `quasiquoted` lists and evaluating the fuzzy sets like `cool`. A second way is to add an `eval` to the function `membership-grade`. We'll opt for that approach. Here is the new function `membership-grade`:

```
; Return overall membership grade of condition based on input-values.
(define (membership-grade condition input-values)
  (cond ((eq? (car condition) 'and)
         (apply min (map (lambda (clause)
                           (membership-grade clause input-values))
                         (rest condition))))
        ((eq? (car condition) 'or)
         (apply max (map (lambda (clause)
                           (membership-grade clause input-values))
                         (rest condition))))
        (else
         (fuzzify (cdr (assoc (first condition) input-values))
           (eval (second condition)))))) )

> (membership-grade (condition rule1) input)
0

> (membership-grade (condition rule2) input)
0.8
```

```
> (outputs (list rule1 rule2) input)
((0.8 (?fan-speed medium)))
```

The final step is to take the outputs and their strengths and create a crisp output value for each output variable. To simplify that operation, we should make two changes to our list of actions. One is to break apart multiple actions from the same rule into different lists. Rules with multiple actions will yield lists like these:

Combining fuzzy actions to produce crisp outputs

```
((0.8 (?distance close) (?fan-speed medium))
 (0.4 (?fan-speed medium) (?distance little-closer)))
```

These actions should be transformed into a simpler list, like this:

```
((0.8 ?distance close)
 (0.8 ?fan-speed medium)
 (0.4 ?fan-speed medium)
 (0.4 ?distance little-closer))
```

```
; Split multiple actions in action-list to list of single actions.
(define (transform action-list)
  (if (null? action-list)
      '()
      (append
        (map (lambda (action) (cons (caar action-list) action) )
          (cdar action-list))
        (transform (rest action-list)))) )
```

The second operation is to only keep the action with the largest strength when there are multiple actions with the same linguistic variable and fuzzy set. For example, given the above four actions

Eliminating unnecessary actions

```
((0.8 ?distance close)
 (0.8 ?fan-speed medium)
 (0.4 ?fan-speed medium)
 (0.4 ?distance little-closer))
```

we would like to get the actions

```
((0.8 ?distance close)
 (0.8 ?fan-speed medium)
 (0.4 ?distance little-closer))
```

This can be done by sequencing through the action list finding all actions that match the current first action. We should only compare the `rests` of the actions, ignoring the strengths. Given a list of matching actions, we form a new action using the largest strength in the list. Then we must recurse with a new action list with all the actions we just processed removed. This can be done simply using `set-difference`.

```scheme
; Reduce duplicate actions to one with the largest strength.
(define (no-duplicates action-list)
  (if (null? action-list)
      '()
      (let ((duplicates
              (keep-if (lambda (action)
                         (equal? (rest action) (cdar action-list)))
                       action-list)))
        (if (null? (rest duplicates))
            (cons (first action-list)
                  (no-duplicates (rest action-list)))
            (cons (cons (apply max (map first duplicates))
                        (cdar action-list))
                  (no-duplicates
                    (set-difference action-list duplicates))))))  )
```

Defuzzifying actions

Once we have the actions in this form, we can defuzzify them into crisp outputs. We'll use a method similar to that used in `no-duplicates` to get a list of actions with the same linguistic variable. Then we'll make a list of the variable name and its crisp value. This is done for each variable. To compute the crisp value we use the formula given previously—the sum of the products of the rule strengths and the maximum values of the fuzzy sets divided by the sum of the rule strengths. To get the maximum value of a fuzzy set, we call `fuzzify` with the message (symbol) `max`:

```scheme
; Defuzzify actions in action-list returning crisp values.
(define (defuzzify action-list)
  (if (null? action-list)
      '()
      (let ((same-var
              (keep-if (lambda (action)
                         (equal? (second action)
                                 (cadar action-list)))
                       action-list)))
        (cons
          (list
            (second (first same-var))
            (/ (apply + (map (lambda (action)
                               (* (first action)
                                  (fuzzify 'max
                                           (eval (third action)))))
                             same-var))
               (apply + (map first same-var))))
          (defuzzify (set-difference action-list same-var)))))  )
```

We can try a contrived example to verify that these functions work. We'll use the fuzzy sets cool and warm that we defined previously. Their maximum values are 60 and 76, respectively.

```
> (transform
  '((0.8 (?x cool))
    (0.3 (?y warm) (?x cool))
    (0.6 (?x warm) (?y warm))
    (0.4 (?y cool) (?x cool))))
((0.8 ?x cool) (0.3 ?y warm) (0.3 ?x cool) (0.6 ?x warm)
 (0.6 ?y warm) (0.4 ?y cool) (0.4 ?x cool))

> (no-duplicates
  '((0.8 ?x cool) (0.3 ?y warm) (0.3 ?x cool) (0.6 ?x warm)
    (0.6 ?y warm) (0.4 ?y cool) (0.4 ?x cool)))
((0.8 ?x cool) (0.6 ?y warm) (0.6 ?x warm) (0.4 ?y cool))

> (defuzzify
  '((0.8 ?x cool) (0.6 ?y warm) (0.6 ?x warm) (0.4 ?y cool)))
((?x 66.857) (?y 69.6))
```

Finally, let's put all the pieces together into one function that takes a list of fuzzy rules and an association list of input values and returns a list of crisp outputs:

```
; Evaluate rules using inputs to produce crisp results.
(define (fuzzy-eval rules inputs)
  (defuzzify
    (no-duplicates
      (transform
        (outputs rules inputs)))) )
```

An alternate inferencing technique comes from Takagi, Sugeno, and Kang. I will refer to this as the TSK method. Premises of rules with the TSK method are the same as was presented earlier, namely nonfuzzy inputs are compared to fuzzy sets. Crisp inputs are compared to fuzzy sets. In the case of multiple conditions in a rule, the membership degrees are multiplied together. This gives the rule strength. The outcomes of the rules do not produce fuzzy sets, but crisp values that are assigned to an output for each rule. This output is the sum of the products of the rule inputs and a collection of parameters. These parameters are adjusted as the rules are developed to produce a working set of rules.

TSK inferencing and rules

Below are some example rules in TSK:

if temperature is high and humidity is low, then $output_1 = p_0^1 + p_1^1 temperature + p_2^1 humidity$

if temperature is medium, then $output_2 = p_0^2 + p_1^2 temperature$

where $p_0^1 \cdots p_n^1$ are the parameters to the first rule.

16.2.4   Fuzzy cheesecake

Let's build a fuzzy logic system to bake a cheesecake.[1] Our system will have two

Sample problem: baking cheesecake

[1.] Mike Clancy provided the inspiration for this problem, along with many delicious cheesecakes.

inputs: the temperature of the oven and the cleanliness of a knife that we insert into the cheesecake. If the knife comes out coated with cheesecake, then it's not ready. If it's clean, then the cake is ready. There are two outputs: the temperature at which the oven should be set, and the time interval between our measurements of the oven's temperature and the knife's cleanliness. We are assuming that we don't use a constant temperature and rely on the oven's thermostat to maintain it, as you normally would do when baking a cheesecake.

Here are the rules to the system. Fuzzy sets are in italics.

Cheesecake rules

1) if the temperature is *cool*, turn the oven *up a lot* and wait a *long time*
2) if the temperature is *warm*, turn the oven *up a little* and wait a *while*
3) if the temperature is *very hot*, turn the oven *down* and wait a *short time*
4) if the temperature is *hot* and the knife is *coated*, keep the oven *the same* and wait a *while*
5) if the temperature is *hot* and the knife is *slightly coated*, keep the oven *the same* and wait a *short time*
6) if the knife is *clean*, turn the oven *down* and wait a *short time*

Here are the rules' Scheme equivalents:

```
(define rules '(
  ((?temperature cool) (?oven up-a-lot) (?wait long-time))
  ((?temperature warm) (?oven up-a-little) (?wait while))
  ((?temperature very-hot) (?oven down) (?wait short-time))
  ((and (?temperature hot) (?knife coated))
    (?oven the-same) (?wait while))
  ((and (?temperature hot) (?knife slightly-coated))
    (?oven the-same) (?wait short-time))
  ((?knife clean) (?oven down) (?wait short-time))))
```

Oven temperature fuzzy sets

We need four collections of fuzzy sets for the different linguistic variables. Here are four fuzzy sets for the temperature input. The numbers are in degrees Fahrenheit.

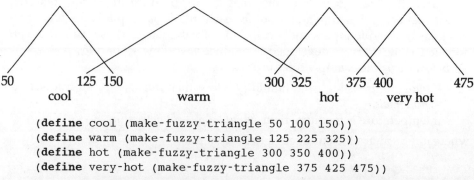

```
(define cool (make-fuzzy-triangle 50 100 150))
(define warm (make-fuzzy-triangle 125 225 325))
(define hot (make-fuzzy-triangle 300 350 400))
(define very-hot (make-fuzzy-triangle 375 425 475))
```

Knife cleanliness fuzzy sets

Here are three fuzzy sets for the knife input. The numbers are on a scale from 0 to 10 of cleanliness, where 0 is very clean and 10 is very coated.

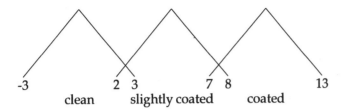

```
(define clean (make-fuzzy-triangle -3 0 3))
(define slightly-coated (make-fuzzy-triangle 2 5 8))
(define coated (make-fuzzy-triangle 7 10 13))
```

Here are four fuzzy sets for setting the oven temperature. The numbers indicate the amount in degrees Fahrenheit that the temperature should be changed.

Change in oven temperature fuzzy sets

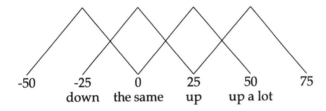

```
(define down (make-fuzzy-triangle -50 -25 0))
(define the-same (make-fuzzy-triangle -25 0 25))
(define up-a-little (make-fuzzy-triangle 0 25 50))
(define up-a-lot (make-fuzzy-triangle 25 50 75))
```

Here are three fuzzy sets for the time to wait between measurements. The numbers are in minutes.

Wait time fuzzy sets

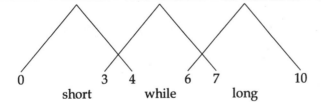

```
(define short-time (make-fuzzy-triangle 0 2 4))
(define while (make-fuzzy-triangle 3 5 7))
(define long-time (make-fuzzy-triangle 6 8 10))
```

To make our fuzzy system more meaningful, we'll build a simulator that simulates the baking of a cheesecake. It will keep track of time and oven temperature and model the energy that goes into the cheesecake. This energy will determine when the cheesecake is done and affect the cleanliness of the knife being stuck in the cheesecake. This won't be an exact system and we'll make many simplifications. Using a cooking temperature of 350 degrees and a time of 30 minutes and multiplying these together, we create an energy amount of 10,500. When the total energy exceeds 10,500 (350 × 30), the cheesecake is done and the

Oven simulator

knife cleanliness reaches zero. The simulator will add a temperature change at each minute to a running energy total. This temperature change is limited to ten degrees each minute.

The process of simulation works as follows:

- Evaluate the fuzzy rules with the current inputs (temperature and cleanliness).
- Adjust the oven temperature according to the *oven* output variable.
- Wait until the *wait* output variable time has elapsed.
- During that wait time, model the temperature changes and energy to the cheesecake.

```
; Model the baking of a cheesecake using fuzzy rules given initial
; temp and energy.  time counts the minutes.
(define (cheesecake rules temp energy time)
  (if (zero? (done energy))
      'eat
      (let* ((output
               (fuzzy-eval rules
                 `((?temperature . ,temp)
                   (?knife . ,(done energy)))))
             (oven (second (assoc '?oven output)))
             (wait (second (assoc '?wait output))))
        (display `(fuzzy output: oven ,oven wait ,wait))
        (newline)
        (let* ((result (bake oven (+ time (truncate wait)) temp
                          energy time))
               (new-temp (first result))
               (new-energy (second result)))
          (cheesecake rules new-temp new-energy
            (+ time (truncate wait))))))) )

; Model baking a cheesecake until time equals stop-time.  oven is
; the temperature change; temp and energy are the current
; temperature and energy levels.
(define (bake oven stop-time temp energy time)
  (if (>= time stop-time)
      (list temp energy)
      (let* ((temp-change
               (if (positive? oven) (min 10 oven) (max -10 oven)))
             (new-energy
               (+ energy (/ (+ temp temp temp-change) 2))))
        (display `(time ,time temp ,(+ temp temp-change)
                    energy ,new-energy knife ,(done new-energy)))
        (newline)
        (bake (- oven temp-change) stop-time (+ temp temp-change)
          new-energy (+ time 1)))) )
```

```
; Helper function for cheesecake.
(define (baking rules oven-temp)
  (cheesecake rules oven-temp 0 1))

; Compute the cleanliness of the knife as a number between 0 and 10.
(define (done energy)
  (- 10 (min 10 (truncate (/ energy 1050)))))
```

Let's run the cheesecake simulator with an initial oven temperature of 300   *Baking simulation*
degrees.

```
> (baking rules 300)
(fuzzy output: oven 25.0 wait 5.0)
(time 1 temp 310.0 energy 305.0 knife 10)
(time 2 temp 320.0 energy 620.0 knife 10)
(time 3 temp 325.0 energy 942.5 knife 10)
(time 4 temp 325.0 energy 1267.5 knife 9)
(time 5 temp 325.0 energy 1592.5 knife 9)
(fuzzy output: oven 0.0 wait 5.0)
(time 6 temp 325.0 energy 1917.5 knife 9)
(time 7 temp 325.0 energy 2242.5 knife 8)
(time 8 temp 325.0 energy 2567.5 knife 8)
(time 9 temp 325.0 energy 2892.5 knife 8)
(time 10 temp 325.0 energy 3217.5 knife 7)
(fuzzy output: oven 0.0 wait 2.0)
(time 11 temp 325.0 energy 3542.5 knife 7)
(time 12 temp 325.0 energy 3867.5 knife 7)
(fuzzy output: oven 0.0 wait 2.0)
(time 13 temp 325.0 energy 4192.5 knife 7)
(time 14 temp 325.0 energy 4517.5 knife 6)
(fuzzy output: oven 0.0 wait 2.0)
(time 15 temp 325.0 energy 4842.5 knife 6)
(time 16 temp 325.0 energy 5167.5 knife 6)
(fuzzy output: oven 0.0 wait 2.0)
(time 17 temp 325.0 energy 5492.5 knife 5)
(time 18 temp 325.0 energy 5817.5 knife 5)
(fuzzy output: oven 0.0 wait 2.0)
(time 19 temp 325.0 energy 6142.5 knife 5)
(time 20 temp 325.0 energy 6467.5 knife 4)
(fuzzy output: oven 0.0 wait 2.0)
(time 21 temp 325.0 energy 6792.5 knife 4)
(time 22 temp 325.0 energy 7117.5 knife 4)
(fuzzy output: oven 0.0 wait 2.0)
(time 23 temp 325.0 energy 7442.5 knife 3)
(time 24 temp 325.0 energy 7767.5 knife 3)
(fuzzy output: oven 0.0 wait 2.0)
(time 25 temp 325.0 energy 8092.5 knife 3)
(time 26 temp 325.0 energy 8417.5 knife 2)
(fuzzy output: oven -25.0 wait 2.0)
(time 27 temp 315.0 energy 8737.5 knife 2)
(time 28 temp 305.0 energy 9047.5 knife 2)
```

```
(fuzzy output: oven -6.25 wait 3.125)
(time 29 temp 298.75 energy 9349.375 knife 2)
(time 30 temp 298.75 energy 9648.125 knife 1)
(time 31 temp 298.75 energy 9946.875 knife 1)
(fuzzy output: oven -10.874 wait 2.848)
(time 32 temp 288.75 energy 10240.625 knife 1)
(time 33 temp 287.876 energy 10528.938 knife 0)
eat
```

*Evaluation of
simulation results*

Let's examine the rules that fired during the simulation. Rule #2 fired first which brought the oven up to 325 degrees, then rule #4 fired once and rule #5 fired eight times. The oven temperature remained constant here. Finally the knife became clean and rule #6 fired which lowered the temperature by 25 degrees. This made the oven warm so rule #2 fired next along with rule #6, and the last two examples showed an interaction between two rules with the system moving toward some balance of temperature reduction and wait time.

*New knife cleanliness
fuzzy sets*

There is very little interaction between the rules. Our problem is that the fuzzy sets are not overlapping enough to give interesting interactions. Instead we are invoking one rule at a time for the most part. Let's change the knife fuzzy sets so they have more overlap.

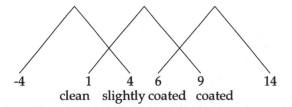

```
(define coated (make-fuzzy-triangle 6 10 14))
(define slightly-coated (make-fuzzy-triangle 1 5 9))
(define clean (make-fuzzy-triangle -4 0 4))
```

Second run

Running our simulator again produces the following output:

```
> (baking rules 300)
(fuzzy output: oven 25.0 wait 5.0)
(time 1 temp 310.0 energy 305.0 knife 10)
(time 2 temp 320.0 energy 620.0 knife 10)
(time 3 temp 325.0 energy 942.5 knife 10)
(time 4 temp 325.0 energy 1267.5 knife 9)
(time 5 temp 325.0 energy 1592.5 knife 9)
(fuzzy output: oven 0.0 wait 5.0)
(time 6 temp 325.0 energy 1917.5 knife 9)
(time 7 temp 325.0 energy 2242.5 knife 8)
(time 8 temp 325.0 energy 2567.5 knife 8)
(time 9 temp 325.0 energy 2892.5 knife 8)
(time 10 temp 325.0 energy 3217.5 knife 7)
(fuzzy output: oven 0.0 wait 3.0)
(time 11 temp 325.0 energy 3542.5 knife 7)
(time 12 temp 325.0 energy 3867.5 knife 7)
```

```
(time 13 temp 325.0 energy 4192.5 knife 7)
(fuzzy output: oven 0.0 wait 3.0)
(time 14 temp 325.0 energy 4517.5 knife 6)
(time 15 temp 325.0 energy 4842.5 knife 6)
(time 16 temp 325.0 energy 5167.5 knife 6)
(fuzzy output: oven 0.0 wait 2.0)
(time 17 temp 325.0 energy 5492.5 knife 5)
(time 18 temp 325.0 energy 5817.5 knife 5)
(fuzzy output: oven 0.0 wait 2.0)
(time 19 temp 325.0 energy 6142.5 knife 5)
(time 20 temp 325.0 energy 6467.5 knife 4)
(fuzzy output: oven 0.0 wait 2.0)
(time 21 temp 325.0 energy 6792.5 knife 4)
(time 22 temp 325.0 energy 7117.5 knife 4)
(fuzzy output: oven 0.0 wait 2.0)
(time 23 temp 325.0 energy 7442.5 knife 3)
(time 24 temp 325.0 energy 7767.5 knife 3)
(fuzzy output: oven -8.333 wait 2.0)
(time 25 temp 316.667 energy 8088.333 knife 3)
(time 26 temp 316.667 energy 8405.0 knife 2)
(fuzzy output: oven -12.5 wait 2.429)
(time 27 temp 306.667 energy 8716.667 knife 2)
(time 28 temp 304.167 energy 9022.083 knife 2)
(fuzzy output: oven -9.211 wait 2.882)
(time 29 temp 294.956 energy 9321.645 knife 2)
(time 30 temp 294.956 energy 9616.601 knife 1)
(fuzzy output: oven -10.699 wait 2.858)
(time 31 temp 284.956 energy 9906.557 knife 1)
(time 32 temp 284.257 energy 10191.163 knife 1)
(fuzzy output: oven -7.399 wait 3.056)
(time 33 temp 276.857 energy 10471.721 knife 1)
(time 34 temp 276.857 energy 10748.578 knife 0)
(time 35 temp 276.857 energy 11025.436 knife 0)
eat
```

Here we see much more interaction between the actions of the rules. The first two fuzzy outputs involve the same rules, but then we see interactions between rules #4 and #5 producing a wait time of three minutes. Then rule #5 alone fires until the knife becomes clean, which happens earlier in this simulation than it did in the last simulation. The last five outputs involve interaction between combinations of rules #2, #5, and #6, which result in nonlinear changes to the wait times and oven temperature changes.

Evaluation of second run

Now let's change the oven temperature fuzzy sets and see what happens. Here are new fuzzy sets for the oven temperature with more overlap between the sets.

New oven temperature fuzzy sets

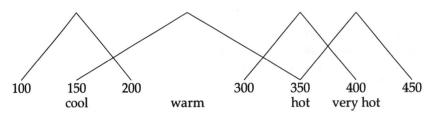

```
(define cool (make-fuzzy-triangle 100 150 200))
(define warm (make-fuzzy-triangle 150 250 350))
(define hot (make-fuzzy-triangle 300 350 400))
(define very-hot (make-fuzzy-triangle 350 400 450))
```

Third run

The results with these new fuzzy sets and the new knife cleanliness fuzzy sets are shown below:

```
> (baking rules 300)
(fuzzy output: oven 25.0 wait 5.0)
(time 1 temp 310.0 energy 305.0 knife 10)
(time 2 temp 320.0 energy 620.0 knife 10)
(time 3 temp 325.0 energy 942.5 knife 10)
(time 4 temp 325.0 energy 1267.5 knife 9)
(time 5 temp 325.0 energy 1592.5 knife 9)
(fuzzy output: oven 8.333 wait 5.0)
(time 6 temp 333.333 energy 1921.667 knife 9)
(time 7 temp 333.333 energy 2255.0 knife 8)
(time 8 temp 333.333 energy 2588.333 knife 8)
(time 9 temp 333.333 energy 2921.667 knife 8)
(time 10 temp 333.333 energy 3255.0 knife 7)
(fuzzy output: oven 6.25 wait 3.0)
(time 11 temp 339.583 energy 3591.458 knife 7)
(time 12 temp 339.583 energy 3931.042 knife 7)
(time 13 temp 339.583 energy 4270.625 knife 6)
(fuzzy output: oven 3.049 wait 2.366)
(time 14 temp 342.632 energy 4611.733 knife 6)
(time 15 temp 342.632 energy 4954.365 knife 6)
(fuzzy output: oven 2.236 wait 2.268)
(time 16 temp 344.868 energy 5298.115 knife 5)
(time 17 temp 344.868 energy 5642.983 knife 5)
(fuzzy output: oven 1.352 wait 2.162)
(time 18 temp 346.221 energy 5988.528 knife 5)
(time 19 temp 346.221 energy 6334.749 knife 4)
(fuzzy output: oven 1.199 wait 2.144)
(time 20 temp 347.420 energy 6681.569 knife 4)
(time 21 temp 347.420 energy 7028.989 knife 4)
(fuzzy output: oven 0.831 wait 2.100)
(time 22 temp 348.251 energy 7376.825 knife 3)
(time 23 temp 348.251 energy 7725.076 knife 3)
(fuzzy output: oven -7.574 wait 2.101)
(time 24 temp 340.678 energy 8069.541 knife 3)
```

```
(time 25 temp 340.678 energy 8410.218 knife 2)
(fuzzy output: oven -12.060 wait 2.471)
(time 26 temp 330.678 energy 8745.896 knife 2)
(time 27 temp 328.617 energy 9075.543 knife 2)
(fuzzy output: oven -7.423 wait 2.899)
(time 28 temp 321.195 energy 9400.449 knife 2)
(time 29 temp 321.195 energy 9721.644 knife 1)
(fuzzy output: oven -11.125 wait 2.832)
(time 30 temp 311.195 energy 10037.838 knife 1)
(time 31 temp 310.069 energy 10348.470 knife 1)
(fuzzy output: oven -7.628 wait 3.042)
(time 32 temp 302.441 energy 10654.725 knife 0)
(time 33 temp 302.441 energy 10957.166 knife 0)
(time 34 temp 302.441 energy 11259.607 knife 0)
eat
```

The first output involves rule #2 only. All others are combinations of rule #2 and other rules. The system increases the oven temperature gradually but less and less each time until the knife becomes clean. In the last five outputs the oven temperature changes oscillate between −7.423 and −12.060. This is a nice example of control in a fuzzy system producing a state of relative equilibrium.

Evaluation of third run

One interesting thing to note is that the cheesecake finished first in the last simulation. At 32 minutes the cheesecake energy exceeded 10,500. The first simulation finished after 33 minutes and the second took 34 minutes. The third simulation finished first because the oven temperature was increased steadily until the knife was clean. The second simulation took the longest because the definition of a clean knife (the fuzzy set) was changed, so the fuzzy system started reducing the oven temperature earlier than the first simulation did.

Comparison of three trials

16.2.5 Exercises

16.1 Modify the cheesecake scenario so that the system stops once the cheesecake is done (i.e., the energy exceeds 10,500) even though there is more wait time in the system. Thus, the three examples would stop at 33, 34, and 32 minutes, respectively. You could do this one of three ways: modify the fuzzy sets dealing with wait times; add new wait time and knife cleanliness fuzzy sets and rules that use them when the cheesecake is almost ready; or modify the driver functions to exit when the energy exceeds 10,500 regardless of the amount of wait time left. Rate the three approaches in implementation difficulty and build a new cheesecake model using one of them.

16.2 Write functions that represent trapezoid or threshold membership functions (those staying at degree of membership 1 after reaching a point).

16.3 What happens in our fuzzy logic system if no rules are applicable? Modify the code so that it returns the symbol no-rules-apply in that case.

16.4   Create fuzzy sets and rules to model some realworld objects. Once you have created these, write a controller that evaluates the fuzzy rules and provides some feedback to the modeled object.

16.5   Modify the fuzzy system to allow hedges to be used in the rules. A hedge is a word or descriptor like *very* or *more or less* that modifies a fuzzy set. Assume that *very* squares the membership grades and that *somewhat* and *more or less* perform a square root on the membership grades. Think of some other hedges and mathematical operations that can be applied to the fuzzy sets that make sense given the semantics of the hedge.

16.6   It is possible to take the negation of a fuzzy set, for example, *not tall*. This is implemented by subtracting the fuzzy set from one. For example, look at the membership grades for the fuzzy sets *tall* and *not tall*.

actual height	*tall* **membership grade**	*not tall* **membership grade**
5′ 3″ or less	0	1
5′ 6″	0.25	0.75
5′ 9″	0.5	0.5
6′	0.75	0.25
6′ 3″ or more	1	0

Modify the fuzzy rule system so that it accepts negations of fuzzy sets.

16.3   Neural Networks

Units and connection weights

Neural networks model the activity of neurons in brains. A neural network (or neural net) simulates a collection of neurons. These artificial neurons are called *units* or *nodes*. Units are highly interconnected with other units to various degrees of strength called *connection weights*. Neural networks take inputs and produce outputs acting like functions in Scheme. However, instead of having Scheme code that maps inputs to outputs, they compute the outputs by *propagating* information up through the network. The output is a function of the input and the weights inside the network. What makes neural networks interesting is the properties they share with brains: the ability to learn, generalize, categorize, and be robust in the face of changes to the network.

Neural nets are often called *artificial neural networks*, as they are artificial models of neurons. *Connectionist* models and *parallel distributed processing systems* are other names that have been used to describe neural networks. The differences are subtle for our level of understanding. In fact, many people tend to use the terms interchangeably.

Layers

Neural networks are typically organized in *layers*, where each layer consists of a group of units. Each unit in a layer is typically not connected to the units in that layer but is connected to all the units in the layers immediately above and below it. In some neural nets the units connect to units in additional layers as well. Look at the following diagram of a simple three-layer network.

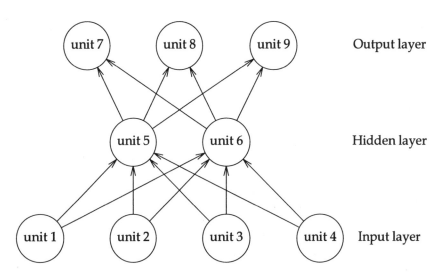

Neural networks are made up of three types of units. *Input units* take values from outside the neural net and pass those values up to other units. *Hidden units* take inputs from input units or other hidden units and pass values to other units. *Output units* take input from input units (in two-layer networks) or hidden units (in three- or more layer networks) and pass values as the output result of the network.

Types of units

The processing of information through a network is called *propagation*. Propagation begins with a collection of input values that are sent to the units of the first or input layer of the network. The other layers (hidden and output) are given new values in a different manner. All the inputs to each of these units are multiplied by connection weights and these products are summed together to make the *net input* to the unit. This is best understood with a diagram.

Propagation through networks

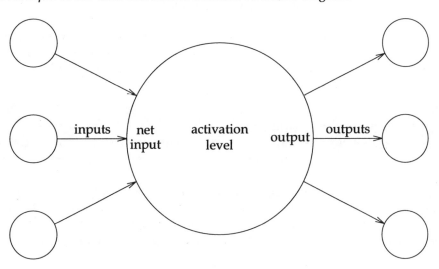

Activation level and sigmoidal function

The net input is converted to an activation level that will be used to produce the output value that the unit sends to the layer of units above it. This conversion typically involves a function that restricts the value of the activation level. A *sigmoidal function* does this, and drawn out, it looks like

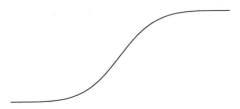

We will use a sigmoidal function that restricts the activation level to be a value between zero and one. Positive net inputs are greater than 0.5 and negative inputs are less than 0.5.

Bias and thresholds

Some neural networks use a *threshold function* in which the unit does not send its activation level to other units unless it exceeds the threshold level. Another method is to use a *bias* value that is associated with each unit and is added to the net input to produce the total input to the unit. A negative bias reduces the inputs from lower units and a positive bias increases it. This acts very much like a threshold function.

Propagation method and formula

When the unit has calculated its activation level, it is sent out to the units it is connected to in the layer above. The activation level is multiplied by each connection weight to the units above and these products are summed with the inputs from other units to form the net inputs to the next layer of units.

The following equation computes unit j's input, $input_j$. We assume that this unit has n units that connect to it. Their activation levels are referred to as $activation_i$. $weight_{ji}$ is the connection weight between $unit_i$ and $unit_j$ above.

$$input_j = \sum_{i=1}^{n} weight_{ji} \times activation_i + bias_j$$

Activation levels are positive numbers between zero and one. Biases and connection weights can be positive or negative and any size. A negative connection weight means that the connection between those two units is *inhibitory*. A positive weight makes an *excitatory* connection.

16.3.1 Learning in neural nets

Adjusting connection weights

A neural network learns through a process of gradual adjustments of the connection weights between units. An increase in a connection weight means that a unit will send a larger value to the node it connects to via that connection weight. A decrease in the connection weight means a smaller value will be sent. Negative connection weights mean negative amounts will be sent that subtract from the net input to the node. Adjusting connection weights changes the effects that nodes have on one another and affects the final output of the network.

The two most common forms of learning are *Hebbian learning* and *back propagation*. Hebbian learning is a simple rule that strengthens the connection between nodes that are simultaneously excited (both have positive activation levels) and weakens connections between units that are simultaneously opposite (different activation levels).

Hebbian learning

Back propagation, or *back-prop* as it is often called, is a more complex type of learning. It reduces the error between the actual output of the network and the desired output by changing the connection weights and biases in such a way that they move slowly toward the correct values. Back-prop is so named because it works in the opposite fashion as the propagation of inputs to outputs we have already seen. Back-prop learning starts at the output nodes comparing the results obtained from forward propagation of inputs to outputs with the desired results. The connection weights and biases are adjusted relative to this difference. A big difference involves a bigger adjustment than a small difference.

Back propagation learning

Back-prop sequences down the network layer by layer using an error measurement calculated from the nodes above. For output units the error measurement is the difference between the actual output of that unit and the desired output value. For input and hidden units, this error measurement is the sum of all the error measurements in the layer above times the respective connection weights between the units.

It takes more than one change of connection weights and biases via back propagation for a network to learn. A training process happens in which a series of forward and back propagations take place. For each of these iterations the accuracy of the network is tested and the weights and biases are adjusted until the difference between outputs and desired results is within some tolerance.

Training a network

Neural networks can be trained to learn a collection of patterns. There is an *input set* representing all the inputs and a *target set* representing all of the desired outputs. Each input is propagated through the network and back propagation is used to update the connection weights and biases. There are different schemes as to when back propagation is done and when the connection weights and biases are changed. Back-prop can be done after each input pattern is propagated through the network, and at each step new connection weights and biases can be calculated. In this scheme the inputs can be *presented* in a fixed order or they can be presented in a random order. Another approach is to delay the changing of connection weights and biases until all the input patterns have been presented. Then the sums of all the weight and bias changes are calculated and the network weights and biases are adjusted accordingly.

Training methods

One of these learning schemes is used for each pass through the input set, an *epoch*. This entire process continues until the total or average of the differences between actual and desired outcomes is less than some threshold.

As a network learns it goes through a process of adjusting weights and biases, settling those values toward some optimum set of values. One can visualize this process as movement along a bumpy terrain. The goal is to go to the lowest spot in this terrain. However, there is always a danger of reaching a low spot that is not the overall low spot. A network can tend to get stuck here in this *local*

Learning failures

minimum and only partially learn the desired patterns.

Failing to learn

There is always a danger that a network cannot learn a collection of patterns. If the network is too small, i.e., it does not have enough hidden units, then it may not be able to learn a pattern just because it is impossible to construct the weights to get the desired outputs. For a simple example of this, imagine that two very similar input patterns are supposed to produce very different outputs. The learning steps conflict with one another so that as the network learns one pattern, it unlearns another. This can be remedied by modifying the network to incorporate enough hidden units or layers to allow the inputs to be differentiated. In general, adding more hidden units allows more complex or larger input sets to be learned. A network with more hidden units can often learn an input set faster (in less training epochs) than a a smaller network can.

Overfitting

There is a down side to using large numbers of hidden units. A large network tends to specialize, or *overfit*, learning its input-to-output mappings exactly. This reduces the network's ability to generalize, producing reasonable outputs given similar inputs to those on which it was trained. The features of neural networks are discussed in the next section.

Neural network plusses

There is a positive side to learning in neural networks. Neural networks usually don't unlearn all they have learned when they learn new information, especially when there is some reinforcement of their previous knowledge. This makes neural networks robust. They tend to have a degree of redundancy so if some weights change or even if some units are removed, the system can still perform close to its prior level. The human mind is similarly robust. As we learn new information, we still maintain old information. We don't forget much considering we loose thousands of neurons each day.

16.3.2   Comparing neural nets with other systems

Contrast of fuzzy systems with neural networks

Neural networks, like fuzzy logic systems, take crisp inputs and produce crisp outputs. Both systems can deal with imprecise values or information and perform reasonably. However, the two systems work in very different ways. Fuzzy logic systems use rules and fuzzy sets that represent vague information. A fuzzy system is developed with general concepts in mind and adjusted to work with specific examples. Similar inputs will produce similar results because of the tolerance inherent in the system.

A neural network has features that tend to smooth out the rough edges that crisp values have. The sigmoidal function that collapses values and the bias that acts as a threshold factor both contribute to this tolerance for a degree of imprecision. Like fuzzy systems, a neural network will yield reasonable results given inputs with which it hasn't been trained but which are similar to trained patterns.

Symbolic versus subsymbolic systems

As fuzzy logic systems are contrasted with crisp systems, neural networks are contrasted with *symbolic systems*. Symbolic systems represent information as symbols, such as words like fish and eat, or query, which could be bound to

```
((interrogative what) (verb is) (noun Mike) (verb saying)
    (prep-phrase (prep to) (article the) (noun computer)))
```

Neural nets are sometimes called *subsymbolic* systems. They work on a level that lies below symbols, dealing with entities that, when combined, can be looked at as more concrete values like symbols. Instead of a specific piece of a neural net representing information like a symbol does, information is distributed throughout many parts of the neural network. If a symbol's value changes, it can have a huge effect on a symbolic system. However, if one weight in a neural network changes, the system performs at about the same level.

Information in a neural network is maintained in a distributed fashion. Don't think of a neural network as a collection of nodes where each node represents a specific piece of information that you can label, such as the height of a person or the number of cars in a city. Instead look at information in a neural network as a certain pattern of activation levels in the nodes. These levels taken as a whole represent information. This is what is meant by information maintained in a distributed fashion. Since no one unit represents an entire fact or concept, neural networks have flexibility in that more than one combination of patterns may produce the same result. And as we've already seen, one network can be trained to learn a collection of patterns because the connection weights between the units each play a partial role in obtaining the final output. Generalization, categorization, handling incomplete inputs, and graceful degradation (performing well even after some of the internal structure has been changed) are all things that neural networks do well but that purely symbolic systems have difficulties with.

Distributed knowledge

Let's look at the properties in which neural networks excel. Neural networks can generalize. Once trained, a network will produce similar outputs for patterns that are close to the learned patterns. If a network is exposed to related patterns during its training, it improves in its ability to generalize. A network is not limited to learning one collection of inputs that map to a particular output. It can learn multiple categories and then classify inputs. The input to a network may be incomplete. For example, if a network is used to recognize patterns of zeroes and ones, there may be a pattern in which we are unsure of some of the digits. Given enough of the input, the proper outcome may still be produced. Lastly, if a unit's weights change or if a unit is removed from a network, the other units and weights may be able to provide enough information to produce the proper results for the trained inputs.

Properties of neural networks

The reason that networks can do these things is due to the distributed nature of the knowledge they maintain and the redundancy in the system. You can view each unit in the network as providing a piece of the eventual answer. If it is slightly wrong or even missing, the other pieces can make up for this because they perform redundant operations or they can make up for the one erroneous or missing piece. In a symbolic system redundancy is rarely built in. Each part is designed to do a specific task with a high degree of precision. There is no room for error; in fact, allowing for a margin of error is a difficult thing to incorporate in a symbolic system.

Redundancy

The artificial intelligence community has been in a raging debate for many years over symbolic versus subsymbolic techniques. Both approaches have their advantages and disadvantages. The debate goes on. In the end neither approach may win out overall, but both may coexist, each suited for a particular class of applications. Here are some of the arguments for each approach.

Arguments supporting subsymbolic systems

The camp supporting neural networks argues that networks can learn any function given a large enough network and enough training sets. The resulting trained network will be able to generalize such that new or incomplete data can be presented to the network and correctly classified. Another advantage to neural nets is that one does not need to analyze the input in any way to custom order or tailor it, categorize it, or in any way understand it as one would have to do when building a decision tree, expert system, or fuzzy logic system.

Arguments supporting symbolic systems

The symbolic AI camp points out that neural networks don't always reach the best decisions (they get stuck in local minima when they learn), or they may never converge on a set of weights. Nets may *overfit* the data, meaning they represent the inputs more or less exactly and lose their ability to generalize or match incomplete inputs. Even when neural nets settle on a working set of weights, one cannot examine the weights and see how the network structured the training data to formulate its categorization. The opacity of the system prevents this. In many systems there is some degree of existing knowledge about the structure of the system to be modeled. It is difficult to represent this like one can in a symbolic system.

16.3.3 History of neural networks

Research with neural nets began with Warren McCullogh and Walter Pitts in the early 1940s. They showed how networks could be used to make calculations. In the late 1940s Donald Hebb theorized that neural networks learned by changing their connection weights. Hebb's learning idea (now referred to as the Hebbian rule) was biologically plausible as well. Simply stated, in Hebbian learning the connection weight between two active units is strengthened.

Perceptrons

In the early 1960s Frank Rosenblatt made very boastful claims about what could be done with *perceptrons*—a simple neural network that has only two layers. He essentially said that a perceptron could learn to perform any type of computation. In response to these strong claims, Marvin Minsky and Seymour Papert wrote a book called *Perceptrons* in 1969. Through rigorous mathematical proofs they showed the limitations of perceptrons. They proved that a perceptron couldn't even solve a problem as simple as an *exclusive or* (often abbreviated as XOR).[2] Minsky and Papert challenged researchers to create a network that could solve this simple problem. *Perceptrons* all but shut down research in neural nets until the mid 1980s.

PDP group

The resurgence of neural networks came about in large part due to the work of the PDP (Parallel Distributed Processing) group—a collection of researchers from U.C. San Diego, including David Rumelhart, James McClelland, Donald Norman, and many other researchers who now form a who's who list of neural

---

[2.] An exclusive or is a logical operation that is true if only one of its arguments is true and false if both are true or both are false.

net researchers and cognitive scientists. The group wrote a three-volume text that came with software to experiment with neural networks that had hidden layers and learning algorithms. They showed that with a single hidden layer, they were able to answer Minsky and Papert's challenge showing a very simple network that solves the XOR problem. We will now develop a neural network that solves this problem as well.

16.3.4 A neural network in Scheme

To best see how neural networks work and get a deeper understanding of their abilities and limitations, we'll build a working model of a network that can learn. A neural network requires a great deal of iteration and this makes it an interesting problem, especially if we take advantage of the capabilities of the applicative operators. The techniques we will use are not the most efficient in terms of memory and speed. If you plan on using this system for large problems, you may consider rewriting it using vectors and destructive operators.

Our system will work with multilayer networks but our examples will be with a simple three-layer network. One layer will be an input layer, another a hidden layer, and the third will be the output layer.

There are many possible representations of a neural network. Nested lists will be the best structure to use to exploit the applicative operators. Each unit can be represented by its activation level (a real number). Each layer is represented as a list of activation levels of the units in that layer. The entire network is a list of layers. By breaking up layers into separate lists, it is easier to apply the output of a given unit to all the units in the next layer up. It will also be easier to implement the learning algorithm.

Representation of units

Connection weights can be represented as lists as well. Since we will need to reference all the weights that connect to each individual unit to sum up its collective inputs, it will be best to use a nested list structure, where each sublist contains all the connection weights between a given unit and the units in the layer below. The biases can be stored in a separate list or within the weight lists. It makes things a bit easier if biases are stored with the weights, especially when returning new weights and biases. The biases will be the first value in each unit's weight list and the weights will make up the rest of the list.

Representing connection weights and biases

We will rely on mapping functions to multiply the outputs of units by their connection weights and to sum these products. As long as there is a one-to-one correspondence of units to connection weights, we don't have to worry about accessing individual weights by their positions in lists. We just sequence through elements of lists.

To get a more concrete idea of what the representation looks like and how it will be used, we'll create an example network. This sample network has three input units, four hidden units, and two output units. The numbers in the circles are the biases of the units. The numbers next to the arrows are the connection weights.

Sample network

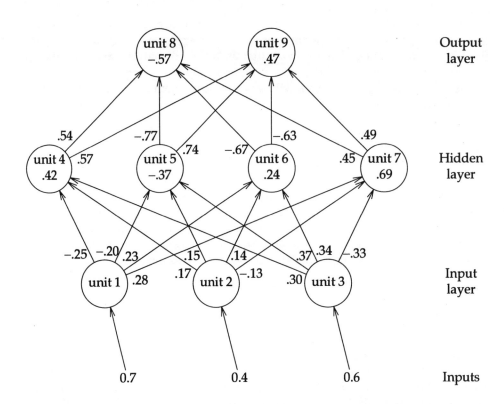

And here is the data representation we can use to model this network:

inputs values:

```
(0.7 0.4 0.6)
```

connection weights and biases for hidden units:

```
((.42 -.25 .17 .30) (-.37 -.20 .15 .37)
 (.24 .23 .14 .34) (.69 .28 -.13 -.33))
```

connection weights and biases for output units:

```
((-.57 .54 -.77 -.67 .45) (.47 .57 .74 -.63 .49))
```

The activation levels of the input layer are set to the inputs. Once we have the activation levels of the input layer, we can compute the outputs that the units in this layer will send up to the next layer. A threshold function is sometimes used that does not send an output unless it is greater than some threshold. We will leave this out and always send the activation level as the output for our neural network.

Computing net inputs   To compute the net input to units in subsequent layers, we must combine the outputs from all the units in the layer below, multiplying each by the connection weight that joins them. This sum is added to the bias of that unit to get the total input to the unit. For example, the total input to unit 7 is calculated as follows:

```
> (+ .69 (apply + (map * '(.7 .4 .6) '(.28 -.13 -.33))))
.636
```

Notice that both lists supplied to `map` are the same length and that the activation of unit 1, 0.7, is multiplied by 0.28, the connection weight between unit 1 and unit 7, and so on for the other units in the input layer.

Let's generalize this to create a function that computes the total input for a hidden or output unit:

```
; Return weighted sum of inputs to a single unit plus bias.
(define (total-input inputs weights)
  (+ (car weights) (apply + (map * inputs (cdr weights)))) )
```

To compute the activation levels of hidden and output layers, we apply the limiting sigmoidal function to the total input to the unit. The sigmoidal function looks like this:

Computing activation levels

$$output_i = \frac{1}{1 + e^{-totalInput_i}}$$

This can be expressed in Scheme with the following function:

```
; Apply the limiting sigmoidal function that restricts the total
; input to be a value between 0 and 1.
(define (sig total-input)
  (/ 1 (+ 1 (expt 2.71828 (- total-input)))) )
```

```
> (sig (total-input '(.7 .4 .6) '(.69 .28 -.13 -.33)))
.654
```

The following function computes the activation levels for all the nodes within a layer. The second parameter, `layer-weights`, represents a list of connection weights for a given layer in the network. It will be a list like the two shown above for hidden or output layer connection weights.

Computing activation levels for entire layers

```
; Return list of activations to nodes in a layer.
(define (act-layer inputs layer-weights)
  (map (lambda (weights) (sig (total-input inputs weights)) )
    layer-weights) )
```

Lastly, we need to propagate activation levels up through all levels of the network starting with inputs to the network. The inputs are passed directly to the input units as their activation levels. Further levels are computed using `act-layer`. A recursive solution works best. Each pass through the recursion computes the activation levels of one layer. We'll need two pieces of information: the weights for all layers of the network and the inputs to the current layer. The weights, `all-weights`, is simply a list of the weights for each layer, which, as shown above, are lists of sublists with weights for each unit. The first item in `all-weights` is the weights between the input layer and the next layer of the network.

Propagating activation throughout the network

The parameter `acts` is a list of the activation levels to be propagated to the next level. The input for each layer (other than the first) is the output of the previous layer (the activation levels of that layer). As the activation level is computed for each layer, it is passed on as the input to the next layer in each recursive call. When the list `all-weights` is empty, `acts` contains the activation levels of the output units.

```
; Return a list of the activation levels in a network beginning with
; the input layer.
(define (propagate all-weights acts)
  (if (null? all-weights)
      (list acts)
      (cons
        acts
        (propagate
          (rest all-weights)
          (act-layer acts (first all-weights)))))) )
```

Using the weights, biases, and input from the previous picture, we can call `propagate` to compute the activation levels for the network:

```
(define weights '(
  ((.42 -.25 .17 .30) (-.37 -.20 .15 .37)
   (.24 .23 .14 .34) (.69 .28 -.13 -.33))
  ((-.57 .54 -.77 -.67 .45) (.47 .57 .74 -.63 .49))))

(define input '(.7 .4 .6))

> (propagate weights input)
((.7 .4 .6) (.621 .443 .659 .654) (.327 .742))
```

Implementing back-prop

The output from this network is 0.327 and 0.742. The next step is to train the network to produce different outputs. Suppose we would like the network to produce 0.4 and 0.9, given the same inputs and initial weights. Through the process of back propagation (back-prop), we can slowly adjust the weights and biases to get the desired outputs.

We won't explain the mathematical derivations of the formulas that back-prop uses. If you are interested in the math, the first volume of the PDP books (see the reference section) gives a good explanation.

Weight change formula

The change in weights of any node in a network is computed using the following formula:

$$weightChange_{ij} = learningRate \times errorSignal_i \times output_j$$
$$+ momentum \times oldWeightChange_{ij}$$

Learning rate and momentum

The subscript ij denotes the weight between $unit_i$ and $unit_j$, where $unit_i$ is in the layer above $unit_j$. The *learningRate* is the speed at which learning takes place. The larger the value of the learning rate, the greater the weights change. However, using a learning rate that is too big can cause the weights to bounce around too much and never converge on a solution. Using 0.5 or 0.25 is a safe starting point for a learning rate. The *momentum* term allows the old weight change to play a role in determining the new weight change. This tends to smooth out oscillations that sometimes occur as the weights move toward the proper values. This term is optional, but with it learning speeds up *a lot*. A good start value for *momentum* is 0.9. Since the learning rate and momentum terms are constants through the back-prop process, we'll make them global variables rather than pass them to a series of functions.

```
(define learn-rate 0.5)
(define momentum 0.9)
```

The error signal represents the difference between the value that the unit should have to produce the output and the actual value it has. *errorSignal_i* is the error signal of the unit in the upper layer. *output_j* is the output of the unit in the lower layer. The error signal of an output unit is the product of two values. The first is the difference between the output we want (the *target*) and the output we get from propagating the input through the network. The second value is the derivative of the sigmoidal function with respect to its input, which is

Error signal

$$output_i(1-output_i)$$

The error signal of output unit *i* is

$$errorSignal_i = (target_i - output_i)output_i(1 - output_i)$$

The error signal of a hidden unit is the sum of all the error signals of the units in the layer above multiplied by their connection weights, all multiplied by the derivative of the activation (sigmoidal) function. For unit *j*, the error signal is

$$errorSignal_j = output_j(1 - output_j)\sum_{i=1}^{n} errorSignal_i \times weight_{ij}$$

The change in a bias is very similar to the change in a weight. It is

Change in bias

$$biasChange_i = learningRate \times errorSignal_i + momentum \times oldBiasChange_i$$

Back propagation begins with the weights connecting the output nodes and moves down layer by layer, ending at the bottom hidden layer's weights. Each hidden layer uses the error signal in the layer above in determining the change in weight. Since we'll need the error signals to compute both the weight change within a layer and the error signals in the layer below, we'll write a function that computes the error signals of a layer and returns them in a list. The output layer's error signals are computed as follows. `targets` is a list of the desired outputs and `outputs` is a list of the actual outputs from the network.

Computing error signals for output layers

```
; Compute error signals for output layer units.
(define (error-sig-output targets outputs)
  (map (lambda (target output)
        (* (- target output) output (- 1 output)) )
    targets outputs) )
```

One important consideration to make is that the weights are accessed differently when doing forward propagation through the network versus backward propagation. In forward propagation when we calculate the total input to a hidden or output layer, we are looking at the weights that feed into that layer from below. With back-prop we are examining the weights that go to the layer above. To make it easier to write the code for back-prop, we should transpose the weights so they are structured as lists of weights to the above layer. We can leave out the biases, as they are not used in computing error signals or bias change values. Looking back at the picture of the network for this example, what we

Transposing weights

need is a list that looks like the following:

```
(((.54 .57) (-.77 .74) (-.67 -.63) (.45 .49))
 ((-.25 -.20 .23 .28) (.17 .15 .14 -.13) (.30 .37 .34 -.33)))
```

The first sublist is a list of the weights that extend above the units in the highest hidden unit to the units in the output unit. To form such a list, we can write a function that transposes the weights and removes the biases. Look at the current form of the weights and biases: ((((.42 -.25 .17 .30) (-.37 -.20 .15 .37)
 (.24 .23 .14 .34) (.69 .28 -.13 -.33))
((-.57 .54 -.77 -.67 .45) (.47 .57 .74 -.63 .49)))

If we map `list` across all the weights in each unit of a layer, we will form new lists of the first elements in each list, the second elements, and so on. Since the weight sublists are in lists for each layer and the number of these sublists varies, the easiest way to construct this mapping is by using `apply` with the list of the weight sublists. The one trick here is that the function `list` must be inserted into the list that `apply` will call `map` with. Another mapping will perform this operation for each layer and will remove the biases. Lastly, we want the weights of the uppermost hidden layer first, so we must reverse the final list we get. The following function does all of this:

```
; Transpose the weights for back-prop.
(define (transpose weights)
  (reverse
    (map (lambda (layer) (cdr (apply map (cons list layer)))) )
      weights)) )
```

Testing this function, we get the following result:

```
> (transpose weights)
(((.54 .57) (-.77 .74) (-.67 -.63) (.45 .49))
 ((-.25 -.20 .23 .28) (.17 .15 .14 -.13) (.30 .37 .34 -.33)))
```

Computing error signals for hidden layers

For hidden layers the error signal is a function of the weights feeding out of the layer, `layer-weights`, the error signals in the layer above, `error-signals`, and the outputs of the units in the layer, `outputs`.

```
; Compute error signals for hidden layer units.
(define (error-sig-inner error-signals layer-weights outputs)
  (map (lambda (output weights)
         (* (apply + (map * error-signals weights))
            output (- 1 output)) )
    outputs layer-weights) )
```

Performing back propagation

The process of back propagation involves computing the error signal of the output nodes and then passing those values down through the network to calculate the error signals in the lower layers. As the error signals are calculated, the change in weights and biases can be determined. The function `back-prop` calls `error-sig-output` to determine the error signals of the output layer and passes those values to `descent`, which moves down through the network calculating error signals and changes in connection weights and biases. The arguments to `back-prop` are the desired outputs, `targets`, the actual outputs from `propagate`, the transposed weights, `trans-weights`, and the prior weight and bias changes, `old-changes`. To facilitate updating the weights and biases, `back-prop` should return the weight and bias changes in the form of the original weights and biases (i.e., not as a transposed list).

```
; Perform back propagation on a network and returns a list of weight
; and bias changes in the form of the original weights and biases.
(define (back-prop target outputs trans-weights old-changes)
  (if (null? outputs)
      'no-outputs
      (reverse
        (descent (error-sig-output target (first outputs))
          (rest outputs) trans-weights old-changes))) )
```

The function `descent` recurses through the network a layer at a time, initially being called with the topmost hidden layer. It calls `calc-weights` to compute the changes in weights connecting the current layer to the one below it. Then it recurses with the error signals of the next layer and continues to compute weights for the layers below. `descent` returns a list of the connection weight and bias changes.

Back propagation through the network

```
; Recurse through a network to compute error signals and return
; connection weight and bias changes.
(define (descent error-signals outputs trans-weights old-changes)
  (if (null? outputs)
      '()
      (cons (calc-weights error-signals (first outputs)
              (first old-changes))
        (descent (error-sig-inner error-signals
                  (first trans-weights) (first outputs))
          (rest outputs) (rest trans-weights)
          (rest old-changes)))) )
```

Calculating the change in connection weights and biases is a straightforward process, given the error signals and the inputs to the units in a layer. We'll use a nested loop where the outer loop handles each node in the layer and the inner loop calculates a weight change for each input going into the node.

Weight and bias changes for a single layer

```
; Compute change in connection weights and biases for all units in
; one layer.  inputs are the activation levels of the units in the
; layer below.
(define (calc-weights error-signals inputs old-change)
  (map (lambda (error change)
         ; insert new bias change
         (cons (+ (* learn-rate error) (* momentum (car change)))
               (map (lambda (input old-weight-change)
                      (+ (* learn-rate error input)
                         (* momentum old-weight-change)) )
                 inputs (cdr change))) )
    error-signals old-change) )
```

Computing new weights and biases

Once the change in weights and biases is determined, we must calculate new connection weights and biases. This is fairly straightforward with a nested loop that adds the appropriate change values to the current weights and biases.

```
; Add the new weight and bias changes to the current weights and
; biases and returns the new weights and biases.
(define (update old-weights weight-change)
  (map (lambda (weight-layer change-layer)
         (map (lambda (weight-unit change-unit)
                (map + weight-unit change-unit) )
              weight-layer change-layer) )
       old-weights weight-change) )
```

Proper learning

That concludes the process of adjusting weights and biases. But back-prop only does a single pass that makes a very small adjustment. If the system makes large adjustments, it can easily overshoot the goal or worse yet, it may undo (or forget) information that it learned earlier because the weights and biases were adjusted so dramatically. The key to learning in a neural network is to make small adjustments and iterate through back propagation many times until the output of the network is within some tolerance of the targets.

Test if finished

To determine when an output has been learned, we'll call avg-square-test, which takes the actual outputs and the desired targets and returns true if they are close enough. If the average of the squares of the differences of the actual and desired outputs is less than .05 squared (.0025), it returns true.

```
; Test if outputs are close enough to target values.
(define (avg-square-test outputs targets)
  (< (/ (apply + (map (lambda (outcome desired)
                        (expt (- outcome desired) 2) )
                      outputs targets))
        (length outputs))
     .0025) )
```

Implementing a training function

We will create a function that learns to produce outputs from inputs. This function takes a list of input patterns, input-set, and a list of corresponding output patterns, target-set, and trains the network to learn all of them. This input and output set is called a *training set*. Once the network has learned the training set, it returns the final connection weights and biases and the number of iterations through the training set, *epochs*, it took to learn. To observe the learning process, we will display the inputs and corresponding outputs from the network and indicate which inputs have been learned. A parameter frequency controls how often this information is displayed.

Our training function will need seven parameters altogether: the input set; the target set; the initial weights and biases; the prior weight and bias changes; learn-func, a function that controls the order in which back-prop is applied to the input set and when the weights are updated; frequency, how often output values are displayed; and the epoch counter. We'll use a helper function that only takes five of these values and sets the old weights and bias changes and the current epoch to zero.

To create a set of weight and bias changes equal to zero, we'll use the function
net-change that returns a new network with each unit adjusted according to the
function passed as an argument.

Initializing weight and bias changes

```
; Return new network with units changed according to func.
(define (net-change func weights)
  (map (lambda (layer)
         (map (lambda (unit) (func unit) ) layer) )
    weights) )
```

Creating the function net-change is an example of programming abstraction.
We could have created a function that only returns a network with weights and
biases equal to zero. But with net-change we can do much more than this. For
example, we can call net-change with **car** to get a list of biases in a network or
with **cdr** to get a list of weights alone.

Programming abstraction

Here is the code to teach a network a training set. Pay close attention to how
learn-func is used. It is passed the entire training set and calls back-prop to get
weight and bias changes. Different variations on learn-func will vary the order
in which the training set is processed and when the weights and biases are
updated. In addition to returning the new weight and bias values, learn-func
must return the most recent weight and bias changes.

```
; Helper function for trainer.
(define (train input-set target-set weights learn-func frequency)
  (trainer input-set target-set weights
    (net-change (lambda (unit)
                  (map (lambda (weight) 0) unit) ) weights)
    learn-func frequency 0) )

; Given training set of inputs and targets, initial weights and
; biases, old weight and bias changes, learning function, display
; frequency, and epoch counter - return the number of epochs to
; train and the new connection weights and biases after learning.
; Print outputs each frequency epochs.
(define (trainer input-set target-set weights old-changes
         learn-func frequency count)
  (let* ((act-set
           (map (lambda (input)
                  (reverse (propagate weights input)) )
             input-set))
         (output-set (map first act-set)))
    (if (zero? (remainder count frequency))
        (print-outputs count input-set output-set target-set))
    (if (every avg-square-test output-set target-set)
        (list count weights)
        (let* ((results (learn-func target-set act-set weights
                          old-changes))
               (weights (first results))
               (changes (second results)))
          (trainer input-set target-set weights changes
            learn-func frequency (+ count 1))))) )
```

Printing outputs

The function below prints the current outputs:

```
; Print the current output value for each input and indicate if
; that input has been learned.
(define (print-outputs count input-set output-set target-set)
  (display count)
  (newline)
  (for-each (lambda (input output target)
              (display input)
              (display " -> ")
              (display output)
              (display " learned: ")
              (display (avg-square-test output target))
              (newline) )
    input-set output-set target-set) )
```

Different learning functions

The following functions can be passed to `trainer` as learning functions. They vary in the order they call `back-prop` with the inputs in the training set and in the time the weights and biases are updated. `adjust-during` processes inputs in the order they occur in the training set and updates the weight and bias changes after each call to `back-prop`.[3] `adjust-after` processes inputs in the order they occur in the training set and accumulates the weight and bias changes and does not adjust the weights or biases until all inputs have gone through back-prop with the original weights and biases.

```
; Pass through the target set and actual outputs using back-prop
; and adjust the weights after each call to back-prop.
(define (adjust-during target-set output-set weights old-changes)
  (if (null? target-set)
      (list weights old-changes)
      (let ((changes (back-prop (first target-set)
                                (first output-set) (transpose weights)
                                (reverse old-changes))))
        (adjust-during (rest target-set) (rest output-set)
          (update weights changes) changes))) )

; Pass through the target set and actual outputs using back-prop
; and adjust the weights after the entire epoch is complete.
(define (adjust-after target-set output-set weights old-changes)
  (after target-set output-set (transpose weights) weights
    old-changes))
```

[3.] Technically, there is a slight bug in `trainer` when used with `adjust-during`: `propagate` is called with the original weights instead of the updated weights. I fixed this and found that with the exclusive or problem, it takes a few more epochs to reach an answer with this "fixed" code. Since the difference is so slight and the code is less efficient because `propagate` is called extra times, I opted to leave the code with this slight bug.

```
(define (after target-set output-set trans-weights new old-changes)
  (if (null? target-set)
      (list new old-changes)
      (let ((changes (back-prop (first target-set)
                                (first output-set) trans-weights
                                (reverse old-changes)))))
        (after (rest target-set) (rest output-set) trans-weights
          (update changes new) changes))) )
```

Rather than assign initial weights and biases, most networks begin with randomly chosen values. Here are functions to create random weights and biases, given the configuration of the network (the number of nodes in each layer):

Creating networks with random weight and bias values

```
; Given a description of a network - a list of numbers indicating
; how many nodes are in each layer beginning with the input layer,
; return a list of random initial connection weights and biases.
(define (random-net net-desc)
  (if (or (null? net-desc) (null? (cdr net-desc)))
      '()
      (cons (make-layer-weights (car net-desc) (second net-desc))
            (random-net (cdr net-desc)))) )

; Return random weights and biases for a layer in a network.
(define (make-layer-weights nodes-below nodes-above)
  (make-list nodes-above
             (lambda (n) (bias-&-weights nodes-below) )) )

; Return random bias and weights for a node in a network.
; The values are in the range -1 to 1.
(define (bias-&-weights num-nodes)
  (make-list (+ num-nodes 1)
             (lambda (n) (- (/ (random 1000) 500) 1) )) )

; Make a list of num-items elements with values based on func.
(define (make-list num-items func)
  (do ((num num-items (- num 1))
       (new-list '() (cons (func num) new-list)))
    ((<= num 0)
     new-list)) )
```

Now we can demonstrate learning in a neural network. We'll train the network we defined earlier to learn the outputs 0.4 and 0.9. Here are the current weights and biases:

Learning trials

```
> weights
(((.42 -.25 .17 .30) (-.37 -.20 .15 .37)
  (.24 .23 .14 .34) (.69 .28 -.13 -.33))
 ((-.57 .54 -.77 -.67 .45) (.47 .57 .74 -.63 .49)))
```

Let's save the activation levels after propagating the inputs 0.7, 0.4, and 0.6 through the network.

```
(define out (propagate weights '(.7 .4 .6)))
```

These activations are

```
> out
((.7 .4 .6) (.621 .443 .659 .654) (.327 .742))
```

Now we can call `back-prop` to get the weight and bias changes after one epoch. The activation levels from `propagate` must be reversed for `back-prop` and the weights must be transposed. The prior weight and bias changes must be initialized to zero, which is what the call to `net-change` does. This list must be reversed as well.

```
> (back-prop '(.4 .9) (reverse out) (transpose weights)
    (reverse (net-change
                 (lambda (unit)
                    (map (lambda (weight) 0) unit)) weights)))
(((.003054 .002138 .001222 .001833)
  (.001226 .000858 .000490 .000736)
  (-.003353 -.002347 -.001341 -.002012)
  (.002498 .001749 .000999 .001499))
 ((.008073 .005012 .003578 .005324 .005279)
  (.015114 .009383 .006699 .009967 .009882)))
```

Training cases

The weight and bias changes are very small. Now let's call `train` to iterate through many epochs until the network has learned. We must list the input and target because `train` takes input and target sets to learn multiple patterns. The last two arguments specify the method with which the weights and biases should be adjusted and the frequency with which epochs should be displayed. We'll adjust the weights after each pattern and print out the outputs after each epoch.

```
> (train '((.7 .4 .6)) '((.4 .9)) weights adjust-during 1)
0
(.7 .4 .6) -> (.327 .742) learned: #f
1
(.7 .4 .6) -> (.331 .750) learned: #f
2
(.7 .4 .6) -> (.340 .763) learned: #f
3
(.7 .4 .6) -> (.352 .780) learned: #f
4
(.7 .4 .6) -> (.367 .800) learned: #f
5
(.7 .4 .6) -> (.383 .819) learned: #f
6
(.7 .4 .6) -> (.399 .838) learned: #t
(6 (((.466 -.218 .188 .327) (-.351 -.187 .158 .382)
     (.193 .197 .121 .312) (.728 .306 -.115 -.307))
    ((-.454 .612 -.718 -.594 .526) (.690 .707 .838 -.486 .635))))
```

Turning momentum off

The targets are learned after six epochs. It's easy to see how the output values slowly move toward the targets. Notice that the changes increase in magnitude from the initial epoch's changes. This is the effect of the momentum term. To see how much longer it takes to learn without the momentum term, let's turn it off.

We will reduce the amount of output by using a larger frequency, 100.

```
(define momentum 0)

> (train '((.7 .4 .6)) '((.4 .9)) weights adjust-during 100)
0
(.7 .4 .6) -> (.327 .742) learned: #f
(23 (((.462 -.220 .187 .325) (-.349 -.185 .158 .382)
      (.200 .202 .124 .316) (.725 .305 -.116 -.309))
     ((-.472 .602 -.726 -.606 .515) (.671 .697 .830 -.499 .623))))
```

With no momentum term the learning slowed down by about a factor of four.

Let's try some larger examples that require learning multiple patterns. We'll start with exclusive or, XOR. First let's reset the momentum term and create a random network with two input nodes, two hidden nodes, and one output.

XOR trials

```
(define momentum 0.9)
(define w (random-net '(2 2 1)))

> w
(((-.536 -.712 -.126) (-.352 -.734 .086)) ((.604 -.994 -.796)))
```

The input and target sets consist of 0s and 1s corresponding to logical false and true. Since 0 and 1 are the extreme values of a node's activation, learning these values is time-consuming. We can speed things up by using 0.1 as 0 and 0.9 as 1.

```
> (train '((0.1 0.1) (0.1 0.9) (0.9 0.1) (0.9 0.9))
    '((0.1) (0.9) (0.9) (0.1)) w adjust-during 100)
0
(.1 .1) -> (.485) learned: #f
(.1 .9) -> (.487) learned: #f
(.9 .1) -> (.540) learned: #f
(.9 .9) -> (.541) learned: #f
100
(.1 .1) -> (.275) learned: #f
(.1 .9) -> (.577) learned: #f
(.9 .1) -> (.578) learned: #f
(.9 .9) -> (.621) learned: #f
200
(.1 .1) -> (.181) learned: #f
(.1 .9) -> (.713) learned: #f
(.9 .1) -> (.713) learned: #f
(.9 .9) -> (.408) learned: #f
(266 (((2.715 -6.175 -6.159) (4.644 -3.452 -3.451))
      ((-2.853 -6.735 6.460))))
```

After 266 epochs XOR is learned. Let's test the other learning method, which adjusts the weights and biases after each epoch:

```
> (train '((0.1 0.1) (0.1 0.9) (0.9 0.1) (0.9 0.9))
    '((0.1) (0.9) (0.9) (0.1)) w adjust-after 100)
0
(.1 .1) -> (.485) learned: #f
(.1 .9) -> (.487) learned: #f
```

```
(.9 .1) -> (.540) learned: #f
(.9 .9) -> (.541) learned: #f
100
(.1 .1) -> (.277) learned: #f
(.1 .9) -> (.578) learned: #f
(.9 .1) -> (.578) learned: #f
(.9 .9) -> (.618) learned: #f
200
(.1 .1) -> (.156) learned: #f
(.1 .9) -> (.806) learned: #f
(.9 .1) -> (.807) learned: #f
(.9 .9) -> (.244) learned: #f
(244 (((2.652 -6.015 -5.985) (4.692 -3.473 -3.470))
     ((-2.856 -6.736 6.442))))
```

In this example adjusting the weights and biases after each epoch produces faster learning. This is not always the case.

Notice that the final weights and biases are about the same with both learning methods. However, this may not always be true. There are many bias and weight configurations that will produce a working XOR solution.

Counting-ones trials

Here is a different problem—*count-ones*. The input set consists of permutations of 0s and 1s (represented as 0.1 and 0.9). The targets are counts (in binary) of the number of 1s in the corresponding input. The numbers 0 through 3 in binary are 00, 01, 10, and 11. This learning task, as well as learning XOR, is difficult because similar inputs produce dissimilar outputs.

```
(define input-set '((0.1 0.1 0.1) (0.1 0.1 0.9) (0.1 0.9 0.1)
  (0.1 0.9 0.9) (0.9 0.1 0.1) (0.9 0.1 0.9) (0.9 0.9 0.1)
  (0.9 0.9 0.9)))

(define target-set '((0.1 0.1) (0.1 0.9) (0.1 0.9) (0.9 0.1)
  (0.1 0.9) (0.9 0.1) (0.9 0.1) (0.9 0.9)))

> (train input-set target-set (random-net '(3 4 2))
    adjust-during 200)
0
(.1 .1 .1) -> (.445 .706) learned: #f
(.1 .1 .9) -> (.425 .666) learned: #f
(.1 .9 .1) -> (.431 .673) learned: #f
(.1 .9 .9) -> (.411 .637) learned: #f
(.9 .1 .1) -> (.443 .724) learned: #f
(.9 .1 .9) -> (.419 .682) learned: #f
(.9 .9 .1) -> (.430 .691) learned: #f
(.9 .9 .9) -> (.409 .652) learned: #f
200
(.1 .1 .1) -> (.005 .286) learned: #f
(.1 .1 .9) -> (.112 .993) learned: #f
(.1 .9 .1) -> (.109 .992) learned: #f
(.1 .9 .9) -> (.931 .352) learned: #f
(.9 .1 .1) -> (.108 .992) learned: #f
(.9 .1 .9) -> (.929 .344) learned: #f
(.9 .9 .1) -> (.930 .337) learned: #f
```

```
(.9 .9 .9) -> (.980 .855) learned: #f
400
(.1 .1 .1) -> (.004 .099) learned: #f
(.1 .1 .9) -> (.109 .904) learned: #t
(.1 .9 .1) -> (.100 .899) learned: #t
(.1 .9 .9) -> (.890 .101) learned: #t
(.9 .1 .1) -> (.099 .899) learned: #t
(.9 .1 .9) -> (.891 .101) learned: #t
(.9 .9 .1) -> (.899 .101) learned: #t
(.9 .9 .9) -> (.951 .896) learned: #t
600
(.1 .1 .1) -> (.009 .100) learned: #f
(.1 .1 .9) -> (.107 .904) learned: #t
(.1 .9 .1) -> (.103 .900) learned: #t
(.1 .9 .9) -> (.893 .100) learned: #t
(.9 .1 .1) -> (.102 .899) learned: #t
(.9 .1 .9) -> (.893 .100) learned: #t
(.9 .9 .1) -> (.899 .100) learned: #t
(.9 .9 .9) -> (.919 .896) learned: #t
(797 (((11.377 -5.812 -5.799 -5.595) (11.131 -7.700 -7.761 -8.281)
      (1.441 -1.207 -1.287 -2.179) (1.767 -5.712 -5.597 -4.592))
    ((2.210 -.120 -4.901 .760 -2.274)
     (2.441 -6.924 8.768 -2.890 -7.994)))))
```

In other learning trials of *count-ones*, I found that the time to learn *count-ones* varied greatly depending on the initial weights and biases. The bottleneck was always in learning the first output of the first pattern. As in this example, the value gets very small and then slowly grows. It's painful to watch but it increases by a slightly larger amount each time.

16.3.5 Exercises

16.7 Compare the effects of adjusting the weights after each epoch versus after each pattern in *count-ones*. Perform different trials and have something to read or do while you wait for the output. Back-prop is very compute-intensive and slow. Which method gives a better learning rate?

16.8 Try improving the speed of learning in the XOR or *count-ones* problems by changing the momentum and learning rates. At some point you may see big oscillations in the output values when the learning goes too fast.

16.9 Write a function that can be used as an argument to train that sequences through the inputs in a random order calling back-prop and adjusting weights after each pattern. How does this function compare to adjust-during and adjust-after in learning XOR or *count-ones*?

16.10 When more hidden units are added to a hidden layer, learning rates often increase. Test this with XOR and *count-ones*.

16.11 Create some interesting input sets and targets and test if they can be learned. Can you create patterns that cannot be learned?

16.12 Modify the learning function and `trainer` so that they incorporate the following two changes: adjust the weights before propagating the next input (this fixes the bug mentioned earlier in the text), and apply back-prop only to outputs that need to be adjusted. Here is an outline of this new approach:

- Propagate the input value to produce an output.
- Compare this output with the target and if it is within the tolerance, continue with the next input in the input set.
- If the output is not close enough to the target, perform back-prop and adjust the weights and biases, then continue with the next input.
- Repeat these steps once all inputs in the pattern have been tested, stopping once all inputs are within the tolerance.

Compare this learning approach with the original `trainer` and `adjust-during`.

16.4 Genetic Algorithms

Populations, chromosomes, genotypes, and phenotypes

Genetic algorithms are models of learning based on evolutionary ideas from biology. These systems represent information on a collection of individual members that make up a *population*. An individual in a genetic system (or *evolutionary system*) is maintained as an artificial *chromosome*. A chromosome is effectively a list of values that encodes information about a particular individual in the population. For example, a chromosome can represent a path to take to reach a goal, as in the traveling salesman problem or the missionaries and cannibals problem. It may represent the membership grades of a fuzzy set or the weights in a neural network. There are many possibilities. It is important to understand that the chromosome is a coded representation of the actual information (e.g., path or weights) in which we are interested. This actual information is called the *phenotype* and the encoded chromosome represents the *genotype*. These terms come from biology.

Evolutionary process

A genetic algorithm begins with an initial (usually randomly chosen) population. This population goes through a process of evolution in which members of the population are chosen according to some *fitness test* and *selection process* and changed by either *crosslinking* or *mutation*. The most fit of these offspring and their parents become the next *generation* of the system. This process continues until some measure of *fitness* has been reached—some members of the population evolve to perform some task at a certain level.

Fitness and selection

The fitness test or fitness measurement is a function that is applied to a chromosome to give it a numerical value of how good it is—its *fitness*. This depends on the particular problem that the genetic algorithm is trying to solve. Once the fitness of chromosomes is determined, the best chromosomes can be chosen for crosslinking or to be passed directly to the next generation. This is the selection

process. Selection may based solely on fitness, *hard selection*, or may be probabil-
istically determined (based on fitness and random luck)—*soft selection*.

Crosslinking

Crosslinking is done by taking two individuals from the population (also
called the *gene pool*) and choosing a random split point between two *genes* in their
chromosomes. A gene is a part of a chromosome. Two new offspring will be produced, each having one piece of one parent's original chromosome. The offspring
may be better or worse than their parents. The following diagram shows how
crosslinking works. The two parents on the left are crosslinked to produce the
two new offspring on the right. The dashed line denotes the crossover point in
each parent.

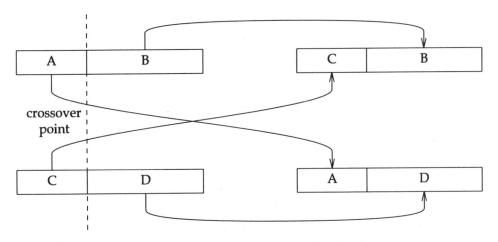

Mutation happens by simply changing a gene of a chromosome to a new randomly chosen value. The value of a gene is called an *allele*. This is a smaller
change to a chromosome than crosslinking but can have a large impact in that it
inserts a random value that may or may not be beneficial. The following diagram
illustrates mutation:

Mutation

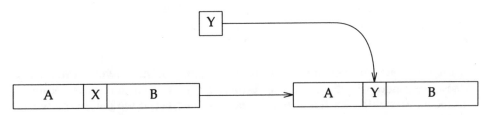

Let's take a closer look at the steps taken in a generation of a genetic algorithm. The first step is to evaluate the members of the population according to
the fitness measurement that gives each member a ranking (fitness) in the population. Then members from the population are selected to be parents to produce a
new generation. An individual may be used only once as a parent or may be
replaced in the population such that it can be a parent more than once in a given
generation.

*Steps taken in one
generation*

Once a collection of parents is created, they are randomly paired up and then "bred" to produce the new generation. Crosslinking is performed to combine one part of one parent's chromosome with another part of another parent's chromosome. Each pair of parents produces a pair of children.

Some parents may pass directly to the next generation. This is called *asexual reproduction*. The number of chromosomes that pass directly to the next generation and the number of chromosomes that are crosslinked are both factors that can be adjusted in a genetic algorithm system.

Mutation may be performed in addition to crosslinking and asexual reproduction. Mutation involves the simple switching of a gene from its current state to another possible state. Only one individual is needed in mutation, unlike crosslinking which requires two. Mutation is usually performed on a smaller part of the population than crosslinking and asexual reproduction.

Stopping the process

Crosslinking, asexual reproduction, and mutation form a collection of new chromosomes. These may be used directly as the next generation, or may be compared with the parent generation and the best members continue on as the next generation. This process of selecting parents, generating new offspring via crosslinking and mutation, and choosing the new generation continues until an offspring is produced that has a large enough fitness to satisfy some stopping criterion. For some problems this is a clear measure and in some problems it isn't. For example, in the missionaries and cannibals problem a chromosome that solves the problem would constitute a stopping criterion. For a problem like the traveling salesman problem in which the cost of the best path is not known, we either have to pick a reasonable guess or stop after a certain number of generations and return the chromosome with the best fit and declare that the best path. Another stopping point occurs when the population has *converged*, when the vast majority of each gene in each chromosome contains the same value (allele). At this point the population does not change much and may have settled to some maximal value.

16.4.1   Building a genetic algorithm in Scheme

Encoding problems into chromosomes

Before we begin to create the code for a genetic algorithm, let's look into how a problem can be encoded into a chromosome representation. For example, if we want to train a neural network using a genetic algorithm instead of back-propagation, our chromosome would be an encoding of the network weights and biases. We cannot directly use the weight structure as a chromosome because a chromosome should be a flat structure, not a nested list. If we flatten the weight and bias list, we form a list of numbers that can be used as a chromosome which can be crosslinked and mutated. Reconstructing the proper list structure reforms the weights and biases so inputs can be propagated to test the fitness compared to the target.

A chromosome does not have to consist of numbers. Characters and symbols can be used. Regardless of which type of gene is used, the legal values for the gene must be specified. This is needed when the initial population is created and when mutation occurs. If this is not done it may be impossible to evaluate the fitness of the offspring.

There are other problems that may arise when evaluating offspring. If our chromosome is a path of cities to visit, crosslinking may produce offspring that include multiple copies of the same city and miss other cities. In a problem like this where genes cannot be repeated in the chromosome, special measures must be taken to fix or ignore such offspring.

Another option to avoid repeating genes is to use different reproduction methods instead of crosslinking. *Reordering* and *inversion* are two such reproductive methods and they require only a single parent. Reordering, as the name suggests, reorders the genes in a chromosome. Inversion reverses the genes in a section of a chromosome. Both of these methods change a chromosome without adding or deleting any of the existing genes and are good for problems in which the exact genes must remain in the chromosomes.

Reordering and inversion

Let's move on to the code. The first step is to create an initial population. We can use make-list (defined in the neural network section) which takes a number of elements and a function of one argument that defines what the elements should be. Using a function instead of a value to define the elements of the list makes make-list a very general function that can be used in many contexts. The function make-list is a good example of procedural abstraction facilitating code reuse. One call to make-list will produce all the chromosomes, and another nested call will produce the genes in a chromosome. The argument create is a function that produces an allele.

Creating an initial population

```
; Randomly create a population of pop-size individuals.
(define (random-pop pop-size chromosome-length create)
  (make-list pop-size
    (lambda (n) (make-list chromosome-length create) )) )

> (random-pop 4 5 (lambda () (random 10)))
((4 3 3 9 7) (9 4 5 3 7) (2 7 2 1 8) (7 3 6 0 7))
```

Our random population can be passed to a function that simulates a generation in our genetic system. In calculating each generation we must carry out the following actions:

- sort the population according to the fitness measure
- test if we have reached our exit criterion with the best individual
- if so, return the generation number and the individual
- otherwise, select the parents to produce the next generation
- perform crosslinking on the parents
- perform mutation according to the mutation probability m-prob
- select the best members from this new generation and the prior generation and pass those along as the next generation

Actions for one generation

```
; Main function for performing genetic algorithms.
(define (generation sorted-pop fitness done? select m-prob create
          count)
  (display sorted-pop)
  (newline)
  (if (done? (first sorted-pop) count)
      (list count (first sorted-pop))
      (let* ((parents (select sorted-pop))
             (children (mutate (crosslink parents) m-prob create))
             (new-pop (subseq (sort fitness
                                    (append sorted-pop children))
                              0 (length sorted-pop))))
        (generation new-pop fitness done? select m-prob create
          (+ count 1)))) )
```

A helper function is a good idea to save the user the bother of passing in the initial counter and sorting the initial random population.

```
; Helper function for generation - sorts population.
(define (gen-algo population fitness done? select m-prob create)
  (generation (sort fitness population) fitness done? select m-prob
    create 0) )
```

Sorting the population

Now let's write the additional functions we need. To sort the population we can use the insertion sort function from Chapter 8, which is repeated here:

```
; Perform insertion sort on a-list according to compare-func.
(define (sort compare-func a-list)
  (if (null? a-list)
      '()
      (insert
        (first a-list)
        (sort compare-func (rest a-list))
        compare-func)) )
```

```
; Insert element into sorted-list using compare-func.
(define (insert element sorted-list compare-func)
  (cond ((null? sorted-list)
           (list element))
        ((compare-func element (first sorted-list))
           (cons element sorted-list))
        (else
           (cons (first sorted-list)
             (insert element (rest sorted-list) compare-func)))) )
```

Selecting parents

The selection function will use two global variables: cross%, the percentage of the population that should be crosslinked, and best%, the percentage of the parents that come from the best of the population ordered by fitness (the remainder are chosen randomly from the rest of the population). From these percentages we can calculate the exact number of parents and the number of parents that come from the best of the sorted population. In making these calculations we should round off the results instead of truncating them. Scheme has a built-in function **round** that can be used for this purpose.

```
; Select parents from the sorted population.
(define (select-parents sorted-pop)
  (let* ((num-parents (round (* (length sorted-pop) cross%)))
         (num-best (round (* num-parents best%))))
    (append (subseq sorted-pop 0 num-best)
      (choose-from (subseq sorted-pop num-best)
        (- num-parents num-best)))) )
```

The function `choose-from` takes a population and a number and randomly picks that many individuals from the population. It does not pick the same individual more than once. To assure this it recurses with the population of all individuals except the one just selected.

```
; Choose num individuals randomly from population.
(define (choose-from pop-list num)
  (if (= 0 num)
      '()
      (let ((elt-pos (random (length pop-list))))
        (cons (list-ref pop-list elt-pos)
              (choose-from (append (subseq pop-list 0 elt-pos)
                                   (subseq pop-list (+ elt-pos 1)))
                (- num 1)))))) )
```

Let's test these functions choosing a crosslink percentage of 60% and taking 75% of the parents for crosslinking from the best (most fit) individuals and the remainder from the rest of the population.

```
(define cross% 0.6)   ; crosslink 60% of the population
(define best% 0.75)   ; 75% of the parents are the best individuals

> (select-parents '((4 5) (2 2) (2 6) (3 0) (3 9) (2 3)))
((4 5) (2 2) (2 6) (3 9))
```

Sixty percent of the population (four individuals) are selected and 75% (three) of these are from the head of the population list. The fourth individual is randomly chosen from the remaining three individuals in the population list, either `(3 0)`, `(3 9)`, or `(2 3)`.

After selecting a set of parents, we must pair and crosslink them. The pairs should be randomly chosen. We can either choose individuals from the population one by one and pair them, or rearrange the entire population and then take pairs in order from this shuffled population. Which approach do you think is easier?

Implementing crosslinking

In the first approach, `choose-from` can be used to get one or two random individuals, but then we'll have to write a "remove one instance" function that removes only one item from the population (there may be duplicates). This sounds easier than shuffling the entire population. However, we can shuffle the population with a single call to `choose-from` using the population size as the number of items to choose. Sometimes the functions we create can have surprising extra benefits. Finally, we must create another function `crosspair` that forms pairs and crosslinks them.

```
; Reorder population then call crosspair to perform crosslinking.
(define (crosslink population)
  (crosspair (choose-from population (length population))) )

; Sequence through pop applying crossover to successive pairs.
(define (crosspair pop)
  (cond ((null? pop) '())
        ((null? (cdr pop)) pop)
        (else (append (crossover (first pop) (second pop))
                      (crosspair (cddr pop)))))) )
```

The crossover point is randomly chosen. We can randomly pick a position in the chromosome and then use subseq to split the chromosomes around the crossover point.

```
; Generate two new offspring by crosslinking two chromosomes.
(define (crossover chromosome1 chromosome2)
  (let ((cross-pos (random (length chromosome1))))
    (list
      (append (subseq chromosome1 0 cross-pos)
              (subseq chromosome2 cross-pos))
      (append (subseq chromosome2 0 cross-pos)
              (subseq chromosome1 cross-pos)))) )
```

Trying out these new functions, we get the following results:

```
> (crosslink '((a b c) (d e f) (1 2 3) (4 5 6)))
((4 b c) (a 5 6) (1 2 3) (d e f))
```

The first pair of genes results from crosslinking (a b c) and (4 5 6). The second pair is from crosslinking (d e f) and (1 2 3). It looks like a crossover did not occur in the second pair, but it did; however, the position was 0, so the crosslinking combines an empty list with the entire second parent. We should fix this by restricting the crossover point to be between 1 and the length of the list minus 1 inclusive. Here is the new code and another trial run:

```
; Generate two new offspring by crosslinking two chromosomes.
(define (crossover chromosome1 chromosome2)
  (let ((cross-pos (+ 1 (random (- (length chromosome1) 1)))))
    (list
      (append (subseq chromosome1 0 cross-pos)
              (subseq chromosome2 cross-pos))
      (append (subseq chromosome2 0 cross-pos)
              (subseq chromosome1 cross-pos)))) )
```

```
> (crosslink '((a b c) (d e f) (1 2 3) (4 5 6)))
((1 e f) (d 2 3) (a b 6) (4 5 c))
```

Try some additional examples to convince yourself that this code actually works.

Implementing mutation

Mutation involves sequencing through all the genes in the population and randomly deciding if they should change according to the mutation probability.

```
; Mutate random genes in population according to probability.
; Use create to produce a new allele.
(define (mutate population probability create)
  (map (lambda (individual)
         (map (lambda (gene)
                (if (< (random 100) (* probability 100))
                    (create)
                    gene) )
           individual) )
    population) )
```

Let's try a sample call with a very high mutation rate of 50%.

```
> (mutate '((4 5) (2 2) (2 6) (3 0) (3 9) (2 3)) 0.50
    (lambda () (random 10)))
((4 8) (2 2) (3 1) (9 0) (0 3) (2 3))
```

Now we are ready to try a sample problem. The task is to find a chromosome with numbers that add up to thirty exactly. Our population size is four and our alleles are numbers between zero and nine. The function to determine if we are done is easy to create.

Sample problem: finding a chromosome that totals thirty

```
; Test if genes in individual sum to 30.
(define (thirty? individual generation)
  (= (apply + individual) 30) )
```

The fitness function should compare the absolute values of the differences between the actual sum in the chromosome and thirty. This way, going over thirty is treated the same as being under thirty.

Fitness function

```
; Fitness comparison between chromosomes c1 and c2.
(define (fit c1 c2)
  (<= (abs (- (apply + c1) 30))
      (abs (- (apply + c2) 30))) )
```

Let's try our genetic algorithm out using a four-member population with chromosomes that are four genes long. We'll use 1% as the mutation rate.

```
> (gen-algo (random-pop 4 4 (lambda () (random 10))) fit thirty?
    select-parents 0.01 (lambda () (random 10)))
((5 5 9 9) (5 1 4 8) (1 6 3 3) (0 1 1 5))
((5 5 9 9) (5 1 9 9) (5 5 4 8) (5 1 4 8))
((5 7 9 9) (5 5 9 9) (5 1 9 9) (5 1 9 9))
(2 (5 7 9 9))
```

Given the values of cross% and best%, the first two chromosomes will be crosslinked each time. In the first generation (5 5 9 9) and (5 1 4 8) are crosslinked and (5 1 9 9) and (5 5 4 8) are produced. In the next generation (5 5 9 9) and (5 1 9 9) are crosslinked producing (5 5 9 9) and (5 1 9 9). Notice that regardless of the crosspoint, the children will be clones of the parents. However, there was a visible mutation and (5 5 9 9) became (5 7 9 9), which totals thirty. This was very lucky. In twelve trials the average time to complete was two-hundred generations.

In the next example we weren't as lucky as we were in the first trial:

```
> (gen-algo (random-pop 4 4 (lambda () (random 10))) fit thirty?
  select-parents 0.01 (lambda () (random 10)))
((8 6 9 6) (9 7 3 6) (5 9 5 2) (2 4 0 2))
((8 6 9 6) (9 7 9 6) (9 7 3 6) (8 6 3 6))
((8 6 9 6) (9 7 9 6) (9 7 9 6) (8 6 9 6))
((8 6 9 6) (9 7 9 6) (9 7 9 6) (8 6 9 6))
((8 6 9 6) (9 7 9 6) (9 7 9 6) (8 6 9 6))
((8 6 9 6) (9 7 9 6) (9 7 9 6) (8 6 9 6))
((8 6 9 6) (9 7 9 6) (9 7 9 6) (8 6 9 6))
((8 6 9 6) (9 7 9 6) (9 7 9 6) (8 6 9 6))
((8 6 9 6) (9 7 9 6) (9 7 9 6) (8 6 9 6))
((8 7 9 6) (9 6 9 6) (8 6 9 6) (9 7 9 6))
(9 (8 7 9 6))
```

Gene and population convergence

This trial is a good example of *gene convergence*. After one generation the last gene in the entire population has the same allele, six. When 95% of the population has the same gene, that gene has converged. After two generations the third and fourth genes have converged. In many of the other trials I ran the entire population converged—all the genes had converged. Crosslinking cannot change the values of these genes, only mutation can.

In the ninth generation (8 6 9 6) and (9 7 9 6) crosslink between the first two genes, producing (8 7 9 6) and (9 6 9 6) which both add to thirty. This trial wasn't too bad. One trial took 552 generations to get the answer.

There are a couple problems lurking here. One is that we have no way to safeguard against population convergence. If we choose larger populations, we can slow this process down because more individuals participate in the crosslinking. In our simple example above only the first two elements of the sorted population are used each time as parents. We can take another measure which is to take the union of the old and new generation in generation instead of appending the two populations. The order of the arguments to union is very important. Look at the code for union in section 7.4 of Chapter 7. It adds elements from the first set onto the second if they don't exist in the second set. We should call union with the offspring as the first argument and the old population as the second argument.

```
; Main function for performing genetic algorithms.
(define (generation sorted-pop fitness done? select m-prob create
         count)
  (display sorted-pop)
  (newline)
  (if (done? (first sorted-pop) count)
      (list count (first sorted-pop))
      (let* ((parents (select sorted-pop))
             (children (mutate (crosslink parents) m-prob create))
             (new-pop (subseq (sort fitness
                                    (union children sorted-pop))
                       0 (length sorted-pop))))
        (generation new-pop fitness done? select m-prob create
          (+ count 1)))) )
```

Below is a trial with this new code. Notice that there are no duplicates in the population.

Retrial of totaling thirty

```
> (gen-algo (random-pop 4 4 (lambda () (random 10))) fit thirty?
    select-parents 0.01 (lambda () (random 10)))
((9 3 8 9) (8 6 5 7) (7 9 6 0) (8 4 2 2))
((9 3 8 9) (8 3 8 9) (9 6 5 7) (8 6 5 7))
((9 3 8 9) (8 3 8 9) (9 6 5 7) (8 6 5 7))
((9 3 8 9) (8 3 8 9) (9 6 5 7) (8 6 5 7))
((9 3 8 9) (8 3 8 9) (9 6 5 7) (8 6 5 7))
((9 3 8 9) (8 3 8 9) (9 6 5 7) (8 6 5 7))
((8 3 9 9) (9 3 8 9) (8 3 8 9) (9 6 5 7))
((9 3 9 9) (8 3 9 9) (9 3 8 9) (8 3 8 9))
(7 (9 3 9 9))
```

This again is one of the faster cases. The average time to reach a solution was just a bit less than with the earlier version of `generation`.

Do genetic algorithms provide an improvement over just randomly generating lists? Let's test this out. Here is a simple, but generic, function that generates and tests chromosomes until a completion test is satisfied. The chromosomes are generated given their size and a gene creation function.

Comparison with randomly generated chromosomes

```
; Randomly make chromosomes until done? is true.  chromosome-size
; and create define the size and gene makeup of the chromosomes.
(define (guess count chromosome-size create done?)
  (let ((try (make-list chromosome-size create)))
    (if (done? try count)
        (list count try)
        (guess (+ count 1) chromosome-size create done?))) )
```

This function is called as follows:

```
(guess 0 4 (lambda (n) (random 10)) thirty?)
```

In sample runs `guess` found the solution in about half the number of cycles or generations as `gen-algo`. So what is the use of creating a genetic algorithm? It has been shown that genetic algorithms should perform better than random trials. We should take a more careful look at our control parameters.

With this problem and the crosslinking parameters used, mutation often plays a big role in generating the final solution. Selection and crosslinking get us close very early on. But crosslinking only the best two members of the population limits the offspring possibilities. We can increase the crosslinking by changing the `cross%` and `best%` values to be 100%, as follows:

Adjusting the crosslinking rate

```
(define cross% 1.0)
(define best% 1.0)
```

There are other possibilities as well. Rather than increase the crosslinking rate by changing the crosslinking variables, we can increase the population and use the old crosslinking values. This will increase the number of crosslinking operations. Or we can take a completely different approach and instead of increasing the crosslinking, we can increase the mutation rate. The table below gives average figures based on a dozen trials for each different configuration. Unless

Adjusting other parameters

indicated, assume the crosslinking is 60% and the mutation rate is 1%.

Summary of trial results

description of GA	average generations to reach goal
original generation	200
new generation	189
random guess	94
100% crosslinking	47
10% mutation	24
population = 10	7
all three above	4

These numbers are somewhat misleading, as they count generations, and with larger population sizes more individuals are tested in each generation. Plus the random guess trials only test one individual at each generation.

Magic square

Let's try a different example that is a variation on the magic square problem. Imagine a three-by-three matrix of numbers like this:

```
4 6 5
7 5 3
4 4 7
```

The goal of this puzzle is to pick numbers for each box such that the sum of each row, column, and diagonal is fifteen. In this example every row and column sums to fifteen, but one diagonal sums to sixteen and the other to fourteen.

Chromosome representation

To build a genetic algorithm to solve this, we'll need to create a fitness function, a function that tests if we are done, and an encoding of the box phenotype into a chromosome. We can take the numbers in row-order (row-by-row) without any nesting and make that our chromosome representation. The example above would be

```
(4 6 5 7 5 3 4 4 7)
```

The fitness and completion functions are similar to the functions in the sum-to-thirty problem except eight sums must be examined. To add up the rows, it is easier to use the phenotype representation

```
((4 6 5) (7 5 3) (4 4 7))
```

Converting from genotype to phenotype

To convert from the genotype to the phenotype, we can use the following function that uses make-list and produces the proper positions of the numbers in the puzzle. This function is general and can work with any size puzzle.

```
; Convert chromosome genotype to phenotype nested list.
(define (decode genotype size)
  (make-list size
    (lambda (row)
      (make-list size
        (lambda (elt) (list-ref genotype
                      (+ (* (- row 1) size) (- elt 1))) )) )) )

> (decode '(4 6 5 7 5 3 4 4 7) 3)
((4 6 5) (7 5 3) (4 4 7))
```

The following function returns a list of the sums of the rows:

Summing rows

```
; Return list of sums of all rows in puzzle.
(define (sum-rows puzzle)
  (map (lambda (row) (apply + row) ) puzzle) )

> (sum-rows '((4 6 5) (7 5 3) (4 4 7)))
(15 15 15)
```

We can use the same function to add up the columns if we convert our puzzle to a list of columns. This can be done with a simplification of the function tran-spose that we used to transpose the weights and biases of a neural network.

Summing columns

```
; Convert puzzle from list of rows to list of columns.
(define (row-to-col puzzle)
  (apply map (cons list puzzle)) )

> (row-to-col '((4 6 5) (7 5 3) (4 4 7)))
((4 7 4) (6 5 4) (5 3 7))

> (sum-rows (row-to-col '((4 6 5) (7 5 3) (4 4 7))))
(15 15 15)
```

To add the diagonals, we can either access the appropriate elements from the chromosome or we can convert the puzzle into a list of two diagonals and pass that to sum-rows. The second approach is slightly more work but is better because our code will be general and can be used for any size puzzle (e.g., four-by-four). We can sequence through the rows using map and extract the proper element from each row. This can be done by constructing a list of positions (0 to the size minus 1).

Summing diagonals

```
; Convert puzzle from list of rows to list of diagonals.
(define (row-to-diag puzzle)
  (let ((pos-list (make-list (length puzzle) (lambda (n) (- n 1)))))
    (list
      (map (lambda (pos row) (list-ref row pos) )
        pos-list puzzle)
      (map (lambda (pos row) (list-ref row pos) )
        (reverse pos-list) puzzle))) )

> (row-to-diag '((4 6 5) (7 5 3) (4 4 7)))
((4 5 7) (5 5 4))

> (sum-rows (row-to-diag '((4 6 5) (7 5 3) (4 4 7))))
(16 14)
```

We can put all of these functions together in one function that returns a fitness value for a puzzle.

Fitness and completion measurements

```
; Return fitness measure for puzzle - sum of absolute values of
; differences between each row, column, and diagonal and 15.
(define (sum-diffs puzzle)
  (apply +
    (map (lambda (sum)
           (abs (- sum 15)) )
      (append (sum-rows puzzle) (sum-rows (row-to-col puzzle))
        (sum-rows (row-to-diag puzzle))))) )
```

Using the fitness measurement, we can write functions to compare two chromosomes and to test if we are done:

```
; Fitness function for chromosomes c1 and c2.
(define (fit8 c1 c2)
  (<= (sum-diffs (decode c1 (truncate (sqrt (length c1)))))
      (sum-diffs (decode c2 (truncate (sqrt (length c2))))) ) )

; Test if puzzle's rows, columns, and diagonals all sum to 15.
(define (all-fifteen? puzzle generation)
  (= (sum-diffs
       (decode puzzle (truncate (sqrt (length puzzle)))))
     0) )
```

Sample trials

Now let's call `gen-algo` to solve this problem. We'll use a population of size twenty and crosslink 75% (fifteen individuals) of the population choosing 60% (nine individuals) from the best of the population. The mutation rate is 1%.

```
(define cross% 0.75)
(define best% 0.6)

(gen-algo (random-pop 20 9 (lambda () (random 10))) fit8
  all-fifteen? select-parents 0.01 (lambda () (random 10)))
```

Here are some of the resulting solutions:

5 5 5	3 7 5	6 5 4	4 7 4	4 4 7	6 1 8	4 3 8
5 5 5	7 5 3	3 5 7	5 5 5	8 5 2	7 5 3	9 5 1
5 5 5	5 3 7	6 5 4	6 3 6	3 6 6	2 9 4	2 7 6

The leftmost result is the simplest solution to this problem. Moving to the right the solutions use three, five, seven, and nine different numbers. The last two solutions are solutions to the true magic square problem in which each number is used only once.

Comparison with randomly generated squares

Given a sample of forty trials, the average number of generations to reach a solution was about 150 generations. Once again we can compare our genetic algorithm with completely randomly generated chromosomes using the `guess` function. These can be generated using the following call:

```
(guess 0 9 (lambda (n) (random 10)) all-fifteen?)
```

If you decide to run this, don't wait for the answer unless you feel really lucky. There are a billion possible chromosomes that can be generated and not too many correct solutions. This call took about ten days (yes days, not minutes) to run and it finally got an answer after 22,651,059 attempts generating the chromosome (4 5 6 7 5 3 4 5 6). Compare this with another probability game—your chances of winning the California lottery where you choose six numbers out of 51 are one in 18,009,460 (not repeating any numbers, and order does not matter). If you are starting to think that soft computing techniques can be used to pick lottery numbers, it is already being done for lottery numbers, stock markets, and international currencies.

16.4.2 Exercises

16.13 The second version of `generation` took the `union` of the offspring and the old population. Why does the order of these two arguments matter in the call to `union`?

16.14 Write functions to carry out reordering and inversion of chromosomes. Define two variables to represent the reordering and inversion rates and change the `generation` function to invoke these for the proper number of parents.

16.15 None of the solutions to the simplified magic square problem had the number zero in the answer. Why do you think this is so?

16.16 All of the solutions to the simplified magic square problem had the number five as the middle gene. Why do you think this is so?

16.17 What do you predict will be the effect of increasing the mutation rate on the simplified magic square problem? Test your hypothesis.

16.18 Do you think that doubling the population will cut the number of generations to solve the simplified magic square problem in half? What about halving the population—will that double the average number of generations to reach a solution?

16.19 Create a new problem and design a way of decoding the phenotypes into chromosomes. Next create gene creation, chromosome fitness, and completion functions and then test out your problem with a genetic algorithm. Compare the solution time using a genetic algorithm to using a call to the function `guess`, which generates purely random chromosomes.

16.5 Mixing Metaphors to Create Better Systems

It is possible to combine fuzzy logic, neural networks, and genetic algorithms to produce systems that perform better than their nonmixed equivalents. Systems are usually mixed to overcome difficult areas that exist within each system.

A fuzzy logic system has difficulties working well until its fuzzy sets are tuned. In the case of TSK systems, the parameters must be tuned as well. This is a difficult process that cannot always be done by human intuition alone. Often a lot

Difficulties in fuzzy logic

of *tweaking* (making fine adjustments) is necessary. This becomes a long, tedious process.

Difficulties in neural networks

Neural networks may be slow in learning (forming a set of connection weights and biases that enable inputs to produce the desired outputs). This is a very time-consuming, compute-intensive process, and for some inputs and desired outputs, the system may never converge on a working set of connection weights.

Difficulties in genetic algorithms

Genetic algorithms have limitations in their ability to evolve to a desirable population. This happens because the crosslinking and mutations may take a great deal of time to yield a good population. When genes or entire chromosomes converge, learning by crosslinking and asexual reproduction slows down and mutation becomes the driving force, but mutation is typically kept to small frequencies for best results when convergence does not occur.

Neuro-fuzzy systems

In all the combinations one system takes on the primary or leading role and the other system or systems take on supporting roles. For example, a *neuro-fuzzy system* may use either the neural network or the fuzzy logic system as its primary model and the other system to support some aspect to make up for the weaknesses in the primary system.

A fuzzy logic system can be combined with a neural network to produce a neuro-fuzzy system. One example of this is a fuzzy expert system that uses a neural network to learn fuzzy set values or parameter values (in the case of TSK systems). For example, a neural network can be trained to learn the relationship of some values and their corresponding membership grades. Then other membership grades for the same fuzzy set can be obtained by passing in their values as inputs and getting the membership grades as outputs from the neural net. The ability of neural nets to generalize is being used to interpolate membership grades.

A different approach is to represent the fuzzy sets as weights in a neural network and update them according to how far the fuzzy system veers from its desired outputs. The weights should not be initialized to random values, but have values based on reasonable estimates. Back propagation will slowly adjust the weights. Rather than propagate inputs forward, the test for correction is to run the inputs through the fuzzy logic system and determine how well the system performs. This is a supervised learning approach.

Another possibility is to use unsupervised learning approaches. These take advantage of neural net's abilities to generalize and categorize. Networks are provided with numerous training sets of expert behavior within the realm that the fuzzy system is trying to perform. Eventually the system groups and categorizes these inputs that are pairs of inputs to the fuzzy system and the outputs desired. By carefully examining these groupings and their degree of fuzziness, fuzzy sets can be created.

Fuzzy-genetic systems

Ideas from fuzzy logic and genetic algorithms can be combined to produce *fuzzy-genetic systems*. Genetic algorithms can use fuzzy rules to choose the parameters of the genetic algorithm like crossover and mutation rate and population size. Another use of fuzzy rules is measuring the fitness of individuals in a population.

Instead of adjusting fuzzy sets or parameters in TSK systems by hand, genetic algorithms can be used in which the fuzzy sets or parameters are chromosomes that undergo crosslinkings and mutations to evolve into better fuzzy sets/parameters. Even entire fuzzy rules can be encoded as chromosomes and adjusted using a genetic algorithm. Their performance is measured by the quality of the fuzzy system.

Just as fuzzy rules can be used to decide crossover and mutation rates, neural networks can be developed to do the same, resulting in *neuro-genetic systems*.

Neuro-genetic systems

A neural net can genetically learn connection weights instead of using Hebbian or back-prop learning approaches. A population of networks is used and the best networks survive. Since genetic algorithms tend to move quickly toward reasonable solutions, this may be a means of speeding up learning in neural networks. After a number of generations, the best weight set can be fine-tuned using a traditional neural network learning approach.

Genetic algorithms can be used to optimize the characteristics of a neural network: the number of units, layers, learning rate, momentum, or tolerance factor in deciding when the actual outputs are close enough to the desired outputs.

16.6 Future Trends

Since soft computing is such a new field, a great deal of the research has been and continues to be in testing soft computing techniques against traditional methods in specific problem areas. This has provided a great deal of information into the general applicability of these techniques. Where weaknesses are encountered, attempts are made to combine soft computing techniques to get around the problems. General methods for doing this are still not well understood.

Fuzzy logic is used in many commercial products. We should expect to see fuzzy logic become more of a buzz word and be accepted technology in many of our consumer electronics goods, although marketing people may find challenges selling fuzzy camera focus mechanisms. The process of creating fuzzy sets is still a difficult problem and a strong contender for improvement through research efforts.

Fuzzy logic in commercial products

Two extensions of fuzzy logic are *information granulation* and *computing with words*. Information granulation can be thought of as fuzzy partitioning, taking objects and dividing them into smaller pieces or into similar or functionally equivalent parts. Granulation can be crisp or fuzzy. For example, a house can be divided into specific rooms (living room, dining room) or into clean rooms versus messy rooms. This second division is fuzzy because clean and messy are fuzzy concepts. For many problems, fuzzy granulation is more practical or natural than crisp granulation.

Information granulation

Computing with words is computation using words as the driving factor. Fuzzy systems take numbers and fuzzify them, then defuzzify the final outcome into crisp values. Computing with words takes fuzzy values and produces fuzzy values. For example, the question "How wealthy is she?" can result in a fuzzy

Computing with words

Neural network
futures

answer (e.g., very rich) instead of a crisp answer like $1,547,842.34. Computing with words converts the fuzzy value wealthy into the fuzzy amount very rich.

Neural networks have not had the commercial success that fuzzy logic systems have, but have done well in complex areas in which the relationships between inputs and outputs are not well understood and do not lend themselves to symbolic representation techniques. Although neural nets can solve such problems, there is great interest in being able to understand networks so that rules can be extracted. There are techniques to do this, but they tend to be complex and limited in how well they work. Rule insertion is desired as well. There are problems that are understood and instead of building a network from random values, being able to create initial approximate weights based on existing knowledge of the system is desired.

Genetic algorithm
futures

Genetic algorithms are perhaps the least exploited of the soft computing fields. They offer great promise as a search technique or as a generation mechanism to create novel solutions. For example, genetic algorithms have been used to make computer paint brushes to create artistically appealing textures. The difficulties with genetic algorithms are in the adjustment of the parameters to get the best performance and in the creation of good fitness functions. As more problems are attempted with genetic algorithms, we should develop better heuristics for using them in a variety of contexts.

16.7 Summary

- Soft computing is a mix of fuzzy logic, neural networks, and probabilistic reasoning of which genetic algorithms is a subfield.
- Fuzzy logic is an extension of conventional logic that allows values that lie between true and false.
- Fuzzy sets represent uncrisp concepts like tall, rich, and fast. A fuzzy set is a mapping between real values like six feet and membership grades that are between zero and one. Membership grades give the degree to which a value represents a fuzzy set.
- Linguistic variables have fuzzy sets as values; for example, height is a linguistic variable that can take values like tall or short.
- Fuzzy expert systems use fuzzy sets and fuzzy rules to represent expert knowledge. They take crisp values and fuzzify them, then find all applicable fuzzy rules and combine them according to the membership grades and produce a new fuzzy set. This fuzzy set is defuzzified to return crisp output values.
- Neural networks are models inspired by neurons in the brain. These networks contain a number of highly interconnected neurons or units. The strength of the connection between two units is called a connection weight.
- Units are organized into layers where the units in each layer are connected to all the units in the layers immediately above and below. The input layer takes inputs and passes them into the network, hidden layers lie between input and output layers, and the output layer gets input from an input or hidden layer

and passes values as the output of the network.

- Propagation is the passing of information through the network from the inputs to the input layer, then to each subsequent layer until the output layer.
- The input to a unit is the sum of all the outputs from the units in the layer below multiplied by the connection weights joining them. This sum is added to the unit's bias and applied to a sigmoidal function to form the activation level of the unit.
- Back propagation and Hebbian learning are used to teach a network to map a collection of inputs to a collection of outputs. Back propagation makes small adjustments to the connection weights and biases until the inputs produce the desired outputs.
- Genetic algorithms are inspired by theories of evolution and genetics. Potential solutions to a problem are encoded as chromosomes (a fixed length list of numbers or characters). Chromosomes are made up of genes.
- The population is ordered according to a fitness measurement. A set of parents is selected from the population and combined via crosslinking.
- Crosslinking switches the genes of two chromosomes around a switch point to form two new chromosomes.
- Mutation changes a single gene in a chromosome.
- Reordering reorders the genes in a chromosome and inversion reverses the genes in a section of a chromosome.
- After the chromosomes are updated through some combination of crosslinking, mutation, reordering, and/or inversion, a new population is chosen based on the fitness measurement of the new offspring and the old population. Then the whole process continues with the new population.
- The genetic algorithm finishes when some member of the population meets a stopping criterion.

16.8 Additional Reading

Fuzzy Logic

Cox, E.D. (1995). *Fuzzy Logic for Business and Industry*, Charles River Media Inc., Rockland, MA.

Kosko, B. (1993). *Fuzzy Thinking: The New Science of Fuzzy Logic*, Hyperion, New York, NY.

Von Altrock, C. (1995). *Fuzzy Logic and NeuroFuzzy Applications Explained*, Prentice Hall PTR, Englewood Cliffs, N.J.

Neural Networks

Kosko, B. (1992). *Neural Networks and Fuzzy Systems: A Dynamical Systems Approach to Machine Intelligence*, Prentice Hall, Englewood Cliffs, NJ.

McClelland, J.L., Rumelhart, D.E., and the PDP Research Group (1986). *Parallel Distributed Processing: Explorations in the Microstructure of Cognition*, Volume 2: Psychological and Biological Models, MIT Press, Cambridge, MA.

Rumelhart, D.E., McClelland, J.L., and the PDP Research Group (1986). *Parallel Distributed Processing: Explorations in the Microstructure of Cognition*, Volume 1: Foundations, MIT Press, Cambridge, MA.

Genetic Algorithms

Goldberg, D.E. (1989). *Genetic Algorithms in Search, Optimization, and Machine Learning*, Addison-Wesley, Reading, MA.

Koza, J.R. (1992). *Genetic Programming: On the Programming of Computers by Means of Natural Selection*, MIT Press, Cambridge, MA.

Michalewicz, Z. (1996). *Genetic Algorithms + Data Structures = Evolution Programs*, Third revision and extended edition, Springer-Verlag, Berlin, Germany.

16.9 Code Listing

Fuzzy expert system code:

```
; Create a function returning the membership grade of a crisp value.
(define (make-fuzzy-triangle left mid right)
  (lambda (crisp-num)
    (cond ((eq? crisp-num 'max) mid)
          ((or (< crisp-num left) (> crisp-num right)) 0)
          ((< crisp-num mid) (/ (- crisp-num left) (- mid left)))
          (else (/ (- right crisp-num) (- right mid)))))) )

; Fuzzify crisp-number based on fuzzy-set.
(define (fuzzify crisp-number fuzzy-set)
  (fuzzy-set crisp-number))

; Return the condition of a rule.
(define (condition rule)
  (first rule))

; Return the actions of a rule.
(define (actions rule)
  (rest rule))
```

```scheme
; Return list of applicable actions and the degree to which they
; should be applied.
(define (outputs rule-list input-values)
  (keep-if
    (lambda (evaled-rule)
      (not (zero? (car evaled-rule))))
    (map (lambda (rule)
           (cons
             (membership-grade (condition rule) input-values)
             (actions rule)))
      rule-list)) )

; Return overall membership grade of condition based on input-values.
(define (membership-grade condition input-values)
  (cond ((eq? (car condition) 'and)
           (apply min (map (lambda (clause)
                             (membership-grade clause input-values))
                      (rest condition))))
        ((eq? (car condition) 'or)
           (apply max (map (lambda (clause)
                             (membership-grade clause input-values))
                      (rest condition))))
        (else
           (fuzzify (cdr (assoc (first condition) input-values))
             (eval (second condition)))))) )

; Split multiple actions in action-list to list of single actions.
(define (transform action-list)
  (if (null? action-list)
      '()
      (append
        (map (lambda (action) (cons (caar action-list) action) )
          (cdar action-list))
        (transform (rest action-list)))) )

; Reduce duplicate actions to one with the largest strength.
(define (no-duplicates action-list)
  (if (null? action-list)
      '()
      (let ((duplicates
              (keep-if (lambda (action)
                         (equal? (rest action) (cdar action-list)))
                action-list)))
        (if (null? (rest duplicates))
            (cons (first action-list)
              (no-duplicates (rest action-list)))
            (cons (cons (apply max (map first duplicates))
                    (cdar action-list))
                  (no-duplicates
                    (set-difference action-list duplicates)))))) )
```

```scheme
; Defuzzify actions in action-list returning crisp values.
(define (defuzzify action-list)
  (if (null? action-list)
      '()
      (let ((same-var
              (keep-if (lambda (action)
                         (equal? (second action)
                           (cadar action-list)))
                action-list)))
        (cons
          (list
            (second (first same-var))
            (/ (apply + (map (lambda (action)
                               (* (first action)
                                 (fuzzify 'max
                                   (eval (third action)))))
                          same-var))
              (apply + (map first same-var))))
          (defuzzify (set-difference action-list same-var)))))) )

; Evaluate rules using inputs to produce crisp results.
(define (fuzzy-eval rules inputs)
  (defuzzify
    (no-duplicates
      (transform
        (outputs rules inputs)))) )
```

Neural network and back propagation code:

```scheme
(define learn-rate 0.5)
(define momentum 0.9)

; Return weighted sum of inputs to a single unit plus bias.
(define (total-input inputs weights)
  (+ (car weights) (apply + (map * inputs (cdr weights)))) )

; Apply the limiting sigmoidal function that restricts the total
; input to be a value between 0 and 1.
(define (sig total-input)
  (/ 1 (+ 1 (expt 2.71828 (- total-input)))) )

; Return list of activations to nodes in a layer.
(define (act-layer inputs layer-weights)
  (map (lambda (weights) (sig (total-input inputs weights)) )
    layer-weights) )
```

```
; Return a list of the activation levels in a network beginning with
; the input layer.
(define (propagate all-weights acts)
  (if (null? all-weights)
      (list acts)
      (cons
        acts
        (propagate
          (rest all-weights)
          (act-layer acts (first all-weights)))))) )

; Compute error signals for output layer units.
(define (error-sig-output targets outputs)
  (map (lambda (target output)
         (* (- target output) output (- 1 output)) )
    targets outputs) )

; Transpose the weights for back-prop.
(define (transpose weights)
  (reverse
    (map (lambda (layer) (cdr (apply map (cons list layer)))) )
      weights)) )

; Compute error signals for hidden layer units.
(define (error-sig-inner error-signals layer-weights outputs)
  (map (lambda (output weights)
         (* (apply + (map * error-signals weights))
            output (- 1 output)) )
    outputs layer-weights) )

; Perform back propagation on a network and returns a list of weight
; and bias changes in the form of the original weights and biases.
(define (back-prop target outputs trans-weights old-changes)
  (if (null? outputs)
      'no-outputs
      (reverse
        (descent (error-sig-output target (first outputs))
          (rest outputs) trans-weights old-changes))) )

; Recurse through a network to compute error signals and return
; connection weight and bias changes.
(define (descent error-signals outputs trans-weights old-changes)
  (if (null? outputs)
      '()
      (cons (calc-weights error-signals (first outputs)
              (first old-changes))
        (descent (error-sig-inner error-signals
                   (first trans-weights) (first outputs))
          (rest outputs) (rest trans-weights)
          (rest old-changes))))) )
```

```scheme
; Compute change in connection weights and biases for all units in
; one layer.  inputs are the activation levels of the units in the
; layer below.
(define (calc-weights error-signals inputs old-change)
  (map (lambda (error change)
           ; insert new bias change
           (cons (+ (* learn-rate error) (* momentum (car change)))
                 (map (lambda (input old-weight-change)
                        (+ (* learn-rate error input)
                           (* momentum old-weight-change)) )
                  inputs (cdr change))) )
     error-signals old-change) )

; Add the new weight and bias changes to the current weights and
; biases and returns the new weights and biases.
(define (update old-weights weight-change)
  (map (lambda (weight-layer change-layer)
           (map (lambda (weight-unit change-unit)
                  (map + weight-unit change-unit) )
            weight-layer change-layer) )
     old-weights weight-change) )

; Test if outputs are close enough to target values.
(define (avg-square-test outputs targets)
  (< (/ (apply + (map (lambda (outcome desired)
                        (expt (- outcome desired) 2) )
                   outputs targets))
        (length outputs))
     .0025) )

; Return new network with units changed according to func.
(define (net-change func weights)
  (map (lambda (layer)
           (map (lambda (unit) (func unit) ) layer) )
     weights) )

; Helper function for trainer.
(define (train input-set target-set weights learn-func frequency)
  (trainer input-set target-set weights
    (net-change (lambda (unit)
                   (map (lambda (weight) 0) unit) ) weights)
    learn-func frequency 0) )
```

```scheme
; Given training set of inputs and targets, initial weights and
; biases, old weight and bias changes, learning function, display
; frequency, and epoch counter - return the number of epochs to
; train and the new connection weights and biases after learning.
; Print outputs each frequency epochs.
(define (trainer input-set target-set weights old-changes
         learn-func frequency count)
  (let* ((act-set
           (map (lambda (input)
                  (reverse (propagate weights input)) )
             input-set))
         (output-set (map first act-set)))
    (if (zero? (remainder count frequency))
        (print-outputs count input-set output-set target-set))
    (if (every avg-square-test output-set target-set)
        (list count weights)
        (let* ((results (learn-func target-set act-set weights
                          old-changes))
               (weights (first results))
               (changes (second results)))
          (trainer input-set target-set weights changes
            learn-func frequency (+ count 1)))))) )

; Print the current output value for each input and indicate if
; that input has been learned.
(define (print-outputs count input-set output-set target-set)
  (display count)
  (newline)
  (for-each (lambda (input output target)
              (display input)
              (display " -> ")
              (display output)
              (display " learned: ")
              (display (avg-square-test output target))
              (newline) )
    input-set output-set target-set) )

; Pass through the target set and actual outputs using back-prop
; and adjust the weights after each call to back-prop.
(define (adjust-during target-set output-set weights old-changes)
  (if (null? target-set)
      (list weights old-changes)
      (let ((changes (back-prop (first target-set)
                       (first output-set) (transpose weights)
                       (reverse old-changes))))
        (adjust-during (rest target-set) (rest output-set)
          (update weights changes) changes))) )
```

```scheme
; Pass through the target set and actual outputs using back-prop
; and adjust the weights after the entire epoch is complete.
(define (adjust-after target-set output-set weights old-changes)
  (after target-set output-set (transpose weights) weights
    old-changes))

(define (after target-set output-set trans-weights new old-changes)
  (if (null? target-set)
      (list new old-changes)
      (let ((changes (back-prop (first target-set)
                        (first output-set) trans-weights
                        (reverse old-changes))))
        (after (rest target-set) (rest output-set) trans-weights
          (update changes new) changes))) )

; Given a description of a network - a list of numbers indicating
; how many nodes are in each layer beginning with the input layer,
; return a list of random initial connection weights and biases.
(define (random-net net-desc)
  (if (or (null? net-desc) (null? (cdr net-desc)))
      '()
      (cons (make-layer-weights (car net-desc) (second net-desc))
            (random-net (cdr net-desc)))) )

; Return random weights and biases for a layer in a network.
(define (make-layer-weights nodes-below nodes-above)
  (make-list nodes-above
            (lambda (n) (bias-&-weights nodes-below) )) )

; Return random bias and weights for a node in a network.
; The values are in the range -1 to 1.
(define (bias-&-weights num-nodes)
  (make-list (+ num-nodes 1)
            (lambda (n) (- (/ (random 1000) 500) 1) )) )

; Make a list of num-items elements with values based on func.
(define (make-list num-items func)
  (do ((num num-items (- num 1))
       (new-list '() (cons (func num) new-list)))
    ((<= num 0)
    new-list)) )
```

Genetic algorithm code:

```scheme
; Randomly create a population of pop-size individuals.
(define (random-pop pop-size chromosome-length create)
  (make-list pop-size
    (lambda (n) (make-list chromosome-length
                    (lambda (n) (create) )) )) )
```

```scheme
; Main function for performing genetic algorithms.
(define (generation sorted-pop fitness done? select m-prob create
          count)
  (display sorted-pop)
  (newline)
  (if (done? (first sorted-pop) count)
      (list count (first sorted-pop))
      (let* ((parents (select sorted-pop))
             (children (mutate (crosslink parents) m-prob create))
             (new-pop (subseq (sort fitness
                                    (union children sorted-pop))
                        0 (length sorted-pop))))
        (generation new-pop fitness done? select m-prob create
          (+ count 1)))) )

; Helper function for generation - sorts population.
(define (gen-algo population fitness done? select m-prob create)
  (generation (sort fitness population) fitness done? select m-prob
    create 0) )

; Perform insertion sort on a-list according to compare-func.
(define (sort compare-func a-list)
  (if (null? a-list)
      '()
      (insert
        (first a-list)
        (sort compare-func (rest a-list))
        compare-func)) )

; Insert element into sorted-list using compare-func.
(define (insert element sorted-list compare-func)
  (cond ((null? sorted-list)
           (list element))
        ((compare-func element (first sorted-list))
           (cons element sorted-list))
        (else
           (cons (first sorted-list)
             (insert element (rest sorted-list) compare-func)))) )

; Select parents from the sorted population.
(define (select-parents sorted-pop)
  (let* ((num-parents (round (* (length sorted-pop) cross%)))
         (num-best (round (* num-parents best%))))
    (append (subseq sorted-pop 0 num-best)
      (choose-from (subseq sorted-pop num-best)
        (- num-parents num-best)))) )
```

```scheme
; Choose num individuals randomly from population.
(define (choose-from pop-list num)
  (if (= 0 num)
      '()
      (let ((elt-pos (random (length pop-list))))
        (cons (list-ref pop-list elt-pos)
              (choose-from (append (subseq pop-list 0 elt-pos)
                                   (subseq pop-list (+ elt-pos 1)))
                  (- num 1))))) )

(define cross% 0.6)   ; crosslink 60% of the population
(define best% 0.75)   ; 75% of the parents are the best individuals

; Reorder population then call crosspair to perform crosslinking.
(define (crosslink population)
  (crosspair (choose-from population (length population))) )

; Sequence through pop applying crossover to successive pairs.
(define (crosspair pop)
  (cond ((null? pop) '())
        ((null? (cdr pop)) pop)
        (else (append (crossover (first pop) (second pop))
                      (crosspair (cddr pop))))) )


; Generate two new offspring by crosslinking two chromosomes.
(define (crossover chromosome1 chromosome2)
  (let ((cross-pos (+ 1 (random (- (length chromosome1) 1)))))
    (list
      (append (subseq chromosome1 0 cross-pos)
              (subseq chromosome2 cross-pos))
      (append (subseq chromosome2 0 cross-pos)
              (subseq chromosome1 cross-pos)))) )

; Mutate random genes in population according to probability.
; Use create to produce a new allele.
(define (mutate population probability create)
  (map (lambda (individual)
         (map (lambda (gene)
                (if (< (random 100) (* probability 100))
                    (create)
                    gene) )
              individual) )
       population) )
```

APPENDIX

1 Scheme Resources

Two items that are helpful for programming in any language are a reference manual and a compiler or interpreter. The reference manual for Scheme is called R4RS (Revised[4] Report on Scheme). It is very terse but covers the entire language. Scheme interpreters and compilers are available commercially or for free. You can get these items and a host of additional information about Scheme by checking out either the following ftp[1] site or web sites.

ftp: `swiss-ftp.ai.mit.edu`
web: `swissnet.ai.mit.edu/scheme-home.html`
        `www.cs.indiana.edu/scheme-repository/home.html`

Connect to the ftp site by specifying "anonymous" as a name and your name as a password. Under the pub directory, you will find various Scheme files and directories including reports on Scheme such as R4RS and implementations of Scheme including scm, PC-Scheme, and MIT Scheme.

The web sites are easier to explore. They have free implementations of Scheme and R4RS in postscript and HTML. In these sites or links from these sites you can find numerous free implementations of Scheme and information about Scheme including a FAQ (frequently asked questions) on Scheme.

Through these different resources you should find Scheme interpreters that run on Windows 3.1, Windows 95, Windows NT, MacOS, Linux and many UNIX platforms.

The code from the examples in this text including the extensions are available on the Web at `www.springer-ny.com/supplements/grillmeyer`. There you can also find corrections to any errors that were found in the text.

You can reach me (Oliver Grillmeyer) via e-mail at `topramen@cs.berkeley.edu`.

[1.] FTP stands for file transfer protocol and is a way of remotely connecting to a computer and receiving or sending information (e.g., programs, text, images).

2   Scheme Reference

As a convenience, the standard Scheme functions including those not covered in this text are listed below by category. Following this section is a listing of the extensions to Scheme used in this text and their implementation.

2.1   Mathematical functions

function	arguments	return value
+	0 or more *nums*	sum of arguments
-	1 or more *nums*	difference of arguments in left to right order
*	0 or more *nums*	product of arguments
/	1 or more *nums*	quotient of arguments in left to right order
<	2 or more *nums*	$num1 < num2 < ... < numN$
>	2 or more *nums*	$num1 > num2 > ... > numN$
=	2 or more *nums*	$num1 = num2 = ... = numN$
<=	2 or more *nums*	$num1 \le num2 \le ... \le numN$
>=	2 or more *nums*	$num1 \ge num2 \ge ... \ge numN$
zero?	*num*	test if $num = 0$
positive?	*num*	test if $num > 0$
negative?	*num*	test if $num < 0$
even?	*num*	test if *num* is an even number
odd?	*num*	test if *num* is an odd number
number?	*num*	test if *num* is a number (integer, real, or ratio)
real?	*num*	test if *num* is a real number
integer?	*num*	test if *num* is an integer
complex?	*num*	test if *num* is a complex number
rational?	*num*	test if *num* is a rational number
exact?	*num*	test if *num* is an exact number
inexact?	*num*	test if *num* is an inexact number
quotient	*num1 num2*	integer division of *num1* and *num2*
max	1 or more *nums*	maximum of arguments
min	1 or more *nums*	minimum of arguments
truncate	*num*	integer part of *num* (digits to the left of the decimal)
round	*num*	rounds *num* to nearest integer
floor	*num*	nearest integer that is less than *num*
ceiling	*num*	nearest integer that is greater than *num*
sqrt	*num*	square root of *num*, $\sqrt{num}$
abs	*num*	absolute value of *num*, $|num|$
expt	*num power*	exponentiation (*num* raised to *power*), num^{power}
remainder	*num1 num2*	remainder of *num1* when divided by *num2*
modulo	*num1 num2*	like `remainder` but differs with negative numbers
numerator	*num*	numerator of *num*
denominator	*num*	denominator of *num*
rationalize	*num1 num2*	simplest rational number within *num2* of *num1*
gcd	0 or more *nums*	greatest common divisor of arguments

`lcm`	0 or more *nums*	least common multiple of arguments
`exp`	*num*	e (2.71828) to the *num* power, e^{num}
`log`	*num*	natural log of *num*
`sin`	*num*	sine of *num*
`cos`	*num*	cosine of *num*
`tan`	*num*	tangent of *num*
`asin`	*num*	arcsine of *num*
`acos`	*num*	arccosine of *num*
`atan`	*num*	arctangent of *num*
`exact->inexact`	*num*	inexact representation of *num*
`inexact->exact`	*num*	exact representation of *num*
`make-rectangular`	*num1 num2*	complex number *num1* + *num2i*
`real-part`	*num*	real part of complex number *num*
`imag-part`	*num*	imaginary part of complex number *num*
`make-polar`	*num1 num2*	complex number $num1 \times e^{inum2}$
`magnitude`	*num*	magnitude of complex number *num*
`angle`	*num*	angle of complex number *num*

2.2   Atom and symbol functions

predicate	arguments	return value
`define`	*variable value*	undefined, binds *variable* to *value*
`set!`	*variable value*	undefined, rebind *variable* to *value*
`eqv?`	*arg1 arg2*	test if atoms *arg1* and *arg2* are the same
`eq?`	*arg1 arg2*	test if symbols *arg1* and *arg2* are the same
`symbol?`	*arg*	test if *arg* is a symbol

2.3   List functions

function	arguments	return value
`length`	*list*	the number of elements in *list*
`car`	*list*	first element of *list*
`cdr`	*list*	rest of *list*
`list-ref`	*list position*	element at position *pos* in *list*
`list-tail`	*list num*	*list* without the first *num* elements
`cons`	*element list*	*list* with *element* inserted at the start
`list`	*el1 ... elN*	the list (*el1 ... elN*)
`append`	*list1 ... listN*	the list formed by concatenating the elements of *list1* through *listN*
`member`	*element list*	the rest of *list* starting with the first occurrence of *element*, `#f` if *element* is not in *list*
`memq`	*element list*	like `member` but uses `eq?` for comparisons
`memv`	*element list*	like `member` but uses `eqv?` for comparisons
`reverse`	*list*	the reverse of the top-level elements of *list*
`assoc`	*element assoc-list*	the first pair in *assoc-list* whose `car` is *element*
`assq`	*element assoc-list*	like `assoc` but uses `eq?` for comparisons

`assv`	*element assoc-list*	like `assoc` but uses `eqv?` for comparisons
`equal?`	*arg1 arg2*	test if *arg1* looks the same as *arg2*
`list?`	*arg*	test if *arg* is a list
`null?`	*arg*	test if *arg* is ( )
`pair?`	*arg*	test if *arg* is a pair
`set-car!`	*list value*	undefined, rebind `car` of *list* to *value*
`set-cdr!`	*list value*	undefined, rebind `cdr` of *list* to *value*

In addition there are combinations of up to four `car` and `cdr` function calls abbreviated with a's and d's sandwiched between a "c" and an "r" (e.g., `cdar`, `cdadr`, `cadaar`).

2.4   Control special forms

```
(if condition
    action
    [ else-action ])
```

If *condition* is true, return *action*. If *condition* is false, return *else-action*. If *condition* is false and there is no *else-action*, return an undefined value.

```
(cond  (condition action1 action2 ... actionN)
       (condition action1 action2 ... actionN)
                        .
                        .
                        .
       (else  action1 action2 ... actionN)
```

Evaluates *condition*s in order and returns the last action, *actionN*, corresponding to the first *condition* that is true. If the are no *actions*, *condition* is returned. If all *condition*s are false, returns *actionN* corresponding to `else`. If all *condition*s are false and there is no `else` clause, `cond` returns an undefined value.

```
(case  key
       ((values1)  action1 action2 ... actionN)
       ((values2)  action1 action2 ... actionN)
                        .
                        .
                        .
       (else  action1 action2 ... actionN)
```

Evaluates *key* and compares it to *values* which are nonquoted atoms (treated literally). If *key* matches any atom in *values*, the corresponding *actions* are evaluated and the last action, *actionN*, is returned. If none of the atoms in any of *valuess* matches *key*, *actionN* of the `else` is returned. Otherwise if there are no matches and no `else` clause, `case` returns an undefined value.

```
(and  condition1 condition2 ... conditionN)
```

Evaluates *condition*s until a false *condition* is found or all *condition*s are true. Returns `#f` if a false *condition* is found, otherwise returns *conditionN*.

```
(or  condition1 condition2 ... conditionN)
```

Evaluates *condition*s until a true *condition* is found or all *condition*s are false. Returns first true *condition* found or `#f` if all *condition*s are false.

2.5 String and character functions

function	arguments	return value
string-length	*string*	number of characters in *string*
string-ref	*string pos*	the character at position *pos* in *string*
string	0 or more *chars*	string consisting of *chars*
make-string	*num char*	string consisting of *num* copies of *char*
string-copy	*string*	a copy of *string*
substring	*string start end*	like subseq but returns part of *string*
string-append	0 or more *strings*	like append but with *strings*
string?	*arg*	test if *arg* is a string
string=?	*str1 str2*	test if *str1* and *str2* are the same
string<?	*str1 str2*	test if *str1* is less than (alphabetically) *str2*
string>?	*str1 str2*	test if *str1* is greater than (alphabetically) *str2*
string<=?	*str1 str2*	test if *str1* is less than or equal to *str2*
string>=?	*str1 str2*	test if *str1* is greater than or equal to *str2*
string-set!	*string pos char*	undefined, rebind element at position *pos* of *string* to *char*
string-fill!	*string char*	undefined, rebind every element of *string* to *char*
char-upcase	*char*	the upper case version of *char*
char-downcase	*char*	the lower case version of *char*
char?	*arg*	test if *arg* is a character
char=?	*char1 char2*	test if *char1* and *char2* are the same
char<?	*char1 char2*	test if *char1* is less than (alphabetically) *char2*
char>?	*char1 char2*	test if *char1* is greater than (alphabetically) *char2*
char<=?	*char1 char2*	test if *char1* is less than or equal to *char2*
char>=?	*char1 char2*	test if *char1* is greater than or equal to *char2*
char-alphabetic?	*char*	test if *char* is alphabetic
char-numeric?	*char*	test if *char* is numeric
char-whitespace?	*char*	test if *char* is a whitespace character
char-upper-case?	*char*	test if *char* is upper case
char-lower-case?	*char*	test if *char* is lower case

There are versions of the ten string and character comparison functions (e.g., string=? and char>=?) that ignore the case of the letters. The letters "-ci" (for case insensitive) are attached to the function names as in string-ci=? and char-ci>=?.

2.6 Vector functions

function	arguments	return value
vector-length	*vector*	number of elements in *vector*
vector-ref	*vector pos*	the element at position *pos* in *vector*
vector	0 or more *elts*	vector consisting of *elts*
make-vector	*num elt*	vector consisting of *num* copies of *elt*
vector?	*arg*	test if *arg* is a vector
vector-set!	*vector pos value*	undefined, rebind element at position *pos* of *vector* to *value*
vector-fill!	*vector value*	undefined, rebind every element of *vector* to *value*

2.7   Conversion functions

function	arguments	return value
symbol->string	*symbol*	string equivalent of *symbol*
string->symbol	*string*	symbol equivalent of *string*
number->string	*number*	string equivalent of *number*
string->number	*string*	number equivalent of *string*
list->string	*list*	string version of the characters in *list*
string->list	*string*	list of characters in *string*
integer->char	*integer*	character equivalent of *integer*
char->integer	*char*	integer equivalent of *char*
list->vector	*list*	vector equivalent of the elements of *list*
vector->list	*vector*	list equivalent of the elements in *vector*

2.8   Functionals

function	arguments	return value
map	*function lists*	list of results from applying *function* to successive elements of *lists*
for-each	*function lists*	undefined, apply *function* to successive elements of *lists*
apply	*function list*	result of applying *function* to elements of *list*

2.9   Additional special forms and functions within Scheme

item	arguments	return value and side-effects
let	*var-value-pairs body*	bind *vars* to *values* and evaluate *body*
let*	*var-value-pairs body*	bind *vars* to *values* in order and evaluate *body*
letrec	*var-value-pairs body*	like let except *vars* can be bound to functions which can be recursive or mutually recursive
quote	*expression*	*expression* unevaluated
quasiquote	*expression*	*expression* unevaluated except for items preceded by "," or ",@"
not	*arg*	the logical opposite of *arg*
boolean?	*arg*	test if *arg* is a boolean (#t or #f)
procedure?	*arg*	test if *arg* is a procedure
begin	1 or more *expressions*	evaluate *expressions* returning result of last one
delay	*expression*	a promise to evaluate *expression* when forced
force	*promise*	result from evaluating *promise* (from a delay)
load	*string*	undefined, load contents of file named *string*
transcript-on	*string*	undefined, save the Scheme interaction in file named *string*
transcript-off	none	undefined, stop saving the Scheme interaction

define can be used to create functions. The syntax for doing this is as follows:

```
(define (function-name parameter-list)
   body)
```

The syntax of let, let*, and letrec is as follows:

```
(let ( (variable-1  value-1)
       (variable-2  value-2)
                .
                .
                .
       (variable-N  value-N)  )
  body)
```

```
(lambda (parameters) body)
```

Creates a function (closure) taking *parameters* with *body* as its actions.

```
(call-with-current-continuation function)
```

The parameter of *function* names an exit function. The body of *function* is evaluated and returns a normal result, unless the exit function is called in which case the argument to the exit function is returned.

2.10   Iteration

```
(do ( (variable1  initial-value1 [ update-value1 ])
      (variable2  initial-value2 [ update-value2 ])
                .
                .
                .
      (variableN  initial-valueN [ update-valueN ])  )
  (test exit-actions)
  body)
```

The *variable*s are bound to *initial-value*s as in let. Next *test* is evaluated and if true *exit-actions* are evaluated and the final action is returned. Otherwise *body* is evaluated and the do repeats the sequence, however *variable*s are bound to *update-value*s on subsequent iterations through the do.

2.11   I/O functions

Input functions

input function	arguments	return value
read	none	the value entered by the user
read-char	none	the character entered by the user
peek-char	none	the next character ready to be read

Output functions

function	arguments	prints out	return value
newline	none	a blank line	undefined
display	*expression*	the value of *expression*	undefined
write	*expression*	the value of *expression*	undefined
write-char	*char*	*char*	undefined

2.12 File functions

function	arguments	return value
`open-input-file`	*string*	open file named *string* for input and return port
`open-output-file`	*string*	open file named *string* for output and return port
`current-input-port`	none	the current input port
`current-output-port`	none	the current output port
`call-with-input-file`	*string function*	call *function* with the input port for *string* if it can be opened
`call-with-output-file`	*string function*	call *function* with the output port for *string* if it can be opened
`with-input-from-file`	*string function*	call *function* with no arguments after opening the file named *string* for input
`with-output-from-file`	*string function*	call *function* with no arguments after opening the file named *string* for output
`close-input-port`	*port*	undefined, close input file associated with *port*
`close-output-port`	*port*	undefined, close output file associated with *port*
`input-port?`	*arg*	test if *arg* is an input-port
`output-port?`	*arg*	test if *arg* is an output-port
`eof-object?`	*arg*	test if *arg* is an eof object
`char-ready?`	*port*	test if if there is a character ready to read on *port*

3 Functions Added as Extensions to Scheme

The following functions are not standard to Scheme, but have been added in this text. They are grouped by the categories used above for the standard functions.

3.1 Mathematical functions

The following two functions have been changed in this text's extensions to always return an exact number even if called with an inexact number.

function	arguments	return value
`truncate`	*num*	exact integer part of *num* (digits to the left of the decimal)
`round`	*num*	rounds *num* to nearest exact integer

3.2 List functions

function	arguments	return value
`first`	*list*	first element of *list*
`second`	*list*	second element of *list*
`third`	*list*	third element of *list*
`fourth`	*list*	fourth element of *list*
`fifth`	*list*	fifth element of *list*
`rest`	*list*	rest of *list* without the first element
`subseq`	*list start*	*list* with elements *start* + 1 to the end of *list*

`subseq`	*list start end*	*list* with elements *start* + 1 through *end*
`position`	*element list*	the position of *element* in *list* (counting from zero), `#f` if *element* is not in *list*
`count`	*element list*	the number of occurrences of *element* in *list*
`remove`	*element list*	*list* with all occurrences of *element* removed
`rassoc`	*element assoc-list*	the first pair in *assoc-list* whose `cdr` is *element*

3.3 Atom and symbol functions

function	arguments	return value
`atom?`	*arg*	*arg* is an atom

3.4 Functionals

function	arguments	return value
`find-if`	*test list*	first element in *list* that satisfies *test*
`find-if-not`	*test list*	first element in *list* that does not satisfy *test*
`count-if`	*test list*	number of elements in *list* that satisfy *test*
`count-if-not`	*test list*	number of elements in *list* that do not satisfy *test*
`remove-if`	*test list*	*list* without elements that satisfy *test*
`keep-if`	*test list*	*list* of elements that satisfy *test*
`every`	*test lists*	final true return value if all successive elements in *lists* satisfy *test*, `#f` otherwise
`any`	*test lists*	first true value from applying *test* to successive elements in *lists*, `#f` otherwise
`accumulate`	*bin-func list*	result of applying *bin-func* to the elements in *list* two at a time

3.5 Additional functions

function	arguments	return value
`random`	*num*	randomly generated number between 0 and *num* − 1
`union`	*set1 set2*	set of elements in either *set1* or *set2*
`intersection`	*set1 set2*	set of elements in both of *set1* and *set2*
`set-difference`	*set1 set2*	set of elements in *set1* that are not in *set2*
`adjoin`	*element set*	*set* with *element* added if its not already in *set*
`subset?`	*set1 set2*	true if all the elements of *set1* are in *set2*?

4 Implementation of Extensions

The definitions of the following extensions differ slightly from those given in the text. The extensions save the values of the functions they use in `let` variables and the extension itself is defined as a `lambda` within the `let`. This way, even if the functions that these extensions use internally are changed, the extensions maintain the old bindings to the functions and they continue to work. For example, if the function `length` were redefined, the extension `subseq` would still work even though it uses `length` because it has saved the initial definition of `length`.

```scheme
; Library files for Exploring Computer Science with Scheme
; Oliver Grillmeyer
; Version 1.5, 10/7/97
;
; Contents
; truncate (redefined to give exact number)
; round (redefined to give exact number)
; first, second, third, fourth, fifth, rest
; subseq
; position, remove, count (all use equal? for comparison)
; atom?
; find-if, find-if-not, count-if, count-if-not, remove-if, keep-if
; rassoc (uses equal? for comparison)
; every, any
; accumulate
; intersection, union, set-difference, subset?, adjoin
; random, init-random
;

; Add the following code if error does not exist in your version of Scheme
; (define error-setup 'init)
;
; (call-with-current-continuation
;    (lambda (stop)
;       (set! error-setup stop)))
;
; Print an error message made up of the arguments to the function.
; (define error
;    (let ( (newline newline) (display display) (car car) (cdr cdr)
;           (for-each for-each) (error-setup error-setup) )
;       (lambda vals
;          (newline)
;          (display "Error: ")
;          (display (car vals))
;          (for-each (lambda (val) (display " ") (display val)) (cdr vals))
;          (error-setup '.) )) )

; Redefine truncate to return an exact integer.
(set! truncate
   (let ( (truncate truncate) (inexact->exact inexact->exact) )
      (lambda (number)
         (inexact->exact (truncate number)) )) )
```

```
; Redefine round to return an exact integer.
(set! round
  (let ( (round round) (inexact->exact inexact->exact) )
    (lambda (number)
      (inexact->exact (round number)) )) )

; Return the first element of a list.
(define first car)

; Return the second element of a list.
(define second cadr)

; Return the third element of a list.
(define third caddr)

; Return the fourth element of a list.
(define fourth cadddr)

; Return the fifth element of a list.
(define fifth
  (let ( (car car) (cddddr cddddr) )
    (lambda (lst)
      (car (cddddr lst)) )) )

; Return the rest of a list.
(define rest cdr)

; Return lst without last num elements.
(define list-head
  (let ( (>= >=) (length length) (= =) (cons cons) (car car)
         (cdr cdr) )
    (lambda (lst num)
      (cond ((>= num (length lst)) '())
            ((= num 0) lst)
            (else (cons (car lst) (list-head (cdr lst) num)))) )) )

; Return subsection of lst from positions start to end-1.
(define subseq
  (let ( (length length) (null? null?) (not not) (<= <=)
         (error error) (list-head list-head) (list-tail list-tail) )
    (lambda (lst start . args)
      (let* ( (len (length lst))
              (end (if (null? args) len (car args))) )
        (cond ((not (<= 0 start len))
                 (error "Improper start value for subseq:" start))
              ((not (<= 0 start end len))
                 (error "Improper end value for subseq:" end))
              (else
                 (list-head (list-tail lst start) (- len end))))) )) )
```

```
; Return the position (base 0) of the first occurrence of elt in lst.
(define position-helper
  (let ( (null? null?) (equal? equal?) (car car) (cdr cdr) (+ +) )
    (lambda (elt lst num)
      (cond ((null? lst) #f)
            ((equal? elt (car lst)) num)
            (else (position-helper elt (cdr lst) (+ num 1))))) )) )

(define position
  (let ( (position-helper position-helper) )
    (lambda (elt lst)
      (position-helper elt lst 0) )) )

; Return lst with all occurrences of elt removed.
(define remove
  (let ( (null? null?) (equal? equal?) (car car) (cdr cdr)
         (cons cons) )
    (lambda (elt lst)
      (cond ((null? lst) '())
            ((equal? elt (car lst)) (remove elt (cdr lst)))
            (else (cons (car lst) (remove elt (cdr lst)))))) )) )

; Return the number of times elt occurs in lst.
(define count
  (let ( (null? null?) (equal? equal?) (car car) (cdr cdr) (+ +) )
    (lambda (elt lst)
      (cond ((null? lst) 0)
            ((equal? elt (car lst))  (+ 1 (count elt (cdr lst))))
            (else (count elt (cdr lst)))) )) )

; Return #t if item is a symbol or a number, #f otherwise.
(define atom?
  (let ( (symbol? symbol?) (number? number?) )
    (lambda (item)
      (or (symbol? item) (number? item)) )) )

; Return the first element in lst that satisfies func, or #f if no
; elements satisfy func.
(define find-if
  (let ( (null? null?) (car car) (cdr cdr) )
    (lambda (func lst)
      (cond ((null? lst) #f)
            ((func (car lst)) (car lst))
            (else (find-if func (cdr lst)))) )) )
```

```
; Return the first element in lst that does not satisfy func, or #f
; if all elements satisfy func.
(define find-if-not
   (let ( (null? null?) (not not) (car car) (cdr cdr) )
      (lambda (func lst)
         (cond ((null? lst) #f)
               ((not (func (car lst))) (car lst))
               (else (find-if-not func (cdr lst)))) )) )

; Return the number of elements in lst that satisfy func.
(define count-if
   (let ( (null? null?) (car car) (cdr cdr) (+ +) )
      (lambda (func lst)
         (cond ((null? lst) 0)
               ((func (car lst)) (+ 1 (count-if func (cdr lst))))
               (else (count-if func (cdr lst)))) )) )

; Return the number of elements in lst that do not satisfy func.
(define count-if-not
   (let ( (null? null?) (not not) (car car) (cdr cdr) (+ +) )
      (lambda (func lst)
         (cond ((null? lst) 0)
               ((not (func (car lst)))
                  (+ 1 (count-if-not func (cdr lst))))
               (else (count-if-not func (cdr lst)))) )) )

; Return lst with all elements satisfying func removed.
(define remove-if
   (let ( (null? null?) (car car) (cdr cdr) (cons cons) )
      (lambda (func lst)
         (cond ((null? lst) '())
               ((func (car lst))
                  (remove-if func (cdr lst)))
               (else
                  (cons (car lst) (remove-if func (cdr lst)))) )) )

; Return lst with all elements satisfying func.
(define keep-if
   (let ( (null? null?) (not not) (car car) (cdr cdr) (cons cons) )
      (lambda (func lst)
         (cond ((null? lst) '())
               ((not (func (car lst)))
                  (keep-if func (cdr lst)))
               (else
                  (cons (car lst) (keep-if func (cdr lst)))) )) )
```

```
; Like assoc but return the first pair whose cdr matches elt.
(define rassoc
   (let ( (find-if find-if) (equal? equal?) (cdr cdr) )
      (lambda (elt assoc-list)
         (find-if (lambda (dotted-pair)
                     (equal? (cdr dotted-pair) elt) )
            assoc-list) )) )

; every and any each take a variable number of lists as arguments
; and apply the function to those N lists using apply and map.
; To make the recursive call, apply is used to convert a list of
; argument lists into separate arguments.

; Return final true return value if all successive elements in lists
; satisfy func, #f otherwise.
(define every
   (let ( (null? null?) (car car) (cdr cdr) (apply apply) (map map)
          (cons cons) (member member) )
      (lambda (func . lists)
         (cond ((member #t (map null? lists)) #t)
               ((member #t (map (lambda (lst) (null? (cdr lst))) lists))
                  (apply func (map car lists)))
               (else
                  (and (apply func (map car lists))
                       (apply every (cons func (map cdr lists))))))) )) )

; Return the first true value from applying func to successive
; elements in lists, or #f if no elements satisfy func.
(define any
   (let ( (null? null?) (car car) (cdr cdr) (apply apply) (map map)
          (cons cons) (member member) )
      (lambda (func . lists)
         (if (member #t (map null? lists))
             #f
             (or (apply func (map first lists))
                 (apply any (cons func (map rest lists)))))) )) )

; Return result of applying func to elements of lst in the following
; manner: func is applied to the first two elements of lst then to
; that result and the third element, then to that result and the
; fourth element, and so on until all elements have been applied.
(define accum-tail
   (let ( (null? null?) (car car) (cdr cdr) )
      (lambda (func lst answer)
         (if (null? lst)
             answer
             (accum-tail func (cdr lst) (func answer (car lst))))) )) )
```

```
(define accumulate
  (let ( (null? null?) (car car) (cdr cdr) (accum-tail accum-tail) )
    (lambda (func lst)
      (if (null? lst)
          (func)
          (accum-tail func (cdr lst) (car lst))) )) )

; Return the elements that set1 and set2 have in common.
(define intersection
  (let ( (null? null?) (member member) (car car) (cdr cdr)
         (cons cons) )
    (lambda (set1 set2)
      (cond ((or (null? set1) (null? set2))
             '())
            ((member (car set1) set2)
             (cons (car set1) (intersection (cdr set1) set2)))
            (else
             (intersection (cdr set1) set2))) )) )

; Return the elements that exist in either set1 or set2.
(define union
  (let ( (null? null?) (member member) (car car) (cdr cdr)
         (cons cons) )
    (lambda (set1 set2)
      (cond ((null? set1)
             set2)
            ((member (car set1) set2)
             (union (cdr set1) set2))
            (else
             (cons (car set1) (union (cdr set1) set2)))) )) )

; Return the elements that exist in set1 but not in set2.
(define set-difference
  (let ( (null? null?) (member member) (car car) (cdr cdr)
         (cons cons) )
    (lambda (set1 set2)
      (cond ((null? set2)
             set1)
            ((null? set1)
             '())
            ((member (car set1) set2)
             (set-difference (cdr set1) set2))
            (else
             (cons (car set1)
                   (set-difference (cdr set1) set2)))) )) )
```

```scheme
; Return #t if all the elements in set1 exist in set2.
(define subset?
  (let ( (null? null?) (member member) (car car) (cdr cdr) )
    (lambda (set1 set2)
      (cond ((null? set1)
                 #t)
            ((null? set2)
                 #f)
            (else
                 (and (member (car set1) set2)
                      (subset? (cdr set1) set2)))) )) )

; Return a new set of item and the elements in set if item does not
; exist in set, otherwise return set.
(define adjoin
  (let ( (member member) (cons cons) )
    (lambda (item set)
      (if (member item set)
          set
          (cons item set)) )) )

; The following code is a modification of a random function used by
; Brian Harvey and Matt Wright in their text "Simply Scheme" which
; they obtained from an old version of the Scheme Library (SLIB)
; written by Aubrey Jaffer.

; random has been modified to allow an initial seed to be created
; using init-random.
(define random 0)

(define (init-random seed)
  (set! random
    (let ( (*seed* seed) (quotient quotient) (modulo modulo)
           (+ +) (- -) (* *) (> >) )
      (lambda (x)
        (let* ((hi (quotient *seed* 127773))
               (low (modulo *seed* 127773))
               (test (- (* 16807 low) (* 2836 hi))))
          (if (> test 0)
              (set! *seed* test)
              (set! *seed* (+ test 2147483647))))
        (modulo *seed* x) ))) )

(init-random 1)
```

INDEX

COLOPHON

I originally wrote the beginning chapters of this book using Common LISP. For a programming language, Common LISP offers a great deal. However, Scheme is better suited and more popular for a first language. Many of the extensions I added to Scheme's built-in functions are based on Common LISP functions.

Rather than rewrite all the examples in the text, I wrote a filter using a UNIX sed script to translate the Common LISP code into Scheme. Where language differences existed or language style required a different approach, I used conditional text within the book's source. Thus I produced two books at the same time; one in Common LISP and another in Scheme. If there is a demand in the future, I will publish the Common LISP version.

This text was typeset using troff, eqn, and pic on a Sun Enterprise server. These tools are challenging to use, but by creating a sound collection of macros, the text was relatively easy to produce and adjust stylistically. However, if I had to do it all over again, I'd use different tools.

UNIX utilities were used extensively to produce this text. All the code examples are preprocessed to embolden the built-in functions and extensions to the language. Each chapter was processed through a series of filters to produce postscript output. Index and table of contents information was redirected to one file and postscript output to another. A makefile was used to handle the complexities of formatting issues. Here is an example to format one chapter:

```
sed -f scheme-translation chapter | sed -f embolden-functions |
pic | eqn | troff -ms 2> index-file > postscript-output
```

The index was produced using a series of UNIX utilities. A multikey sort arranged the index entries in the proper order and then an awk script produced the final index file to be typeset with troff.

The main body of the text is typeset in 10 point Palatino. The code examples and function names are given in 9 point Courier. Section headings and margin notes are set in Helvetica. The page headers are in 10 point Times bold italic. Chapter titles are in 24 point Bookman.